V. I. LENIN

SELECTED WORKS

One-Volume Edition

V. I. LENIN
Selected Works

One-Volume Edition

INTERNATIONAL PUBLISHERS

New York

Acknowledgments

Writings included in this volume are taken from works previously published in the United States and England and are protected either by U.S. Copyright or under the Universal Copyright Convention, or both. Permission to quote or reprint any portion of the present volume, outside of reasonable usage for review purposes, should be requested from International Publishers, 381 Park Avenue South, New York, N.Y. 10016.

ISBN 0-7178-0300-7

Library of Congress Catalog Card Number: 75-175177

Printed in the United States of America

CONTENTS

PUBLISHER'S PREFACE

The present volume presents essential aspects of Lenin's contribution to the development of revolutionary Marxism into the 20th century. To do this in a single volume is a formidable task, for he left a vast and rich literary heritage. During the thirty years from 1893 to 1923 he wrote hundreds of books and pamphlets, as well as thousands of articles and letters, and delivered numerous speeches and reports at Party congresses, political conferences and meetings. His *Selected Works* in three volumes (1967) gives a fuller presentation. The present selections, also taken from the entire range of Lenin's writings, provide the reader with a more easily accessible introduction to his general thinking.

As a creative thinker and Communist leader, Lenin responded to a great variety of problems arising from revolutionary practice and from every turn in events. He was sensitive to every ideological nuance and was always deeply engaged in philosophy and theory; he followed closely revolutionary movements throughout the world; he was concerned with new scientific and cultural developments. No area of human and social endeavor escaped his attention. He was a painstaking scholar, as his many studies attest, but a scholar with close ties to life and struggle, always strongly, even fiercely, partisan.

Dogmatism of any kind was foreign to him. He inveighed against any attempt to revise or distort the underlying principles of Marxism, but like Marx and Engels he kept these principles alive by using them to digest new experience and thereby opening new theoretical ground. As an innovator, as the leader of the first great socialist revolution in history, he was impatient with any effort to fossilize Marxism, the very nature of which demands the constant study of changing reality, the specifics of any given situation. It was Lenin's supreme capacity to apply the Marxist approach to the specifics of tsarist Russia and of the new epoch of world capitalism which produced the Leninist stage of Marxist theory, commonly known as Marxism-Leninism. It is the Marxism of the epoch of imperialism and of the transition to socialism.

Efforts have been made to separate Lenin from Marx and Engels, to deny the continuity of Marxism as represented by Lenin. The aim is to present Lenin, and with him the October Revolution, as a break from Marxism, as a product of peculiar Russian conditions, so unique as to preclude the emergence under those conditions of a new stage of Marxism with universal validity. Lenin was the first to affirm that the Russian socialist revolution has characteristics distinctively its own and that it would be harmful to generalize the peculiarities (see, for example, his

"Left-Wing" Communism). But as with every really profound revolution that opens a new epoch (as with the Great French Revolution in the 19th century), the Russian socialist revolution and the entire body of theory associated with it could not help but have a universal impact, as events in the past half century have demonstrated. And Lenin's development of Marxism, in the broadest sense, is integral to it.

Lenin would also be the first to say that this theoretical heritage, as with the heritage of Marx and Engels, should not be fossilized, but should, on the contrary, be employed with full regard for the specifics of each situation, in place and in time. It is with this in mind, that the present volume of selections should be studied. There is much that can be learned here, in two major respects: First, as regards the dynamics of the revolutionary movement in Russia before the October Revolution and during the first five years of Soviet power; and second, the new theoretical stature of Marxism achieved in the entire course of that revolutionary development. Obviously, both aspects are interwoven, one being impossible without the other; and it is equally obvious that Lenin is concerned at all times with both aspects simultaneously—with the theoretical implications of the practical and with the practical implications of the theoretical: the unity of theory and practice, of Marxism and the working-class movement. This is his unique quality. The theoretical tasks he sets himself are dictated by the requirements of the actual revolutionary movement, and he performs these tasks rigorously, without tailoring his theory to the limits set by current political slogans or ideology. And conversely, he does not permit theoretical presuppositions to hamper his freedom of observation of new phenomena or his flexibility in tactics. That is why it is always so exciting and rewarding to read Lenin: for one has a sense of being present at the solution, the new departure, the innovation of new concepts, in the very midst of the events that Lenin confronts and digests.

The first three essays present in capsule form the basic Marxist doctrine and its "historical destiny" as seen by Lenin, and his struggle to save it from revisionism. The opening sentence of the first article summarizes his central theme: "The chief thing in the doctrine of Marx is that it brings out the historic role of the proletariat as the builder of socialist society." In his essay on "The Three Sources" (German philosophy, English classical political economy, and French socialism) he presents another cardinal aspect of his approach: "there is nothing resembling 'sectarianism' in Marxism, in the sense of its being a hide-bound, petrified doctrine, a doctrine which arose *away from* the highroad of the development of world civilization." And in his essay on revisionism he strikes another keynote of his thinking when he writes of Bernstein's "catch-phrase"— "the movement is everything, the ultimate aim is nothing"—this "expresses the substance of revisionism better than many long disquisitions."

Aside from the three introductory essays, the rest of the selections are arranged in chronological order, beginning with "Our Programme" (1899). In this, and in the two articles that follow, Lenin deals with the necessity for conscious political activity as opposed to dependence upon spontaneity, in other words, with the need for a vanguard proletarian party. His concept of the party, one of Lenin's major contributions to Marxism, is also touched upon elsewhere in this volume, but it is most fully presented in his *What Is To Be Done?* (not included here).

Perhaps his view of the party as vanguard can best be understood in relation to what may be termed his theory of socialist revolution, in which the hegemony of the proletariat is central. His "Two Tactics" (here printed in full), written at the beginning of the Revolution of 1905, is a work of extraordinary significance, a cardinal contribution to Marxism. It set the course for the Bolsheviks in that Revolution and beyond that in the March 1917 revolution against tsarism and in the socialist victory of November. It may be considered the first scientific treatment of the nature of bourgeois-democratic revolution in the imperialist epoch, its development into the socialist revolution, and of the role of the working class in both stages of the revolution. In it, Lenin sets forth the pivotal role of the worker-peasant alliance in the development of the revolution over its entire course. His theory of socialist revolution, as presented in this and other writings, was confirmed by the success of the socialist revolution in Russia, by the emergence of socialism in other countries since the second world war, and by the collapse of colonialism and the striving toward socialism in formerly dependent countries. To the present day, this work continues to provide deep insights into the problems of national liberation movements and into the concept of phases or stages of revolutionary movements in general.

It is noteworthy that two of his classical works which have a direct bearing upon the revolutionary epoch opened in Russia were written before the November seizure of power—"Imperialism: The Last Stage of Capitalism," composed in the midst of the first world war, in 1916, and "The State and Revolution," finished in August-September 1917 from notes made abroad the year before, both of which are given here in full.

The first was the culmination of years of study devoted to the analysis of modern capitalism (Lenin's *Notebooks on Imperialism* contain notes on 148 books in German, French, English and Russian and on 232 articles). In this work Lenin singles out the new features of monopoly capitalism or imperialism that distinguish it from the earlier stage of "free competition" as analyzed by Marx in *Capital*. It is a core work, the source for a new level of theoretical, strategic and tactical concepts. Among the conclusions drawn by Lenin from this study which had far-reaching implications was his recognition of the effects of the uneven development of capitalism in sharpening the contradictions among the

13

imperialist powers. From this there emerged the concept of the imperialist chain breaking at "the weakest link," making possible the victory of socialism in a group of countries or a single country, and not necessarily the most developed, and also the possibility of exploiting inter-imperialist rivalries to defend socialism once established. At another level, Lenin showed the bond between imperialism and opportunism in the labor movement, which explains the betrayal by Social Democracy during the first world war, and indicates the approach which was to lead to the formation of the Third International.

In "The State and Revolution" Lenin rescued Marx's and Engels' teachings on the state from the revisionists, restored the concept of the dictatorship of the proletariat to its prime place in these teachings, and cleared the theoretical path for the establishment of Soviet power, which occurred three months after the book was completed. Thus, Lenin had worked out in theory, in advance, both the analysis of the world setting in which the revolution was to occur and the character of the working-class state that was to emerge; what remained was to grasp firmly the "specifics" that would make the taking of power possible.

Among other selections from the period preceding the October Revolution special mention should be made of "The Socialist Revolution and the Right of Nations to Self-Determination." Concerned largely with the complex national question in the Russian empire and in Europe, this work clarifies the basic principles of working-class parties with respect to national movements. Lenin gets behind the general phrases about the "equality of nations" to the concrete historical setting of the problem, its relation to the fight for democracy and to the class struggle, the role of chauvinism and bourgeois nationalism, and the differentiated responsibilities of the working class of the oppressor nation and that of the oppressed nation. The approach worked out here and in numerous other writings provided the principles for the formation of the USSR as a multi-national state.

The group of selections devoted to the preparations for the seizure of power, aside from indicating the nature of the inner debates, are of primary importance for consideration of what constitutes a revolutionary situation at its apex, the difference between adventurism and appropriate armed uprising, and the choice of the "right moment." Included here in full is Lenin's daring and confident pamphlet "Can the Bolsheviks Retain State Power?" which appeared a few weeks before they actually took power—and then retained it.

The second half of the book, beginning with the famous "The Immediate Tasks of the Soviet Government" (April 1918), is largely devoted to the revolution in progress—the transition to socialism, in the midst of civil war and imperialist intervention, poverty and famine, capitalist encirclement, illiteracy and cultural deprivation, and the prevading peasant economy. The theoretical aspects of the transition—the necessity of a transition period, the characteristics of the dictatorship of the proletariat in Russia, the role of petty commodity production, class relations during the transition—are discussed notably in "Economics and Politics in the Era of the Dictatorship of the Proletariat" and in "A Great Beginning." In the "The Immediate Tasks" Lenin had already set forth key principles for scientific socialist planning and the initial steps for organization and management of the economy.

Of special interest in revealing the obstacles and conflicts surrounding the fulfillment of the "immediate tasks" is Lenin's article, "Left-Wing Childishness and the Petty-Bourgeois Mentality" (May 1918). It is directed against Communists who opposed the separate peace with Germany (the Brest-Litovsk Treaty) and favored a "revolutionary war," while on the domestic front opposing Lenin's New Economic Policy. The latter gave concessions to the peasantry as private traders, as Lenin explained, to gain time and resources for the advance to socialism, while strengthening the worker-peasant alliance. As is the case generally with Lenin's writings which deal with specific situations, here too will be found important theoretical clarifications and extensions. Thus the reader will be struck by his treatment, in the midst of polemic, of the role of state capitalism under a working-class government in facilitating the transition to socialism. Or to cite another example, his illuminating explanation—at the same time a telling blow at his opponents—of the difference between confiscation or nationalisation and real socialisation, the revolutionary process of transforming society. As always, Lenin is not taken in by phrases, as revolutionary-sounding as they may seem. He goes directly to the essence, with both the existing reality and the goal firmly grasped, and is therefore able to make even serious compromises (such as the Brest-Litovsk Peace and the NEP) because he sees them as temporary retreats to make possible great strides forward. This flexibility in tactics arises from his keen understanding of the relation of forces and his uncompromising stand against revisionism in principle. It is the difference between the science of socialist revolution and mere adventurism or dilettantism at worst, or swaying to the right and to the left at best.

Throughout these selections it is clear that Lenin saw the progress of the Russian revolution not only in terms of the internal aspects, although these were decisive, but also in the context of world developments, and primarily in relation to the prospects of the international revolutionary movement. He saw the socialist revolution in Russia as opening a new, the socialist, epoch of world history, and Soviet economic achievements as having great significance for the emergence of socialism on a global scale. In this respect, special attention should be called to the final group of five articles, beginning with "Letter to the Congress," which has come to be known as his political testament. The key to understanding the separate

15

themes discussed here, their relation to Lenin's general perspective in the last four months of his life, is to be found in his assessment of the stage of the revolution in Soviet Russia in relation to the divisions and contradictions in world capitalism (see the last part of "Better Fewer, But Better"). To take full advantage of the opportunity of that particular conjuncture, he emphasises the need for unity in the party based on maintaining agreement between the workers and peasants with the workers playing the leading role, complete renovation of the old state apparatus, education and the cultural revolution to prepare the people for socialism, stronger links between town and country, trade cooperatives especially to involve the peasantry, and industrial development as central. It is here that he also stresses the new revolutionary storm rising in the East.

Other selections deal with the international revolutionary movement, including in full " 'Left-Wing' Communism: An Infantile Disorder" and "Letter to American Workers." His articles on youth, philosophy, proletarian culture and other topics indicate Lenin's comprehensive interests and leadership.

Lenin's speech at the Moscow Soviet, November 20, 1922, was his last public appearance. It was down to earth, characteristically without rhetoric, full of confidence yet placing things the way they are: "We must not approach socialism as if it were an icon painted in festive colors. . . . We have brought socialism into everyday life and must here see how matters stand. That is the task of our day, the task of our epoch."

The present text is a reproduction of the anthology as published by Progress Publishers, Moscow, 1968. It has extensive explanatory notes, a biographical index, and a subject index.

July 1971 INTERNATIONAL PUBLISHERS

THE HISTORICAL DESTINY
OF THE DOCTRINE OF KARL MARX[1]

The chief thing in the doctrine of Marx is that it brings out the historic role of the proletariat as the builder of socialist society. Has the course of events all over the world confirmed this doctrine since it was expounded by Marx? Marx first advanced it in 1844. The *Communist Manifesto* of Marx and Engels, published in 1848, gave an integral and systematic exposition of this doctrine, an exposition which has remained the best to this day. Since then world history has clearly been divided into three main periods: 1) from the revolution of 1848[2] to the Paris Commune (1871)[3]; 2) from the Paris Commune to the Russian revolution (1905); 3) since the Russian revolution.

Let us see what has been the destiny of Marx's doctrine in each of these periods.

I

At the beginning of the first period Marx's doctrine by no means dominated. It was only one of the very numerous groups or trends of socialism. The forms of socialism that did dominate were in the main akin to our Narodism[4]: incomprehension of the materialist basis of historical movement, inability to single out the role and significance of each class in capitalist society, concealment of the bourgeois nature of democratic reforms under diverse, quasi-socialist phrases about the "people", "justice", "right", and so on.

The revolution of 1848 struck a deadly blow at all these vociferous, motley and ostentatious forms of *pre*-Marxian socialism. In all countries, the revolution revealed the various classes of society *in action*. The shooting of the workers by the republican bourgeoisie in Paris in the June days of 1848 finally revealed that the proletariat *alone* was socialist by nature. The liberal bourgeoisie dread-

ed the independence of this class a hundred times more than it
did any kind of reaction. The craven liberals grovelled before reaction. The peasantry were content with the abolition of the survivals of feudalism and joined the supporters of order, wavering but
occasionally between *workers' democracy and bourgeois liberalism*. All doctrines of *non*-class socialism and *non*-class politics
proved to be sheer nonsense.

The Paris Commune (1871) completed this development of bourgeois changes; the republic, i.e., the form of political organisation
in which class relations appear in their most unconcealed form,
owed its consolidation solely to the heroism of the proletariat.

In all the other European countries, a more tangled and less
complete development led to the same result—a bourgeois society
that had taken definite shape. Towards the end of the first period
(1848-71), a period of storms and revolutions, pre-Marxian socialism was *dead*. Independent *proletarian* parties came into being:
the First International (1864-72)[5] and the German Social-Democratic Party.

II

The second period (1872-1904) was distinguished from the first
by its "peaceful" character, by the absence of revolutions. The
West had finished with bourgeois revolutions. The East had not
yet risen to them.

The West entered a phase of "peaceful" preparations for the
changes to come. Socialist parties, basically proletarian, were formed
everywhere, and learned to use bourgeois parliamentarism and
to found their own daily press, their educational institutions, their
trade unions and their co-operative societies. Marx's doctrine gained
a complete victory and *began to spread*. The selection and mustering of the forces of the proletariat and its preparation for
the coming battles made slow but steady progress.

The dialectics of history were such that the theoretical victory of
Marxism compelled its enemies to *disguise themselves* as Marxists.
Liberalism, rotten within, tried to revive itself in the form of socialist *opportunism*. They interpreted the period of preparing the forces
for great battles as renunciation of these battles. Improvement
of the conditions of the slaves to fight against wage-slavery they
took to mean the sale by the slaves of their right to liberty for a
few pence. They cravenly preached "social peace" (i.e., peace with
the slave-owners), renunciation of the class struggle, etc. They had
very many adherents among socialist members of parliament.
various officials of the working-class movement. and the "sympathising" intelligentsia.

III

However, the opportunists had scarcely congratulated them-selves on "social peace" and on the non-necessity of storms under "democracy" when a new source of great world storms opened up in Asia. The Russian revolution was followed by revolutions in Turkey, Persia and China.[6] It is in this era of storms and their "repercussions" in Europe that we are now living. No matter what the fate of the great Chinese republic, against which various "civilised" hyenas are now whetting their teeth, no power on earth can restore the old serfdom in Asia or wipe out the heroic democracy of the masses in the Asiatic and semi-Asiatic countries.

Certain people who were inattentive to the conditions for pre-paring and developing the mass struggle were driven to despair and to anarchism by the lengthy delays in the decisive struggle against capitalism in Europe. We can now see how short-sighted and faint-hearted this anarchist despair is.

The fact that Asia, with its population of eight hundred million, has been drawn into the struggle for these same European ideals should inspire us with optimism and not despair.

The Asiatic revolutions have again shown us the spinelessness and baseness of liberalism, the exceptional importance of the in-dependence of the democratic masses, and the pronounced demar-cation between the proletariat and the bourgeoisie of all kinds. After the experience both of Europe and Asia, anyone who speaks of non-class politics and non-class socialism, ought simply to be put in a cage and exhibited alongside the Australian kangaroo or something like that.

After Asia, Europe has also begun to stir, although not in the Asiatic way. The "peaceful" period of 1872-1904 has passed, never to return. The high cost of living and the tyranny of the trusts are leading to an unprecedented sharpening of the economic struggle, which has set into movement even the British workers who have been most corrupted by liberalism. We see a political crisis brew-ing even in the most "diehard", bourgeois-Junker country, Ger-many. The frenzied arming and the policy of imperialism are turn-ing modern Europe into a "social peace" which is more like a gun-powder barrel. Meanwhile the decay of all the bourgeois parties and the maturing of the proletariat are making steady progress.

Since the appearance of Marxism, each of the three great periods of world history has brought Marxism new confirmation and new triumphs. But a still greater triumph awaits Marxism, as the doctrine of the proletariat, in the coming period of history.

Pravda No. 50, March 1, 1913
Signed: *V. I.*

Collected Works, Vol. 18

THE THREE SOURCES
AND THREE COMPONENT PARTS OF MARXISM[7]

Throughout the civilised world the teachings of Marx evoke the utmost hostility and hatred of all bourgeois science (both official and liberal), which regards Marxism as a kind of "pernicious sect". And no other attitude is to be expected, for there can be no "impartial" social science in a society based on class struggle. In one way or another, *all* official and liberal science *defends* wage slavery, whereas Marxism has declared relentless war on that slavery. To expect science to be impartial in a wage-slave society is as foolishly naïve as to expect impartiality from manufacturers on the question of whether workers' wages ought not to be increased by decreasing the profits of capital.

But this is not all. The history of philosophy and the history of social science show with perfect clarity that there is nothing resembling "sectarianism" in Marxism, in the sense of its being a hidebound, petrified doctrine, a doctrine which arose *away from* the highroad of the development of world civilisation. On the contrary, the genius of Marx consists precisely in his having furnished answers to questions already presented by the foremost minds of mankind. His doctrine emerged as the direct and immediate *continuation* of the teachings of the greatest representatives of philosophy, political economy and socialism.

The Marxist doctrine is omnipotent because it is true. It is comprehensive and harmonious, and provides men with an integral world outlook irreconcilable with any form of superstition, reaction, or defence of bourgeois oppression. It is the legitimate successor to the best that man produced in the nineteenth century, as represented by German philosophy, English political economy and French socialism.

It is these three sources of Marxism, which are also its component parts, that we shall outline in brief.

I

The philosophy of Marxism is *materialism.* Throughout the modern history of Europe, and especially at the end of the eighteenth century in France, where a resolute struggle was conducted against every kind of medieval rubbish, against serfdom in institutions and ideas, materialism has proved to be the only philosophy that is consistent, true to all the teachings of natural science and hostile to superstition, cant and so forth. The enemies of democracy have, therefore, always exerted all their efforts to "refute", undermine and defame materialism, and have advocated various forms of philosophical idealism, which always, in one way or another, amounts to the defence or support of religion.

Marx and Engels defended philosophical materialism in the most determined· manner and repeatedly explained how profoundly erroneous is every deviation from this basis. Their views are most clearly and fully expounded in the works of Engels, *Ludwig Feuerbach* and *Anti-Dühring,*[8] which, like the *Communist Manifesto,* are handbooks for every class-conscious worker.

But Marx did not stop at eighteenth century materialism: he developed philosophy to a higher level. He enriched it with the achievements of German classical philosophy, especially of Hegel's system, which in its turn had led to the materialism of Feuerbach. The main achievement was *dialectics,* i.e., the doctrine of development in its fullest, deepest and most comprehensive form, the doctrine of the relativity of the human knowledge that provides us with a reflection of eternally developing matter. The latest discoveries of natural science—radium, electrons, the transmutation of elements—have been a remarkable confirmation of Marx's dialectical materialism despite the teachings of the bourgeois philosophers with their "new" reversions to old and decadent idealism.

Marx deepened and developed philosophical materialism to the full, and extended the cognition of nature to include the cognition of *human society.* His *historical materialism* was a great achievement in scientific thinking. The chaos and arbitrariness that had previously reigned in views on history and politics were replaced by a strikingly integral and harmonious scientific theory, which shows how, in consequence of the growth of productive forces, out of one system of social life another and higher system develops—how capitalism, for instance, grows out of feudalism.

Just as man's knowledge reflects nature (i.e., developing matter), which exists independently of him, so man's *social knowledge* (i.e., his various views and doctrines—philosophical, religious, political and so forth) reflects the *economic system* of society. Political institutions are a superstructure on the economic foundation. We see, for example, that the various political forms of the modern

European states serve to strengthen the domination of the bourgeoisie over the proletariat.

Marx's philosophy is a consummate philosophical materialism which has provided mankind, and especially the working class, with powerful instruments of knowledge.

II

Having recognised that the economic system is the foundation on which the political superstructure is erected, Marx devoted his greatest attention to the study of this economic system. Marx's principal work, *Capital,* is devoted to a study of the economic system of modern, i.e., capitalist, society.

Classical political economy, before Marx, evolved in England, the most developed of the capitalist countries. Adam Smith and David Ricardo, by their investigations of the economic system, laid the foundations of the *labour theory of value.* Marx continued their work; he provided a proof of the theory and developed it consistently. He showed that the value of every commodity is determined by the quantity of socially necessary labour time spent on its production.

Where the bourgeois economists saw a relation between things (the exchange of one commodity for another) Marx revealed a *relation between people.* The exchange of commodities expresses the connection between individual producers through the market. *Money* signifies that the connection is becoming closer and closer, inseparably uniting the entire economic life of the individual producers into one whole. *Capital* signifies a further development of this connection: man's labour power becomes a commodity. The wage worker sells his labour power to the owner of land, factories and instruments of labour. The worker spends one part of the day covering the cost of maintaining himself and his family (wages), while the other part of the day he works without remuneration, creating for the capitalist *surplus value,* the source of profit, the source of the wealth of the capitalist class.

The doctrine of surplus value is the cornerstone of Marx's economic theory.

Capital, created by the labour of the worker, crushes the worker, ruining small proprietors and creating an army of unemployed. In industry, the victory of large-scale production is immediately apparent, but the same phenomenon is also to be observed in agriculture, where the superiority of large-scale capitalist agriculture is enhanced, the use of machinery increases and the peasant economy, trapped by money-capital, declines and falls into ruin under the burden of its backward technique. The decline of small-scale production assumes different forms in agriculture, but the decline itself is an indisputable fact.

By destroying small-scale production, capital leads to an increase in productivity of labour and to the creation of a monopoly position for the associations of big capitalists. Production itself becomes more and more social—hundreds of thousands and millions of workers become bound together in a regular economic organism—but the product of this collective labour is appropriated by a handful of capitalists. Anarchy of production, crises, the furious chase after markets and the insecurity of existence of the mass of the population are intensified.

By increasing the dependence of the workers on capital, the capitalist system creates the great power of united labour.

Marx traced the development of capitalism from embryonic commodity economy, from simple exchange, to its highest forms, to large-scale production.

And the experience of all capitalist countries, old and new, year by year demonstrates clearly the truth of this Marxian doctrine to increasing numbers of workers.

Capitalism has triumphed all over the world, but this triumph is only the prelude to the triumph of labour over capital.

III

When feudalism was overthrown, and *"free"* capitalist society appeared in the world, it at once became apparent that this freedom meant a new system of oppression and exploitation of the working people. Various socialist doctrines immediately emerged as a reflection of and protest against this oppression. Early socialism, however, was *utopian* socialism. It criticised capitalist society, it condemned and damned it, it dreamed of its destruction, it had visions of a better order and endeavoured to convince the rich of the immorality of exploitation.

But utopian socialism could not indicate the real solution. It could not explain the real nature of wage-slavery under capitalism, it could not reveal the laws of capitalist development, or show what *social force* is capable of becoming the creator of a new society.

Meanwhile, the stormy revolutions which everywhere in Europe, and especially in France, accompanied the fall of feudalism, of serfdom, more and more clearly revealed the *struggle of classes* as the basis and the driving force of all development.

Not a single victory of political freedom over the feudal class was won except against desperate resistance. Not a single capitalist country evolved on a more or less free and democratic basis except by a life-and-death struggle between the various classes of capitalist society.

The genius of Marx lies in his having been the first to deduce from this the lesson world history teaches and to apply that lesson consistently. The deduction he made is the doctrine of the *class struggle*.

People always have been the foolish victims of deception and self-deception in politics, and they always will be until they have learnt to seek out the *interests* of some class or other behind all moral, religious, political and social phrases, declarations and promises. Champions of reforms and improvements will always be fooled by the defenders of the old order until they realise that every old institution, however barbarous and rotten it may appear to be, is kept going by the forces of certain ruling classes. And there is *only one* way of smashing the resistance of those classes, and that is to find, in the very society which surrounds us, the forces which can—and, owing to their social position, *must*—constitute the power capable of sweeping away the old and creating the new, and to enlighten and organise those forces for the struggle.

Marx's philosophical materialism alone has shown the proletariat the way out of the spiritual slavery in which all oppressed classes have hitherto languished. Marx's economic theory alone has explained the true position of the proletariat in the general system of capitalism.

Independent organisations of the proletariat are multiplying all over the world, from America to Japan and from Sweden to South Africa. The proletariat is becoming enlightened and educated by waging its class struggle; it is ridding itself of the prejudices of bourgeois society; it is rallying its ranks ever more closely and is learning to gauge the measure of its successes; it is steeling its forces and is growing irresistibly.

Prosveshcheniye No. 3, March 1913   *Collected Works*, Vol. 19
Signed: *V. I.*

MARXISM AND REVISIONISM

There is a well-known saying that if geometrical axioms affected human interests attempts would certainly be made to refute them. Theories of natural history which conflicted with the old prejudices of theology provoked, and still provoke, the most rabid opposition. No wonder, therefore, that the Marxian doctrine, which directly serves to enlighten and organise the advanced class in modern society, indicates the tasks facing this class and demonstrates the inevitable replacement (by virtue of economic development) of the present system by a new order—no wonder that this doctrine has had to fight for every step forward in the course of its life.

Needless to say, this applies to bourgeois science and philosophy, officially taught by official professors in order to befuddle the rising generation of the propertied classes and to "coach" it against internal and foreign enemies. This science will not even hear of Marxism, declaring that it has been refuted and annihilated. Marx is attacked with equal zest by young scholars who are making a career by refuting socialism, and by decrepit elders who are preserving the tradition of all kinds of outworn "systems". The progress of Marxism, the fact that its ideas are spreading and taking firm hold among the working class, inevitably increase the frequency and intensity of these bourgeois attacks on Marxism, which becomes stronger, more hardened and more vigorous every time it is "annihilated" by official science.

But even among doctrines connected with the struggle of the working class, and current mainly among the proletariat, Marxism by no means consolidated its position all at once. In the first half-century of its existence (from the 1840s on) Marxism was engaged in combating theories fundamentally hostile to it. In the early forties Marx and Engels settled accounts with the radical Young Hegelians[9] whose viewpoint was that of philosophical idealism. At the end of the forties the struggle began in the field of economic doctrine, against Proudhonism.[10] The fifties saw the completion of

this struggle in criticism of the parties and doctrines which manifested themselves in the stormy year of 1848. In the sixties the
struggle shifted from the field of general theory to one closer to
the direct labour movement: the ejection of Bakuninism from the
International.[11] In the early seventies the stage in Germany was occupied for a short while by the Proudhonist Mühlberger, and in
the late seventies by the positivist Dühring. But the influence of
both on the proletariat was already absolutely insignificant. Marxism was already gaining an unquestionable victory over all other
ideologies in the labour movement.

By the nineties this victory was in the main completed. Even
in the Latin countries, where the traditions of Proudhonism held
their ground longest of all, the workers' parties in effect built their
programmes and their tactics on Marxist foundations. The revived
international organisation of the labour movement—in the shape
of periodical international congresses—from the outset, and almost
without a struggle, adopted the Marxist standpoint in all essentials. But after Marxism had ousted all the more or less integral
doctrines hostile to it, the tendencies expressed in those doctrines
began to seek other channels. The forms and causes of the struggle
changed, but the struggle continued. And the second half-century
of the existence of Marxism began (in the nineties) with the
struggle of a trend hostile to Marxism within Marxism itself.

Bernstein, a one-time orthodox Marxist, gave his name to this
trend, by coming forward with the most noise and with the most
purposeful expression of amendments to Marx, revision of Marx,
revisionism. Even in Russia where—owing to the economic backwardness of the country and the preponderance of a peasant population weighed down by the relics of serfdom—non-Marxist
socialism has naturally held its ground longest of all, it is plainly
passing into revisionism before our very eyes. Both in the agrarian
question (the programme of the municipalisation of all land) and
in general questions of programme and tactics, our Social-Narodniks are more and more substituting "amendments" to Marx for
the moribund and obsolescent remnants of their old system,
which in its own way was integral and fundamentally hostile to
Marxism.

Pre-Marxist socialism has been defeated. It is continuing the
struggle, no longer on its own independent ground, but on the
general ground of Marxism, as revisionism. Let us, then, examine
the ideological content of revisionism.

In the sphere of philosophy revisionism followed in the wake
of bourgeois professorial "science". The professors went "back to
Kant"—and revisionism dragged along after the neo-Kantians.[12]
The professors repeated the platitudes that priests have uttered a
thousand times against philosophical materialism—and the revi-

sionists, smiling indulgently, mumbled (word for word after the latest *Handbuch*) that materialism had been "refuted" long ago. The professors treated Hegel as a "dead dog", and while themselves preaching idealism, only an idealism a thousand times more petty and banal than Hegel's, contemptuously shrugged their shoulders at dialectics—and the revisionists floundered after them into the swamp of philosophical vulgarisation of science, replacing "artful" (and revolutionary) dialectics by "simple" (and tranquil) "evolution". The professors earned their official salaries by adjusting both their idealist and their "critical" systems to the dominant medieval "philosophy" (i.e., to theology)—and the revisionists drew close to them, trying to make religion a "private affair", not in relation to the modern state, but in relation to the party of the advanced class.

What such "amendments" to Marx really meant in class terms need not be stated: it is self-evident. We shall simply note that the only Marxist in the international Social-Democratic movement to criticise the incredible platitudes of the revisionists from the standpoint of consistent dialectical materialism was Plekhanov. This must be stressed all the more emphatically since profoundly mistaken attempts are being made at the present time to smuggle in old and reactionary philosophical rubbish disguised as a criticism of Plekhanov's tactical opportunism.*

Passing to political economy, it must be noted first of all that in this sphere the "amendments" of the revisionists were much more comprehensive and circumstantial; attempts were made to influence the public by "new data on economic development". It was said that concentration and the ousting of small-scale production by large-scale production do not occur in agriculture at all, while they proceed very slowly in commerce and industry. It was said that crises had now become rarer and weaker, and that cartels and trusts would probably enable capital to eliminate them altogether. It was said that the "theory of collapse" to which capitalism is heading was unsound, owing to the tendency of class antagonisms to become milder and less acute. It was said, finally, that it would not be amiss to correct Marx's theory of value, too, in accordance with Böhm-Bawerk.

The fight against the revisionists on these questions resulted in as fruitful a revival of the theoretical thought in international socialism as did Engels's controversy with Dühring twenty years

---

* See *Studies in the Philosophy of Marxism* by Bogdanov, Bazarov and others. This is not the place to discuss the book, and I must at present confine myself to stating that in the very near future I shall prove in a series of articles, or in a separate pamphlet, that *everything* I have said in the text about neo-Kantian revisionists essentially applies also to these "new" neo-Humist and neo-Berkeleyan revisionists.[13] (See *Collected Works*, Vol. 14.—*Ed.*)

earlier. The arguments of the revisionists were analysed with the help of facts and figures. It was proved that the revisionists were systematically painting a rose-coloured picture of modern small-scale production. The technical and commercial superiority of large-scale *production* over small-scale production not only in industry, but also in agriculture, is proved by irrefutable facts. But commodity production is far less developed in agriculture, and modern statisticians and economists are, as a rule, not very skilful in picking out the special branches (sometimes even the operations) in agriculture which indicate that agriculture is being progressively drawn into the process of *exchange* in world economy. Small-scale production maintains itself on the ruins of natural economy by constant worsening of diet, by chronic starvation, by lengthening of the working day, by deterioration in the quality and the care of cattle, in a word, by the very methods whereby handicraft production maintained itself against capitalist manufacture. Every advance in science and technology inevitably and relentlessly undermines the foundations of small-scale production in capitalist society; and it is the task of socialist political economy to investigate this process in all its forms, often complicated and intricate, and to demonstrate to the small producer the impossibility of his holding his own under capitalism, the hopelessness of peasant farming under capitalism, and the necessity for the peasant to adopt the standpoint of the proletarian. On this question the revisionists sinned, in the scientific sense, by superficial generalisations based on facts selected one-sidedly and without reference to the system of capitalism as a whole. From the political point of view, they sinned by the fact that they inevitably, whether they wanted to or not, invited or urged the peasant to adopt the attitude of a small proprietor (i.e., the attitude of the bourgeoisie) instead of urging him to adopt the point of view of the revolutionary proletarian.

The position of revisionism was even worse as regards the theory of crises and the theory of collapse. Only for a very short time could people, and then only the most short-sighted, think of refashioning the foundations of Marx's theory under the influence of a few years of industrial boom and prosperity. Realities very soon made it clear to the revisionists that crises were not a thing of the past: prosperity was followed by a crisis. The forms, the sequence, the picture of particular crises changed, but crises remained an inevitable component of the capitalist system. While uniting production, the cartels and trusts at the same time, and in a way that was obvious to all, aggravated the anarchy of production, the insecurity of existence of the proletariat and the oppression of capital, thereby intensifying class antagonisms to an unprecedented degree. That capitalism is heading for a breakdown

—in the sense both of individual political and economic crises and of the complete collapse of the entire capitalist system—has been made particularly clear, and on a particularly large scale, precisely by the new giant trusts. The recent financial crisis in America and the appalling increase of unemployment all over Europe, to say nothing of the impending industrial crisis to which many symptoms are pointing—all this has resulted in the recent "theories" of the revisionists having been forgotten by everybody, including, apparently, many of the revisionists themselves. But the lessons which this instability of the intellectuals had given the working class must not be forgotten.

As to the theory of value, it need only be said that apart from the vaguest of hints and sighs, à la Böhm-Bawerk, the revisionists have contributed absolutely nothing, and have therefore left no traces whatever on the development of scientific thought.

In the sphere of politics, revisionism did really try to revise the foundation of Marxism, namely, the doctrine of the class struggle. Political freedom, democracy and universal suffrage remove the ground for the class struggle—we were told—and render untrue the old proposition of the *Communist Manifesto* that the working men have no country. For, they said, since the "will of the majority" prevails in a democracy, one must neither regard the state as an organ of class rule, nor reject alliances with the progressive, social-reform bourgeoisie against the reactionaries.

It cannot be disputed that these arguments of the revisionists amounted to a fairly well-balanced system of views, namely, the old and well-known liberal-bourgeois views. The liberals have always said that bourgeois parliamentarism destroys classes and class divisions, since the right to vote and the right to participate in the government of the country are shared by all citizens without distinction. The whole history of Europe in the second half of the nineteenth century, and the whole history of the Russian revolution in the early twentieth, clearly show how absurd such views are. Economic distinctions are not mitigated but aggravated and intensified under the freedom of "democratic" capitalism. Parliamentarism does not eliminate, but lays bare the innate character even of the most democratic bourgeois republics as organs of class oppression. By helping to enlighten and to organise immeasurably wider masses of the population than those which previously took an active part in political events, parliamentarism does not make for the elimination of crises and political revolutions, but for the maximum intensification of civil war during such revolutions. The events in Paris in the spring of 1871 and the events in Russia in the winter of 1905 showed as clearly as could be how inevitably this intensification comes about. The French bourgeoisie without a moment's hesitation made a deal with the enemy of the whole

h the foreign army which had ruined its country, in
и٤.	ush the proletarian movement. Whoever does not under-
stand the inevitable inner dialectics of parliamentarism and bourgeois democracy—which leads to an even sharper decision of the
argument by mass violence than formerly—will never be able on
the basis of this parliamentarism to conduct propaganda and agitation consistent in principle, really preparing the working-class masses
for victorious participation in such "arguments". The experience
of alliances, agreements and blocs with the social-reform liberals
in the West and with the liberal reformists (Cadets[14]) in the Russian revolution, has convincingly shown that these agreements only
blunt the consciousness of the masses, that they do not enhance
but weaken the actual significance of their struggle, by linking
fighters with elements who are least capable of fighting and most
vacillating and treacherous. Millerandism[15] in France—the biggest
experiment in applying revisionist political tactics on a wide, a
really national scale—has provided a practical appraisal of revisionism that will never be forgotten by the proletariat all over the
world.

A natural complement to the economic and political tendencies
of revisionism was its attitude to the ultimate aim of the socialist
movement. "The movement is everything, the ultimate aim is nothing"—this catch-phrase of Bernstein's expresses the substance of
revisionism better than many long disquisitions. To determine its
conduct from case to case, to adapt itself to the events of the day
and to the chopping and changing of petty politics, to forget the
primary interests of the proletariat and the basic features of the
whole capitalist system, of all capitalist evolution, to sacrifice these
primary interests for the real or assumed advantages of the moment—such is the policy of revisionism. And it patently follows from
the very nature of this policy that it may assume an infinite variety
of forms, and that every more or less "new" question, every more
or less unexpected and unforeseen turn of events, even though
it changes the basic line of development only to an insignificant
degree and only for the briefest period, will always inevitably give
rise to one variety of revisionism or another.

The inevitability of revisionism is determined by its class roots
in modern society. Revisionism is an international phenomenon.
No thinking socialist who is in the least informed can have the
slightest doubt that the relation between the orthodox and the Bernsteinians in Germany, the Guesdists and the Jaurèsists (and now
particularly the Broussists) in France,[16] the Social-Democratic
Federation[17] and the Independent Labour Party in Great Britain,[18]
Brouckère and Vandervelde in Belgium, the Integralists and the
Reformists in Italy,[19] the Bolsheviks and the Mensheviks in Russia,[20] is everywhere essentially similar, notwithstanding the immense

variety of national conditions and historical factors in the present state of all these countries. In reality, the "division" within the present international socialist movement is now proceeding along the *same* lines in all the various countries of the world, which testifies to a tremendous advance compared with thirty or forty years ago, when heterogeneous trends in the various countries were struggling within the one international socialist movement. And that "revisionism from the Left" which has taken shape in the Latin countries as "revolutionary syndicalism",[21] is also adapting itself to Marxism, "amending" it: Labriola in Italy and Lagardelle in France frequently appeal from Marx who is understood wrongly to Marx who is understood rightly.

We cannot stop here to analyse the ideological content of *this* revisionism, which as yet is far from having developed to the same extent as opportunist revisionism: it has not yet become international, has not yet stood the test of a single big practical battle with a socialist party in any single country. We confine ourselves therefore to that "revisionism from the Right" which was described above.

Wherein lies its inevitability in capitalist society? Why is it more profound than the differences of national peculiarities and of degrees of capitalist development? Because in every capitalist country, side by side with the proletariat, there are always broad strata of the petty bourgeoisie, small proprietors. Capitalism arose and is constantly arising out of small production. A number of new "middle strata" are inevitably brought into existence again and again by capitalism (appendages to the factory, work at home, small workshops scattered all over the country to meet the requirements of big industries, such as the bicycle and automobile industries, etc.). These new small producers are just as inevitably being cast again into the ranks of the proletariat. It is quite natural that the petty-bourgeois world outlook should again and again crop up in the ranks of the broad workers' parties. It is quite natural that this should be so and always will be so, right up to the changes of fortune that will take place in the proletarian revolution. For it would be a profound mistake to think that the "complete" proletarianisation of the majority of the population is essential for bringing about such a revolution. What we now frequently experience only in the domain of ideology, namely, disputes over theoretical amendments to Marx; what now crops up in practice only over individual partial issues of the labour movement, as tactical differences with the revisionists and splits on this basis—is bound to be experienced by the working class on an incomparably larger scale when the proletarian revolution will sharpen all disputed issues, will focus all differences on points which are of the most immediate importance in determining the conduct of the masses, and will make it necessary in the heat of the fight to distinguish enemies from friends, and to cast out bad allies in order to deal decisive blows at the enemy.

The ideological struggle waged by revolutionary Marxism against revisionism at the end of the nineteenth century is but the prelude to the great revolutionary battles of the proletariat, which is marching forward to the complete victory of its cause despite all the waverings and weaknesses of the petty bourgeoisie.

Written in late March—
not later than April 3 (16), 1908

Collected Works, Vol. 15

Published between
September 25 and October 2
(October 8 and 15), 1908
in the symposium:
Karl Marx (1818-1883)
by O. and M. Kedrov Publishers
Signed: *VI. Ilyin*

OUR PROGRAMME

International Social-Democracy is at present in a state of ideological wavering. Hitherto the doctrines of Marx and Engels were considered to be the firm foundation of revolutionary theory, but voices are now being raised everywhere to proclaim these doctrines inadequate and obsolete. Whoever declares himself to be a Social-Democrat and intends to publish a Social-Democratic organ must define precisely his attitude to a question that is preoccupying the attention of the German Social-Democrats and not of them alone. We take our stand entirely on the Marxist theoretical position: Marxism was the first to transform socialism from a utopia into a science, to lay a firm foundation for this science, and to indicate the path that must be followed in further developing and elaborating it in all its parts. It disclosed the nature of modern capitalist economy by explaining how the hire of the labourer, the purchase of labour power, conceals the enslavement of millions of propertyless people by a handful of capitalists, the owners of the land, factories, mines, and so forth. It showed that all modern capitalist development displays the tendency of large-scale production to eliminate petty production and creates conditions that make a socialist system of society possible and necessary. It taught us how to discern, beneath the pall of rooted customs, political intrigues, abstruse laws, and intricate doctrines—the *class struggle,* the struggle between the propertied classes in all their variety and the propertyless mass, the *proletariat,* which is at the head of all the propertyless. It made clear the real task of a revolutionary socialist party: not to draw up plans for refashioning society, not to preach to the capitalists and their hangers-on about improving the lot of the workers, not to hatch conspiracies, *but to organise the class struggle of the proletariat and to lead this struggle, the ultimate aim of which is the conquest of political power by the proletariat and the organisation of a socialist society.*

And we now ask: Has anything new been introduced into this theory by its loud-voiced "renovators" who are raising so much noise in our day and have grouped themselves around the German socialist Bernstein? *Absolutely nothing.* Not by a single step have they advanced the science which Marx and Engels enjoined us to develop; they have not taught the proletariat any new methods of struggle; they have only retreated, borrowing fragments of backward theories and preaching to the proletariat, not the theory of struggle, but the theory of concession—concession to the most vicious enemies of the proletariat, the governments and bourgeois parties who never tire of seeking new means of baiting the socialists. Plekhanov, one of the founders and leaders of Russian Social-Democracy, was entirely right in ruthlessly criticising Bernstein's latest "critique"; the views of Bernstein have now been rejected by the representatives of the German workers as well (at the Hannover Congress).[22]

We anticipate a flood of accusations for these words; the shouts will rise that we want to convert the socialist party into an order of "true believers" that persecutes "heretics" for deviations from "dogma", for every independent opinion, and so forth. We know about all these fashionable and trenchant phrases. Only there is not a grain of truth or sense in them. There can be no strong socialist party without a revolutionary theory which unites all socialists, from which they draw all their convictions, and which they apply in their methods of struggle and means of action. To defend such a theory, which to the best of your knowledge you consider to be true, against unfounded attacks and attempts to corrupt, it is not to imply that you are an enemy of *all* criticism. We do not regard Marx's theory as something completed and inviolable; on the contrary, we are convinced that it has only laid the foundation stone of the science which socialists *must* develop in all directions if they wish to keep pace with life. We think that an *independent* elaboration of Marx's theory is especially essential for Russian socialists; for this theory provides only general *guiding* principles, which, *in particular,* are applied in England differently than in France, in France differently than in Germany, and in Germany differently than in Russia. We shall therefore gladly afford space in our paper for articles on theoretical questions and we invite all comrades openly to discuss controversial points.

What are the main questions that arise in the application to Russia of the programme common to all Social-Democrats? We have stated that the essence of this programme is to organise the class struggle of the proletariat and to lead this struggle, the ultimate aim of which is the conquest of political power by the proletariat and the establishment of a socialist society. The class struggle of the proletariat comprises the economic struggle (struggle against individual capitalists or against individual groups of capitalists for the improvement of the workers' condition) and the political struggle (struggle against the government for the broadening of the people's rights, i.e., for democracy, and for the broadening of the political power of the proletariat). Some Russian Social-Democrats (among them apparently those who direct *Rabochaya Mysl*[23]) regard the economic struggle as incomparably the more important and almost go so far as to relegate the political struggle to the more or less distant future. This standpoint is utterly false. All Social-Democrats are agreed that it is necessary to organise the economic struggle of the working class, that it is necessary to carry on agitation among the workers on this basis, i.e., to help the workers in their day-to-day struggle against the employers, to draw their attention to every form and every case of oppression and in this way to make clear to them the necessity for combination. But to forget the political struggle for the economic would mean to depart from the basic principle of international Social-Democracy, it would mean to forget what the entire history of the labour movement teaches us. The confirmed adherents of the bourgeoisie and of the government which serves it have even made repeated attempts to organise purely economic unions of workers and to divert them in this way from "politics", from socialism. It is quite possible that the Russian Government, too, may undertake something of the kind, as it has always endeavoured to throw some paltry sops or, rather, sham sops, to the people, only to turn their thoughts away from the fact that they are oppressed and without rights. No economic struggle can bring the workers any lasting improvement, or can even be conducted on a large scale, unless the workers have the right freely to organise meetings and unions, to have their own newspapers, and to send their representatives to the national assemblies, as do the workers in Germany and all other European countries (with the exception of Turkey and Russia). But in order to win these rights it is necessary to wage a *political struggle*. In Russia, not only the workers, but all citizens are deprived of political rights. Russia is an absolute and unlimited monarchy. The tsar alone promulgates laws, appoints officials and controls them. For this reason, *it seems* as though in Russia the tsar and the tsarist government are independent of all classes and accord equal treatment to all. But *in reality* all officials are chosen exclusively from the propertied class and all are subject to the influence of the big capitalists, who make the ministers dance to their tune and who achieve whatever they want. The Russian working class is burdened by a double yoke; it is robbed and plundered by the capitalists and the landlords, and to prevent it from fighting them, the police bind it hand and foot, gag it, and every attempt to defend the rights of the people is persecuted. Every strike against a capitalist results in the military and police being let loose on the workers. Every economic struggle necessa-

rily becomes a political struggle, and Social-Democracy must in-
dissolubly combine the one with the other into a *single class struggle of the proletariat*. The first and chief aim of such a struggle
must be the conquest of political rights, *the conquest of political
liberty*. If the workers of St. Petersburg alone, with a little help
from the socialists, have rapidly succeeded in wringing a concession from the government—the adoption of the law on the reduction of the working day[24]—then the Russian working class as a
whole, led by a single Russian Social-Democratic Labour Party,
will be able, in persistent struggle, to win incomparably more
important concessions.

The Russian working class is able to wage its economic and
political struggle alone, even if no other class comes to its aid. But
in the political struggle the workers do not stand alone. The people's complete lack of rights and the savage lawlessness of the
bashi-bazouk officials rouse the indignation of all honest educated
people who cannot reconcile themselves to the persecution of free
thought and free speech; they rouse the indignation of the persecuted Poles, Finns, Jews, and Russian religious sects; they rouse
the indignation of the small merchants, manufacturers, and peasants, who can nowhere find protection from the persecution of
officials and police. All these groups of the population are incapable, separately, of carrying on a persistent political struggle. But
when the working class raises the banner of this struggle, it will
receive support from all sides. Russian Social-Democracy will place
itself at the head of all fighters for the rights of the people, of all
fighters for democracy, and it will prove invincible!

These are our fundamental views, and we shall develop them
systematically and from every aspect in our paper. We are convinced that in this way we shall tread the path which has been
indicated by the Russian Social-Democratic Labour Party in its
published *Manifesto*.[25]

Written not earlier than   *Collected Works*, Vol. 4
   October 1899

First published in 1925
in *Lenin Miscellany III*

WHERE TO BEGIN?

In recent years the question of "what is to be done" has confronted Russian Social-Democrats with particular insistence. It is not a question of what path we must choose (as was the case in the late eighties and early nineties), but of what practical steps we must take upon the known path and how they shall be taken. It is a question of a system and plan of practical work. And it must be admitted that we have not yet solved this question of the character and the methods of struggle, fundamental for a party of practical activity, that it still gives rise to serious differences of opinion which reveal a deplorable ideological instability and vacillation. On the one hand, the "Economist"[26] trend, far from being dead, is endeavouring to clip and narrow the work of political organisation and agitation. On the other, unprincipled eclecticism is again rearing its head, aping every new "trend", and is incapable of distinguishing immediate demands from the main tasks and permanent needs of the movement as a whole. This trend, as we know, has ensconced itself in *Rabocheye Dyelo*.[27] This journal's latest statement of "programme", a bombastic article under the bombastic title "A Historic Turn" (*"Listok" Rabochego Dyela*, No. 6[28]), bears out with special emphasis the characterisation we have given. Only yesterday there was a flirtation with "Economism", a fury over the resolute condemnation of *Rabochaya Mysl,* and Plekhanov's presentation of the question of the struggle against autocracy was being toned down. But today Liebknecht's words are being quoted: "If the circumstances change within twenty-four hours, then tactics must be changed within twenty-four hours." There is talk of a "strong fighting organisation" for direct attack, for storming the autocracy; of "broad revolutionary political agitation among the masses" (how energetic we are now—both revolutionary and political!); of "ceaseless calls for street protests"; of "street demonstrations of a pronounced (*sic!*) political character"; and so on, and so forth.

We might perhaps declare ourselves happy at *Rabocheye Dyelo*'s quick grasp of the programme we put forward in the first issue of *Iskra*,[29] calling for the formation of a strong well-organised party, whose aim is not only to win isolated concessions but to storm the fortress of the autocracy itself; but the lack of any set point of view in these individuals can only dampen out happiness.

Rabocheye Dyelo, of course, mentions Liebknecht's name in vain. The tactics of agitation in relation to some special question, or the tactics with regard to some detail of party organisation may be changed in twenty-four hours; but only people devoid of all principle are capable of changing, in twenty-four hours, or, for that matter, in twenty-four months, their view on the necessity—in general, constantly, and absolutely—of an organisation of struggle and of political agitation among the masses. It is ridiculous to plead different circumstances and a change of periods: the building of a fighting organisation and the conduct of political agitation are essential under any "drab, peaceful" circumstances, in any period, no matter how marked by a "declining revolutionary spirit"; moreover, it is precisely in such periods and under such circumstances that work of this kind is particularly necessary, since it is too late to form the organisation in times of explosion and outbursts; the party must be in a state of readiness to launch activity at a moment's notice. "Change the tactics within twenty-four hours!" But in order to change tactics it is first necessary to have tactics; without a strong organisation skilled in waging political struggle under all circumstances and at all times, there can be no question of that systematic plan of action, illumined by firm principles and steadfastly carried out, which alone is worthy of the name of tactics. Let us, indeed, consider the matter; we are now being told that the "historic moment" has presented our Party with a "completely new" question—the question of terror. Yesterday the "completely new" question was political organisation and agitation; today it is terror. Is it not strange to hear people who have so grossly forgotten their principles holding forth on a radical change in tactics?

Fortunately, *Rabocheye Dyelo* is in error. The question of terror is not a new question at all; it will suffice to recall briefly the established views of Russian Social-Democracy on the subject.

In principle we have never rejected,. and cannot reject, terror. Terror is one of the forms of military action that may be perfectly suitable and even essential at a definite juncture in the battle, given a definite state of the troops and the existence of definite conditions. But the important point is that terror, at the present time, is by no means suggested as an operation for the army in the field, an operation closely connected with and integrated into the entire system of struggle, but as an independent form of occasional attack unrelated to any army. Without a central body and with the weakness of local revolutionary organisations, this, in fact, is all that terror can be. We, therefore, declare emphatically that under the present conditions such a means of struggle is inopportune and unsuitable; that it diverts the most active fighters from their real task, the task which is most important from the standpoint of the interests of the movement as a whole; and that it disorganises the forces, not of the government, but of the revolution. We need but recall the recent events. With our own eyes we saw that the mass of workers and "common people" of the towns pressed forward in struggle, while the revolutionaries lacked a staff of leaders and organisers. Under such conditions, is there not the danger that, as the most energetic revolutionaries go over to terror, the fighting contingents, in whom alone it is possible to place serious reliance, will be weakened? Is there not the danger of rupturing the contact between the revolutionary organisations and the disunited masses of the discontented, the protesting, and the disposed to struggle, who are weak precisely because they are disunited? Yet it is this contact that is the sole guarantee of our success. Far be it from us to deny the significance of heroic individual blows, but it is our duty to sound a vigorous warning against becoming infatuated with terror, against taking it to be the chief and basic means of struggle, as so many people strongly incline to do at present. Terror can never be a regular military operation; at best it can only serve as one of the methods employed in a decisive assault. But can we *issue the call* for such a decisive assault at the present moment? *Rabocheye Dyelo* apparently thinks we can. At any rate, it exclaims: "Form assault columns!" But this, again, is more zeal than reason. The main body of our military forces consists of volunteers and insurgents. We possess only a few small units of regular troops, and these are not even mobilised; they are not connected with one another, nor have they been trained to form columns of any sort, let alone assault columns. In view of all this, it must be clear to anyone who is capable of appreciating the general conditions of our struggle and who is mindful of them at every "turn" in the historical course of events that at the present moment our slogan cannot be "To the assault", but has to be, "Lay siege to the enemy fortress". In other words, the immediate task of our Party is not to summon all available forces for the attack right now, but to call for the formation of a revolutionary organisation capable of uniting all forces and guiding the movement in actual practice and not in name alone, that is, an organisation ready at any time to support every protest and every outbreak and use it to build up and consolidate the fighting forces suitable for the decisive struggle.

The lesson of the February and March events[30] has been so impressive that no disagreement in principle with this conclusion is now likely to be encountered. What we need at the present moment, however, is not a solution of the problem in principle but a practical solution. We should not only be clear on the nature of the organisation that is needed and its precise purpose, but we must elaborate a definite *plan* for an organisation, so that its formation may be undertaken from all aspects. In view of the pressing importance of the question, we, on our part, take the liberty of submitting to the comrades a skeleton plan to be developed in greater detail in a pamphlet now in preparation for print.[31]

In our opinion, the starting-point of our activities, the first step towards creating the desired organisation, or, let us say, the main thread which, if followed, would enable us steadily to develop, deepen, and extend that organisation, should be the founding of an All-Russian political newspaper. A newspaper is what we most of all need; without it we cannot conduct that systematic, all-round propaganda and agitation, consistent in principle, which is the chief and permanent task of Social-Democracy in general and, in particular, the pressing task of the moment, when interest in politics and in questions of socialism has been aroused among the broadest strata of the population. Never has the need been felt so acutely as today for reinforcing dispersed agitation in the form of individual action, local leaflets, pamphlets, etc., by means of generalised and systematic agitation that can only be conducted with the aid of the periodical press. It may be said without exaggeration that the frequency and regularity with which a newspaper is printed (and distributed) can serve as a precise criterion of how well this cardinal and most essential sector of our militant activities is built up. Furthermore, our newspaper must be all-Russian. If we fail, and as long as we fail, to combine our efforts to influence the people and the government by means of the printed word, it will be utopian to think of combining other means, more complex, more difficult, but also more decisive, for exerting influence. Our movement suffers in the first place, ideologically, as well as in practical and organisational respects, from its state of fragmentation, from the almost complete immersion of the overwhelming majority of Social-Democrats in local work, which narrows their outlook, the scope of their activities, and their skill in the maintenance of secrecy and their preparedness. It is precisely in this state of fragmentation that one must look for the deepest roots of the instability and the waverings noted above. The *first* step towards eliminating this shortcoming, towards transforming diverse local movements into a single, all-Russian movement, must be the founding of an all-Russian newspaper. Lastly, what we need is definitely a *political* newspaper. Without a political organ, a political movement deserving that name is inconceivable in the Europe of today. Without such a newspaper we cannot possibly fulfil our task—that of concentrating all the elements of political discontent and protest, of vitalising thereby the revolutionary movement of the proletariat. We have taken the first step, we have aroused in the working class a passion for "economic", factory exposures; we must now take the next step, that of arousing in every section of the population that is at all politically conscious a passion for *political* exposure. We must not be discouraged by the fact that the voice of political exposure is today so feeble, timid, and infrequent. This is not because of a wholesale submission to police despotism, but because those who are able and ready to make exposures have no tribune from which to speak, no eager and encouraging audience, they do not see anywhere among the people that force to which it would be worth while directing their complaint against the "omnipotent" Russian Government. But today all this is rapidly changing. There is such a force—it is the revolutionary proletariat, which has demonstrated its readiness, not only to listen to and support the summons to political struggle, but boldly to engage in battle. We are now in a position to provide a tribune for the nation-wide exposure of the tsarist government, and it is our duty to do this. That tribune must be a Social-Democratic newspaper. The Russian working class, as distinct from the other classes and strata of Russian society, displays a constant interest in political knowledge and manifests a constant and extensive demand (not only in periods of intensive unrest) for illegal literature. When such a mass demand is evident, when the training of experienced revolutionary leaders has already begun, and when the concentration of the working class makes it virtual master in the working-class districts of the big cities and in the factory settlements and communities, it is quite feasible for the proletariat to found a political newspaper. Through the proletariat the newspaper will reach the urban petty bourgeoisie, the rural handicraftsmen, and the peasants, thereby becoming a real people's political newspaper.

The role of a newspaper, however, is not limited solely to the dissemination of ideas, to political education, and to the enlistment of political allies. A newspaper is not only a collective propagandist and a collective agitator, it is also a collective organiser. In this last respect it may be likened to the scaffolding round a building under construction, which marks the contours of the structure and facilitates communication between the builders, enabling them to distribute the work and to view the common results achieved by their organised labour. With the aid of the newspaper, and through it, a permanent organisation will naturally take shape that will engage, not only in local activities, but in regular general work, and will train its members to follow political events carefully, appraise their significance and their effect on the various strata of the population, and develop effective means for the revolutionary party to influence those events. The mere technical task of regularly supplying the newspaper with copy and of promoting regular distribution will necessitate a network of local agents of the united party, who will maintain constant contact with one another, know the general state of affairs, get accustomed to performing regularly their detailed functions in the all-Russian work, and test their strength in the organisation of various revolutionary actions. This network of agents* will form the skeleton of precisely the kind of organisation we need—one that is sufficiently large to embrace the whole country; sufficiently broad and many-sided to effect a strict and detailed division of labour; sufficiently well tempered to be able to conduct steadily *its own* work under any circumstances, at all "sudden turns", and in face of all contingencies; sufficiently flexible to be able, on the one hand, to avoid an open battle against an overwhelming enemy, when the enemy has concentrated all his forces at one spot, and yet, on the other, to take advantage of his unwieldiness and to attack him when and where he least expects it. Today we are faced with the relatively easy task of supporting student demonstrations in the streets of big cities; tomorrow we may, perhaps, have the more difficult task of supporting, for example, the unemployed movement in some particular area, and the day after to be at our posts in order to play a revolutionary part in a peasant uprising. Today we must take advantage of the tense political situation arising out of the government's campaign against the Zemstvo[32]; tomorrow we may have to support popular indignation against some tsarist bashi-bazouk on the rampage and help, by means of boycott, indictment, demonstrations, etc., to make things so hot for him as to force him into open retreat. Such a degree of combat readiness can be developed only through the constant activity of regular troops. If we join forces to produce a common newspaper, this work will train and bring into the foreground, not only the most skilful propagandists, but the most capable organisers, the most talented political party leaders capable, at the right moment, of releasing the slogan for the decisive struggle and of taking the lead in that struggle.

In conclusion, a few words to avoid possible misunderstanding. We have spoken continuously of systematic, planned preparation, yet it is by no means our intention to imply that the autocracy can

---

* It will be understood, of course, that these agents could work successfully only in the closest contact with the local committees (groups, study circles) of our Party. In general, the entire plan we project can, of course, be implemented only with the most active support of the committees which have on repeated occasions attempted to unite the Party and which, we are sure, will achieve this unification—if not today, then tomorrow, if not in one way, then in another.

be overthrown only by a regular siege or by organised assault. Such a view would be absurd and doctrinaire. On the contrary, it is quite possible, and historically much more probable, that the autocracy will collapse under the impact of one of the spontaneous outbursts or unforeseen political complications which constantly threaten it from all sides. But no political party that wishes to avoid adventurous gambles can base its activities on the anticipation of such outbursts and complications. We must go our own way, and we must steadfastly carry on our regular work, and the less our reliance on the unexpected, the less the chance of our being caught unawares by any "historic turns".

Written May 1901

Published in May 1901
in newspaper *Iskra* No. 4

Collected Works, Vol. 5

A TALK WITH DEFENDERS OF ECONOMISM

Below we publish in full, as received from one of our representatives,

"A letter to the Russian Social-Democratic Press.

"In response to the suggestion made by our comrades in exile that we express our views on *Iskra*, we have resolved to state the reasons for our disagreement with that organ.

"While recognising that the appearance of a special Social-Democratic organ specially devoted to questions of the political struggle is entirely opportune, we do not think that *Iskra*, which has undertaken this task, has performed it satisfactorily. The principal drawback of the paper, which runs like a scarlet thread through its columns, and which is the cause of all its other defects, large and small, is the exaggerated importance it attaches to the influence which the ideologists of the movement exert upon its various tendencies. At the same time, *Iskra* gives too little consideration to the material elements and the material environment of the movement, whose interaction creates a definite type of labour movement and determines its path, the path from which the ideologists, despite all their efforts, are incapable of diverting it, even if they are inspired by the finest theories and programmes.

"This defect becomes most marked when *Iskra* is compared with *Yuzhny Rabochy*,[33] which, like *Iskra*, raises the banner of political struggle but connects it with the preceding phase of the South-Russian working-class movement. Such a presentation of the question is alien to *Iskra*. It has set itself the task of fanning 'the spark into a great conflagration', but it forgets that necessary inflammable material and favourable environmental conditions are required for such a task. In dissociating itself completely from the 'Economists', *Iskra* loses sight of the fact that their activity prepared the ground for the workers' participation in the February and March events, upon which *Iskra* lays so much stress and, to all appearances, greatly exaggerates. While criticising adversely the activity of the Social-Democrats of the late nineties, *Iskra* ignores the fact that at that time the conditions were lacking for any work other than the struggle for minor demands, and ignores also the enormous educational significance of that struggle. *Iskra* is entirely wrong and unhistorical in its appraisement of that period and of the direction of the activities of the Russian Social-Democrats at the time, in identifying their tactics with those of Zubatov, in failing to differentiate between the 'struggle for minor demands', which widens and deepens the labour movement, and 'minor concessions', whose purpose was to paralyse every struggle and every movement.

"Thoroughly imbued with the sectarian intolerance so characteristic of ideologists in the infantile period of social movements, *Iskra* is ready to brand every disagreement with it, not only as a departure from Social-Democratic principles, but as desertion to the camp of the enemy. Of such a nature is its extremely indecent and most reprehensible attack upon *Rabochaya Mysl*, contained in the article on Zubatov, in which the latter's success among a certain section of the working class was attributed to that publication. Negatively disposed to the other Social-Democratic organisations, which differ from it in their views on the progress and the tasks of the Russian labour movement, *Iskra*, in the heat of controversy, at times forgets the truth and, picking on isolated unfortunate expressions, attributes to its opponents views they do not hold, emphasises points of disagreement that are frequently of little material importance, and obstinately ignores the numerous points of contact in views. We have in mind *Iskra*'s attitude towards *Rabocheye Dyelo*.

"*Iskra*'s excessive predilection for controversy is due primarily to its exaggerating the role of 'ideology' (programmes, theories ...) in the movement, and is partly an echo of the internecine squabbles that have flared up among Russian political exiles in Western Europe, of which they have hastened to inform the world in a number of polemical pamphlets and articles. In our opinion, these disagreements exercise almost no influence upon the actual course of the Russian Social-Democratic movement, except perhaps to damage it by bringing an undesirable schism into the midst of the comrades working in Russia. For this reason, we cannot but express our disapproval of *Iskra*'s fervent polemics, particularly when it oversteps the bounds of decency.

"This basic drawback of *Iskra* is also the cause of its inconsistency on the question of the attitude of Social-Democracy to the various social classes and tendencies. By theoretical reasoning, *Iskra* solved the problem of the immediate transition to the struggle against absolutism. In all probability it senses the difficulty of such a task for the workers under the present state of affairs but lacking the patience to wait until the workers will have gathered sufficient forces for this struggle, *Iskra* begins to seek allies in the ranks of the liberals and intellectuals. In this quest, it not infrequently departs from the class point of view obscures class antagonisms, and puts into the forefront the common nature of the discontent with the government, although the causes and the degree of the discontent vary considerably among the 'allies'. Such, for example, is *Iskra*'s attitude towards the Zemstvo. It tries to fan into flames of political struggle the Zemstvo's Frondian demonstrations, which are frequently called forth by the fact that the government pays more attention to the protection of industry than to the agrarian aspirations of the Zemstvo gentry,* and it promises the nobles that are dissatisfied with the government's sops the assistance of the working class, but it does not say a word about the class antagonism that exists between these social strata. It may be conceded that it is admissible to say that the Zemstvo is being roused and that it is an element fighting the government; but this must be stated so clearly and distinctly that no doubt will be left as to the character of a possible agreement with such elements. *Iskra*, however, approaches the question of our attitude towards the Zemstvo in a way that to our mind can only dim class-consciousness; for in this matter, like the advocates of liberalism and of the various cultural endeavours, *Iskra* goes against the fundamental task of Social-Democratic literature, which is, not to obscure class antagonism, but to criticise the bourgeois system and explain the class interests that divide it. Such, too, is *Iskra*'s attitude towards the student movement. And yet in other articles *Iskra* sharply condemns all 'compromise' and defends, for instance, the intolerant conduct of the Guesdists.

"We shall refrain from dwelling upon *Iskra*'s minor defects and blunders, but in conclusion we think it our duty to observe that we do not in the least desire by our criticism to belittle the significance which *Iskra* can acquire, nor do we

---

* Lenin's reference is to the liberal landlords, members of the Zemstvo Boards.—*Tr.*

close our eyes to its merits. We welcome it as a political. Social-Democratic newspaper in Russia. We regard one of its greatest merits to be its able explanation of the question of terror to which it devoted a number of timely articles. Finally, we cannot refrain from noting the exemplary, literary style in which Iskra is written, a thing so rare in illegal publications, its regular appearance, and the abundance of fresh and interesting material which it publishes.

"A group of comrades"

"September 1901

In the first place, we should like to say that we cordially welcome the straightforwardness and frankness of the authors of this letter. It is high time to stop playing at hide-and-seek, concealing one's Economist *"credo"* (as is done by a section of the Odessa Committee from which the "politicians" broke away), or declaring, as if in mockery of the truth, that at the present time "not a single Social-Democratic organisation is guilty of the sin of Economism" (*Two Conferences*, p. 32, published by *Rabocheye Dyelo*). And now to the matter.

The authors of the letter fall into the very same fundamental error as that made by *Rabocheye Dyelo* (see particularly issue No. 10). They are muddled over the question of the relations between the "material" (spontaneous, as *Rabocheye Dyelo* puts it) elements of the movement and the ideological (conscious, operating "according to plan"). They fail to understand that the "ideologist" is worthy of the name only when he *precedes* the spontaneous movement, points out the road, and is able ahead of all others to solve all the theoretical, political, tactical, and organisational questions which the "material elements" of the movement spontaneously encounter. In order truly to give "consideration to the material elements of the movement", one must view them critically, one must be able to point out the dangers and defects of spontaneity and *to elevate* it to the level of consciousness. To say, however, that ideologists (i.e., politically conscious leaders) cannot divert the movement from the path determined by the interaction of environment and elements is to ignore the simple truth that the conscious element *participates* in this interaction and in the determination of the path. Catholic and monarchist labour unions in Europe are also an inevitable result of the interaction of environment and elements, but it was the consciousness of priests and Zubatovs and not that of socialists that participated in this interaction. The theoretical views of the authors of this letter (like those of *Rabocheye Dyelo)* do not represent Marxism, but that parody of it which is nursed by our "Critics" and Bernsteinians who are unable to connect spontaneous evolution with conscious revolutionary activity.

In the prevailing circumstances of today this profound theoretical error inevitably leads to a great tactical error, which has brought incalculable damage to Russian Social-Democracy. It is a fact that the spontaneous awakening of the masses of the workers and (due to their influence) of other social strata has been taking place with astonishing rapidity during the past few years. The "material elements" of the movement have grown enormously even as compared with 1898,[34] but *the conscious leaders* (the Social-Democrats) *lag behind this growth.* This is the main cause of the crisis which Russian Social-Democracy is now experiencing. The mass (spontaneous) movement lacks "ideologists" sufficiently trained theoretically to be proof against all vacillations; it lacks leaders with such a broad political outlook, such revolutionary energy, and such organisational talent as to create a militant political party on the basis of the new movement.

All this in itself would, however, be but half the evil. Theoretical knowledge, political experience, and organising ability are things that can be acquired. If only the desire exists to study and acquire these qualities. But since the end of 1897, particularly since the autumn of 1898, there have come forward in the Russian Social-Democratic movement individuals and periodicals that not only close their eyes to this drawback, but that have declared it to be a special virtue, that have elevated the worship of, and servility towards, spontaneity to the dignity of a theory and are preaching that Social-Democrats must not march ahead of the movement, but should drag along *at the tail-end.* (These periodicals include not only *Rabochaya Mysl,* but *Rabocheye Dyelo,* which began with the "stages theory" and ended with the defence, as a matter of principle, of spontaneity, of the "full rights of the movement of the moment", of "tactics-as-process", etc.)

This was, indeed, a sad situation. It meant the emergence of a *separate trend,* which is usually designated as Economism (in the broad sense of the word), the principal feature of which is its incomprehension, even *defence, of lagging,* i.e., as we have explained, the lagging of the conscious leaders behind the spontaneous awakening of the masses. The characteristic features of this trend express themselves in the following: with respect to principles, in a vulgarisation of Marxism and in helplessness in the face of modern "criticism", that up-to-date species of opportunism; with respect to politics, in the striving to restrict political agitation and political struggle or to reduce them to petty activities, in the failure to understand that unless Social-Democrats take the leadership of the general democratic movement in *their own* hands, they will never be able to overthrow the autocracy; with respect to tactics, in utter instability (last spring *Rabocheye Dyelo* stood in amazement before the "new" question of terror, and only six months later, after considerable wavering and, as always, dragging along at the tail-end of the movement, did it express itself against terror, in a very ambiguous resolution); and with respect to organisation, in the failure

to understand that the mass character of the movement does not
diminish, but increases, our obligation to establish a strong and
centralised organisation of revolutionaries capable of leading the
preparatory struggle, every unexpected outbreak, and, finally, the
decisive assault. Against this trend we have conducted and will continue to conduct an irreconcilable struggle. The authors of the letter apparently
belong to this trend. They tell us that the economic struggle prepared the ground for the workers' participation in the demonstrations. True enough; but we appreciated sooner and more profoundly than all others the importance of this preparation, when, as
early as December 1900, in our first issue, we opposed the stages
theory,* and when, in February, in our second issue, immediately
after the drafting of the students into the army, and prior to the
demonstrations, we called upon the workers to come to the aid of
the students.** The February and March events did not "refute
the fears and alarms of *Iskra*" (as Martynov, who thereby displays
his utter failure to understand the question, thinks—*Rabocheye
Dyelo,* No. 10, p. 53), but wholly confirmed them, for the leaders
lagged behind the spontaneous rise of the masses and proved to be
unprepared for the fulfilment of their duties as leaders. Even at
the present time the preparations are far from adequate, and for
that reason all talk about "exaggerating the role of ideology" or
the role of the conscious element as compared with the spontaneous
element, etc., continues to exercise a most baneful influence upon
our Party.

No less harmful is the influence exerted by the talk, allegedly in
defence of the class point of view, about the need to lay less stress
on the general character of discontent manifested by the various
strata of the population against the government. On the contrary,
we are proud of the fact that *Iskra* rouses political discontent
among *all* strata of the population, and the only thing we regret
is that we are unable to do this on a much wider scale. It is not
true to say that in doing so, we obscure the class point of view; the
authors of the letter have not pointed to a single concrete instance
in evidence of this, nor can they do so. Social-Democracy, as the
vanguard in the struggle for democracy, must (notwithstanding the
opinion expressed in *Rabocheye Dyelo,* No. 10, p. 41) lead the activities of the various oppositional strata, explain to them the general political significance of their partial and professional conflicts
with the government, rally them to the support of the revolutionary party, and train from its own ranks leaders capable of exercising political influence upon all oppositional strata. Any renuncia-

---

* See *Collected Works*, Vol. 4, pp. 366-71.—*Ed.*
** Ibid., pp. 414-19.—*Ed.*

tion of this function, however florid the phrases about close, organic contact with the proletarian struggle, etc., with which it may deck itself, is tantamount to a fresh "defence of lagging", the defence of lagging behind the nation-wide democratic movement on the part of Social-Democrats; it is tantamount to a surrender of the leadership to bourgeois democracy. Let the authors of the letter ponder over the question as to why the events of last spring served so strongly to stimulate non-Social-Democratic revolutionary tendencies, instead of raising the authority and prestige of Social-Democracy.

Nor can we refrain from protesting against the astonishing short-sightedness displayed by the authors of the letter in regard to the controversies and internecine squabbles among the political exiles. They repeat the stale nonsense about the "indecency" of devoting to *Rabochaya Mysl* an article on Zubatov. Do they wish to deny that the spreading of Economism facilitates the tasks of the Zubatovs? In asserting this, however, we do not in the slightest "identify" the tactics of the Economists with those of Zubatov. As for the "political exiles" (if the authors of the letter were not so unpardonably careless concerning the continuity of ideas in the Russian Social-Democratic movement, they would have known that the warning about Economism sounded by the "political exiles", to be precise, by the Emancipation of Labour group,[35] has been strikingly confirmed!), note the manner in which Lassalle, who was active among the Rhine workers in 1852, judged the controversies of the exiles in London. Writing to Marx, he said:

"...The publication of your work against the 'big men', Kinkel, Ruge, etc., should hardly meet with any difficulties on the part of the police.... For, in my opinion, the government is not averse to the publication of such works, because it thinks that 'the revolutionaries will cut one another's throats'. Their bureaucratic logic neither suspects nor fears the fact that it is precisely internal Party struggles that lend a party strength and vitality; that the greatest proof of a party's weakness is its diffuseness and the blurring of clear demarcations; and that a party becomes stronger by purging itself" (letter from Lassalle to Marx, June 24, 1852).

Let the numerous complacent opponents of severity, irreconcilability, and fervent polemics, etc., take note!

In conclusion, we shall observe that in these remarks we have been able to deal only briefly with the questions in dispute. We intend to devote a special pamphlet to the analysis of these questions, which we hope will appear in the course of six weeks.

TWO TACTICS OF SOCIAL-DEMOCRACY IN THE DEMOCRATIC REVOLUTION[36]

PREFACE

In a revolutionary period it is very difficult to keep abreast of events which provide an astonishing amount of new material for an appraisal of the tactical slogans of revolutionary parties. The present pamphlet was written before the Odessa events.* We have already pointed out in *Proletary*[38] (No. 9—"Revolution Teaches")** that these events have forced even those Social-Democrats who created the "uprising-as-process" theory and who rejected propaganda for a provisional revolutionary government actually to go over, or begin to go over, to their opponents' side. Revolution undoubtedly teaches with a rapidity and thoroughness which appear incredible in peaceful periods of political development. And, what is particularly important, it teaches not only the leaders, but the masses as well.

There is not the slightest doubt that the revolution will teach Social-Democratism to the masses of the workers in Russia. The revolution will confirm the programme and tactics of Social-Democracy in actual practice by demonstrating the true nature of the various classes of society, by demonstrating the bourgeois character of our democracy and the real aspirations of the peasantry, who, while being revolutionary in the bourgeois-democratic sense, carry within themselves not the idea of "socialisation", but the seeds of a new class.struggle between the peasant bourgeoisie and the rural proletariat. The old illusions of the old Narodism, so clearly visible, for instance, in the draft programme of the "Socialist-Revolutionary Party"[39] on the question of the development of capitalism in Russia, the question of the democratic character of our "society", and the question of the significance of a complete victory of a peasant uprising—all these illusions will be completely and mercilessly dispelled by the revolution. For the

---

* The reference is to the mutiny on the armoured cruiser *Potemkin*.[37] (Author's note to the 1907 edition.—*Ed.*)
** See *Collected Works*, Vol. 9, p. 148.—*Ed.*

first time, the various classes will be given their real political baptism. These classes will emerge from the revolution with a definite political physiognomy, for they will have revealed themselves not only in the programme and tactical slogans of their ideologists but also in open political action by the masses.

Undoubtedly, the revolution will teach us, and will teach the masses of the people. But the question that now confronts a militant political party is: shall we be able to teach the revolution anything? Shall we be able to make use of the correctness of our Social-Democratic doctrine, of our bond with the only thoroughly revolutionary class, the proletariat, to put a proletarian imprint on the revolution, to carry the revolution to a real and decisive victory, not in word but in deed, and to paralyse the instability, half-heartedness, and treachery of the democratic bourgeoisie?

It is to this end that we must direct all our efforts, and the achievement of that end will depend, on the one hand, on the accuracy of our appraisal of the political situation and the correctness of our tactical slogans, and, on the other hand, on whether these slogans will be backed by the real fighting strength of the masses of the workers. All the usual, regular, and current work of all organisations and groups of our Party, the work of propaganda, agitation, and organisation, is directed towards strengthening and expanding the ties with the masses. Necessary as this work always is it cannot be considered adequate at a time of revolution. In such a contingency the working class feels an instinctive urge for open revolutionary action, and we must learn to set the aims of this action correctly, and then make these aims as widely known and understood as possible. It must not be forgotten that the current pessimism about our ties with the masses very often serves as a screen for bourgeois ideas regarding the proletariat's role in the revolution. Undoubtedly, we still have a great deal to do in educating and organising the working class; but now the gist of the matter is: where should we place the main political emphasis in this work of education and organisation? On the trade unions and legally existing associations, or on an insurrection, on the work of creating a revolutionary army and a revolutionary government? Both serve to educate and organise the working class. Both are, of course, necessary. But in the present revolution the problem amounts to this: which is to be emphasised in the work of educating and organising the working class, the former or the latter?

The outcome of the revolution depends on whether the working class will play the part of a subsidiary to the bourgeoisie, a subsidiary that is powerful in the force of its onslaught against the autocracy, but impotent politically, or whether it will play the part of leader of the people's revolution. The more intelligent representatives of the bourgeoisie are perfectly aware of this. That is why

Osvobozhdeniye[40] praises Akimovism, Economism in Social-Democracy, the trend which is *now* bringing the trade unions and legally existing associations to the forefront. That is why Mr. Struve (in *Osvobozhdeniye*, No. 72) welcomes the Akimovist tendency in the new-*Iskra*[41] ideas. That is why he comes down so heavily on the detested revolutionary narrowness of the decisions of the Third Congress of the Russian Social-Democratic Labour Party.[42]

It is exceptionally important at the present time for Social-Democrats to have correct tactical slogans for leading the masses. There is nothing more dangerous in a revolutionary period than belittling the importance of tactical slogans that are sound in principle. For example, *Iskra* in No. 104 actually goes over to the side of its opponents in the Social-Democratic movement, and yet, at the same time, it disparages the importance of slogans and tactical decisions that are ahead of the times and indicate the path along which the movement is proceeding, though with a number of failures, errors, etc. On the contrary, preparation of correct tactical decisions is of immense importance for a party which desires to lead the proletariat in the spirit of sound Marxist principles, and not merely to lag in the wake of events. In the resolutions of the Third Congress of the Russian Social-Democratic Labour Party and of the conference of the section that has split away from the Party,* we have the most precise, most carefully considered, and most complete expression of tactical views—views not casually expressed by individual writers, but accepted by the responsible representatives of the Social-Democratic proletariat. Our Party is in advance of all the others, for it has a precise and generally accepted programme. It must also set the other parties an example of a principled attitude to its tactical resolutions, as distinct from the opportunism of the democratic *Osvobozhdeniye* bourgeoisie, and the revolutionary phrase-mongering of the Socialist-Revolutionaries. It was only during the revolution that they suddenly thought of coming forward with a "draft" programme and of investigating for the first time whether it is a bourgeois revolution that is going on before their eyes.

That is why we think it the most urgent task of the revolutionary Social-Democrats carefully to study the tactical resolutions of the Third Congress of the Russian Social-Democratic Labour Party and of the Conference, define what deviations from the principles

---

* The Third Congress of the Russian Social-Democratic Labour Party (London, May 1905) was attended only by Bolsheviks, while Mensheviks alone participated in the "Conference" (Geneva, time the same). In the present pamphlet the latter are frequently referred to as the "new-*Iskra* group" because, while continuing to publish *Iskra*, they declared through their then adherent Trotsky that there was a gulf between the old and the new *Iskra*. (Author's note to the 1907 edition.—*Ed.*)

of Marxism they contain, and get a clear understanding of the Social-Democratic proletariat's concrete tasks in a democratic revolution. It is to this work that the present pamphlet is devoted.

The testing of our tactics from the standpoint of the principles of Marxism and of the lessons of the revolution is also necessary for those who really desire to pave the way for unity of tactics as a basis for the future complete unity of the whole Russian Social-Democratic Labour Party, and not to confine themselves solely to verbal admonitions.

N. Lenin

July 1905

1. AN URGENT POLITICAL QUESTION

At the present revolutionary juncture the question of the convocation of a popular constituent assembly is on the order of the
day. Opinions are divided as to how this question should be solved.
Three political trends are taking shape. The tsarist government
admits the necessity of convening representatives of the people, but
under no circumstances does it want to permit their assembly to
be popular and constituent. It seems willing to agree, if we are to
believe the newspaper reports on the work of the Bulygin Commission,[43] to a consultative assembly, which is to be elected without
freedom of agitation, and by a system of restrictive qualifications
or one that is restricted to certain social estates. Since it is led by
the Social-Democratic Party, the revolutionary proletariat demands
complete transfer of power to a constituent assembly, and for this
purpose strives to achieve not only universal suffrage and complete
freedom to conduct agitation, but also the immediate overthrow
of the tsarist government and its replacement by a provisional
revolutionary government. Finally, the liberal bourgeoisie, expressing its wishes through the leaders of the so-called "Constitutional-
Democratic Party", does not demand the overthrow of the tsarist
government; nor does it advance the slogan of a provisional government, or insist on real guarantees that the elections will be
absolutely free and fair and that the assembly of representatives
will be genuinely popular and genuinely constituent. As a matter
of fact, the liberal bourgeoisie, the only serious social support of
the *Osvobozhdeniye* trend, is striving to effect as peaceful a deal
as possible between the tsar and the revolutionary people, a deal,
moreover, that would give a maximum of power to itself, the bourgeoisie, and a minimum to the revolutionary people—the proletariat and the peasantry.

Such is the political situation at the present time. Such are the
three main political trends, corresponding to the three main social
forces in contemporary Russia. We have already shown on more

than one occasion in *Proletary* (Nos. 3, 4, 5)* how the *Osvobozhdeniye* group use pseudo-democratic phrases to cover up their half-hearted, or, to put it more bluntly and plainly, their treacherous, perfidious policy towards the revolution. Let us now see how the Social-Democrats appraise the tasks of the moment. Excellent material for this is provided by the two resolutions quite recently adopted by the Third Congress of the Russian Social-Democratic Labour Party and by the "Conference" of the Party's break-away section. The question as to which of these resolutions appraises the political situation more correctly and defines the tactics of the revolutionary proletariat more correctly is of enormous importance, and every Social-Democrat who is anxious to perform his duties intelligently as propagandist, agitator, and organiser must study this question with the closest attention disregarding all irrelevant considerations.

By the Party's tactics we mean the Party's political conduct, or the character, direction, and methods of its political activity. Tactical resolutions are adopted by Party congresses in order to accurately define the political conduct of the Party as a whole with regard to new tasks or in view of a new political situation. Such a new situation has been created by the revolution that has started in Russia, i.e., the complete, decisive, and open break between the overwhelming majority of the people and the tsarist government. The new question concerns the practical methods of convening a genuinely popular and a genuinely constituent assembly (the theoretical question concerning such an assembly was officially settled by Social-Democracy long ago, before all other parties, in its Party programme). Since the people have broken with the government and the masses realise the necessity of setting up a new order, the party which set itself the object of overthrowing the government must necessarily consider what government should replace the old, deposed government. There arises a *new* question concerning a provisional revolutionary government. To give a complete answer to this question the party of the class-conscious proletariat must clarify: 1) the *significance* of a provisional revolutionary government in the revolution now in progress and in the entire struggle of the proletariat in general; 2) its *attitude* towards a provisional revolutionary government; 3) the precise conditions of Social-Democratic *participation* in this government; 4) the conditions under which pressure is to be brought to bear on this government *from below*, i.e., in the event of there being no Social-Democrats in it. Only when all these questions have been clarified, will the political conduct of the party in this sphere be principled, clear, and firm.

---

* See *Collected Works*, Vol. 8, pp. 486-94, 511-25.—*Ed.*

Let us now consider how the resolution of the Third Congress of the Russian Social-Democratic Labour Party answers these questions. The following is the full text of the resolution:

"*Resolution on a Provisional Revolutionary Government*

"Whereas:

1) both the direct interests of the proletariat and those of its struggle for the ultimate aims of socialism require the fullest possible measure of political freedom, and, consequently, the replacement of the autocratic form of government by the democratic republic;

2) the establishment of a democratic republic in Russia is possible only as a result of a victorious popular insurrection whose organ will be a provisional revolutionary government, which alone will be capable of securing complete freedom of agitation during the election campaign and of convening a constituent assembly that will really express the will of the people, an assembly elected on the basis of universal and equal suffrage, direct elections and secret ballot;

3) under the present social and economic order this democratic revolution in Russia will not weaken but strengthen the domination of the bourgeoisie which at a certain juncture will inevitably go to any length to take away from the Russian proletariat as many of the gains of the revolutionary period as possible:

"Therefore the Third Congress of the Russian Social-Democratic Labour Party resolves:

a) that it is necessary to spread among the working class a concrete idea of the most probable course of the revolution, and of the necessity, at a certain moment in the revolution, for the appearance of a provisional revolutionary government, from which the proletariat will demand the realisation of all the immediate political and economic demands of our programme (the minimum programme);

b) that subject to the alignment of forces and other factors which cannot be exactly predetermined, representatives of our Party may participate in the provisional revolutionary government for the purpose of waging a relentless struggle against all counter-revolutionary attempts and of defending the independent interests of the working class;

c) that an indispensable condition for such participation is strict control of its representatives by the Party, and the constant safeguarding of the independence of Social-Democracy which strives for the complete socialist revolution, and, consequently, is irreconcilably opposed to all the bourgeois parties;

d) that irrespective of whether participation of Social-Democrats in the provisional revolutionary government is possible or not, we must propagate among the broadest sections of the proletariat the idea that the armed proletariat, led by the Social-Democratic Party, must bring to bear constant pressure on the provisional government for the purpose of defending, consolidating, and extending the gains of the revolution."

2. WHAT CAN WE LEARN FROM THE RESOLUTION OF THE THIRD CONGRESS OF THE R.S.D.L.P. ON A PROVISIONAL REVOLUTIONARY GOVERNMENT?

As is evident from its title, the resolution of the Third Congress of the Russian Social-Democratic Labour Party is devoted wholly and exclusively to the question of a provisional revolutionary government. Hence, the participation of Social-Democrats in a provisional revolutionary government constitutes part of that question. On the other hand, the resolution deals with a provisional revolutionary government only, and with nothing else; consequently, the question of the "conquest of power" in general, etc., does not at all come into the picture. Was the Congress right in eliminating this and similar questions? Undoubtedly it was, because the political situation in Russia does not by any means turn such questions into immediate issues. On the contrary, the whole people have now raised the issue of the overthrow of the autocracy and the convocation of a constituent assembly. Party congresses should take up and decide not issues which this or that writer has happened to mention opportunely or inopportunely, but such as are of vital political importance by reason of the prevailing conditions and the objective course of social development.

Of what significance is a provisional revolutionary government in the present revolution and in the general struggle of the proletariat? The resolution of the congress explains this by pointing at the very outset to the need for the "fullest possible measure of political liberty", both from the standpoint of the immediate interests of the proletariat and from the standpoint of the "final aims of socialism". And complete political liberty requires that the tsarist autocracy be replaced by a democratic republic, as our Party programme has already recognised. The stress the congress resolution lays on the slogan of a democratic republic is necessary both as a matter of logic and in point of principle, for it is precisely complete liberty that the proletariat, as the foremost champion of democracy, is striving to attain. Moreover, it is all the more advisable to stress this at the present time, because right now the monarchists, namely, the so-called Constitutional-"Democratic" or the *Osvobozhdeniye* Party in our country, are flying the flag of "democracy". To establish a republic it is absolutely necessary to have an assembly of people's representatives, which must be a popular (i.e., elected on the basis of universal and equal suffrage, direct elections, and secret ballot) and constituent assembly. That is exactly what is recognised further on in the congress resolution. However, the resolution does not stop at that. To establish a new order "that will really express the will of the people" it is not enough to term a representative assembly a constituent assembly. Such an assembly must have the authority and power to "constitute". Conscious of this the congress resolution does not confine itself to the formal slogan of a "constituent assembly", but adds the material conditions which alone will enable such an assembly to carry out its task properly. This specification of the conditions enabling an assembly that is constituent in name to become one in fact is imperatively necessary, for, as we have more than once pointed out, the liberal bourgeoisie, as represented by the Constitutional-Monarchist Party, is deliberately distorting the slogan of a popular constituent assembly, and reducing it to a hollow phrase.

The congress resolution states that a provisional revolutionary government *alone*, and one, moreover, that will be the organ of a victorious popular insurrection, can secure full freedom to conduct an election campaign and convene an assembly that will really express the will of the people. Is this thesis correct? Whoever took it into his head to dispute it would have to assert that it is possible for the tsarist government not to side with reaction, that it is capable of being neutral during the elections, that it will see to it that the will of the people really finds expression. Such assertions are so absurd that no one would venture to defend them openly; but they are being surreptitiously smuggled in under liberal colours by our *Osvobozhdeniye* gentry. Somebody must convene the constituent assembly; somebody must guarantee the freedom and fairness of the elections; somebody must invest such an assembly with full power and authority. Only a revolutionary government, which is the organ of the insurrection, can desire this in all sincerity, and be capable of doing all that is required to achieve this. The tsarist government will inevitably oppose it. A liberal government which has come to terms with the tsar and which does not rely in full on the popular uprising cannot sincerely desire this, and could not accomplish it, even if it most sincerely desired to. Therefore, the Congress resolution gives the only correct and entirely consistent democratic slogan.

But an appraisal of a provisional revolutionary government's significance would be incomplete and wrong if the class nature of the democratic revolution were lost sight of. The resolution, therefore, adds that a revolution will strengthen the rule of the bourgeoisie. This is inevitable under the present, i.e., capitalist, social and economic, system. And the strengthening of the bourgeoisie's rule over a proletariat that has secured some measure of political liberty must inevitably lead to a desperate struggle between them for power, must lead to desperate attempts on the part of the bourgeoisie "to take away from the proletariat the gains of the revolutionary period". Therefore, the proletariat, which is in the van of the struggle for democracy and heads that struggle, must not for a single moment forget the new antagonisms inherent in bourgeois democracy, or the new struggle.

Thus, the section of the resolution which we have just reviewed fully appraises the significance of a provisional revolutionary government both in its relation to the struggle for freedom and for a republic, in its relation to a constituent assembly, and in its relation to the democratic revolution which clears the ground for a new class struggle.

The next question is that of the proletariat's attitude in general towards a provisional revolutionary government. The congress resolution answers this first of all by directly advising the Party to spread among the working class the conviction that a provisional revolutionary government is necessary. The working class must be made aware of this necessity. Whereas the "democratic" bourgeoisie keeps in the background the question of the overthrow of the tsarist government, we must bring it to the fore and insist on the need for a provisional revolutionary government. Moreover, we must outline for such a government a programme of action that will conform with the objective conditions of the present period and with the aims of proletarian democracy. This programme is the *entire* minimum programme of our Party, the programme of the immediate political and economic reforms which, on the one hand, can be fully realised on the basis of the existing social and economic relationships and, on the other hand, are requisite for the next step forward, for the achievement of socialism.

Thus, the resolution clearly defines the nature and the purpose of a provisional revolutionary government. In origin and basic character such a government must be the organ of a popular uprising. Its formal purpose must be to serve as an instrument for convening a national constituent assembly. The content of its activities must be the implementation of the minimum programme of proletarian democracy, the only programme capable of safeguarding the interests of a people that has risen in revolt against the autocracy.

It might be argued that a provisional government, being only provisional, cannot carry out a constructive programme that has not yet received the approval of the entire people. Such an argument would merely be the sophistry of reactionaries and "absolutists". To refrain from carrying out a constructive programme means tolerating the existence of the feudal regime of a corrupt autocracy. Such a regime could be tolerated only by a government of traitors to the cause of the revolution, but not by a government that is the organ of a popular insurrection. It would be mockery for anyone to propose that we should refrain from exercising freedom of assembly pending the confirmation of such freedom by a constituent assembly, on the plea that the constituent assembly might not confirm freedom of assembly. It is equal mockery to object to the immediate execution of the minimum programme by a provisional revolutionary government.

Finally, we will note that the resolution, by making implementation of the minimum programme the provisional revolutionary government's task, eliminates the absurd and semi-anarchist ideas of giving immediate effect to the maximum programme, and the conquest of power for a socialist revolution. The degree of Russia's economic development (an objective condition), and the degree of class-consciousness and organisation of the broad masses of the proletariat (a subjective condition inseparably bound up with the objective condition) make the immediate and complete emancipation of the working class impossible. Only the most ignorant people can close their eyes to the bourgeois nature of the democratic revolution which is now taking place; only the most naïve optimists can forget how little as yet the masses of the workers are informed about the aims of socialism and the methods of achieving it. We are all convinced that the emancipation of the working classes must be won by the working classes themselves; a socialist revolution is out of the question unless the masses become class-conscious and organised, trained and educated in an open class struggle against the entire bourgeoisie. Replying to the anarchists' objections that we are putting off the socialist revolution, we say: we are not putting it off, but are taking the first step towards it in the only possible way, along the only correct path, namely, the path of a democratic republic. Whoever wants to reach socialism by any other path than that of political democracy, will inevitably arrive at conclusions that are absurd and reactionary both in the economic and the political sense. If any workers ask us at the appropriate moment why we should not go ahead and carry out our maximum programme we shall answer by pointing out how far from socialism the masses of the democratically-minded peoples still are, how undeveloped class antagonisms still are, and how unorganised the proletarians still are. Organise hundreds of thousands of workers all over Russia; get the millions to sympathise with our programme! Try to do this without confining yourselves to high-sounding but hollow anarchist phrases—and you will see at once that achievement of this organisation and the spread of this socialist enlightenment depend on the fullest possible achievement of democratic transformations.

Let us continue. Once the significance of a provisional revolutionary government and the attitude of the proletariat toward it have been made clear, the following question arises: is it permissible for us to participate in such a government (action from above) and, if so, under what conditions? What should be our action from below? The resolution supplies precise answers to both these questions. It emphatically declares that it is *permissible* in principle for Social-Democrats to participate in a provisional revolutionary government (during the period of a democratic revolution, the period of struggle for a republic). By this declaration we once and for all dissociate ourselves both from the anarchists, who answer this question in the negative in principle, and from the tail-enders in Social-Democracy (like Martynov and the new-*Iskra* supporters), who have *tried to frighten* us with the prospect of a situation in which it might prove necessary for us to participate in such a government. By this declaration the Third Congress of the Russian Social-Democratic Labour Party irrevocably rejected the new-*Iskra* idea that the participation of Social-Democrats in a provisional revolutionary government would be a variety of Millerandism, that it is impermissible in principle, as sanctifying the bourgeois order. etc.

It stands to reason, however, that the question of permissibility in principle does not solve the question of practical expediency. Under what conditions is this new form of struggle—the struggle "from above", recognised by the Party Congress—expedient? It goes without saying that it is impossible at present to speak of concrete conditions, such as the relation of forces, etc., and the resolution, naturally, refrains from defining these conditions in advance. No intelligent person would venture at present to predict anything on this subject. What we can and must do is to determine the nature and aim of our participation. That is what is done in the resolution, which points to the two purposes for which we participate: 1) a relentless struggle against counter-revolutionary attempts, and 2) the defence of the independent interests of the working class. At a time when the liberal bourgeoisie is beginning to talk with such zeal about the psychology of reaction (see Mr. Struve's most instructive "Open Letter" in *Osvobozhdeniye*, No. 71) in an attempt to frighten the revolutionary people and induce it to show compliance towards the autocracy—at such a time it is particularly appropriate for the party of the proletariat to call attention to the task of waging a real war against counter-revolution. In the final analysis force alone settles the great problems of political liberty and the class struggle, and it is our business to prepare and organise this force and to employ it actively, not only for defence but also for attack. The long reign of political reaction in Europe, which has lasted almost uninterruptedly since the days of the Paris Commune, has made us too greatly accustomed to the idea that action can proceed only "from below", has too greatly

inured us to seeing only defensive struggles. We have now undoubtedly entered a new era—a period of political upheavals and
revolutions has begun. In a period such as that which Russia is
now passing through, it is impermissible to confine ourselves to
old, stereotyped formulas. We must propagate the idea of action
from above, must prepare for the most energetic, offensive action,
and must study the conditions for and forms of such action. The
congress resolution brings two of these conditions into the forefront: one refers to the formal aspect of Social-Democratic participation in a provisional revolutionary government (strict control
by the Party over its representatives), the other to the nature of
such participation (without for an instant losing sight of the aim
of effecting a complete socialist revolution).

Having thus explained all aspects of the Party's policy with
regard to action "from above"—this new, hitherto almost unprecedented method of struggle—the resolution also provides for the
eventuality that we shall not be able to act from above. We must
in any case exercise pressure on the provisional revolutionary
government from below. To be able to exercise this pressure from
below, the proletariat must be armed—for in a revolutionary situation matters develop with exceptional rapidity to the stage of open
civil war—and must be led by the Social-Democratic Party. The
object of its armed pressure is "to defend, consolidate, and extend
the gains of the revolution", i.e., those gains which from the standpoint of the proletariat's interests must consist in fulfilling the
whole of our minimum programme.

With this, we conclude our brief analysis of the Third Congress
resolution on a provisional revolutionary government. As the reader
will see, the resolution explains the importance of this new question, the attitude of the party of the proletariat toward it, and the
policy the party must pursue both within a provisional revolutionary government and outside it.

Let us now consider the corresponding resolution of the "Conference".

3. WHAT IS MEANT BY "THE REVOLUTION'S DECISIVE VICTORY OVER TSARISM"?

The resolution of the "Conference" is devoted to the question:
*"The conquest of power and participation in a provisional govern-
ment."** As we have already pointed out, there is confusion in the
very manner in which the question is presented. On the one hand,

---

* The full text of this resolution can be reconstructed by the reader from the
quotations given on pp. 400, 403, 407, 431 and 433 of the pamphlet. (Author's note
to the 1907 edition. See pp. 63, 68, 72, 99, 102-103 of the present volume.—*Ed.*)

the question is presented in a narrow way: it deals only with our participation in a provisional government and not with the Party's tasks in regard to a provisional revolutionary government in general. On the other hand, two totally different questions are confused, viz., the question of our participation in one of the stages of the *democratic* revolution and the question of the *socialist* revolution. Indeed, the "conquest of power" by Social-Democracy is precisely a socialist revolution, nor can it be anything else if we use these words in their direct and usual meaning. If, however, we are to understand these words to mean the conquest of power for a democratic revolution and not for a socialist revolution, then what is the point in talking not only about participation in a provisional revolutionary government but also about the "conquest of power" *in general*? Obviously our "conferees" were themselves not very certain as to what they shóuld talk about—the democratic or the socialist revolution. Those who have followed the literature on this question know that this confusion was started by Comrade Martynov in his notorious *Two Dictatorships*; the new-Iskrists are reluctant to recall the manner in which this question was presented (even before January 9)[44] in that model of tail-ender writing. Nevertheless, there can be no doubt that it exerted an ideological influence on the conference.

But enough about the title of the resolution. Its contents reveal errors incomparably more serious and profound. Here is the first part:

"A decisive victory of the revolution over tsarism may be marked either by the establishment of a provisional government, which will emerge from a victorious popular insurrection, or by the revolutionary initiative of a representative institution of one kind or another, which, under direct revolutionary pressure from the people, decides to set up a popular constituent assembly."

Thus, we are told that a decisive victory of the revolution over tsarism may be marked either by a victorious insurrection, or ... by a representative institution's decisiun to set up a constituent assembly! What does that mean? How are we to understand it? A decisive victory may be marked by a "decision" to set up a constituent assembly?? And such a "victory" is put side by side with the establishment of a provisional government which will "emerge from a victorious popular insurrection"!! The conference failed to note that a *victorious* popular insurrection and the *establishment* of a provisional government would signify the victory of the revolution *in actual fact*, whereas a "decision" to set up a constituent assembly would signify a victory of the revolution *in words* only.

The conference of the new-*Iskra* Mensheviks fell into the very error that the liberals, the *Osvobozhdeniye* group, are constantly making. The *Osvobozhdeniye* group prattle about a "constituent" assembly, bashfully shutting their eyes to the fact that power and authority remain in the hands of the tsar and forgetting that to "constitute" one must possess the *power* to do so. The conference also forgot that it is a far cry from a "decision" adopted by representatives—no matter who they are—to the fulfilment of that decision. The conference also forgot that while power remains in the hands of the tsar all decisions of any representatives whatsoever will remain empty and miserable prattle, as was the case with the "decisions" of the Frankfort Parliament,[45] famous in the history of the German Revolution of 1848. In his *Neue Rheinische Zeitung*[46] Marx, the representative of the revolutionary proletariat, castigated the Frankfort *Osvobozhdeniye*-type liberals with merciless sarcasm, precisely because they uttered fine words, adopted all sorts of democratic "decisions", "constituted" all kinds of liberties, while in fact they left power in the hands of the king and failed to organise an armed struggle against the military forces at the king's disposal. And while the Frankfort-*Osvobozhdeniye* liberals were prattling, the king bided his time and consolidated his military forces, and the counter-revolution relying on real force utterly routed the democrats, with all their fine "decisions".

The conference put on a par with a decisive victory the very thing that lacks the essential condition for victory. How was it possible for Social-Democrats, who recognise the republican programme of our Party, to commit such an error? To understand this strange phenomenon we must turn to the Third Congress's resolution on the break-away section of the Party.* This resolution

* We cite this resolution in full. "The congress places on record that since the time of the Party's fight against Economism certain trends have survived in the R.S.D.L.P. which are akin to Economism in varying degrees and respects, and betray a common tendency to belittle the importance of the class-conscious elements in the proletarian struggle and to subordinate it to the element of spontaneity. On questions of organisation the representatives of these trends put forward, in theory, the organisation-as-process principle which is out of harmony with methodically conducted Party work, while in practice they systematically deviate from Party discipline in very many cases, and in other cases preach to the least enlightened section of the Party the idea of a wide application of the elective principle, without taking into consideration the objective conditions of Russian life, and so strive to undermine the only basis for Party ties that is possible at the present time. In tactical questions they betray a striving to narrow the scope of Party work, declaring their opposition to the Party pursuing completely independent tactics in relation to the liberal-bourgeois parties, denying that it is possible and desirable for our Party to assume the role of organiser in the people's insurrection and opposing the participation of the Party in a provisional democratic-revolutionary government under any conditions whatsoever.

"The congress instructs all Party members everywhere to conduct an energetic ideological struggle against such partial deviations from the principles of revolutionary Social-Democracy; at the same time, however, it is of the opinion that persons who share such views to any degree may belong to Party organisations on the indispensable condition that they recognise the Party congresses and the Party Rules and wholly submit to Party discipline." (Author's note to the 1907 edition.—*Ed.*)

refers to the fact that various trends "akin to Economism" exist in our Party. Our "conferees" (it is not fortuitous that they are under the ideological guidance of Martynov) talk of the revolution in exactly the same way as the Economists talked of the political struggle or the eight-hour day. The Economists immediately brought forward the "theory of stages": 1) the struggle for rights, 2) political agitation, 3) political struggle; or, 1) a ten-hour day, 2) a nine-hour day, 3) an eight-hour day. The results of this "tactics-as-process" are sufficiently well known to all. Now we are invited to make a preliminary and neat division of the revolution as well into the following stages: 1) the tsar convenes a representative institution; 2) this institution "decides" under pressure of the "people" to set up a constituent assembly; 3) ... the Mensheviks have not yet agreed among themselves as to the third stage; they have forgotten that the revolutionary pressure of the people will meet with the counter-revolutionary pressure of tsarism and that therefore either the "decision" will remain unfulfilled or the issue will be decided after all by the victory or the defeat of a popular insurrection. The conference resolution duplicates the following Economist reasoning: a decisive victory of the workers may be marked either by the realisation of the eight-hour day in a revolutionary way, or by the granting of a ten-hour day and a "decision" to go over to a nine-hour day.... The duplication is perfect.

The objection may be made to us that the authors of the resolution did not mean *to place on a par* the victory of an insurrection and the "decision" of a representative institution convened by the tsar, and that they only wanted to provide for the Party's tactics in either case. To this we shall answer: 1) The text of the resolution plainly and unambiguously describes the *decision* of a representative institution as "a decisive victory of the revolution over tsarism". Perhaps that is the result of careless wording; perhaps it could be corrected after consulting the minutes, but, until corrected, the present wording can have only one meaning, and that meaning is entirely in keeping with the *Osvobozhdeniye* line of reasoning. 2) The *Osvobozhdeniye* line of reasoning into which the authors of the resolution have drifted stands out in far greater relief in other literary productions of the new-*Iskra* group. For instance, in its article "The Zemsky Sobor* and our Tactics", *Sotsial-Demokrat*,[47] organ of the Tiflis Committee (published in the Georgian language; praised by *Iskra* in No. 100), goes so far as to say that "tactics" "which would make the Zemsky Sobor our centre of action" (about the convocation of which, we may add, nothing definite is known as yet!) "*are more to our advantage*" than the "tactics" of insurrection and the establishment of a provisional

* National Assembly.—*Ed.*

revolutionary government. We shall again refer to this article later.
3) No objection can be made to a preliminary discussion of the
tactics the Party should adopt both in the event of the victory of
the revolution and in the event of its defeat, both in the event of
a successful insurrection and in the event of the insurrection failing to develop into a serious force. It is possible that the tsarist
government will succeed in convening a representative assembly
for the purpose of striking a deal with the liberal bourgeoisie; providing for that eventuality, the Third Congress resolution speaks
plainly about "hypocritical policy", "pseudo-democracy", "a travesty of popular representation, such as the so-called Zemsky
Sobor".* But the whole point is that this is not said in a resolution
on a provisional revolutionary government, for it had nothing to
do with a provisional revolutionary government. This eventuality
defers the problem of the insurrection and of the establishment of
a provisional revolutionary government; it alters this problem, etc.
The point at issue today is not that all kinds of combinations are
possible, that both victory and defeat are possible or that there
may be direct or circuitous paths; the point is that it is impermissible for a Social-Democrat to cause confusion in workers' minds

---

* The following is the text of this resolution on the attitude towards the
tactics of the government on the eve of the revolution:
"Whereas for purposes of self-preservation, the government, during the present
revolutionary period, while intensifying the usual measures of repression directed
mainly against the class-conscious elements of the proletariat, at the same time
1) tries by means of concessions and promises of reform to corrupt the working
class politically and thereby to divert it from the revolutionary struggle; 2) with
the same object clothes its hypocritical policy of concessions in pseudo-democratic
forms, ranging from an invitation to the workers to elect their representatives
to commissions and conferences, to the establishment of a travesty of popular
representation, such as the so-called Zemsky Sobor; 3) organises the so-called
Black Hundreds and incites against the revolution all those elements of the
people in general who are reactionary, ignorant, or blinded by racial or religious
hatred:
"The Third Congress of the R.S.D.L.P resolves to call on all Party organisations:
a) while exposing the reactionary purpose of the government's concessions to
emphasise in their propaganda and agitation the fact that, on the one hand,
these concessions were wrested by force, and, on the other, that it is absolutely
impossible for the autocracy to grant reforms satisfactory to the proletariat;
b) taking advantage of the election campaign to explain to the workers
the real significance of these governmental measures and to show that it is
necessary for the proletariat to convene by revolutionary means a constituent
assembly on the basis of universal and equal suffrage, direct elections and a
secret ballot;
c) to organise the proletariat for the immediate realisation in a revolutionary
way of the eight-hour working day and of the other immediate demands of the
working class;
d) to organise armed resistance to the actions of the Black Hundreds and,
in general, of all reactionary elements led by the government." (Author's note
to the 1907 edition.—*Ed.*)

as to which is the genuinely revolutionary path; that it is impermissible to describe as a decisive victory, as *Osvobozhdeniye* does, something which lacks the *main* condition for victory. It is possible that we shall win even the eight-hour day, not at one stroke, but only in a long and roundabout way; but what would you say of a man who calls such impotence, such weakness as renders the proletariat *incapable* of counteracting procrastination, delays, haggling, treachery, and reaction—a victory for the workers? It is possible that the Russian revolution will end in an "abortive constitution", as was once stated in *Vperyod*,* but can this justify a Social-Democrat, who on the eve of a decisive struggle would call this abortion a "decisive victory over tsarism"? It is possible that at worst we shall not only fail to win a republic but that even the constitution will be illusory, a constitution "*à la* Shipov",[48] but would it be pardonable for a Social-Democrat to tone down our republican slogan?

Of course, the new-Iskrists have not as yet gone so far as to tone it down. But the degree to which the revolutionary spirit has abandoned them, the degree to which lifeless pedantry has blinded them to the militant tasks of the moment, is most vividly shown by the fact that in their resolution they, of all things, *forgot* to say a word about the republic. This is incredible but it is a fact. All the slogans of Social-Democracy were endorsed, repeated, explained, and presented in detail in the various resolutions of the conference—even the election of shop-stewards and deputies by the workers was not forgotten, but they simply found no occasion to mention the republic in a resolution on a provisional revolutionary government. To talk of the "victory" of the people's insurrection, of the establishment of a provisional government without indicating what these "steps" and acts have to do with winning a republic amounts to writing a resolution with the intention of crawling along in the wake of the proletarian movement, and not of giving guidance to the proletariat's struggle.

To sum up: the first part of the resolution 1) gave no explanation whatever of the significance of a provisional revolutionary government from the standpoint of the struggle for a republic and of securing a genuinely popular and genuinely constituent assembly; 2) quite confused the democratic consciousness of the prole-

---

* The newspaper *Vperyod*, which was published in Geneva, began to appear in January 1905 as the organ of the Bolshevik section of the Party. From January to May eighteen issues appeared. In May by virtue of the decision of the Third Congress of the Russian Social-Democratic Labour Party, *Proletary* replaced *Vperyod* as the Central Organ of the R.S.D.L.P. (This congress took place in London, in May; the Mensheviks did not appear there but organised their own "conference" in Geneva.) (Author's note to the 1907 edition.—*Ed*.)

tariat by placing on a par with revolution's decisive victory over tsarism a state of affairs in which precisely the main condition for a real victory is lacking.

4. THE ABOLITION OF THE MONARCHY. THE REPUBLIC

Let us go over to the next section of the resolution:

"... in either case such a victory will inaugurate a new phase in the revolutionary epoch.

"The final abolition of the entire regime of the monarchy and social estates in the process of mutual struggle between the elements of politically emancipated bourgeois society for the satisfaction of their social interests and for the direct acquisition of power—such is the task in this new phase which the objective conditions of social development spontaneously evoke.

"Therefore, a provisional government that would undertake to carry out the tasks of this revolution, bourgeois in its historical nature, would, in regulating the mutual struggle between antagonistic classes of a nation in the process of emancipation, not only have to advance revolutionary development, but also to combat factors in that development threatening the foundations of the capitalist system."

Let us examine this section which forms an independent part of the resolution. The basic idea in the arguments quoted above coincides with the one set forth in the third clause of the congress resolution. However, collation of these parts of the two resolutions will at once reveal the following radical difference between them. The congress resolution, which briefly describes the social and economic basis of the revolution, concentrates attention entirely on the clear-cut struggle of classes for definite gains, and places in the forefront the militant tasks of the proletariat. The resolution of the conference, which carries a long, nebulous, and confused description of the socio-economic basis of the revolution, speaks very vaguely about a struggle for definite gains, and leaves the militant tasks of the proletariat completely in the background. The resolution of the conference speaks of the abolition of the old order in the process of mutual struggle among the various elements of society. The congress resolution says that we, the party of the proletariat, must effect this abolition; that only the establishment of a democratic republic signifies genuine abolition of the old order; that we must win that republic; that we shall fight for it and for complete liberty, not only against the autocracy, but also against the bourgeoisie, when it attempts (and it will surely do so) to wrest our gains from us. The congress resolution calls on a definite class to wage a struggle for a precisely defined immediate aim. The conference resolution discourses on the mutual struggle of various forces. One resolution expresses the psychology of active struggle, the other that of the passive onlooker; one resounds with the call for live action, the other is steeped in lifeless pedantry. Both resolutions state that the present revolution is only our first step, which will be followed by a second; but from this, one resolution draws the conclusion that we must take this first step all the sooner, get it over all the sooner, win a republic, mercilessly crush the counter-revolution, and prepare the ground for the second step. The other resolution, however, oozes, so to speak, with verbose descriptions of the first step and (excuse the crude expression) simply masticates it. The congress resolution takes the old, yet eternally new, ideas of Marxism (the bourgeois nature of a democratic revolution) as a preface or first premise, whence it draws conclusions as to the progressive tasks of the progressive class, which is fighting both for the democratic and for the socialist revolution. The conference resolution does not go beyond the preface chewing it over and over again, and trying to be clever about it.

This is the very distinction which has long divided the Russian Marxists into two wings: the moralising and the militant wings of the old days of "legal Marxism", and the economic and political wings of the period of the nascent mass movement. From the correct Marxist premise concerning the deep economic roots of the class struggle in general and of the political struggle in particular, the Economists have drawn the singular conclusion that we must turn our backs on the political struggle and retard its development, narrow its scope, and reduce its aims. The political wing, on the contrary, has drawn a different conclusion from these same premises, namely, that the deeper the roots of our present struggle, the more widely, the more boldly, the more resolutely, and with greater initiative must we wage this struggle. We have the very same controversy before us now, only under different circumstances and in a different form. From the premises that a democratic revolution is far from being a socialist revolution, that the poor and needy are by no means the only ones to be "interested" in it, that it is deeply rooted in the inescapable needs and requirements of the *whole* of bourgeois society—from these premises we draw the conclusion that the advanced class must formulate its democratic aims all the more boldly, express them all the more sharply and completely, put forward the immediate slogan of a republic, and popularise the idea of the need to establish a provisional revolutionary government and to crush the counter-revolution ruthlessly. Our opponents, the new-*Iskra* group, however, deduce from these very same premises that the democratic conclusions should not be expressed fully, that the republic may be omitted from the practical slogans, that we can refrain from popularising the idea of the need for a provisional revolutionary government, that a mere decision to convene a constituent assembly can be termed a decisive victory,

that there is no need to advance the task of combating counter-
revolution as our active aim, so that it may be submerged in a
nebulous (and, as we shall presently see, wrongly formulated)
reference to a "process of mutual struggle". This is not the language
of political leaders, but of archive fogeys.

The more closely one examines the various formulations in the
resolution of the new-*Iskra* group, the clearer its aforementioned
basic features become. We are told, for instance, of a "process of
mutual struggle between the elements of politically emancipated
bourgeois society". Bearing in mind the subject this resolution
deals with (a provisional revolutionary government) one asks in
astonishment, "If you are referring to the process of mutual struggle, how can you keep silent about the elements which are politically *enslaving* bourgeois society? Do the 'conferees' really imagine
that, since they have assumed the revolution will be victorious,
these elements have already disappeared?" Such an idea would be
absurd in general and an expression of the greatest political naïveté
and political short-sightedness in particular. After the revolution's
victory over counter-revolution the latter will not disappear; on
the contrary, it will inevitably start a new and even more desperate struggle. Since the purpose of our resolution is to analyse the
tasks that will confront us when the revolution is victorious, it is
our duty to devote tremendous attention to the tasks of repelling
counter-revolutionary attacks (as is done in the congress resolution), and not to submerge these immediate, urgent, and vital
political tasks of a militant party in general discussions on what
will happen *after* the present revolutionary period, or what will
happen when a "politically *emancipated* society" already exists.
Just as the Economists would, by repeating the truism that politics
are subordinated to economics, cover up their incapacity to understand urgent political tasks, so the new-*Iskra* group, by repeating
the truism that struggles will take place in a politically *emancipated* society, cover up their incapacity to understand the urgent
revolutionary tasks of that society's political *emancipation*.

Take the expression "the final abolition of the whole regime of
the monarchy and the social-estates". In plain language the final
abolition of the monarchist system means the establishment of a
democratic republic. But our good Martynov and his admirers
think that this expression is far too clear and simple. They insist
on making it "deeper" and putting it more "cleverly". As a result,
we get, on the one hand, ridiculous and vain efforts to appear
profound; on the other hand, we get a description instead of a
slogan, a kind of melancholy retrospection instead of a stirring
appeal to march forward. We get the impression not of living
people eager to fight for a republic here and now, but of so many

withered mummies who, *sub specie aeternitatis,** consider the question from the *plusquamperfectum* viewpoint.

Let us continue: "... the provisional government ... would undertake to carry out the tasks of this ... bourgeois revolution". ... Here we at once see the result of our conferees having overlooked a concrete question confronting the proletariat's political leaders. The concrete question of a provisional revolutionary government has been obscured from their field of vision by the question of the future series of governments which will carry out the aims of the bourgeois revolution in general. If you want to consider the question "historically", the example of any European country will show you that it was a series of governments, by no means "provisional", that carried out the historical aims of the bourgeois revolution, that even governments which defeated the revolution were nevertheless forced to carry out the historical aims of that defeated revolution. But what you speak of is not called a "provisional revolutionary government": that is the name given to the government of a revolutionary epoch, one that immediately replaces the overthrown government and rests on the people's insurrection, and not on some kind of representative institution coming from the people. A provisional revolutionary government is the organ of struggle for the immediate victory of the revolution, for the immediate repulsion of attempts at counter-revolution, and not at all an organ for the implementation of the historical aims of the bourgeois revolution in general. Let us leave it to the future historians of a future *Russkaya Starina*[49] to determine exactly what aims of the bourgeois revolution we, or some government or other, shall have achieved—there will be time enough to do that thirty years from now; at present we must put forward slogans and give practical directives for the struggle for a republic and for the proletariat's most active participation in that struggle.

For the reasons stated, the final propositions in the foregoing section of the resolution quoted above are also unsatisfactory. The expression that the provisional government would have to "regulate" the mutual struggle among the antagonistic classes is most inapt, or at any rate awkwardly put; Marxists should not use such liberal-*Osvobozhdeniye* formulas, which would have us believe that it is possible to have governments which serve not as organs of the class struggle but as its "regulators".... The government would "not only have to advance revolutionary development but also to combat factors in that development threatening the foundations of the capitalist system". But it is the proletariat, in whose name the resolution speaks, that constitutes this "factor"! Instead of indicating just how the proletariat should "advance revolutionary

---

* From the viewpoint of eternity (Latin).—*Ed.*

development" at the present time (advance it farther than the constitutionalist bourgeoisie would care to go), instead of advice to make definite preparations for the struggle against the bourgeoisie when the latter turns against the conquests of the revolution, we are offered a general description of a process, a description which says nothing about the concrete aims of *our* activity. The new-*Iskra* manner of expressing its views reminds one of Marx's opinion (stated in his famous Theses on Feuerbach)[50] of the old materialism, which was alien to the ideas of dialectics. The philosophers have only *interpreted* the world in various ways, said Marx; the point, however, is to *change* it. Similarly, the new-*Iskra* group can give a tolerable description and explanation of the process of struggle taking place before their eyes, but they are altogether incapable of giving a correct slogan for this struggle. Good marchers but poor leaders, they disparage the materialist conception of history by ignoring the active, leading, and guiding part which can and must be played in history by parties that have realised the material prerequisites of a revolution and have placed themselves at the head of the progressive classes.

5. HOW SHOULD "THE REVOLUTION BE ADVANCED"?

Let us quote the next section of the resolution:

"Under such conditions, Social-Democracy must strive to maintain throughout the revolution a position which will best of all ensure it the possibility of advancing the revolution, will not tie the hands of Social-Democracy in its struggle against the inconsistent and self-seeking policy of the bourgeois parties, and will preserve it from being dissolved in bourgeois democracy.

"Therefore, Social-Democracy must not set itself the aim of seizing or sharing power in the provisional government, but must remain the party of extreme revolutionary opposition."

The advice to occupy a position which best ensures the possibility of advancing the revolution pleases us very much indeed. We would only desire that this piece of good advice should be accompanied by a direct indication as to how Social-Democracy should further advance the revolution right now, in the present political situation, in a period of rumours, conjectures, and talk and schemes about the convocation of the people's representatives. Can the revolution now be further advanced by those who fail to understand the danger of the *Osvobozhdeniye* theory of "compromise" between the people and the tsar, by those who call a mere "decision" to convene a constituent assembly a victory, who do not set themselves the task of carrying on active propaganda of the idea of the need for a provisional revolutionary government, or who leave the slogan of a democratic republic in the background? Such people actually *pull the revolution back*, because, as far as *practical politics* are concerned, they have stopped at the level of the *Osvobozhdeniye* stand. What is the use of their recognising a programme which demands that the autocracy be replaced by a republic, if in a resolution on tactics that defines the Party's present and immediate tasks in the period of revolution they omit the slogan of a struggle for a republic? It is the *Osvobozhdeniye* position, the position of the constitutionalist bourgeoisie, that is now actually characterised by the fact that a decision to convene a popular constituent assembly is considered a decisive victory, while a prudent silence is maintained on the subject of a provisional revolutionary government and a republic! To *advance* the revolution, to take it beyond the limits to which the monarchist bourgeoisie advances it, it is necessary actively to produce, emphasise, and bring into the forefront slogans that will *preclude* the "inconsistency" of bourgeois democracy. At present there are *only two* such slogans: 1) a provisional revolutionary government, and 2) a republic, because the slogan of a popular constituent assembly *has been accepted* by the monarchist bourgeoisie (see the programme of the *Osvobozhdeniye* League) and accepted for the very purpose of devitalising the revolution, preventing its complete victory, and enabling the big bourgeoisie to strike a huckster's bargain with tsarism. And now we see that of the two slogans, which alone are capable of advancing the revolution, the conference completely forgot the slogan of a republic, and plainly put the slogan of a provisional revolutionary government on a par with the *Osvobozhdeniye* slogan of a popular constituent assembly, calling both the one and the other "a decisive victory of the revolution"!!

Indeed, such is the undoubted fact, which, we are sure, will serve as a landmark for the future historian of Russian Social-Democracy. The conference of Social-Democrats held in May 1905 passed a resolution which contains fine words about the necessity of advancing the democratic revolution, but in fact pulls it back and goes no farther than the democratic slogans of the monarchist bourgeoisie.

The new-*Iskra* group likes to accuse us of ignoring the danger of the proletariat becoming dissolved in bourgeois democracy. We should like to see the person who would undertake to prove this charge on the basis of the text of the resolutions passed by the Third Congress of the Russian Social-Democratic Labour Party. Our reply to our opponents is—a Social-Democratic Party which operates in a bourgeois society cannot take part in politics without marching, in certain cases, *side by side* with bourgeois democracy. The difference between us in this respect is that we march side by side with the revolutionary and republican bourgeoisie, without merging with it, whereas you march side by side with the *liberal* and the monarchist bourgeoisie, without merging with it either. That is how matters stand.

The tactical slogans you have formulated in the name of the conference coincide with the slogans of the "Constitutional-Democratic" Party, i.e., the party of the monarchist bourgeoisie; moreover, you have not even noticed or realised this coincidence, thus actually following in the wake of the Osvobozhdeniye fraternity.

The tactical slogans we have formulated in the name of the Third Congress of the Russian Social-Democratic Labour Party coincide with the slogans of the democratic-revolutionary and republican bourgeoisie. In Russia this bourgeoisie and petty bourgeoisie have not yet formed themselves into a big people's party.* But only one who is utterly ignorant of what is now taking place in Russia can doubt that elements of such a party exist. We intend to guide (if the great Russian revolution makes progress) not only the proletariat, organised by the Social-Democratic Party, but also this petty bourgeoisie, which is capable of marching side by side with us.

Through its resolution the conference unconsciously descends to the level of the liberal and monarchist bourgeoisie. Through its resolution, the Party Congress consciously raises to its own level those elements of revolutionary democracy that are capable of waging a struggle, and not acting as brokers.

Such elements are mostly to be found among the peasants. In classifying the big social groups according to their political tendencies we can, without danger of serious error, identify revolutionary and republican democracy with the mass of the peasants—of course, in the same sense and with the same reservations and implied conditions that we can identify the working class with Social-Democracy. In other words, we can formulate our conclusions in the following terms as well: in a revolutionary period the conference, through its nation-wide** political slogans, unconsciously descends to the level of the mass of the landlords. Through its country-wide political slogans, the Party Congress raises the mass of the peasants to a revolutionary level. To anyone who, because of this conclusion, would accuse us of a penchant for paradoxes, we issue the following challenge: let him refute the proposition that, if we are not strong enough to bring the revolution to a successful conclusion, if the revolution ends in a "decisive victory" in the Osvobozhdeniye sense, i.e., only in the form of a representative assembly convened by the tsar, one that could be

---

* The Socialist-Revolutionaries are a terrorist group of intellectuals rather than the embryo of such a party, although the objective significance of this group's activities can be reduced to this very task of achieving the aims of the revolutionary and republican bourgeoisie.

** We are not referring here to the special peasant slogans which have been dealt with in separate resolutions.

called a constituent assembly only in derision—then that will be a revolution in which the *landlord and big bourgeois* element will preponderate. On the other hand, if we are destined to live through a really great revolution, if history does not allow a "miscarriage" this time, if we are strong enough to carry the revolution to a successful conclusion, to a decisive victory, not in the *Osvobozhdeniye* or the new-*Iskra* sense of the word, then that will be a revolution in which the peasant and proletarian element will preponderate.

Some people may, perhaps, interpret our admission that such a preponderance is possible as renunciation of the view that the impending revolution will be bourgeois in character. This is very likely, considering how this concept is misused in *Iskra*. For this reason it will not be at all superfluous to dwell on this question.

6. WHENCE IS THE PROLETARIAT THREATENED WITH THE DANGER OF FINDING ITSELF WITH ITS HANDS TIED IN THE STRUGGLE AGAINST THE INCONSISTENT BOURGEOISIE?

Marxists are absolutely convinced of the bourgeois character of the Russian revolution. What does that mean? It means that the democratic reforms in the political system, and the social and economic reforms that have become a necessity for Russia, do not in themselves imply the undermining of capitalism, the undermining of bourgeois rule; on the contrary, they will, for the first time, really clear the ground for a wide and rapid, European, and not Asiatic, development of capitalism; they will, for the first time, make it possible for the bourgeoisie to rule as a class. The Socialist-Revolutionaries cannot grasp this idea, for they do not know the ABC of the laws of development of commodity and capitalist production; they fail to see that even the complete success of a peasant insurrection, even the redistribution of the whole of the land in favour of the peasants and in accordance with their desires ("general redistribution"[51] or something of the kind) will not destroy capitalism at all, but will, on the contrary, give an impetus to its development and hasten the class disintegration of the peasantry itself. Failure to grasp this truth makes the Socialist-Revolutionaries unconscious ideologists of the petty bourgeoisie. Insistence on this truth is of enormous importance for Social-Democracy not only from the standpoint of theory but also from that of practical politics, for it follows therefrom that complete class independence of the party of the proletariat in the present "general democratic" movement is an indispensable condition.

But it does not by any means follow that a *democratic* revolution (bourgeois in its social and economic essence) would not be of *enormous* interest to the proletariat. It does not follow that the democratic revolution could not take place both in a form advantageous mainly to the big capitalist, the financial magnate, and the "enlightened" landlord, and in a form advantageous to the peasant and the worker.

The new-*Iskra* group completely misunderstands the meaning and significance of bourgeois revolution as a category. The idea that is constantly running through their arguments is that a bourgeois revolution is one that can be advantageous only to the bourgeoisie. And yet nothing can be more erroneous than such an idea. A bourgeois revolution is a revolution which does not depart from the framework of the bourgeois, i.e., capitalist, socio-economic system. A bourgeois revolution expresses the needs of capitalist development, and, far from destroying the foundations of capitalism, it effects the contrary—it broadens and deepens them. This revolution, therefore, expresses the interests not only of the working class but of the entire bourgeoisie as well. Since the rule of the bourgeoisie over the working class is inevitable under capitalism, it can well be said that a bourgeois revolution expresses the interests not so much of the proletariat as of the bourgeoisie. But it is quite absurd to think that a bourgeois revolution does not at all express proletarian interests. This absurd idea boils down either to the hoary Narodnik theory that a bourgeois revolution runs counter to the interests of the proletariat, and that, therefore, we do not need bourgeois political liberty; or to anarchism which denies any participation of the proletariat in bourgeois politics, in a bourgeois revolution and in bourgeois parliamentarism. From the standpoint of theory this idea disregards the elementary propositions of Marxism concerning the inevitability of capitalist development on the basis of commodity production. Marxism teaches us that at a certain stage of its development a society which is based on commodity production and has commercial intercourse with civilised capitalist nations must inevitably take the road of capitalism. Marxism has irrevocably broken with the Narodnik and anarchist gibberish that Russia, for instance, can bypass capitalist development, escape from capitalism, or skip it in some way other than that of the class struggle, on the basis and within the framework of this same capitalism.

All these principles of Marxism have been proved and explained in minute detail in general and with regard to Russia in particular. And from these principles it follows that the idea of seeking salvation for the working class in anything save the further development of capitalism is *reactionary*. In countries like Russia the working class suffers not so much from capitalism as from the insufficient development of capitalism. The working class is, therefore, *most certainly interested* in the broadest, freest, and most rapid development of capitalism. The removal of all the remnants of the old order which hamper the broad, free, and rapid development of capitalism is of absolute *advantage* to the working class. The bourgeois revolution is precisely an upheaval that most resolutely sweeps away survivals of the past, survivals of the serf-owning system (which include not only the autocracy but the monarchy as well), and most fully guarantees the broadest, freest, and most rapid development of capitalism.

That is why a *bourgeois* revolution is *in the highest degree advantageous to the proletariat.* A bourgeois revolution is *absolutely* necessary in the interests of the proletariat. The more complete, determined, and consistent the bourgeois revolution, the more assured will the proletariat's struggle be against the bourgeoisie and for socialism. Only those who are ignorant of the ABC of scientific socialism can regard this conclusion as new, strange, or paradoxical. And from this conclusion, among other things, follows the thesis that *in a certain sense* a bourgeois revolution is *more advantageous* to the proletariat than to the bourgeoisie. This thesis is unquestionably correct in the following sense: it is to the advantage of the bourgeoisie to rely on certain remnants of the past, as against the proletariat, for instance, on the monarchy, the standing army, etc. It is to the advantage of the bourgeoisie for the bourgeois revolution not to sweep away all remnants of the past too resolutely, but keep some of them, i.e., for this revolution not to be fully consistent, not to be complete, and not to be determined and relentless. Social-Democrats often express this idea somewhat differently by stating that the bourgeoisie betrays its own self, that the bourgeoisie betrays the cause of liberty, that the bourgeoisie is incapable of being consistently democratic. It is of greater advantage to the bourgeoisie for the necessary changes in the direction of bourgeois democracy to take place more slowly, more gradually, more cautiously, less resolutely, by means of reforms and not by means of revolution; for these changes to spare the "venerable" institutions of the serf-owning system (such as the monarchy) as much as possible; for these changes to develop as little as possible the independent revolutionary activity, initiative, and energy of the common people, i.e., the peasantry and especially the workers, for otherwise it will be easier for the workers, as the French say, "to change the rifle from one shoulder to the other", i.e., to turn against the bourgeoisie the weapon the bourgeois revolution will supply them with, the liberty the revolution will bring, and the democratic institutions that will spring up on the ground cleared of the serf-owning system.

On the other hand, it is more advantageous to the working class for the necessary changes in the direction of bourgeois democracy to take place by way of revolution and not by way of reform, because the way of reform is one of delay, procrastination, the painfully slow decomposition of the putrid parts of the national organism. It is the proletariat and the peasantry that suffer first of all and most of all from that putrefaction. The revolutionary path is one of rapid amputation, which is the least painful to the proletariat, the path of the immediate removal of what is putrescent, the path of least compliance with and consideration for the monarchy and the abominable, vile, rotten, and noxious institutions that go with it.

So it is not only because of the censorship, not only "for fear of the Jews", that our bourgeois-liberal press deplores the possibility of the revolutionary path, fears the revolution, tries to frighten the tsar with the bogey of revolution, seeks to avoid revolution, and grovels and toadies for the sake of miserable reforms as the foundation of the reformist path. This standpoint is shared not only by *Russkiye Vedomosti, Syn Otechestva, Nasha Zhizn,* and *Nashi Dni,*[52] but also by the illegal, uncensored *Osvobozhdeniye.* The very position the bourgeoisie holds as a class in capitalist society inevitably leads to its inconsistency in a democratic revolution. The very position the proletariat holds as a class compels it to be consistently democratic. The bourgeoisie looks backward in fear of democratic progress which threatens to strengthen the proletariat. The proletariat has nothing to lose but its chains, but with the aid of democratism it has the whole world to win. That is why the more consistent the bourgeois revolution is in achieving its democratic transformations, the less will it limit itself to what is of advantage exclusively to the bourgeoisie. The more consistent the bourgeois revolution, the more does it guarantee the proletariat and the peasantry the benefits accruing from the democratic revolution.

Marxism teaches the proletarian not to keep aloof from the bourgeois revolution, not to be indifferent to it, not to allow the leadership of the revolution to be assumed by the bourgeoisie but, on the contrary, to take a most energetic part in it, to fight most resolutely for consistent proletarian democratism, for the revolution to be carried to its conclusion. We cannot get out of the bourgeois-democratic boundaries of the Russian revolution, but we can vastly extend these boundaries, and within these boundaries we can and must fight for the interests of the proletariat, for its immediate needs and for conditions that will make it possible to prepare its forces for the future complete victory. There is bourgeois democracy and bourgeois democracy. The Zemstvo monarchist who favours an upper chamber and "asks" for universal suffrage, while secretly, on the sly, striking a bargain with tsarism for a docked constitution, is a bourgeois democrat too. The peasant, who has taken up arms

against the landlords and the   government officials, and with a
"naïve republicanism" proposes "to send the tsar packing",* is also
a bourgeois democrat. There are bourgeois-democratic regimes like
the one in Germany, and also like the one in England; like the one
in Austria and also like those   in America and Switzerland. He
would be a fine Marxist indeed, who in a period of democratic revolution failed to see this difference between the degrees of democratism and the difference between its forms, and confined himself to
"clever" remarks to the effect that, after all, this is "a bourgeois
revolution", the fruit of "bourgeois revolution".

Our new-Iskrists are just such clever fellows, who actually flaunt
their short-sightedness. They confine themselves to disquisitions
on the bourgeois character of revolution, just when and where it
is necessary to be able to draw a distinction between republican-
revolutionary and monarchist-liberal bourgeois democracy, to say
nothing of the distinction between inconsistent bourgeois democratism and consistent proletarian democratism. They are satisfied
—as if they had really become like the "man in the muffler"[53]—
with doleful talk about a "process of mutual struggle of antagonistic classes", when the question is one of providing *democratic
leadership* in the present revolution, of emphasising *progressive
democratic* slogans, as distinct from the treacherous slogans of Mr.
Struve and Co., of bluntly and straightforwardly stating the immediate aims of the really revolutionary struggle of the proletariat
and the peasantry, as distinct from the liberal haggling of the landlords and manufacturers. Such now is the gist of the matter, which
you, gentlemen, have missed, namely: will our revolution result
in a real, immense victory, or merely in a wretched deal; will it
go so far as the revolutionary-democratic dictatorship of the
proletariat and the peasantry, or will it "peter out" in a liberal
constitution *à la* Shipov?

At first sight it may appear that in raising this question we are
deviating entirely from our subject. However, that may appear so
only at first sight. As a matter of fact, it is precisely this question
that lies at the root of the difference in principle which has already
become clearly marked between the Social-Democratic tactics of
the Third Congress of the Russian Social-Democratic Labour Party
and the tactics initiated by the conference of the new-*Iskra* supporters. The latter have already taken not two but three steps back
resurrecting the mistakes of Economism in solving problems that
are incomparably more complex, more important, and more vital
to the workers' party, viz., questions of its tactics in time of revolution. That is why we must analyse the question we have raised
with all due attention.

---

* See *Osvobozhdeniye*, No. 71, p. 337, footnote 2.

The above-quoted section of the new-Iskrists' resolution points to the danger of Social-Democracy tying its own hands in the struggle against the inconsistent policy of the bourgeoisie, of its becoming dissolved in bourgeois democracy. The thought of this danger pervades all specifically new-Iskrist literature; it lies at the very heart of the principle involved in our Party split (ever since the bickering in the split was completely overshadowed by the turn towards Economism). Without any equivocation we admit that this danger really exists, that just at the present time, at the height of the Russian revolution, this danger has become particularly grave. The pressing and extremely responsible duty that devolves on all of us theoreticians or—as I should prefer to say of myself—publicists of Social-Democracy is to find out *from what direction* this danger actually threatens. For the source of our disagreement is not a dispute as to whether such a danger exists, but the dispute as to whether it is caused by the so-called tail-ism of the "Minority" or the so-called revolutionism of the "Majority".

To remove all misinterpretations and misunderstandings let us first of all note that the danger to which we are referring lies not in the subjective, but in the objective aspect of the matter, not in the formal stand which Social-Democracy will take in the struggle, but in the material outcome of the entire present revolutionary struggle. The question is not whether this or that Social-Democratic group will want to dissolve in bourgeois democracy, or whether they realise that they are doing so. Nobody suggests that. We do not suspect any Social-Democrat of harbouring such a desire, and this is not at all a matter of desire. Nor is it a question of whether this or that Social-Democratic group will formally retain its separate identity, individuality, and independence of bourgeois democracy throughout the course of the revolution. They may not merely proclaim such "independence", but may even retain it formally, and yet *it may turn out* that their hands will nevertheless be tied in the struggle against the inconsistency of the bourgeoisie. The ultimate political outcome of the revolution may prove to be that, despite the formal "independence" of Social-Democracy, despite its complete organisational individuality as a separate party, it will in fact not be independent; it will not be able to place the imprint of its proletarian independence on the course of events; it will prove so weak that, on the whole and in the last analysis, its "dissolution" in bourgeois democracy will nevertheless be a historical fact.

That is what constitutes the real danger. Now let us see from what direction the danger threatens—from the deviation of Social-Democracy, as represented by the new *Iskra*, to the Right, as we believe; or from the deviation of Social-Democracy, as represented by the "Majority", *Vperyod*, etc., to the Left—as the new-*Iskra* group believes.

The answer to this question, as we have pointed out, is determined by the objective combination of the operation of the various social forces. The character of these forces has been defined theoretically by the Marxist analysis of Russian life; at present it is being determined in practice by open action by groups and classes in the course of the revolution. Now the entire theoretical analysis made by the Marxists long before the period we are now passing through, as well as all the practical observations of the development of revolutionary events, show that, from the standpoint of objective conditions, there are two possible courses and two possible outcomes of the revolution in Russia. The transformation of the economic and political system in Russia along bourgeois-democratic lines is inevitable and inescapable. No power on earth can prevent such a transformation, but the combined action of the existing forces which are effecting it may result in either of two things, may bring about either of two forms of that transformation. Either 1) matters will end in "the revolution's decisive victory over tsarism", or 2) the forces will be inadequate for a decisive victory, and matters will end in a deal between tsarism and the most "inconsistent" and most "self-seeking" elements of the bourgeoisie. By and large, all the infinite variety of details and combinations, which no one is able to foresee, lead to one outcome or the other.

Let us now consider these two possibilities, first, from the standpoint of their social significance and, secondly, from the standpoint of the position of Social-Democracy (its "dissolution" or "having its hands tied") in one outcome or the other.

What is meant by "the revolution's decisive victory over tsarism"? We have already seen that in using this expression the new-*Iskra* group fail to grasp even its immediate political significance. Still less do they seem to understand the class essence of this concept. Surely, we Marxists must not under any circumstances allow ourselves to be deluded by *words,* such as "revolution" or "the great Russian revolution", as do many revolutionary democrats (of the Gapon type). We must be perfectly certain in our minds as to what real social forces are opposed to "tsarism" (which is a real force perfectly intelligible to all) and are capable of gaining a "decisive victory" over it. The big bourgeoisie, the landlords, the factory owners, the "society" which follows the *Osvobozhdeniye* lead, cannot be such a force. We see that they do not even want a decisive victory. We know that owing to their class position they are incapable of waging a decisive struggle against tsarism; they are too heavily fettered by private property, by capital and land to enter into a decisive struggle. They stand in too great need of tsarism, with its bureaucratic, police, and military forces for use against the proletariat and the peasantry, to want it to be destroyed. No, the only force capable of gaining "a decisive victory over tsarism" is the *people,* i.e., the proletariat and the peasantry, if we take the main, big forces, and distribute the rural and urban petty bourgeoisie (also part of "the people") between the two. "The revolution's decisive victory over tsarism" means the establishment of the *revolutionary-democratic dictatorship of the proletariat and the peasantry.* Our new-*Iskra* group cannot escape from this conclusion, which *Vperyod* indicated long ago. No other force is capable of gaining a decisive victory over tsarism.

And such a victory will be precisely a dictatorship, i.e., it must inevitably rely on military force, on the arming of the masses, on an insurrection, and not on institutions of one kind or another established in a "lawful" or "peaceful" way. It can be only a dictatorship, for realisation of the changes urgently and absolutely indispensable to the proletariat and the peasantry will evoke desperate resistance from the landlords, the big bourgeoisie, and tsarism. Without a dictatorship it is impossible to break down that resistance and repel counter-revolutionary attempts. But of course it will be a democratic, not a socialist dictatorship. It will be unable (without a series of intermediary stages of revolutionary development) to affect the foundations of capitalism. At best, it may bring about a radical redistribution of landed property in favour of the peasantry, establish consistent and full democracy, including the formation of a republic, eradicate all the oppressive features of Asiatic bondage, not only in rural but also in factory life, lay the foundation for a thorough improvement in the conditions of the workers and for a rise in their standard of living, and—last but not least—carry the revolutionary conflagration into Europe. Such a victory will not yet by any means transform our bourgeois revolution into a socialist revolution; the democratic revolution will not immediately overstep the bounds of bourgeois social and economic relationships; nevertheless, the significance of such a victory for the future development of Russia and of the whole world will be immense. Nothing will raise the revolutionary energy of the world proletariat so much, nothing will shorten the path leading to its complete victory to such an extent, as this decisive victory of the revolution that has now started in Russia.

How far such a victory is probable is another question. We are not in the least inclined to be unreasonably optimistic on that score; we do not for a moment forget the immense difficulties of this task, but, since we are out to fight, we must desire victory and be able to point out the right road to it. Trends capable of leading to such a victory undoubtedly exist. True, our influence on the masses of the proletariat—the Social-Democratic influence—is as yet very, very inadequate; the revolutionary influence on the mass of the peasantry is quite insignificant; the proletarians, and especially the peasants, are still frightfully disunited, backward, and ignorant.

However, revolution unites rapidly and enlightens rapidly. Every step in its development rouses the masses and attracts them with irresistible force to the side of the revolutionary programme, as the only programme that fully and consistently expresses their real and vital interests.

According to a law of mechanics, action and reaction are always equal. In history too, the destructive force of a revolution is to a considerable degree dependent on how strong and protracted the suppression of the striving for liberty has been, and how profound is the contradiction between the outmoded "superstructure" and the living forces of our times. The international political situation, too, is in many respects taking shape in a way most advantageous to the Russian revolution. The workers' and peasants' insurrection has already begun; it is sporadic, spontaneous, and weak, but it unquestionably and undoubtedly proves the existence of forces capable of waging a decisive struggle and marching towards a decisive victory.

If these forces prove inadequate tsarism will have time to conclude a deal, which is already being prepared at the two extremes by the Bulygins and the Struves. Then the whole matter will end in a docked constitution, or, if the worst comes to the worst, even in a travesty of a constitution. This, too, will be a "bourgeois revolution", but it will be a miscarriage, a premature birth, an abortion. Social-Democracy entertains no illusions on that score; it knows the treacherous nature of the bourgeoisie; it will not lose heart or abandon its persistent, patient, and sustained work of giving the proletariat class training, even in the most drab, humdrum days of bourgeois-constitutional "Shipov" bliss. Such an outcome would be more or less similar to that of almost all the nineteenth-century democratic revolutions in Europe, and our Party development would then proceed along the arduous, long, but familiar and beaten track.

The question now arises: in which outcome of the two possible will Social-Democracy find its hands actually tied in the struggle against the inconsistent and self-seeking bourgeoisie, find itself actually "dissolved", or almost so, in bourgeois democracy?

It is sufficient to put this question clearly to have a reply without a moment's difficulty.

If the bourgeoisie succeeds in frustrating the Russian revolution by coming to terms with tsarism, Social-Democracy will find its hands actually tied in the struggle against the inconsistent bourgeoisie; Social-Democracy will find itself "dissolved" in bourgeois democracy in the sense that the proletariat will not succeed in placing its clear imprint on the revolution, will not succeed in settling accounts with tsarism in the proletarian or, as Marx once said, "in the plebeian manner".

If the revolution gains a decisive victory—then we shall settle accounts with tsarism in the Jacobin, or, if you like, in the plebeian way. "The whole French terrorism," wrote Marx in 1848 in the famous *Neue Rheinische Zeitung,* "was nothing but a plebeian manner of settling accounts with the enemies of the bourgeoisie, with absolutism, feudalism, and philistinism" (see Marx, *Nachlass,* Mehring's edition, Vol. III, p. 211).[54] Have those people who in a period of a democratic revolution try to frighten the Social-Democratic workers in Russia with the bogey of "Jacobinism" ever given thought to the significance of these words of Marx?

The new-*Iskra* group, the Girondists[55] of contemporary Russian Social-Democracy, does not merge with the *Osvobozhdeniye* group, but actually, by reason of the nature of its slogans, it follows in the wake of the latter. And the *Osvobozhdeniye* group, i.e., the representatives of the liberal bourgeoisie, wishes to settle accounts with the autocracy in a reformist manner, gently and compliantly, so as not to offend the aristocracy, the nobles, or the Court—cautiously, without breaking anything—kindly and politely as befits gentlemen in white gloves (like the ones Mr. Petrunkevich borrowed from a bashi-bazouk to wear at the reception of "representatives of the people" [?] held by Nicholas the Bloodstained,[56] see *Proletary,* No. 5*).

The Jacobins of contemporary Social-Democracy—the Bolsheviks, the *Vperyod* supporters, the "Congress" group, *Proletary* supporters—or whatever else we may call them—wish by their slogans to raise the revolutionary and republican petty bourgeoisie, and especially the peasantry, to the level of the consistent democratism of the proletariat, which fully retains its individuality as a class. They want the people, i.e., the proletariat and the peasantry, to settle accounts with the monarchy and the aristocracy in the "plebeian way", ruthlessly destroying the enemies of liberty, crushing their resistance by force, making no concessions whatever to the accursed heritage of serf-ownership, Asiatic barbarism, and human degradation.

This, of course, does not mean that we necessarily propose to imitate the Jacobins of 1793, and borrow their views, programme, slogans, and methods of action. Nothing of the kind. Our programme is not an old one but a new—the minimum programme of the Russian Social-Democratic Labour Party.[57] We have a new slogan: the revolutionary-democratic dictatorship of the proletariat and the peasantry. If we live to see the real victory of the revolution we shall also have new methods of action in keeping with the nature and aims of the working-class party that is striving for a complete socialist revolution. By our parallel we merely want to

---

* See *Collected Works,* Vol. 8, pp. 526-30.—*Ed.*

explain that the representatives of the progressive class of the twentieth century, the proletariat, i.e., the Social-Democrats, are divided into two wings (the opportunist and the revolutionary) similar to those into which the representatives of the progressive class of the eighteenth century, the bourgeoisie, were divided, i.e., the Girondists and the Jacobins.

Only in the event of a complete victory of the democratic revolution will the proletariat have its hands free in the struggle against the inconsistent bourgeoisie; only in that event will it not become "dissolved" in bourgeois democracy, but will leave its proletarian, or rather proletarian-peasant, imprint on the whole revolution.

In a word, to avoid finding itself with its hands tied in the struggle against the inconsistent bourgeois democracy the proletariat must be class-conscious and strong enough to rouse the peasantry to revolutionary consciousness, guide its assault, and thereby independently pursue the line of consistent proletarian democratism.

That is how matters stand in the question—so ineptly dealt with by the new-*Iskra* group—of the danger of our hands being tied in the struggle against the inconsistent bourgeoisie. The bourgeoisie will always be inconsistent. There is nothing more naïve and futile than attempts to set forth conditions and points* which, if satisfied, would enable us to consider that the bourgeois democrat is a sincere friend of the people. Only the proletariat can be a consistent fighter for democracy. It can become a victorious fighter for democracy only if the peasant masses join its revolutionary struggle. If the proletariat is not strong enough for this the bourgeoisie will be at the head of the democratic revolution and will impart an inconsistent and self-seeking nature to it. Nothing but a revolutionary-democratic dictatorship of the proletariat and the peasantry can prevent this.

Thus, we arrive at the indubitable conclusion that it is the new-*Iskra* tactics which, by its objective significance, is *playing into the hands of the bourgeois democrats*. The preaching of organisational diffuseness which goes to the length of plebiscites, the principle of compromise, and the divorcement of Party literature from the Party; belittling of the aims of insurrection; confusing of the popular political slogans of the revolutionary proletariat with those of the monarchist bourgeoisie; distortion of the requisites for "revolution's decisive victory over tsarism"—all these taken together produce that very policy of tail-ism in a revolutionary period, which bewilders the proletariat, disorganises it, confuses its understanding, and belittles the tactics of Social-Democracy instead of pointing

---

* As was attempted by Starover in his resolution,[58] annulled by the Third Congress, and as the conference attempts in an equally poor resolution.

out the only way to victory and getting all the revolutionary and republican elements of the people to   adhere to the proletariat's slogan.

––––

To bear out this conclusion, reached by us through analysis of the resolution, let us approach this same question from other angles. Let us first see how in the Georgian *Sotsial-Demokrat* a naïve and outspoken Menshevik illustrates the new-*Iskra* tactics. Secondly, let us see who is actually making use of the new-*Iskra* slogans in the present political situation.

7. THE TACTICS OF "ELIMINATING THE CONSERVATIVES FROM THE GOVERNMENT"

The article in the organ of the Tiflis Menshevik "Committee" (*Sotsial-Demokrat,* No. 1), to which we have just referred, is entitled "The Zemsky Sobor and Our Tactics". Its author has not yet entirely forgotten our programme; he advances the slogan of a republic, but this is how he discusses tactics:

"It is possible to point to two ways of achieving this goal" (a republic): "either completely ignore the Zemsky Sobor that is being convened by the government and defeat the government by force of arms, form a revolutionary government and convene a constituent assembly, or declare the Zemsky Sobor the centre of our action, influencing its composition and activities by force of arms, forcibly compelling it to declare itself a constituent assembly, or convene a constituent assembly through it. These two tactics differ very sharply from each other. Let us see which of them is of more advantage to us."

This is how the Russian new-Iskrists set forth ideas subsequently incorporated in the resolution we have analysed. Note that this was written before the battle of Tsushima,[59] when the Bulygin "scheme" had not yet seen the light of day. Even the liberals were losing patience and voicing their distrust from the pages of the legal press; however, a Social-Democrat of the new-*Iskra* brand has proved more credulous than the liberals. He declares that the Zemsky Sobor "is being convened" and trusts the tsar so much that he proposes to make this as yet non-existent Zemsky Sobor (or, possibly, "State Duma" or "Advisory Legislative Assembly"?) the centre of our action. Being more outspoken and straightforward than the authors of the resolution adopted at the conference, our Tiflisian does not put the two "tactics" (which he expounds with inimitable naïveté) on a par, but declares that the second is of greater "advantage". Just listen:

"The first tactic. As you know, the coming revolution is a bourgeois revolution, i.e., its purpose is to effect such changes in the present system as are of interest not only to the proletariat but to the whole of bourgeois society. All classes are opposed to the government, even the capitalists themselves. The militant proletariat and the militant bourgeoisie are in a certain sense marching together and jointly attacking the autocracy from different sides. The government is completely isolated and has no public sympathy. For this reason it is very easy to destroy it. The Russian proletariat, as a whole, is not yet sufficiently class-conscious and organised to be able to carry out the revolution by itself. And even if it were able to do so it would carry through a proletarian (socialist) revolution and not a bourgeois revolution. Hence, it is in our interest that the government should remain without allies, that it should be unable to divide the opposition, join hands with the bourgeoisie, and leave the proletariat in isolation...."

So it is in the interests of the proletariat that the tsarist government should be unable to divide the bourgeoisie and the proletariat! Is it not by mistake that this Georgian organ is called *Sotsial-Demokrat* instead of *Osvobozhdeniye*? And note its peerless philosophy of democratic revolution! Is it not obvious that this poor Tiflisian is hopelessly confused by the pedantic tail-ist interpretation of the concept "bourgeois revolution"? He discusses the question of the possible isolation of the proletariat in a democratic revolution, and *forgets* ... forgets a trifle ... the peasantry! Of the possible allies of the proletariat he knows and favours the Zemstvo landlords, but is not aware of the peasants. And this in the Caucasus! Well, were we not right when we said that in its reasoning the new *Iskra* was sinking to the level of the monarchist bourgeoisie instead of raising the revolutionary peasantry to the position of our ally?

"... Otherwise the defeat of the proletariat and the victory of the government are inevitable. This is just what the autocracy is striving for. In its Zemsky Sobor it will undoubtedly attract to its side representatives of the nobility, the Zemstvos, the cities, the universities, and similar bourgeois institutions. It will try to appease them with petty concessions, and thereby reconcile them to itself. Strengthened in this way, it will direct all its blows against the working people, who will have been isolated. It is our duty to prevent such an unfortunate outcome. But can this be done by the first method? Let us assume that we paid no attention whatever to the Zemsky Sobor, but started to prepare for insurrection ourselves, and one fine day came out in the streets armed and ready for battle. The result would be that we would be confronted not with one but with two enemies: the government and the Zemsky Sobor. While we were preparing, they were able to come to terms, enter into an agreement with each other, draw up a constitution advantageous to themselves, and divide power between them. This tactic is of direct advantage to the government, and we must reject it in the most energetic fashion...."

Now this is frank! So we must resolutely reject the "tactics" of preparing an insurrection because "meanwhile" the government would come to terms with the bourgeoisie. Can one find in the old literature of the most rabid Economism anything that would even approximate such a disgrace to revolutionary Social-Democracy? It is a fact that insurrections and outbreaks by workers and peasants are occurring, first in one place and then in another. The Zemsky Sobor, however, is a Bulygin promise. And the *Sotsial-Demokrat* of the city of Tiflis decides that the tactic of preparing an insurrection should be rejected, and a "centre of influence" should be awaited—the Zemsky Sobor....

"...The second tactic, on the contrary, consists in bringing the Zemsky Sobor under our supervision, in not giving it the opportunity to act according to its own will, and enter into an agreement with the government.*

"We support the Zemsky Sobor inasmuch as it fights the autocracy, and we fight it whenever it becomes reconciled with the autocracy. By energetic intervention and by force we shall bring about a split among the deputies,** rally the radicals to our side, eliminate the conservatives from the government, and thus put the whole Zemsky Sobor on the path of revolution. Thanks to such tactics, the government will always remain isolated, the opposition will be strong, and the establishment of a democratic system will thereby be facilitated."

Well, well! Let anyone now say that we exaggerate the new-Iskrists' turn to the most vulgar semblance of Economism. This is positively like the famous powder for exterminating flies: first you catch your fly, stick it on the flypaper, and the fly will die. Bring about a split among the deputies of the Zemsky Sobor by *force,* "eliminate the conservatives from the government"—and the *whole* Zemsky Sobor will take *the path of revolution....* No "Jacobin" armed insurrection of any sort, but just like that, in genteel, almost parliamentary fashion, "influencing" *the members of the Zemsky Sobor.*

Poor Russia! It has been said that she always wears the old-fashioned bonnets that Europe has discarded. We have no parliament as yet, even Bulygin has not yet promised one, but we have any amount of parliamentary cretinism.[60]

"...How should this intervention be effected? First of all, we shall demand that the Zemsky Sobor be convened on the basis of universal and equal suffrage, direct elections by secret ballot. Simultaneously with the announcement*** of this electoral procedure, complete freedom to carry on the election campaign, i.e., freedom of assembly, speech, and the press, the inviolability of electors and candidates, and the release of all political prisoners, must be made law.**** The elections themselves must be fixed as late as possible, to give us sufficient time to inform and prepare the people. And since the drafting of the regulations governing the convocation of the Sobor has been entrusted to a commission headed by Bulygin, Minister of the Interior, we should also exert pressure on this commission and on its members.***** If the Bulygin Commission refuses to satisfy

---

* By what means can the Zemstvo people be deprived of their own will? Perhaps by use of a special sort of litmus-paper?

** Heavens! This is certainly rendering tactics "profound"! There are no forces available to fight in the streets, but it is possible "to bring about a split among the deputies" "by force". Listen, comrade from Tiflis, lie if you must, but there's a limit....

*** In *Iskra*?

**** By Nicholas?

***** So this is what is meant by the tactic of "eliminating the conservatives from the government"!

our demands* and grants suffrage only to property owners, then we must intervene in these elections and by revolutionary means make the voters elect progressive candidates and in the Zemsky Sobor demand a constituent assembly. Finally, we must by all possible measures—demonstrations, strikes, and insurrection if need be—compel the Zemsky Sobor to convene a constituent assembly or declare itself to be such. The armed proletariat must be the defender of the constituent assembly, and together** both will march forward to a democratic republic.

"Such is the Social-Democratic tactics, and it alone will secure us victory."

Let not the reader imagine that this incredible nonsense comes from some new-*Iskra* maiden writer, a man with no authority or influence. No, this is stated in the *organ* of an entire committee of new-*Iskra* supporters, the Tiflis Committee. More than that. This nonsense has been *openly endorsed by "Iskra"*, in No. 100 of which we read the following about that issue of the *Sotsial-Demokrat*:

"The first issue is edited in a lively and talented manner. The experienced hand of a capable editor and writer is perceptible.... It may be said with all confidence that the newspaper will carry out brilliantly the task it has set itself."

Yes! If that task is to show clearly to all and sundry the utter ideological decay of the new-*Iskra* trend, then it has indeed been carried out "brilliantly". No one could have expressed new-*Iskra* degradation to liberal bourgeois opportunism in a more "lively, talented, and capable" manner.

8. THE *OSVOBOZHDENIYE* AND NEW-*ISKRA* TRENDS

Let us now proceed to another striking confirmation of the political significance of the new-*Iskra* trend.

In a splendid, remarkable, and most instructive article, entitled "How to Find Oneself" (*Osvobozhdeniye*, No. 71), Mr. Struve wages war against the "programmatic revolutionism" of our extreme parties. Mr. Struve is particularly displeased with me personally.*** As far as I am concerned, Mr. Struve could not have

---

* But surely such a thing cannot happen if we follow this correct and profound tactic!

** Both the armed proletariat and the conservatives "eliminated from the government"?

*** "In comparison with the revolutionism of Mr. Lenin and his associates the revolutionism of the West-European Social-Democracy of Bebel, and even of Kautsky, is opportunism; but the foundations of even this already toned-down revolutionism have been undermined and washed away by history." A most irate thrust. Only Mr. Struve should not think he can lay all the blame on me, as he could on an opponent no longer alive. I have only to challenge Mr. Struve, though I am sure he will never accept such a challenge, to answer the following questions. When and where did I call the "revolutionism of Bebel and Kautsky" opportunism? When and where did I ever claim to have created any sort of special trend in International Social-Democracy *not identical* with the

pleased me more: I could not wish for a better ally in the fight against the renascent Economism of the new-*Iskra* group and the absence of principles displayed by the Socialist-Revolutionaries. On some other occasion we shall relate how Mr. Struve and *Osvobozhdeniye* have proved in practice how utterly reactionary are the "amendments" to Marxism made in the Socialist-Revolutionaries' draft programme. We have already repeatedly* spoken of the honest, faithful and real service rendered to me by Mr. Struve whenever he approved of the new-*Iskra* trend *in principle,* and we shall now speak of that once more.

Mr. Struve's article contains a number of very interesting statements, which we can note here only in passing. He intends "to create Russian democracy by relying on class collaboration and not on class struggle", in which case "the socially privileged intelligentsia" (something like the "cultured nobility" to which Mr. Struve makes obeisance with the grace of a true high-society ... lackey) will bring "the weight of its social position" (the weight of its money-bags) to this "non-class" party. Mr. Struve expresses the desire to acquaint the youth with the worthlessness "of the hackneyed radical opinion that the bourgeoisie has become frightened and has betrayed the proletariat and the cause of liberty". (We welcome this desire with all our heart. Nothing can confirm

---

trend of Bebel and Kautsky? When and where have there been brought to light differences between me, on the one hand, and Bebel and Kautsky, on the other—differences even slightly approximating in gravity the differences between Bebel and Kautsky, for instance, on the agrarian question in Breslau?[61] Let Mr. Struve try to answer these three questions.

To our readers we say: the liberal bourgeoisie *everywhere* and *always* resorts to the method of assuring its adherents in a given country that the Social-Democrats of that country are most unreasonable, whereas their comrades in a neighbouring country are "goody-goodies". The German bourgeoisie has *hundreds of times* held up "goody-goody" French socialists as models for the Bebels and the Kautskys. The French bourgeoisie quite recently pointed to "goody-goody" Bebel as a model for the French socialists. That is an old trick, Mr. Struve! You will find only children and ignoramuses swallowing such bait. The complete unanimity of international revolutionary Social-Democracy on all major questions of programme and tactics is a most incontrovertible fact.

* Let us remind the reader that the article "What Should Not Be Done" (*Iskra*, No. 52) was vociferously hailed by *Osvobozhdeniye* as a "noteworthy turn" towards concessions to the opportunists. The principles underlying the new-*Iskra* ideas were especially lauded by *Osvobozhdeniye* in an item on the split among Russian Social-Democrats. Commenting on Trotsky's pamphlet, *Our Political Tasks*, *Osvobozhdeniye* noted the similarity between this author's ideas and what was once written and said by the *Rabocheye Dyelo* writers Krichevsky, Martynov, Akimov (see the leaflet entitled "An Obliging Liberal" published by *Vperyod*) (*Collected Works*, Vol. 7, pp. 486-89). *Osvobozhdeniye* welcomed Martynov's pamphlet on the two dictatorships (see the item in *Vperyod*, No. 9) (*Collected Works*, Vol. 8, pp. 221-22). Finally, Starover's belated complaints about the old slogan of the old *Iskra*, "first draw a line of demarcation and then unite", met with particular sympathy from *Osvobozhdeniye*.

the correctness of this Marxist "hackneyed opinion" better than a war waged against it by Mr. Struve. Please, Mr. Struve, don't put off this splendid plan of yours!)

For the purposes of our subject it is important to note the *practical* slogans now being warred against by this politically sensitive representative of the Russian bourgeoisie who is so responsive to the slightest change in the weather. First, he is warring against the slogan of republicanism. Mr. Struve is firmly convinced that this slogan is "incomprehensible and foreign to the mass of the people" (he has forgotten to add: comprehensible to, but not to the advantage of, the bourgeoisie!). We should like to see what reply Mr. Struve would get from the workers in our study circles and at our mass meetings. Or perhaps the workers are not the people? And what about the peasants? They are sometimes given to what Mr. Struve calls "naïve republicanism" ("to send the tsar packing") —yet the liberal bourgeoisie believes that *naïve* republicanism will be replaced not by enlightened republicanism, but by enlightened monarchism! *Ça dépend*, Mr. Struve; it will depend on circumstances. Both tsarism and the bourgeoisie cannot but oppose a radical improvement in the condition of the peasantry at the expense of the landed estates, whereas the working class cannot but assist the peasantry in this respect.

Secondly, Mr. Struve asserts that "in a civil war the attacker is always in the wrong". This idea verges closely on the above-mentioned new-*Iskra* trends. We will not say, of course, that in civil war it is *always* advantageous to attack; no, sometimes defensive tactics is obligatory *for the time being*. But to apply to the Russia of 1905 a proposition like the one Mr. Struve has made means precisely to demonstrate a little of the "hackneyed radical opinion" ("the bourgeoisie takes fright and betrays the cause of liberty"). Whoever now refuses to attack the autocracy and reaction, whoever fails to prepare for such an attack, and whoever does not advocate it, has no right to call himself an adherent of revolution.

Mr. Struve condemns the slogans: "secrecy" and "rioting" (a riot being "an insurrection in miniature"). Mr. Struve despises both of these—and he does so from the standpoint of "the approach to the masses". We should like to ask Mr. Struve whether he can point to any passage in, for instance, *What Is To Be Done?**—the work, from his standpoint, of an extreme revolutionary—which advocates rioting. As regards "secrecy", is there really much difference between, for example, us and Mr. Struve? Are we not both working on "illegal" newspapers which are being smuggled into Russia "secretly" and serve the "secret" groups of either the *Osvobozhdeniye* League or the R.S.D.L.P.? Our workers' mass meetings are often

---

* See *Collected Works*, Vol. 5, pp. 347-529.—*Ed.*

held "secretly"—we do commit that sin. But what about the meetings held by gentlemen of the *Osvobozhdeniye* League? Have you any grounds to brag, Mr. Struve, and look down upon contemptible partisans of contemptible secrecy?

True, strict secrecy is required in supplying the workers with arms. On this point Mr. Struve is rather more outspoken. Just listen: "As regards insurrection, or a revolution in the technical sense, only mass propaganda in favour of a democratic programme can create the socio-psychological conditions for a general armed uprising. Thus, even from the point of view of an insurrection being the *inevitable* consummation of the present struggle for emancipation— a view I do not share—the imbuing of the masses with ideas of democratic reform is a most fundamental and most necessary task."

Mr. Struve tries to evade the issue. He speaks of the inevitability of an insurrection instead of speaking of its necessity for the victory of the revolution. An insurrection—unprepared, spontaneous, sporadic—has already begun. No one can positively vouch that it will develop into a full-fledged and integral insurrection of the people, for that depends on the state of the revolutionary forces (which can be fully gauged only in the course of the struggle itself), on the behaviour of the government and the bourgeoisie, and on a number of other circumstances, which cannot be estimated with precision. It is pointless to speak of inevitability, in the meaning of absolute certainty with regard to some concrete event, to which Mr. Struve would reduce the matter. What you must speak of, if you would be a partisan of revolution, is whether insurrection is *necessary for the victory* of the revolution, whether it is necessary to proclaim it vigorously, to advocate it and make immediate and energetic preparations for it. Mr. Struve cannot fail to understand this difference: he does not, for instance, obscure the question of the need for universal suffrage—which to a democrat is indisputable—by questioning the inevitability of its attainment in the course of the present revolution—which, to people engaged in political activity, is disputable and of little account. By evading the issue of the need for an insurrection, Mr. Struve reveals the innermost essence of the liberal bourgeoisie's political stand. In the first place, the bourgeoisie would prefer to come to terms with the autocracy rather than crush it; secondly, the bourgeoisie, in all cases, shifts the armed struggle on to the workers' shoulders. That is the *real* meaning of Mr. Struve's evasiveness. That is why he *backs out* of the question of the need for an insurrection, towards the question of its "socio-psychological conditions", and preliminary "propaganda". Just as in the Frankfort Parliament of 1848 the bourgeois windbags were busy drawing up resolutions, declarations, and decisions, engaging in "mass propaganda" and preparing the "socio-psychological conditions", when it was a matter of repelling the government's armed forces, when the movement had "led to the necessity" of an armed struggle, when verbal persuasion alone (which is a hundredfold necessary during the preparatory period) had become banal, bourgeois inactivity and cowardice—so Mr. Struve also evades the question of insurrection, and takes cover behind *phrases*. Mr. Struve shows us revealingly what many Social-Democrats turn a blind eye to, namely, that a revolutionary period differs from ordinary, everyday, preparatory periods in history in that the temper, excitement, and convictions of the masses must and do express themselves in *action*.

Vulgar revolutionism fails to see that words are action, too; this proposition is indisputable when applied to history *in general,* or to those periods of history when no open political mass action takes place. No putches of any sort can replace or artificially evoke such action. Tail-ist revolutionaries fail to understand that when a revolutionary period has set in, when the old "superstructure" has cracked from top to bottom, when open political action by the classes and masses that are creating a new superstructure for themselves has become a fact, and when civil war has begun—it is apathy, lifelessness, pedantry, or else betrayal of the revolution and treachery to it to confine oneself to "words" *in the old way*, without advancing the *direct slogan* on the need to pass over to "action", and to try to avoid action by pleading the need for "psychological conditions" and "propaganda" in general. The democratic bourgeoisie's Frankfort windbags are a memorable historical example of just such treachery or of just such pedantic stupidity.

Would you like an instance provided by the history of the Social-Democratic movement in Russia to explain this difference between vulgar revolutionism and tail-ism in revolutionaries? We shall provide you with such an explanation. Call to mind the years 1901 and 1902, which are so recent, but already seem ancient history to us today. Demonstrations had begun. Vulgar revolutionism had raised a wail about "assault tactics" (*Rabocheye Dyelo*), "bloodthirsty leaflets" were being issued (of Berlin origin, if my memory does not fail me), and attacks were being made on the "literary pretentiousness" and armchair nature of the idea of agitation being conducted on a country-wide scale through a newspaper (Nadezhdin). On the contrary, revolutionaries' tail-ism found expression at the time in the teaching that "the economic struggle is the *best* means of political agitation". How did the revolutionary Social-Democrats behave? They attacked both these trends. They condemned pyrotechnic methods and the cries about assault tactics, for it was, or should have been, obvious to all that open mass action was a matter of the morrow. They condemned tail-ism and openly issued the slogan *even* of a popular insurrection, not in the meaning of a direct appeal (Mr. Struve would not discover any appeal to "riot" in our utterances of that period), but in the meaning of a *necessary* deduction, the meaning of "propaganda" (of which Mr. Struve has only now bethought himself—our worthy Mr. Struve is always several years behind the times), in the sense of preparing those very "socio-psychological conditions" on which the representatives of the bewildered and huckstering bourgeoisie are now "sadly and inappropriately" holding forth. *At that time* propaganda and agitation, agitation and propaganda were really brought to the fore by the objective state of affairs. *At the time* work on an all-Russia political newspaper, the weekly publication of which seemed an ideal, could be proposed (and was proposed in *What Is To Be Done?*) as the touchstone of the work of preparing for an insurrection. *At that time* slogans advocating mass agitation *instead of* direct armed action, preparation of the socio-psychological conditions for insurrection *instead of* pyrotechnics were revolutionary Social-Democracy's only correct slogans. *At the present time* these slogans have been overtaken by events; the movement has left them behind; they have become tatters, rags fit only to cover *Osvobozhdeniye* hypocrisy and new-*Iskra* tail-ism!

Or perhaps I am mistaken? Perhaps the revolution has not yet begun? Perhaps the time has not yet arrived for open political action by the classes? Perhaps there is no civil war yet, and the criticism of weapons should not yet be the *necessary* and obligatory successor, heir, trustee, and consummator of the weapon of criticism?

Get out of your study, look about you, and seek your answer in the streets. Has not the government itself started civil war by everywhere shooting down crowds of peaceful and unarmed citizens? Have not the armed Black Hundreds[62] come out as an "argument" of the autocracy? Has not the bourgeoisie—even the bourgeoisie—recognised the need for a citizens' militia? Does not Mr. Struve himself, the ideally moderate and punctilious Mr. Struve, say (alas, he does so only to evade the issue!) that "the open nature of revolutionary action" (that's what we are like today!) "is now one of the most important conditions for exerting an educational influence upon the mass of the people"?

Those who have eyes to see can have no doubt as to how the question of an insurrection must now be presented by partisans of revolution. Examine the *three* presentations of this question provided in those organs of the free press that are at all capable of influencing the *masses*.

Presentation one. The resolution of the Third Congress of the Russian Social-Democratic Labour Party.* It is publicly acknow-

---

* The following is the text in full:
"1) Whereas the proletariat, being, by virtue of its position, the foremost

ledged and declared that the general democratic revolutionary movement *has already brought about the necessity* of an insurrection.
The organisation of the proletariat for an insurrection has been
placed on the order of the day as one of the essential, principal,
and *indispensable* tasks of the Party. Instructions have been issued
for *most energetic* measures to be taken to arm the proletariat and
ensure the possibility of direct leadership of the insurrection.

Presentation two. An article in *Osvobozhdeniye,* with a statement
of principles, by the "leader of the Russian constitutionalists" (as
Mr. Struve was recently described by so influential an organ of the
European bourgeoisie as *Frankfurter Zeitung*[63]) or the leader of the
Russian progressive bourgeoisie. He does not share the opinion that
an insurrection is inevitable. Secret activity and rioting are the
specific methods of unreasonable revolutionism. Republicanism is
the method of stunning. An insurrection is really a mere technical
question, whereas "the fundamental and most necessary task" is to
carry on mass propaganda and to prepare the socio-psychological
conditions.

Presentation three. The resolution of the new-*Iskra* conference.
Our task is to prepare an insurrection. A planned insurrection is
out of the question. Favourable conditions for an insurrection are
created by the disorganisation of the government, by our agitation,

---

and only consistently revolutionary class, is therefore called upon to play the
leading role in the general democratic revolutionary movement in Russia;

"2) Whereas this movement at the present time has already led to the
necessity of an armed uprising;

"3) Whereas the proletariat will inevitably take the most energetic part in
this uprising, which participation will decide the destiny of the revolution
in Russia;

"4) Whereas the proletariat can play the leading role in this revolution only
if it is united in a single and independent political force under the banner of
the Social-Democratic Labour Party, which directs its struggle both ideologically and practically;

"5) Whereas only the performance of this role will ensure to the proletariat
the most advantageous conditions for the struggle for socialism, against the
propertied classes of bourgeois-democratic Russia;

"Therefore the Third Congress of the R.S.D.L.P. holds that the task of organising the proletariat for direct struggle against the autocracy by means of
the armed uprising is one of the major and most urgent tasks of the Party
at the present revolutionary moment.

"Accordingly, the congress instructs all Party organisations:

"a) to explain to the proletariat by means of propaganda and agitation, not
only the political significance, but the practical organisational aspect of the
impending armed uprising;

"b) to explain in that propaganda and agitation the role of mass political
strikes, which may be of great importance at the beginning and during the
progress of the uprising, and

"c) to take the most energetic steps towards arming the proletariat, as
well as drawing up a plan of the armed uprising and of direct leadership thereof,
for which purpose special groups of Party workers should be formed as and
when necessary." (Author's note to the 1907 edition.—*Ed.*)

and by our organisation. Only then "can technical combat preparations acquire more or less serious significance".

Is that all? Yes, that is all. Whether insurrection has become necessary is something the new-*Iskra* leaders of the proletariat do not yet know. Whether the task of organising the proletariat for the immediate struggle is an urgent one is not yet clear to them. It is not necessary to urge the adoption of the most energetic measures; it is far more important (in 1905, and not in 1902) to explain in general outline under what conditions these measures "may" acquire "more or less serious" significance. . . .

Do you see now, comrades of the new *Iskra,* where your turn to Martynovism has led you? Do you realise that your political philosophy has proved a rehash of the *Osvobozhdeniye* philosophy? —that (against your will, and without your being aware of it) you are following in the wake of the monarchist bourgeoisie? It is now clear to you that, while repeating stale truths and perfecting yourselves in sophistry, you have lost sight of the fact that—in the memorable words of Pyotr Struve's memorable article—"the open nature of revolutionary *action* is now one of the most important conditions for exerting an educational influence upon the mass of the people"?

9. WHAT IS MEANT BY BEING A PARTY OF EXTREME OPPOSITION IN TIME OF REVOLUTION?

Let us return to the resolution on a provisional government. We have shown that new-Iskrist tactics does not push the revolution forward—the possibility of which they would like to ensure by their resolution—but pull it back. We have shown that it is precisely this tactics that *ties the hands* of Social-Democracy in the struggle against the inconsistent bourgeoisie and does not prevent its being dissolved in bourgeois democracy. The false premises of the resolution naturally lead to the following false conclusion: "Therefore, Social-Democracy must not set itself the aim of seizing or sharing power in the provisional government, but must remain the party of extreme revolutionary opposition." Consider the first half of this conclusion, which contains a statement of aims. Do the new-Iskrists declare that the revolution's decisive victory over tsarism is the aim of Social-Democratic activity? They do. They are unable correctly to formulate the conditions of a decisive victory, and lapse into the *Osvobozhdeniye* formulation, but they do set themselves this aim. Further, do they associate a provisional government with insurrection? Yes, they do so directly by stating that a provisional government "will emerge from a victorious popular insurrection". Finally, do they set themselves the aim of guiding the insurrection? Yes, they do. Like Mr. Struve they evade the admission that an insurrection is an urgent necessity, but at the same time, unlike Mr. Struve, they say that "Social-Democracy strives to *subordinate* it (the insurrection) to its influence and *leadership* and to use it in the interests of the working class".

How nicely this hangs together, does it not? We set ourselves the *aim* of subordinating the insurrection of both the proletarian and *non-proletarian* masses to our influence and our leadership, and of using it in our interests. Hence, we set ourselves the aim of leading, in the insurrection, both the proletariat, and the revolutionary bourgeoisie and petty bourgeoisie ("the non-proletarian groups"), i.e., of "*sharing*" the leadership of the insurrection between the Social-Democracy and the revolutionary bourgeoisie. We set ourselves the aim of securing *victory* for the insurrection, which is to lead to the establishment of a provisional government ("which will emerge from a victorious popular insurrection"). *Therefore* ... therefore we must not set ourselves the aim of seizing power or of sharing it in a provisional revolutionary government!!

Our friends cannot make their arguments dovetail. They vacillate between the standpoint of Mr. Struve, who evades the issue of an insurrection, and the standpoint of revolutionary Social-Democracy, which calls upon us to undertake this urgent task. They vacillate between anarchism, which on principle condemns all participation in a provisional revolutionary government as betrayal of the proletariat, and Marxism, which demands such participation, given Social-Democracy's guiding influence in the insurrection.* They have no independent stand whatever: neither that of Mr. Struve, who wants to come to terms with tsarism and is, therefore, compelled to resort to evasions and subterfuges on the question of insurrection, nor that of the anarchists, who condemn all action "from above" and all participation in a bourgeois revolution. The new-*Iskra* group confuses a deal with tsarism and a victory over the latter. They want to take part in a bourgeois revolution. They have gone somewhat beyond Martynov's *Two Dictatorships*. They even consent to lead an insurrection of the people—in order to renounce that leadership immediately after victory is won (or, perhaps, immediately before the victory?), i.e., *in order not to avail themselves of the fruits of victory*, but to turn all these fruits over *entirely to the bourgeoisie*. This is what they call "using the insurrection in the interests of the working class. ..."

There is no need to dwell on this muddle any longer. It will be more useful to examine how this muddle *originated* in the formulation which reads: "remain the party of extreme revolutionary opposition".

---

* See *Proletary*, No. 3, "On the Provisional Revolutionary Government", article two, 1905. (See *Collected Works*, Vol. 8, pp. 474-81.—*Ed.*)

This is one of the familiar propositions of international revolutionary Social-Democracy. It is a perfectly correct proposition. It has become a common place to all opponents of revisionism or opportunism in parliamentary countries. It has become generally accepted as the legitimate and necessary rebuff to "parliamentary cretinism", to Millerandism, Bernsteinism, and Italian reformism of the Turati brand. Our good new-Iskrists have learned this excellent proposition by heart and are zealously applying it ... *quite inappropriately*. Categories of the parliamentary struggle are introduced into resolutions written for conditions   in which no parliament exists. The concept "opposition", which is the reflection and the expression of a political situation in which no one seriously speaks of an *insurrection,* is meaninglessly applied to a situation in which insurrection *has begun* and in which all supporters of revolution are thinking and talking about leadership in it. The desire to *"remain"* with the old methods, i.e., action only "from below", is voiced with pomp and clamour *precisely at a time* when the revolution has confronted us with the necessity, in the event of a victorious insurrection, of acting *from above.*

No, our new-*Iskra* group is decidedly out of luck! Even when they formulate a correct Social-Democratic proposition they do not know how to apply it correctly. They have failed to understand that when the revolution gets under way, and there are civil war and insurrectionary outbursts, but still no parliament, terms and concepts of parliamentary struggle undergo a transformation and turn into their opposites. They do not realise that in the conditions under examination amendments are introduced by means of street demonstrations, interpellations are made by means of offensive action by armed citizens, and opposition to the government is effected by the forcible overthrow of that government.

Just as the well-known hero of our folk epos repeated good advice when it was out of place, our admirers of Martynov repeat the lessons of peaceful parliamentarism at a time when, as they themselves state, actual hostilities have begun. There is nothing more ridiculous than this pompous advancement of the slogan of "extreme opposition" in a resolution which begins by referring to a "decisive victory of the revolution" and to a "popular insurrection"! Try to conceive, gentlemen, what it means to · be the "extreme opposition" in a period of insurrection. Does it mean exposing the government, or deposing it? Does it mean voting against the government, or defeating its armed forces in open battle? Does it mean refusing to replenish the government's exchequer, or the revolutionary seizure of that exchequer for the needs of the uprising, to arm the workers and peasants, and to convoke a constituent assembly? Are you not beginning to understand, gentlemen, that the term "extreme opposition" expresses only negative actions

—exposing, voting against, refusing? Why is that so? Because this term applies only to the parliamentary struggle and, moreover, in a period when no one makes "decisive victory" the immediate object of the struggle. Are you not beginning to understand that things change cardinally in this respect, from the moment the politically oppressed people launch a determined attack along the whole front in desperate struggle for victory?

The workers ask us: Must the urgent business of insurrection be energetically begun? What is to be done to make the incipient insurrection victorious? What use should be made of victory? What programme can and should then be implemented? The new-Iskrists, who are making Marxism more profound, answer: we must remain the party of extreme revolutionary opposition.... Well, were we not right in calling these knights past masters of philistinism?

10. "REVOLUTIONARY COMMUNES" AND THE REVOLUTIONARY-DEMOCRATIC DICTATORSHIP OF THE PROLETARIAT AND THE PEASANTRY

The Conference of the new-*Iskra* group did not keep to the anarchist stand into which the new *Iskra* had talked itself (action only "from below", not "from below and from above"). The absurdity of admitting the possibility of an insurrection and not admitting the possibility of victory and participation in a provisional revolutionary government was too glaring. The resolution, therefore, introduced certain reservations and restrictions into the Martynov-Martov solution of the question. Let us consider these reservations, as stated in the following section of the resolution:

"This tactic" ("to remain the party of extreme revolutionary opposition") "does not, of course, in any way exclude the expediency of a partial and episodic seizure of power and the establishment of revolutionary communes in one city or another, or in one district or another, exclusively for the purpose of helping to spread the insurrection and of disrupting the government."

If that is the case, it means the admission in principle of action not only from below, but also from above. It means that the proposition laid down in L. Martov's well-known *feuilleton* in *Iskra* (No. 93) is discarded, and that the tactics of *Vperyod*, i.e., not only "from below", but also "from above", is acknowledged as correct.

Further, the seizure of power (even if partial, episodic, etc.) obviously presupposes participation not only of Social-Democrats, and not only of the proletariat. This follows from the fact that it is not the proletariat alone that is interested and takes an active part in a democratic revolution. It follows from the insurrection being a "popular" one, as is stated at the beginning of the resolution under examination, with "non-proletarian groups" (the words used in the conference resolution on the uprising), i.e., the bourgeoisie, also taking part in it. Hence, the principle that any participation of socialists in a provisional revolutionary government jointly with the petty bourgeoisie is betrayal of the working class *was thrown overboard by the conference*, which is what *Vperyod* sought to achieve. "Betrayal" does not cease to be betrayal because the action constituting it is partial, episodic, local, etc. Hence, the idea that participation in a provisional revolutionary government is tantamount to vulgar Jaurèsism *was thrown overboard* by the conference, which is what *Vperyod* sought to achieve. A government does not cease to be a government because its power extends not to many cities but to a single city, not to many districts but to a single district, or because of the name it bears. Thus, *the theoretical presentation of this question*, as attempted by the new *Iskra, was discarded by the conference.*

Let us see whether the restrictions the conference imposed on the formation of revolutionary governments and on participation in them, which are now admitted in principle, are reasonable. We are not aware of the distinction between "episodic" and "provisional".* We are afraid that the former word, which is "new" and foreign, is merely a screen for lack of clear thinking. It *seems* "more profound", but actually it is only more obscure and confused. What is the difference between the "expediency" of a partial "seizure of power" in a city or district, and participation in a provisional revolutionary government of the entire state? Do not "cities" include a city like St. Petersburg where the events of January 9 took place? Do not districts include the Caucasus, which is bigger than many a state? Will not the problems (which at one time embarrassed the new *Iskra*) of what to do with the prisons, the police, the treasury, etc., confront us the moment we "seize power" even in a single city, let alone in a district? No one will deny, of course, that if we lack sufficient forces, if the insurrection is not wholly successful, or if the victory is indecisive, provisional revolutionary governments may possibly be set up in individual localities, in individual cities and the like. But what has all that got to do with the point at issue, gentlemen? Do not you yourselves, in the beginning of the resolution, speak of a "decisive victory of the revolution", a "victorious popular insurrection"?? Since when have Social-Democrats taken over the job of the anarchists: splitting the attention and the aims of the proletariat, and directing its attention to the "partial", instead of the general, the single, the integral, and the complete? While presupposing "seizure of power"

---

* The first word was in scholarly use at the time, while the second was, and still is, colloquial Russian.—*Tr.*

in a city, you yourselves speak of "extending the insurrection"—to another city, may we venture to think?—to all cities, may we dare to hope? Your conclusions, gentlemen, are as unsound and haphazard, as contradictory and confused, as your premises. The Third Congress of the R.S.D.L.P. gave an exhaustive and clear answer to the question of a provisional revolutionary government in general. This answer covers all cases of local provisional governments as well. However, by artificially and arbitrarily isolating a *part* of the question, the conference's answer merely *evades* the issue as a whole (and that unsuccessfully), and creates confusion.

What is meant by "revolutionary communes"? Does this concept differ from "a provisional revolutionary government", and, if so, in what respect? The gentlemen of the conference do not know themselves. Confusion of revolutionary thought leads them, as very often happens, to *revolutionary phrase-mongering*. Indeed, the use of the words "revolutionary commune" in a resolution passed by representatives of Social-Democracy is revolutionary phrase-mongering and nothing else. Marx often condemned such phrase-mongering in which some "charming" terms from the *outworn past* are used to conceal the tasks of the future. In such cases the charm of a term which has already played its part in history becomes so much useless and harmful tinsel, a child's rattle. We must give the workers and the whole people a clear and unambiguous notion as to *why* we want a provisional revolutionary government to be set up, and *exactly what changes* we shall bring about if we exercise decisive influence on the government on the very day following the victory of the popular insurrection which has already commenced. These are questions confronting political leaders.

The Third Congress of the R.S.D.L.P. replied to these questions with absolute clarity, and drew up a complete programme of these changes—our Party's minimum programme. The word "commune", however, gives no answer at all; it only confuses people's minds with the distant echo of a sonorous phrase or empty rhetoric. The more we cherish, for instance, the memory of the Paris Commune of 1871, the less permissible is it to refer to it offhand, without analysing its mistakes and the special conditions attending it. To do so would mean repeating the absurd example of the Blanquists—whom Engels ridiculed—who (in 1874, in their *Manifesto*) paid homage to every act of the Commune.[64] What reply will a conferee give to a worker who asks him about *this* "revolutionary commune", the one that is mentioned in the resolution? He will only be able to tell him that this is the name by which a certain workers' government is known in history, a government that was unable to, and could not, at that time, distinguish between the elements of a democratic revolution and a socialist revolution, a government that confused the tasks of fighting for a republic with those of fighting for socialism, was unable to launch an energetic military offensive against Versailles,[65] made a mistake in failing to seize the Bank of France, etc. In short, whether in your answer you refer to the Paris Commune or to some other commune, your answer will be: it was a government *such as ours should not be.* A fine answer, indeed! Does it not testify to pedantic moralising and impotence on the part of a revolutionary, when a resolution says nothing about the practical programme of the Party and inappropriately begins giving lessons from history? Does this not reveal the very mistake we have unsuccessfully been accused of, i.e., confusing a democratic revolution with a socialist revolution, between which none of the "communes" was able to distinguish?

Extending the insurrection and disorganising the government are presented as the "exclusive" aim of a provisional government (so inappropriately termed a "commune"). Taken in its literal sense, the word "exclusive" eliminates all other aims; it is an echo of the absurd theory of "only from below". Such elimination of other aims is another instance of short-sightedness and lack of reflection. A "revolutionary commune", i.e., a revolutionary government, even if only in a single city, will inevitably have to administer (even if provisionally, "partly, episodically") all affairs of state, and it is the height of folly to hide one's head under one's wing and refuse to see this. This government will have to enact an eight-hour working day, establish workers' inspection of factories, institute free universal education, introduce the election of judges, set up peasant committees, etc.; in a word, it will certainly have to carry out a number of reforms. To designate these reforms as "helping to spread the insurrection" would be playing with words and deliberately causing greater confusion in a matter that calls for absolute clarity.

————

The concluding part of the new-*Iskra* conference resolution provides no fresh material for a criticism of basic Economist trends that have been revived in our Party, but it does illustrate, from a somewhat different angle, what has been said above.

Here is that concluding part:

"Only in one event should Social-Democracy on its own initiative direct its efforts towards seizing power and holding it as long as possible—namely, in the event of the revolution spreading to the advanced countries of Western Europe, where conditions for the achievement of socialism have already reached a certain [?] degree of maturity. In that event the limited historical scope of the Russian revolution can be considerably widened and the possibility will arise of entering on the path of socialist reforms.

"By basing its tactics on the expectation that during the entire revolutionary period the Social-Democratic Party will retain its stand of extreme revolutionary opposition to all governments that may succeed one another in the course of the revolution, Social-Democracy will best be able to prepare itself to utilise governmental power if it falls [??] into its hands."

The basic idea here is the one repeatedly formulated by *Vperyod*, which has stated that we must not be afraid (as Martynov is) of Social-Democracy's complete victory in a democratic revolution, i.e., of a revolutionary-democratic dictatorship of the proletariat and the peasantry, for such a victory will enable us to rouse Europe; after throwing off the yoke of the bourgeoisie, the socialist proletariat of Europe will in its turn help us to accomplish the socialist revolution. But see how the new-*Iskra* rendering impairs this idea. We shall not dwell on details; on the absurd assumption that power could "fall" into the hands of a class-conscious party which considers seizure of power harmful tactics; on the fact that in Europe the conditions for socialism have reached not a certain degree of maturity, but maturity in general; on the fact that our Party programme knows no socialist reforms, but only the socialist revolution. Let us take the principal and basic difference between *Vperyod*'s idea and the one presented in the resolution. *Vperyod* set the revolutionary proletariat of Russia an active task: winning the battle for democracy and using this victory to bring the revolution into Europe. The resolution fails to grasp this link between our "decisive victory" (not in the new-*Iskra* sense) and the revolution in Europe, and, therefore, it does not speak of the tasks of the proletariat or the prospects of the *latter*'s victory, but of one of the possibilities in general: "in the event of the revolution spreading...." *Vperyod* pointedly and definitely indicated—and this was incorporated in the resolution of the Third Congress of the Russian Social-Democratic Labour Party—how "governmental power" can and must "be utilised" in the interests of the proletariat, bearing in mind what can be achieved immediately, at a given stage of social development, and what must first be achieved as a democratic prerequisite of the struggle for socialism. Here, too, the resolution lags hopelessly behind when it states: "will be able to prepare itself to utilise", but fails to say *how* it will be able, *how* it will prepare itself, and to utilise *for what purpose*. We have no doubt, for instance, that the new-Iskrists may be "able to prepare themselves to utilise" their leading position in the Party, but the point is that so far their experience of that utilisation, their preparation, does not hold out much hope of possibility becoming reality....

Vperyod stated quite definitely wherein lies the real "possibility of retaining power"—namely, in the revolutionary-democratic dictatorship of the proletariat and the peasantry; in their joint mass strength, which is capable of outweighing all the forces of counter-revolution; in the inevitable concurrence of their interests in *demo-*

cratic reforms. Here, too, the resolution of the conference gives us nothing positive; it merely evades the issue. Surely, the possibility of retaining power in Russia must be determined by the composition of the social forces in Russia herself, by the circumstances of the democratic revolution now taking place in our country. A victory of the proletariat in Europe (it is still quite a far cry from bringing the revolution into Europe to the victory of the proletariat) will give rise to a desperate counter-revolutionary struggle on the part of the Russian bourgeoisie—yet the resolution of the new-Iskrists does not say a word about this counter-revolutionary force whose significance was appraised in the resolution of the R.S.D.L.P.'s Third Congress. If, in our fight for a republic and democracy, we could not rely upon the peasantry as well as upon the proletariat, the prospect of our "retaining power" would be hopeless. But if it is not hopeless, if the "revolution's decisive victory over tsarism" opens up such a possibility, then we must indicate it, call actively for its transformation into reality, and issue practical slogans not only *for the contingency* of the revolution being brought into Europe, but also *for the purpose* of taking it there. The reference made by tail-ist Social-Democrats to the "limited historical scope of the Russian revolution" merely serves to cover up their limited understanding of the aims of this democratic revolution, and of the proletariat's leading role in it!

One of the objections raised to the slogan of "the revolutionary-democratic dictatorship of the proletariat and the peasantry" is that dictatorship presupposes a "single will" (*Iskra*, No. 95), and that there can be no single will of the proletariat and the petty bourgeoisie. This objection is unsound, for it is based on an abstract, "metaphysical" interpretation of the term "single will". There may be a single will in one respect and not in another. The absence of unity on questions of socialism and in the struggle for socialism does not preclude singleness of will on questions of democracy and in the struggle for a republic. To forget this would be tantamount to forgetting the logical and historical difference between a democratic revolution and a socialist revolution. To forget this would be tantamount to forgetting the character of the democratic revolution as one *of the whole people*: if it is "of the whole people", that means that there *is* "singleness of will" precisely in so far as this revolution meets the needs and requirements of the whole people. Beyond the bounds of democratism there can be no question of the proletariat and the peasant bourgeoisie having a single will. Class struggle between them is inevitable, but it is in a democratic republic that this struggle will be the most thoroughgoing and widespread struggle of the people *for socialism*. Like everything else in the world, the revolutionary-democratic dictatorship of the proletariat and the peasantry has a past and a future. Its past is autocracy, serfdom, monarchy, and privilege. In the struggle against this past, in the struggle against counter-revolution, a "single will" of the proletariat and the peasantry is possible, for here there is unity of interests.

Its future is the struggle against private property, the struggle of the wage-worker against the employer, the struggle for socialism. Here singleness of will is impossible.* Here the path before us lies not from autocracy to a republic, but from a petty-bourgeois democratic republic to socialism.

Of course, in actual historical circumstances, the elements of the past become interwoven with those of the future; the two paths cross. Wage-labour with its struggle against private property exists under the autocracy as well; it arises even under serfdom. But this does not in the least prevent us from logically and historically distinguishing between the major stages of development. We all contrapose bourgeois revolution and socialist revolution; we all insist on the absolute necessity of strictly distinguishing between them; however, can it be denied that in the course of history individual, *particular* elements of the two revolutions become interwoven? Has the period of democratic revolutions in Europe not been familiar with a number of socialist movements and attempts to establish socialism? And will not the future socialist revolution in Europe still have to complete a great deal left undone in the field of democratism?

A Social-Democrat must never for a moment forget that the proletariat will inevitably have to wage a class struggle for socialism even against the most democratic and republican bourgeoisie and petty bourgeoisie. This is beyond doubt. Hence, the absolute necessity of a separate, independent, strictly class party of Social-Democracy. Hence, the temporary nature of our tactics of "striking a joint blow" with the bourgeoisie and the duty of keeping a strict watch "over our ally, as over an enemy", etc. All this also leaves no room for doubt. However, it would be ridiculous and reactionary to deduce from this that we must forget, ignore, or neglect tasks which, although transient and temporary, are vital at the present time. The struggle against the autocracy is a temporary and transient task for socialists, but to ignore or neglect this task in any way amounts to betrayal of socialism and service to reaction. The revolutionary-democratic dictatorship of the proletariat and the peasantry is unquestionably only a transient, temporary socialist aim, but to ignore this aim in the period of a democratic revolution would be downright reactionary.

---

* The development of capitalism, more extensive and rapid in conditions of liberty, will inevitably soon put an end to singleness of will; that will take place the sooner, the earlier counter-revolution and reaction are crushed.

Concrete political aims must be set in concrete circumstances. All things are relative, all things flow, and all things change. German Social-Democracy does not put into its programme the demand for a republic. The situation in Germany is such that this question can in practice hardly be separated from that of socialism (although with regard to Germany, too, Engels in his comments on the draft of the Erfurt Programme in 1891[66] warned against belittling the importance of a republic and of the struggle for a republic!). In Russian Social-Democracy the question of eliminating the demand for a republic from its programme and its agitation has never even arisen, for in our country there can be no talk of an indissoluble link between the question of a republic and that of socialism. It was quite natural for a German Social-Democrat of 1898 not to place special emphasis on the question of a republic, and this evokes neither surprise nor condemnation. But in 1848 a German Social-Democrat who would have relegated to the background the question of a republic would have been a downright traitor to the revolution. There is no such thing as abstract truth. Truth is always concrete.

The time will come when the struggle against the Russian autocracy will end, and the period of democratic revolution will have passed in Russia; it will then be ridiculous even to speak of "singleness of will" of the proletariat and the peasantry, about a democratic dictatorship, etc. When that time comes we shall deal directly with the question of the socialist dictatorship of the proletariat and speak of it in greater detail. At present the party of the advanced class cannot but strive most energetically for the democratic revolution's decisive victory over tsarism. And a decisive victory means nothing else than the revolutionary-democratic dictatorship of the proletariat and the peasantry.

Note

1) We would remind the reader that in the polemic between *Iskra* and *Vperyod*, the former referred, among other things, to Engels's letter to Turati,[67] in which Engels warned the (future) leader of the Italian reformists against confusing the democratic revolution with the socialist. The impending revolution in Italy, Engels wrote about the political situation in Italy in 1894, would be a petty-bourgeois, democratic and not a socialist revolution. *Iskra* reproached *Vperyod* with having departed from the principle laid down by Engels. This reproach was unjustified, because, on the whole, *Vperyod* (No. 14) fully acknowledged the correctness of Marx's theory of the distinction between the three main forces in nineteenth century revolutions.* According to this theory, the

---

* See *Collected Works*, Vol. 8, pp. 275-92.—*Ed.*

following forces take a stand against the old order, against the autocracy, feudalism, and the serf-owning system: 1) the liberal big bourgeoisie, 2) the radical petty bourgeoisie, 3) the proletariat. The first fights for nothing more than a constitutional monarchy; the second, for a democratic republic; the third, for a socialist revolution. To confuse the petty bourgeoisie's struggle for a complete democratic revolution with the proletariat's struggle for a socialist revolution threatens the socialist with political bankruptcy. Marx's warning to this effect is quite justified. It is, however, precisely for this very reason that the slogan of "revolutionary communes" is erroneous, because the very mistake made by the communes known to history was that of confusing the democratic revolution with the socialist revolution. On the other hand, our slogan—a revolutionary democratic dictatorship of the proletariat and the peasantry—fully safeguards us against this mistake. While recognising the incontestably bourgeois nature of a revolution incapable of *directly* overstepping the bounds of a mere democratic revolution our slogan *advances* this particular revolution and strives to give it forms most advantageous to the proletariat; consequently, it strives to make the utmost of the democratic revolution in order to attain the greatest success in the proletariat's further struggle for socialism.

11. A CURSORY COMPARISON BETWEEN SEVERAL OF THE RESOLUTIONS OF THE THIRD CONGRESS OF THE R.S.D.L.P. AND THOSE OF THE "CONFERENCE"

The question of the provisional revolutionary government is at present the pivotal tactical question of the Social-Democratic movement. It is neither possible nor necessary to dwell in similar detail on the other resolutions of the conference. We shall confine ourselves merely to referring briefly to several points which confirm the difference in principle, analysed above, between the tactical trend in the resolutions of the Third Congress of the R.S.D.L.P. and that in the conference resolutions.

Take the question of the attitude towards the government's tactics on the eve of revolution. Once again you will find a comprehensive answer to this question in a resolution of the Third Congress of the R.S.D.L.P. This resolution takes into account all the multifarious conditions and tasks of the particular moment: exposure of the hypocrisy of the government's concessions; utilisation of "travesties of popular representation"; the revolutionary realisation of the working class's urgent demands (the principal one being the eight-hour working day), and, finally, resistance to the Black Hundreds. In the conference resolutions this question is dealt with piecemeal in several sections: "resistance to the evil forces of reaction" is mentioned only in the preamble to the resolution on the attitude towards other parties. Participation in elections to representative bodies is considered apart from tsarism's "compromises" with the bourgeoisie. Instead of calling for the achievement of an eight-hour working day by revolutionary means a special resolution with the pretentious title "On the Economic Struggle" merely repeats (after high-flown and very stupid phrases about "the central place occupied by the labour question in Russian public life") the old slogan of campaigning for "the legislative institution of an eight-hour day". The inadequacy and the belatedness of this slogan at the present time are too obvious to require proof.

The question of open political action. The Third Congress takes into consideration the impending *radical* change in our activities. Secret activities and the development of the underground organisation must on no account be abandoned: this would be playing into the hands of the police and be of the utmost advantage to the government. But at the same time we must give thought to open action as well. Expedient forms of such action and, consequently, special bodies—less secret—must be *prepared* immediately for this purpose. Legal and semi-legal associations must be made use of with a view to transforming them, as far as possible, into bases for the future open Social-Democratic Labour Party in Russia.

Here, too, the conference splits up the issue and fails to bring forward any integral slogans. What strikes the eye is the ridiculous instruction to the Organising Committee to see to the "placement" of legally functioning publicists. Then there is the totally absurd decision "to subordinate to our influence the democratic newspapers that set themselves the aim of rendering assistance to the working-class movement". This is the professed aim of all our legal liberal newspapers, nearly all of which are of the *Osvobozhdeniye* trend. Why should not the *Iskra* Editorial Board themselves make a start in carrying out their advice and give us an example of how to subordinate *Osvobozhdeniye* to Social-Democratic influence? Instead of the slogan of utilising legally existing associations so as to establish bases for the *Party*, we are given, first, a particular piece of advice about "trade" unions only (Party members must be active in them), and, secondly, advice to guide "the revolutionary organisations of the workers"="unofficially constituted organisations"="revolutionary workers' clubs". How these "clubs" have come to be classed as unofficially constituted organisations, and what these "clubs" really are—goodness only knows. Instead of definite and clear instructions from a supreme Party body we have some thoughts jotted down at random and some rough drafts made by men of letters. There is no complete picture of the beginning of the Party's transition to an entirely new basis in all its work. The "peasant question" was presented in entirely different ways by the Party Congress and the conference. The congress drew up a resolution on the "attitude to the peasant movement"; the conference—on "work among the peasants". In the one case prominence is given to the task of guiding the entire revolutionary-democratic movement in the general national interests of the struggle against tsarism. In the other case the question is reduced to mere "work" among a particular section of society. In the one case a central practical slogan for our agitation is advanced calling for the immediate organisation of revolutionary peasant committees in order to carry out all democratic changes. In the other, a "demand for the organisation of committees" is to be presented to a constituent assembly. Why should we wait for this constituent assembly? Will it really be constituent? Will it be stable without the preliminary and simultaneous establishment of revolutionary peasant committees? The conference has lost sight of all these questions. Its decisions all reflect the general idea which we have been following up—namely, that in the bourgeois revolution we must do only our own special work, without pursuing the aim of guiding the entire democratic movement, and of conducting that movement independently. Just as the Economists were constantly falling into the fallacy that the economic struggle is for the Social-Democrats, while the political struggle is for the liberals, so the new-*Iskra* supporters, in all their reasonings, keep falling into the idea that we should modestly sit in a corner out of the way of the bourgeois revolution, with the bourgeoisie doing the active work of carrying out the revolution.

Finally, note must also be taken of the resolution on the attitude toward other parties. The resolution of the Third Congress of the R.S.D.L.P. speaks of exposing all limitedness and inadequacy in the bourgeois movement for emancipation, without entertaining the naïve idea of enumerating, from congress to congress, every possible instance of such limitedness, or of drawing a line of distinction between bad bourgeois and good bourgeois. Repeating the mistake made by Starover the conference persistently searched for that line and developed the famous "litmus-paper" theory. Starover proceeded from a very good idea—that of presenting the severest possible conditions to the bourgeoisie. Only he forgot that any attempt to separate in advance bourgeois democrats that deserve approval, agreements, etc., from those that do not deserve them leads to a "formula" which is immediately scrapped by developments and introduces confusion into proletarian class-consciousness. From real unity in the struggle the emphasis is shifted to declarations, promises, and slogans. Starover held that "universal and equal suffrage, direct elections and the secret ballot" was such a radical slogan. Hardly had two years elapsed when the "litmus-paper" proved its uselessness and the slogan of universal suffrage was taken over by the *Osvobozhdeniye* group, who thereby not only came no closer to Social-Democracy, but, on the contrary, tried by means of that very slogan to mislead the workers and divert them from socialism.

Now the new-Iskrists are presenting "conditions" that are even "severer". They are "demanding" from the enemies of tsarism "energetic and unequivocal [!?] support of every determined action by the organised proletariat", etc., up to, and including, "active participation in the self-arming of the people". The line has been carried much further—but nevertheless this line is *again already obsolete*, at once revealing its uselessness. Why, for instance, is there no slogan for a republic? How is it that the Social-Democrats—in the interests of "relentless revolutionary war against all the foundations of the system of social estates and the monarchy" —"demand" from the bourgeois democrats anything you like except the struggle for a republic?

That this question is not mere captiousness, that the new-Iskrists' mistake is of vital political significance is proved by the Russian Liberation Union (see *Proletary*, No. 4).* These "enemies of tsarism" will meet in full all the "requirements" of the new-*Iskra* supporters. And yet we have shown that the *Osvobozhdeniye* spirit reigns in the programme (or lack of programme) of this "Russian Liberation Union", and that the *Osvobozhdeniye* group can easily take it in tow. However, in the concluding section of the resolution the conference declares that "Social-Democracy will continue to oppose, as *hypocritical friends of the people*, all those political parties which, though they display a liberal and democratic banner, refuse to render genuine support to the revolutionary struggle of the proletariat". The Russian Liberation Union not only does not withhold this support, but offers it most insistently. Is that a guarantee that the leaders of this union are not "hypocritical friends of the people", even though they are "liberationists"?

You see: by inventing "conditions" in advance, and presenting "demands" that are ludicrous by reason of their redoubtable impotence, the new-Iskrists immediately put themselves in a ridiculous position. Their conditions and demands immediately prove

---

* *Proletary*, No. 4, which appeared on June 4, 1905, contained a lengthy article entitled "A New Revolutionary Workers' Association" (see *Collected Works*, Vol. 8, pp. 499-510.—*Ed.*). The article gives the contents of the appeals issued by this union, which assumed the name of the "Russian Liberation Union" and set itself the aim of convening a constituent assembly with the aid of an insurrection. Further, the article defines the attitude of Social-Democrats to such non-party unions. In what measure this union really existed and what its fate was in the revolution is absolutely unknown to us. (Author's note to the 1907 edition.—*Ed.*)

inadequate when it comes to an appraisal of living realities. Their chase after formulas is hopeless, for no formula can embrace all the various manifestations of hypocrisy, inconsistency, and narrow-mindedness displayed by the bourgeois democrats. It is not a question of "litmus-paper", formulas, or written and printed demands, nor is it a question of drawing, in advance, a line of distinction between hypocritical and sincere "friends of the people"; it is a question of real unity in the struggle, of the Social-Democrats unabatingly criticising every "uncertain" step taken by bourgeois democracy. What is needed for "genuine consolidation of all the social forces interested in democratic change" is not the "points" over which the conference laboured so assiduously and so vainly, but the ability to put forward genuinely revolutionary slogans. For this slogans are needed that will raise the revolutionary and republican bourgeoisie to the level of the proletariat, and not lower the aims of the proletariat to the level of the monarchist bourgeoisie. What is needed for this is the most energetic participation in the insurrection, not sophistical evasion of the urgent task of an insurrection.

12. WILL THE SWEEP OF THE DEMOCRATIC REVOLUTION BE DIMINISHED IF THE BOURGEOISIE RECOILS FROM IT?

The foregoing lines were already written when a copy came to hand of the resolutions adopted by the Caucasian Conference of the new-Iskrists, and published by *Iskra*. Even if we tried we could not invent anything better *pour la bonne bouche* (as a titbit).

The editors of *Iskra* remark with full justice: "On the fundamental question of tactics the Caucasian Conference also arrived at a decision *analogous*" (in truth!) "to that adopted by the All-Russia Conference" (i.e., of the new-*Iskra* group). "The question of Social-Democracy's attitude towards a provisional revolutionary government has been settled by the Caucasian comrades in the spirit of most outspoken opposition to the new method advocated by the *Vperyod* group and the delegates of the so-called congress who joined it." "It must be admitted that the formulation of the proletarian party's tactics in a bourgeois revolution, as given by the conference, is *most apt.*"

What is true is true. No one could have given a more "apt" formulation of the fundamental error of the new-*Iskra* group. We shall quote this formulation in full, first mentioning parenthetically the blossoms, and then, at the end, the fruit.

Here is the resolution on a provisional government adopted by the Caucasian Conference of new-*Iskra* supporters:

"Whereas we consider it to be our task to take advantage of the revolutionary situation so as to deepen [of course! They should have added: "à la Martynov!"] Social-Democratic consciousness in the proletariat [only to render the consciousness more profound, and not to win a republic? What a "profound" conception of revolution!] and in order to secure for the Party complete freedom to criticise the nascent bourgeois-state system [it is not our business to secure a republic! Our business is only to secure freedom of criticism. Anarchist ideas engender anarchist language: "bourgeois-state" system!], the conference declares itself against the formation of a Social-Democratic provisional government, and entering such a government [recall the resolution passed by the Bakuninists ten months before the Spanish revolution and referred to by Engels: see *Proletary*, No. 3], and considers it to be the most expedient course to exercise pressure from without [from below and not from above] upon the bourgeois provisional government in order to secure a feasible measure [!?] of democratisation of the state system. The conference believes that the formation of a provisional government by Social-Democrats, or their entering such a government would lead, on the one hand, to the masses of the proletariat becoming disappointed in the Social-Democratic Party and abandoning it, because the Social-Democrats, despite the seizure of power, would not be able to satisfy the pressing needs of the working class, including the establishment of socialism [a republic is not a pressing need! The authors in their innocence do not notice that they are speaking purely anarchist language, as if they were repudiating participation in bourgeois revolutions!], and, on the other hand, *would cause the bourgeois classes to recoil from the revolution and thus diminish its sweep*."

That is the crux of the matter. That is where anarchist ideas become interwoven (as is constantly the case among the West-European Bernsteinians too) with the sheerest opportunism. Just imagine: these people will not enter a provisional government because that would cause the bourgeoisie to recoil from the revolution, thereby diminishing the sweep of the revolution! Here, indeed, we have the new-*Iskra* philosophy as a whole, in a pure and consistent form: since the revolution is a bourgeois revolution, we must bow to bourgeois philistinism and make way for it. If we are even in part, even for a moment, guided by the consideration that our participation may cause the bourgeoisie to recoil, we thereby simply hand over leadership of the revolution entirely to the bourgeois classes. We thereby place the proletariat entirely under the tutelage of the bourgeoisie (while retaining complete "freedom of criticism"!!), compelling the proletariat to be moderate and meek, so that the bourgeoisie should not recoil. We emasculate the most vital needs of the proletariat, namely, its political needs—which the Economists and their imitators have never properly understood—so as not to

make the bourgeoisie recoil. We go over completely from the platform of revolutionary struggle for the achievement of democracy to
the extent required by the proletariat, to a platform of chaffering
with the bourgeoisie, buying the bourgeoisie's voluntary consent
("so that it should not recoil") at the price of our principles, by
betraying the revolution.

In two short lines, the Caucasian new-Iskrists managed to express
the gist of the tactic of betraying revolution and converting the proletariat into a wretched appendage of the bourgeois classes. That
which we deduced above from the errors of the new-*Iskra* tendency
we now see elevated to a clear and definite principle, viz., following
in the wake of the monarchist bourgeoisie. Since the establishment
of a republic would make the bourgeoisie recoil (and is already doing so—Mr. Struve is an example), down with the fight for a republic. Since every energetic and consistent democratic demand on the
part of the proletariat makes the bourgeoisie recoil, always and
everywhere in the world—hide in your lairs, working men; act only
from without; do not dream of using, in the interests of the revolution, the instruments and weapons of the "bourgeois-state" system;
reserve for yourselves "freedom of criticism"!

The fundamental fallacy in their very conception of the term
"bourgeois revolution" has come to the surface. The Martynov or
new-*Iskra* "conception" of this term leads directly to the proletariat's
cause being betrayed to the bourgeoisie.

Those who have forgotten the old Economism and do not study
or remember it will find it difficult to understand the present resur-
gence of Economism. Call to mind the Bernsteinian *Credo*. From
"purely proletarian" views and programmes its authors drew the
following conclusion: we Social-Democrats must concern ourselves
with economics, with the real working-class cause, with freedom to
criticise all political chicanery, with really rendering Social-Democratic work more profound. Politics are for the liberals. God save us
from falling into "revolutionism": that will make the bourgeoisie
recoil. Those who will re-read the whole *Credo*[68] or the Separate
Supplement to No. 9 of *Rabochaya Mysl* (September 1899) will
discern the entire course of this reasoning.

Today we have the same thing, only on a large scale, applied to
an appraisal of the whole of the "great" Russian revolution—alas,
vulgarised and reduced in advance to a travesty by the theoreticians
of orthodox philistinism! We Social-Democrats must concern
ourselves with freedom of criticism, with making class-consciousness
more profound, with action from without. They, the bourgeois
classes, must have freedom to act, a free field for revolutionary
(read: liberal) leadership, freedom to effect "reforms" from above.

These vulgarisers of Marxism have never given thought to what
Marx said about the need to replace the weapon of criticism by the

criticism of weapons.[69] Taking the name of Marx in vain they, in actual fact, draw up resolutions on tactics wholly in the spirit of the Frankfort bourgeois windbags, who freely criticised absolutism and deepened democratic consciousness, but failed to understand that a time of revolution is a time of action, of action from both above and below. By turning Marxism into sophistry they have turned the ideology of the advanced, the most determined, and energetic revolutionary class into an ideology of its most backward strata, of those who shrink from difficult revolutionary-democratic tasks, and leave them to Messrs. the Struves to take care of.

If the bourgeois classes recoil from revolution because Social-Democrats enter a revolutionary government they will thereby "diminish the sweep" of the revolution.

Listen to that, Russian workers: the sweep of the revolution will be the mightier if it is effected by the Struves, who are not scared of the Social-Democrats, and do not want victory over tsarism, but want to come to terms with it. The sweep of the revolution will be the mightier if the first of the two possible outcomes outlined above eventuates, i.e., if the monarchist bourgeoisie comes to terms with the autocracy on a "constitution" *à la* Shipov!

Social-Democrats, who write such disgraceful things in resolutions for the guidance of the whole Party, or who approve of such "apt" resolutions, are so blinded by sophistry, which has utterly driven the living spirit out of Marxism, that they fail to notice that these resolutions turn all their other fine words into empty phrases. Take any of their articles in *Iskra*, or even the notorious pamphlet written by our notorious Martynov—there you will read about a *popular* insurrection, about carrying the revolution to *completion*, about striving to rely upon the *common people* in the struggle against the inconsistent bourgeoisie. However, all these excellent things become miserable phrases as soon as you accept or approve the idea that "the sweep of the revolution" will be "diminished" as a consequence of the bourgeoisie's alienation. These are the alternatives, gentlemen: either we, together with the people, must strive to carry out the revolution and win complete victory over tsarism *despite* the inconsistent, self-seeking, and cowardly bourgeoisie, or else we do not accept this "despite", and are afraid that the bourgeoisie may "recoil" from the revolution; in the second case we are betraying the proletariat and the people to the bourgeoisie—the inconsistent, self-seeking, and cowardly bourgeoisie.

Don't take it into your heads to misinterpret my words. Don't shrill that you are being accused of deliberate treachery. No, you have always crawled towards the marsh, and have at last crawled into it, just as unconsciously as the Economists of old, who were irresistibly and irrevocably drawn down the inclined plane of "deeper" Marxism, until it at last became an anti-revolutionary, soulless, and lifeless intellectual pose.

Have you, gentlemen, ever given thought to real social forces that determine "the sweep of the revolution"? Let us disregard the foreign political forces, the international combinations, which have developed very favourably for us at the present time, but which we all leave out of the discussion, and rightly so, inasmuch as we are concerned with the question of Russia's internal forces. Examine these internal social forces. Aligned against the revolution are the autocracy, the imperial court, the police, the bureaucracy, the army, and a handful of the aristocracy. The deeper the indignation of the people grows, the less reliable the troops become, and the more the bureaucracy wavers. Moreover, the bourgeoisie, on the whole, is now in favour of revolution, zealously speechifying about liberty and holding forth more and more frequently in the name of the people and even in the name of the revolution.* But we Marxists all know from theory and from daily and hourly observation of our liberals, Zemstvo people, and *Osvobozhdeniye* supporters that the bourgeoisie is inconsistent, self-seeking, and cowardly in its support of the revolution. The bourgeoisie, in the mass, will inevitably turn towards counter-revolution, towards the autocracy, against the revolution, and against the people, as soon as its narrow, selfish interests are met, as soon as it "recoils" from consistent democracy (*and it is already recoiling from it!*). There remains the "people", that is, the proletariat and the peasantry: the proletariat alone can be relied on to march on to the end, for it goes far beyond the democratic revolution. That is why the proletariat fights in the forefront for a republic and contemptuously rejects stupid and unworthy advice to take into account the possibility of the bourgeoisie recoiling. The peasantry includes a great number of semi-proletarian as well as petty-bourgeois elements. This makes it also unstable, compelling the proletariat to rally in a strictly class party. However, the instability of the peasantry dif ers radically from that of the bourgeoisie, for at present the peasantry is interested not so much in the absolute preservation of private property as in the confiscation of the landed estates, one of the principal forms of private property. Without thereby becoming socialist, or ceasing to be petty-bourgeois, the peasantry is capable of becoming a wholehearted and most radical adherent of the democratic revolution. The peasantry will inevitably become such if only the course of revolutionary events, which brings it enlightenment, is not prematurely cut short by the treachery of the bourgeoisie and the defeat of the proletariat. Subject to this

---

* Of interest in this connection is Mr. Struve's open letter to Jaurès recently published by the latter in *L'Humanité*[70] and by Mr. Struve in *Osvobozhdeniye*, No. 72.

condition the peasantry will inevitably become a bulwark of the revolution and the republic, for only a completely victorious revolution can give the peasantry *everything* in the sphere of agrarian reforms —*everything* that the peasants desire, dream of, and truly need (not for the abolition of capitalism as the "Socialist-Revolutionaries" imagine, but) in order to emerge from the mire of semi-serfdom, from the gloom of oppression and servitude, in order to improve their living conditions, as much as they can be improved within the system of commodity production.

Moreover, it is not only by the prospect of radical agrarian reform that the peasantry is attached to the revolution, but by all its general and permanent interests as well. Even when fighting with the proletariat, the peasantry stands in need of democracy, for only a democratic system is capable of accurately expressing its interests and ensuring its predominance as a mass, as the majority. The more enlightened the peasantry becomes (and since the war with Japan[71] it is becoming enlightened at a pace unsuspected by many who are accustomed to measure enlightenment with the school yardstick), the more consistently and resolutely will it stand for a thoroughgoing democratic revolution; for, unlike the bourgeoisie, it has nothing to fear from the people's supremacy, but on the contrary stands to gain by it. A democratic republic will become the peasantry's ideal as soon as it begins to throw off its naïve monarchism, because the conscious monarchism of the bourgeois stockjobbers (with an upper chamber, etc.) implies for the peasantry the same absence of rights and the same oppression and ignorance as it suffers today, only slightly polished over with the varnish of European constitutionalism.

That is why, as a class, the bourgeoisie naturally and inevitably tends to come under the wing of the liberal-monarchist party, while the peasantry, in the mass, tends to come under the leadership of the revolutionary and republican party. That is why the bourgeoisie is incapable of carrying through the democratic revolution to its consummation, while the peasantry is capable of doing so, and we must exert all our efforts to help it do so.

The objection may be raised that this goes without saying, is all ABC, something that all Social-Democrats understand perfectly well. No, that is not the case; it is not understood by those who can talk about "the diminishing sweep" of the revolution as a consequence of the bourgeoisie falling away from it. Such people repeat the words of our agrarian programme, which they have learned by rote without understanding their meaning, for otherwise they would not be frightened by the concept of the revolutionary-democratic dictatorship of the proletariat and the peasantry, which inevitably follows from the entire Marxist world outlook and from our programme; otherwise they would not restrict the sweep of the great Russian revolution to the limits to which the bourgeoisie is prepared to go. Such people defeat their abstract Marxist revolutionary phrases by their concrete anti-Marxist and anti-revolutionary resolutions.

Those who really understand the role of the peasantry in a victorious Russian revolution would not dream of saying that the sweep of the revolution will be diminished if the bourgeoisie recoils from it. For, in actual fact, the Russian revolution will begin to assume its real sweep, and will really assume the widest revolutionary sweep possible in the epoch of bourgeois-democratic revolution, only when the bourgeoisie recoils from it and when the masses of the peasantry come out as active revolutionaries side by side with the proletariat. To be consistently carried through to the end, our democratic revolution must rely on forces capable of paralysing the inevitable inconsistency of the bourgeoisie (i.e., capable precisely of "making it recoil from the revolution", which the Caucasian adherents of *Iskra* fear so much because of their thoughtlessness).

The proletariat must carry the democratic revolution to completion, allying to itself the mass of the peasantry in order to crush the autocracy's resistance by force and paralyse the bourgeoisie's instability. The proletariat must accomplish the socialist revolution, allying to itself the mass of the semi-proletarian elements of the population, so as to crush the bourgeoisie's resistance by force and paralyse the instability of the peasantry and the petty bourgeoisie. Such are the tasks of the proletariat, so narrowly presented by the new-*Iskra* group in all their arguments and resolutions on the sweep of the revolution.

One circumstance, however, should not be forgotten, one that is frequently lost sight of in discussions about the "sweep" of the revolution. It should not be forgotten that it is not a question of the difficulties presented by this problem, but of the way in which its solution is to be sought and attained. It is not a question of whether it is easy or difficult to render the sweep of the revolution mighty and invincible, but of how to act so as to make that sweep more powerful. It is on the fundamental nature of our activities, the direction they should follow, that our views differ. We emphasise this because inattentive and unscrupulous people only too frequently confuse two different problems, viz., that of the direction to be followed, i.e., the choice of one of two different roads, and that of the ease of attaining our goal, or the nearness of its attainment along a given road.

In the foregoing we have not dealt with this last problem at all because it has not evoked any disagreement or differences in the Party. The problem itself is, of course, extremely important and deserving of the most serious attention from all Social-Democrats. It would be unforgivable optimism to forget the difficulties involved in drawing into the movement the masses not only of the working class, but also of the peasantry. These difficulties have more than once wrecked efforts to carry through a democratic revolution to completion, the inconsistent and self-seeking bourgeoisie triumphing most of all, because it has "made capital" in the shape of monarchist protection against the people, at the same time "preserving the virginity" of liberalism ... or of the *Osvobozhdeniye* trend. However, difficulty does not imply impossibility. The important thing is to be confident that the path chosen is the right one, this confidence multiplying a hundredfold revolutionary energy and revolutionary enthusiasm, which can perform miracles.

The depth of the rift among present-day Social-Democrats on the question of the path to be chosen can at once be seen by comparing the Caucasian resolution of the new-*Iskra* supporters with the resolution of the Third Congress of the Russian Social-Democratic Labour Party. The Congress resolution says: the bourgeoisie is inconsistent and will without fail try to deprive us of the gains of the revolution. Therefore, make more energetic preparations for the fight, comrades and workers! Arm yourselves, win the peasantry over to your side! We shall not, without a struggle, surrender our revolutionary gains to the self-seeking bourgeoisie. The resolution of the Caucasian new-*Iskra* supporters says: the bourgeoisie is inconsistent and may recoil from the revolution. Therefore, comrades and workers, please do not think of joining a provisional government, for, if you do, the bourgeoisie will certainly recoil, and the sweep of the revolution will thereby be diminished!

One side says: advance the revolution to its consummation despite resistance or passivity on the part of the inconsistent bourgeoisie.

The other side says: do not think of independently advancing the revolution to completion, for if you do, the inconsistent bourgeoisie will recoil from it.

Are these not two diametrically opposite paths? Is it not obvious that one set of tactics absolutely excludes the other, that the first tactics is the only correct tactics of revolutionary Social-Democracy, while the second is in fact purely *Osvobozhdeniye* tactics?

13. CONCLUSION. DARE WE WIN?

People who are superficially acquainted with the state of affairs in Russian Social-Democracy, or who judge as mere onlookers, with no knowledge of the whole history of our inner-Party struggle since the days of Economism, very often dismiss the disagreements on tactics which have now taken shape, especially after the Third Congress, with the simple argument that there are two natural, inevitable and quite reconcilable trends in every Social-Democratic movement. One side, they say, lays special emphasis on the ordinary, current, and everyday work, on the necessity of developing propaganda and agitation, of preparing forces, deepening the movement, etc., while the other side lays emphasis on the militant, general political, revolutionary tasks of the movement, points to the necessity of insurrection, and advances the slogans of a revolutionary-democratic dictatorship and a provisional revolutionary government. Neither side should exaggerate, they say; extremes are bad in both cases (and, generally speaking, everywhere in the world), etc., etc.

The cheap truism of the pedestrian (and "political" in quotation marks) wisdom undoubtedly contained in such arguments, too often conceals an inability to understand the urgent and acute needs of the Party. Take the present-day tactical differences among Russian Social-Democrats. Of course, the special emphasis on the everyday, routine aspect of the work, such as we see in the new-*Iskra* arguments about tactics, could not of itself present any danger or give rise to any divergence of opinion regarding tactical slogans. But it is sufficient to compare the resolutions of the Third Congress of the Russian Social-Democratic Labour Party with the conference resolutions for this divergence to become striking.

What, then, is the trouble? In the first place, it is not enough to speak in the abstract of two currents in the movement, and of the harmfulness of extremes. One must know concretely what ails a given movement at a given time, and what constitutes the real political danger to the Party at the present time. Secondary, one must know what real political forces profit by the tactical slogans advanced—or perhaps by the absence of certain slogans. If one were to listen to the new-Iskrists one would arrive at the conclusion that the Social-Democratic Party is threatened with the danger of throwing overboard propaganda and agitation, the economic struggle, and criticism of bourgeois democracy, the danger of becoming inordinately absorbed in military preparations, armed attacks, the seizure of power, etc. Actually, however, real danger is threatening the Party from an entirely different quarter. Anyone who is at all familiar with the state of the movement, anyone who follows it carefully and thoughtfully, cannot fail to see the ridiculous aspect of the new-Iskrists' fears. The entire work of the Russian Social-Democratic Labour Party has already taken definite and unvarying shape, which absolutely guarantees that our main attention will be fixed on propaganda and agitation, extemporaneous and mass meetings, the distribution of leaflets and pamphlets, assisting in the economic struggle and championing the slogans of that struggle. There is not a single Party committee, not a single district committee, not a single central delegates' meeting or a single factory group where ninety-nine per cent of all the attention, energy, and time is not always and invariably devoted to these functions, which have become firmly established ever since the middle of the nineties. Only those who are entirely unfamiliar with the movement do not know that. Only very naïve or ill-informed people will accept new *Iskra*'s repetition of stale truths at their face value, when that is done with an air of great importance.

The fact is that, far from displaying excessive zeal with regard to the tasks of insurrection, to general political slogans and to giving leadership to the entire popular revolution, we, on the contrary, display a most striking *backwardness* in this very respect, a backwardness which constitutes our greatest weakness and is a real danger to the movement, which may degenerate, and in some places is degenerating, from one that is revolutionary in deed into one that is revolutionary in word. Among the many, many hundreds of organisations, groups, and circles that are conducting the work of the Party you will not find one which has not, since its very inception, conducted the kind of day-by-day work the new-*Iskra* wiseacres now talk of with the air of people who have discovered new truths. On the other hand, you will find only an insignificant percentage of groups and circles that have understood the tasks an insurrection entails, have begun to carry them out, and have realised the necessity of leading the entire popular revolution against tsarism, the necessity of advancing certain definite progressive slogans and no others, for that purpose.

We have incredibly fallen behind our progressive and genuinely revolutionary tasks; in very many instances we have not even become aware of them; here and there we have failed to notice that revolutionary-bourgeois democracy has gained strength owing to our backwardness in this respect. But, with their backs turned to the course of events and the requirements of the times, the new-*Iskra* writers keep insistently repeating: "Don't forget the old! Don't let yourselves be carried away by the new!" This is the unvarying *leitmotiv* in all the important resolutions of the conference; whereas in the congress resolutions you just as unvaryingly read: while confirming the old (but not stopping to masticate it over and over again precisely because it *is* old and has already been settled and recorded in literature, in resolutions and by experience), we bring forward a new task, draw attention to it, issue a new slogan, and demand that genuinely revolutionary Social-Democrats immediately set to work to put it into effect.

That is how matters really stand with regard to the question of the two trends in Social-Democratic tactics. The revolutionary period has presented new tasks, which only the totally blind can fail to see. Some Social-Democrats unhesitatingly recognise these tasks and place them on the order of the day, declaring: the armed uprising brooks no delay; prepare yourselves for it immediately and energetically; remember that it is indispensable for a decisive victory; bring forward slogans for a republic, for a provisional government, for a revolutionary-democratic dictatorship of the proletariat and the peasantry. Other Social-Democrats, however, draw back, mark time, write prefaces instead of giving slogans; instead of seeing what is new, while confirming what is old, they masticate the latter tediously and at great length, inventing pretexts to avoid the new, unable to determine the conditions for a decisive victory or to bring forward slogans which alone are in line with a striving to achieve full victory.

The political outcome of this tail-ism stares us in the face. The fable about a *rapprochement* between the "majority" of the Russian Social-Democratic Labour Party and revolutionary bourgeois democracy remains a fable unconfirmed by a single political fact, by a single important resolution of the "Bolsheviks" or a single document of the Third Congress of the Russian Social-Democratic Labour Party. On the other hand, the opportunist, monarchist bourgeoisie, as represented by the *Osvobozhdeniye*, has long been *welcoming* the trends in the "principles" advocated by the new-*Iskra* group, and is now actually using their stream to drive its mill and is adopting their catchwords and "ideas", which are directed against "secrecy" and "riots", against exaggerating the "technical" aspect of the revolution, against openly proclaiming the slogan of insurrection, against the "revolutionism" of extreme demands, etc., etc. The resolution of an entire conference of "Menshevik" Social-Democrats in the Caucasus and the endorsement of that resolution by the editors of the new *Iskra* sums up the whole matter politically in no mistakable way: what if the bourgeoisie should recoil in case the proletariat takes part in a revolutionary-democratic dictatorship! This puts the matter in a nutshell and gives the finishing touches to the proletariat's transformation into an appendage to the monarchist bourgeoisie. The *political significance* of the new *Iskra's* tail-ism is thereby proved in fact—not by a casual observation from some individual but by a resolution especially endorsed by an entire trend.

Anyone who gives thought to these facts will understand the real significance of stock references to two sides and two trends in the Social-Democratic movement. For a full-scale study of these trends one should take Bernsteinism. In exactly the same way the Bernsteinians have been dinning into our ears that it is they who understand the proletariat's true needs and the tasks of building up its forces, the task of deepening all the work, preparing the elements of a new society, and the task of propaganda and agitation. Bernstein says: we demand a frank recognition of that which is, thus sanctifying "movement" *without* any "ultimate aim", sanctifying defensive tactics alone, preaching the tactics of fear "lest the bourgeoisie recoil". So the Bernsteinians raised an outcry against the "Jacobinism" of the revolutionary Social-Democrats, against "publicists" who fail to understand the "workers' initiative", etc., etc. In reality, as everyone knows, revolutionary Social-Democrats have never even thought of abandoning day-by-day, petty work, the mustering of forces, etc., etc. All they demanded was a clear understanding of the ultimate aim, a clear presentation of the revolutionary tasks; they wanted to raise the semi-proletarian and semi-petty-bourgeois strata to the revolutionary level of the proletariat—not to reduce the latter level to that of opportunist considerations such as "lest the bourgeoisie recoil". Perhaps the most vivid expression of this rift between the intellectual-opportunist wing and the proletarian-revolutionary wing of the Party was the question: *dürfen wir siegen?* "Dare we win?" Is it permissible for us to win? Would it not be dangerous for us to win? Ought we to win? This question, so strange at first sight, was however raised and had to be raised, because the opportunists were afraid of victory, were frightening the proletariat away from it, predicting that trouble would come of it and ridiculing slogans that straightforwardly called for it.

The same fundamental division into an intellectual-opportunist and proletarian-revolutionary trend exists among us too, with the very material difference, however, that here we are faced with the question of a democratic, not of a socialist revolution. The question "dare we win?", which seems so absurd at first sight, has been raised among us as well. It has been raised by Martynov in his *Two Dictatorships*, wherein he prophesies dire misfortune if we prepare well for an insurrection, and carry it out quite successfully. The question has been raised in all the new-*Iskra* literature dealing with a provisional revolutionary government, and persistent if futile efforts have all the time been made to liken Millerand's participation in a bourgeois-opportunist government to Varlin's[72] participation in a petty-bourgeois revolutionary government. It is embodied in the resolution: "lest the bourgeoisie recoil". And although Kautsky, for instance, now tries to wax ironical and says that our dispute about a provisional revolutionary government is like sharing out the meat before the bear is killed, this irony only proves that even clever and revolutionary Social-Democrats are liable to put their foot in it when they talk about something they know of only by hearsay. German Social-Democracy is not yet so near to killing its bear (carrying out a socialist revolution), but the dispute as to whether we "dare" kill the bear has been of enormous importance from the point of view of principles and of practical politics. Russian Social-Democrats are not yet so close to being able to "kill their bear" (carry out a democratic revolution), but the question as to whether we "dare" kill it is of extreme importance to the whole future of Russia and that of Russian Social-Democracy. An army cannot be energetically and successfully mustered and led unless we are sure that we "dare" win.

Take our old Economists. They, too, clamoured that their opponents were conspirators and Jacobins (see *Rabocheye Dyelo*, especially No. 10, and Martynov's speech at the Second Congress, in the debate on the programme[73]), that by plunging into politics they were divorcing themselves from the masses, that they were losing sight of the fundamentals of the working-class movement, ignoring the workers' initiative, etc., etc. In reality these supporters of "workers' initiative" were opportunist intellectuals, who tried to foist on the workers their own narrow and philistine conception of the tasks of the proletariat. In reality the opponents of Economism, as everyone can see from the old *Iskra*, did not neglect or relegate into the background any of the aspects of Social-Democratic work, nor did they in the least forget the economic struggle; at the same time they were able to present the urgent and immediate political tasks in their full scope and thus opposed the transformation of the workers' party into an "economic" appendage to the liberal bourgeoisie.

The Economists learned by rote that politics are based on economics and "understood" this to mean that the political struggle should be reduced to the level of the economic struggle. The new-Iskrists have learned by rote that in its economic essence, the democratic revolution is a bourgeois revolution, and "understand" this to mean that the democratic aims of the proletariat should be lowered to the level of bourgeois moderation, a level beyond which "the bourgeoisie will recoil". On the pretext of deepening their work, on the pretext of rousing the workers' initiative and pursuing a purely class policy, the Economists were actually delivering the working class into the hands of the liberal-bourgeois politicians, i.e., were leading the Party along a path whose objective significance was exactly such. On the same pretexts the new-Iskrists are actually betraying to the bourgeoisie the interests of the proletariat in the democratic revolution, i.e., are leading the Party along a path whose objective significance is exactly such. The Economists thought that leadership in the political struggle was not the concern of Social-Democrats, but, properly speaking, that of the liberals. The new-Iskrists think that the active conduct of the democratic revolution is no concern of Social-Democrats, but, properly speaking, that of the democratic bourgeoisie, for, they argue, the proletariat's guidance and pre-eminent part will "diminish the sweep" of the revolution.

In short, the new-Iskrists are imitators of Economism, not only in having their origin at the Second Party Congress, but also in the manner in which they now present the tactical tasks of the proletariat in the democratic revolution. They, too, constitute an intellectual-opportunist wing of the Party. In the sphere of organisation they made their *début* with the anarchist individualism of intellectuals and ended up with "disorganisation-as-process", establishing in the "Rules" adopted by the conference the separation of Party publishing activities from the Party organisation, and an indirect and practically four-stage system of elections, a system of Bonapartist plebiscites instead of democratic representation, and finally the principle of "agreements" between the part and the whole. In Party tactics they slid down the same inclined plane. In the "plan of the Zemstvo campaign"[74] they declared that addresses to the Zemstvo-ists were "the highest type of demonstration", and discerned only two active forces on the political scene (on the eve of January 9!)—the government and the bourgeois democrats. They made the urgent task of arming the people "more profound" by replacing a direct and practical slogan with a call to arm the people with a burning desire to arm themselves. In their official resolutions they have distorted and emasculated the tasks connected with an insurrection, with the establishment of a provisional government, and with a revolutionary-democratic dictatorship. "Lest the bourgeoisie recoil"—this final chord of their latest resolution throws clear light on the question of where their path is leading the Party.

In its social and economic essence, the democratic revolution in Russia is a bourgeois revolution. It is, however, not enough merely to repeat this correct Marxist proposition. It has to be properly understood and properly applied to political slogans. In general, all political liberty founded on present-day, i.e., capitalist, relations of production is bourgeois liberty. The demand for liberty expresses primarily the interests of the bourgeoisie. Its representatives were the first to raise this demand. Its supporters have everywhere used like masters the liberty they acquired, reducing it to moderate and meticulous bourgeois doses, combining it with the most subtle suppression of the revolutionary proletariat in peaceful times, and with savage suppression in times of storm.

But only rebel Narodniks, anarchists, and Economists could conclude therefrom that the struggle for liberty should be negated or disparaged. These intellectualist-philistine doctrines could be foisted on the proletariat only for a time and against its will. The proletariat has always realised instinctively that it needs political liberty, needs it more than anyone else, although the immediate effect of that liberty will be to strengthen and organise the bourgeoisie. It is not by evading the class struggle that the proletariat expects to find its salvation, but by developing it, by extending its scope, its consciousness, organisation, and resoluteness. Whoever disparages the tasks of the political struggle transforms the Social-Democrat from a tribune of the people into a trade union secretary. Whoever disparages the proletarian tasks in a democratic bourgeois revolution transforms the Social-Democrat from a leader of the people's revolution into a leader of a free labour union.

Yes, the *people*'s revolution. Social-Democracy has fought, and is quite rightly fighting, against the bourgeois-democratic abuse of the word "people". It demands that this word shall not be used to cover up failure to understand class antagonisms within the people. It insists categorically on the need for complete class independence for the party of the proletariat. However, it does not divide the "people" into "classes" so that the advanced class will become locked up within itself, will confine itself within narrow limits, and emasculate its activity for fear that the economic rulers of the world will recoil; it does that so that the advanced class, which does not suffer from the half-heartedness, vacillation, and indecision of the intermediate classes, should fight with all the greater energy and enthusiasm for the cause of the whole people, at the head of the whole people.

That is what the present-day new-Iskrists so often fail to understand, people who substitute for active political slogans in the democratic revolution a mere pedantic repetition of the word "class", declined in all cases and genders!

The democratic revolution is bourgeois in nature. The slogan of a general redistribution, or "land and freedom"—that most widespread slogan of the peasant masses, downtrodden and ignorant, yet passionately yearning for light and happiness—is a bourgeois slogan. But we Marxists should know that there is not, nor can there be, any other path to real freedom for the proletariat and the peasantry, than the path of bourgeois freedom and bourgeois progress. We must not forget that there is not, nor can there be at the present time, any other means of bringing socialism nearer, than complete political liberty, than a democratic republic, than the revolutionary-democratic dictatorship of the proletariat and the peasantry. As representatives of the advanced and only revolutionary class, revolutionary without any reservations, doubts, or looking back, we must confront the whole of the people with the tasks of the democratic revolution as extensively and boldly as possible and with the utmost initiative. To disparage these tasks means making a travesty of theoretical Marxism, distorting it in philistine fashion, while in practical politics it means placing the cause of the revolution into the hands of the bourgeoisie, which will inevitably recoil from the task of consistently effecting the revolution. The difficulties that lie on the road to complete victory of the revolution are very great. No one will be able to blame the proletariat's representatives if, when they have done everything in their power, their efforts are defeated by the resistance of reaction, the treachery of the bourgeoisie, and the ignorance of the masses. But everybody, and, above all, the class-conscious proletariat, will condemn Social-Democracy if it curtails the revolutionary energy of the democratic revolution and dampens revolutionary ardour because it is afraid to win, because it is actuated by the consideration: lest the bourgeoisie recoil.

Revolutions are the locomotives of history, said Marx.[75] Revolutions are festivals of the oppressed and the exploited. At no other time are the mass of the people in a position to come forward so actively as creators of a new social order, as at a time of revolution. At such times the people are capable of performing miracles, if judged by the limited, philistine yardstick of gradualist progress. But it is essential that leaders of the revolutionary parties, too, should advance their aims more comprehensively and boldly at such a time, so that their slogans shall always be in advance of the revolutionary initiative of the masses, serve as a beacon, reveal to them our democratic and socialist ideal in all its magnitude and splendour, and show them the shortest and most direct route to complete, absolute, and decisive victory. Let us leave to the opportunists of the *Osvobozhdeniye* bourgeoisie the task of inventing roundabout, circuitous paths of compromise, out of fear of the revolution and of the direct path. If we are forcibly compelled to drag ourselves along such paths we shall be able to fulfil our duty in petty, everyday work also. But first let the choice of path be decided in ruthless struggle. We shall be traitors, betrayers of the revolution, if we do not use this festive energy of the masses and their revolutionary ardour to wage a ruthless and self-sacrificing struggle for the direct and decisive path. Let the bourgeois opportunists contemplate the future reaction with craven fear. The workers will not be intimidated either by the thought that reaction intends to be terrible, or that the bourgeoisie proposes to recoil. The workers do not expect to make deals; they are not asking for petty concessions. What they are striving towards is ruthlessly to crush the reactionary forces, i.e., to set up a *revolutionary-democratic dictatorship of the proletariat and the peasantry*.

Of course, in stormy times greater dangers threaten the ship of our Party than in periods of the smooth "sailing" of liberal progress, which means the painfully steady sucking of the working class's life-blood by its exploiters. Of course, the tasks of the revolutionary-democratic dictatorship are infinitely more difficult and more complex than the tasks of an "extreme opposition", or of an exclusively parliamentary struggle. But whoever is consciously capable of preferring smooth sailing and the course of safe "opposition" in the present revolutionary situation had better abandon Social-Democratic work for a while, had better wait until the revolution is over, until the festive days have passed, when humdrum, everyday life starts again, and his narrow routine standards no longer strike such an abominably discordant note, or constitute such an ugly distortion of the tasks of the advanced class.

At the head of the whole people, and particularly of the peasantry —for complete freedom, for a consistent democratic revolution, for a republic! At the head of all the toilers and the exploited—for socialism! Such in practice must be the policy of the revolutionary proletariat, such is the class slogan which must permeate and determine the solution of every tactical problem, every practical step of the workers' party during the revolution.

EPILOGUE

ONCE AGAIN THE *OSVOBOZHDENIYE* TREND, ONCE AGAIN THE NEW-*ISKRA* TREND

Osvobozhdeniye, Nos. 71-72, and *Iskra*, Nos. 102-103, provide a wealth of additional material on the question dealt with in Chapter 8 of our pamphlet. Since it is quite impossible here to make use of all this rich material we shall confine ourselves to the most important points only: firstly, the kind of "realism" in Social-Democracy that *Osvobozhdeniye* praises, and why the latter should praise it; secondly, the relationship between the concepts of revolution and dictatorship.

I. WHY DO BOURGEOIS LIBERAL REALISTS PRAISE SOCIAL-DEMOCRATIC "REALISTS"?

Articles entitled "The Split in Russian Social-Democracy" and "The Triumph of Common Sense" (*Osvobozhdeniye*, No. 72) express an opinion on Social-Democracy held by representatives of the liberal bourgeoisie, an opinion of remarkable value to class-conscious proletarians. We cannot too strongly recommend to every Social-Democrat that he should read these articles in full and *ponder over* every sentence in them. We shall first of all reproduce the most important propositions in these two articles.

"It is fairly difficult," writes *Osvobozhdeniye*, "for an outside observer to grasp the real political meaning of the differences that have split the Social-Democratic Party into two factions. A definition of the 'Majority' faction as the more radical and unswerving, as distinct from the 'Minority' which allows of certain compromises in the interests of the cause, is not quite exact, and in any case does not provide an exhaustive characterisation. At any rate the traditional dogmas of Marxist orthodoxy are observed by the Minority faction with even greater zeal, perhaps, than by the Lenin faction. The following characterisation would appear to us to be more accurate. The fundamental political temper of the 'Majority' is abstract revolutionism, rebelliousness, and eagerness to stir up insurrection among the popular masses by any and every means and to immediately seize power on their behalf; to a certain extent this brings the 'Leninists' close to the Socialist-Revolutionaries and makes the idea of a Russian revolution of the whole people overshadow in their minds the idea of the class struggle. While in practice abjuring much of the narrow-mindedness of the Social-Democratic doctrine, the 'Leninists' are, on the other hand, thoroughly imbued with the narrow-mindedness of revolutionism; they renounce all practical work except the preparation of an immediate insurrection, ignore on principle all forms of legal and semi-legal agitation and any kind of practically useful compromise with other oppositional trends. On the contrary, the Minority, while steadfastly adhering to the doctrine of Marxism, at the same time preserves the realistic elements of the Marxist world outlook. Contraposing the interests of the 'proletariat' to those of the bourgeoisie is the fundamental idea of this group. On the other hand, however, the proletariat's struggle is conceived—of course within certain bounds dictated by the immutable dogmas of Social-Democracy—in realistically sober fashion, with a clear realisation of all the concrete conditions and aims of this struggle. Neither of the two factions pursues its basic point of view quite consistently, for in their ideological and political activities they are bound by the stringent formulas of the Social-Democratic catechism, which prevent the 'Leninists' from becoming unswerving rebels after the fashion of, at least, some Socialist-Revolutionaries, and the '*Iskra* group' from becoming practical leaders of the real political movement of the working class."

After quoting the contents of the most important resolutions the *Osvobozhdeniye* writer goes on to illustrate his general "ideas" with several concrete remarks about them. In comparison with the Third Congress, he says, "the Minority Conference takes a totally different attitude towards an insurrection". "In connection with the attitude towards an insurrection" there is a difference in the respective resolutions on a provisional government. "A similar difference is revealed with regard to the workers' trade unions. In their resolution the 'Leninists' have not said a single word about this most important starting-point in the political education and organisation of the working class. The Minority, on the contrary, drew up a very weighty resolution." With regard to the liberals, both factions, he says, see eye to eye, but the Third Congress "repeats almost word for word the Plekhanov resolution on the attitude towards the liberals, adopted at the Second Congress, and rejects the Starover resolution adopted by the same congress, which was more favourably inclined towards the liberals". Although the congress and the conference resolutions on the peasant movement coincide on the whole, "the 'Majority' lays more emphasis on the idea of the revolutionary confiscation of the landlords' estates and other land, while the 'Minority' wants to make the demand for democratic state and administrative reforms the basis of its agitation".

Finally, *Osvobozhdeniye* cites from No. 100 of *Iskra* a Menshevik resolution, whose main clause reads as follows: "Since underground work alone does not at present secure adequate participation of the masses in Party life, and in some degree leads to the masses as such being contraposed to the Party as an illegal organisation, the latter must assume leadership of the trade union struggle of the workers on a legal basis, strictly linking up this struggle with the Social-Democratic tasks." Commenting on this resolution *Osvobozhdeniye* exclaims: "We heartily welcome this resolution as a triumph of common sense, as evidence that a definite section of the Social-Democratic Party is beginning to see the light with regard to tactics."

The reader now has before him all the noteworthy opinions of *Osvobozhdeniye*. It would, of course, be a most grave error to regard these opinions as correct in the sense of corresponding to the objective truth. Mistakes in them will easily be detected by every Social-Democrat at every step. It would be naïve to forget that these opinions are thoroughly imbued with the liberal bourgeoisie's interests and points of view, and that in this sense they are utterly biased and tendentious. They reflect the Social-Democrats' views in the same way as objects are reflected in a concave or convex mirror. It would, however, be an even greater mistake to forget that in the final analysis these bourgeois-distorted opinions reflect the actual interests of the bourgeoisie, which, as a class, undoubtedly understands correctly which trends in Social-Democracy are advantageous, close, akin, and agreeable to it, and which trends are harmful, distant, alien, and antipathetic. A bourgeois philosopher or a bourgeois publicist will never understand Social-Democracy properly, whether it is Menshevik or Bolshevik Social-Democracy. But if he is at all a sensible publicist, his class instinct will not fail him, and he will always grasp the essence of what one trend or another in the Social Democratic movement may mean to the bourgeoisie, although he may present it in a distorted way. That is why our enemy's class instinct, his class opinion always deserves the closest attention from every class-conscious proletarian.

What, then, does the Russian bourgeoisie's class instinct, as voiced by *Osvobozhdeniye* adherents, tell us?

It quite definitely expresses its satisfaction with the trend represented by the new *Iskra*, praising it for realism, sober-mindedness, the triumph of common sense, the soundness of its resolutions, its having begun to see the light on questions of tactics, its practicalness, etc.—and it expresses dissatisfaction with the trend of the Third Congress, censuring it for its narrow-mindedness, revolutionism, rebelliousness, its repudiation of practically useful compromises, etc. The class instinct of the bourgeoisie suggests to it exactly what has been repeatedly proved in our literature with the aid of most precise facts, namely, that the new-*Iskra* supporters are the opportunist wing of the present-day Russian Social-Democratic movement, and their opponents—the revolutionary wing. The liberals cannot but sympathise with the trends in the former, and cannot but censure the trends in the latter. As ideologists of the bourgeoisie the liberals understand perfectly well that the bourgeoisie stands to gain by the "practicalness, sober-mindedness, and soundness" of the working class, by actually restricting its field of activity within the framework of capitalism, reforms, the trade union struggle, etc. The proletariat's "revolutionary narrow-mindedness", its endeavours to win the leadership in a popular Russian revolution in order to promote its own class aims—these things are dangerous and frightening to the bourgeoisie.

That this is the actual significance of the word "realism" in its *Osvobozhdeniye* sense is evident, among other things, from the way it was previously used by *Osvobozhdeniye* and by Mr. Struve. *Iskra* itself could not but admit that *such* was the significance of *Osvobozhdeniye*'s "realism". Take, for instance, the article entitled "High Time!" in the supplement to *Iskra*, No. 73-74. The author of this article (a consistent exponent of the views of the "Marsh" at

the Second Congress of the Russian Social-Democratic Labour
Party) frankly expressed the opinion that "at the Congress Akimov
played the part of the ghost of opportunism rather than of its real
representative". And the editors of *Iskra* were forthwith obliged
to correct the author of the article "High Time!" by stating in a
note:

"This opinion cannot be agreed with. Comrade Akimov's views on the programme bear the clear imprint of opportunism, which fact is admitted even by
the *Osvobozhdeniye* critic, who—in one of its recent issues—stated that Comrade
Akimov is an adherent of the 'realist'—read: revisionist—tendency."

Thus, *Iskra* itself is perfectly aware that *Osvobozhdeniye's*
"realism" is simply opportunism and nothing else. If in attacking
"liberal realism" *(Iskra*, No. 102) *Iskra* now says nothing about *its
having been praised by the liberals* for its realism, this silence is
explained by the circumstance that such praise is bitterer than any
censure. Such praise (which *Osvobozhdeniye* uttered not by mere
chance and not for the first time) actually proves the affinity between liberal realism and those tendencies of Social-Democratic
"realism" (read: opportunism) that stand out in every resolution of
the new-Iskrists, in consequence of the fallacy of their entire
tactical stand.

Indeed, the Russian bourgeoisie has already fully revealed its inconsistency and cupidity in the "popular" revolution—has revealed
it in Mr. Struve's arguments, in the entire tenor and content of
the bulk of liberal newspapers, and in the nature of the political
utterances of most Zemstvo members, the bulk of the intellectuals,
and in general of all the adherents of Messrs. Trubetskoi, Petrunkevich, Rodichev, and Co. Of course, the bourgeoisie does not always
reveal a clear understanding, but by and large, its class instinct
enables it to realise perfectly well that, on the one hand, the proletariat and the "people" are useful for *its* revolution as cannon
fodder, as a battering-ram against the autocracy, but that, on the
other hand, the proletariat and the revolutionary peasantry will be
terribly dangerous to it if they win a "decisive victory over tsarism"
and carry the democratic revolution to completion. That is why the
bourgeoisie strains every effort to induce the proletariat to be
content with a "modest" role in the revolution, to be more sober-
minded, practical, and realistic, and let its activities be guided by
the principle, "lest the bourgeoisie recoil".

Intellectual bourgeois know full well that they will not be able
to get rid of the working-class movement. That is why they do not
at all come out against the working-class movement as such, or
against the proletariat's class struggle as such—no, they even pay
lip-service to the right to strike and to a genteel class struggle, since
they understand the working-class movement and the class struggle

in the Brentano or Hirsch-Duncker sense. In other words they are fully prepared to "yield" to the workers the right to strike and freedom of association (which in fact has already been almost won by the workers themselves), if only the workers renounce their "rebelliousness", their "narrow-minded revolutionism", their hostility to "compromises of practical use", their claims and aspirations to place upon the "revolution of the whole Russian people" the imprint of *their* class struggle, the imprint of proletarian consistency, proletarian determination, and "plebeian Jacobinism". That is why intellectual bourgeois all over Russia are exerting every effort, resorting to thousands of ways and means—books,* lectures, speeches, talks, etc., etc.—to imbue the workers with the ideas of (bourgeois) sober-mindedness, (liberal) practicalness, (opportunist) realism, (Brentano) class struggle,[76] (Hirsch-Duncker) trade unions,[77] etc. The last two slogans are particularly convenient for the bourgeois of the "Constitutional-Democratic" party, the *Osvobozhdeniye* party, since in appearance they coincide with Marxist slogans, and, with some minor omissions and slight distortions, can easily be confused with and sometimes even passed off as Social-Democratic slogans. For instance, the legal liberal newspaper *Rassvet*[78] (which we shall some day try to discuss in greater detail with *Proletary* readers) frequently says such "outspoken" things about the class struggle, the possible deception of the proletariat by the bourgeoisie, the working-class movement, the proletariat's initiative, etc., etc., that the inattentive reader or unenlightened worker might easily be led to believe that its "Social-Democratism" is genuine. Actually, however, it is a bourgeois imitation of Social-Democratism, an opportunist distortion and perversion of the concept of the class struggle.

At the root of all this gigantic bourgeois subterfuge (gigantic in the extent of its influence on the masses) lies an urge to reduce the working-class movement mainly to a trade union movement, to keep it as far away as possible from an independent policy (i.e., one that is revolutionary and directed towards a democratic dictatorship), "to make the idea of the class struggle overshadow, in the workers' minds, the idea of a Russian revolution of the whole people".

As the reader will perceive, we have turned the *Osvobozhdeniye* formulation upside down. This is an excellent formulation, one that excellently expresses two views upon the proletariat's role in a democratic revolution—the bourgeois view and the Social-Democratic view. The bourgeoisie wants to confine the proletariat to the trade union movement, and thereby to "make the idea of the (*Brentano*) class struggle overshadow in its mind the idea of a Russian revolu-

---

* Cf. Prokopovich, *The Labour Question in Russia*.

tion of the whole people"—fully in the spirit of the Bernsteinian authors of the *Credo*, who tried to make the idea of a "purely working-class movement" overshadow in the workers' minds the idea of political struggle. On the contrary, Social-Democracy wants to develop the proletariat's class struggle to the level of leadership in the Russian revolution of the whole people, i.e., to bring that revolution to the democratic dictatorship of the proletariat and the peasantry.

The revolution in our country is one of the whole people, says the bourgeoisie to the proletariat. As a separate class, you should, therefore, confine yourselves to your class struggle; in the name of "common sense" you should devote your attention mainly to the trade unions and their legalisation; you should consider these trade unions as "the most important starting-point in your political educa-tion and organisation"; in a revolutionary situation you should for the most part draw up "sound" resolutions like the new-*Iskra* resolution; you should give heed to resolutions "more favourably in-clined towards the liberals"; you should show preference for leaders with a tendency to become "practical leaders of the real political movement of the working class", and should "preserve the realistic elements of the Marxist world outlook" (if you have unfortunately already become infected with the "stringent formulas" of this "un-scientific" catechism).

The revolution in our country is one of the whole people, the Social-Democrats say to the proletariat. As the most progressive and the only thoroughly revolutionary class, you should strive to play not merely a most active part in it, but the leading part as well. Therefore, you must not confine yourself within a narrowly con-ceived framework of the class struggle, understood mainly as the trade union movement; on the contrary, you must strive to extend the framework and the content of your class struggle so as to make it *include* not only *all* the aims of the present, democratic Russian revolution of the whole people, but the aims of the subsequent socialist revolution as well. Therefore, without ignoring the trade union movement, or refusing to take advantage of even the slightest legal opportunities, you must in a revolutionary period bring into the forefront the tasks of an insurrection and the formation of a revolutionary army and a revolutionary government, as being the only way to the people's complete victory over tsarism, to the achievement of a democratic republic and genuine political freedom.

It would be superfluous to speak about the half-hearted and in-consistent stand, naturally so pleasing to the bourgeoisie, taken on this question by the new-*Iskra* resolutions because of their mistaken "line".

II. COMRADE MARTYNOV AGAIN GIVES "PROFUNDITY" TO THE QUESTION

Let us pass on to Martynov's articles in Nos. 102 and 103 of *Iskra*. We shall, of course, make no reply to Martynov's attempts to prove the incorrectness of our interpretation, and the correctness of his own interpretation, of a number of quotations from Engels and Marx. These attempts are so trivial, Martynov's subterfuges so obvious, and the question so clear that it would be of no interest to dwell on this point again. Every thoughtful reader will be able easily to see through the simple wiles employed by Martynov in his full retreat, especially when the complete translations of Engels's pamphlet *The Bakuninists at Work* and Marx's *Address of the Central Committee to the Communist League* of March 1850, now being prepared by a group of *Proletary* collaborators, are published. A single quotation from Martynov's article will suffice to make his retreat clear to the reader.

"*Iskra* 'admits'," says Martynov in No. 103, "that setting up a provisional government is a possible and expedient way of furthering the revolution, but denies the expediency of Social-Democrats participating in a *bourgeois* provisional government, precisely so as to be able, in the future, to gain complete control of the state machinery for a socialist revolution." In other words, *Iskra* now admits the absurdity of all its fears concerning a revolutionary government's responsibility for the exchequer and the banks, concerning the danger and impossibility of taking over the "prisons", etc. But *Iskra* is only muddling things as previously, confusing democratic with socialist dictatorship. This muddle is unavoidable; it is a means to cover up the retreat.

But among the muddle-heads of the new *Iskra* Martynov stands out as Muddle-head No. 1, as a muddle-head of talent, if one might say so. By confusing the question by his laboured efforts to "give it profundity", he almost invariably "arrives" at new formulations which lay bare all the falseness of the stand he has taken. You will remember how in the days of Economism he rendered Plekhanov "more profound" and created the formulation: "economic struggle against the employers and the government". In all Economist literature it would be difficult to find a more apt expression of this trend's falseness. It is the same today. Martynov serves the new *Iskra* zealously and almost every time he opens his mouth he furnishes us with new and excellent material for an appraisal of the new *Iskra*'s false position. In No. 102 he says that Lenin "has imperceptibly put the concept of dictatorship in place of that of revolution" (p. 3, col. 2).

In essence, all the accusations the new-Iskrists have levelled at us can be reduced to this one. Indeed, we are grateful to Martynov for this accusation! He has rendered us most invaluable service in the struggle against the new-*Iskra* ideas by formulating his accusation in this way! We must positively beg the editors of *Iskra* to let Martynov loose against us more often for the purpose of making the attacks on *Proletary* "more profound", and for a "truly principled" formulation of these attacks. For the more Martynov exerts himself to argue on the plane of principles, the worse do his arguments appear, and the more clearly does he reveal the gaps in the new-*Iskra* trend, the more successfully does he perform on himself and on his friends the useful *reductio ad absurdum* pedagogical operation (reducing the principles of the new *Iskra* to an absurdity).

Vperyod and *Proletary* use the concepts of dictatorship and revolution "interchangeably". *Iskra* does not want such "interchangeability". Just so, most esteemed Comrade Martynov! You have unwittingly stated a great truth. With this *new* formulation you have confirmed our contention that *Iskra* is lagging behind the revolution and straying into an *Osvobozhdeniye* formulation of its tasks, whereas *Vperyod* and *Proletary* are issuing slogans that advance the democratic revolution.

Is this something you don't understand, Comrade Martynov? In view of the importance of the question we shall try to give you a detailed explanation.

The bourgeois character of the democratic revolution expresses itself, among other things, in the facts that a number of classes, groups, and sections of society which fully stand for recognition of private property and commodity production and are incapable of going beyond these bounds, are compelled by force of circumstances to recognise the uselessness of the autocracy and of the whole feudal order in general, and join in the demand for liberty. The bourgeois character of *this* liberty, which is demanded by "society" and advocated in a flood of words (and only words!) from the landowners and the capitalists, is manifesting itself more and more clearly. At the same time the radical difference between the workers' and the bourgeoisie's struggle for liberty, between proletarian and liberal democratism, is also becoming more palpable. The working class and its class-conscious representatives are marching forward and carrying this struggle forward, not only unafraid of bringing it to completion, but striving to go far beyond the uttermost limits of the democratic revolution. Inconsistent and selfish, the bourgeoisie accepts the slogans of liberty hypocritically and only in part. Doomed to inevitable failure are all attempts to establish, by some particular line or by drawing up particular "points" (like those in Starover's resolution or that of the conferees), the limits beyond which this hypocrisy of the bourgeois friends of liberty, or, rather, this betrayal of liberty by its bourgeois friends, begins. That is because the bourgeoisie, caught between two fires (the autocracy and the proletariat), is capable of changing its position and slogans by a thousand ways and means, adapting itself by moving an inch to the left or an inch to the right, haggling and chaffering all the time. The task of proletarian democratism is not to invent such lifeless "points", but to criticise the developing political situation ceaselessly, to expose the ever new and unforeseeable inconsistencies and betrayals on the part of the bourgeoisie.

Recall the history of Mr. Struve's political pronouncements in the illegal press, the history of Social-Democracy's war with him, and you will clearly see how these tasks have been carried out by Social-Democracy, the champion of proletarian democratism. Mr. Struve began with a purely Shipov slogan: "Rights and an Authoritative Zemstvo" (see my article in *Zarya*,[79] "The Persecutors of the Zemstvo and the Hannibals of Liberalism"*). Social-Democracy exposed him and drove him towards a definitely constitutionalist programme. When these "shoves" took effect, thanks to the particularly rapid progress of revolutionary events, the struggle shifted to the *next* problem of democratism: not merely a constitution in general, but one providing for universal and equal suffrage, direct elections, and a secret ballot. When we "captured" this new position from the "enemy" (the adoption of universal suffrage by the *Osvobozhdeniye* League) we began to press further; we showed up the hypocrisy and falseness of a two-chamber system, and the fact that universal suffrage had not been fully recognised by the *Osvobozhdeniye* League; we pointed to their *monarchism* and showed up the huckstering nature of their democratism, or, in other words, the *bartering away* of the interests of the great Russian revolution by these *Osvobozhdeniye* heroes of the money-bag.

Finally, the autocracy's obduracy, the tremendous progress of the civil war, and the hopelessness of the plight to which the monarchists have reduced Russia have begun to penetrate into even the thickest of skulls. The revolution became a *fact*. It was no longer necessary to be a revolutionary to acknowledge the revolution. The autocratic government has actually been disintegrating before our eyes. As has justly been remarked in the legal press by a certain liberal (Mr. Gredeskul), actual disobedience to this government has set in. Notwithstanding its apparent might the autocracy has proved impotent; the events attending the developing revolution have simply begun to thrust aside this parasitic organism, which is rotting alive. Compelled to base their activities (or, to put it more correctly, their shady political deals) on relationships as they are actually taking shape, the liberal bourgeois *have begun to see the necessity of recognising the revolution.* They do so not because they are revolutionaries, but despite the fact that they are *not* revolutionaries.

---

* See *Collected Works*, Vol. 5, pp. 31-80.—*Ed.*

They do so of necessity and against their will, glaring angrily at the success of the revolution, and levelling the accusation of revolutionism against the autocracy, which does not want to strike a bargain, but wants a life-and-death struggle. Born hucksters, they hate struggle and revolution, but circumstances force them to stand on the ground of revolution, for there is no other ground under their feet.

We are witnessing a highly instructive and highly comical spectacle. The bourgeois liberal prostitutes are trying to drape themselves in the toga of revolution. The *Osvobozhdeniye* people—*risum teneatis, amici!**—the *Osvobozhdeniye* people are beginning to speak in the name of the revolution! They are beginning to assure us that they "do not fear revolution" (Mr. Struve in *Osvobozhdeniye*, No. 72)!!! They are voicing their claim "to be at the head of the revolution"!!!

This is a most significant phenomenon, one that characterises not only an advance in bourgeois liberalism, but even more so the advance of the real successes of the revolutionary movement, which has *compelled* recognition. Even the bourgeoisie is beginning to feel that it is more to its advantage to take its stand on the side of the revolution, for the autocracy is so shaky. On the other hand, however, this phenomenon, which testifies to the new and higher level reached by the entire movement, sets us new and higher tasks as well. The bourgeoisie's recognition of the revolution cannot be sincere, irrespective of the personal integrity of one bourgeois ideologist or another. The bourgeoisie cannot but bring selfishness and inconsistency, the spirit of chaffering and petty reactionary dodges even into this higher stage of the movement. We must now formulate the immediate *concrete* tasks of the revolution in a *different* way, in the name of our programme, and in amplification of our programme. What was adequate yesterday is *inadequate today*. Yesterday, perhaps, the demand for the recognition of the revolution was adequate as an advanced democratic slogan. Today that is not enough. The revolution has forced even Mr. Struve to recognise it. The advanced class must now define exactly *the very content* of the urgent and pressing tasks of this revolution. While recognising the revolution, Messrs. the Struves again and again show their asses' ears and strike up the old tune about the possibility of a peaceful outcome, about *Nicholas* calling on the *Osvobozhdeniye* group to take power, etc., etc. The *Osvobozhdeniye* people recognise the revolution so as to emasculate and betray it the more safely for themselves. It is now our duty to show the proletariat and the whole people the inadequacy of the slogan of "revolution"; we must show how necessary it is to have a clear and unambiguous, consistent, and determined definition of *the very*

---

* Restrain your laughter, friends!

content of the revolution. And this definition is provided by the one slogan that is capable of correctly expressing a "decisive victory" of the revolution, the slogan of the revolutionary-democratic dictatorship of the proletariat and the peasantry.

Abuse of terms is a most common practice in politics. The name "socialist", for example, has often been appropriated by supporters of English bourgeois liberalism ("We are all socialists now,"* said Harcourt), by supporters of Bismarck, and by friends of Pope Leo XIII. The term "revolution" also fully lends itself to abuse, and, at a certain stage in the development of the movement, such abuse is inevitable. When Mr. Struve began to speak in the name of revolution we could not but recall Thiers. A few days before the February revolution this monstrous gnome, this most perfect embodiment of the bourgeoisie's political venality sensed that a storm was brewing among the people, and announced from the parliamentary tribune that he *was of the party of revolution*! (See Marx's *The Civil War in France*.) The political significance of *Osvobozhdeniye*'s joining the party of revolution is *exactly the same as* Thiers's. When the Russian Thiers begin to speak of their belonging to the party of revolution, that means that the slogan of revolution has become inadequate, is meaningless, and defines no tasks since the revolution has become a fact, and the most diverse elements are going over to its side.

Indeed, what is revolution from the Marxist point of view? The forcible demolition of the obsolete political superstructure, the contradiction between which and the new relations of production have caused its collapse at a certain moment. The contradiction between the autocracy and the entire structure of capitalist Russia and all the needs of her bourgeois-democratic development has now caused its collapse, all the more severe owing to the lengthy period in which this contradiction was artificially sustained. The superstructure is cracking at every joint, is yielding to pressure, and growing weaker. Through the representatives of the most diverse classes and groups, the people must now, by their own efforts, build themselves a new superstructure. At a certain stage of development, the uselessness of the old superstructure becomes obvious to all; the revolution is recognised by all. The task now is to define *which* classes must build the new superstructure, and *how* they are to build it. If this is not defined the slogan of revolution is empty and meaningless at the present time; for the feebleness of the autocracy makes "revolutionaries" even of the Grand Dukes and of *Moskovskiye Vedomosti*[80]! If this is not defined there can be no talk about the advanced democratic tasks of the advanced class. The slogan "the democratic dictatorship of the proletariat and the peasantry" provides

---

* These words are in English in the original.—*Ed.*

that definition. This slogan defines the classes upon which the new "builders" of the new superstructure can and must rely, the character of the new superstructure (a "democratic" as distinct from a socialist dictatorship), and how it is to be built (dictatorship, i.e., the forcible suppression of resistance by force and the arming of the revolutionary classes of the people). Whoever now refuses to recognise this slogan of revolutionary-democratic dictatorship, the slogan of a revolutionary army, of a revolutionary government, and of revolutionary peasant committees, either hopelessly fails to understand the tasks of the revolution, is unable to define the new and higher tasks evoked by the present situation, or is deceiving the people, betraying the revolution, and misusing the slogan of "revolution". Comrade Martynov and his friends are instances of the former, and Mr. Struve and the whole of the "Constitutional-Democratic" Zemstvo party—of the latter case.

Comrade Martynov was so sharp and shrewd that he charged us with having made the concepts of dictatorship and revolution "interchangeable" just at a time when the development of the revolution required that its tasks be defined by the slogan of dictatorship. Comrade Martynov has again been so unlucky as to be left behind, stranded at the stage before the last, *at the level reached by Osvobozhdeniye*; for recognition of "revolution" (in word) and refusal to recognise the democratic dictatorship of the proletariat and the peasantry (i.e., revolution in deed) today amounts to taking the political stand of *Osvobozhdeniye*, i.e., is to the interests of the liberal monarchist bourgeoisie. Through Mr. Struve the liberal bourgeoisie is now expressing itself in favour of revolution. Through the revolutionary Social-Democrats the class-conscious proletariat is demanding a dictatorship of the proletariat and the peasantry. And at this stage the new-*Iskra* wiseacre intervenes in the controversy and yells: "Don't dare make the ideas of dictatorship and revolution 'interchangeable'!" Well, is it not true that the false stand taken by the new-Iskrists dooms them to be constantly dragging along at the tail end of *Osvobozhdeniye* trend?

We have shown that the *Osvobozhdeniye* people are ascending (not without prodding from the Social-Democrats) step by step in the matter of recognising democratism. At first, the issue in dispute between us was: Shipovism (rights and an authoritative Zemstvo) or constitutionalism? Then it was: limited suffrage or universal suffrage? Later: recognition of the revolution or a huckster's bargain with the autocracy? Finally, it is now: recognition of the revolution without the dictatorship of the proletariat and the peasantry, or recognition of the demand for a dictatorship of these classes in the democratic revolution? It is possible and probable that the *Osvobozhdeniye* people (it makes no difference whether these are present ones, or their successors in the Left wing of the bourgeois democrats) will ascend another step, i.e., recognise in due course (perhaps by the time Comrade Martynov ascends another step) the slogan of dictatorship as well. This will inevitably be the case if the Russian revolution continues to forge ahead, and achieves a decisive victory. What will the position of Social-Democracy then be? The complete victory of the present revolution will mark the end of the democratic revolution and the beginning of a determined struggle for a socialist revolution. Satisfaction of the present-day demands of the peasantry, the utter rout of reaction and the achievement of a democratic republic will mark the utter limit of the revolutionism of the bourgeoisie, and even that of the petty bourgeoisie, and the beginning of the proletariat's real struggle for socialism. The more complete the democratic revolution, the sooner, the more widespread, the cleaner, and the more determined will the development of this new struggle be. The slogan of a "democratic" dictatorship express the historically limited nature of the present revolution and the necessity of a new struggle on the basis of the new order for the complete emancipation of the working class from all oppression and all exploitation. In other words, when the democratic bourgeoisie or petty bourgeoisie ascends another step, when not only the revolution but the complete victory of the revolution becomes an accomplished fact, we shall "change" (perhaps amid the horrified cries of new and future Martynovs) the slogan of the democratic dictatorship to the slogan of a socialist dictatorship of the proletariat, i.e., of a full socialist revolution.

III. THE VULGAR BOURGEOIS
AND THE MARXIST VIEWS ON DICTATORSHIP

In his notes to Marx's articles from the *Neue Rheinische Zeitung* of 1848, which he published, Mehring tells us that one of the reproaches levelled at this newspaper by bourgeois publications was that it had allegedly demanded "the immediate introduction of a dictatorship as the sole means of achieving democracy" (Marx, *Nachlass*, Vol. III, p. 53). From the vulgar bourgeois standpoint the terms dictatorship and democracy are mutually exclusive. Failing to understand the theory of class struggle and accustomed to seeing in the political arena the petty squabbling of the various bourgeois circles and coteries, the bourgeois understands by dictatorship the annulment of all liberties and guarantees of democracy, arbitrariness of every kind, and every sort of abuse of power in a dictator's personal interests. In fact, it is precisely this vulgar bourgeois view that is manifested in the writings of our Martynov, who winds up his "new campaign" in the new *Iskra* by attributing the partiality of *Vperyod* and *Proletary* for the slogan of dictatorship to Lenin's "passionate desire to try his luck" (*Iskra*, No. 103, p. 3, col. 2). This charming explanation is wholly on a level with the bourgeois charges against the *Neue Rheinische Zeitung* and against the preaching of dictatorship. Thus Marx too was accused (by bourgeois liberals, not Social-Democrats) of "supplanting" the concepts of revolution and dictatorship. In order to explain to Martynov the meaning of the term class dictatorship, as distinct from personal dictatorship, and the tasks of a democratic dictatorship, as distinct from those of a socialist dictatorship, it would not be amiss to dwell on the views of the *Neue Rheinische Zeitung*.

"After a revolution," wrote the *Neue Rheinische Zeitung* on September 14, 1848, "every provisional organisation of the state requires a dictatorship and an energetic dictatorship at that. From the very beginning we have reproached Camphausen" (the head of the Ministry after March 18, 1848) "for not acting dictatorially, for not having immediately smashed up and eliminated the remnants of the old institutions. And while Herr Camphausen was lulling himself with constitutional illusions the defeated party (i.e., the party of reaction) strengthened its positions in the bureaucracy and in the army, and here and there even began to venture upon open struggle."[81]

These words, Mehring justly remarks, sum up in a few propositions all that was propounded in detail in the *Neue Rheinische Zeitung* in long articles on the Camphausen Ministry. What do these words of Marx tell us? That a provisional revolutionary government *must* act dictatorially (a proposition which *Iskra* was totally unable to grasp since it was fighting shy of the slogan of dictatorship), and that the task of such a dictatorship is to destroy the remnants of the old institutions (which is precisely what was clearly stated in the resolution of the Third Congress of the Russian Social-Democratic Labour Party on the struggle against counter-revolution and was omitted in the resolution of the conference, as shown above). Thirdly, and lastly, it follows from these words that Marx castigated the bourgeois democrats for entertaining "constitutional illusions" in a period of revolution and open civil war. The meaning of these words becomes particularly obvious from the article in the *Neue Rheinische Zeitung* of June 6, 1848. "A constituent national assembly," Marx wrote, "must first of all be an active, revolutionary-active assembly. The Frankfort Assembly, however, is busying itself with school exercises in parliamentarism while allowing the government to act. Let us assume that this learned assembly succeeds, after mature consideration, in evolving the best possible agenda and the best constitution, but what is the use of the best possible agenda and of the best possible constitution, if the German governments have in the meantime placed the bayonet on the agenda?"[82]

That is the meaning of the slogan: dictatorship. We can judge from this what Marx's attitude would have been towards resolutions which call a "decision to organise a constituent assembly" a decisive victory, or which invite us to "remain the party of extreme revolutionary opposition"!

Major questions in the life of nations are settled only by force. The reactionary classes themselves are usually the first to resort to violence, to civil war; they are the first to "place the bayonet on the agenda", as the Russian autocracy has systematically and unswervingly been doing everywhere ever since January 9. And since such a situation has arisen, since the bayonet has really become the main point on the political agenda, since insurrection has proved imperative and urgent—constitutional illusions and school exercises in parliamentarism become merely a screen for the bourgeois betrayal of the revolution, a screen to conceal the fact that the bourgeoisie is "recoiling" from the revolution. It is precisely the slogan of dictatorship that the genuinely revolutionary class must advance in that case.

On the question of the tasks of this dictatorship Marx wrote in the *Neue Rheinische Zeitung*: "The National Assembly should have acted dictatorially against the reactionary attempts of the obsolete governments, and thus gained for itself the power of public opinion against which all bayonets and rifle butts would have been shattered.... But this Assembly bores the German people instead of carrying them with it or being carried away by them."[83] In Marx's opinion, the National Assembly should have "eliminated from the regime actually existing in Germany everything that contradicted the principle of the sovereignty of the people", and then it should have "consolidated the revolutionary ground on which it stands in order to make the sovereignty of the people, won by the revolution, secure against all attacks."[84]

Consequently, in their content, the tasks which Marx set a revolutionary government or dictatorship in 1848 amounted first and foremost to a *democratic* revolution: defence against counter-revolution and the actual elimination of everything that contradicted the sovereignty of the people. That is nothing else than a revolutionary-democratic dictatorship.

To proceed: which classes, in Marx's opinion, could and should have achieved this task (to fully exercise in deed the principle of the people's sovereignty and beat off the attacks of the counter-revolution)? Marx speaks of the "people". But we know that he always fought ruthlessly against petty-bourgeois illusions about the unity of the "people" and the absence of a class struggle within the people. In using the word "people" Marx did not thereby gloss over class distinctions, but united definite elements capable of bringing the revolution to completion.

After the victory of the Berlin proletariat on March 18, the *Neue Rheinische Zeitung* wrote, the results of the revolution proved two-fold: "On the one hand, the arming of the people, the right of asso-ciation, the actual achievement of the sovereignty of the people; on the other hand, the retention of the monarchy and the Camp-hausen-Hansemann Ministry, i.e., the government of representatives of the big bourgeoisie. Thus, the revolution had two series of results, which had inevitably to diverge. The people had achieved victory; they had won liberties of a decisively democratic nature, but im-mediate power did not pass into their hands, but into the hands of the big bourgeoisie. In short, the revolution was not consummated. The people let representatives of the big bourgeoisie form a min-istry, and these representatives of the big bourgeoisie at once showed what they were after by offering an alliance to the old Prussian nobility and bureaucracy. Arnim, Canitz, and Schwerin joined the ministry.

"The upper bourgeoisie, ever anti-revolutionary, concluded a defensive and offensive alliance with the reactionaries for fear of the people, that is to say, the workers and the democratic bour-geoisie." (Italics ours.)[85]

Thus, not only a "decision to organise a constituent assembly", but even its actual convocation is insufficient for a decisive victory of the revolution! Even after a partial victory in an armed struggle (the victory of the Berlin workers over the troops on March 18, 1848) an "incomplete" revolution, a revolution "that has not been carried to completion", is possible. On what, then, does its comple-tion depend? It depends on whose hands immediate power passes into, into the hands of the Petrunkeviches and Rodichevs, that is to say, the Camphausens and the Hansemanns, or into the hands of the *people*, i.e., the workers and the democratic bourgeoisie. In the first instance, the bourgeoisie will possess power, and the pro-letariat—"freedom of criticism", freedom to "remain the party of extreme revolutionary opposition". Immediately after the victory the bourgeoisie will conclude an alliance with the reactionaries (this would inevitably happen in Russia too, if, for example, the St. Pe-tersburg workers gained only a partial victory in street fighting with the troops and left it to Messrs. Petrunkeviches and Co. to form a government). In the second instance, a revolutionary-democratic dictatorship, i.e., the complete victory of the revolution, would be possible.

It now remains to define more precisely what Marx really meant by "democratic bourgeoisie" (*demokratische Bürgerschaft*), which, together with the workers, he called the people, in contradistinction to the big bourgeoisie.

A clear answer to this question is supplied by the following passage from an article in the *Neue Rheinische Zeitung* of July 29, 1848: "...The German Revolution of 1848 is only a parody of the French Revolution of 1789.

"On August 4, 1789, three weeks after the storming of the Bastille, the French people in a single day prevailed over all feudal burdens.

"On July 11, 1848, four months after the March barricades, the feudal burdens prevailed over the German people. *Teste Gierke cum Hansemanno.**

"The French bourgeoisie of 1789 did not for a moment leave its allies, the peasants, in the lurch. It knew that its rule was grounded in the destruction of feudalism in the countryside, the creation of a free landowning (*grundbesitzenden*) peasant class.

"The German bourgeoisie of 1848 is, without the least compunction, betraying the peasants, who are its most natural allies, the flesh of its flesh, and without whom it is powerless against the aristocracy.

"The continuance of feudal rights, their sanction under the guise of (illusory) redemption—such is the result of the German revolution of 1848. The mountain brought forth a mouse."[86]

This is a very instructive passage, which provides us with four important propositions: 1) The uncompleted German revolution differs from the completed French revolution in that the German bourgeoisie betrayed not only democracy in general, but also the peasantry in particular. 2) The creation of a free class of peasants is the foundation for the consummation of a democratic revolution. 3) The creation of such a class means the abolition of feudal services, the destruction of feudalism, but does not yet mean a socialist revolution. 4) The peasants are the "most natural" allies of the bourgeoisie, that is to say, of the democratic bourgeoisie, which without them is "powerless" against reaction.

With the proper allowances for concrete national peculiarities and with serfdom substituted for feudalism, all these propositions are fully applicable to the Russia of 1905. There is no doubt that by learning from the experience of Germany as elucidated by Marx, we can arrive at no other slogan for a decisive victory of the revolution than: a revolutionary-democratic dictatorship of the proletariat and the peasantry. There is no doubt that the proletariat

---

* "Witnesses: Herr Gierke together with Herr Hansemann." Hansemann was a Minister who represented the party of the big bourgeoisie (Russian counterpart: Trubetskoi or Rodichev, and the like); Gierke was Minister of Agriculture in the Hansemann Cabinet, who drew up a plan, a "bold" plan for "abolishing feudal burdens", professedly "without compensation", but in fact for abolishing only the minor and unimportant burdens, while preserving or granting compensation for the more essential ones. Herr Gierke was something like the Russian Kablukovs, Manuilovs, Hertzensteins, and similar bourgeois liberal friends of the muzhik, who desire the "extension of peasant landownership" but do not wish to offend the landlords.

and the peasantry are the chief components of the "people" as contrasted by Marx in 1848 to the resisting reactionaries and the treacherous bourgeoisie. There is no doubt that in Russia, too, the liberal bourgeoisie and the gentlemen of the *Osvobozhdeniye* League are betraying and will betray the peasantry, i.e., will confine themselves to a pseudo-reform and take the side of the landlords in the decisive battle between them and the peasantry. In this struggle only the proletariat is capable of supporting the peasantry to the end. There is no doubt, finally, that in Russia, too, the success of the peasants' struggle, i.e., the transfer of the whole of the land to the peasantry, will signify a complete democratic revolution, and constitute the social basis of the revolution carried through to its completion, but this will by no means be a socialist revolution, or the "socialisation" that the ideologists of the petty bourgeoisie, the Socialist-Revolutionaries, talk about. The success of the peasant insurrection, the victory of the democratic revolution will merely clear the way for a genuine and decisive struggle for socialism, on the basis of a democratic republic. In this struggle the peasantry, as a landowning class, will play the same treacherous, unstable part as is now being played by the bourgeoisie in the struggle for democracy. To forget this is to forget socialism, to deceive oneself and others, regarding the real interests and tasks of the proletariat.

In order to leave no gaps in the presentation of the views held by Marx in 1848, it is necessary to note one essential difference between German Social-Democracy of the time (or the Communist Party of the proletariat, to use the language of that period) and present-day Russian Social-Democracy. Here is what Mehring says:

"The *Neue Rheinische Zeitung* appeared in the political arena as the 'organ of democracy'. There is no mistaking the trend running through all its articles. But in the direct sense it championed the interests of the bourgeois revolution against absolutism and feudalism more than the interests of the proletariat against those of the bourgeoisie. Very little is to be found in its columns about an independent working-class movement during the years of the revolution, although one should not forget that along with it there appeared, twice a week, under the editorship of Moll and Schapper, a special organ of the Cologne Workers' League.[87] At any rate, the present-day reader will be struck by the little attention the *Neue Rheinische Zeitung* paid to the German working-class movement of its day, although Stephan Born, its most capable mind, was a pupil of Marx and Engels in Paris and Brussels, and in 1848 was their newspaper's Berlin correspondent. In his *Memoirs* Born says that Marx and Engels never expressed a single word in disapproval of his agitation among the workers. However, subsequent statements by Engels make it appear quite probable that they were at least dissatisfied with the methods of this agitation. Their dissatisfaction

was justified inasmuch as Born was obliged to make many concessions to the as yet totally undeveloped class-consciousness of the
proletariat in the greater part of Germany, concessions which do
not stand the test of criticism from the viewpoint of the *Communist Manifesto*. Their dissatisfaction was unjustified inasmuch as
Born managed nonetheless to maintain his agitation on a relatively
high plane.... Without doubt, Marx and Engels were historically
and politically right in thinking that the primary interest of the
working class was to drive the bourgeois revolution as far forward
as possible.... Nevertheless, remarkable proof of how the elementary instinct of the working-class movement is able to correct con-
ceptions of the most brilliant thinkers is provided by the fact that
in April 1849 they declared in favour of a specific workers' organisation and decided to participate in a workers' congress which was
being prepared especially by the East Elbe (Eastern Prussia) proletariat."

Thus, it was only in April 1849, after a revolutionary newspaper
had been appearing for almost a year (the *Neue Rheinische Zeitung*
began publication on June 1, 1848), that Marx and Engels declared
in favour of a special workers' organisation! Until then they were
merely running an "organ of democracy" unlinked by any organisational ties with an independent workers' party. This fact, monstrous and improbable as it may appear from our present-day standpoint, clearly shows us the enormous difference between the German
Social-Democratic Party of those days and the Russian Social-
Democratic Labour Party of today. This fact shows how much less
the proletarian features of the movement, the proletarian current
within it, were in evidence in the German democratic revolution
(because of the backwardness of Germany in 1848 both economically
and politically—its disunity as a state). This should not be forgotten (as it is forgotten, for instance, by Plekhanov) in appraising
Marx's repeated declarations during this period and somewhat later
about the need for organising an independent proletarian party.
Marx arrived at this practical conclusion only as a result of the experience of the democratic revolution, almost a year later—so philistine, so petty-bourgeois was the whole atmosphere in Germany
at the time. To us this conclusion is the well-known and solid
gain of half a century's experience of international Social-
Democracy—a gain on the basis of which we *began* to organise the
Russian Social-Democratic Labour Party. In our case there can be
no question, for instance, of revolutionary proletarian newspapers
standing outside the Social-Democratic Party of the proletariat, or
of their appearing even for a moment simply as "organs of
democracy".

But the contrast which hardly began to reveal itself between Marx
and Stephan Born exists in our case in a form which is the more

developed by reason of the more powerful manifestation of the proletarian current in the democratic stream of our revolution. Speaking of the probable dissatisfaction of Marx and Engels with the
agitation conducted by Stephan Born, Mehring expresses himself
too mildly and too evasively. Here is what Engels wrote of Born
in 1885 (in his preface to the *Enthüllungen über den Kommunisten-
prozess zu Köln*, Zürich, 1885*):

"The members of the Communist League[88] everywhere stood at
the head of the extreme democratic movement, proving thereby
that the League was an excellent school of revolutionary activity.
The compositor Stephan Born, who had worked in Brussels and
Paris as an active member of the League, founded a Workers'
Brotherhood [*Arbeiterverbrüderung*] in Berlin which became fairly
widespread and existed until 1850. Born, a very talented young
man, who, however, was too much in a hurry to become a political
figure, 'fraternised' with the most miscellaneous ragtag and bobtail
[*Krethi und Plethi*] in order to get a crowd together, and was not
at all the man who could bring unity into the conflicting tendencies,
light into the chaos. Consequently, in the official publications of the
association the views represented in the *Communist Manifesto* were
mingled hodge-podge with guild recollections and guild aspirations,
fragments of Louis Blanc and Proudhon, protectionism, etc.; in
short, they wanted to please everybody [*allen alles sein*]. *In particular, strikes, trade unions, and producers' co-operatives were set
going, and it was forgotten that above all it was a question of first
conquering, by means of political victories, the field* in which alone
such things could be realised on a lasting basis, [italics mine]. When,
afterwards, the victories of the reaction made the leaders of the
Brotherhood realise the necessity of taking a direct part in the
revolutionary struggle, they were naturally left in the lurch by the
confused mass which they had grouped around themselves. Born
took part in the Dresden uprising in May 1849, and had a lucky
escape. But, in contrast to the great political movement of the
proletariat, the Workers' Brotherhood proved to be a pure *Sonder-
bund* (separate league), which to a large extent existed only on
paper and played such a subordinate role that the reaction did not
find it necessary to suppress it until 1850, and its surviving branches
until several years later. Born, whose real name was Buttermilch,**

---

* *Revelations About the Cologne Communist Trial*, Zürich, 1885.—*Ed.*
** In translating Engels I made a mistake in the first edition by taking the
word *Buttermilch* to be not a proper noun but a common noun. This mistake
naturally afforded great delight to the Mensheviks. Koltsov wrote that I had
"rendered Engels more profound" (reprinted in *Two Years*, a collection of
articles) and Plekhanov even now recalls this mistake in *Tovarishch*[89]—in short,
it afforded *an excellent pretext to slur over the question of the two tendencies
in the working-class movement* of 1848 in Germany, the Born tendency (akin

has not become a political figure but a petty Swiss professor, who no longer translates Marx into guild language, but the meek Renan into his own fulsome German."[90]

That is how Engels judged the two tactics of Social-Democracy in the democratic revolution!

Our new-Iskrists are also leaning towards Economism, and with such unreasonable zeal as to earn the praises of the monarchist bourgeoisie for "seeing the light". They too gather a motley crowd around themselves, flattering the Economists, demagogically attracting the undeveloped masses by the slogans of "initiative", "democracy", "autonomy", etc., etc.; their workers' unions, too, often exist only on the pages of the Khlestakov-type new *Iskra*. Their slogans and resolutions betray a similar failure to understand the tasks of the "great political movement of the proletariat".

Written June-July 1905

Published in July 1905
in Geneva
in pamphlet form
by C.C., R.S.D.L.P.

Collected Works, Vol. 9

---

to our Economists) and the Marxist tendency. To take advantage of the mistake of an opponent, even if it concerns Born's name, is more than natural. But to use a correction to a translation to slur over the substance of the question of the two tactics is to dodge the real issue. (Author's note to the 1907 edition.—*Ed.*)

PARTY ORGANISATION AND PARTY LITERATURE

The new conditions for Social-Democratic work in Russia which have arisen since the October Revolution[91] have brought the question of party literature to the fore. The distinction between the illegal and the legal press, that melancholy heritage of the epoch of feudal, autocratic Russia, is beginning to disappear. It is not yet dead, by a long way. The hypocritical government of our Prime Minister is still running amuck, so much so that *Izvestia Soveta Rabochikh Deputatov*[92] is printed "illegally"; but apart from bringing disgrace on the government, apart from striking further moral blows at it, nothing comes of the stupid attempts to "prohibit" that which the government is powerless to thwart.

So long as there was a distinction between the illegal and the legal press, the question of the party and non-party press was decided extremely simply and in an extremely false and abnormal way. The entire illegal press was a party press, being published by organisations and run by groups which in one way or another were linked with groups of practical party workers. The entire legal press was non-party—since parties were banned—but it "gravitated" towards one party or another. Unnatural alliances, strange "bedfellows" and false cover-devices were inevitable. The forced reserve of those who wished to express party views merged with the immature thinking or mental cowardice of those who had not risen to these views and who were not, in effect, party people.

An accursed period of Aesopian language, literary bondage, slavish speech, and ideological serfdom! The proletariat has put an end to this foul atmosphere which stifled everything living and fresh in Russia. But so far the proletariat has won only half freedom for Russia.

The revolution is not yet completed. While tsarism is *no longer* strong enough to defeat the revolution, the revolution is *not yet* strong enough to defeat tsarism. And we are living in times when everywhere and in everything there operates this unnatural combination of open, forthright, direct and consistent party spirit with an underground, covert, "diplomatic" and dodgy "legality". This un-natural combination makes itself felt even in our newspaper: for all Mr. Guchkov's witticisms about Social-Democratic tyranny for-bidding the publication of moderate liberal-bourgeois newspapers, the fact remains that *Proletary*, the Central Organ of the Russian Social-Democratic Labour Party, still remains outside the locked doors of *autocratic*, police-ridden Russia.

Be that as it may, the half-way revolution compels all of us to set to work at once organising the whole thing on new lines. Today literature, even that published "legally", can be nine-tenths party literature. It must become party literature. In contradistinction to bourgeois customs, to the profit-making, commercialised bourgeois press, to bourgeois literary careerism and individualism, "aristoc-ratic anarchism" and drive for profit, the socialist proletariat must put forward the principle of *party literature*, must develop this prin-ciple and put it into practice as fully and completely as possible.

What is this principle of party literature? It is not simply that, for the socialist proletariat, literature cannot be a means of en-riching individuals or groups: it cannot, in fact, be an individual undertaking, independent of the common cause of the proletariat. Down with non-partisan writers! Down with literary supermen! Literature must become *part* of the common cause of the proletar-iat, "a cog and a screw" of one single great Social-Democratic mechanism set in motion by the entire politically-conscious vanguard of the entire working class. Literature must become a component of organised, planned and integrated Social-Democratic Party work.

"All comparisons are lame," says a German proverb. So is my comparison of literature with a cog, of a living movement with a mechanism. And I daresay there will ever be hysterical intellectuals to raise a howl about such a comparison, which degrades, deadens, "bureaucratises" the free battle of ideas, freedom of criticism, freedom of literary creation, etc., etc. Such outcries, in point of fact, would be nothing more than an expression of bourgeois-intel-lectual individualism. There is no question that literature is least of all subject to mechanical adjustment or levelling, to the rule of the majority over the minority. There is no question, either, that in this field greater scope must undoubtedly be allowed for personal initiative, individual inclination, thought and fantasy, form and content. All this is undeniable; but all this simply shows that the literary side of the proletarian party cause cannot be mechanically identified with its other sides. This, however, does not in the least refute the proposition, alien and strange to the bourgeoisie and bourgeois democracy, that literature must by all means and neces-sarily become an element of Social-Democratic Party work, in-separably bound up with the other elements. Newspapers must become the organs of the various party organisations, and their writers must by all means become members of these organisations. Publishing and distributing centres, bookshops and reading-rooms, libraries and similar establishments—must all be under party control. The organised socialist proletariat must keep an eye on all this work, supervise it in its entirety, and, from beginning to end, without any exception, infuse into it the life-stream of the living proletarian cause, thereby cutting the ground from under the old, semi-Oblomov, semi-shopkeeper Russian principle: the writer does the writing, the reader does the reading.

We are not suggesting, of course, that this transformation of literary work, which has been defiled by the Asiatic censorship and the European bourgeoisie, can be accomplished all at once. Far be it from us to advocate any kind of standardised system, or a solution by means of a few decrees. Cut-and-dried schemes are least of all applicable here. What is needed is that the whole of our Party, and the entire politically conscious Social-Democratic proletariat throughout Russia, should become aware of this new problem, specify it clearly and everywhere set about solving it. Emerging from the captivity of the feudal censorship, we have no desire to become, and shall not become, prisoners of bourgeois-shopkeeper literary relations. We want to establish, and we shall establish, a free press, free not simply from the police, but also from capital, from careerism, and what is more, free from bourgeois-anarchist individualism.

These last words may sound paradoxical, or an affront to the reader. What! some intellectual, an ardent champion of liberty, may shout. What, you want to impose collective control on such a delicate, individual matter as literary work! You want workmen to decide questions of science, philosophy, or aesthetics by a majority of votes! You deny the absolute freedom of absolutely individual ideological work!

Calm yourselves, gentlemen! First of all, we are discussing party literature and its subordination to party control. Everyone is free to write and say whatever he likes, without any restrictions. But every voluntary association (including a party) is also free to expel members who use the name of the party to advocate anti-party views. Freedom of speech and the press must be complete. But then freedom of association must be complete too. I am bound to accord you, in the name of free speech, the full right to shout, lie and write to your heart's content. But you are bound to grant me, in the name of freedom of association, the right to enter into, or withdraw from, association with people advocating this or that view. The party is a voluntary association, which would inevitably break up, first ideologically and then physically, if it did not cleanse itself of people advocating anti-party views. And to define the

border-line between party and anti-party there is the party programme, the party's resolutions on tactics and its rules and, lastly,
the entire experience of international Social-Democracy, the voluntary international associations of the proletariat, which has constantly brought into its parties individual elements and trends not
fully consistent, not completely Marxist and not altogether correct
and which, on the other hand, has constantly conducted periodical
"cleansings" of its ranks. So it will be with us too, supporters of
bourgeois "freedom of criticism", *within* the Party. We are now
becoming a mass party all at once, changing abruptly to an open
organisation, and it is inevitable that we shall be joined by many
who are inconsistent (from the Marxist standpoint), perhaps we
shall be joined even by some Christian elements, and even by some
mystics. We have sound stomachs and we are rock-like Marxists.
We shall digest those inconsistent elements. Freedom of thought
and freedom of criticism within the Party will never make us forget about the freedom of organising people into those voluntary
associations known as parties.

Secondly, we must say to you bourgeois individualists that your
talk about absolute freedom is sheer hypocrisy. There can be no
real and effective "freedom" in a society based on the power of
money, in a society in which the masses of working people live in
poverty and the handful of rich live like parasites. Are you free
in relation to your bourgeois publisher, Mr. Writer, in relation to
your bourgeois public, which demands that you provide it with pornography in frames* and paintings, and prostitution as a "supplement" to "sacred" scenic art? This absolute freedom is a bourgeois
or an anarchist phrase (since, as a world outlook, anarchism is
bourgeois philosophy turned inside out). One cannot live in
society and be free from society. The freedom of the bourgeois
writer, artist or actress is simply masked (or hypocritically masked)
dependence on the money-bag, on corruption, on prostitution.

And we socialists expose this hypocrisy and rip off the false
labels, not in order to arrive at a non-class literature and art (that
will be possible only in a socialist extra-class society), but to contrast
this hypocritically free literature, which is in reality linked to the
bourgeoisie, with a really free one that will be *openly* linked to the
proletariat.

It will be a free literature, because the idea of socialism and sympathy with the working people, and not greed or careerism, will
bring ever new forces to its ranks. It will be a free literature, because it will serve, not some satiated heroine, not the bored "upper
ten thousand" suffering from fatty degeneration, but the millions

---

* There must be a misprint in the source, which says *ramkakh* (frames),
while the context suggests *romanakh* (novels).—*Ed.*

and tens of millions of working people—the flower of the country, its strength and its future. It will be a free literature, enriching the last word in the revolutionary thought of mankind with the experience and living work of the socialist proletariat, bringing about permanent interaction between the experience of the past (scientific socialism, the completion of the development of socialism from its primitive, utopian forms) and the experience of the present (the present struggle of the worker comrades).

To work, then, comrades! We are faced with a new and difficult task. But it is a noble and grateful one—to organise a broad, multiform and varied literature inseparably linked with the Social-Democratic working-class movement. All Social-Democratic literature must become Party literature. Every newspaper, journal, publishing house, etc., must immediately set about reorganising its work, leading up to a situation in which it will, in one form or another, be integrated into one Party organisation or another. Only then will "Social-Democratic" literature really become worthy of that name, only then will it be able to fulfil its duty and, even within the framework of bourgeois society, break out of bourgeois slavery and merge with the movement of the really advanced and thoroughly revolutionary class.

Novaya Zhizn, No. 12
November 13, 1905
Signed: *N. Lenin*

Collected Works, Vol. 10

ON THE SLOGAN
FOR A UNITED STATES OF EUROPE

In No. 40 of *Sotsial-Demokrat*[93] we reported that a conference of our Party's groups abroad[94] had decided to defer the question of the "United States of Europe" slogan pending a discussion, in the press, on the *economic* aspect of the matter.*

At our conference the debate on this question assumed a purely political character. Perhaps this was partly caused by the Central Committee's Manifesto having formulated this slogan as a forthright political one ("the immediate *political* slogan...", as it says there); not only did it advance the slogan of a republican United States of Europe, but expressly emphasised that this slogan is meaningless and false "without the revolutionary overthrow of the German, Austrian and Russian monarchies".

It would be quite wrong to object to such a presentation of the question *within the limits* of a political appraisal of this slogan— e.g., to argue that it obscures or weakens, etc., the slogan of a socialist revolution. Political changes of a truly democratic nature, and especially political revolutions, can under no circumstances whatsoever either obscure or weaken the slogan of a socialist revolution. On the contrary, they always bring it closer, extend its basis, and draw new sections of the petty bourgeoisie and the semi-proletarian masses into the socialist struggle. On the other hand, political revolutions are inevitable in the course of the socialist revolution. which should not be regarded as a single act, but as a period of turbulent political and economic upheavals, the most intense class struggle, civil war, revolutions, and counter-revolutions.

But while the slogan of a republican United States of Europe—if accompanied by the revolutionary overthrow of the three most reactionary monarchies in Europe, headed by the Russian—is quite invulnerable as a political slogan, there still remains the highly important question of its economic content and significance. From the standpoint of the economic conditions of imperialism—i.e., the

---

* See *Collected Works*, Vol. 21, p. 158.—*Ed.*

export of capital and the division of the world by the "advanced" and "civilised" colonial powers—a United States of Europe, under capitalism, is either impossible or reactionary.

Capital has become international and monopolist. The world has been carved up by a handful of Great Powers, i.e., powers successful in the great plunder and oppression of nations. The four Great Powers of Europe—Britain, France, Russia and Germany, with an aggregate population of between 250,000,000 and 300,000,000, and an area of about 7,000,000 square kilometres—possess colonies with a population of *almost 500 million* (494,500,000) and an area of 64,600,000 square kilometres, i.e., almost half the surface of the globe (133,000,000 square kilometres, exclusive of Arctic and Antarctic regions). Add to this the three Asian states—China, Turkey and Persia, now being rent piecemeal by thugs that are waging a war of "liberation", namely, Japan, Russia, Britain and France. Those three Asian states, which may be called semi-colonies (in reality they are now 90 per cent colonies), have a total population of 360,000,000 and an area of 14,500,000 square kilometres (almost one and a half times the area of all Europe).

Furthermore, Britain, France and Germany have invested capital abroad to the value of no less than 70,000 million rubles. The business of securing "legitimate" profits from this tidy sum—these exceed 3,000 million rubles annually—is carried out by the national committees of the millionaires, known as governments, which are equipped with armies and navies and which provide the sons and brothers of the millionaires with jobs in the colonies and semi-colonies as viceroys, consuls, ambassadors, officials of all kinds, clergymen, and other leeches.

That is how the plunder of about a thousand million of the earth's population by a handful of Great Powers is organised in the epoch of the highest development of capitalism. No other organisation is possible under capitalism. Renounce colonies, "spheres of influence", and the export of capital? To think that it is possible means coming down to the level of some snivelling parson who every Sunday preaches to the rich on the lofty principles of Christianity and advises them to give the poor, well, if not millions, at least several hundred rubles yearly.

A United States of Europe under capitalism is tantamount to an agreement on the partition of colonies. Under capitalism, however, no other basis and no other principle of division are possible except force. A multi-millionaire cannot share the "national income" of a capitalist country with anyone otherwise than "in proportion to the capital invested" (with a bonus thrown in, so that the biggest capital may receive more than its share). Capitalism is private ownership of the means of production, and anarchy in production. To advocate a "just" division of income on such a basis is sheer Proudhonism, stupid philistinism. No division can be effected otherwise than in "proportion to strength", and strength changes with the course of economic development. Following 1871, the rate of Germany's accession of strength was three or four times as rapid as that of Britain and France, and of Japan about ten times as rapid as Russia's. There is and there can be no other way of testing the real might of a capitalist state than by war. War does not contradict the fundamentals of private property—on the contrary, it is a direct and inevitable outcome of those fundamentals. Under capitalism the smooth economic growth of individual enterprises or individual states is impossible. Under capitalism, there are no other means of restoring the periodically disturbed equilibrium than crises in industry and wars in politics.

Of course, *temporary* agreements are possible between capitalists and between states. In this sense a United States of Europe is possible as an agreement between the *European* capitalists ... but to what end? Only for the purpose of jointly suppressing socialism in Europe, of jointly protecting colonial booty *against* Japan and America, who have been badly done out of their share by the present partition of colonies, and the increase of whose might during the last fifty years has been immeasurably more rapid than that of backward and monarchist Europe, now turning senile. Compared with the United States of America, Europe as a whole denotes economic stagnation. On the present economic basis, i.e., under capitalism, a United States of Europe would signify an organisation of reaction to retard America's more rapid development. The times when the cause of democracy and socialism was associated only with Europe alone have gone for ever.

A United States of the World (not of Europe alone) is the state form of the unification and freedom of nations which we associate with socialism—until the time when the complete victory of communism brings about the total disappearance of the state, including the democratic. As a separate slogan, however, the slogan of a United States of the World would hardly be a correct one, first, because it merges with socialism; second, because it may be wrongly interpreted to mean that the victory of socialism in a single country is impossible, and it may also create misconceptions as to the relations of such a country to the others.

Uneven economic and political development is an absolute law of capitalism. Hence, the victory of socialism is possible first in several or even in one capitalist country alone. After expropriating the capitalists and organising their own socialist production, the victorious proletariat of that country will arise *against* the rest of the world—the capitalist world—attracting to its cause the oppressed classes of other countries, stirring uprisings in those countries against the capitalists, and in case of need using even armed force against the exploiting classes and their states. The political form of a society wherein the proletariat is victorious in overthrowing the bourgeoisie will be a democratic republic, which will more and more concentrate the forces of the proletariat of a given nation or nations, in the struggle against states that have not yet gone over to socialism. The abolition of classes is impossible without a dictatorship of the oppressed class, of the proletariat. A free union of nations in socialism is impossible without a more or less prolonged and stubborn struggle of the socialist republics against the backward states.

It is for these reasons and after repeated discussions at the conference of R.S.D.L.P. groups abroad, and following that conference, that the Central Organ's editors have come to the conclusion that the slogan for a United States of Europe is an erroneous one.

Sotsial-Demokrat No. 44,   *Collected Works,* Vol. 21
     August 23, 1915

THE SOCIALIST REVOLUTION
AND THE RIGHT OF NATIONS TO SELF-DETERMINATION
(THESES)

1. IMPERIALISM, SOCIALISM AND THE LIBERATION OF OPPRESSED NATIONS

Imperialism is the highest stage in the development of capitalism. In the foremost countries capital has outgrown the bounds of national states, has replaced competition by monopoly and has created all the objective conditions for the achievement of socialism. In Western Europe and in the United States, therefore, the revolutionary struggle of the proletariat for the overthrow of capitalist governments and the expropriation of the bourgeoisie is on the order of the day. Imperialism forces the masses into this struggle by sharpening class contradictions on a tremendous scale, by worsening the conditions of the masses both economically—trusts, high cost of living—and politically—the growth of militarism, more frequent wars, more powerful reaction, the intensification and expansion of national oppression and colonial plunder. Victorious socialism must necessarily establish a full democracy and, consequently, not only introduce full equality of nations but also realise the right of the oppressed nations to self-determination, i.e., the right to free political separation. Socialist parties which did not show by all their activity, both now, during the revolution, and after its victory, that they would liberate the enslaved nations and build up relations with them on the basis of a free union—and free union is a false phrase without the right to secede—these parties would be betraying socialism.

Democracy, of course, is also a form of state which must disappear when the state disappears, but that will only take place in the transition from conclusively victorious and consolidated socialism to full communism.

2. THE SOCIALIST REVOLUTION AND THE STRUGGLE FOR DEMOCRACY

The socialist revolution is not a single act, it is not one battle on one front, but a whole epoch of acute class conflicts, a long series of battles on all fronts, i.e., on all questions of economics and politics, battles that can only end in the expropriation of the bourgeoisie. It would be a radical mistake to think that the struggle for democracy was capable of diverting the proletariat from the socialist revolution or of hiding, overshadowing it, etc. On the contrary, in the same way as there can be no victorious socialism that does not practise full democracy, so the proletariat cannot prepare for its victory over the bourgeoisie without an all-round, consistent and revolutionary struggle for democracy.

It would be no less a mistake to remove one of the points of the democratic programme, for example, the point on the self-determination of nations, on the grounds of it being "impracticable" or "illusory" under imperialism. The contention that the right of nations to self-determination is impracticable within the bounds of capitalism can be understood either in the absolute, economic sense, or in the conditional, political sense.

In the first case it is radically incorrect from the standpoint of theory. First, in that sense, such things as, for example, labour money, or the abolition of crises, etc., are impracticable under capitalism. It is absolutely untrue that the self-determination of nations is *equally* impracticable. Secondly, even the one example of the secession of Norway from Sweden in 1905 is sufficient to refute "impracticability" in that sense. Thirdly, it would be absurd to deny that some slight change in the political and strategic relations of, say, Germany and Britain, might today or tomorrow make the formation of a new Polish, Indian and other similar state fully "practicable". Fourthly, finance capital, in its drive to expand, can "freely" buy or bribe the freest democratic or republican government and the elective officials of any, even an "independent", country. The domination of finance capital and of capital in general is not to be abolished by *any* reforms in the sphere of political democracy; and self-determination belongs wholly and exclusively to this sphere. This domination of finance capital, however, does not in the least nullify the significance of political democracy as a freer, wider and clearer *form* of class oppression and class struggle. Therefore all arguments about the "impracticability", in the economic sense, of one of the demands of political democracy under capitalism are reduced to a theoretically incorrect definition of the general and basic relationships of capitalism and of political democracy as a whole.

In the second case the assertion is incomplete and inaccurate. This is because not only the right of nations to self-determination, but *all* the fundamental demands of political democracy are only partially "practicable" under imperialism, and then in a distorted form and by way of exception (for example, the secession of Norway from Sweden in 1905). The demand for the immediate liberation of the colonies that is put forward by all revolutionary Social-

Democrats is also "impracticable" under capitalism without a series of revolutions. But from this it does not by any means follow that Social-Democracy should reject the immediate and most determined struggle for *all* these demands—such a rejection would only play into the hands of the bourgeoisie and reaction—but, on the contrary, it follows that these demands must be formulated and put through in a revolutionary and not a reformist manner, going beyond the bounds of bourgeois legality, breaking them down, going beyond speeches in parliament and verbal protests, and drawing the masses into decisive action, extending and intensifying the struggle for every fundamental democratic demand up to a direct proletarian onslaught on the bourgeoisie, i.e., up to the socialist revolution that expropriates the bourgeoisie. The socialist revolution may flare up not only through some big strike, street demonstration or hunger riot or a military insurrection or colonial revolt, but also as a result of a political crisis such as the Dreyfus case[95] or the Zabern incident,[96] or in connection with a referendum on the secession of an oppressed nation, etc.

Increased national oppression under imperialism does not mean that Social-Democracy should reject what the bourgeoisie call the "utopian" struggle for the freedom of nations to secede but, on the contrary, it should make greater use of the conflicts that arise in this sphere, *too*, as grounds for mass action and for revolutionary attacks on the bourgeoisie.

3. THE SIGNIFICANCE OF THE RIGHT TO SELF-DETERMINATION AND ITS RELATION TO FEDERATION

The right of nations to self-determination implies exclusively the right to independence in the political sense, the right to free political separation from the oppressor nation. Specifically, this demand for political democracy implies complete freedom to agitate for secession and for a referendum on secession by the seceding nation. This demand, therefore, is not the equivalent of a demand for separation, fragmentation and the formation of small states. It implies only a consistent expression of struggle against all national oppression. The closer a democratic state system is to complete freedom to secede the less frequent and less ardent will the desire for separation be in practice, because big states afford indisputable advantages, both from the standpoint of economic progress and from that of the interests of the masses and, furthermore, these advantages increase with the growth of capitalism. Recognition of self-determination is not synonymous with recognition of federation as a principle. One may be a determined opponent of that principle and a champion of democratic centralism but still prefer federation to national inequality as the only way to full democratic centralism. It was from this standpoint that Marx, who was a centralist, preferred even the federation of Ireland and England to the forcible subordination of Ireland to the English.

The aim of socialism is not only to end the division of mankind into tiny states and the isolation of nations in any form, it is not only to bring the nations closer together but to integrate them. And it is precisely in order to achieve this aim that we must, on the one hand, explain to the masses the reactionary nature of Renner and Otto Bauer's idea of so-called "cultural and national autonomy"[97] and, on the other, demand the liberation of oppressed nations in a clearly and precisely formulated political programme that takes special account of the hypocrisy and cowardice of socialists in the oppressor nations, and not in general nebulous phrases, not in empty declamations and not by way of "relegating" the question until socialism has been achieved. In the same way as mankind can arrive at the abolition of classes only through a transition period of the dictatorship of the oppressed class, it can arrive at the inevitable integration of nations only through a transition period of the complete emancipation of all oppressed nations, i.e., their freedom to secede.

4. THE PROLETARIAN-REVOLUTIONARY PRESENTATION OF THE QUESTION OF THE SELF-DETERMINATION OF NATIONS

The petty bourgeoisie had put forward not only the demand for the self-determination of nations but all the points of our democratic minimum programme long before, as far back as the seventeenth and eighteenth centuries. They are still putting them all forward in a utopian manner because they fail to see the class struggle and its increased intensity under democracy, and because they believe in "peaceful" capitalism. That is the exact nature of the utopia of a peaceful union of equal nations under imperialism which deceives the people and which is defended by Kautsky's followers. The programme of Social-Democracy, as a counter-balance to this petty-bourgeois, opportunist utopia, must postulate the division of nations into oppressor and oppressed as basic, significant and inevitable under imperialism.

The proletariat of the oppressor nations must not confine themselves to general, stereotyped phrases against annexation and in favour of the equality of nations in general, such as any pacifist bourgeois will repeat. The proletariat cannot remain silent on the question of the *frontiers* of a state founded on national oppression, a question so "unpleasant" for the imperialist bourgeoisie. The proletariat must struggle against the enforced retention of oppressed nations within the bounds of the given state, which means that they must fight for the right to self-determination. The proletariat must demand freedom of political separation for the colonies and nations oppressed by "their own" nation. Otherwise, the internationalism of the proletariat would be nothing but empty words; neither confidence nor class solidarity would be possible between the workers of the oppressed and the oppressor nations; the hypocrisy of the reformists and Kautskyites, who defend self-determination but remain silent about the nations oppressed by "their own" nation and kept in "their own" state by force, would remain unexposed.

On the other hand, the socialists of the oppressed nations must, in particular, defend and implement the full and unconditional unity, including organisational unity, of the workers of the oppressed nation and those of the oppressor nation. Without this it is impossible to defend the independent policy of the proletariat and their class solidarity with the proletariat of other countries in face of all manner of intrigues, treachery and trickery on the part of the bourgeoisie. The bourgeoisie of the oppressed nations persistently utilise the slogans of national liberation to deceive the workers; in their internal policy they use these slogans for reactionary agreements with the bourgeoisie of the dominant nation (for example, the Poles in Austria and Russia who come to terms with reactionaries for the oppression of the Jews and Ukrainians); in their foreign policy they strive to come to terms with one of the rival imperialist powers for the sake of implementing their predatory plans (the policy of the small Balkan states, etc.).

The fact that the struggle for national liberation against one imperialist power may, under certain conditions, be utilised by another "great" power for its own, equally imperialist, aims, is just as unlikely to make the Social-Democrats refuse to recognise the right of nations to self-determination as the numerous cases of bourgeois utilisation of republican slogans for the purpose of political deception and financial plunder (as in the Romance countries, for example) are unlikely to make the Social-Democrats reject their republicanism.*

---

* It would, needless to say, be quite ridiculous to reject the right to self-determination on the grounds that it implies "defence of the fatherland". With equal right, i.e., with equal lack of seriousness, the social-chauvinists of 1914-16 refer to any of the demands of democracy (to its republicanism, for example) and to any formulation of the struggle against national oppression in order to justify "defence of the fatherland". Marxism deduces the defence of the fatherland in wars, for example, in the great French Revolution or the wars of Garibaldi, in Europe, and the renunciation of defence of the fatherland in the imperialist war of 1914-16, from an analysis of the concrete historical peculiarities of each individual war and never from any "general principle", or any one point of a programme.

5. MARXISM AND PROUDHONISM
ON THE NATIONAL QUESTION

In contrast to the petty-bourgeois democrats, Marx regarded every democratic demand without exception not as an absolute, but as an historical expression of the struggle of the masses of the people, led by the bourgeoisie, against feudalism. There is not one of these demands which could not serve and has not served, under certain circumstances, as an instrument in the hands of the bourgeoisie for deceiving the workers. To single out, in this respect, one of the demands of political democracy, specifically, the self-determination of nations, and to oppose it to the rest, is fundamentally wrong in theory. In practice, the proletariat can retain its independence only by subordinating its struggle for all democratic demands, not excluding the demand for a republic, to its revolutionary struggle for the overthrow of the bourgeoisie.

On the other hand, in contrast to the Proudhonists who "denied" the national problem "in the name of social revolution", Marx, mindful in the first place of the interests of the proletarian class struggle in the advanced countries, put the fundamental principle of internationalism and socialism in the foreground—namely, that no nation can be free if it oppresses other nations. It was from the standpoint of the interests of the German workers' revolutionary movement that Marx in 1848 demanded that victorious democracy in Germany should proclaim and grant freedom to the nations oppressed by the Germans. It was from the standpoint of the revolutionary struggle of the English workers that Marx, in 1869, demanded the separation of Ireland from England, and added: "... even if federation should follow upon separation."[98] Only by putting forward this demand was Marx really educating the English workers in the spirit of internationalism. Only in this way could he counterpose the opportunists and bourgeois reformism—which even to this day, half a century later, has not carried out the Irish "reform"—with a revolutionary solution of the given historical task. Only in this way could Marx maintain—in contradiction to the apologists of capital who shout that the freedom of small nations to secede is utopian and impracticable and that not only economic but also political concentration is progressive—that this concentration is progressive when it is *non*-imperialist, and that nations should not be brought together by force, but by a free union of the proletarians of all countries. Only in this way could Marx, in opposition to the merely verbal, and often hypocritical, recognition of the equality and self-determination of nations, advocate the revolutionary action of the masses in the settlement of national questions *as well*. The imperialist war of 1914-16, and the Augean stables[99] of hypocrisy on the part of the opportunists and Kautskyites that it has exposed, have strikingly confirmed the correctness of Marx's policy, which should serve as a model for all advanced countries, for all of them are now oppressing other nations.*

6. THREE TYPES OF COUNTRIES WITH RESPECT TO THE SELF-DETERMINATION OF NATIONS

In this respect, countries must be divided into three main types. First, the advanced capitalist countries of Western Europe and the United States. In these countries progressive bourgeois national movements came to an end long ago. Every one of these "great" nations oppresses other nations both in the colonies and at home. The tasks of the proletariat of these ruling nations are the same as those of the proletariat in England in the nineteenth century in relation to Ireland.**

Secondly, Eastern Europe: Austria, the Balkans and particularly Russia. Here it was the twentieth century that particularly developed the bourgeois-democratic national movements and intensified the national struggle. The tasks of the proletariat in these countries, both in completing their bourgeois-democratic reforms, and rendering assistance to the socialist revolution in other countries, cannot be carried out without championing the right of nations to self-determination. The most difficult and most important task in this is to unite the class struggle of the workers of the oppressor nations with that of the workers of the oppressed nations.

---

* Reference is often made—e.g., recently by the German chauvinist Lensch in *Die Glocke*[100] Nos. 8 and 9—to the fact that Marx's objection to the national movement of certain peoples, to that of the Czechs in 1848, for example, refutes the necessity of recognising the self-determination of nations from the Marxist standpoint. But this is incorrect, for in 1848 there were historical and political grounds for drawing a distinction between "reactionary" and revolutionary-democratic nations. Marx was right to condemn the former and defend the latter. The right to self-determination is one of the demands of democracy which must naturally be subordinated to its general interests. In 1848 and the following years these general interests consisted primarily in combating tsarism.

** In some small states which have kept out of the war of 1914-16—Holland and Switzerland, for example—the bourgeoisie makes extensive use of the "self-determination of nations" slogan to justify participation in the imperialist war. This is a motive inducing the Social-Democrats in such countries to repudiate self-determination. Wrong arguments are being used to defend a correct proletarian policy, the repudiation of "defence of the fatherland" in an *imperialist* war. This results in a distortion of Marxism in theory, and in practice leads to a peculiar small-nation narrow-mindedness, neglect of the *hundreds of millions* of people in nations that are enslaved by the "dominant" nations. Comrade Gorter, in his excellent pamphlet *Imperialism, War and Social-Democracy* wrongly rejects the principle of self-determination of nations, but correctly *applies* it, when he demands the *immediate* granting of "political and *national* independence" to the Dutch Indies and exposes the Dutch opportunists who refuse to put forward this demand and to fight for it.

Thirdly, the semi-colonial countries, such as China, Persia and Turkey, and all the colonies, which have a combined population of 1,000 million. In these countries the bourgeois-democratic movements either have hardly begun, or have still a long way to go. Socialists must not only demand the unconditional and immediate liberation of the colonies without compensation—and this demand in its political expression signifies nothing else than the recognition of the right to self-determination; they must also render determined support to the more revolutionary elements in the bourgeois-democratic movements for national liberation in these countries and assist their uprising—or revolutionary war, in the event of one—against the imperialist powers that oppress them.

7. SOCIAL-CHAUVINISM AND THE SELF-DETERMINATION OF NATIONS

The imperialist epoch and the war of 1914-16 has laid special emphasis on the struggle against chauvinism and nationalism in the leading countries. There are two main trends on the self-determination of nations among the social-chauvinists, that is, among the opportunists and Kautskyites, who hide the imperialist, reactionary nature of the war by applying to it the "defence of the fatherland" concept.

On the one hand, we see quite undisguised servants of the bourgeoisie who defend annexation on the plea that imperialism and political concentration are progressive, and who deny what they call the utopian, illusory, petty-bourgeois, etc., right to self-determination. This includes Cunow, Parvus and the extreme opportunists in Germany, some of the Fabians[101] and trade union leaders in England, and the opportunists in Russia: Semkovsky, Liebman, Yurkevich, etc.

On the other hand, we see the Kautskyites, among whom are Vandervelde, Renaudel, many pacifists in Britain and France, and others. They favour unity with the former and in practice are completely identified with them; they defend the right to self-determination hypocritically and by words alone: they consider "excessive" ("zu viel verlangt": Kautsky in Die Neue Zeit,[102] May 21, 1915) the demand for free political separation, they do not defend the necessity for revolutionary tactics on the part of the socialists of the oppressor nations in particular but, on the contrary, obscure their revolutionary obligations, justify their opportunism, make easy for them their deception of the people, and avoid the very question of the frontiers of a state forcefully retaining under-privileged nations within its bounds, etc.

Both are equally opportunist, they prostitute Marxism, having lost all ability to understand the theoretical significance and practical urgency of the tactics which Marx explained with Ireland as an example.

As for annexations, the question has become particularly urgent in connection with the war. But what is annexation? It is quite easy to see that a protest against annexations either boils down to recognition of the self-determination of nations or is based on the pacifist phrase that defends the *status quo* and is hostile to *any*, even revolutionary, violence. Such a phrase is fundamentally false and incompatible with Marxism.

8. THE CONCRETE TASKS OF THE PROLETARIAT IN THE IMMEDIATE FUTURE

The socialist revolution may begin in the very near future. In this case the proletariat will be faced with the immediate task of winning power, expropriating the banks and effecting other dictatorial measures. The bourgeoisie—and especially the intellectuals of the Fabian and Kautskyite type—will, at such a moment, strive to split and check the revolution by foisting limited, democratic aims on it. Whereas *any* purely democratic demands are in a certain sense liable to act as a hindrance to the revolution, provided the proletarian attack on the pillars of bourgeois power has begun, the necessity to proclaim and grant liberty to *all* oppressed peoples (i.e., their right to self-determination) will be as urgent in the socialist revolution as it was for the victory of the bourgeois-democratic revolution in, say, Germany in 1848, or Russia in 1905.

It is possible, however, that five, ten or more years will elapse before the socialist revolution begins. This will be the time for the revolutionary education of the masses in a spirit that will make it impossible for socialist-chauvinists and opportunists to belong to the working-class party and gain a victory, as was the case in 1914-16. The socialists must explain to the masses that British socialists who do not demand freedom to separate for the colonies and Ireland, German socialists who do not demand freedom to separate for the colonies, the Alsatians, Danes and Poles, and who do not extend their revolutionary propaganda and revolutionary mass activity directly to the sphere of struggle against national oppression, or who do not make use of such incidents as that at Zabern for the broadest illegal propaganda among the proletariat of the oppressor nation, for street demonstrations and revolutionary mass action—Russian socialists who do not demand freedom to separate for Finland, Poland, the Ukraine, etc., etc.—that such socialists act as chauvinists and lackeys of bloodstained and filthy imperialist monarchies and the imperialist bourgeoisie.

9. THE ATTITUDE OF RUSSIAN AND POLISH SOCIAL-DEMOCRATS AND OF THE SECOND INTERNATIONAL TO SELF-DETERMINATION

The differences between the revolutionary Social-Democrats of Russia and the Polish Social-Democrats on the question of self-determination came out into the open as early as 1903, at the congress which adopted the Programme of the R.S.D.L. Party, and which, despite the protest by the Polish Social-Democrat delegation, inserted Clause 9, recognising the right of nations to self-determination. Since then the Polish Social-Democrats have on no occasion repeated, in the name of their party, the proposal to remove Clause 9 from our Party's Programme, or to replace it by some other formula.

In Russia, where the oppressed nations account for no less than 57 per cent of the population, or over 100 million, where they occupy mostly the border regions, where some of them are more highly cultured than the Great Russians, where the political system is especially barbarous and medieval, where the bourgeois-democratic revolution has not been consummated—there, in Russia, recognition of the right of nations oppressed by tsarism to free secession from Russia is absolutely obligatory for Social-Democrats, for the furtherance of their democratic and socialist aims. Our Party, re-established in January 1912,[103] adopted a resolution in 1913 reaffirming the right to self-determination and explaining it in precisely the above concrete sense.[104] The rampage of Great-Russian chauvinism in 1914-16 both among the bourgeoisie and among the opportunist socialists (Rubanovich, Plekhanov, *Nashe Dyelo*,[105] etc.) has given us even more reason to insist on this demand and to regard those who deny it as actual supporters of Great-Russian chauvinism and tsarism. Our Party declares that it most emphatically declines to accept any responsibility for such actions against the right to self-determination.

The latest formulation of the position of the Polish Social-Democrats on the national question (the declaration of the Polish Social-Democrats at the Zimmerwald Conference[106]) contains the following ideas:

The declaration condemns the German and other governments that regard the "Polish regions" as a pawn in the forthcoming compensation game, "*depriving the Polish people of the opportunity of deciding their own fate themselves*". "Polish Social-Democrats resolutely and solemnly protest against the *carving up and parcelling out of a whole country*".... They flay the socialists who left it to the Hohenzollerns "*to liberate the oppressed peoples*". They express the conviction that only participation in the approaching struggle of the international revolutionary proletariat, the struggle for socialism, "*will break the fetters of national oppression* and destroy *all forms of foreign* rule, will ensure for *the Polish people* the possibility of free all-round development as an *equal* member of a concord of nations". The declaration recognises that *"for the Poles"* the war is *"doubly* fratricidal". (*Bulletin of the International Socialist Committee*[107] No. 2, September 27, 1915, p. 15. Russian translation in the symposium *The International and the War*, p. 97.)

These propositions do not differ in substance from recognition of the right of nations to self-determination, although their political formulations are even vaguer and more indeterminate than those of most programmes and resolutions of the Second International.[108] Any attempt to express these ideas as precise political formulations and to define their applicability to the capitalist system or only to the socialist system will show even more clearly the mistake the Polish Social-Democrats make in denying the self-determination of nations.

The decision of the London International Socialist Congress of 1896, which recognised the self-determination of nations, should be supplemented on the basis of the above theses by specifying: 1) the particular urgency of this demand under imperialism, 2) the political conventionalism and class content of all the demands of political democracy, the one under discussion included, 3) the necessity to distinguish the concrete tasks of the Social-Democrats of the oppressor nations from those of the Social-Democrats of the oppressed nations, 4) the inconsistent, purely verbal recognition of self-determination by the opportunists and the Kautskyites, which is, therefore, hypocritical in its political significance, 5) the actual identity of the chauvinists and those Social-Democrats, especially those of the Great Powers (Great Russians, Anglo-Americans, Germans, French, Italians, Japanese, etc.), who do not uphold the freedom to secede for colonies and nations oppressed by "their own" nations, 6) the necessity to subordinate the struggle for the demand under discussion and for all the basic demands of political democracy directly to the revolutionary mass struggle for the overthrow of the bourgeois governments and for the achievement of socialism.

The introduction into the International of the viewpoint of certain small nations, especially that of the Polish Social-Democrats, who have been led by their struggle against the Polish bourgeoisie, which deceives the people with its nationalist slogans, to the incorrect denial of self-determination, would be a theoretical mistake, a substitution of Proudhonism for Marxism implying in practice involuntary support for the most dangerous chauvinism and opportunism of the Great-Power nations.

Editorial Board of "Sotsial-Demokrat",
Central Organ of R.S.D.L.P.

Postscript. In *Die Neue Zeit* for March 3, 1916, which has just appeared, Kautsky openly holds out the hand of Christian reconciliation to Austerlitz, a representative of the foulest German chauvinism, rejecting freedom of separation for the oppressed nations of Hapsburg Austria but recognising it for *Russian* Poland, as a menial service to Hindenburg and Wilhelm II. One could not have wished for a better self-exposure of Kautskyism!

Written January-February 1916

Published in April 1916
in the magazine *Vorbote* No. 2

First published in Russian
in October 1916
in *Sbornik Sotsial-Demokrata*
No. 1

Collected Works, Vol. 22

IMPERIALISM, THE HIGHEST STAGE OF CAPITALISM[109]

(A POPULAR OUTLINE)

PREFACE

The pamphlet here presented to the reader was written in the spring of 1916, in Zurich. In the conditions in which I was obliged to work there I naturally suffered somewhat from a shortage of French and English literature and from a serious dearth of Russian literature. However, I made use of the principal English work on imperialism, the book by J. A. Hobson, with all the care that, in my opinion, that work deserves.

This pamphlet was written with an eye to the tsarist censorship. Hence, I was not only forced to confine myself strictly to an exclusively theoretical, specifically economic analysis of facts, but to formulate the few necessary observations on politics with extreme caution, by hints, in an allegorical language—in that accursed Aesopian language—to which tsarism compelled all revolutionaries to have recourse whenever they took up the pen to write a "legal" work.

It is painful, in these days of liberty, to re-read the passages of the pamphlet which have been distorted, cramped, compressed in an iron vice on account of the censor. That the period of imperialism is the eve of the socialist revolution; that social-chauvinism (socialism in words, chauvinism in deeds) is the utter betrayal of socialism, complete desertion to the side of the bourgeoisie; that this split in the working-class movement is bound up with the objective conditions of imperialism, etc.—on these matters I had to speak in a "slavish" tongue, and I must refer the reader who is interested in the subject to the articles I wrote abroad in 1914-17, a new edition of which is soon to appear. Special attention should be drawn to a passage on pages 119-20.* In order to show the reader, in a guise acceptable to the censors, how shamelessly untruthful the capitalists and the social-chauvinists who have deserted to their side (and whom Kautsky opposes so inconsistently) are on the question of annexations; in order to show how shamelessly they *screen* the

---

* See p. 259 of the present volume.—*Ed.*

annexations of *their* capitalists, I was forced to quote as an example
—Japan! The careful reader will easily substitute Russia for Japan,
and Finland, Poland, Courland, the Ukraine, Khiva, Bokhara, Estonia or other regions peopled by non-Great Russians, for Korea.

I trust that this pamphlet will help the reader to understand the
fundamental economic question, that of the economic essence of
imperialism, for unless this is studied, it will be impossible to understand and appraise modern war and modern politics.

                                                              Author

Petrograd, April 26, 1917

PREFACE TO THE FRENCH AND GERMAN EDITIONS

I

As was indicated in the preface to the Russian edition, this pamphlet was written in 1916, with an eye to the tsarist censorship, I am unable to revise the whole text at the present time, nor, perhaps, would this be advisable, since the main purpose of the book was, and remains, to present, on the basis of the summarised returns of irrefutable bourgeois statistics, and the admissions of bourgeois scholars of all countries, a *composite picture* of the world capitalist system in its international relationships at the beginning of the twentieth century—on the eve of the first world imperialist war.

To a certain extent it will even be useful for many Communists in advanced capitalist countries to convince themselves by the example of this pamphlet, *legal from the standpoint of the tsarist censor*, of the possibility, and necessity, of making use of even the slight remnants of legality which still remain at the disposal of the Communists, say, in contemporary America or France, after the recent almost wholesale arrests of Communists, in order to explain the utter falsity of social-pacifist views and hopes for "world democracy". The most essential of what should be added to this censored pamphlet I shall try to present in this preface.

II

It is proved in the pamphlet that the war of 1914-18 was imperialist (that is, an annexationist, predatory, war of plunder) on the part of both sides; it was a war for the division of the world, for the partition and repartition of colonies and spheres of influence of finance capital, etc.

Proof of what was the true social, or rather, the true class character of the war is naturally to be found, not in the diplomatic history of the war, but in an analysis of the *objective* position of the ruling *classes* in *all* the belligerent countries. In order to depict this objective position one must not take examples or isolated data (in view of the extreme complexity of the phenomena of social life it is always possible to select any number of examples or separate data to prove any proposition), but *all* the data on the *basis* of economic life in *all* the belligerent countries and the *whole* world.

It is precisely irrefutable summarised data of this kind that I quoted in describing the *partition of the world* in 1876 and 1914 (in Chapter VI) and the division of the world's *railways* in 1890 and 1913 (in Chapter VII). Railways are a summation of the basic capitalist industries, coal, iron and steel; a summation and the most striking index of the development of world trade and bourgeois-democratic civilisation. How the railways are linked up with large-scale industry, with monopolies, syndicates, cartels, trusts, banks and the financial oligarchy is shown in the preceding chapters of the book. The uneven distribution of the railways, their uneven development—sums up, as it were, modern monopolist capitalism on a world-wide scale. And this summary proves that imperialist wars are absolutely inevitable under *such* an economic system, *as long as* private property in the means of production exists.

The building of railways seems to be a simple, natural, democratic, cultural and civilising enterprise; that is what it is in the opinion of the bourgeois professors who are paid to depict capitalist slavery in bright colours, and in the opinion of petty-bourgeois philistines. But as a matter of fact the capitalist threads, which in thousands of different intercrossings bind these enterprises with private property in the means of production in general, have converted this railway construction into an instrument for oppressing *a thousand million* people (in the colonies and semi-colonies) that is, more than half the population of the globe that inhabits the dependent countries, as well as the wage slaves of capital in the "civilised" countries.

Private property based on the labour of the small proprietor, free competition, democracy, all the catchwords with which the capitalists and their press deceive the workers and the peasants—are things of the distant past. Capitalism has grown into a world system of colonial oppression and of the financial strangulation of the overwhelming majority of the population of the world by a handful of "advanced" countries. And this "booty" is shared between two or three powerful world plunderers armed to the teeth (America, Great Britain, Japan), who are drawing the whole world into *their* war over the division of *their* booty.

III

The Treaty of Brest-Litovsk[110] dictated by monarchist Germany, and the subsequent much more brutal and despicable Treaty of Versailles[111] dictated by the "democratic" republics of America and France and also by "free" Britain, have rendered a most useful service to humanity by exposing both imperialism's hired coolies of the pen and petty-bourgeois reactionaries who, although they call themselves pacifists and socialists, sang praises to "Wilsonism",[112] and insisted that peace and reforms were possible under imperialism.

The tens of millions of dead and maimed left by the war—a war to decide whether the British or German group of financial plunderers is to receive the most booty—and those two "peace treaties", are with unprecedented rapidity opening the eyes of the millions and tens of millions of people who are downtrodden, oppressed, deceived and duped by the bourgeoisie. Thus, out of the universal ruin caused by the war a world-wide revolutionary crisis is arising which, however prolonged and arduous its stages may be, cannot end otherwise than in a proletarian revolution and in its victory.

The Basle Manifesto[113] of the Second International, which in 1912 gave an appraisal of the very war that broke out in 1914 and not of war in general (there are different kinds of wars, including revolutionary wars)—this Manifesto is now a monument exposing to the full the shameful bankruptcy and treachery of the heroes of the Second International.

That is why I reproduce this Manifesto as a supplement to the present edition, and again and again I urge the reader to note that the heroes of the Second International are as assiduously avoiding the passages of this Manifesto which speak precisely, clearly and definitely of the connection between that impending war and the proletarian revolution, as a thief avoids the scene of his crime.

IV

Special attention has been devoted in this pamphlet to a criticism of Kautskyism, the international ideological trend represented in all countries of the world by the "most prominent theoreticians", the leaders of the Second International (Otto Bauer and Co. in Austria, Ramsay MacDonald and others in Britain, Albert Thomas in France, etc., etc.) and a multitude of socialists, reformists, pacifists, bourgeois democrats and parsons.

This ideological trend is, on the one hand, a product of the disintegration and decay of the Second International, and, on the other hand, the inevitable fruit of the ideology of the petty bourgeoisie, whose entire way of life holds them captive to bourgeois and democratic prejudices.

The views held by Kautsky and his like are a complete renunciation of those same revolutionary principles of Marxism that writer has championed for decades, especially, by the way, in his struggle against socialist opportunism (of Bernstein, Millerand, Hyndman,

Gompers, etc.). It is not a mere accident, therefore, that Kautsky's followers all over the world have now united in practical politics with the extreme opportunists (through the Second, or Yellow International[114]) and with the bourgeois governments (through bourgeois coalition governments in which socialists take part).

The growing world proletarian revolutionary movement in general, and the communist movement in particular, cannot dispense with an analysis and exposure of the theoretical errors of Kautskyism. The more so since pacifism and "democracy" in general, which lay no claim to Marxism whatever, but which, like Kautsky and Co., are obscuring the profundity of the contradictions of imperialism and the inevitable revolutionary crisis to which it gives rise, are still very widespread all over the world. To combat these tendencies is the bounden duty of the party of the proletariat, which must win away from the bourgeoisie the small proprietors who are duped by them, and the millions of working people who enjoy more or less petty-bourgeois conditions of life.

V

A few words must be said about Chapter VIII, "Parasitism and Decay of Capitalism". As already pointed out in the text, Hilferding, ex-"Marxist", and now a comrade-in-arms of Kautsky and one of the chief exponents of bourgeois, reformist policy in the Independent Social-Democratic Party of Germany,[115] has taken a step backward on this question compared with the *frankly* pacifist and reformist Englishman, Hobson. The international split of the entire working-class movement is now quite evident (the Second and the Third Internationals[116]). The fact that armed struggle and civil war is now raging between the two trends is also evident—the support given to Kolchak and Denikin in Russia by the Mensheviks and Socialist-Revolutionaries against the Bolsheviks; the fight the Scheidemanns and Noskes have conducted in conjunction with the bourgeoisie against the Spartacists[117] in Germany; the same thing in Finland, Poland, Hungary, etc. What is the economic basis of this world-historical phenomenon?

It is precisely the parasitism and decay of capitalism, characteristic of its highest historical stage of development, i.e., imperialism. As this pamphlet shows, capitalism has now singled out a *handful* (less than one-tenth of the inhabitants of the globe; less than one-fifth at a most "generous" and liberal calculation) of exceptionally rich and powerful states which plunder the whole world simply by "clipping coupons". Capital exports yield an income of eight to ten thousand million francs per annum, at pre-war prices and according to pre-war bourgeois statistics. Now, of course, they yield much more.

Obviously, out of such enormous *superprofits* (since they are obtained over and above the profits which capitalists squeeze out of the workers of their "own" country) it is *possible to bribe* the labour leaders and the upper stratum of the labour aristocracy. And that is just what the capitalists of the "advanced" countries are doing: they are bribing them in a thousand different ways, direct and indirect, overt and covert.

This stratum of workers turned bourgeois, or the labour aristocracy, who are quite philistine in their mode of life, in the size of their earnings and in their entire outlook, is the principal prop of the Second International, and in our days, the principal *social* (not military) *prop of the bourgeoisie*. For they are the real *agents of the bourgeoisie in the working-class* movement, the labour lieutenants of the capitalist class, real vehicles of reformism and chauvinism. In the civil war between the proletariat and the bourgeoisie they inevitably, and in no small numbers, take the side of the bourgeoisie, the "Versaillais"[118] against the "Communards".

Unless the economic roots of this phenomenon are understood and its political and social significance is appreciated, not a step can be taken toward the solution of the practical problems of the communist movement and of the impending social revolution.

Imperialism is the eve of the social revolution of the proletariat. This has been confirmed since 1917 on a world-wide scale.

N. Lenin

July 6, 1920

During the last fifteen to twenty years, especially since the Spanish-American War (1898) and the Anglo-Boer War (1899-1902),[119] the economic and also the political literature of the two hemispheres has more and more often adopted the term "imperialism" in order to describe the present era. In 1902, a book by the English economist J. A. Hobson, *Imperialism*, was published in London and New York. This author, whose point of view is that of bourgeois social-reformism and pacifism which, in essence, is identical with the present point of view of the ex-Marxist, Karl Kautsky, gives a very good and comprehensive description of the principal specific economic and political features of imperialism. In 1910, there appeared in Vienna the work of the Austrian Marxist, Rudolf Hilferding, *Finance Capital* (Russian edition, Moscow, 1912). In spite of the mistake the author makes on the theory of money, and in spite of a certain inclination on his part to reconcile Marxism with opportunism, this work gives a very valuable theoretical analysis of "the latest phase of capitalist development", as the subtitle runs. Indeed, what has been said of imperialism during the last few years, especially in an enormous number of magazine and newspaper articles, and also in the resolutions, for example, of the Chemnitz[120] and Basle congresses which took place in the autumn of 1912, has scarcely gone beyond the ideas expounded, or more exactly, summed up by the two writers mentioned above....

Later on, I shall try to show briefly, and as simply as possible, the connection and relationships between the *principal* economic features of imperialism. I shall not be able to deal with the non-economic aspects of the question, however much they deserve to be dealt with. References to literature and other notes which, perhaps, would not interest all readers, are to be found at the end of this pamphlet.

I. CONCENTRATION OF PRODUCTION AND MONOPOLIES

The enormous growth of industry and the remarkably rapid concentration of production in ever-larger enterprises are one of the most characteristic features of capitalism. Modern porduction censuses give most complete and most exact data on this process.

In Germany, for example, out of every 1,000 industrial enterprises, large enterprises, i.e., those employing more than 50 workers,
numbered three in 1882, six in 1895 and nine in 1907; and out of
every 100 workers employed, this group of enterprises employed 22,
30 and 37, respectively. Concentration of production, however, is
much more intense than the concentration of workers, since labour
in the large enterprises is much more productive. This is shown by
the figures on steam-engines and electric motors. If we take what in
Germany is called industry in the broad sense of the term, that is,
including commerce, transport, etc., we get the following picture.
Large-scale enterprises, 30,588 out of a total of 3,265,623, that is to
say, 0.9 per cent. These enterprises employ 5,700,000 workers out of
a total of 14,400,000, i.e., 39.4 per cent; they use 6,600,000 steam
horse power out of a total of 8,800,000, i.e., 75.3 per cent, and
1,200,000 kilowatts of electricity out of a total of 1,500,000, i.e., 77.2
per cent.

Less than one-hundredth of the total number of enterprises utilise
more than three-fourths of the total amount of steam and electric
power! Two million nine hundred and seventy thousand small enterprises (employing up to five workers), constituting 91 per cent of the
total, utilise only 7 per cent of the total amount of steam and electric
power! Tens of thousands of huge enterprises are everything; millions of small ones are nothing.

In 1907, there were in Germany 586 establishments employing one
thousand and more workers, nearly *one-tenth* (1,380,000) of the total
number of workers employed in industry, and they consumed
almost one-third (32 per cent) of the total amount of steam and
electric power.* As we shall see, money capital and the banks make
this superiority of a handful of the largest enterprises still more
overwhelming, in the most literal sense of the word, i.e., millions of
small, medium and even some big "proprietors" are in fact in complete subjection to some hundreds of millionaire financiers.

In another advanced country of modern capitalism, the United
States of America, the growth of the concentration of production is
still greater. Here statistics single out industry in the narrow sense
of the word and classify enterprises according to the value of their
annual output. In 1904 large-scale enterprises with an output valued
at one million dollars and overnumbered 1,900 (out of 216,180, i.e.,
0.9 per cent). These employed 1,400,000 workers (out of 5,500,000,
i.e., 25.6 per cent) and the value of their output amounted to
$5,600,000,000 (out of $14,800,000,000, i.e., 38 per cent). Five years
later, in 1909, the corresponding figures were: 3,060 enterprises (out
of 268,491, i.e., 1.1 per cent) employing 2,000,000 workers (out of

---

* Figures taken from *Annalen des deutschen Reichs*, 1911, Zahn.

6,600,000, i.e., 30.5 per cent) with an output valued at $9,000,000,000 (out of $20,700,000,000, i.e., 43.8 per cent).*

Almost half the total production of all the enterprises of the country was carried on by *one-hundredth part* of these enterprises! These 3,000 giant enterprises embrace 258 branches of industry. From this it can be seen that, at a certain stage of its development concentration itself, as it were, leads straight to monopoly, for a score or so of giant enterprises can easily arrive at an agreement, and on the other hand, the hindrance to competition, the tendency towards monopoly, arises from the huge size of the enterprises. This transformation of competition into monopoly is one of the most important—if not the most important—phenomena of modern capitalist economy, and we must deal with it in greater detail. But first we must clear up one possible misunderstanding.

American statistics speak of 3,000 giant enterprises in 250 branches of industry, as if there were only a dozen enterprises of the largest scale for each branch of industry.

But this is not the case. Not in every branch of industry are there large-scale enterprises; and moreover, a very important feature of capitalism in its highest stage of development is so-called *combination* of production, that is to say, the grouping in a single enterprise of different branches of industry, which either represent the consecutive stages in the processing of raw materials (for example, the smelting of iron ore into pig-iron, the conversion of pig-iron into steel, and then, perhaps, the manufacture of steel goods)—or are auxiliary to one another (for example, the utilisation of scrap, or of by-products, the manufacture of packing materials, etc.).

"Combination," writes Hilferding, "levels out the fluctuations of trade and therefore assures to the combined enterprises a more stable rate of profit. Secondly, combination has the effect of eliminating trade. Thirdly, it has the effect of rendering possible technical improvements, and, consequently, the acquisition of superprofits over and above those obtained by the 'pure' [i.e., non-combined] enterprises. Fourthly, it strengthens the position of the combined enterprises relative to the 'pure' enterprises, strengthens them in the competitive struggle in periods of serious depression, when the fall in prices of raw materials does not keep pace with the fall in prices of manufactured goods."**

The German bourgeois economist, Heymann, who has written a book especially on "mixed", that is, combined, enterprises in the German iron industry, says: "Pure enterprises perish, they are crushed between the high price of raw material and the low price of the finished product." Thus we get the following picture: "There

---

* *Statistical Abstract of the United States, 1912*, p. 202.
** *Finance Capital*, Russ. ed., pp. 286-87.

remain, on the one hand, the big coal companies, producing millions of tons yearly, strongly organised in their coal syndicate, and on the other, the big steel plants, closely allied to the coal mines, having their own steel syndicate. These giant enterprises, producing 400,000 tons of steel per annum, with a tremendous output of ore and coal and producing finished steel goods, employing 10,000 workers quartered in company houses, and sometimes owning their own railways and ports, are the typical representatives of the German iron and steel industry. And concentration goes on further and further. Individual enterprises are becoming larger and larger. An ever-increasing number of enterprises in one, or in several different industries, join together in giant enterprises, backed up and directed by half a dozen big Berlin banks. In relation to the German mining industry, the truth of the teachings of Karl Marx on concentration is definitely proved; true, this applies to a country where industry is protected by tariffs and freight rates. The German mining industry is ripe for expropriation."[*]

Such is the conclusion which a bourgeois economist who, by way of exception is conscientious, had to arrive at. It must be noted that he seems to place Germany in a special category because her industries are protected by higher tariffs. But this is a circumstance which only accelerates concentration and the formation of monopolist manufacturers' associations, cartels, syndicates, etc. It is extremely important to note that in free-trade Britain, concentration *also* leads to monopoly, although somewhat later and perhaps in another form. Professor Hermann Levy, in his special work of research entitled *Monopolies, Cartels and Trusts*, based on data on British economic development, writes as follows:

"In Great Britain it is the size of the enterprise and its high technical level which harbour a monopolist tendency. This, for one thing, is due to the great investment of capital per enterprise, which gives rise to increasing demands for new capital for the new enterprises and thereby renders their launching more difficult. Moreover (and this seems to us to be the more important point), every new enterprise that wants to keep pace with the gigantic enterprises that have been formed by concentration would here produce such an enormous quantity of surplus goods that it could dispose of them only by being able to sell them profitably as a result of an enormous increase in demand; otherwise, this surplus would force prices down to a level that would be unprofitable both for the new enterprise and for the monopoly combines." Britain differs from other countries where protective tariffs facilitate the formation of cartels in that monopolist manufacturers' associations, cartels and trusts arise in

---

[*] Hans Gideon Heymann, *Die gemischten Werke im deutschen Grosseisengewerbe* (*Combined Plants in the German Big Iron Industry*), Stuttgart, 1904 (S. 256, 278-279).

the majority of cases only when the number of the chief competing enterprises has been reduced to "a couple of dozen or so". "Here the influence of concentration on the formation of large industrial monopolies in a whole sphere of industry stands out with crystal clarity."*

Half a century ago, when Marx was writing *Capital,* free competition appeared to the overwhelming majority of economists to be a "natural law". Official science tried, by a conspiracy of silence, to kill the works of Marx, who by a theoretical and historical analysis of capitalism had proved that free competition gives rise to the concentration of production, which, in turn, at a certain stage of development, leads to monopoly. Today, monopoly has become a fact. Economists are writing mountains of books in which they describe the diverse manifestations of monopoly, and continue to declare in chorus that "Marxism is refuted". But facts are stubborn things, as the English proverb says, and they have to be reckoned with, whether we like it or not. The facts show that differences between capitalist countries, e.g., in the matter of protection or free trade, only give rise to insignificant variations in the form of monopolies or in the moment of their appearance; and that the rise of monopolies, as the result of the concentration of production, is a general and fundamental law of the present stage of development of capitalism.

For Europe, the time when the new capitalism *definitely* superseded the old can be established with fair precision; it was the beginning of the twentieth century. In one of the latest compilations on the history of the "formation of monopolies", we read:

"Isolated examples of capitalist monopoly could be cited from the period preceding 1860; in these could be discerned the embryo of the forms that are so common today; but all this undoubtedly represents the prehistory of the cartels. The real beginning of modern monopoly goes back, at the earliest, to the sixties. The first important period of development of monopoly commenced with the international industrial depression of the seventies and lasted until the beginning of the nineties." "If we examine the question on a European scale, we will find that the development of free competition reached its apex in the sixties and seventies. It was then that Britain completed the construction of her old-style capitalist organisation. In Germany, this organisation had entered into a fierce struggle with handicraft and domestic industry, and had begun to create for itself its own forms of existence."

"The great revolution, commenced with the crash of 1873, or rather, the depression which followed it and which, with hardly discernible interruptions in the early eighties, and the unusually violent, but short-lived boom round about 1889, marks twenty-two

---

* Hermann Levy, *Monopole, Kartelle und Trusts,* Jena, 1909, S. 286, 290, 298.

years of European economic history." "During the short boom of 1889-90, the system of cartels was widely resorted to in order to take advantage of favourable business conditions. An ill-considered policy drove prices up still more rapidly and still higher than would have been the case if there had been no cartels, and nearly all these cartels perished ingloriously in the smash. Another five-year period of bad trade and low prices followed, but a new spirit reigned in industry; the depression was no longer regarded as something to be taken for granted; it was regarded as nothing more than a pause before another boom.

"The cartel movement entered its second epoch: instead of being a transitory phenomenon, the cartels have become one of the foundations of economic life. They are winning one field of industry after another, primarily, the raw materials industry. At the beginning of the nineties the cartel system had already acquired— in the organisation of the coke syndicate on the model of which the coal syndicate was later formed—a cartel technique which has hardly been improved on. For the first time the great boom at the close of the nineteenth century and the crisis of 1900-03 occurred entirely—in the mining and iron industries at least—under the aegis of the cartels. And while at that time it appeared to be something novel, now the general public takes it for granted that large spheres of economic life have been, as a general rule, removed from the realm of free competition."[*]

Thus, the principal stages in the history of monopolies are the following: 1) 1860-70, the highest stage, the apex of development of free competition; monopoly is in the barely discernible, embryonic stage. 2) After the crisis of 1873, a lengthy period of development of cartels; but they are still the exception. They are not yet durable. They are still a transitory phenomenon. 3) The boom at the end of the nineteenth century and the crisis of 1900-03. Cartels become one of the foundations of the whole of economic life. Capitalism has been transformed into imperialism.

Cartels come to an agreement on the terms of sale, dates of payment, etc. They divide the markets among themselves. They fix the quantity of goods to be produced. They fix prices. They divide the profits among the various enterprises, etc.

The number of cartels in Germany was estimated at about 250 in 1896 and at 385 in 1905, with about 12,000 firms participating.[**]

---

[*] Th. Vogelstein, "Die finanzielle Organisation der kapitalistischen Industrie und die Monopolbildungen" in *Grundriss der Sozialökonomik*, VI. Abt., Tübingen, 1914. Cf., also by the same author: *Organisationsformen der Eisenindustrie und Textilindustrie in England und Amerika*, Bd. I, Lpz., 1910.

[**] Dr. Riesser, *Die deutschen Großbanken und ihre Konzentration im Zusammenhange mit der Entwicklung der Gesamtwirtschaft in Deutschland*, 4. Aufl., 1912, S. 149; Robert Liefmann, *Kartelle und Trusts und die Weiterbildung der volkswirtschaftlichen Organisation*, 2. Aufl., 1910, S. 25.

But it is generally recognised that these figures are underestimations. From the statistics of German industry for 1907 we quoted above, it is evident that even these 12,000 very big enterprises probably consume more than half the steam and electric power used in the country. In the United States of America, the number of trusts in 1900 was estimated at 185 and in 1907, 250. American statistics divide all industrial enterprises into those belonging to individuals, to private firms or to corporations. The latter in 1904 comprised 23.6 per cent, and in 1909, 25.9 per cent, i.e., more than one-fourth of the total industrial enterprises in the country. These employed in 1904, 70.6 per cent, and in 1909, 75.6 per cent, i.e., more than three-fourths of the total wage-earners. Their output at these two dates was valued at $10,900,000,000 and $16,300,000,000, i.e., 73.7 per cent and 79.0 per cent of the total, respectively.

At times cartels and trusts concentrate in their hands seven- or eight-tenths of the total output of a given branch of industry. The Rhine-Westphalian Coal Syndicate, at its foundation in 1893, concentrated 86.7 per cent of the total coal output of the area, and in 1910 it already concentrated 95.4 per cent.* The monopoly so created assures enormous profits, and leads to the formation of technical production units of formidable magnitude. The famous Standard Oil Company in the United States was founded in 1900: "It has an authorised capital of $150,000,000. It issued $100,000,000 common and $106,000,000 preferred stock. From 1900 to 1907 the following dividends were paid on the latter: 48, 48, 45, 44, 36, 40, 40, 40 per cent in the respective years, i.e., in all, $367,000,000. From 1882 to 1907, out of total net profits amounting to $889,000,000, $606,000,000 were distributed in dividends, and the rest went to reserve capital."** "In 1907 the various works of the United States Steel Corporation employed no less than 210,180 people. The largest enterprise in the German mining industry, Gelsenkirchener Bergwerksgesellschaft, in 1908 had a staff of 46,048 workers and office employees."*** In 1902, the United States Steel Corporation already produced 9,000,000 tons of steel.**** Its output constituted in 1901, 66.3 per cent, and in 1908, 56.1 per cent of the total output of steel in the United States.**** The output of ore was 43.9 per cent and 46.3 per cent, respectively.

The report of the American Government Commission on Trusts states: "Their superiority over competitors is due to the magnitude

---

* Dr. Fritz Kestner, *Der Organisationszwang. Eine Untersuchung über die Kämpfe zwischen Kartellen und Aussenseitern*, Berlin, 1912, S. 11.
** R. Liefmann, *Beteilgungs- und Finanzierungsgesellschaften. Eine Studie über den modernen Kapitalismus und das Effektenwesen*, 1. Aufl., Jena, 1909, S. 212.
*** Ibid., S. 218.
**** Dr. S. Tschierschky, *Kartell und Trust*, Göttingen, 1903, S. 13.
***** Th. Vogelstein, *Organisationsformen*, S. 275.

of their enterprises and their excellent technical equipment. Since its inception, the Tobacco Trust has devoted all its efforts to the universal substitution of mechanical for manual labour. With this end in view it has bought up all patents that have anything to do with the manufacture of tobacco and has spent enormous sums for this purpose. Many of these patents at first proved to be of no use, and had to be modified by the engineers employed by the trust. At the end of 1906, two subsidiary companies were formed solely to acquire patents. With the same object in view, the trust has built its own foundries, machine shops and repair shops. One of these establishments, that in Brooklyn, employs on the average 300 workers; here experiments are carried out on inventions concerning the manufacture of cigarettes, cheroots, snuff, tinfoil for packing, boxes, etc. Here, also, inventions are perfected."* "Other trusts also employ what are called development engineers whose business it is to devise new methods of production and to test technical improvements. The United States Steel Corporation grants big bonuses to its workers and engineers for all inventions that raise technical efficiency, or reduce cost of production."**

In German large-scale industry, e.g., in the chemical industry, which has developed so enormously during these last few decades, the promotion of technical improvement is organised in the same way. By 1908 the process of concentration of production had already given rise to two main "groups" which, in their way, were also in the nature of monopolies. At first these groups constituted "dual alliances" of two pairs of big factories, each having a capital of from twenty to twenty-one million marks—on the one hand, the former Meister Factory in Höchst and the Casella Factory in Frankfurt am Main; and on the other hand, the aniline and soda factory at Ludwigshafen and the former Bayer Factory at Elberfeld. Then, in 1905, one of these groups, and in 1908 the other group, each concluded an agreement with yet another big factory. The result was the formation of two "triple alliances", each with a capital of from forty to fifty million marks. And these "alliances" have already begun to "approach" each other, to reach "an understanding" about prices, etc.***

Competition becomes transformed into monopoly. The result is immense progress in the socialisation of production. In particular,

---

* *Report of the Commissioner of Corporations on the Tobacco Industry*, Washington, 1909, p. 266, cited according to Dr. Paul Tafel, *Die nordamerikanischen Trusts und ihre Wirkungen auf den Fortschritt der Technik*, Stuttgart, 1913, S. 48.
** Dr. P. Tafel, ibid., S. 48.
*** Riesser, op. cit., third edition, p. 547 et seq. The newspapers (June 1916) report the formation of a new gigantic trust which combines the chemical industry of Germany.

the process of technical invention and improvement becomes socialised.

This is something quite different from the old free competition between manufacturers, scattered and out of touch with one another, and producing for an unknown market. Concentration has reached the point at which it is possible to make an approximate estimate of all sources of raw materials (for example, the iron ore deposits) of a country and even, as we shall see, of several countries, or of the whole world. Not only are such estimates made, but these sources are captured by gigantic monopolist associations. An approximate estimate of the capacity of markets is also made, and the associations "divide" them up amongst themselves by agreement. Skilled labour is monopolised, the best engineers are engaged; the means of transport are captured—railways in America, shipping companies in Europe and America. Capitalism in its imperialist stage leads directly to the most comprehensive socialisation of production; it, so to speak, drags the capitalists, against their will and consciousness, into some sort of a new social order, a transitional one from complete free competition to complete socialisation.

Production becomes social, but appropriation remains private. The social means of production remain the private property of a few. The general framework of formally recognised free competition remains, and the yoke of a few monopolists on the rest of the population becomes a hundred times heavier, more burdensome and intolerable.

The German economist, Kestner, has written a book especially devoted to "the struggle between the cartels and outsiders", i.e., the capitalists outside the cartels. He entitled his work *Compulsory Organisation*, although, in order to present capitalism in its true light, he should, of course, have written about compulsory submission to monopolist associations. It is instructive to glance at least at the list of the methods the monopolist associations resort to in the present-day, the latest, the civilised struggle for "organisation": 1) stopping supplies of raw materials (..."one of the most important methods of compelling adherence to the cartel"); 2) stopping the supply of labour by means of "alliances" (i.e., of agreements between the capitalists and the trade unions by which the latter permit their members to work only in cartelised enterprises); 3) stopping deliveries; 4) closing trade outlets; 5) agreements with the buyers, by which the latter undertake to trade only with the cartels; 6) systematic price cutting (to ruin "outside" firms, i.e., those which refuse to submit to the monopolists. Millions are spent in order to sell goods for a certain time below their cost price; there were instances when the price of petrol was thus reduced from 40 to 22 marks, i.e., almost by half!); 7) stopping credits; 8) boycott.

Here we no longer have competition between small and large, between technically developed and backward enterprises. We see here the monopolists throttling those who do not submit to them, to their yoke, to their dictation. This is how this process is reflected in the mind of a bourgeois economist:

"Even in the purely economic sphere," writes Kestner, "a certain change is taking place from commercial activity in the old sense of the word towards organisational-speculative activity. The greatest success no longer goes to the merchant whose technical and commercial experience enables him best of all to estimate the needs of the buyer, and who is able to discover and, so to speak, 'awaken' a latent demand; it goes to the speculative genius [?!] who knows how to estimate, or even only to sense in advance, the organisational development and the possibilities of certain connections between individual enterprises and the banks. . . ."

Translated into ordinary human language this means that the development of capitalism has arrived at a stage when, although commodity production still "reigns" and continues to be regarded as the basis of economic life, it has in reality been undermined and the bulk of the profits go to the "geniuses" of financial manipulation. At the basis of these manipulations and swindles lies socialised production; but the immense progress of mankind, which achieved this socialisation, goes to benefit . . . the speculators. We shall see later how "on these grounds" reactionary, petty-bourgeois critics of capitalist imperialism dream of going *back* to "free", "peaceful", and "honest" competition.

"The prolonged raising of prices which results from the formation of cartels," says Kestner, "has hitherto been observed only in respect of the most important means of production, particularly coal, iron and potassium, but never in respect of manufactured goods. Similarly, the increase in profits resulting from this raising of prices has been limited only to the industries which produce means of production. To this observation we must add that the industries which process raw materials (and not semi-manufactures) not only secure advantages from the cartel formation in the shape of high profits, to the detriment of the finished goods industry, but have also secured a *dominating position* over the latter, which did not exist under free competition."[*]

The words which I have italicised reveal the essence of the case which the bourgeois economists admit so reluctantly and so rarely, and which the present-day defenders of opportunism, led by Kautsky, so zealously try to evade and brush aside. Domination, and the violence that it associated with it, such are the relationships that are typical of the "latest phase of capitalist development";

---

[*] Kestner, op. cit., S. 254.

this is what inevitably had to result, and has resulted, from the formation of all-powerful economic monopolies.

I shall give one more example of the methods employed by the cartels. Where it is possible to capture all or the chief sources of raw materials, the rise of cartels and formation of monopolies is particularly easy. It would be wrong, however, to assume that monopolies do not arise in other industries in which it is impossible to corner the sources of raw materials. The cement industry, for instance, can find its raw materials everywhere. Yet in Germany this industry too is strongly cartelised. The cement manufacturers have formed regional syndicates: South German, Rhine-Westphalian, etc. The prices fixed are monopoly prices: 230 to 280 marks a car-load, when the cost price is 180 marks! The enterprises pay a dividend of from 12 to 16 per cent—and it must not be forgotten that the "geniuses" of modern speculation know how to pocket big profits besides what they draw in dividends. In order to prevent competition in such a profitable industry, the monopolists even resort to various stratagems: they spread false rumours about the bad situation in their industry; anonymous warnings are published in the newspapers, like the following: "Capitalists, don't invest your capital in the cement industry!"; lastly, they buy up "outsiders" (those outside the syndicates) and pay them compensation of 60,000, 80,000 and even 150,000 marks.* Monopoly hews a path for itself everywhere without scruple as to the means, from paying a "modest" sum to buy off competitors, to the American device of employing dynamite against them.

The statement that cartels can abolish crises is a fable spread by bourgeois economists who at all costs desire to place capitalism in a favourable light. On the contrary, the monopoly created in *certain* branches of industry increases and intensifies the anarchy inherent in capitalist production *as a whole*. The disparity between the development of agriculture and that of industry, which is characteristic of capitalism in general, is increased. The privileged position of the most highly cartelised, so-called *heavy* industry, especially coal and iron, causes "a still greater lack of co-ordination" in other branches of industry—as Jeidels, the author of one of the best works on "the relationship of the German big banks to industry", admits.**

"The more developed an economic system is," writes Liefmann, an unblushing apologist of capitalism, "the more it resorts to risky enterprises, or enterprises in other countries, to those which need a great deal of time to develop, or finally, to those which are only

---

* L. Eschwege, "Zement" in *Die Bank*,[121] 1909, 1, S. 115 et seq.
** Jeidels, *Das Verhältnis der deutschen Grossbanken zur Industrie mit besonderer Berücksichtigung der Eisenindustrie*, Leipzig, 1905, S. 271.

of local importance."* The increased risk is connected in the long run with a prodigious increase of capital, which, as it were, overflows the brim, flows abroad, etc. At the same time the extremely rapid rate of technical progress gives rise to increasing elements of disparity between the various spheres of national economy, to anarchy and crises. Liefmann is obliged to admit that: "In all probability mankind will see further important technical revolutions in the near future which will also affect the organisation of the economic system" ... electricity and aviation.... "As a general rule, in such periods of radical economic change, speculation develops on a large scale"....**

Crises of every kind—economic crises most frequently, but not only these—in their turn increase very considerably the tendency towards concentration and towards monopoly. In this connection, the following reflections of Jeidels on the significance of the crisis of 1900, which, as we have already seen, marked the turning-point in the history of modern monopoly, are exceedingly instructive:

"Side by side with the gigantic plants in the basic industries, the crisis of 1900 still found many plants organised on lines that today would be considered obsolete, the 'pure' (non-combined) plants, which were brought into being at the height of the industrial boom. The fall in prices and the falling off in demand put these 'pure' enterprises in a precarious position, which did not affect the gigantic combined enterprises at all or only affected them for a very short time. As a consequence of this the crisis of 1900 resulted in a far greater concentration of industry than the crisis of 1873: the latter crisis also produced a sort of selection of the best-equipped enterprises, but owing to the level of technical development at that time, this selection could not place the firms which successfully emerged from the crisis in a position of monopoly. Such a durable monopoly exists to a high degree in the gigantic enterprises in the modern iron and steel and electrical industries owing to their very complicated technique, far-reaching organisation and magnitude of capital, and, to a lesser degree, in the engineering industry, certain branches of the metallurgical industry, transport, etc."***

Monopoly! This is the last word in the "latest phase of capitalist development". But we shall only have a very insufficient, incomplete, and poor notion of the real power and the significance of modern monopolies if we do not take into consideration the part played by the banks.

---

* Liefmann, *Beteilgungs- und Finanzierungsgesellschaften*, S. 434.
** Ibid., S. 465-466.
*** Jeidels, op. cit., S. 108.

II. BANKS AND THEIR NEW ROLE

The principal and primary function of banks is to serve as middlemen in the making of payments. In so doing they transform inactive money capital into active, that is, into capital yielding a profit; they collect all kinds of money revenues and place them at the disposal of the capitalist class.

As banking develops and becomes concentrated in a small number of establishments, the banks grow from modest middlemen into powerful monopolies having at their command almost the whole of the money capital of all the capitalists and small businessmen and also the larger part of the means of production and sources of raw materials in any one country and in a number of countries. This transformation of numerous modest middlemen into a handful of monopolists is one of the fundamental processes in the growth of capitalism into capitalist imperialism; for this reason we must first of all examine the concentration of banking.

In 1907-08, the combined deposits of the German joint-stock banks, each having a capital of more than a million marks, amounted to 7,000 million marks; in 1912-13, these deposits already amounted to 9,800 million marks, an increase of 40 per cent in five years; and of the 2,800 million increase, 2,750 million was divided among 57 banks, each having a capital of more than 10 million marks. The distribution of the deposits between big and small banks was as follows:*

Percentage of Total Deposits

	In 9 big Berlin banks	In the other 48 banks with a capital of more than 10 million marks	In 115 banks with a capital of 1-10 million marks	In small banks (with a capital of less than million marks)
1907-08	47	32.5	16.5	4
1912-13	49	36	12	3

The small banks are being squeezed out by the big banks, of which only nine concentrate in their hands almost half the total deposits. But we have left out of account many important details, for instance, the transformation of numerous small banks into actual branches of the big banks, etc. Of this I shall speak later on.

At the end of 1913, Schulze-Gaevernitz estimated the deposits in the nine big Berlin banks at 5,100 million marks, out of a total of about 10,000 million marks. Taking into account not only the deposits, but the total bank capital, this author wrote: "At the end

---

* Alfred Lansburgh, "Fünf Jahre deutsches Bankwesen" in *Die Bank*, 1913, No. 8, S. 728.

of 1909, the nine big Berlin banks, *together with their affiliated banks*, controlled 11,300 million marks, that is, about 83 per cent of the total German bank capital. The Deutsche Bank, which *together with its affiliated banks* controls nearly 3,000 million marks, represents, parallel to the Prussian State Railway Administration, the biggest and also the most decentralised accumulation of capital in the Old World."*

I have emphasised the reference to the "affiliated" banks because it is one of the most important distinguishing features of modern capitalist concentration. The big enterprises, and the banks in particular, not only completely absorb the small ones, but also "annex" them, subordinate them, bring them into their "own" group or "concern" (to use the technical term) by acquiring "holdings" in their capital, by purchasing or exchanging shares, by a system of credits, etc., etc. Professor Liefmann has written a voluminous "work" of about 500 pages describing modern "holding and finance companies",** unfortunately adding very dubious "theoretical" reflections to what is frequently undigested raw material. To what results this "holding" system leads in respect of concentration is best illustrated in the book written on the big German banks by Riesser, himself a banker. But before examining his data, let us quote a concrete example of the "holding" system.

The Deutsche Bank "group" is one of the biggest, if not the biggest, of the big banking groups. In order to trace the main threads which connect all the banks in this group, a distinction must be made between holdings of the first and second and third degree, or what amounts to the same thing, between dependence (of the lesser banks on the Deutsche Bank) in the first, second and third degree. We then obtain the following picture***: (See Table on p. 190.)

Included in the eight banks "occasionally" dependent on the Deutsche Bank in the "first degree", are three foreign banks: one Austrian (the Wiener Bankverein) and two Russian (the Siberian Commercial Bank and the Russian Bank for Foreign Trade). Altogether, the Deutsche Bank group comprises, directly and indirectly, partially and totally, 87 banks; and the total capital—its own and that of others which it controls—is estimated at between two and three thousand million marks.

---

* Schulze-Gaevernitz, "Die deutsche Kreditbank" in *Grundriß der Sozialökonomik*, Tübingen, 1915, S. 12 und 137.
** R. Liefmann, *Beteiligungs- und Finanzierungsgesellschaften. Eine Studie über den modernen Kapitalismus und das Effektenwesen*, 1 Aufl., Jena, 1909, S. 212.
*** Alfred Lansburgh, "Das Beteiligungssystem im deutschen Bankwesen" in *Die Bank*, 1910, 1, S. 500.

		Direct or 1st degree dependence:	2nd degree dependence:	3rd degree dependence:
The Deutsche Bank has holdings	permanently . . .	in 17 other banks;	9 of the 17 have holdings in 34 other banks	4 of the 9 have holdings in 7 other banks
	for an indefinite period . . .	in 5 " "	—	—
	occasionally . . .	in 8 " "	5 of the 8 have holdings in 14 other banks	2 of the 5 have holdings in 2 other banks
	Total . . .	in 30 " "	14 of the 30 have holdings in 48 other banks	6 of the 14 have holdings in 9 other banks

It is obvious that a bank which stands at the head of such a group, and which enters into agreement with half a dozen other banks only slightly smaller than itself for the purpose of conducting exceptionally big and profitable financial operations like floating state loans, has already outgrown the part of "middleman" and has become an association of a handful of monopolists.

The rapidity with which the concentration of banking proceeded in Germany at the turn of the twentieth century is shown by the following data which we quote in an abbreviated form from Riesser:

Six Big Berlin Banks

Year	Branches in Germany	Deposit banks and exchange offices	Constant holdings in German joint-stock banks	Total establishments
1895	16	14	1	42
1900	21	40	8	80
1911	104	276	63	450

We see the rapid expansion of a close network of channels which cover the whole country, centralising all capital and all revenues, transforming thousands and thousands of scattered economic enterprises into a single national capitalist, and then into a world capitalist economy. The "decentralisation" that Schulze-Gaevernitz, as an exponent of present-day bourgeois political economy, speaks of in the passage previously quoted, really means the subordination to a single centre of an increasing number of formerly relatively "independent", or rather, strictly local economic units. In reality it is *centralisation*, the enhancement of the role, importance and power of monopolist giants.

In the older capitalist countries this "banking network" is still more close. In Great Britain and Ireland, in 1910, there were in all

7,151 branches of banks. Four big banks had more than 400 branches each (from 447 to 689); four had more than 200 branches each, and eleven more than 100 each.

In France, *three* very big banks, Crédit Lyonnais, the Comptoir National and the Société Générale, extended their operations and their network of branches in the following manner.*

	Number of branches and offices			Capital (000,000 francs)	
	In the provinces	In Paris	Total	Own capital	Deposits used as capital
1870	47	17	64	200	427
1890	192	66	258	265	1,245
1909	1,033	196	1,229	887	4,363

In order to show the "connections" of a big modern bank, Riesser gives the following figures of the number of letters dispatched and received by the Disconto-Gesellschaft, one of the biggest banks in Germany and in the world (its capital in 1914 amounted to 300 million marks):

	Letters received	Letters dispatched
1852 . , . . .	6,135	6,292
1870	85,800	87,513
1900	533,102	626,043

The number of accounts of the big Paris bank, the Crédit Lyonnais, increased from 28,535 in 1875 to 633,539 in 1912.**

These simple figures show perhaps better than lengthy disquisitions how the concentration of capital and the growth of bank turnover are radically changing the significance of the banks. Scattered capitalists are transformed into a single collective capitalist. When carrying the current accounts of a few capitalists, a bank, as it were, transacts a purely technical and exclusively auxiliary operation. When, however, this operation grows to enormous dimensions we find that a handful of monopolists subordinate to their will all the operations, both commercial and industrial, of the whole of capitalist society; for they are enabled—by means of their bank-

---

* Eugen Kaufmann, *Das französische Bankwesen*, Tübingen, 1911, S. 356 und 362.
** Jean Lescure, *L'épargne en France*, Paris, 1914, p. 52.

ing connections, their current accounts and other financial operations—first, to *ascertain exactly* the financial position of the various capitalists, then to *control* them, to influence them by restricting or enlarging, facilitating or hindering credits, and finally to *entirely determine* their fate, determine their income, deprive them of capital, or permit them to increase their capital rapidly and to enormous dimensions, etc.

We have just mentioned the 300 million marks capital of the Disconto-Gesellschaft of Berlin. This increase of the capital of the bank was one of the incidents in the struggle for hegemony between two of the biggest Berlin banks—the Deutsche Bank and the Disconto. In 1870, the first was still a novice and had a capital of only 15 million marks, while the second had a capital of 30 million marks. In 1908, the first had a capital of 200 million, while the second had 170 million. In 1914, the first increased its capital to 250 million and the second, by merging with another first-class big bank, the Schaaffhausenscher Bankverein, increased its capital to 300 million. And, of course, this struggle for hegemony went hand in hand with the more and more frequent conclusion of "agreements" of an increasingly durable character between the two banks. The following are the conclusions that this development forces upon banking specialists who regard economic questions from a standpoint which does not in the least exceed the bounds of the most moderate and cautious bourgeois reformism.

Commenting on the increase of the capital of the Disconto-Gesellschaft to 300 million marks, the German review, *Die Bank*, wrote: "Other banks will follow this same path and in time the three hundred men, who today govern Germany economically, will gradually be reduced to fifty, twenty-five or still fewer. It cannot be expected that this latest move towards concentration will be confined to banking. The close relations that exist between individual banks naturally lead to the bringing together of the industrial syndicates which these banks favour.... One fine morning we shall wake up in surprise to see nothing but trusts before our eyes, and to find ourselves faced with the necessity of substituting state monopolies for private monopolies. However, we have nothing to reproach ourselves with, except that we have allowed things to follow their own course, slightly accelerated by the manipulation of stocks."*

This is an example of the impotence of bourgeois journalism which differs from bourgeois science only in that the latter is less sincere and strives to obscure the essence of the matter, to hide the forest behind the trees. To be "surprised" at the results of con-

---

* A. Lansburgh, "Die Bank mit den 300 Millionen" in *Die Bank*, 1914, 1, S. 426.

centration, to "reproach" the government of capitalist Germany, or capitalist "society" ("ourselves"), to fear that the introduction of stocks and shares might "accelerate" concentration in the same way as the German "cartel" specialist Tschierschky fears the American trusts and "prefers" the German cartels on the grounds that they "may not, like the trusts, excessively accelerate technical and economic progress"*—is not all this a sign of impotence?

But facts remain facts. There are no trusts in Germany; there are "only" cartels—but Germany is *governed* by not more than three hundred magnates of capital, and the number of these is constantly diminishing. At all events, banks greatly intensify and accelerate the process of concentration of capital and the formation of monopolies in all capitalist countries, notwithstanding all the differences in their banking laws.

The banking system "possesses, indeed, the form of universal book-keeping and distribution of means of production on a social scale, but solely the form", wrote Marx in *Capital* half a century ago (Russ. trans., Vol. III, part II, p. 144[122]). The figures we have quoted on the growth of bank capital, on the increase in the number of the branches and offices of the biggest banks, the increase in the number of their accounts, etc., present a concrete picture of this "universal book-keeping" of the *whole* capitalist class; and not only of the capitalists, for the banks collect, even though temporarily, all kinds of money revenues—of small businessmen, office clerks, and of a tiny upper stratum of the working class. "Universal distribution of means of production"—that, from the formal aspect, is what *grows* out of the modern banks, which, numbering some three to six of the biggest in France, and six to eight in Germany, control millions and millions. In *substance*, however, the distribution of means of production is not at all "universal", but private, i.e., it conforms to the interests of big capital, and primarily, of huge, monopoly capital, which operates under conditions in which the masses live in want, in which the whole development of agriculture hopelessly lags behind the development of industry, while within industry itself the "heavy industries" exact tribute from all other branches of industry.

In the matter of socialising capitalist economy the savings-banks and post-offices are beginning to compete with the banks; they are more "decentralised", i.e., their influence extends to a greater number of localities, to more remote places, to wider sections of the population. Here is the data collected by an American commission on the comparative growth of deposits in banks and savings-banks**:

---

* S. Tschierschky, op. cit., S. 128.
** *Statistics of the National Monetary Commission*, quoted in *Die Bank*, 1910, 2, S. 1200.

Deposits (000,000,000 marks)

	Britain		France		Germany		
	Banks	Sa-vings-banks	Banks	Sa-vings-banks	Banks	Credit societies	Savings-banks
1880	8.4	1.6	?	0.9	0.5	0.4	2.6
1888	12.4	2.0	1.5	2.1	1.1	0.4	4.5
1908	23.2	4.2	3.7	4.2	7.1	2.2	13.9

As they pay interest at the rate of 4 per cent and $4^1/_4$ per cent on deposits, the savings-banks must seek "profitable" investments for their capital, they must deal in bills, mortgages, etc. The boundaries between the banks and the savings-banks "become more and more obliterated". The Chambers of Commerce of Bochum and Erfurt, for example, demand that savings-banks be "prohibited" from engaging in "purely" banking business, such as discounting bills; they demand the limitation of the "banking" operations of the post-office.* The banking magnates seem to be afraid that state monopoly will steal upon them from an unexpected quarter. It goes without saying, however, that this fear is no more than an expression of the rivalry, so to speak, between two department managers in the same office; for, on the one hand, the millions entrusted to the savings-banks are in the final analysis actually controlled by *these very same* bank capital magnates, while, on the other hand, state monopoly in capitalist society is merely a means of increasing and guaranteeing the income of millionaires in some branch of industry who are on the verge of bankruptcy.

The change from the old type of capitalism, in which free competition predominated, to the new capitalism, in which monopoly reigns, is expressed, among other things, by a decline in the importance of the Stock Exchange. The review, *Die Bank*, writes: "The Stock Exchange has long ceased to be the indispensable medium of circulation that it formerly was when the banks were not yet able to place the bulk of new issues with their clients."**

"'Every bank is a Stock Exchange', and the bigger the bank, and the more successful the concentration of banking, the truer does this modern aphorism ring."*** "While formerly, in the seventies, the Stock Exchange, flushed with the exuberance of youth" (a "subtle" allusion to the Stock Exchange crash of 1873, the company promotion scandals,[123] etc.), "opened the era of the industrialisation of Germany, nowadays the banks and industry are able to

---

* *Die Bank,* 1913, S. 811, 1022; 1914, S. 713.
** *Die Bank,* 1914, 1, S. 316.
*** Dr. Oscar Stillich, *Geld- und Bankwesen,* Berlin, 1907, S. 169.

'manage it alone'. The domination of our big banks over the Stock Exchange ... is nothing else than the expression of the completely organised German industrial state. If the domain of the automatically functioning economic laws is thus restricted, and if the domain of conscious regulation by the banks is considerably enlarged, the national economic responsibility of a few guiding heads is immensely increased," so writes the German Professor Schulze-Gaevernitz,* an apologist of German imperialism, who is regarded as an authority by the imperialists of all countries, and who tries to gloss over the "mere detail" that the "conscious regulation" of economic life by the banks consists in the fleecing of the public by a handful of "completely organised" monopolists. The task of a bourgeois professor is not to lay bare the entire mechanism, or to expose all the machinations of the bank monopolists, but rather to present them in a favourable light.

In the same way, Riesser, a still more authoritative economist and himself a banker, makes shift with meaningless phrases in order to explain away undeniable facts: "... the Stock Exchange is steadily losing the feature which is absolutely essential for national economy as a whole and for the circulation of securities in particular—that of being not only a most exact measuring-rod, but also an almost automatic regulator of the economic movements which converge on it."**

In other words, the old capitalism, the capitalism of free competition with its indispensable regulator, the Stock Exchange, is passing away. A new capitalism has come to take its place, bearing obvious features of something transient, a mixture of free competition and monopoly. The question naturally arises: *into what* is this new capitalism "developing"? But the bourgeois scholars are afraid to raise this question.

"Thirty years ago, businessmen, freely competing against one another, performed nine-tenths of the work connected with their business other than manual labour. At the present time, nine-tenths of this 'brain work' is performed by *employees*. Banking is in the forefront of this evolution."*** This admission by Schulze-Gaevernitz brings us once again to the question: into what is this new capitalism, capitalism in its imperialist stage, developing?

Among the few banks which remain at the head of all capitalist economy as a result of the process of concentration, there is naturally to be observed an increasingly marked tendency towards monopolist agreements, towards a *bank trust*. In America, not nine, but *two* very big banks, those of the multimillionaires Rockefeller

---

* Schulze-Gaevernitz, "Die deutsche Kreditbank" in *Grundriß der Sozialökonomik*, Tübingen, 1915, S. 101.
** Riesser, op. cit., 4th ed., S. 629.
*** Schulze-Gaevernitz, "Die deutsche Kreditbank" in *Grundriß der Sozialökonomik*, Tübingen, 1915, S. 151.

and Morgan, control a capital of eleven thousand million marks.* In Germany the absorption of the Schaaffhausenscher Bankverein by the Disconto-Gesellschaft to which I referred above, was commented on in the following terms by the *Frankfurter Zeitung*, an organ of Stock Exchange interests:

"The concentration movement of the banks is narrowing the circle of establishments from which it is possible to obtain credits, and is consequently increasing the dependence of big industry upon a small number of banking groups. In view of the close connection between industry and the financial world, the freedom of movement of industrial companies which need banking capital is restricted. For this reason, big industry is watching the growing trustification of the banks with mixed feelings. Indeed, we have repeatedly seen the beginnings of certain agreements between the individual big banking concerns, which aim at restricting competition."**

Again and again, the final word in the development of banking is monopoly.

As regards the close connection between the banks and industry, it is precisely in this sphere that the new role of the banks is, perhaps, most strikingly felt. When a bank discounts a bill for a firm, opens a current account for it, etc., these operations, taken separately, do not in the least diminish its independence, and the bank plays no other part than that of a modest middleman. But when such operations are multiplied and become an established practice, when the bank "collects" in its own hands enormous amounts of capital, when the running of a current account for a given firm enables the bank—and this is what happens—to obtain fuller and more detailed information about the economic position of its client, the result is that the industrial capitalist becomes more completely dependent on the bank.

At the same time a personal link-up, so to speak, is established between the banks and the biggest industrial and commercial enterprises, the merging of one with another through the acquisition of shares, through the appointment of bank directors to the Supervisory Boards (or Boards of Directors) of industrial and commercial enterprises, and vice versa. The German economist, Jeidels, has compiled most detailed data on this form of concentration of capital and of enterprises. Six of the biggest Berlin banks were represented by their directors in *344* industrial companies; and by their board members in *407* others, making a total of *751* companies. In *289* of these companies they either had two of their representatives on each of the respective Supervisory Boards, or held the posts of chairmen. We find these industrial and commercial com-

---

* *Die Bank,* 1912, 1, S. 435.
** Quoted by Schulze-Gaevernitz, op. cit., S. 155.

panies in the most diverse branches of industry: insurance, transport, restaurants, theatres, art industry, etc. On the other hand, on the Supervisory Boards of these six banks (in 1910) were fifty-one of the biggest industrialists, including the director of Krupp, of the powerful "Hapag" (Hamburg-Amerika Line), etc., etc. From 1895 to 1910, each of these six banks participated in the share and bond issues of many hundreds of industrial companies (the number ranging from 281 to 419).*

The "personal link-up" between the banks and industry is supplemented by the "personal link-up" between both of them and the government. "Seats on Supervisory Boards," writes Jeidels, "are freely offered to persons of title, also to ex-civil servants, who are able to do a great deal to facilitate [!!] relations with the authorities."... "Usually, on the Supervisory Board of a big bank, there is a member of parliament or a Berlin city councillor."

The building and development, so to speak, of the big capitalist monopolies is therefore going on full steam ahead in all "natural" and "supernatural" ways. A sort of division of labour is being systematically developed amongst the several hundred kings of finance who reign over modern capitalist society:

"Simultaneously with this widening of the sphere of activity of certain big industrialists [joining the boards of banks, etc.] and with the assignment of provincial bank managers to definite industrial regions, there is a growth of specialisation among the directors of the big banks. Generally speaking, this specialisation is only conceivable when banking is conducted on a large scale, and particularly when it has widespread connections with industry. This division of labour proceeds along two lines: on the one hand, relations with industry as a whole are entrusted to one director, as his special function; on the other, each director assumes the supervision of several separate enterprises, or of a group of enterprises in the same branch of industry or having similar interests.... [Capitalism has already reached the stage of organised *supervision* of individual enterprises.] One specialises in German industry, sometimes even in West German industry alone [the West is the most industrialised part of Germany], others specialise in relations with foreign states and foreign industry, in information on the characters of industrialists and others, in Stock Exchange questions, etc. Besides, each bank director is often assigned a special locality or a special branch of industry; one works chiefly on Supervisory Boards of electric companies, another, on chemical, brewing, or beet sugar plants, a third, in a few isolated industrial enterprises, but at the same time works on the Supervisory Boards of insurance companies.... In short, there can be no doubt that the growth in the

---

* Jeidels, op. cit.; Riesser, op. cit.

dimensions and diversity of the big banks' operations is accompanied by an increase in the division of labour among their directors with the object (and result) of, so to speak, lifting them somewhat out of pure banking and making them better experts, better judges of the general problems of industry and the special problems of each branch of industry, thus making them more capable of acting within the respective bank's industrial sphere of influence. This system is supplemented by the banks' endeavours to elect to their Supervisory Boards men who are experts in industrial affairs, such as industrialists, former officials, especially those formerly in the railway service or in mining," etc.*

We find the same system only in a slightly different form in French banking. For instance, one of the three biggest French banks, the Crédit Lyonnais, has organised a financial research service (*service des études financières*), which permanently employs over fifty engineers, statisticians, economists, lawyers, etc. This costs from six to seven hundred thousand francs annually. The service is in turn divided into eight departments: one specialises in collecting information on industrial establishments, another studies general statistics, a third, railway and steamship companies, a fourth, securities, a fifth, financial reports, etc.**

The result is, on the one hand, the ever-growing merger, or, as N. I. Bukharin aptly calls it, coalescence, of bank and industrial capital and, on the other hand, the growth of the banks into institutions of a truly "universal character". On this question I find it necessary to quote the exact terms used by Jeidels, who has best studied the subject:

"An examination of the sum total of industrial relationships reveals the universal *character* of the financial establishments working on behalf of industry. Unlike other kinds of banks, and contrary to the demand sometimes expressed in the literature that banks should specialise in one kind of business or in one branch of industry in order to prevent the ground from slipping from under their feet—the big banks are striving to make their connections with industrial enterprises as varied as possible in respect of the locality or branches of industry and are striving to eliminate the unevenness in the distribution of capital among localities and branches of industry resulting from the historical development of individual enterprises." "One tendency is to make the connections with industry general; another tendency is to make them durable and close. In the six big banks both these tendencies are realised, not in full, but to a considerable extent and to an equal degree."

---

* Jeidels, op. cit., S. 157-158.
** An article by Eug. Kaufmann on French banks in *Die Bank,* 1909, 2, S. 851 et seq.

Quite often industrial and commercial circles complain of the "terrorism" of the banks. And it is not surprising that such complaints are heard, for the big banks "command", as will be seen from the following example. On November 19, 1901, one of the big, so-called Berlin "D" banks (the names of the four biggest banks begin with letter D) wrote to the Board of Directors of the German Central Northwest Cement Syndicate in the following terms: "As we learn from the notice you published in a certain newspaper of the 18th inst., we must reckon with the possibility that the next general meeting of your syndicate, to be held on the 30th of this month, may decide on measures which are likely to effect changes in your enterprise which are unacceptable to us. We deeply regret that, for these reasons, we are obliged henceforth to withdraw the credit which had hitherto been allowed you.... But if the said next general meeting does not decide upon measures which are unacceptable to us, and if we receive suitable guarantees on this matter for the future, we shall be quite willing to open negotiations with you on the grant of a new credit."*

As a matter of fact, this is small capital's old complaint about being oppressed by big capital, but in this case it was a whole syndicate that fell into the category of "small" capital! The old struggle between small and big capital is being resumed at a new and immeasurably higher stage of development. It stands to reason that the big banks' enterprises, worth many millions, can accelerate technical progress with means that cannot possibly be compared with those of the past. The banks, for example, set up special technical research societies, and, of course, only "friendly" industrial enterprises benefit from their work. To this category belong the Electric Railway Research Association, the Central Bureau of Scientific and Technical Research, etc.

The directors of the big banks themselves cannot fail to see that new conditions of national economy are being created; but they are powerless in the face of these phenomena.

"Anyone who has watched, in recent years," writes Jeidels, "the changes of incumbents of directorships and seats on the Supervisory Boards of the big banks, cannot fail to have noticed that power is gradually passing into the hands of men who consider the active intervention of the big banks in the general development of industry to be necessary and of increasing importance. Between these new men and the old bank directors, disagreements on this subject of a business and often of a personal nature are growing. The issue is whether or not the banks, as credit institutions, will suffer from this intervention in industry, whether they are sacrificing tried principles and an assured profit to engage in a field of activity which

---

* Dr. Oscar Stillich, *Geld- und Bankwesen*, Berlin, 1907, S. 147.

has nothing in common with their role as middlemen in providing credit, and which is leading the banks into a field where they are more than ever before exposed to the blind forces of trade fluctuations. This is the opinion of many of the older bank directors, while most of the young men consider active intervention in industry to be a necessity as great as that which gave rise, simultaneously with big modern industry, to the big banks and modern industrial banking. The two parties are agreed only on one point: that there are neither firm principles nor a concrete aim in the new activities of the big banks."*

The old capitalism has had its day. The new capitalism represents a transition towards something. It is hopeless, of course, to seek for "firm principles and a concrete aim" for the purpose of "reconciling" monopoly with free competition. The admission of the practical men has quite a different ring from the official praises of the charms of "organised" capitalism sung by its apologists, Schulze-Gaevernitz, Liefmann and similar "theoreticians".

At precisely what period were the "new activities" of the big banks finally established? Jeidels gives us a fairly exact answer to this important question:

"The connections between the banks and industrial enterprises, with their new content, their new forms and their new organs, namely, the big banks which are organised on both a centralised and a decentralised basis, were scarcely a characteristic economic phenomenon before the nineties; in one sense, indeed, this initial date may be advanced to the year 1897, when the important 'mergers' took place and when, for the first time, the new form of decentralised organisation was introduced to suit the industrial policy of the banks. This starting-point could perhaps be placed at an even later date, for it was the crisis of 1900 that enormously accelerated and intensified the process of concentration of industry and of banking, consolidated that process, for the first time transformed the connection with industry into the actual monopoly of the big banks, and made this connection much closer and more active."**

Thus, the twentieth century marks the turning-point from the old capitalism to the new, from the domination of capital in general to the domination of finance capital.

III. FINANCE CAPITAL AND THE FINANCIAL OLIGARCHY

"A steadily increasing proportion of capital in industry," writes Hilferding, "ceases to belong to the industrialists who employ it. They obtain the use of it only through the medium of the banks

---

* Jeidels, op. cit., S. 183-184.
** Ibid., S. 181.

which, in relation to them, represent the owners of the capital. On the other hand, the bank is forced to sink an increasing share of its funds in industry. Thus, to an ever greater degree the banker is being transformed into an industrial capitalist. This bank capital, i.e., capital in money form, which is thus actually transformed into industrial capital, I call 'finance capital'." "Finance capital is capital controlled by banks and employed by industrialists."*

This definition is incomplete insofar as it is silent on one extremely important fact—on the increase of concentration of production and of capital to such an extent that concentration is leading, and has led, to monopoly. But throughout the whole of his work, and particularly in the two chapters preceding the one from which this definition is taken, Hilferding stresses the part played by *capitalist monopolies*.

The concentration of production; the monopolies arising therefrom; the merging or coalescence of the banks with industry—such is the history of the rise of finance capital and such is the content of that concept.

We now have to describe how, under the general conditions of commodity production and private property, the "business operations" of capitalist monopolies inevitably lead to the domination of a financial oligarchy. It should be noted that German—and not only German—bourgeois scholars, like Riesser, Schulze-Gaevernitz, Liefmann and others, are all apologists of imperialism and of finance capital. Instead of revealing the "mechanics" of the formation of an oligarchy, its methods, the size of its revenues "impeccable and peccable", its connections with parliaments, etc., etc., they obscure or gloss over them. They evade these "vexed questions" by pompous and vague phrases, appeals to the "sense of responsibility" of bank directors, by praising "the sense of duty" of Prussian officials, giving serious study to the petty details of absolutely ridiculous parliamentary bills for the "supervision" and "regulation" of monopolies, playing spillikins with theories, like, for example, the following "scholarly" definition, arrived at by Professor Liefmann: *"Commerce is an occupation having for its object the collection, storage and supply of goods."** (The Professor's bold-face italics.) From this it would follow that commerce existed in the time of primitive man, who knew nothing about exchange, and that it will exist under socialism!

But the monstrous facts concerning the monstrous rule of the financial oligarchy are so glaring that in all capitalist countries, in America, France and Germany, a whole literature has sprung up, written from the *bourgeois* point of view, but which, nevertheless,

---

* R. Hilferding, *Finance Capital*, Moscow, 1912 (in Russian), pp. 338-39.
** R. Liefmann, op. cit., S. 476.

gives a fairly truthful picture and criticism—petty-bourgeois, naturally—of this oligarchy.

Paramount importance attaches to the "holding system", already briefly referred to above. The German economist, Heymann, probably the first to call attention to this matter, describes the essence of it in this way:

"The head of the concern controls the principal company [literally: the "mother company"]; the latter reigns over the subsidiary companies ["daughter companies"] which in their turn control still other subsidiaries ["grandchild companies"], etc. In this way, it is possible with a comparatively small capital to dominate immense spheres of production. Indeed, if holding 50 per cent of the capital is always sufficient to control a company, the head of the concern needs only one million to control eight million in the second subsidiairies. And if this 'interlocking' is extended, it is possible with one million to control sixteen million, thirty-two million, etc."*

As a matter of fact, experience shows that it is sufficient to own 40 per cent of the shares of a company in order to direct its affairs,** since in practice a certain number of small, scattered shareholders find it impossible to attend general meetings, etc. The "democratisation" of the ownership of shares, from which the bourgeois sophists and opportunist so-called "Social-Democrats" expect (or say that they expect) the "democratisation of capital", the strengthening of the role and significance of small-scale production, etc., is, in fact, one of the ways of increasing the power of the financial oligarchy. Incidentally, this is why, in the more advanced, or in the older and more "experienced" capitalist countries, the law allows the issue of shares of smaller denomination. In Germany, the law does not permit the issue of shares of less than one thousand marks denomination, and the magnates of German finance look with an envious eye at Britain, where the issue of one-pound shares (= 20 marks, about 10 rubles) is permitted. Siemens, one of the biggest industrialists and "financial kings" in Germany, told the Reichstag on June 7, 1900, that "the one-pound share is the basis of British imperialism".*** This merchant has a much deeper and more "Marxist" understanding of imperialism than a certain disreputable writer who is held to be one of the founders of Russian Marxism[124] and believes that imperialism is a bad habit of a certain nation....

But the "holding system" not only serves enormously to increase the power of the monopolists; it also enables them to resort with impunity to all sorts of shady and dirty tricks to cheat the public,

---

* Hans Gideon Heymann, *Die gemischten Werke im deutschen Großeisengewerbe*, Stuttgart, 1904, S. 268-69.
** Liefmann, *Beteiligungsgesellschaften, etc.*, S. 258 of the first edition.
*** Schulze-Gaevernitz in *Grundriß der Sozialökonomik*, V. 2, S. 110.

because formally the directors of the "mother company" are not legally responsible for the "daughter company", which is supposed to be "independent", and *through the medium* of which they can "pull off" *anything*. Here is an example taken from the German review, *Die Bank*, for May 1914:

"The Spring Steel Company of Kassel was regarded some years ago as being one of the most profitable enterprises in Germany. Through bad management its dividends fell from 15 per cent to nil. It appears that the Board, without consulting the shareholders, had loaned *six million marks* to one of its 'daughter companies', the Hassia Company, which had a nominal capital of only some hundreds of thousands of marks. This commitment, amounting to nearly treble the capital of the 'mother company' was never mentioned in its balance-sheets. This ommission was quite legal and could be hushed up for two whole years because it did not violate any point of company law. The chairman of the Supervisory Board, who as the responsible head had signed the false balance-sheets, was, and still is, the president of the Kassel Chamber of Commerce. The shareholders only heard of the loan to the Hassia Company, long afterwards, when it had been proved to be a mistake"... (the writer should put this word in inverted commas) ... "and when Spring Steel shares dropped nearly 100 per cent, because those in the know were getting rid of them. ...

"*This typical example of balance-sheet jugglery, quite common* in joint-stock companies, explains why their Boards of Directors are willing to undertake risky transactions with a far lighter heart than individual businessmen. Modern methods of drawing up balance-sheets not only make it possible to conceal doubtful undertakings from the ordinary shareholder, but also allow the people most concerned to escape the consequence of unsuccessful speculation by selling their shares in time when the individual businessman risks his own skin in everything he does. ...

"The balance-sheets of many joint-stock companies put us in mind of the palimpsests of the Middle Ages from which the visible inscription had first to be erased in order to discover beneath it another inscription giving the real meaning of the document. [Palimpsests are parchment documents from which the original inscription has been erased and another inscription imposed.]

"The simplest and, therefore, most common procedure for making balance-sheets indecipherable is to divide a single business into several parts by setting up 'daughter companies'—or by annexing them. The advantages of this system for various purposes—legal and illegal—are so evident that big companies which do not employ it are quite the exception."*

---

* L. Eschwege, "Tochtergesellschaften" in *Die Bank*, 1914, 1, S. 545.

As an example of a huge monopolist company that extensively employs this system, the author quotes the famous General Electric Company (the A.E.G., to which I shall refer again later on). In 1912, it was calculated that this company held shares in *175* to *200* other companies, dominating them, of course, and thus controlling a total capital of about 1,500 *million marks.**

None of the rules of control, the publication of balance-sheets, the drawing up of balance-sheets according to a definite form, the public auditing of accounts, etc., the things about which well-intentioned professors and officials—that is, those imbued with the good intention of defending and prettifying capitalism—discourse to the public, are of any avail; for private property is sacred, and no one can be prohibited from buying, selling, exchanging or hypothecating shares, etc.

The extent to which this "holding system" has developed in the big Russian banks may be judged by the figures given by E. Agahd, who for fifteen years was an official of the Russo-Chinese Bank and who, in May 1914, published a book, not altogether correctly entitled *Big Banks and the World Market.*** The author divides the big Russian banks into two main groups: *a*) banks that come under the "holding system", and *b*) "independent" banks—"independence", however, being arbitrarily taken to mean independence of *foreign* banks. The author divides the first group into three subgroups: 1) German holdings, 2) British holdings, and 3) French holdings, having in view the "holdings" and domination of the big foreign banks of the particular country mentioned. The author divides the capital of the banks into "productively" invested capital (industrial and commercial undertakings), and "speculatively" invested capital (in Stock Exchange and financial operations), assuming, from his petty-bourgeois reformist point of view, that it is possible, under capitalism, to separate the first form of investment from the second and to abolish the second form.

Here are the figures he supplies: (See Table on p. 205.)

According to these figures, of the approximately 4,000 million rubles making up the "working" capital of the big banks, *more than three-fourths*, more than 3,000 million, belonged to banks which in reality were only "daughter companies" of foreign banks, and chiefly of Paris banks (the famous trio: Union Parisienne, Paris et Pays-Bas and Société Générale), and of Berlin banks (particularly the Deutsche Bank and Disconto-Gesellschaft). Two of the biggest

---

* Kurt Heinig, "Der Weg des Elektrotrusts" in *Die Neue Zeit,* 1912, 30. Jahrg., 2, S. 484.

** E. Agahd, *Großbanken und Weltmarkt. Die wirtschaftliche und politische Bedeutung der Großbanken im Weltmarkt unter Berücksichtigung ihres Einflusses auf Rußlands Volkswirtschaft und die deutsche-russischen Beziehungen,* Berlin, 1914.

Bank Assets
(According to Reports for October-November 1913)
000,000 rubles

Groups of Russian banks	Capital invested		
	productively	speculatively	total
a 1) 4 banks: Siberian Commercial, Russian, International, and Discount Bank	413.7	859.1	1,272.8
a 2) 2 banks: Commercial and Industrial, and Russo-British	239.3	169.1	408.4
a 3) 5 banks: Russian-Asiatic, St.Petersburg Private,Azov-Don,Union Moscow, Russo-French Commercial . .	711.8	661.2	1,373.0
(11 banks) *Total*: . . . . . *a)*=	1,364.8	1,689.4	3,054.2
b) 8 banks: Moscow Merchants, Volga-Kama, Junker and Co., St. Petersburg Commercial (formerly Wawelberg), Bank of Moscow (formerly Ryabushinsky), Moscow Discount, Moscow Commercial, Moscow Private .	504.2	391.1	895.3
(19 banks) *Total*	1,869.0	2,080.5	3,949.5

Russian banks, the Russian (Russian Bank for Foreign Trade) and the International (St. Petersburg International Commercial Bank), between 1906 and 1912 increased their capital from 44 to 98 million rubles, and their reserves from 15 million to 39 million "employing three-fourths German capital". The first bank belongs to the Berlin Deutsche Bank "concern" and the second to the Berlin Disconto-Gesellschaft. The worthy Agahd is deeply indignant at the majority of the shares being held by the Berlin banks, so that the Russian shareholders are, therefore, powerless. Naturally, the country which exports capital skims the cream; for example, the Berlin Deutsche Bank, before placing the shares of the Siberian Commercial Bank on the Berlin market, kept them in its portfolio for a whole year, and then sold them at the rate of 193 for 100, that is, at nearly twice their nominal value, "earning" a profit of nearly six million rubles, which Hilferding calls "promoter's profits".

Our author puts the total "capacity" of the principal St. Petersburg banks at 8,235 million rubles, well over 8,000 million, and the "holdings", or rather, the extent to which foreign banks dominated them, he estimates as follows: French banks, 55 per cent; British, 10 per cent; German, 35 per cent. The author calculates that of the total of 8,235 million rubles of functioning capital, 3,687 million rubles, or over 40 per cent, fall to the share of the Produgol and Prodamet syndicates[125] and the syndicates in the oil, metallurgical and cement industries. Thus, owing to the formation of capitalist monopolies, the merging of bank and industrial capital has also made enormous strides in Russia.

Finance capital, concentrated in a few hands and exercising a virtual monopoly, exacts enormous and ever-increasing profits from the floating of companies, issue of stock, state loans, etc., strengthens the domination of the financial oligarchy and levies tribute upon the whole of society for the benefit of monopolists. Here is an example, taken from a multitude of others, of the "business" methods of the American trusts, quoted by Hilferding. In 1887, Havemeyer founded the Sugar Trust by amalgamating fifteen small firms, whose total capital amounted to 6,500,000 dollars. Suitably "watered", as the Americans say, the capital of the trust was declared to be 50 million dollars. This "over-capitalisation" anticipated the monopoly profits, in the same way as the United States Steel Corporation anticipates its monopoly profits in buying up as many iron ore fields as possible. In fact, the Sugar Trust set up monopoly prices, which secured it such profits that it could pay 10 per cent dividend on capital "watered" *sevenfold, or about 70 per cent on the capital actually invested at the time the trust was formed!* In 1909, the capital of the Sugar Trust amounted to 90 million dollars. In twenty-two years, it had increased its capital more than tenfold.

In France the domination of the "financial oligarchy" (*Against the Financial Oligarchy in France*, the title of the well-known book by Lysis, the fifth edition of which was published in 1908) assumed a form that was only slightly different. Four of the most powerful banks enjoy, not a relative, but an "absolute monopoly" in the issue of bonds. In reality, this is a "trust of big banks". And monopoly ensures monopoly profits from bond issues. Usually a borrowing country does not get more than 90 per cent of the sum of the loan, the remaining 10 per cent goes to the banks and other middlemen. The profit made by the banks out of the Russo-Chinese loan of 400 million francs amounted to 8 per cent; out of the Russian (1904) loan of 800 million francs the profit amounted to 10 per cent; and out of the Moroccan (1904) loan of 62,500,000 francs it amounted to 18.75 per cent. Capitalism, which began its development with petty usury capital, is ending its development with gigantic usury capital. "The French," says Lysis, "are the usurers of Europe." All the conditions of economic life are being profoundly modified by this transformation of capitalism. With a stationary population, and stagnant industry, commerce and shipping, the "country" can grow rich by usury. "Fifty persons, representing a capital of eight million francs, can control *2,000 million* francs deposited in four banks." The "holding system", with which we are already familiar, leads to the same result. One of the biggest banks, the Société Générale, for instance, issues 64,000 bonds for its "daughter company", the Egyptian Sugar Refineries. The bonds are issued at 150 per cent, i.e., the bank gains 50 centimes on the franc. The dividends of the new company were found to be fictitious, the "public" lost from 90 to 100 million francs. "One of the directors of the Société Générale was a member of the board of directors of the Sugar Refineries." It is not surprising that the author is driven to the conclusion that "the French Republic is a financial monarchy"; "it is the complete domination of the financial oligarchy; the latter dominates over the press and the government".*

The extraordinarily high rate of profit obtained from the issue of bonds, which is one of the principal functions of finance capital, plays a very important part in the development and consolidation of the financial oligarchy. "There is not a single business of this type within the country that brings in profits even approximately equal to those obtained from the flotation of foreign loans," says *Die Bank.***

"No banking operation brings in profits comparable with those obtained from the issue of securities!" According to the *German Economist*, the average annual profits made on the issue of industrial stock were as follows:

1895—38.6%	1898—67.7%
1896—36.1%	1899—66.9%
1897—66.7%	1900—55.2%

"In the ten years from 1891 to 1900, *more than a thousand million marks* were 'earned' by issuing German industrial stock."***

During periods of industrial boom, the profits of finance capital are immense, but during periods of depression, small and unsound businesses go out of existence, and the big banks acquire "holdings" in them by buying them up for a mere song, or participate in profitable schemes for their "reconstruction" and "reorganisation". In the "reconstruction" of undertakings which have been running at a loss, "the share capital is written down, that is, profits are distributed on a smaller capital and continue to be calculated on this smaller basis. Or, if the income has fallen to zero, new capital is called in, which, combined with the old and less remunerative capital, will bring in an adequate return. "Incidentally," adds Hilferd-

---

* Lysis, *Contre l'oligarchie financière en France*, 5 éd. Paris, 1908, pp. 11, 12, 26, 39, 40, 48.
** *Die Bank*, 1913, No. 7, S. 630.
*** Stillich, op. cit., S. 143. also W. Sombart, *Die deutsche Volkswirtschaft im 19. Jahrhundert*, 2, Aufl., 1909, S. 526, Anlage 8.

ing, "all these reorganisations and reconstructions have a twofold significance for the banks: first, as profitable transactions; and secondly, as opportunities for securing control of the companies in difficulties."*

Here is an instance. The Union Mining Company of Dortmund was founded in 1872. Share capital was issued to the amount of nearly 40 million marks and the market price of the shares rose to 170 after it had paid a 12 per cent dividend for its first year. Finance capital skimmed the cream and earned a trifle of something like 28 million marks. The principal sponsor of this company was that very big German Disconto-Gesellschaft which so successfully attained a capital of 300 million marks. Later, the dividends of the Union declined to nil; the shareholders had to consent to a "writing down" of capital, that is, to losing some of it in order not to lose it all. By a series of "reconstructions", more than 73 million marks were written off the books of the Union in the course of thirty years. "At the present time, the original shareholders of the company possess only 5 per cent of the nominal value of their shares"** but the banks "earned something" out of every "reconstruction".

Speculation in land situated in the suburbs of rapidly growing big towns is a particularly profitable operation for finance capital. The monopoly of the banks merges here with the monopoly of ground-rent and with monopoly of the means of communication, since the rise in the price of land and the possibility of selling it profitably in lots, etc., is mainly dependent on good means of communication with the centre of the town; and these means of communication are in the hands of large companies which are connected with these same banks through the holding system and the distribution of seats on the boards. As a result we get what the German writer, L. Eschwege, a contributor to *Die Bank* who has made a special study of real estate business and mortgages, etc., calls a "bog". Frantic speculation in suburban building lots; collapse of building enterprises like the Berlin firm of Boswau and Knauer, which acquired as much as 100 million marks with the help of the "sound and solid" Deutsche Bank—the latter, of course, acting through the holding system, i.e., secretly, behind the scenes—and got out of it with a loss of "only" 12 million marks, then the ruin of small proprietors and of workers who get nothing from the fictitious building firms, fraudulent, deals with the "honest" Berlin police and administration for the purpose of gaining control of the issue of cadastral certificates, building licences, etc., etc.***

"American ethics", which the European professors and well-

---

* *Finance Capital*, p. 172.
** Stillich, op. cit., S. 138 und Liefmann, S. 51.
*** In *Die Bank*, 1913, S. 952, L. Eschwege, *Der Sumpf*; ibid., 1912, 1, S. 223 et seq.

meaning bourgeois so hypocritically deplore, have, in the age of finance capital, become the ethics of literally every large city in any country.

At the beginning of 1914, there was talk in Berlin of the formation of a "transport trust", i.e., of establishing "community of interests" between the three Berlin transport undertakings: the city electric railway, the tramway company and the omnibus company. "We have been aware," wrote *Die Bank*, "that this plan was contemplated ever since it became known that the majority of the shares in the bus company had been acquired by the other two transport companies.... We may fully believe those who are pursuing this aim when they say that by uniting the transport services, they will secure economies, part of which will in time benefit the public. But the question is complicated by the fact that behind the transport trust that is being formed are the banks, which, if they desire, can subordinate the means of transportation, which they have monopolised, to the interests of their real estate business. To be convinced of the reasonableness of such a conjecture, we need only recall that the interests of the big bank that encouraged the formation of the Electric Railway Company were already involved in it at the time the company was formed. That is to say: the interests of this transport undertaking were interlocked with the real estate interests. The point is that the eastern line of this railway was to run across land which these banks sold at an enormous profit for itself and for several partners in the transactions when it became certain the line was to be laid down."*

A monopoly, once it is formed and controls thousands of millions, inevitably penetrates into *every* sphere of public life, regardless of the form of government and all other "details". In German economic literature one usually comes across obsequious praise of the integrity of the Prussian bureaucracy, and allusions to the French Panama scandal[126] and to political corruption in America. But the fact is that *even* bourgeois literature devoted to German banking matters constantly has to go far beyond the field of purely banking operations; it speaks, for instance, about "the attraction of the banks" in reference to the increasing frequency with which public officials take employment with the banks, as follows: "How about the integrity of a state official who in his innermost heart is aspiring to a soft job in the Behrenstrasse?"** (The Berlin street where the head office of the Deutsche Bank is situated.) In 1909, the publisher of *Die Bank*, Alfred Lansburgh, wrote an article entitled "The Economic Significance of Byzantinism", in which he incidentally referred to Wilhelm II's tour of Palestine, and to "the

---

* "Verkehrstrust" in *Die Bank*, 1914, 1, S. 89.
** "Der Zug zur Bank" in *Die Bank*, 1909, 1, S. 79.

immediate result of this journey, the construction of the Baghdad railway, that fatal 'great product of German enterprise', which is more responsible for the 'encirclement' than all our political blunders put together".* (By encirclement is meant the policy of Edward VII to isolate Germany and surround her with an imperialist anti-German alliance.) In 1911, Eschwege, the contributor to this same magazine to whom I have already referred, wrote an article entitled "Plutocracy and Bureaucracy", in which he exposed, for example, the case of a German official named Völker, who was a zealous member of the Cartel Committee and who, it turned out some time later, obtained a lucrative post in the biggest cartel, the Steel Syndicate. Similar cases, by no means casual, forced this bourgeois author to admit that "the economic liberty guaranteed by the German Constitution has become in many departments of economic life, a meaningless phrase" and that under the existing rule of the plutocracy, "even the widest political liberty cannot save us from being converted into a nation of unfree people".**

As for Russia, I shall confine myself to one example. Some years ago, all the newspapers announced that Davydov, the director of the Credit Department of the Treasury, had resigned his post to take employment with a certain big bank at a salary which, according to the contract, would total over one million rubles in the course of several years. The Credit Department is an institution, the function of which is to "co-ordinate the activities of all the credit institutions of the country" and which grants subsidies to banks in St. Petersburg and Moscow amounting to between 800 and 1,000 million rubles.***

It is characteristic of capitalism in general that the ownership of capital is separated from the application of capital to production, that money capital is separated from industrial or productive capital, and that the rentier who lives entirely on income obtained from money capital, is separated from the entrepreneur and from all who are directly concerned in the management of capital. Imperialism, or the domination of finance capital, is that highest stage of capitalism in which this separation reaches vast proportions. The supremacy of finance capital over all other forms of capital means the predominance of the rentier and of the financial oligarchy; it means that a small number of financially "powerful" states stand out among all the rest. The extent to which this process is going on may be judged from the statistics on emissions, i.e., the issue of all kinds of securities.

In the *Bulletin of the International Statistical Institute,*

---

* Ibid., S. 301.
** Ibid., 1911, 2, 825; 1913, 2, S. 962.
*** E. Agahd, op. cit., S. 202.

A. Neymarck* has published very comprehensive, complete and comparative figures covering the issue of securities all over the world, which have been repeatedly quoted in part in economic literature. The following are the totals he gives for four decades:

Total Issues in Francs per Decade

(000,000,000)

1871-1880	76.1
1881-1890	64.5
1891-1900	100.4
1901-1910	197.8

In the 1870s the total amount of issues for the whole world was high, owing particularly to the loans floated in connection with the Franco-Prussian War, and the company-promotion boom which set in in Germany after the war. On the whole, the increase was relatively not very rapid during the three last decades of the nineteenth century, and only in the first ten years of the twentieth century is an enormous increase of almost 100 per cent to be observed. Thus the beginning of the twentieth century marks the turning-point, not only in the growth of monopolies (cartels, syndicates, trusts), of which we have already spoken, but also in the growth of finance capital.

Neymarck estimates the total amount of issued securities current in the world in 1910 at about 815,000 million francs. Deducting from this sum amounts which might have been duplicated, he reduces the total to 575,000-600,000 million, which is distributed among the various countries as follows (I take 600,000 million):

Financial Securities Current in 1910

(000,000,000 francs)

Great Britain	142 ⎫	Holland	12.5
United States	132 ⎬ 479	Belgium	7.5
France	110 ⎭	Spain	7.5
Germany	95	Switzerland	6.25
Russia	31	Denmark	3.75
Austria-Hungary	24	Sweden, Norway,	
Italy	14	Rumania, etc.	2.5
Japan	12		
		Total	600

From these figures we at once see standing out in sharp relief four of the richest capitalist countries, each of which holds secu-

* *Bulletin de l'institut international de statistique*, t. XIX, livr. II, La Haye, 1912. Data concerning small states, second column, are estimated by adding 20 per cent to the 1902 figures.

rities to amounts ranging approximately from 100,000 to 150,000 million francs. Of these four countries, two, Britain and France, are the oldest capitalist countries, and, as we shall see, possess the most colonies; the other two, the United States and Germany, are capitalist countries leading in the rapidity of development and the degree of extension of capitalist monopolies in industry. Together, these four countries own 479,000 million francs, that is, nearly 80 per cent of the world's finance capital. In one way or another, nearly the whole of the rest of the world is more or less the debtor to and tributary of the international banker countries, these four "pillars" of world finance capital.

It is particularly important to examine the part which the export of capital plays in creating the international network of dependence on and connections of finance capital.

IV. EXPORT OF CAPITAL

Typical of the old capitalism, when free competition held undivided sway, was the export of *goods*. Typical of the latest stage of capitalism, when monopolies rule, is the export of *capital*.

Capitalism is commodity production at its highest stage of development, when labour power itself becomes a commodity. The growth of internal exchange, and, particularly, of international exchange, is a characteristic feature of capitalism. The uneven and spasmodic development of individual enterprises, individual branches of industry and individual countries is inevitable under the capitalist system. England became a capitalist country before any other, and by the middle of the nineteenth century, having adopted free trade, claimed to be the "workshop of the world", the supplier of manufactured goods to all countries, which in exchange were to keep her provided with raw materials. But in the last quarter of the nineteenth century, *this* monopoly was already undermined; for other countries, sheltering themselves with "protective" tariffs, developed into independent capitalist states. On the threshold of the twentieth century we see the formation of a new type of monopoly. firstly, monopolist associations of capitalists in all capitalistically developed countries; secondly, the monopolist position of a few very rich countries, in which the accumulation of capital has reached gigantic proportions. An enormous "surplus of capital" has arisen in the advanced countries.

It goes without saying that if capitalism could develop agriculture, which today is everywhere lagging terribly behind industry, if it could raise the living standards of the masses, who in spite of the amazing technical progress are everywhere still half-starved and poverty-stricken, there could be no question of a surplus of capital. This "argument" is very often advanced by the petty-bourgeois critics of capitalism. But if capitalism did these things it would not be capitalism; for both uneven development and a semi-starvation level of existence of the masses are fundamental and inevitable conditions and constitute premises of this mode of production. As long as capitalism remains what it is, surplus capital will be utilised not for the purpose of raising the standard of living of the masses in a given country, for this would mean a decline in profits for the capitalists, but for the purpose of increasing profits by exporting capital abroad to the backward countries. In these backward countries profits are usually high, for capital is scarce, the price of land is relatively low, wages are low, raw materials are cheap. The export of capital is made possible by a number of backward countries having already been drawn into world capitalist intercourse; main railways have either been or are being built in those countries, elementary conditions for industrial development have been created, etc. The need to export capital arises from the fact that in a few countries capitalism has become "overripe" and (owing to the backward state of agriculture and the poverty of the masses) capital cannot find a field for "profitable" investment.

Here are approximate figures showing the amount of capital invested abroad by the three principal countries*:

Capital Invested Abroad
(000,000,000 francs)

Year	Great Britain	France	Germany
1862 . . .	3.6	—	—
1872 . . .	15.0	10(1869)	—
1882 . . .	22.0	15(1880)	?
1893 . . .	42.0	20(1890)	?
1902 . . .	62.0	27-37	12.5
1914 . . .	75-100.0	60	44.0

This table shows that the export of capital reached enormous dimensions only at the beginning of the twentieth century. Before the war the capital invested abroad by the three principal countries amounted to between 175,000 million and 200,000 million francs.

---

* Hobson, *Imperialism*, London, 1902, p. 58; Riesser, op. cit., S. 395 und 404; P. Arndt in *Weltwirtschaftliches Archiv*, Bd. 7, 1916, S. 35; Neymarck in *Bulletin*; Hilferding, *Finance Capital*, p. 492; Lloyd George, Speech in the House of Commons, May 4, 1915, reported in the *Daily Telegraph*, May 5, 1915; B. Harms, *Probleme der Weltwirtschaft*, Jena, 1912, S. 235 et seq.; Dr. Siegmund Schilder, *Entwicklungstendenzen der Weltwirtschaft*, Berlin, 1912, Band I, S. 150; George Paish, "Great Britain's Capital Investments, etc.", in *Journal of the Royal Statistical Society*, Vol. LXXIV, 1910-1911, p. 167 et seq.; Georges Diouritch, *L'Expansion des banques allemandes à l'étranger, ses rapports avec le développement économique de l'Allemagne*, Paris, 1909, p. 84.

At the modest rate of 5 per cent, the income from this sum should reach from 8,000 to 10,000 million francs a year—a sound basis for the imperialist oppression and exploitation of most of the countries and nations of the world, for the capitalist parasitism of a handful of wealthy states!

How is this capital invested abroad distributed among the various countries? *Where* is it invested? Only an approximate answer can be given to these questions, but it is one sufficient to throw light on certain general relations and connections of modern imperialism.

Distribution (Approximate) of Foreign Capital
in Different Parts of the Globe (circa 1910)

	Great Britain	France	Germany	Total
		(000,000,000 marks)		
Europe	4	23	18	45
America	37	4	10	51
Asia, Africa and Australia	29	8	7	44
Total	70	35	35	140

The principal spheres of investment of British capital are the British colonies, which are very large also in America (for example, Canada), not to mention Asia, etc. In this case, enormous exports of capital are bound up most closely with vast colonies, of the importance of which for imperialism I shall speak later. In the case of France the situation is different. French capital exports are invested mainly in Europe, primarily in Russia (at least ten thousand million francs). This is mainly *loan* capital, government loans, and not capital invested in industrial undertakings. Unlike British colonial imperialism, French imperialism might be termed usury imperialism. In the case of Germany, we have a third type; colonies are inconsiderable, and German capital invested abroad is divided most evenly between Europe and America.

The export of capital influences and greatly accelerates the development of capitalism in those countries to which it is exported. While, therefore, the export of capital may tend to a certain extent to arrest development in the capital-exporting countries, it can only do so by expanding and deepening the further development of capitalism throughout the world.

The capital-exporting countries are nearly always able to obtain certain "advantages", the character of which throws light on the peculiarity of the epoch of finance capital and monopoly. The following passage, for instance, appeared in the Berlin review, *Die Bank*, for October 1913:

"A comedy worthy of the pen of Aristophanes is lately being played on the international capital market. Numerous foreign countries, from Spain to the Balkan states, from Russia to Argentina, Brazil and China, are openly or secretly coming into the big money market with demands, sometimes very persistent, for loans. The money markets are not very bright at the moment and the political outlook is not promising. But not a single money market dares to refuse a loan for fear that its neighbour may forestall it, consent to grant a loan and so secure some reciprocal service. In these international transactions the creditor nearly always manages to secure some extra benefit: a favourable clause in a commercial treaty, a coaling station, a contract to construct a harbour, a fat concession, or an order for guns."[*]

Finance capital has created the epoch of monopolies, and monopolies introduce everywhere monopolist principles: the utilisation of "connections" for profitable transactions takes the place of competition on the open market. The most usual thing is to stipulate that part of the loan granted shall be spent on purchases in the creditor country, particularly on orders for war materials, or for ships, etc. In the course of the last two decades (1890-1910), France has very often resorted to this method. The export of capital thus becomes a means of encouraging the export of commodities. In this connection, transactions between particularly big firms assume a form which, as Schilder[**] "mildly" puts it, "borders on corruption". Krupp in Germany, Schneider in France, Armstrong in Britain are instances of firms which have close connections with powerful banks and governments and which cannot easily be "ignored" when a loan is being arranged.

France, when granting loans to Russia, "squeezed" her in the commercial treaty of September 16, 1905, stipulating for certain concessions to run till 1917. She did the same in the commercial treaty with Japan of August 19, 1911. The tariff war between Austria and Serbia, which lasted, with a seven months' interval, from 1906 to 1911, was partly caused by Austria and France competing to supply Serbia with war materials. In January 1912, Paul Deschanel stated in the Chamber of Deputies that from 1908 to 1911 French firms had supplied war materials to Serbia to the value of 45 million francs.

A report from the Austro-Hungarian Consul at Sao-Paulo (Brazil) states: "The Brazilian railways are being built chiefly by French, Belgian, British and German capital. In the financial operations connected with the construction of these railways the countries involved stipulate for orders for the necessary railway materials."

Thus finance capital, literally, one might say, spreads its net over all countries of the world. An important role in this is played by

---

[*] *Die Bank*, 1913, 2, S. 1024-1025.
[**] Schilder, op. cit., S. 346, 350, 371.

banks founded in the colonies and by their branches. German imperialists look with envy at the "old" colonial countries which have been particularly "successful" in providing for themselves in this respect. In 1904, Great Britain had 50 colonial banks with 2,279 branches (in 1910 there were 72 banks with 5,449 branches); France had 20 with 136 branches; Holland, 16 with 68 branches; and Germany had "only" 13 with 70 branches.* The American capitalists, in their turn, are jealous of the English and German: "In South America," they complained in 1915, "five German banks have forty branches and five British banks have seventy branches.... Britain and Germany have invested in Argentina, Brazil, and Uruguay in the last twenty-five years approximately four thousand million dollars, and as a result together enjoy 46 per cent of the total trade of these three countries."**

The capital-exporting countries have divided the world among themselves in the figurative sense of the term. But finance capital has led to the *actual* division of the world.

V. DIVISION OF THE WORLD
AMONG CAPITALIST ASSOCIATIONS

Monopolist capitalist associations, cartels, syndicates and trusts first divided the home market among themselves and obtained more or less complete possession of the industry of their own country. But under capitalism the home market is inevitably bound up with the foreign market. Capitalism long ago created a world market. As the export of capital increased, and as the foreign and colonial connections and "spheres of influence" of the big monopolist associations expanded in all ways, things "naturally" gravitated towards an international agreement among these associations, and towards the formation of international cartels.

This is a new stage of world concentration of capital and production, incomparably higher than the preceding stages. Let us see how this supermonopoly develops.

The electrical industry is highly typical of the latest technical achievements and is most typical of capitalism at the *end* of the nineteenth and the beginning of the twentieth centuries. This industry has developed most in the two leaders of the new capitalist countries, the United States and Germany. In Germany, the crisis of

---

* Riesser, op. cit., 4th ed., S. 375; Diouritch, p. 283.

** *The Annals of the American Academy of Political and Social Science*, Vol. LIX, May 1915, p. 301. In the same volume on p. 331, we read that the well-known statistician Paish, in the last issue of the financial magazine *The Statist*, estimated the amount of capital exported by Britain, Germany, France, Belgium and Holland at $40,000 million, i.e., 200,000 million francs.

1900 gave a particularly strong impetus to its concentration. During the crisis, the banks, which by that time had become fairly well merged with industry, enormously accelerated and intensified the ruin of relatively small firms and their absorption by the large ones. "The banks," writes Jeidels, "refused a helping hand to the very firms in greatest needs of capital, and brought on first a frenzied boom and then the hopeless failure of the companies which have not been connected with them closely enough."*

As a result, after 1900, concentration in Germany progressed with giant strides. Up to 1900 there had been seven or eight "groups" in the electrical industry. Each consisted of several companies (altogether there were 28) and each was backed by from 2 to 11 banks. Between 1908 and 1912 all these groups were merged into two, or one. The following diagram shows the process:

Groups in the Electrical Industry:

Prior to 1900:	Felten & Guillaume	Lahmeyer	Union A.E.G.	Siemens & Halske	Schuckert & Co.	Berg- mann	Kum- mer
	Felten & Lahmeyer		A.E.G. (G.E.C.)	Siemens & Halske-Schuckert		Berg- mann	Failed in 1900
By 1912:	A.E.G. (G.E.C.)			Siemens & Halske-Schuckert			

(In close "co-operation" since 1908)

The famous A.E.G. (General Electric Company), which grew up in this way, controls 175 to 200 companies (through the "holding" system), and a total capital of approximately 1,500 *million* marks. Of direct agencies abroad alone, it has thirty-four, of which twelve are joint-stock companies, in more than ten countries. As early as 1904 the amount of capital invested abroad by the German electrical industry was estimated at 233 million marks. Of this sum, 62 million were invested in Russia. Needless to say, the A.E.G. is a huge "combine"—its manufacturing companies alone number no less than sixteen—producing the most diverse articles, from cables and insulators to motor-cars and flying machines.

But concentration in Europe was also a component part of the process of concentration in America, which developed in the following way:

---

* Jeidels, op. cit., S. 232.

General Electric Company

United States:	Thomson-Houston Co. establishes a firm in Europe	Edison Co. establishes in Europe the French Edison Co. which transfers its patents to the German firm
Germany:	Union Electric Co.	General Electric Co. (A.E.G.)

General Electric Co. (A.E.G.)

Thus, *two* electrical "great powers" were formed: "there are no other electrical companies in the world *completely* independent of them," wrote Heining in his article "The Path of the Electric Trust". An idea, although far from complete, of the turnover and the size of the enterprises of the two "trusts" can be obtained from the following figures:

		Turnover (000,000 marks)	Number of employees	Net profits (000,000 marks)
America: General Electric Co. (G.E.C.) . . .	1907:	252	28,000	35.4
	1910:	298	32,000	45.6
Germany: General Electric Co. (A.E.G.) . . .	1907:	216	30,700	14.5
	1911:	362	60,800	21.7

And then, in 1907, the German and American trusts concluded an agreement by which they divided the world between them. Competition between them ceased. The American General Electric Company (G.E.C.) "got" the United States and Canada. The German General Electric Company (A.E.G.) "got" Germany, Austria, Russia, Holland, Denmark, Switzerland, Turkey and the Balkans. Special agreements, naturally secret, were concluded regarding the penetration of "daughter companies" into new branches of industry, into "new" countries formally not yet allotted. The two trusts were to exchange inventions and experiments.*

The difficulty of competing against this trust, actually a single world-wide trust controlling a capital of several thousand million, with "branches", agencies, representatives, connections, etc., in every

---

* Riesser, op. cit.; Diouritch, op. cit., p. 239; Kurt Heinig, op. cit.

corner of the world, is self-evident. But the division of the world between two powerful trusts does not preclude *redivision* if the relation of forces changes as a result of uneven development, war, bankruptcy, etc.

An instructive example of an attempt at such a redivision, of the struggle for redivision, is provided by the oil industry.

"The world oil market," wrote Jeidels in 1905, "is even today still divided between two great financial groups—Rockefeller's American Standard Oil Co., and Rothschild and Nobel, the controlling interests of the Russian oilfields in Baku. The two groups are closely connected. But for several years five enemies have been threatening their monopoly"*: 1) the exhaustion of the American oilfields; 2) the competition of the firm of Mantashev of Baku; 3) the Austrian oilfields; 4) the Rumanian oilfields; 5) the overseas oilfields, particularly in the Dutch colonies (the extremely rich firms, Samuel, and Shell, also connected with British capital). The three last groups are connected with the big German banks, headed by the huge Deutsche Bank. These banks independently and systematically developed the oil industry in Rumania, for example, in order to have a foothold of their "own". In 1907, the foreign capital invested in the Rumanian oil industry was estimated at 185 million francs, of which 74 million was German capital.**

A struggle began for the "division of the world", as, in fact, it is called in economic literature. On the one hand, the Rockefeller "oil trust" wanted to lay its hands on *everything*; it formed a "daughter company" *right in* Holland, and bought up oilfields in the Dutch Indies, in order to strike at its principal enemy, the Anglo-Dutch Shell trust. On the other hand, the Deutsche Bank and the other German banks aimed at "retaining" Rumania "for themselves" and at uniting her with Russia against Rockefeller. The latter possessed far more capital and an excellent system of oil transportation and distribution. The struggle had to end, and did end in 1907, with the utter defeat of the Deutsche Bank, which was confronted with the alternative: either to liquidate its "oil interests" and lose millions, or submit. It chose to submit, and concluded a very disadvantageous agreement with the "oil trust". The Deutsche Bank agreed "not to attempt anything which might injure American interests". Provision was made, however, for the annulment of the agreement in the event of Germany establishing a state oil monopoly.

Then the "comedy of oil" began. One of the German finance kings, von Gwinner, a director of the Deutsche Bank, through his private secretary, Stauss, launched a campaign *for* a state oil monopoly. The gigantic machine of the huge German bank and all its wide

---

* Jeidels, op. cit., S. 192-193.
** Diouritch, op. cit., p. 245-246.

"connections" were set in motion. The press bubbled over with "patriotic" indignation against the "yoke" of the American trust, and, on March 15, 1911, the Reichstag, by an almost unanimous vote, adopted a motion asking the government to introduce a bill for the establishment of an oil monopoly. The government seized upon this "popular" idea, and the game of the Deutsche Bank, which hoped to cheat its American counterpart and improve its business by a state monopoly, appeared to have been won. The German oil magnates already saw visions of enormous profits, which would not be less than those of the Russian sugar refiners.... But, firstly, the big German banks quarrelled among themselves over the division of the spoils. The Disconto-Gesellschaft exposed the covetous aims of the Deutsche Bank; secondly, the government took fright at the prospect of a struggle with Rockefeller, for it was very doubtful whether Germany could be sure of obtaining oil from other sources (the Rumanian output was small); thirdly, just at that time the 1913 credits of a thousand million marks were voted for Germany's war preparations. The oil monopoly project was postponed. The Rockefeller "oil trust" came out of the struggle, for the time being, victorious.

The Berlin review, *Die Bank*, wrote in this connection that Germany could fight the oil trust only by establishing an electricity monopoly and by converting water-power into cheap electricity. "But," the author added, "the electricity monopoly will come when the producers need it, that is to say, when the next great crash in the electrical industry is imminent, and when the gigantic, expensive power stations now being put up at great cost everywhere by private electrical concerns, which are already obtaining certain franchises from towns, from states, etc., can no longer work at a profit. Water-power will then have to be used. But it will be impossible to convert it into cheap electricity at state expense; it will also have to be handed over to a 'private monopoly controlled by the state', because private industry has already concluded a number of contracts and has stipulated for heavy compensation.... So it was with the nitrate monopoly, so it is with the oil monopoly, so it will be with the electric power monopoly. It is time our state socialists, who allow themselves to be blinded by a beautiful principle, understood, at last, that in Germany the monopolies have never pursued the aim, nor have they had the result, of benefiting the consumer, or even of handing over to the state part of the promoter's profits; they have served only to facilitate, at the expense of the state, the recovery of private industries which were on the verge of bankruptcy."[*]

Such are the valuable admissions which the German bourgeois economists are forced to make. We see plainly here how private

---

[*] *Die Bank*, 1912, 2, S. 629, 1036; 1913; 1, 388.

and state monopolies are interwoven in the epoch of finance capital; how both are but separate links in the imperialist struggle between the big monopolists for the division of the world.

In merchant shipping, the tremendous development of concentration has ended also in the division of the world. In Germany two powerful companies have come to the fore: the Hamburg-Amerika and the Norddeutscher Lloyd, each having a capital of 200 million marks (in stocks and bonds) and possessing shipping tonnage to the value of 185 to 189 million marks. On the other hand, in America, on January 1, 1903, the International Mercantile Marine Co., known as the Morgan trust was formed; it united nine American and British steamship companies, and possessed a capital of 120 million dollars (480 million marks). As early as 1903, the German giants and this American-British trust concluded an agreement to divide the world with a consequent division of profits. The German companies undertook not to compete in the Anglo-American traffic. Which ports were to be "allotted" to each was precisely stipulated; a joint committee of control was set up, etc. This agreement was concluded for twenty years, with the prudent provision for its annulment in the event of war.*

Extremely instructive also is the story of the formation of the International Rail Cartel. The first attempt of the British, Belgian and German rail manufacturers to form such a cartel was made as early as 1884, during a severe industrial depression. The manufacturers agreed not to compete with one another in the home markets of the countries involved, and they divided the foreign markets in the following quotas: Great Britain, 66 per cent; Germany, 27 per cent; Belgium, 7 per cent. India was reserved entirely for Great Britain. Joint war was declared against a British firm which remained outside the cartel, the cost of which was met by a percentage levy on all sales. But in 1886 the cartel collapsed when two British firms retired from it. It is characteristic that agreement could not be achieved during subsequent boom periods.

At the beginning of 1904, the German steel syndicate was formed. In November 1904, the International Rail Cartel was revived, with the following quotas: Britain, 53.5 per cent; Germany, 28.83 per cent; Belgium, 17.67 per cent. France came in later and received 4.8 per cent, 5.8 per cent and 6.4 per cent in the first, second and third year respectively, over and above the 100 per cent limit, i.e., out of a total of 104.8 per cent, etc. In 1905, the United States Steel Corporation entered the cartel; then Austria and Spain. "At the present time," wrote Vogelstein in 1910, "the division of the world is complete, and the big consumers, primarily the state railways— since the world has been parcelled out without consideration for

---

* Riesser, op. cit., S. 125.

their interests—can now dwell like the poet in the heavens of Jupiter."*

Let me also mention the International Zinc Syndicate which was established in 1909 and which precisely apportioned output among five groups of factories: German, Belgian, French, Spanish and British; and also the International Dynamite Trust, which, Liefmann says, is "quite a modern, close alliance of all the German explosives manufacturers who, with the French and American dynamite manufacturers, organised in a similar manner, have divided the whole world among themselves, so to speak".**

Liefmann calculated that in 1897 there were altogether about forty international cartels in which Germany had a share, while in 1910 there were about a hundred. Certain bourgeois writers (now joined by Karl Kautsky, who has completely abandoned the Marxist position he had held, for example, in 1909) have expressed the opinion that international cartels, being one of the most striking expressions of the internationalisation of capital, give the hope of peace among nations under capitalism. Theoretically, this opinion is absolutely absurd, while in practice it is sophistry and a dishonest defence of the worst opportunism. International cartels show to what point capitalist monopolies have developed, and *the object* of the struggle between the various capitalist associations. This last circumstance is the most important; it alone shows us the historico-economic meaning of what is taking place; for the *forms* of the struggle may and do constantly change in accordance with varying, relatively specific and temporary causes, but the *substance* of the struggle, its class *content*, positively *cannot* change while classes exist. Naturally, it is in the interests of, for example, the German bourgeoisie, to whose side Kautsky has in effect gone over in his theoretical arguments (I shall deal with this later), to obscure the *substance* of the present economic struggle (the division of the world) and to emphasise now this and now another *form* of the struggle. Kautsky makes the same mistake. Of course, we have in mind not only the German bourgeoisie, but the bourgeoisie all over the world. The capitalists divide the world, not out of any particular malice, but because the degree of concentration which has been reached forces them to adopt this method in order to obtain profits. And they divide it "in proportion to capital", "in proportion to strength", because there cannot be any other method of division under commodity production and capitalism. But strength varies with the degree of economic and political development. In order to understand what is taking place, it is necessary to know what questions are settled by the changes in strength. The question as to whether these changes are

---

* Vogelstein, *Organisationsformen*, S. 100.
** Liefmann, *Kartelle und Trusts*, 2, A., S. 161.

"purely" economic or *non*-economic (e.g., military) is a secondary one, which cannot in the least affect fundamental views on the latest epoch of capitalism. To substitute the question of the form of the struggle and agreements (today peaceful, tomorrow warlike, the next day warlike again) for the question of the *substance* of the struggle and agreements between capitalist associations is to sink to the role of a sophist.

The epoch of the latest stage of capitalism shows us that certain relations between capitalist associations grow up, *based* on the economic division of the world; while parallel to and in connection with it, certain relations grow up between political alliances, between states, on the basis of the territorial division of the world, of the struggle for colonies, of the "struggle for spheres of influence".

VI. DIVISION OF THE WORLD AMONG THE GREAT POWERS

In his book, on "the territorial development of the European colonies", A. Supan,* the geographer, gives the following brief summary of this development at the end of the nineteenth century:

Percentage of Territory Belonging to the European
Colonial Powers
(Including the United States)

	1876	1900	Increase or decrease
Africa	10.8	90.4	+79.6
Polynesia	56.8	98.9	+42.1
Asia	51.5	56.6	+ 5.1
Australia	100.0	100.0	—
America	27.5	27.2	— 0.3

"The characteristic feature of this period," he concludes, "is, therefore, the division of Africa and Polynesia." As there are no unoccupied territories—that is, territories that do not belong to any state—in Asia and America, it is necessary to amplify Supan's conclusion and say that the characteristic feature of the period under review is the final partitioning of the globe—final, not in the sense that *repartition* is impossible; on the contrary, repartitions are possible and inevitable—but in the sense that the colonial policy of the capitalist countries has *completed* the seizure of the unoccupied territories on our planet. For the first time the world is completely divided up, so that in the future *only* redivision is possible, i.e., ter-

---

* A. Supan, *Die territoriale Entwicklung der europäischen Kolonien*, 1906, S. 254.

ritories can only pass from one "owner" to another, instead of passing as ownerless territory to an "owner".

Hence, we are living in a peculiar epoch of world colonial policy, which is most closely connected with the "latest stage in the development of capitalism", with finance capital. For this reason, it is essential first of all to deal in greater detail with the facts, in order to ascertain as exactly as possible what distinguishes this epoch from those preceding it, and what the present situation is. In the first place, two questions of fact arise here: is an intensification of colonial policy, a sharpening of the struggle for colonies, observed precisely in the epoch of finance capital? And how, in this respect, is the world divided at the present time?

The American writer, Morris, in his book on the history of colonisation,* made an attempt to sum up the data on the colonial possessions of Great Britain, France and Germany during different periods of the nineteenth century. The following is a brief summary of the results he has obtained:

Colonial Possessions

Year	Great Britain		France		Germany	
	Area (000,000 sq. m.)	Pop. (000,000)	Area (000,000 sq. m.)	Pop. (000,000)	Area (000,000 sq. m.)	Pop. (000,000)
1815-1830	?	126.4	0.02	0.5	—	—
1860	2.5	145.1	0.2	3.4	--	—
1880	7.7	267.9	0.7	7.5	—	—
1899	9.3	309.0	3.7	56.4	1.0	14.7

For Great Britain, the period of the enormous expansion of colonial conquests was that between 1860 and 1880, and it was also very considerable in the last twenty years of the nineteenth century. For France and Germany this period falls precisely in these twenty years. We saw above that the development of pre-monopoly capitalism, of capitalism in which free competition was predominant, reached its limit in the 1860s and 1870s. We now see that it is *precisely after that period* that the tremendous "boom" in colonial conquests begins, and that the struggle for the territorial division of the world becomes extraordinarily sharp. It is beyond doubt, therefore, that capitalism's transition to the stage of monopoly capitalism, to finance capital, *is connected* with the intensification of the struggle for the partitioning of the world.

Hobson, in his work on imperialism, marks the years 1884-1900 as the epoch of intensified "expansion" of the chief European states. According to his estimate, Great Britain during these years acquired

---

* Henry C. Morris, *The History of Colonisation*, New York, 1900, Vol. II, p. 88; Vol. I, p. 419; Vol. II, p. 304.

3,700,000 square miles of territory with 57,000,000 inhabitants; France, 3,600,000 square miles with 36,500,000; Germany, 1,000,000 square miles with 14,700,000; Belgium, 900,000 square miles with 30,000,000; Portugal, 800,000 square miles with 9,000,000 inhabitants. The scramble for colonies by all the capitalist states at the end of the nineteenth century and particularly since the 1880s is a commonly known fact in the history of diplomacy and of foreign policy.

In the most flourishing period of free competition in Great Britain, i.e., between 1840 and 1860, the leading British bourgeois politicians were *opposed* to colonial policy and were of the opinion that the liberation of the colonies, their complete separation from Britain, was inevitable and desirable. M. Beer, in an article, "Modern British Imperialism",* published in 1898, shows that in 1852, Disraeli, a statesman who was generally inclined towards imperialism, declared: "The colonies are millstones round our necks." But at the end of the nineteenth century the British heroes of the hour were Cecil Rhodes and Joseph Chamberlain, who openly advocated imperialism and applied the imperialist policy in the most cynical manner!

It is not without interest to observe that even then these leading British bourgeois politicians saw the connection between what might be called the purely economic and the socio-political roots of modern imperialism. Chamberlain advocated imperialism as a "true, wise and economical policy", and pointed particularly to the German, American and Belgian competition which Great Britain was encountering in the world market. Salvation lies in monopoly, said the capitalists as they formed cartels, syndicates and trusts. Salvation lies in monopoly, echoed the political leaders of the bourgeoisie, hastening to appropriate the parts of the world not yet shared out. And Cecil Rhodes, we are informed by his intimate friend, the journalist Stead, expressed his imperialist views to him in 1895 in the following terms: "I was in the East End of London [a working-class quarter] yesterday and attended a meeting of the unemployed. I listened to the wild speeches, which were just a cry for 'bread! bread!' and on my way home I pondered over the scene and I became more than ever convinced of the importance of imperialism.... My cherished idea is a solution for the social problem, i.e., in order to save the 40,000,000 inhabitants of the United Kingdom from a bloody civil war, we colonial statesmen must acquire new lands to settle the surplus population, to provide new markets for the goods produced in the factories and mines. The Empire, as I have always said, is a bread and butter question. If you want to avoid civil war, you must become imperialists."**

---

* *Die Neue Zeit*, XVI, I, 1898, S. 302.
** Ibid., S. 304.

That was said in 1895 by Cecil Rhodes, millionaire, a king of finance, the man who was mainly responsible for the Anglo-Boer War. True, his defence of imperialism is crude and cynical, but in substance it does not differ from the "theory" advocated by Messrs. Maslov, Südekum, Potresov, David, the founder of Russian Marxism and others. Cecil Rhodes was a somewhat more honest social-chauvinist....

To present as precise a picture as possible of the territorial division of the world and of the changes which have occurred during the last decades in this respect, I shall utilise the data furnished by Supan in the work already quoted on the colonial possessions of all the powers of the world. Supan takes the years 1876 and 1900; I shall take the year 1876—a year very aptly selected, for it is precisely by that time that the pre-monopolist stage of development of West-European capitalism can be said to have been, in the main, completed—and the year 1914, and instead of Supan's figures I shall quote the more recent statistics of Hübner's *Geographical and Statistical Tables*. Supan gives figures only for colonies; I think it useful, in order to present a complete picture of the division of the world, to add brief data on non-colonial and semi-colonial countries, in which category I place Persia, China and Turkey: the first of these countries is already almost completely a colony, the second and third are becoming such.

We thus get the following result:

Colonial Possessions of the Great Powers
(000,000 square kilometres and 000,000 inhabitants)

	Colonies				Metropolitan countries		Total	
	1876		1914		1914		1914	
	Area	Pop.	Area	Pop.	Area	Pop.	Area	Pop.
Great Britain	22.5	251.9	33.5	393.5	0.3	46.5	33.8	440.0
Russia. . .	17.0	15.9	17.4	33.2	5,4	136.2	22.8	169.4
France . .	0.9	6.0	10.6	55.5	0.5	39.6	11.1	95.1
Germany . .	—	—	2.9	12.3	0.5	64.9	3.4	77.2
United States	—	—	0.3	9.7	9.4	97.0	9.7	106.7
Japan. . .	—	—	0.3	19.2	0.4	53.0	0.7	72.2
Total for 6 Great Powers	40.4	273.8	65.0	523.4	16.5	437.2	81.5	960.6

Colonies of other powers (Belgium, Holland, etc.) 9.9 45.3
Semi-colonial countries (Persia, China, Turkey) 14.5 361.2
Other countries 28.0 289.9

Total for the world 133.9 1,657.0

We clearly see from these figures how "complete" was the partition of the world at the turn of the twentieth century. After 1876 colonial possessions increased to enormous dimensions, by more than fifty per cent, from 40,000,000 to 65,000,000 square kilometres for the six biggest powers; the increase amounts to 25,000,000 square kilometres, fifty per cent more than the area of the metropolitan countries (16,500,000 square kilometres). In 1876 three powers had no colonies, and a fourth, France, had scarcely any. By 1914 these four powers had acquired colonies with an area of 14,100,000 square kilometres, i.e., about half as much again as the area of Europe, with a population of nearly 100,000,000. The unevenness in the rate of expansion of colonial possessions is very great. If, for instance, we compare France, Germany and Japan, which do not differ very much in area and population, we see that the first has acquired almost three times as much colonial territory as the other two combined. In regard to finance capital, France, at the beginning of the period we are considering, was also, perhaps, several times richer than Germany and Japan put together. In addition to, and on the basis of, purely economic conditions, geographical and other conditions also affect the dimensions of colonial possessions. However strong the process of levelling the world, of levelling the economic and living conditions in different countries, may have been in the past decades as a result of the pressure of large-scale industry, exchange and finance capital, considerable differences still remain; and among the six countries mentioned we see, firstly, young capitalist countries (America, Germany, Japan) whose progress has been extraordinarily rapid; secondly, countries with an old capitalist development (France and Great Britain), whose progress lately has been much slower than that of the previously mentioned countries, and thirdly, a country most backward economically (Russia), where modern capitalist imperialism is enmeshed, so to speak, in a particularly close network of pre-capitalist relations.

Alongside the colonial possessions of the Great Powers, we have placed the small colonies of the small states, which are, so to speak, the next objects of a possible and probable "redivision" of colonies. These small states mostly retain their colonies only because the big powers are torn by conflicting interests, friction, etc., which prevent them from coming to an agreement on the division of the spoils. As to the "semi-colonial" states, they provide an example of the transitional forms which are to be found in all spheres of nature and society. Finance capital is such a great, such a decisive, you might say, force in all economic and in all international relations, that it is capable of subjecting, and actually does subject, to itself even states enjoying the fullest political independence; we shall shortly see examples of this. Of course, finance capital finds most "convenient", and derives the greatest profit from, a *form* of subjection which involves the loss of the political independence of the subjected countries and peoples. In this respect, the semi-colonial countries provide a typical example of the "middle stage". It is natural that the struggle for these semi-dependent countries should have become particularly bitter in the epoch of finance-capital, when the rest of the world has already been divided up.

Colonial policy and imperialism existed before the latest stage of capitalism, and even before capitalism. Rome, founded on slavery, pursued a colonial policy and practised imperialism. But "general" disquisitions on imperialism, which ignore, or put into the background, the fundamental difference between socio-economic formations, inevitably turn into the most vapid banality or bragging, like the comparison: "Greater Rome and Greater Britain."* Even the capitalist colonial policy of *previous* stages of capitalism is essentially different from the colonial policy of finance capital.

The principal feature of the latest stage of capitalism is the domination of monopolist associations of big employers. These monopolies are most firmly established when *all* the sources of raw materials are captured by one group, and we have seen with what zeal the international capitalist associations exert every effort to deprive their rivals of all opportunity of competing, to buy up, for example, iron-fields, oilfields, etc. Colonial possession alone gives the monopolies complete guarantee against all contingencies in the struggle against competitors, including the case of the adversary wanting to be protected by a law establishing a state monopoly. The more capitalism is developed, the more strongly the shortage of raw materials is felt, the more intense the competition and the hunt for sources of raw materials throughout the whole world, the more desperate the struggle for the acquisition of colonies.

"It may be asserted," writes Schilder, "although it may sound paradoxical to some, that in the more or less foreseeable future the growth of the urban and industrial population is more likely to be hindered by a shortage of raw materials for industry than by a shortage of food." For example, there is a growing shortage of timber—the price of which is steadily rising—of leather, and of raw materials for the textile industry. "Associations of manufacturers are making efforts to create an equilibrium between agriculture and industry in the whole of world economy; as an example of this we might mention the International Federation of Cotton Spinners' Associations in several of the most important industrial countries, founded in 1904, and the European Federation of Flax Spinners' Associations, founded on the same model in 1910."**

---

* C. P. Lucas, *Greater Rome and Greater Britain*, Oxford, 1912, or the Earl of Cromer, *Ancient and Modern Imperialism*, London, 1910.
** Schilder, op. cit., S. 38-42.

Of course, the bourgeois reformists, and among them particularly the present-day adherents of Kautsky, try to belittle the importance of facts of this kind by arguing that raw materials "could be" obtained in the open market without a "costly and dangerous" colonial policy; and that the supply of raw materials "could be" increased enormously by "simply" improving conditions in agriculture in general. But such arguments become an apology for imperialism, an attempt to paint it in bright colours, because they ignore the principal feature of the latest stage of capitalism: monopolies. The free market is becoming more and more a thing of the past; monopolist syndicates and trusts are restricting it with every passing day, and "simply" improving conditions in agriculture means improving the conditions of the masses, raising wages and reducing profits. Where, except in the imagination of sentimental reformists, are there any trusts capable of concerning themselves with the condition of the masses instead of the conquest of colonies?

Finance capital is interested not only in the already discovered sources of raw materials but also in potential sources, because present-day technical development is extremely rapid, and land which is useless today may be improved tomorrow if new methods are devised (to this end a big bank can equip a special expedition of engineers, agricultural experts, etc.), and if large amounts of capital are invested. This also applies to prospecting for minerals, to new methods of processing up and utilising raw materials, etc., etc. Hence, the inevitable striving of finance capital to enlarge its spheres of influence and even its actual territory. In the same way that the trusts capitalise their property at two or three times its value, taking into account its "potential" (and not actual) profits and the further results of monopoly, so finance capital in general strives to seize the largest possible amount of land of all kinds in all places, and by every means, taking into account potential sources of raw materials and fearing to be left behind in the fierce struggle for the last remnants of independent territory, or for the repartition of those territories that have been already divided.

The British capitalists are exerting every effort to develop cotton growing in *their* colony, Egypt (in 1904, out of 2,300,000 hectares of land under cultivation, 600,000, or more than one-fourth were under cotton); the Russians are doing the same in *their* colony, Turkestan, because in this way they will be in a better position to defeat their foreign competitors, to monopolise the sources of raw materials and form a more economical and profitable textile trust in which *all* the processes of cotton production and manufacturing will be "combined" and concentrated in the hands of one set of owners.

The interests pursued in exporting capital also give an impetus to the conquest of colonies, for in the colonial market it is easier to employ monopoly methods (and sometimes they are the only methods that can be employed) to eliminate competition, to ensure supplies, to secure the necessary "connections", etc.

The non-economic superstructure which grows up on the basis of finance capital, its politics and its ideology, stimulates the striving for colonial conquest. "Finance capital does not want liberty, it wants domination," as Hilferding very truly says. And a French bourgeois writer, developing and supplementing, as it were, the ideas of Cecil Rhodes quoted above,* writes that social causes should be added to the economic causes of modern colonial policy: "Owing to the growing complexities of life and the difficulties which weigh not only on the masses of the workers, but also on the middle classes, 'impatience, irritation and hatred are accumulating in all the countries of the old civilisation and are becoming a menace to public order; the energy which is being hurled out of the definite class channel must be given employment abroad in order to avert an explosion at home'."**

Since we are speaking of colonial policy in the epoch of capitalist imperialism, it must be observed that finance capital and its foreign policy, which is the struggle of the great powers for the economic and political division of the world, give rise to a number of *transitional* forms of state dependence. Not only are the two main groups of countries, those owning colonies, and the colonies themselves, but also the diverse forms of dependent countries which, politically, are formally independent, but in fact, are enmeshed in the net of financial and diplomatic dependence, are typical of this epoch. We have already referred to one form of dependence—the semi-colony. An example of another is provided by Argentina.

"South America, and especially Argentina," writes Schulze-Gaevernitz in his work on British imperialism, "is so dependent financially on London that it ought to be described as almost a British commercial colony."*** Basing himself on the reports of the Austro-Hungarian Consul at Buenos Aires for 1909, Schilder estimated the amount of British capital invested in Argentina at 8,750 million francs. It is not difficult to imagine what strong connections British finance capital (and its faithful "friend", diplomacy) thereby acquires with the Argentine bourgeoisie, with the circles that control the whole of that country's economic and political life.

A somewhat different form of financial and diplomatic dependence, accompanied by political independence, is presented by Por-

---

* See pp. 225-26 of the present volume.—*Ed.*
** Wahl, *La France aux colonies* quoted by Henri Russier, *Le Partage de l'Océanie*, Paris, 1905, p. 165.
*** Schulze-Gaevernitz, *Britischer Imperialismus und englischer Freihandel zu Beginn des 20-ten Jahrhunderts*, Leipzig, 1906, S. 318. Sartorius v. Waltershausen says the same in *Das volkswirtschaftliche System der Kapitalanlage im Auslande*, Berlin, 1907, S. 46.

tugal. Portugal is an independent sovereign state, but actually, for more than two hundred years, since the war of the Spanish Succession (1701-14), it has been a British protectorate. Great Britain has protected Portugal and her colonies in order to fortify her own positions in the fight against her rivals, Spain and France. In return Great Britain has received commercial privileges, preferential conditions for importing goods and especially capital into Portugal and the Portuguese colonies, the right to use the ports and islands of Portugal, her telegraph cables, etc., etc.* Relations of this kind have always existed between big and little states, but in the epoch of capitalist imperialism they become a general system, they form part of the sum total of "divide the world" relations and become links in the chain of operations of world finance capital.

In order to finish with the question of the division of the world, I must make the following additional observation. This question was raised quite openly and definitely not only in American literature after the Spanish-American War, and in English literature after the Anglo-Boer War, at the very end of the nineteenth century and the beginning of the twentieth; not only has German literature, which has "most jealously" watched "British imperialism", systematically given its appraisal of this fact. This question has also been raised in French bourgeois literature as definitely and broadly as is thinkable from the bourgeois point of view. Let me quote Driault, the historian, who, in his book, *Political and Social Problems at the End of the Nineteenth Century*, in the chapter "The Great Powers and the Division of the World", wrote the following: "During the past few years, all the free territory of the globe, with the exception of China, has been occupied by the powers of Europe and North America. This has already brought about several conflicts and shifts of spheres of influence, and these foreshadow more terrible upheavals in the near future. For it is necessary to make haste. The nations which have not yet made provision for themselves run the risk of never receiving their share and never participating in the tremendous exploitation of the globe which will be one of the most essential features of the next century [i.e., the twentieth]. That is why all Europe and America have lately been afflicted with the fever of colonial expansion, of 'imperialism', that most noteworthy feature of the end of the nineteenth century." And the author added: "In this partition of the world, in this furious hunt for the treasures and the big markets of the globe, the relative strength of the empires founded in this nineteenth century is totally out of proportion to the place occupied in Europe by the nations which founded them. The dominant powers in Europe, the arbiters of her destiny, are *not* equally preponderant in the whole world. And, as colonial might,

---

* Schilder, op. cit., Vol. I, S. 160-161.

the hope of controlling as yet unassessed wealth, will evidently react upon the relative strength of the European powers, the colonial question—'imperialism', if you will—which has already modified the political conditions of Europe itself, will modify them more and more."*

VII. IMPERIALISM AS A SPECIAL STAGE OF CAPITALISM

We must now try to sum up, to draw together the threads of what has been said above on the subject of imperialism. Imperialism emerged as the development and direct continuation of the fundamental characteristics of capitalism in general. But capitalism only became capitalist imperialism at a definite and very high stage of its development, when certain of its fundamental characteristics began to change into their opposites, when the features of the epoch of transition from capitalism to a higher social and economic system had taken shape and revealed themselves in all spheres. Economically, the main thing in this process is the displacement of capitalist free competition by capitalist monopoly. Free competition is the basic feature of capitalism, and of commodity production generally; monopoly is the exact opposite of free competition, but we have seen the latter being transformed into monopoly before our eyes, creating large-scale industry and forcing out small industry, replacing large-scale by still larger-scale industry, and carrying concentration of production and capital to the point where out of it has grown and is growing monopoly: cartels, syndicates and trusts, and merging with them, the capital of a dozen or so banks, which manipulate thousands of millions. At the same time the monopolies, which have grown out of free competition, do not eliminate the latter, but exist above it and alongside it, and thereby give rise to a number of very acute, intense antagonisms, frictions and conflicts. Monopoly is the transition from capitalism to a higher system.

If it were necessary to give the briefest possible definition of imperialism we should have to say that imperialism is the monopoly stage of capitalism. Such a definition would include what is most important, for, on the one hand, finance capital is the bank capital of a few very big monopolist banks, merged with the capital of the monopolist associations of industrialists; and, on the other hand, the division of the world is the transition from a colonial policy which has extended without hindrance to territories unseized by any capitalist power, to a colonial policy of monopolist posses-

---

* J.-E. Driault, *Problèmes politiques et sociaux*, Paris, 1900, p. 299.

sion of the territory of the world, which has been completely divided up.

But very brief definitions, although convenient, for they sum up the main points, are nevertheless inadequate, since we have to deduce from them some especially important features of the phenomenon that has to be defined. And so, without forgetting the conditional and relative value of all definitions in general, which can never embrace all the concatenations of a phenomenon in its full development, we must give a definition of imperialism that will include the following five of its basic features:

1) the concentration of production and capital has developed to such a high stage that it has created monopolies which play a decisive role in economic life; 2) the merging of bank capital with industrial capital, and the creation, on the basis of this "finance capital", of a financial oligarchy; 3) the export of capital as distinguished from the export of commodities acquires exceptional importance; 4) the formation of international monopolist capitalist associations which share the world among themselves, and 5) the territorial division of the whole world among the biggest capitalist powers is completed. Imperialism is capitalism at that stage of development at which the dominance of monopolies and finance capital is established; in which the export of capital has acquired pronounced importance; in which the division of the world among the international trusts has begun, in which the division of all territories of the globe among the biggest capitalist powers has been completed.

We shall see later that imperialism can and must be defined differently if we bear in mind not only the basic, purely economic concepts—to which the above definition is limited—but also the historical place of this stage of capitalism in relation to capitalism in general, or the relation between imperialism and the two main trends in the working-class movement. The thing to be noted at this point is that imperialism, as interpreted above, undoubtedly represents a special stage in the development of capitalism. To enable the reader to obtain the most well-grounded idea of imperialism, I deliberately tried to quote as extensively as possible *bourgeois* economists who have to admit the particularly incontrovertible facts concerning the latest stage of capitalist economy. With the same object in view, I have quoted detailed statistics which enable one to see to what degree bank capital, etc., has grown, in what precisely the transformation of quantity into quality, of developed capitalism into imperialism, was expressed. Needless to say, of course, all boundaries in nature and in society are conventional and changeable, and it would be absurd to argue, for example, about the particular year or decade in which imperialism "definitely" became established.

In the matter of defining imperialism, however, we have to enter into controversy, primarily, with Karl Kautsky, the principal Marxist theoretician of the epoch of the so-called Second International—that is, of the twenty-five years between 1889 and 1914. The fundamental ideas expressed in our definition of imperialism were very resolutely attacked by Kautsky in 1915, and even in November 1914, when he said that imperialism must not be regarded as a "phase" or stage of economy, but as a policy, a definite policy "preferred" by finance capital; that imperialism must not be "identified" with "present-day capitalism"; that if imperialism is to be understood to mean "all the phenomena of present-day capitalism"—cartels, protection, the domination of the financiers, and colonial policy—then the question as to whether imperialism is necessary to capitalism becomes reduced to the "flattest tautology", because, in that case, "imperialism is naturally a vital necessity for capitalism", and so on. The best way to present Kautsky's idea is to quote his own definition of imperialism, which is diametrically opposed to the substance of the ideas which I have set forth (for the objections coming from the camp of the German Marxists, who have been advocating similar ideas for many years already, have been long known to Kautsky as the objections of a definite trend in Marxism).

Kautsky's definition is as follows:

"Imperialism is a product of highly developed industrial capitalism. It consists in the striving of every industrial capitalist nation to bring under its control or to annex all large areas of *agrarian* [Kautsky's italics] territory, irrespective of what nations inhabit it."*

This definition is of no use at all because it one-sidedly, i.e., arbitrarily, singles out only the national question (although the latter is extremely important in itself as well as in its relation to imperialism), it arbitrarily and *inaccurately* connects this question *only* with industrial capital in the countries which annex other nations, and in an equally arbitrary and inaccurate manner pushes into the forefront the annexation of agrarian regions.

Imperialism is a striving for annexations—this is what the *political* part of Kautsky's definition amounts to. It is correct, but very incomplete, for politically, imperialism is, in general, a striving towards violence and reaction. For the moment, however, we are interested in the *economic* aspect of the question, which Kautsky *himself* introduced into *his* definition. The inaccuracies in Kautsky's definition are glaring. The characteristic feature of imperialism is *not* industrial *but* finance capital. It is not an accident that in France it was precisely the extraordinarily rapid development of *finance*

---

* *Die Neue Zeit*, 1914, 2 (B. 32), S. 909, Sept. 11, 1914; cf. 1915, 2, S. 107 et seq.

capital, and the weakening of industrial capital, that from the eighties onwards, gave rise to the extreme intensification of annexationist (colonial) policy. The characteristic feature of imperialism is precisely that it strives to annex *not only* agrarian territories, but even most highly industrialised regions (German appetite for Belgium; French appetite for Lorraine), because (1) the fact that the world is already partitioned obliges those contemplating a *redivision* to reach out for *every kind* of territory, and (2) an essential feature of imperialism is the rivalry between several great powers in the striving for hegemony, i.e., for the conquest of territory, not so much directly for themselves as to weaken the adversary and undermine *his* hegemony. (Belgium is particularly important for Germany as a base for operations against Britain; Britain needs Baghdad as a base for operations against Germany, etc.)

Kautsky refers especially—and repeatedly—to English writers who, he alleges, have given a purely political meaning to the word "imperialism" in the sense that he, Kautsky, understands it. We take up the work by the English writer Hobson, *Imperialism*, which appeared in 1902, and there we read:

"The new imperialism differs from the older, first, in substituting for the ambition of a single growing empire the theory and the practice of competing empires, each motivated by similar lusts of political aggrandizement and commercial gain; secondly, in the dominance of financial or investing over mercantile interests."*

We see that Kautsky is absolutely wrong in referring to English writers generally (unless he meant the vulgar English imperialists, or the avowed apologists for imperialism). We see that Kautsky, while claiming that he continues to advocate Marxism, as a matter of fact takes a step backward compared with the *social-liberal* Hobson, who *more correctly* takes into account two "historically concrete" (Kautsky's definition is a mockery of historical concreteness!) features of modern imperialism: 1) the competition between *several* imperialisms, and 2) the predominance of the financier over the merchant. If it is chiefly a question of the annexation of agrarian countries by industrial countries, then the role of the merchant it put in the forefront.

Kautsky's definition is not only wrong and un-Marxist. It serves as a basis for a whole system of views which signify a rupture with Marxist theory and Marxist practice all along the line. I shall refer to this later. The argument about words which Kautsky raises as to whether the latest stage of capitalism should be called imperialism or the stage of finance capital is not worth serious attention. Call it what you will, it makes no difference. The essence of the matter is that Kautsky detaches the politics of imperialism from

---

* Hobson, *Imperialism*, London, 1902, p. 324.

its economics, speaks of annexations as being a policy "preferred" by finance capital, and opposes to it another bourgeois policy which, he alleges, is possible on this very same basis of finance capital. It follows, then, that monopolies in the economy are compatible with non-monopolistic, non-violent, non-annexationist methods in politics. It follows, then, that the territorial division of the world, which was completed during this very epoch of finance capital, and which constitutes the basis of the present peculiar forms of rivalry between the biggest capitalist states, is compatible with a non-imperialist policy. The result is a slurring-over and a blunting of the most profound contradictions of the latest stage of capitalism, instead of an exposure of their depth; the result is bourgeois reformism instead of Marxism.

Kautsky enters into controversy with the German apologist of imperialism and annexations, Cunow, who clumsily and cynically argues that imperialism is present-day capitalism; the development of capitalism is inevitable and progressive; therefore imperialism is progressive; therefore, we should grovel before it and glorify it! This is something like the caricature of the Russian Marxists which the Narodniks drew in 1894-95. They argued: if the Marxists believe that capitalism is inevitable in Russia, that it is progressive, then they ought to open a tavern and begin to implant capitalism! Kautsky's reply to Cunow is as follows: imperialism is not present-day capitalism; it is only one of the forms of the policy of present-day capitalism. This policy we can and should fight, fight imperialism, annexations, etc.

The reply seems quite plausible, but in effect it is a more subtle and more disguised (and therefore more dangerous) advocacy of conciliation with imperialism, because a "fight" against the policy of the trusts and banks that does not affect the economic basis of the trusts and banks is mere bourgeois reformism and pacifism, the benevolent and innocent expression of pious wishes. Evasion of existing contradictions, forgetting the most important of them, instead of revealing their full depth—such is Kautsky's theory, which has nothing in common with Marxism. Naturally, such a "theory" can only serve the purpose of advocating unity with the Cunows!

"From the purely economic point of view," writes Kautsky, "it is not impossible that capitalism will yet go through a new phase, that of the extension of the policy of the cartels to foreign policy, the phase of ultra-imperialism,"* i.e., of a superimperialism, of a union of the imperialisms of the whole world and not struggles among them, a phase when wars shall cease under capitalism, a

---

* *Die Neue Zeit*, 1914, 2 (B. 32), S. 921, Sept. 11, 1914. Cf. 1915, 2. S. 107 et seq.

phase of "the joint exploitation of the world by internationally united finance capital".*

We shall have to deal with this "theory of ultra-imperialism" later on in order to show in detail how decisively and completely it breaks with Marxism. At present, in keeping with the general plan of the present work, we must examine the exact economic data on this question. "From the purely economic point of view", is "ultra-imperialism" possible, or is it ultra-nonsense?

If the purely economic point of view is meant to be a "pure" abstraction, then all that can be said reduces itself to the following proposition: development is proceeding towards monopolies, hence, towards a single world monopoly, towards a single world trust. This is indisputable, but it is also as completely meaningless as is the statement that "development is proceeding" towards the manufacture of foodstuffs in laboratories. In this sense the "theory" of ultra-imperialism is no less absurd than a "theory of ultra-agriculture" would be.

If, however, we are discussing the "purely economic" conditions of the epoch of finance capital as a historically concrete epoch which began at the turn of the twentieth century, then the best reply that one can make to the lifeless abstractions of "ultra-imperialism" (which serve exclusively a most reactionary aim: that of diverting attention from the depth of *existing* antagonisms) is to contrast them with the concrete economic realities of the present-day world economy. Kautsky's utterly meaningless talk about ultra-imperialism encourages, among other things, that profoundly mistaken idea which only brings grist to the mill of the apologists of imperialism, i.e., that the rule of finance capital *lessens* the unevenness and contradictions inherent in the world economy, whereas in reality it *increases* them.

R. Calwer, in his little book, *An Introduction to the World Economy*,** made an attempt to summarise the main, purely economic data that enable one to obtain a concrete picture of the internal relations of the world economy at the turn of the twentieth century. He divides the world into five "main economic areas", as follows: 1) Central Europe (the whole of Europe with the exception of Russia and Great Britain); 2) Great Britain; 3) Russia; 4) Eastern Asia; 5) America; he includes the colonies in the "areas" of the states to which they belong and "leaves aside" a few countries not distributed according to areas, such as Persia, Afghanistan, and Arabia in Asia, Morocco and Abyssinia in Africa, etc.

Here is a brief summary of the economic data he quotes on these regions:

---

* *Die Neue Zeit*, 1915, 1, S. 144, April 30, 1915.
** R. Calwer, *Einführung in die Weltwirtschaft*, Berlin, 1906.

| | Area (000,000 sq. km.) | Population (000,000) | Transport | | Trade | Industry Output | | |
Principal economic areas			Railways (000 km.)	Mercantile fleet (000,000 tons)	Imports and exports (000,000,000 marks)	Coal	Iron	Number of cotton spindles (000,000)
						(000,000 tons)		
1) Central Europe . . .	27.6 (23.6)*	388 (146)	204	8	41	251	15	26
2) Britain	28.9 (28.6)*	398 (355)	140	11	25	249	9	51
3) Russia	22	131	63	1	3	16	3	7
4) Eastern Asia	12	389	8	1	2	8	0.02	2
5) America	30	148	379	6	14	245	14	19

We see three areas of highly developed capitalism (high development of means of transport, of trade and of industry): the Central European, the British and the American areas. Among these are three states which dominate the world: Germany, Great Britain, and the United States. Imperialist rivalry and the struggle between these countries have become extremely keen because Germany has only an insignificant area and few colonies; the creation of "Central Europe" is still a matter for the future, it is being born in the midst of a desperate struggle. For the moment the distinctive feature of the whole of Europe is political disunity. In the British and American areas, on the other hand, political concentration is very highly developed, but there is a vast disparity between the immense colonies of the one and the insignificant colonies of the other. In the colonies, however, capitalism is only beginning to develop. The struggle for South America is becoming more and more acute.

There are two areas where capitalism is little developed: Russia and Eastern Asia. In the former, the population is extremely sparse, in the latter it is extremely dense; in the former political concentration is high, in the latter it does not exist. The partitioning of China is only just beginning, and the struggle for it between Japan, the U.S., etc., is continually gaining in intensity.

Compare this reality—the vast diversity of economic and political conditions, the extreme disparity in the rate of development of the various countries, etc., and the violent struggles among the imperialist states—with Kautsky's silly little fable about "peaceful" ultra-imperialism. Is this not the reactionary attempt of a frightened philistine to hide from stern reality? Are not the international

---

* The figures in parentheses show the area and population of the colonies.

cartels which Kautsky imagines are the embryos of "ultra-imperialism" (in the same way as one "can" describe the manufacture of tablets in a laboratory as ultra-agriculture in embryo) an example of the division *and the redivision* of the world, the transition from peaceful division to non-peaceful division and vice versa? Is not American and other finance capital, which divided the whole world peacefully with Germany's participation in, for example, the international rail syndicate, or in the international mercantile shipping trust, now engaged in *redividing* the world on the basis of a new relation of forces that is being changed by methods *anything but* peaceful?

Finance capital and the trusts do not diminish but increase the differences in the rate of growth of the various parts of the world economy. Once the relation of forces is changed, what other solution of the contradictions can be found *under capitalism* than that of *force*? Railway statistics* provide remarkably exact data on the different rates of growth of capitalism and finance capital in world economy. In the last decades of imperialist development, the total length of railways has changed as follows:

	Railways (000 kilometres)		
	1890	1913	+
Europe	224	346	+122
U. S.	268	411	+143
All colonies	82 ⎫	210 ⎫	+128 ⎫
Independent and semi-independent states of Asia and America . . .	43 ⎭ 125	137 ⎭ 347	+ 94 ⎭ +222
Total . . .	617	1,104	

Thus, the development of railways has been most rapid in the colonies and in the independent (and semi-independent) states of Asia and America. Here, as we know, the finance capital of the four or five biggest capitalist states holds undisputed sway. Two hundred thousand kilometres of new railways in the colonies and in the other countries of Asia and America represent a capital of more than 40,000 million marks newly invested on particularly advantageous terms, with special guarantees of a good return and with profitable orders for steel works, etc., etc.

---

* *Statistisches Jahrbuch für das deutsche Reich, 1915*; *Archiv für Eisenbahnwesen, 1892.* Minor details for the distribution of railways among the colonies of the various countries in 1890 had to be estimated approximately.

Capitalism is growing with the greatest rapidity in the colonies and in overseas countries. Among the latter, *new* imperialist powers are emerging (e.g., Japan). The struggle among the world imperialisms is becoming more acute. The tribute levied by finance capital on the most profitable colonial and overseas enterprises is increasing. In the division of this "booty", an exceptionally large part goes to countries which do not always stand at the top of the list in the rapidity of the development of their productive forces. In the case of the biggest countries, together with their colonies, the total length of railways was as follows:

	(000 kilometres)		
	1890	1913	
U.S	268	413	+ 145
British Empire	107	208	+ 101
Russia	32	78	+ 46
Germany	43	68	+ 25
France	41	63	+ 22
Total for 5 powers .	491	830	+ 339

Thus, about 80 per cent of the total existing railways are concentrated in the hands of the five biggest powers. But the concentration of the *ownership* of these railways, the concentration of finance capital, is immeasurably greater since the French and British millionaires, for example, own an enormous amount of shares and bonds in American, Russian and other railways.

Thanks to her colonies, Great Britain has increased the length of "her" railways by 100,000 kilometres, four times as much as Germany. And yet, it is well known that the development of productive forces in Germany, and especially the development of the coal and iron industries, has been incomparably more rapid during this period than in Britain—not to speak of France and Russia. In 1892, Germany produced 4,900,000 tons of pig-iron and Great Britain produced 6,800,000 tons; in 1912, Germany produced 17,600,000 tons and Great Britain, 9,000,000 tons. Germany, therefore, had an overwhelming superiority over Britain in this respect.* The question is: what means other than war could there be *under capitalism* to overcome the disparity between the development of productive forces and the accumulation of capital on the one side, and the division of colonies and spheres of influence for finance capital on the other?

* Cf. also Edgar Crammond, "The Economic Relations of the British and German Empires" in *The Journal of the Royal Statistical Society*, July 1914, p. 777 et seq.

VIII. PARASITISM AND DECAY OF CAPITALISM

We now have to examine yet another significant aspect of imperialism to which most of the discussions on the subject usually attach insufficient importance. One of the shortcomings of the Marxist Hilferding is that on this point he has taken a step backward compared with the non-Marxist Hobson. I refer to parasitism, which is characteristic of imperialism.

As we have seen, the deepest economic foundation of imperialism is monopoly. This is capitalist monopoly, i.e., monopoly which has grown out of capitalism and which exists in the general environment of capitalism, commodity production and competition, in permanent and insoluble contradiction to this general environment. Nevertheless, like all monopoly, it inevitably engenders a tendency to stagnation and decay. Since monopoly prices are established, even temporarily, the motive cause of technical and, consequently, of all other progress disappears to a certain extent and, further, the *economic* possibility arises of deliberately retarding technical progress. For instance, in America, a certain Owens invented a machine which revolutionised the manufacture of bottles. The German bottle-manufacturing cartel purchased Owens's patent, but pigeon-holed it, refrained from utilising it. Certainly, monopoly under capitalism can never completely, and for a very long period of time, eliminate competition in the world market (and this, by the by, is one of the reasons why the theory of ultra-imperialism is so absurd). Certainly, the possibility of reducing the cost of production and increasing profits by introducing technical improvements operates in the direction of change. But the *tendency* to stagnation and decay, which is characteristic of monopoly, continues to operate, and in some branches of industry, in some countries, for certain periods of time, it gains the upper hand.

The monopoly ownership of very extensive, rich or well-situated colonies, operates in the same direction.

Further, imperialism is an immense accumulation of money capital in a few countries, amounting, as we have seen, to 100,000-150,000 million francs in securities. Hence the extraordinary growth of a class, or rather, of a stratum of rentiers, i.e., people who live by "clipping coupons", who take no part in any enterprise whatever, whose profession is idleness. The export of capital, one of the most essential economic bases of imperialism, still more completely isolates the rentiers from production and sets the seal of parasitism on the whole country that lives by exploiting the labour of several overseas countries and colonies.

"In 1893," writes Hobson, "the British capital invested abroad represented about 15 per cent of the total wealth of the United

Kingdom."* Let me remind the reader that by 1915 this capital had increased about two and a half times. "Aggressive imperialism," says Hobson further on, "which costs the tax-payer so dear, which is of so little value to the manufacturer and trader ... is a source of great gain to the investor.... The annual income Great Britain derives from commissions in her whole foreign and colonial trade, import and export, is estimated by Sir R. Giffen at £18,000,000 [nearly 170 million rubles] for 1899, taken at 2½ per cent, upon a turnover of £800,000,000." Great as this sum is, it cannot explain the aggressive imperialism of Great Britain, which is explained by the income of £90 million to £100 million from "invested" capital, the income of the rentiers.

The income of the rentiers is *five times greater* than the income obtained from the foreign trade of the biggest "trading" country in the world! This is the essence of imperialism and imperialist parasitism.

For that reason the term "rentier state" (Rentnerstaat), or usurer state, is coming into common use in the economic literature that deals with imperialism. The world has become divided into a handful of usurer states and a vast majority of debtor states. "At the top of the list of foreign investments," says Schulze-Gaevernitz, "are those placed in politically dependent or allied countries: Great Britain grants loans to Egypt, Japan, China and South America. Her navy plays here the part of bailiff in case of necessity. Great Britain's political power protects her from the indignation of her debtors."** Sartorius von Waltershausen in his book, *The National Economic System of Capital Investments Abroad*, cites Holland as the model "rentier state" and points out that Great Britain and France are now becoming such.*** Schilder is of the opinion that five industrial states have become "definitely pronounced creditor countries": Great Britain, France, Germany, Belgium and Switzerland. He does not include Holland in this list simply because she is "industrially little developed."**** The United States is a creditor only of the American countries.

"Great Britain," says Schulze-Gaevernitz, "is gradually becoming transformed from an industrial into a creditor state. Notwithstanding the absolute increase in industrial output and the export of manufactured goods, there is an increase in the relative importance of income from interest and dividends, issues of securities, commissions and speculation in the whole of the national economy. In my opinion it is precisely this that forms the economic basis of

---

* Hobson, op. cit., pp. 59, 62.
** Schulze-Gaevernitz, *Britischer Imperialismus*, S. 320 et seq.
*** Sartorius von Waltershausen, *Das volkswirtschaftliche System, etc.*, Berlin, 1907, Buch IV.
**** Schilder, op. cit., S. 393.

imperialist ascendancy. The creditor is more firmly attached to the debtor than the seller is to the buyer."* In regard to Germany, A. Lansburgh, the publisher of the Berlin *Die Bank*, in 1911, in an article entitled "Germany—a Rentier State", wrote the following: "People in Germany are ready to sneer at the yearning to become rentiers that is observed in France. But they forget that as far as the bourgeoisie is concerned the situation in Germany is becoming more and more like that in France."**

The rentier state is a state of parasitic, decaying capitalism, and this circumstance cannot fail to influence all the socio-political conditions of the countries concerned, in general, and the two fundamental trends in the working-class movement, in particular. To demonstrate this in the clearest possible manner let me quote Hobson, who is a most reliable witness, since he cannot be suspected of leaning towards Marxist orthodoxy; on the other hand, he is an Englishman who is very well acquainted with the situation in the country which is richest in colonies, in finance capital, and in imperialist experience.

With the Anglo-Boer War fresh in his mind, Hobson describes the connection between imperialism and the interests of the "financiers", their growing profits from contracts, supplies, etc., and writes: "While the directors of this definitely parasitic policy are capitalists, the same motives appeal to special classes of the workers. In many towns most important trades are dependent upon government employment or contracts; the imperialism of the metal and shipbuilding centres is attributable in no small degree to this fact." Two sets of circumstances, in this writer's opinion, have weakened the old empires: 1) "economic parasitism", and 2) the formation of armies recruited from subject peoples. "There is first the habit of economic parasitism, by which the ruling state has used its provinces, colonies, and dependencies in order to enrich its ruling class and to bribe its lower classes into acquiescence." And I shall add that the economic possibility of such bribery, whatever its form may be, requires high monopolist profits.

As for the second circumstance, Hobson writes: "One of the strangest symptoms of the blindness of imperialism is the reckless indifference with which Great Britain, France and other imperial nations are embarking on this perilous dependence. Great Britain has gone farthest. Most of the fighting by which we have won our Indian Empire has been done by natives; in India, as more recently in Egypt, great standing armies are placed under British commanders; almost all the fighting associated with our African dominions, except in the southern part, has been done for us by natives."

* Schulze-Gaevernitz, op. cit., S. 122.
** *Die Bank,* 1911, 1, S. 10-11.

Hobson gives the following economic appraisal of the prospect of the partitioning of China: "The greater part of Western Europe might then assume the appearance and character already exhibited by tracts of country in the South of England, in the Riviera, and in the tourist-ridden or residential parts of Italy and Switzerland, little clusters of wealthy aristocrats drawing dividends and pensions from the Far East, with a somewhat larger group of professional retainers and tradesmen and a larger body of personal servants and workers in the transport trade and in the final stages of production of the more perishable goods; all the main arterial industries would have disappeared, the staple foods and manufactures flowing in as tribute from Asia and Africa.... We have foreshadowed the possibility of even a larger alliance of Western states, a European federation of great powers which, so far from forwarding the cause of world civilisation, might introduce the gigantic peril of a Western parasitism, a group of advanced industrial nations, whose upper classes drew vast tribute from Asia and Africa, with which they supported great tame masses of retainers, no longer engaged in the staple industries of agriculture and manufacture, but kept in the performance of personal or minor industrial services under the control of a new financial aristocracy. Let those who would scout such a theory [it would be better to say: prospect] as undeserving of consideration examine the economic and social condition of districts in Southern England today which are already reduced to this condition, and reflect upon the vast extension of such a system which might be rendered feasible by the subjection of China to the economic control of similar groups of financiers, investors, and political and business officials, draining the greatest potential reservoir of profit the world has ever known, in order to consume it in Europe. The situation is far too complex, the play of world forces far too incalculable, to render this or any other single interpretation of the future very probable; but the influences which govern the imperialism of Western Europe today are moving in this direction, and, unless counteracted or diverted, make towards some such consummation."*

The author is quite right: *if* the forces of imperialism had not been counteracted they would have led precisely to what he has described. The significance of a "United States of Europe" in the present imperialist situation is correctly appraised. He should have added, however, that, also *within* the working-class movement, the opportunists, who are for the moment victorious in most countries, are "working" systematically and undeviatingly in this very direction. Imperialism, which means the partitioning of the world, and the exploitation of other countries besides China, which means high

---

* Hobson, op. cit., pp. 103, 205, 144, 335, 386.

monopoly profits for a handful of very rich countries, makes it economically possible to bribe the upper strata of the proletariat, and thereby fosters, gives shape to, and strengthens opportunism. We must not, however, lose sight of the forces which counteract imperialism in general, and opportunism in particular, and which, naturally, the social-liberal Hobson is unable to perceive.

The German opportunist, Gerhard Hildebrand, who was once expelled from the Party for defending imperialism, and who could today be a leader of the so-called "Social-Democratic" Party of Germany, supplements Hobson well by his advocacy of a "United States of Western Europe" (without Russia) for the purpose of "joint" action ... against the African Negroes, against the "great Islamic movement", for the maintenance of a "powerful army and navy", against a "Sino-Japanese coalition",* etc.

The description of "British imperialism" in Schulze-Gaevernitz's book reveals the same parasitical traits. The national income of Great Britain approximately doubled from 1865 to 1898, while the income "from abroad" increased *ninefold* in the same period. While the "merit" of imperialism is that it "trains the Negro to habits of industry" (you cannot manage without coercion...), the "danger" of imperialism lies in that "Europe will shift the burden of physical toil—first agricultural and mining, then the rougher work in industry—on to the coloured races, and itself be content with the role of rentier, and in this way, perhaps, pave the way for the economic, and later, the political emancipation of the coloured races".

An increasing proportion of land in England is being taken out of cultivation and used for sport, for the diversion of the rich. As far as Scotland—the most aristocratic place for hunting and other sports—is concerned, it is said that "it lives on its past and on Mr. Carnegie" (the American multimillionaire). On horse racing and fox hunting alone England annually spends £14,000,000 (nearly 130 million rubles). The number of rentiers in England is about one million. The percentage of the productively employed population to the total population is declining:

	Population England and Wales (000,000)	Workers in basic industries (000,000)	Per cent of total population
1851	17.9	4.1	23
1901	32.5	4.9	15

---

* Gerhard Hildebrand, *Die Erschütterung der Industrieherrschaft und des Industriesozialismus*, 1910, S. 229 et seq.

And in speaking of the British working class the bourgeois student of "British imperialism at the beginning of the twentieth century" is obliged to distinguish systematically between the "*upper stratum*" of the workers and the "*lower stratum of the proletariat proper*". The upper stratum furnishes the bulk of the membership of co-operatives, of trade unions, of sporting clubs and of numerous religious sects. To this level is adapted the electoral system, which in Great Britain is still "*sufficiently restricted to exclude the lower stratum of the proletariat proper*"! In order to present the condition of the British working class in a rosy light, only this upper stratum—which constitutes a *minority* of the proletariat—is usually spoken of. For instance, "the problem of unemployment is mainly a London problem and that of the lower proletarian stratum, *to which the politicians attach little importance....*"* He should have said: to which the bourgeois politicians and the "socialist" opportunists attach little importance.

One of the special features of imperialism connected with the facts I am describing, is the decline in emigration from imperialist countries and the increase in immigration into these countries from the more backward countries where lower wages are paid. As Hobson observes, emigration from Great Britain has been declining since 1884. In that year the number of emigrants was 242,000, while in 1900, the number was 169,000. Emigration from Germany reached the highest point between 1881 and 1890, with a total of 1,453,000 emigrants. In the course of the following two decades, it fell to 544,000 and to 341,000. On the other hand, there was an increase in the number of workers entering Germany from Austria, Italy, Russia and other countries. According to the 1907 census, there were 1,342,294 foreigners in Germany, of whom 440,800 were industrial workers and 257,329 agricultural workers.** In France, the workers employed in the mining industry are, "in great part", foreigners: Poles, Italians and Spaniards.*** In the United States, immigrants from Eastern and Southern Europe are engaged in the most poorly paid jobs, while American workers provide the highest precentage of overseers or of the better-paid workers.**** Imperialism has the tendency to create privileged sections also among the workers, and to detach them from the broad masses of the proletariat.

It must be observed that in Great Britain the tendency of imperialism to split the workers, to strengthen opportunism among them and to cause temporary decay in the working-class movement, revealed itself much earlier than the end of the nineteenth

---

* Schulze-Gaevernitz, *Britischer Imperialismus*, S. 301.
** *Statistik des Deutschen Reichs*, Bd. 211.
*** Henger, *Die Kapitalsanlage der Franzosen*, Stuttgart, 1913.
**** Hourwich, *Immigration and Labour*, New York, 1913.

and the beginning of the twentieth centuries; for two important distinguishing features of imperialism were already observed in Great Britain in the middle of the nineteenth century—vast colonial possessions and a monopolist position in the world market. Marx and Engels traced this connection between opportunism in the working-class movement and the imperialist features of British capitalism systematically, during the course of several decades. For example, on October 7, 1858, Engels wrote to Marx: "The English proletariat is actually becoming more and more bourgeois, so that this most bourgeois of all nations is apparently aiming ultimately at the possession of a bourgeois aristocracy and a bourgeois proletariat *alongside* the bourgeoisie. For a nation which exploits the whole world this is of course to a certain extent justifiable." Almost a quarter of a century later, in a letter dated August 11, 1881, Engels speaks of the "worst English trade unions which allow themselves to be led by men sold to, or at least paid by, the middle class". In a letter to Kautsky, dated September 12, 1882, Engels wrote: "You ask me what the English workers think about colonial policy. Well, exactly the same as they think about politics in general. There is no workers' party here, there are only Conservatives and Liberal-Radicals, and the workers gaily share the feast of England's monopoly of the world market and the colonies."* (Engels expressed similar ideas in the press in his preface to the second edition of *The Condition of the Working Class in England,* which appeared in 1892.)

This clearly shows the causes and effects. The causes are: 1) exploitation of the whole world by this country; 2) its monopolist position in the world market; 3) its colonial monopoly. The effects are: 1) a section of the British proletariat becomes bourgeois; 2) a section of the proletariat allows itself to be led by men bought by, or at least paid by, the bourgeoisie. The imperialism of the beginning of the twentieth century completed the division of the world among a handful of states, each of which today exploits (in the sense of drawing superprofits from) a part of the "whole world" only a little smaller than that which England exploited in 1858; each of them occupies a monopolist position in the world market thanks to trusts, cartels, finance capital and creditor and debtor relations; each of them enjoys to some degree a colonial monopoly (we have seen that out of the total of 75,000,000 sq. km., which comprise the *whole* colonial world, *65,000,000* sq. km., or 86 per cent, belong to six powers; *61,000,000* sq. km., or 81 per cent, belong to three powers).

---

* Briefwechsel von Marx und Engels, Bd. II, S. 290; IV, 433.—Karl Kautsky, *Sozialismus und Kolonialpolitik*, Berlin, 1907, S. 79; this pamphlet was written by Kautsky in those infinitely distant days when he was still a Marxist.

The distinctive feature of the present situation is the prevalence of such economic and political conditions that are bound to increase the irreconcilability between opportunism and the general and vital interests of the working-class movement: imperialism has grown from an embryo into the predominant system; capitalist monopolies occupy first place in economics and politics; the division of the world has been completed; on the other hand, instead of the undivided monopoly of Great Britain, we see a few imperialist powers contending for the right to share in this monopoly, and this struggle is characteristic of the whole period of the early twentieth century. Opportunism cannot now be completely triumphant in the working-class movement of one country for decades as it was in Britain in the second half of the nineteenth century; but in a number of countries it has grown ripe, overripe, and rotten, and has become completely merged with bourgeois policy in the form of "social-chauvinism".*

IX. CRITIQUE OF IMPERIALISM

By the critique of imperialism, in the broad sense of the term, we mean the attitude of the different classes of society towards imperialist policy in connection with their general ideology.

The enormous dimensions of finance capital concentrated in a few hands and creating an extraordinarily dense and widespread network of relationships and connections which subordinates not only the small and medium, but also the very small capitalists and small masters, on the one hand, and the increasingly intense struggle waged against other national state groups of financiers for the division of the world and domination over other countries, on the other hand, cause the propertied classes to go over entirely to the side of imperialism. "General" enthusiasm over the prospects of imperialism, furious defence of it and painting it in the brightest colours—such are the signs of the times. Imperialist ideology also penetrates the working class. No Chinese Wall separates it from the other classes. The leaders of the present-day, so-called, "Social-Democratic" Party of Germany are justly called "social-imperialists", that is, socialists in words and imperialists in deeds; but as early as 1902, Hobson noted the existence in Britain of "Fabian imperialists" who belonged to the opportunist Fabian Society.

Bourgeois scholars and publicists usually come out in defence of imperialism in a somewhat veiled form; they obscure its

---

* Russian social-chauvinism in its overt form, represented by the Potresovs, Chkhenkelis, Maslovs, etc., and in its covert form (Chkheidze, Skobelev, Axelrod, Martov, etc.), also emerged from the Russian variety of opportunism, namely, liquidationism.[127]

complete domination and its deep-going roots, strive to push specific and secondary details into the forefront and do their very best to distract attention from essentials by means of absolutely ridiculous schemes for "reform", such as police supervision of the trusts or banks, etc. Cynical and frank imperialists who are bold enough to admit the absurdity of the idea of reforming the fundamental characteristics of imperialism are rarer phenomenon.

Here is an example. The German imperialists attempt, in the magazine *Archives of World Economy*, to follow the national emancipation movements in the colonies, particularly, of course, in colonies other than those belonging to Germany. They note the unrest and the protest movements in India, the movement in Natal (South Africa), in the Dutch East Indies, etc. One of them, commenting on an English report of a conference held on June 28-30, 1910. of representatives of various subject nations and races, of peoples of Asia, Africa and Europe who are under foreign rule, writes as follows in appraising the speeches delivered at this conference: "We are told that we must fight imperialism; that the ruling states should recognise the right of subject peoples to independence; that an international tribunal should supervise the fulfilment of treaties concluded between the great powers and weak peoples. Further than the expression of these pious wishes they do not go. We see no trace of understanding of the fact that imperialism is inseparably bound up with capitalism in its present form and that, therefore [!!], an open struggle against imperialism would be hopeless, unless, perhaps, the fight were to be confined to protests against certain of its especially abhorrent excesses."* Since the reform of the basis of imperialism is a deception, a "pious wish", since the bourgeois representatives of the oppressed nations go no "further" forward, the bourgeois representative of an oppressing nation goes "further" *backward*, to servility towards imperialism under cover of the claim to be "scientific". That is also "logic"!

The questions as to whether it is possible to reform the basis of imperialism, whether to go forward to the further intensification and deepening of the antagonisms which it engenders, or backward, towards allaying these antagonisms, are fundamental questions in the critique of imperialism. Since the specific political features of imperialism are reaction everywhere and increased national oppression due to the oppression of the financial oligarchy and the elimination of free competition, a petty-bourgeois-democratic opposition to imperialism arose at the beginning of the twentieth century in nearly all imperialist countries. Kautsky not only did not trouble to oppose, was not only unable to oppose this petty-bourgeois reformist opposition, which is really reactionary in its economic basis,

---

* *Weltwirtschaftliches Archiv*, Bd. II, S. 193.

but became merged with it in practice, and this is precisely where Kautsky and the broad international Kautskyan trend deserted Marxism.

In the United States, the imperialist war waged against Spain in 1898 stirred up the opposition of the "anti-imperialists", the last of the Mohicans of bourgeois democracy who declared this war to be "criminal", regarded the annexation of foreign territories as a violation of the Constitution, declared that the treatment of Aguinaldo, leader of the Filipinos (the Americans promised him the independence of his country, but later landed troops and annexed it), was "Jingo treachery", and quoted the words of Lincoln: "When the white man governs himself, that is self-government; but when he governs himself and also governs others, it is no longer self-government; it is despotism."* But as long as all this criticism shrank from recognising the inseverable bond between imperialism and the trusts, and, therefore, between imperialism and the foundations of capitalism, while it shrank from joining the forces engendered by large-scale capitalism and its development—it remained a "pious wish".

This is also the main attitude taken by Hobson in his critique of imperialism. Hobson anticipated Kautsky in protesting against the "inevitability of imperialism" argument, and in urging the necessity of "increasing the consuming capacity" of the people (under capitalism!). The petty-bourgeois point of view in the critique of imperialism, the omnipotence of the banks, the financial oligarchy, etc., is adopted by the authors I have often quoted, such as Agahd, A. Lansburgh, L. Eschwege, and among the French writers Victor Berard, author of a superficial book entitled *England and Imperialism* which appeared in 1900. All these authors, who make no claim to be Marxists, contrast imperialism with free competition and democracy, condemn the Baghdad railway scheme, which is leading to conflicts and war, utter "pious wishes" for peace, etc. This applies also to the compiler of international stock and share issue statistics, A. Neymarck, who, after calculating the thousands of millions of francs representing "international" securities, exclaimed in 1912: "Is it possible to believe that peace may be disturbed . . . that, in the face of these enormous figures, anyone would risk starting a war?"**

Such simple-mindedness on the part of the bourgeois economists is not surprising; moreover, *it is in their interest* to pretend to be so naïve and to talk "seriously" about peace under imperialism. But what remains of Kautsky's Marxism, when, in 1914, 1915 and 1916, he takes up the same bourgeois-reformist point of view and affirms

---

* J. Patouillet, *L'impérialisme américain*, Dijon, 1904, p. 272.
** *Bulletin de l'institut international de statistique*, T. XIX, livr. II, p. 225.

that "everybody is agreed" (imperialists, pseudo-socialists and social-pacifists) on the matter of peace? Instead of an analysis of imperialism and an exposure of the depths of its contradictions, we have nothing but a reformist "pious wish" to wave them aside, to evade them.

Here is a sample of Kautsky's economic criticism of imperialism. He takes the statistics of the British export and import trade with Egypt for 1872 and 1912; it seems that this export and import trade has grown more slowly than British foreign trade as a whole. From this Kautsky concludes that "we have no reason to suppose that without military occupation the growth of British trade with Egypt would have been less, simply as a result of the mere operation of economic factors". "The urge of capital to expand ... can be best promoted, not by the violent methods of imperialism, but by peaceful democracy."*

This argument of Kautsky's, which is repeated in every key by his Russian armour-bearer (and Russian shielder of the social-chauvinists), Mr. Spectator, constitutes the basis of Kautskyan critique of imperialism, and that is why we must deal with it in greater detail. We will begin with a quotation from Hilferding, whose conclusions Kautsky on many occasions, and notably in April 1915, has declared to have been "unanimously adopted by all socialist theoreticians".

"It is not the business of the proletariat," writes Hilferding, "to contrast the more progressive capitalist policy with that of the now bygone era of free trade and of hostility towards the state. The reply of the proletariat to the economic policy of finance capital, to imperialism, cannot be free trade, but socialism. The aim of proletarian policy cannot today be the ideal of restoring free competition—which has now become a reactionary ideal—but the complete elimination of competition by the abolition of capitalism."**

Kautsky broke with Marxism by advocating in the epoch of finance capital a "reactionary ideal", "peaceful democracy", "the mere operation of economic factors", for *objectively* this ideal drags us back from monopoly to non-monopoly capitalism, and is a reformist swindle.

Trade with Egypt (or with any other colony or semi-colony) "would have grown more" *without* military occupation, without imperialism, and without finance capital. What does this mean? That capitalism would have developed more rapidly if free competition had not been restricted by monopolies in general, or by the "connections", yoke (i.e., also the monopoly) of finance capital, or by the monopolist possession of colonies by certain countries?

---

* Kautsky, *Nationalstaat, imperialistischer Staat und Staatenbund*, Nürnberg, 1915, S. 72 und 70.
** *Finance Capital*, p. 567.

Kautsky's argument can have no other meaning; and *this* "meaning" is meaningless. Let us assume that free competition, without any sort of monopoly, *would* have developed capitalism and trade more rapidly. But the more rapidly trade and capitalism develop, the greater is the concentration of production and capital which *gives rise* to monopoly. And monopolies have *already* arisen—precisely *out of* free competition! Even if monopolies have now begun to retard progress, it is not an argument in favour of free competition, which has become impossible after it has given rise to monopoly.

Whichever way one turns Kautsky's argument, one will find nothing in it except reaction and bourgeois reformism.

Even if we correct this argument and say, as Spectator says, that the trade of the colonies with Britain is now developing more slowly than their trade with other countries, it does not save Kautsky; for it is *also* monopoly, *also* imperialism that is beating Great Britain, only it is the monopoly and imperialism of another country (America, Germany). It is known that the cartels have given rise to a new and peculiar form of protective tariffs, i.e., goods suitable for export are protected (Engels noted this in Vol. III of *Capital*[128]). It is known, too, that the cartels and finance capital have a system peculiar to themselves, that of "exporting goods at cut-rate prices", or "dumping", as the English call it: within a given country the cartel sells its goods at high monopoly prices, but sells them abroad at a much lower price to undercut the competitor, to enlarge its own production to the utmost, etc. If Germany's trade with the British colonies is developing more rapidly than Great Britain's, it only proves that German imperialism is younger, stronger and better organised than British imperialism, is superior to it; but it by no means proves the "superiority" of free trade, for it is not a fight between free trade and protection and colonial dependence, but between two rival imperialisms, two monopolies, two groups of finance capital. The superiority of German imperialism over British imperialism is more potent than the wall of colonial frontiers or of protective tariffs: to use this as an "argument" *in favour* of free trade and "peaceful democracy" is banal, it means forgetting the essential features and characteristics of imperialism, substituting petty-bourgeois reformism for Marxism.

It is interesting to note that even the bourgeois economist, A. Lansburgh, whose criticism of imperialism is as a petty-bourgeois as Kautsky's, nevertheless got closer to a more scientific study of trade statistics. He did not compare one single country, chosen at random, and one single colony with the other countries; he examined the export trade of an imperialist country: 1) with countries which are financially dependent upon it, and borrow money from it; and 2) with countries which are financially independent. He obtained the following results:

Export Trade of Germany (000,000 marks)

		1889	1908	Per cent increase
To countries financially dependent on Germany	Rumania	48.2	70.8	47
	Portugal	19.0	32.8	73
	Argentina	60.7	147.0	143
	Brazil	48.7	84.5	73
	Chile	28.3	52.4	85
	Turkey	29.9	64.0	114
	Total	*234.8*	*451.5*	*92*
To countries financially independent of Germany	Great Britain	651.8	997.4	53
	France	210.2	437.9	108
	Belgium	137.2	322.8	135
	Switzerland	177.4	401.1	127
	Australia	21.2	64.5	205
	Dutch East Indies	8.8	40.7	363
	Total	*1,206.6*	*2,264.4*	*87*

Lansburgh did not draw *conclusions* and therefore, strangely enough, failed to observe that *if* the figures prove anything at all, they prove that *he is wrong*, for the exports to countries financially dependent on Germany have grown *more rapidly*, if only slightly, than exports to the countries which are financially independent. (I emphasise the "if", for Lansburgh's figures are far from complete.)

Tracing the connection between exports and loans, Lansburgh writes:

"In 1890-91, a Rumanian loan was floated through the German banks, which had already in previous years made advances on this loan. It was used chiefly to purchase railway materials in Germany. In 1891, German exports to Rumania amounted to 55 million marks. The following year they dropped to 39.4 million marks and, with fluctuations, to 25.4 million in 1900. Only in very recent years have they regained the level of 1891, thanks to two new loans.

"German exports to Portugal rose, following the loans of 1888-89, to 21,100,000 (1890); then, in the two following years, they dropped to 16,200,000 and 7,400,000, and regained their former level only in 1903.

"The figures of German trade with Argentina are still more striking. Loans were floated in 1888 and 1890; German exports to

Argentina reached 60,700,000 marks (1889). Two years later they amounted to only 18,600,000 marks, less than one-third of the previous figure. It was not until 1901 that they regained and surpassed the level of 1889, and then only as a result of new loans floated by the state and by municipalities, with advances to build power stations, and with other credit operations.

"Exports to Chile, as a consequence of the loan of 1889, rose to 45,200,000 marks (in 1892), and a year later dropped to 22,500,000 marks. A new Chilean loan floated by the German banks in 1906 was followed by a rise of exports to 84,700,000 marks in 1907, only to fall again to 52,400,000 marks in 1908."*

From these facts Lansburgh draws the amusing petty-bourgeois moral of how unstable and irregular export trade is when it is bound up with loans, how bad it is to invest capital abroad instead of "naturally" and "harmoniously" developing home industry, how "costly" are the millions in bakhshish that Krupp has to pay in floating foreign loans, etc. But the facts tell us clearly: the increase in exports is connected with *just these* swindling tricks of finance capital, which is not concerned with bourgeois morality, but with skinning the ox twice—first, it pockets the profits from the loan; then it pockets other profits from the *same* loan which the borrower uses to make purchases from Krupp, or to purchase railway material from the Steel Syndicate, etc.

I repeat that I do not by any means consider Lansburgh's figures to be perfect; but I had to quote them because they are more scientific than Kautsky's and Spectator's and because Lansburgh showed the correct way to approach the question. In discussing the significance of finance capital in regard to exports, etc., one must be able to single out the connection of exports especially and solely with the tricks of the financiers, especially and solely with the sale of goods by cartels, etc. Simply to compare colonies with non-colonies, one imperialism with another imperialism, one semi-colony or colony (Egypt) with all other countries, is to evade and to obscure the very *essence* of the question.

Kautsky's theoretical critique of imperialism has nothing in common with Marxism and serves only as a preamble to propaganda for peace and unity with the opportunists and the social-chauvinists, precisely for the reason that it evades and obscures the very profound and fundamental contradictions of imperialism: the contradictions between monopoly and free competition which exists side by side with it, between the gigantic "operations" (and gigantic profits) of finance capital and "honest" trade in the free market, the contradiction between cartels and trusts, on the one hand, and non-cartelised industry, on the other, etc.

---

* *Die Bank*, 1909, 2, S. 819 et seq.

The notorious theory of "ultra-imperialism", invented by Kautsky, is just as reactionary. Compare his arguments on this subject in 1915, with Hobson's arguments in 1902.

Kautsky: ". . . Cannot the present imperialist policy be supplanted by a new, ultra-imperialist policy, which will introduce the joint exploitation of the world by internationally united finance capital in place of the mutual rivalries of national finance capitals? Such a new phase of capitalism is at any rate conceivable. Can it be achieved? Sufficient premises are still lacking to enable us to answer this question."*

Hobson: "Christendom thus laid out in a few great federal empires, each with a retinue of uncivilised dependencies, seems to many the most legitimate development of present tendencies, and one which would offer the best hope of permanent peace on an assured basis of inter-Imperialism."

Kautsky called ultra-imperialism or super-imperialism what Hobson, thirteen years earlier, described as inter-imperialism. Except for coining a new and clever catchword, replacing one Latin prefix by another, the only progress Kautsky has made in the sphere of "scientific" thought is that he gave out as Marxism what Hobson, in effect, described as the cant of English parsons. After the Anglo-Boer War it was quite natural for this highly honourable caste to exert their main efforts to *console* the British middle class and the workers who had lost many of their relatives on the battlefields of South Africa and who were obliged to pay higher taxes in order to guarantee still higher profits for the British financiers. And what better consolation could there be than the theory that imperialism is not so bad; that it stands close to inter- (or ultra-) imperialism, which can ensure permanent peace? No matter what the good intentions of the English parsons, or of sentimental Kautsky, may have been, the only objective, i.e., real, social significance of Kautsky's "theory" is this: it is a most reactionary method of consoling the masses with hopes of permanent peace being possible under capitalism, by distracting their attention from the sharp antagonisms and acute problems of the present times, and directing it towards illusory prospects of an imaginary "ultra-imperialism" of the future. Deception of the masses—that is all there is in Kautsky's "Marxist" theory.

Indeed, it is enough to compare well-known and indisputable facts to become convinced of the utter falsity of the prospects which Kautsky tries to conjure up before the German workers (and the workers of all lands). Let us consider India, Indo-China and China. It is known that these three colonial and semi-colonial countries, with a population of six to seven hundred million, are subjected to

---

* *Die Neue Zeit*, April 30, 1915, S. 144.

the exploitation of the finance capital of several imperialist powers: Great Britain, France, Japan, the U.S.A., etc. Let us assume that these imperialist countries form alliances against one another in order to protect or enlarge their possessions, their interests and their spheres of influence in these Asiatic states; these alliances will be "inter-imperialist", or "ultra-imperialist" alliances. Let us assume that *all* the imperialist countries conclude an alliance for the "peaceful" division of these parts of Asia; this alliance would be an alliance of "internationally united finance capital". There are actual examples of alliances of this kind in the history of the twentieth century—the attitude of the powers to China,[129] for instance. We ask, is it "conceivable", assuming that the capitalist system remains intact—and this is precisely the assumption that Kautsky does make —that such alliances would be more than temporary, that they would eliminate friction, conflicts and struggle in every possible form?

The question has only to be presented clearly for any other than a negative answer to be impossible. This is because the only conceivable basis under capitalism for the division of spheres of influence, interests, colonies, etc., is a calculation of the *strength* of those participating, their general economic, financial, military strength, etc. And the strength of these participants in the division does not change to an equal degree, for the *even* development of different undertakings, trusts, branches of industry, or countries is impossible under capitalism. Half a century ago Germany was a miserable, insignificant country, if her capitalist strength is compared with that of the Britain of that time; Japan compared with Russia in the same way. It is "conceivable" that in ten or twenty years' time the relative strength of the imperialist powers will have remained *un*changed? It is out of the question.

Therefore, in the realities of the capitalist system, and not in the banal philistine fantasies of English parsons, or of the German "Marxist", Kautsky, "inter-imperialist" or "ultra-imperialist" alliances, no matter what form they may assume, whether of one imperialist coalition against another, or of a general alliance embracing *all* the imperialist powers, are *inevitably* nothing more than a "truce" in periods between wars. Peaceful alliances prepare the ground for wars, and in their turn grow out of wars; the one conditions the other, producing alternating forms of peaceful and non-peaceful struggle on *one and the same* basis of imperialist connections and relations within world economics and world politics. But in order to pacify the workers and reconcile them with the social-chauvinists who have deserted to the side of the bourgeoisie, over-wise Kautsky *separates* one link of a single chain from another, separates the present peaceful (and ultra-imperialist, nay, ultra-ultra-imperialist) alliance of *all* the powers for the "pacification" of China (remember the suppression of the Boxer Rebellion[130]) from the non-peaceful conflict of tomorrow, which will prepare the ground for another "peaceful" general alliance for the partition, say, of Turkey, on the day after tomorrow, *etc., etc.* Instead of showing the living connection between periods of imperialist peace and periods of imperialist war, Kautsky presents the workers with a lifeless abstraction in order to reconcile them to their lifeless leaders.

An American writer, Hill, in his *A History of the Diplomacy in the International Development of Europe* refers in his preface to the following periods in the recent history of diplomacy: 1) the era of revolution; 2) the constitutional movement; 3) the present era of "commercial imperialism".* Another writer divides the history of Great Britain's "world policy" since 1870 into four periods: 1) the first Asiatic period (that of the struggle against Russia's advance in Central Asia towards India); 2) the African period (approximately 1885-1902): that of the struggle against France for the partition of Africa (the "Fashoda incident" of 1898[131] which brought her within a hair's breadth of war with France); 3) the second Asiatic period (alliance with Japan against Russia); and 4) the "European" period, chiefly anti-German.** "The political patrol clashes take place on the financial field," wrote the banker, Riesser, in 1905 in showing how French finance capital operating in Italy was preparing the way for a political alliance of these countries, and how a conflict was developing between Germany and Great Britain over Persia, between all the European capitalists over Chinese loans, etc. Behold, the living reality of peaceful "ultra-imperialist" alliances in their inseverable connection with ordinary imperialist conflicts!

Kautsky's obscuring of the deepest contradictions of imperialism, which inevitably boils down to painting imperialism in bright colours, leaves its traces in this writer's criticism of the political features of imperialism. Imperialism is the epoch of finance capital and of monopolies, which introduce everywhere the striving for domination, not for freedom. Whatever the political system the result of these tendencies is everywhere reaction and an extreme intensification of antagonisms in this field. Particularly intensified become the yoke of national oppression and the striving for annexations, i.e., the violation of national independence (for annexation is nothing but the violation of the right of nations to self-determination). Hilferding rightly notes the connection between imperialism and the intensification of national oppression. "In the newly opened-up

---

* David Jayne Hill, *A History of the Diplomacy in the International Development of Europe*, Vol. I, p. 10.
** Schilder, op. cit., S. 178.

countries," he writes, "the capital imported into them intensifies antagonisms and excites against the intruders the constantly growing resistance of the peoples who are awakening to national consciousness; this resistance can easily develop into dangerous measures against foreign capital. The old social relations become completely revolutionised, the age-long agrarian isolation of 'nations without history' is destroyed and they are drawn into the capitalist whirlpool. Capitalism itself gradually provides the subjugated with the means and resources for their emancipation and they set out to achieve the goal which once seemed highest to the European nations: the creation of a united national state as a means to economic and cultural freedom. This movement for national independence threatens European capital in its most valuable and most promising fields of exploitation, and European capital can maintain its domination only by continually increasing its military forces."[*]

To this must be added that it is not only in newly opened-up countries, but also in the old, that imperialism is leading to annexation, to increased national oppression, and, consequently, also to increasing resistance. While objecting to the intensification of political reaction by imperialism, Kautsky leaves in the shade a question that has become particularly urgent, viz., the impossibility of unity with the opportunists in the epoch of imperialism. While objecting to annexations, he presents his objections in a form that is most acceptable and least offensive to the opportunists. He addresses himself to a German audience, yet he obscures the most topical and important point, for instance, the annexation of Alsace-Lorraine by Germany. In order to appraise this "mental aberration" of Kautsky's I shall take the following example. Let us suppose that a Japanese condemns the annexation of the Philippines by the Americans. The question is: will many believe that he does so because he has a horror of annexations as such, and not because he himself has a desire to annex the Philippines? And shall we not be constrained to admit that the "fight" the Japanese is waging against annexations can be regarded as being sincere and politically honest only if he fights against the annexation of Korea by Japan, and urges freedom for Korea to secede from Japan?

Kautsky's theoretical analysis of imperialism, as well as his economic and political critique of imperialism, are permeated *through and through* with a spirit, absolutely irreconcilable with Marxism, of obscuring and glossing over the fundamental contradictions of imperialism and with a striving to preserve at all costs the crumbling unity with opportunism in the European working-class movement.

---

[*] *Finance Capital*, p. 487.

X. THE PLACE OF IMPERIALISM IN HISTORY

We have seen that in its economic essence imperialism is monopoly capitalism. This in itself determines its place in history, for monopoly that grows out of the soil of free competition, and precisely out of free competition, is the transition from the capitalist system to a higher socio-economic order. We must take special note of the four principal types of monopoly, or principal manifestations of monopoly capitalism, which are characteristic of the epoch we are examining.

Firstly, monopoly arose out of the concentration of production at a very high stage. This refers to the monopolist capitalist associations, cartels, syndicates and trusts. We have seen the important part these play in present-day economic life. At the beginning of the twentieth century, monopolies had acquired complete supremacy in the advanced countries, and although the first steps towards the formation of the cartels were taken by countries enjoying the protection of high tariffs (Germany, America), Great Britain, with her system of free trade, revealed the same basic phenomenon, only a little later, namely, the birth of monopoly out of the concentration of production.

Secondly, monopolies have stimulated the seizure of the most important sources of raw materials, especially for the basic and most highly cartelised industries in capitalist society: the coal and iron industries. The monopoly of the most important sources of raw materials has enormously increased the power of big capital, and has sharpened the antagonism between cartelised and non-cartelised industry.

Thirdly, monopoly has sprung from the banks. The banks have developed from modest middleman enterprises into the monopolists of finance capital. Some three to five of the biggest banks in each of the foremost capitalist countries have achieved the "personal link-up" between industrial and bank capital, and have concentrated in their hands the control of thousands upon thousands of millions which form the greater part of the capital and income of entire countries. A financial oligarchy, which throws a close network of dependence relationships over all the economic and political institutions of present-day bourgeois society without exception—such is the most striking manifestation of this monopoly.

Fourthly, monopoly has grown out of colonial policy. To the numerous "old" motives of colonial policy, finance capital has added the struggle for the sources of raw materials, for the export of capital, for spheres of influence, i.e., for spheres for profitable deals, concessions, monopoly profits and so on, economic territory in general. When the colonies of the European powers, for instance, comprised only one-tenth of the territory of Africa (as was the case in 1876), colonial policy was able to develop by methods other than those of monopoly—by the "free grabbing" of territories, so to speak. But when nine-tenths of Africa had been seized (by 1900), when the whole world had been divided up, there was inevitably ushered in the era of monopoly possession of colonies and, consequently, of particularly intense struggle for the division and the redivision of the world.

The extent to which monopolist capital has intensified all the contradictions of capitalism is generally known. It is sufficient to mention the high cost of living and the tyranny of the cartels. This intensification of contradictions constitutes the most powerful driving force of the transitional period of history, which began from the time of the final victory of world finance capital.

Monopolies, oligarchy, the striving for domination and not for freedom, the exploitation of an increasing number of small or weak nations by a handful of the richest or most powerful nations—all these have given birth to those distinctive characteristics of imperialism which compel us to define it as parasitic or decaying capitalism. More and more prominently there emerges, as one of the tendencies of imperialism, the creation of the "rentier state", the usurer state, in which the bourgeoisie to an ever-increasing degree lives on the proceeds of capital exports and by "clipping coupons". It would be a mistake to believe that this tendency to decay precludes the rapid growth of capitalism. It does not. In the epoch of imperialism, certain branches of industry, certain strata of the bourgeoisie and certain countries betray, to a greater or lesser degree, now one and now another of these tendencies. On the whole, capitalism is growing far more rapidly than before; but this growth is not only becoming more and more uneven in general, its unevenness also manifests itself, in particular, in the decay of the countries which are richest in capital (Britain).

In regard to the rapidity of Germany's economic development, Riesser, the author of the book on the big German banks, states: "The progress of the preceding period (1848-70), which had not been exactly slow, compares with the rapidity with which the whole of Germany's national economy, and with it German banking, progressed during this period (1870-1905) in about the same way as the speed of the mail coach in the good old days compares with the speed of the present-day automobile ... which is whizzing past so fast that it endangers not only innocent pedestrians in its path, but also the occupants of the car." In its turn, this finance capital which has grown with such extraordinary rapidity is not unwilling, precisely because it has grown so quickly, to pass on to a more "tranquil" possession of colonies which have to be seized—and not only by peaceful methods—from richer nations. In the United States, economic development in the last decades has been even more rapid than in Germany, *and for this very reason*, the parasitic features of modern American capitalism have stood out with particular prominence. On the other hand, a comparison of, say, the republican American bourgeoisie with the monarchist Japanese or German bourgeoisie shows that the most pronounced political distinction diminishes to an extreme degree in the epoch of imperialism—not because it is unimportant in general, but because in all these cases we are talking about a bourgeoisie which has definite features of parasitism.

The receipt of high monopoly profits by the capitalists in one of the numerous branches of industry, in one of the numerous countries, etc., makes it economically possible for them to bribe certain sections of the workers, and for a time a fairly considerable minority of them, and win them to the side of the bourgeoisie of a given industry or given nation against all the others. The intensification of antagonisms between imperialist nations for the division of the world increases this urge. And so there is created that bond between imperialism and opportunism, which revealed itself first and most clearly in Great Britain, owing to the fact that certain features of imperialist development were observable there much earlier than in other countries. Some writers, L. Martov, for example, are prone to wave aside the connection between imperialism and opportunism in the working-class movement—a particularly glaring fact at the present time—by resorting to "official optimism" (*à la* Kautsky and Huysmans) like the following: the cause of the opponents of capitalism would be hopeless if it were progressive capitalism that led to the increase of opportunism, or, if it were the best-paid workers who were inclined towards opportunism, etc. We must have no illusions about "optimism" of this kind. It is optimism in respect of opportunism; it is optimism which serves to conceal opportunism. As a matter of fact the extraordinary rapidity and the particularly revolting character of the development of opportunism is by no means a guarantee that its victory will be durable: the rapid growth of a painful abscess on a healthy body can only cause it to burst more quickly and thus relieve the body of it. The most dangerous of all in this respect are those who do not wish to understand that the fight against imperialism is a sham and humbug unless it is inseparably bound up with the fight against opportunism.

From all that has been said in this book on the economic essence of imperialism, it follows that we must define it as capitalism in transition, or, more precisely, as moribund capitalism. It is very instructive in this respect to note that bourgeois economists, in describing modern capitalism, frequently employ catchwords and phrases like "interlocking", "absence of isolation", etc.; "in conformity with their functions and course of development", banks are "not purely private business enterprises; they are more and more outgrowing the sphere of purely private business regulation". And this very Riesser, whose words I have just quoted, declares with all seriousness that the "prophecy" of the Marxists concerning "socialisation" has "not come true"!

What then does this catchword "interlocking" express? It merely expresses the most striking feature of the process going on before our eyes. It shows that the observer counts the separate trees, but cannot see the wood. It slavishly copies the superficial, the fortuitous, the chaotic. It reveals the observer as one who is overwhelmed by the mass of raw material and is utterly incapable of appreciating its meaning and importance. Ownership of shares, the relations between owners of private property "interlock in a haphazard way". But underlying this interlocking, its very base, are the changing social relations of production. When a big enterprise assumes gigantic proportions, and, on the basis of an exact computation of mass data, organises according to plan the supply of primary raw materials to the extent of two-thirds, or three-fourths, of all that is necessary for tens of millions of people; when the raw materials are transported in a systematic and organised manner to the most suitable places of production, sometimes situated hundreds or thousands of miles from each other; when a single centre directs all the consecutive stages of processing the material right up to the manufacture of numerous varieties of finished articles; when these products are distributed according to a single plan among tens and hundreds of millions of consumers (the marketing of oil in America and Germany by the American oil trust)—then it becomes evident that we have socialisation of production, and not mere "interlocking"; that private economic and private property relations constitute a shell which no longer fits its contents, a shell which must inevitably decay if its removal is artificially delayed, a shell which may remain in a state of decay for a fairly long period (if, at the worst, the cure of the opportunist abscess is protracted), but which will inevitably be removed.

The enthusiastic admirer of German imperialism, Schulze-Gaevernitz, exclaims:

"Once the supreme management of the German banks has been entrusted to the hands of a dozen persons, their activity is even today more significant for the public good than that of the majority of the Ministers of State.... [The "interlocking" of bankers, ministers, magnates of industry and rentiers is here conveniently forgotten.] If we imagine the development of those tendencies we have noted carried to their logical conclusion we will have: the money capital of the nation united in the banks; the banks themselves combined into cartels; the investment capital of the nation cast in the shape of securities. Then the forecast of that genius

Saint-Simon will be fulfilled: 'The present anarchy of production, which corresponds to the fact that economic relations are developing without uniform regulation, must make way for organisation in production. Production will no longer be directed by isolated manufacturers, independent of each other and ignorant of man's economic needs; that will be done by a certain public institution. A central committee of management, being able to survey the large field of social economy from a more elevated point of view, will regulate it for the benefit of the whole of society, will put the means of production into suitable hands, and above all will take care that there be constant harmony between production and consumption. Institutions already exist which have assumed as part of their functions a certain organisation of economic labour, the banks.' We are still a long way from the fulfilment of Saint-Simon's forecast, but we are on the way towards it: Marxism, different from what Marx imagined, but different only in form."*

A crushing "refutation" of Marx, indeed, which retreats a step from Marx's precise, scientific analysis to Saint-Simon's guess-work, the guess-work of a genius, but guess-work all the same.

Written January-June 1916   *Collected Works*, Vol. 22

First published in pamphlet
form in the middle of 1917
by the Publishing House
Zhizn i Znaniye, Petrograd;
Preface to the French and German
editions was published in 1921
in the magazine
Kommunisticheski Internatsional
No. 18

---

* *Grundriβ der Sozialökonomik*, S. 146.

THE STATE AND REVOLUTION[132]
THE MARXIST THEORY OF THE STATE AND THE TASKS OF THE PROLETARIAT IN THE REVOLUTION

PREFACE TO THE FIRST EDITION

The question of the state is now acquiring particular importance both in theory and in practical politics. The imperialist war has immensely accelerated and intensified the process of transformation of monopoly capitalism into state-monopoly capitalism. The monstrous oppression of the working people by the state, which is merging more and more with the all-powerful capitalist associations, is becoming increasingly monstrous. The advanced countries—we mean their hinterland—are becoming military convict prisons for the workers.

The unprecedented horrors and miseries of the protracted war are making the people's position unbearable and increasing their anger. The world proletarian revolution is clearly maturing. The question of its relation to the state is acquiring practical importance.

The elements of opportunism that accumulated over the decades of comparatively peaceful development have given rise to the trend of social-chauvinism which dominates the official socialist parties throughout the world. This trend—socialism in words and chauvinism in deeds (Plekhanov, Potresov, Breshkovskaya, Rubanovich, and, in a slightly veiled form, Tsereteli, Chernov and Co. in Russia; Scheidemann, Legien, David and others in Germany; Renaudel, Guesde and Vandervelde in France and Belgium; Hyndman and the Fabians in England, etc., etc.)—is conspicuous for the base, servile adaptation of the "leaders of socialism" to the interests not only of "their" national bourgeoisie, but of "their" state, for the majority of the so-called Great Powers have long been exploiting and enslaving a whole number of small and weak nations. And the imperialist war is a war for the division and redivision of this kind of booty. The struggle to free the working people from the influence of the bourgeoisie in general, and of the imperialist bourgeoisie in particular, is impossible without a struggle against opportunist prejudices concerning the "state".

First of all we examine the theory of Marx and Engels of the state, and dwell in particular detail on those aspects of this theory which are ignored or have been distorted by the opportunists. Then we deal specially with the one who is chiefly responsible for these distortions, Karl Kautsky, the best-known leader of the Second International (1889-1914), which has met with such miserable bankruptcy in the present war. Lastly, we sum up the main results of the experience of the Russian revolutions of 1905 and particularly of 1917. Apparently, the latter is now (early August 1917) completing the first stage of its development; but this revolution as a whole can only be understood as a link in a chain of socialist proletarian revolutions being caused by the imperialist war. The question of the relation of the socialist proletarian revolution to the state, therefore, is acquiring not only practical political importance, but also the significance of a most urgent problem of the day, the problem of explaining to the masses what they will have to do before long to free themselves from capitalist tyranny.

The Author

August 1917

PREFACE TO THE SECOND EDITION

The present, second edition is published virtually unaltered, except that section 3 has been added to Chapter II.

The Author

Moscow
December 17, 1918

CHAPTER I

CLASS SOCIETY AND THE STATE

1. THE STATE—A PRODUCT OF THE IRRECONCILABILITY OF CLASS ANTAGONISMS

What is now happening to Marx's theory has, in the course of history, happened repeatedly to the theories of revolutionary thinkers and leaders of oppressed classes fighting for emancipation. During the lifetime of great revolutionaries, the oppressing classes constantly hounded them, received their theories with the most savage malice, the most furious hatred and the most unscrupulous campaigns of lies and slander. After their death, attempts are made to convert them into harmless icons, to canonise them, so to say, and to hallow their *names* to a certain extent for the "consolation" of the oppressed classes and with the object of duping the latter, while at the same time robbing the revolutionary theory of its *substance,* blunting its revolutionary edge and vulgarising it. Today, the bourgeoisie and the opportunists within the labour movement concur in this doctoring of Marxism. They omit, obscure or distort the revolutionary side of this theory, its revolutionary soul. They push to the foreground and extol what is or seems acceptable to the bourgeoisie. All the social-chauvinists are now "Marxists" (don't laugh!). And more and more frequently German bourgeois scholars, only yesterday specialists in the annihilation of Marxism, are speaking of the "national-German" Marx, who, they claim, educated the labour unions which are so splendidly organised for the purpose of waging a predatory war!

In these circumstances, in view of the unprecedentedly widespread distortion of Marxism, our prime task is to *re-establish* what Marx really taught on the subject of the state. This will necessitate a number of long quotations from the works of Marx and Engels themselves. Of course, long quotations will render the text cumbersome and not help at all to make it popular reading, but we cannot possibly dispense with them. All, or at any rate all the most essential passages in the works of Marx and Engels on the subject of the state must by all means be quoted as fully as possible so that the reader may form an independent opinion of the totality of the views of the founders of scientific socialism, and of the evolution of those views, and so that their distortion by the "Kautskyism" now prevailing may be documentarily proved and clearly demonstrated.

Let us begin with the most popular of Engels's works, *The Origin of the Family, Private Property, and the State,* the sixth edition of which was published in Stuttgart as far back as 1894. We shall have to translate the quotations from the German originals, as the Russian translations, while very numerous, are for the most part either incomplete or very unsatisfactory.

Summing up his historical analysis, Engels says:

> "The state is, therefore, by no means a power forced on society from without; just as little is it 'the reality of the ethical idea', 'the image and reality of reason', as Hegel maintains. Rather, it is a product of society at a certain stage of development; it is the admission that this society has become entangled in an insoluble contradiction with itself, that it has split into irreconcilable antagonisms which it is powerless to dispel. But in order that these antagonisms, these classes with conflicting economic interests might not consume themselves and society in fruitless struggle, it became necessary to have a power, seemingly standing above society, that would alleviate the conflict and keep it within the bounds of 'order'; and this power, arisen out of society but placing itself above it, and alienating itself more and more from it, is the state." (Pp. 177-78, sixth German edition.)[133]

This expresses with perfect clarity the basic idea of Marxism with regard to the historical role and the meaning of the state. The state is a product and a manifestation of the *irreconcilability* of class antagonisms. The state arises where, when and insofar as class antagonisms objectively *cannot* be reconciled. And, conversely, the existence of the state proves that the class antagonisms are irreconcilable.

It is on this most important and fundamental point that the distortion of Marxism, proceeding along two main lines, begins.

On the one hand, the bourgeois, and particularly the petty-bourgeois, ideologists, compelled under the weight of indisputable historical facts to admit that the state only exists where there are class antagonisms and a class struggle, "correct" Marx in such a way as to make it appear that the state is an organ for the *reconciliation* of classes. According to Marx, the state could neither have arisen nor maintained itself had it been possible to reconcile classes. From what the petty-bourgeois and philistine professors and publicists say, with quite frequent and benevolent references to Marx, it appears that the state does reconcile classes. According to Marx, the state is an organ of class *rule*, an organ for the *oppression of one class by another*; it is the creation of "order", which legalises and perpetuates this oppression by moderating the conflict between the classes. In the opinion of the petty-bourgeois politicians, however, order means the reconciliation of classes, and not the oppression of one class by another; to alleviate the conflict means reconciling classes and not depriving the oppressed classes of definite means and methods of struggle to overthrow the oppressors.

For instance, when, in the revolution of 1917, the question of the significance and role of the state arose in all its magnitude as a practical question demanding immediate action, and, moreover, action on a mass scale, all the Socialist-Revolutionaries and Mensheviks descended at once to the petty-bourgeois theory that the "state" "reconciles" classes. Innumerable resolutions and articles by politicians of both these parties are thoroughly saturated with this petty-bourgeois and philistine "reconciliation" theory. That the state is an organ of the rule of a definite class which *cannot* be reconciled with its antipode (the class opposite to it) is something the petty-bourgeois democrats will never be able to understand. Their attitude to the state is one of the most striking manifestations of the fact that our Socialist-Revolutionaries and Mensheviks are not socialists at all (a point that we Bolsheviks have always maintained), but petty-bourgeois democrats using near-socialist phraseology.

On the other hand, the "Kautskyite" distortion of Marxism is far more subtle. "Theoretically", it is not denied that the state is an organ of class rule, or that class antagonisms are irreconcilable. But what is overlooked or glossed over is this: if the state is the product of the irreconcilability of class antagonisms, if it is a power standing *above* society and "*alienating* itself *more and more* from it", it is clear that the liberation of the oppressed class is impossible not only without a violent revolution, *but also without the destruction* of the apparatus of state power which was created by the ruling class and which is the embodiment of this "alienation". As we shall see later, Marx very explicitly drew this theoretically self-evident conclusion on the strength of a concrete historical analysis of the tasks of the revolution. And—as we shall show in detail further on—it is this conclusion which Kautsky has "forgotten" and distorted.

2. SPECIAL BODIES OF ARMED MEN, PRISONS, ETC.

Engels continues:

> "As distinct from the old gentile [tribal or clan] order,[134] the state, first, divides its subjects *according to territory*...."

This division seems "natural" to us, but it cost a prolonged struggle against the old organisation according to generations or tribes.

"The second distinguishing feature is the establishment of a *public power* which no longer directly coincides with the population organising itself as an armed force. This special, public power is necessary because a self-acting armed organisation of the population has become impossible since the split into classes.... This public power exists in every state; it consists not merely of armed men but also of material adjuncts, prisons, and institutions of coercion of all kinds, of which gentile [clan] society knew nothing...."

Engels elucidates the concept of the "power" which is called the state, a power which arose from society but places itself above it and alienates itself more and more from it. What does this power mainly consist of? It consists of special bodies of armed men having prisons, etc., at their command.

We are justified in speaking of special bodies of armed men, because the public power which is an attribute of every state "does not directly coincide" with the armed population, with its "self-acting armed organisation".

Like all great revolutionary thinkers, Engels tries to draw the attention of the class-conscious workers to what prevailing philistinism regards as least worthy of attention, as the most habitual thing, hallowed by prejudices that are not only deep-rooted but, one might say, petrified. A standing army and police are the chief instruments of state power. But how can it be otherwise?

From the viewpoint of the vast majority of Europeans of the end of the nineteenth century whom Engels was addressing, and who had not gone through or closely observed a single great revolution, it could not have been otherwise. They could not understand at all what a "self-acting armed organisation of the population" was. When asked why it became necessary to have special bodies of armed men placed above society and alienating themselves from it (police and a standing army), the West-European and Russian philistines are inclined to utter a few phrases borrowed from Spencer or Mikhailovsky, to refer to the growing complexity of social life, the differentiation of functions, and so on.

Such a reference seems "scientific", and effectively lulls the ordinary person to sleep by obscuring the important and basic fact, namely, the split of society into irreconcilably antagonistic classes.

Were it not for this split, the "self-acting armed organisation of the population" would differ from the primitive organisation of a stick-wielding herd of monkeys, or of primitive men, or of men united in clans, by its complexity, its high technical level, and so on. But such an organisation would still be possible.

It is impossible because civilised society is split into antagonistic, and, moreover, irreconcilably antagonistic, classes, whose "self-acting" arming would lead to an armed struggle between them. A state arises, a special power is created, special bodies of armed men, and every revolution, by destroying the state apparatus, shows us the naked class struggle, clearly shows us how the ruling class strives to restore the special bodies of armed men which serve *it*, and how the oppressed class strives to create a new organisation of this kind, capable of serving the exploited instead of the exploiters.

In the above argument, Engels raises theoretically the very same question which every great revolution raises before us in practice, palpably and, what is more, on a scale of mass action, namely, the question of the relationship between "special" bodies of armed men and the "self-acting armed organisation of the population". We shall see how this question is specifically illustrated by the experience of the European and Russian revolutions.

But to return to Engels's exposition.

He points out that sometimes—in certain parts of North America, for example—this public power is weak (he has in mind a rare exception in capitalist society, and those parts of North America in its pre-imperialist days where the free colonist predominated), but that, generally speaking, it grows stronger:

> "It [the public power] grows stronger, however, in proportion as class antagonisms within the state become more acute, and as adjacent states become larger and more populous. We have only to look at our present-day Europe, where class struggle and rivalry in conquest have tuned up the public power to such a pitch that it threatens to swallow the whole of society and even the state."

This was written not later than the early nineties of the last century, Engels's last preface being dated June 16, 1891. The turn towards imperialism—meaning the complete domination of the trusts, the omnipotence of the big banks, a grand-scale colonial policy, and so forth—was only just beginning in France, and was even weaker in North America and in Germany. Since then "rivalry in conquest" has taken a gigantic stride, all the more because by the beginning of the second decade of the twentieth century the world had been completely divided up among these "rivals in conquest", i.e., among the predatory Great Powers. Since then, military and naval armaments have grown fantastically and the predatory war of 1914-17 for the domination of the world by Britain or Germany, for the division of the spoils, has brought the "swallowing" of all the forces of society by the rapacious state power close to complete catastrophe.

Engels could, as early as 1891, point to "rivalry in conquest" as one of the most important distinguishing features of the foreign policy of the Great Powers, while the social-chauvinist scoundrels have ever since 1914, when this rivalry, many times intensified, gave rise to an imperialist war, been covering up the defence of the predatory interests of "their own" bourgeoisie with phrases about "defence of the fatherland", "defence of the republic and the revolution", etc.!

3. THE STATE—AN INSTRUMENT FOR THE EXPLOITATION OF THE OPPRESSED CLASS

The maintenance of the special public power standing above society requires taxes and state loans.

"...Having public power and the right to levy taxes," Engels writes, "the officials now stand, as organs of society, *above society*. The free, voluntary respect that was accorded to the organs of the gentile [clan] constitution does not satisfy them, even if they could gain it...." Special laws are enacted proclaiming the sanctity and immunity of the officials. "The shabbiest police servant" has more "authority" than the representatives of the clan, but even the head of the military power of a civilised state may well envy the elder of a clan the "unstrained respect" of society.

The question of the privileged position of the officials as organs of state power is raised here. The main point indicated is: what is it that places them *above* society? We shall see how this theoretical question was answered in practice by the Paris Commune in 1871 and how it was obscured from a reactionary standpoint by Kautsky in 1912.

"...Because the state arose from the need to hold class antagonisms in check, but because it arose, at the same time, in the midst of the conflict of these classes, it is, as a rule, the state of the most powerful, economically dominant class, which, through the medium of the state, becomes also the politically dominant class, and thus acquires new means of holding down and exploiting the oppressed class...." The ancient and feudal states were organs for the exploitation of the slaves and serfs; likewise, "the modern representative state is an instrument of exploitation of wage labour by capital. By way of exception, however, periods occur in which the warring classes balance each other so nearly that the state power as ostensible mediator acquires, for the moment, a certain degree of independence of both...." Such were the absolute monarchies of the seventeenth and eighteenth centuries, the Bonapartism[135] of the First and Second Empires in France, and the Bismarck regime in Germany.

Such, we may add, is the Kerensky government in republican Russia since it began to persecute the revolutionary proletariat, at a moment when, owing to the leadership of the petty-bourgeois democrats, the Soviets have *already* become impotent, while the bourgeoisie are not *yet* strong enough simply to disperse them.

In a democratic republic, Engels continues, "wealth exercises its power indirectly, but all the more surely", first, by means of the "direct corruption of officials" (America); secondly, by means of an "alliance of the government and the Stock Exchange" (France and America).

At present, imperialism and the domination of the banks have "developed" into an exceptional art both these methods of upholding and giving effect to the omnipotence of wealth in democratic republics of all descriptions. Since, for instance, in the very first months of the Russian democratic republic, one might say during the honeymoon of the "socialist" S.R.s and Mensheviks joined in wedlock to the bourgeoisie, in the coalition government, Mr. Palchinsky obstructed every measure intended for curbing the capitalists and their marauding practices, their plundering of the state by means of war contracts; and since later on Mr. Palchinsky, upon resigning from the Cabinet (and being, of course, replaced by another quite similar Palchinsky), was "rewarded" by the capitalists with a lucrative job with a salary of 120,000 rubles per annum— what would you call that? Direct or indirect bribery? An alliance of the government and the syndicates, or "merely" friendly relations? What role do the Chernovs, Tseretelis, Avksentyevs and Skobelevs play? Are they the "direct" or only the indirect allies of the millionaire treasury-looters?

Another reason why the omnipotence of "wealth" is more *certain* in a democratic republic is that it does not depend on defects in the political machinery or on the faulty political shell of capitalism. A democratic republic is the best possible political shell for capitalism, and, therefore, once capital has gained possession of this very best shell (through the Palchinskys, Chernovs, Tseretelis and Co.), it establishes its power so securely, so firmly, that *no* change of persons, institutions or parties in the bourgeois-democratic republic can shake it.

We must also note that Engels is most explicit in calling universal suffrage as well an instrument of bourgeois rule. Universal suffrage, he says, obviously taking account of the long experience of German Social-Democracy, is "the gauge of the maturity of the working class. It cannot and never will be anything more in the present-day state".

The petty-bourgeois democrats, such as our Socialist-Revolutionaries and Mensheviks, and also their twin brothers, all the social-chauvinists and opportunists of Western Europe, expect just this "more" from universal suffrage. They themselves share, and instil into the minds of the people, the false notion that universal suffrage "in the *present-day* state" is really capable of revealing the will of the majority of the working people and of securing its realisation.

Here we can only indicate this false notion, only point out that Engels's perfectly clear, precise and concrete statement is distorted at every step in the propaganda and agitation of the "official" (i.e., opportunist) socialist parties. A detailed exposure of the utter falsity of this notion which Engels brushes aside here is given in our further account of the views of Marx and Engels on the "*present-day*" state.

Engels gives a general summary of his views in the most popular of his works in the following words:

> "The state, then, has not existed from all eternity. There have been societies that did without it, that had no idea of the state and state power. At a certain stage of economic development, which was necessarily bound up with the split of society into classes, the state became a necessity owing to this split. We are now rapidly approaching a stage in the development of production at which the existence of these classes not only will have ceased to be a necessity, but will become a positive hindrance to production. They will fall as inevitably as they arose at an earlier stage. Along with them the state will inevitably fall. Society, which will reorganise production on the basis of a free and equal association of the producers, will put the whole machinery of state where it will then belong: into a museum of antiquities, by the side of the spinning-wheel and the bronze axe."

We do not often come across this passage in the propaganda and agitation literature of the present-day Social-Democrats. Even when we do come across it, it is mostly quoted in the same manner as one bows before an icon, i.e., it is done to show official respect for Engels, and no attempt is made to gauge the breadth and depth of the revolution that this relegating of "the whole machinery of state to a museum of antiquities" implies. In most cases we do not even find an understanding of what Engels calls the state machine.

4. THE "WITHERING AWAY" OF THE STATE, AND VIOLENT REVOLUTION

Engels's words regarding the "withering away" of the state are so widely known, they are so often quoted, and so clearly reveal the essence of the customary adaptation of Marxism to opportunism that we must deal with them in detail. We shall quote the whole argument from which they are taken.

"*The proletariat seizes state power and turns the means of production into state property to begin with.* But thereby it abolishes itself as the proletariat, abolishes all class distinctions and class antagonisms, and abolishes also the state as state. Society thus far, operating amid class antagonisms, needed the state, that is, an organisation of the particular exploiting class, for the maintenance of its external conditions of production, and, therefore, especially, for the purpose of forcibly keeping the exploited class in the conditions of oppression determined by the given mode of production (slavery, serfdom or bondage, wage-labour). The state was the official representative of society as a whole, its concentration in a a visible corporation. But it was this only insofar as it was the state of that class which itself represented, for its own time, society as a whole: in ancient times, the state of slave-owning citizens; in the Middle Ages, of the feudal nobility; in our own time, of the bourgeoisie. When at last it becomes the real representative of the whole of society, it renders itself unnecessary. As soon as there is no longer any social class to be held in subjection, as soon as class rule, and the individual struggle for existence based upon the present anarchy in production, with the collisions and excesses arising from this struggle, are removed, nothing more remains to be held in subjection—nothing necessitating a special coercive force, a state. The first act by which the state really comes forward as the representative of the whole of society—the taking possession of the means of production in the name of society—is also its last independent act as a state. State interference in social relations becomes, in one domain after another, superfluous, and then dies down of itself. The government of persons is replaced by the administration of things, and by the conduct of processes of production. The state is not 'abolished'. *It withers away.* This gives the measure of the value of the phrase 'a free people's state', both as to its justifiable use for a time from an agitational point of view, and as to its ultimate scientific insufficiency; and also of the so-called anarchists' demand that the state be abolished overnight." (*Herr Eugen Dühring's Revolution in Science* [*Anti-Dühring*], pp. 301-03, third German edition.)[136]

It is safe to say that of this argument of Engels's, which is so remarkably rich in ideas, only one point has become an integral part of socialist thought among modern socialist parties, namely, that according to Marx the state "withers away"—as distinct from the anarchist doctrine of the "abolition" of the state. To prune Marxism to such an extent means reducing it to opportunism, for this "interpretation" only leaves a vague notion of a slow, even, gradual change, of absence of leaps and storms, of absence of revolution. The current, widespread, popular, if one may say so, conception of the "withering away" of the state undoubtedly means obscuring, if not repudiating, revolution.

Such an "interpretation", however, is the crudest distortion of Marxism, advantageous only to the bourgeoisie. In point of theory, it is based on disregard for the most important circumstances and considerations indicated in, say, Engels's "summary" argument we have just quoted in full.

In the first place, at the very outset of his argument, Engels says that, in seizing state power, the proletariat thereby "abolishes the state as state". It is not done to ponder over the meaning of this. Generally, it is either ignored altogether, or is considered to be something in the nature of "Hegelian weakness" on Engels's part. As a matter of fact, however, these words briefly express the experience of one of the greatest proletarian revolutions, the Paris Commune of 1871, of which we shall speak in greater detail in its proper place. As a matter of fact, Engels speaks here of the pro-letarian revolution "abolishing" the *bourgeois* state, while the words about the state withering away refer to the remnants of the *proletarian* state *after* the socialist revolution. According to Engels, the bourgeois state does not "wither away", but is "*abolished*" by the proletariat in the course of the revolution. What withers away after this revolution is the proletarian state or semi-state.

Secondly, the state is a "special coercive force". Engels gives this splendid and extremely profound definition here with the utmost lucidity. And from it follows that the "special coercive force" for the suppression of the proletariat by the bourgeoisie, of millions of working people by handfuls of the rich, must be replaced by a "special coercive force" for the suppression of the bourgeoisie by the proletariat (the dictatorship of the proletariat). This is precisely what is meant by "abolition of the state as state". This is precisely the "act" of taking possession of the means of production in the name of society. And it is self-evident that *such* a replacement of one (bourgeois) "special force" by another (proletarian) "special force" cannot possibly take place in the form of "withering away".

Thirdly, in speaking of the state "withering away", and the even more graphic and colourful "dying down of itself", Engels refers quite clearly and definitely to the period *after* "the state has taken possession of the means of production in the name of the whole of society", that is, *after* the socialist revolution. We all know that the political form of the "state" at that time is the most complete democracy. But it never enters the head of any of the opportunists, who shamelessly distort Marxism, that Engels is consequently speaking here of *democracy* "dying down of itself", or "withering away". This seems very strange at first sight. But it is "incomprehensible" only to those who have not thought about democracy *also* being a state and, consequently, also disappearing when the state disappears. Revolution alone can "abolish" the bourgeois state. The state in general, i.e., the most complete democracy, can only "wither away".

Fourthly, after formulating his famous proposition that "the state withers away", Engels at once explains specifically that this proposition is directed against both the opportunists and the anarchists. In doing this, Engels puts in the forefront that conclusion, drawn from the proposition that "the state withers away", which is directed against the opportunists.

One can wager that out of every 10,000 persons who have read or heard about the "withering away" of the state, 9,990 are completely unaware, or do not remember, that Engels directed his conclusions from that proposition *not* against the anarchists *alone*. And of the remaining ten, probably nine do not know the meaning of a "free people's state" or why an attack on this slogan means an attack on the opportunists. This is how history is written! This is how a great revolutionary teaching is imperceptibly falsified and adapted to prevailing philistinism. The conclusion directed against the anarchists has been repeated thousands of times; it has been vulgarised, and rammed into people's heads in the shallowest form, and has acquired the strength of a prejudice, whereas the conclusion directed against the opportunists has been obscured and "forgotten"!

The "free people's state" was a programme demand and a catchword current among the German Social-Democrats in the seventies. This catchword is devoid of all political content except that it describes the concept of democracy in a pompous philistine fashion. Insofar as it hinted in a legally permissible manner at a democratic republic, Engels was prepared to "justify" its use "for a time" from an agitational point of view. But it was an opportunist catchword, for it amounted to something more than prettifying bourgeois democracy, and was also failure to understand the socialist criticism of the state in general. We are in favour of a democratic republic as the best form of state for the proletariat under capitalism. But we have no right to forget that wage slavery is the lot of the people even in the most democratic bourgeois republic. Furthermore, every state is a "special force" for the suppression of the oppressed class. Consequently, *every* state is *not* "free" and *not* a "people's state". Marx and Engels explained this repeatedly to their party comrades in the seventies.

Fifthly, the same work of Engels's, whose argument about the withering away of the state everyone remembers, also contains an argument of the significance of violent revolution. Engels's historical analysis of its role becomes a veritable panegyric on violent revolution. This "no one remembers". It is not done in modern socialist parties to talk or even think about the significance of this idea, and it plays no part whatever in their daily propaganda and agitation among the people. And yet it is inseparably bound up with the "withering away" of the state into one harmonious whole.

Here is Engels's argument:

> "...That force, however, plays yet another role [other than that of a diabolical power] in history, a revolutionary role; that, in the words of Marx, it is the midwife of every old society which is pregnant with a new one, that it is the instrument with which social movement forces its way through and shatters the dead, fossilised political forms—of this there is not a word in Herr Dühring. It is only with sighs and groans that he admits the possibility that force will perhaps be necessary for the overthrow of an economy based on exploitation— unfortunately, because all use of force demoralises, he says, the person who uses it. And this in spite of the immense moral and spiritual impetus which has been given by every victorious revolution! And this in Germany, where a violent collision— which may, after all, be forced on the people—would at least have the advantage of wiping out the servility which has penetrated the nation's mentality following the humiliation of the Thirty Years' War.[137] And this parson's mode of thought— dull, insipid and impotent—presumes to impose itself on the most revolutionary party that history has known!" (P. 193, third German edition, Part II, end of Chap. IV.)[138]

How can this panegyric on violent revolution, which Engels insistently brought to the attention of the German Social-Democrats between 1878 and 1894, i.e., right up to the time of his death, be combined with the theory of the "withering away" of the state to form a single theory?

Usually the two are combined by means of eclecticism, by an unprincipled or sophistic selection made arbitrarily (or to please the powers that be) of first one, then another argument, and in ninety-nine cases out of a hundred, if not more, it is the idea of the "withering away" that is placed in the forefront. Dialectics are replaced by eclecticism—this is the most usual, the most widespread practice to be met with in present-day official Social-Democratic literature in relation to Marxism. This sort of substitution is, of course, nothing new; it was observed even in the history of classical Greek philosophy. In falsifying Marxism in opportunist fashion, the substitution of eclecticism for dialectics is the easiest way of deceiving the people. It gives an illusory satisfaction; it seems to take into account all sides of the process, all trends of development, all the conflicting influences, and so forth, whereas in reality it provides no integral and revolutionary conception of the process of social development at all.

We have already said above, and shall show more fully later, that the theory of Marx and Engels of the inevitability of a violent revolution refers to the bourgeois state. The latter *cannot* be superseded by the proletarian state (the dictatorship of the proletariat) through the process of "withering away", but, as a general rule, only through a violent revolution. The panegyric Engels sang in its honour, and which fully corresponds to Marx's repeated statements (see the concluding passages of *The Poverty of Philosophy* and the *Communist Manifesto*,[139] with their proud and open proclamation of the inevitability of a violent revolution; see what Marx wrote nearly thirty years later, in criticising the Gotha Programme of 1875, when he mercilessly castigated the opportunist character of that programme)—this panegyric is by no means a mere "impulse", a mere declamation or a polemical sally. The necessity of systematically imbuing the masses with *this* and precisely this view of violent revolution lies at the root of the *entire* theory of Marx and Engels. The betrayal of their theory by the now prevailing social-chauvinist and Kautskyite trends expresses itself strikingly in both these trends ignoring *such* propaganda and agitation.

The supersession of the bourgeois state by the proletarian state is impossible without a violent revolution. The abolition of the proletarian state, i.e., of the state in general, is impossible except through the process of "withering away".

A detailed and concrete elaboration of these views was given by Marx and Engels when they studied each particular revolutionary situation, when they analysed the lessons of the experience of each particular revolution. We shall now pass to this, undoubtedly the most important, part of their theory.

CHAPTER II

THE STATE AND REVOLUTION. THE EXPERIENCE OF 1848-51

1. THE EVE OF THE REVOLUTION

The first works of mature Marxism—*The Poverty of Philosophy* and the *Communist Manifesto*—appeared just on the eve of the revolution of 1848. For this reason, in addition to presenting the general principles of Marxism, they reflect to a certain degree the concrete revolutionary situation of the time. It will, therefore, be more expedient, perhaps, to examine what the authors of these works said about the state immediately before they drew conclusions from the experience of the years 1848-51.

In *The Poverty of Philosophy*, Marx wrote:

> "...The working class, in the course of development, will substitute for the old bourgeois society an association which will preclude classes and their antagonism, and there will be no more political power proper, since political power is precisely the official expression of class antagonism in bourgeois society." (P. 182, German edition, 1885.)[140]

It is instructive to compare this general exposition of the idea of the state disappearing after the abolition of classes with the exposition contained in the *Communist Manifesto*, written by Marx and Engels a few months later—in November 1847, to be exact:

> "...In depicting the most general phases of the development of the proletariat, we traced the more or less veiled civil war, raging within existing society up to the point where that war breaks out into open revolution, and where the violent overthrow of the bourgeoisie lays the foundation for the sway of the proletariat....
>
> "...We have seen above that the first step in the revolution by the working class is to raise the proletariat to the position of ruling class, to win the battle of democracy.
>
> "The proletariat will use its political supremacy to wrest, by degrees, all capital from the bourgeoisie, to centralise all instruments of production in the hands of the state, i.e., of the proletariat organised as the ruling class; and to increase the total of productive forces as rapidly as possible." (Pp. 31 and 37, seventh German edition, 1906.)[141]

Here we have a formulation of one of the most remarkable and most important ideas of Marxism on the subject of the state. namely, the idea of the "dictatorship of the proletariat" (as Marx and Engels began to call it after the Paris Commune); and also, a highly interesting definition of the state, which is also one of the "forgotten words" of Marxism: *"the state, i.e., the proletariat organised as the ruling class"*.

This definition of the state has never been explained in the prevailing propaganda and agitation literature of the official Social-Democratic parties. More than that, it has been deliberately ignored, for it is absolutely irreconcilable with reformism, and is a slap in the face for the common opportunist prejudices and philistine illusions about the "peaceful development of democracy".

The proletariat needs the state—this is repeated by all the opportunists, social-chauvinists and Kautskyites, who assure us that this is what Marx taught. But they "*forget*" to add that, in the first place, according to Marx, the proletariat needs only a state which is withering away, i.e., a state so constituted that it begins to wither away immediately, and cannot but wither away. And, secondly, the working people need a "state, i.e., the proletariat organised as the ruling class".

The state is a special organisation of force: it is an organisation of violence for the suppression of some class. What class must the the proletariat suppress? Naturally, only the exploiting class, i.e., the bourgeoisie. The working people need the state only to suppress the resistance of the exploiters, and only the proletariat can direct this suppression, can carry it out. For the proletariat is the only class that is consistently revolutionary, the only class that can unite all the working and exploited people in the struggle against the bourgeoisie, in completely removing it.

The exploiting classes need political rule to maintain exploitation, i.e., in the selfish interests of an insignificant minority against the vast majority of the people. The exploited classes need political rule in order to completely abolish all exploitation, i.e., in the interests of the vast majority of the people, and against the insignificant minority consisting of the modern slave-owners—the land-owners and capitalists.

The petty-bourgeois democrats, those sham socialists who replaced the class struggle by dreams of class harmony, even pictured the socialist transformation in a dreamy fashion—not as the overthrow of the rule of the exploiting class, but as the peaceful submission of the minority to the majority which has become aware of its aims. This petty-bourgeois utopia, which is inseparable from the idea of the state being above classes, led in practice to the betrayal of the interests of the working classes, as was shown, for example, by the history of the French revolutions of 1848 and 1871, and by the experience of "socialist" participation in bourgeois Cabinets in Britain, France, Italy and other countries at the turn of the century.

All his life Marx fought against this petty-bourgeois socialism, now revived in Russia by the Socialist-Revolutionary and Menshevik parties. He developed his theory of the class struggle consistently, down to the theory of political power, of the state.

The overthrow of bourgeois rule can be accomplished only by the proletariat, the particular class whose economic conditions of existence prepare it for this task and provide it with the possibility and the power to perform it. While the bourgeoisie break up and disintegrate the peasantry and all the petty-bourgeois groups, they weld together, unite and organise the proletariat. Only the proletariat—by virtue of the economic role it plays in large-scale production—is capable of being the leader of *all* the working and exploited people, whom the bourgeoisie exploit, oppress and crush, often not less but more than they do the proletarians, but who are incapable of waging an *independent* struggle for their emancipation.

The theory of the class struggle, applied by Marx to the question of the state and the socialist revolution, leads as a matter of course to the recognition of the *political rule* of the proletariat, of its dictatorship, i.e., of undivided power directly backed by the armed force of the people. The overthrow of the bourgeoisie can be achieved only by the proletariat becoming the *ruling class*, capable of crushing the inevitable and desperate resistance of the bourgeoisie, and of organising *all* the working and exploited people for the new economic system.

The proletariat needs state power, a centralised organisation of force, an organisation of violence, both to crush the resistance of the exploiters and to *lead* the enormous mass of the population—the peasants, the petty bourgeoisie, and semi-proletarians—in the work of organising a socialist economy.

By educating the workers' party, Marxism educates the vanguard of the proletariat, capable of assuming power and *leading the whole people* to socialism, of directing and organising the new system, of being the teacher, the guide, the leader of all the working and exploited people in organising their social life without the bourgeoisie and against the bourgeoisie. By contrast, the opportunism now prevailing trains the members of the workers' party to be the representatives of the better-paid workers, who lose touch with the masses, "get along" fairly well under capitalism, and sell their birthright for a mess of pottage, i.e., renounce their role as revolutionary leaders of the people against the bourgeoisie.

Marx's theory of "the state, i.e., the proletariat organised as the ruling class", is inseparably bound up with the whole of his doctrine of the revolutionary role of the proletariat in history. The culmination of this role is the proletarian dictatorship, the political rule of the proletariat.

But since the proletariat needs the state as a *special* form of organisation of violence *against* the bourgeoisie, the following conclusion suggests itself: is it conceivable that such an organisation can be created without first abolishing, destroying the state machine created by the bourgeoisie *for themselves*? The *Communist Manifesto* leads straight to this conclusion, and it is of this conclusion that Marx speaks when summing up the experience of the revolution of 1848-51.

2. THE REVOLUTION SUMMED UP

Marx sums up his conclusions from the revolution of 1848-51, on the subject of the state we are concerned with, in the following argument contained in *The Eighteenth Brumaire of Louis Bonaparte*:

"... But the revolution is thoroughgoing. It is still journeying through purgatory. It does its work methodically. By December 2, 1851 [the day of Louis Bonaparte's coup d'état], it had completed one half of its preparatory work. It is now completing the other half. First it perfected the parliamentary power, in order to be able to overthrow it. Now that it has attained this, it is perfecting the *executive power*, reducing it to its purest expression, isolating it, setting it up against itself as the sole object, *in order to concentrate all its forces of destruction against it* [italics ours]. And when it has done this second half of its preliminary work, Europe will leap from its seat and exultantly exclaim: well grubbed, old mole!

"This executive power with its enormous bureaucratic and military organisation, with its vast and ingenious state machinery, with a host of officials numbering half a million, besides an army of another half million, this appalling parasitic body, which enmeshes the body of French society and chokes all its pores, sprang up in the days of the absolute monarchy, with the decay of the feudal system, which it helped to hasten." The first French Revolution developed centralisation, "but at the same time" it increased "the extent, the attributes and the number of agents of governmental power. Napoleon completed this state machinery". The legitimate monarchy and the July monarchy "added nothing but a greater division of labour....

"... Finally, in its struggle against the revolution, the parliamentary republic found itself compelled to strengthen, along with repressive measures, the resources and centralisation of governmental power. All revolutions perfected this machine instead of smashing it [italics ours]. The parties that contended in turn for domination regarded the possession of this huge state edifice as the principal spoils of the victor." (*The Eighteenth Brumaire of Louis Bonaparte*, pp. 98-99, fourth edition, Hamburg, 1907.)[142]

In this remarkable argument Marxism takes a tremendous step forward compared with the *Communist Manifesto*. In the latter the question of the state is still treated in an extremely abstract manner, in the most general terms and expressions. In the above-quoted passage. the question is treated in a concrete manner, and the conclusion is extremely precise, definite, practical and palpable:

Is Lenin stretching Marx's point?

all previous revolutions perfected the state machine, whereas it must be broken, smashed.

This conclusion is the chief and fundamental point in the Marxist theory of the state. And it is precisely this fundamental point which has been completely *ignored* by the dominant official Social-Democratic parties and, indeed, *distorted* (as we shall see later) by the foremost theoretician of the Second International, Karl Kautsky.

The *Communist Manifesto* gives a general summary of history, which compels us to regard the state as the organ of class rule and leads us to the inevitable conclusion that the proletariat cannot overthrow the bourgeoisie without first winning political power, without attaining political supremacy, without transforming the state into the "proletariat organised as the ruling class"; and that this proletarian state will begin to wither away immediately after its victory because the state is unnecessary and cannot exist in a society in which there are no class antagonisms. The question as to how, from the point of view of historical development, the replacement of the bourgeois by the proletarian state is to take place is not raised here.

This is the question Marx raises and answers in 1852. True to his philosophy of dialectical materialism, Marx takes as his basis the historical experience of the great years of revolution, 1848 to 1851. Here, as everywhere else, his theory is a *summing up of experience*, illuminated by a profound philosophical conception of the world and a rich knowledge of history.

The problem of the state is put specifically: How did the bourgeois state, the state machine necessary for the rule of the bourgeoisie, come into being historically? What changes did it undergo, what evolution did it perform in the course of bourgeois revolutions and in the face of the independent actions of the oppressed classes? What are the tasks of the proletariat in relation to this state machine?

The centralised state power that is peculiar to bourgeois society came into being in the period of the fall of absolutism. Two institutions most characteristic of this state machine are the bureaucracy and the standing army. In their works, Marx and Engels repeatedly show that the bourgeoisie are connected with these institutions by thousands of threads. Every worker's experience illustrates this connection in an extremely graphic and impressive manner. From its own bitter experience, the working class learns to recognise this connection. That is why it so easily grasps and so firmly learns the doctrine which shows the inevitability of this connection, a doctrine which the petty-bourgeois democrats either ignorantly and flippantly deny, or still more flippantly admit "in general", while forgetting to draw appropriate practical conclusions.

The bureaucracy and the standing army are a "parasite" on the body of bourgeois society—a parasite created by the internal antagonisms which rend that society, but a parasite which "chokes" all its vital pores. The Kautskyite opportunism now prevailing in official Social-Democracy considers the view that the state is a *parasitic organism* to be the peculiar and exclusive attribute of anarchism. It goes without saying that this distortion of Marxism is of vast advantage to those philistines who have reduced socialism to the unheard-of disgrace of justifying and prettifying the imperialist war by applying to it the concept of "defence of the fatherland"; but it is unquestionably a distortion, nevertheless.

The development, perfection and strengthening of the bureaucratic and military apparatus proceeded during all the numerous bourgeois revolutions which Europe has witnessed since the fall of feudalism. In particular, it is the petty bourgeoisie who are attracted to the side of the big bourgeoisie and are largely subordinated to them through this apparatus, which provides the upper sections of the peasants, small artisans, tradesmen and the like with comparatively comfortable, quiet and respectable jobs raising their holders *above* the people. Consider what happened in Russia during the six months following February 27, 1917. The official posts which formerly were given by preference to the Black Hundreds[143] have now become the spoils of the Cadets, Mensheviks and Socialist-Revolutionaries. Nobody has really thought of introducing any serious reforms. Every effort has been made to put them off "until the Constituent Assembly meets", and to steadily put off its convocation until after the war![144] But there has been no delay, no waiting for the Constituent Assembly, in the matter of dividing the spoils, of getting the lucrative jobs of ministers, deputy ministers, governors-general, etc., etc.! The game of combinations that has been played in forming the government has been, in essence, only an expression of this division and redivision of the "spoils", which has been going on above and below, throughout the country, in every department of central and local government. The six months between February 27 and August 27, 1917, can be summed up, objectively summed up beyond all dispute, as follows: reforms shelved, distribution of official jobs accomplished and "mistakes" in the distribution corrected by a few redistributions.

But the more the bureaucratic apparatus is "redistributed" among the various bourgeois and petty-bourgeois parties (among the Cadets, Socialist-Revolutionaries and Mensheviks in the case of Russia), the more keenly aware the oppressed classes, and the proletariat at their head, become of their irreconcilable hostility to the *whole* of bourgeois society. Hence the need for all bourgeois parties, even for the most democratic and "revolutionary-democratic" among them, to intensify repressive measures against the revolutionary proletariat, to strengthen the apparatus of coercion, i.e., the state machine. This course of events compels the revolution *"to concentrate all its forces of destruction"* against the state power, and to set itself the aim, not of improving the state machine, but of *smashing and destroying* it.

It was not logical reasoning, but actual developments, the actual experience of 1848-51, that led to the matter being presented in this way. The extent to which Marx held strictly to the solid ground of historical experience can be seen from the fact that, in 1852, he did not yet specifically raise the question of *what* was to take the place of the state machine to be destroyed. Experience had not yet provided material for dealing with this question, which history placed on the agenda later on, in 1871. In 1852, all that could be established with the accuracy of scientific observation was that the proletarian revolution *had approached* the task of "concentrating all its forces of destruction" against the state power, of "smashing" the state machine.

Here the question may arise: is it correct to generalise the experience, observations and conclusions of Marx, to apply them to a field that is wider than the history of France during the three years 1848-51? Before proceeding to deal with this question, let us recall a remark made by Engels and then examine the facts. In his introduction to the third edition of *The Eighteenth Brumaire*, Engels wrote:

> "... France is the country where, more than anywhere else, the historical class struggles were each time fought out to a finish, and where, consequently, the changing political forms within which they move and in which their results are summarised have been stamped in the sharpest outlines. The centre of feudalism in the Middle Ages, the model country, since the Renaissance, of a unified monarchy based on social estates, France demolished feudalism in the Great Revolution and established the rule of the bourgeoisie in a classical purity unequalled by any other European land. And the struggle of the upward-striving proletariat against the ruling bourgeoisie appeared here in an acute form unknown elsewhere." (P. 4, 1907 edition.)[145]

The last remark is out of date inasmuch as since 1871 there has been a lull in the revolutionary struggle of the French proletariat, although, long as this lull may be, it does not at all preclude the possibility that in the coming proletarian revolution France may show herself to be the classic country of the class struggle to a finish.

Let us, however, cast a general glance over the history of the advanced countries at the turn of the century. We shall see that the same process went on more slowly, in more varied forms, in a much wider field: on the one hand, the development of "parliamentary power" both in the republican countries (France, America, Switzerland), and in the monarchies (Britain, Germany to a certain extent, Italy, the Scandinavian countries, etc.); on the other hand, a struggle for power among the various bourgeois and pettybourgeois parties which distributed and redistributed the "spoils" of office, with the foundations of bourgeois society unchanged; and, lastly, the perfection and consolidation of the "executive power", of its bureaucratic and military apparatus.

There is not the slightest doubt that these features are common to the whole of the modern evolution of all capitalist states in general. In the three years 1848-51 France displayed, in a swift, sharp, concentrated form, the very same processes of development which are peculiar to the whole capitalist world.

Imperialism—the era of bank capital, the era of gigantic capitalist monopolies, of the development of monopoly capitalism into state-monopoly capitalism—has clearly shown an extraordinary strengthening of the "state machine" and an unprecedented growth in its bureaucratic and military apparatus in connection with the intensification of repressive measures against the proletariat both in the monarchical and in the freest, republican countries.

World history is now undoubtedly leading, on an incomparably larger scale than in 1852, to the "concentration of all the forces" of the proletarian revolution on the "destruction" of the state machine.

What the proletariat will put in its place is suggested by the highly instructive material furnished by the Paris Commune.

3. THE PRESENTATION OF THE QUESTION BY MARX IN 1852[*]

In 1907, Mehring, in the magazine *Neue Zeit* (Vol. XXV, 2, p. 164), published extracts from Marx's letter to Weydemeyer dated March 5, 1852. This letter, among other things, contains the following remarkable observation:

"And now as to myself, no credit is due to me for discovering the existence of classes in modern society or the struggle between them. Long before me bourgeois historians had described the historical development of this class struggle and bourgeois economists, the economic anatomy of the classes. What I did that was new was to prove: 1) that the *existence of classes* is only bound up with *particular, historical phases in the development of production* (historische Entwicklungsphasen der Produktion), 2) that the class struggle necessarily

---

[*] Added in the second edition.

leads to the *dictatorship of the proletariat*, 3) that this dictatorship itself only constitutes the transition to the *abolition of all classes* and to a *classless society*...."[146]

In these words, Marx succeeded in expressing with striking clarity, first, the chief and radical difference between his theory and that of the foremost and most profound thinkers of the bourgeoisie; and, secondly, the essence of his theory of the state.

It is often said and written that the main point in Marx's theory is the class struggle. But this is wrong. And this wrong notion very often results in an opportunist distortion of Marxism and its falsification in a spirit acceptable to the bourgeoisie. For the theory of the class struggle was created *not* by Marx, *but* by the bourgeoisie *before* Marx, and, generally speaking, it is *acceptable* to the bourgeoisie. Those who recognise *only* the class struggle are not yet Marxists; they may be found to be still within the bounds of bourgeois thinking and bourgeois politics. To confine Marxism to the theory of the class struggle means curtailing Marxism, distorting it, reducing it to something acceptable to the bourgeoisie. Only he is a Marxist who *extends* the recognition of the class struggle to the recognition of the *dictatorship of the proletariat*. This is what constitutes the most profound distinction between the Marxist and the ordinary petty (as well as big) bourgeois. This is the touchstone on which the *real* understanding and recognition of Marxism should be tested. And it is not surprising that when the history of Europe brought the working class face to face with this question as a *practical* issue, not only all the opportunists and reformists, but all the Kautskyites (people who vacillate between reformism and Marxism) proved to be miserable philistines and petty-bourgeois democrats *repudiating* the dictatorship of the proletariat. Kautsky's pamphlet, *The Dictatorship of the Proletariat*, published in August 1918, i.e., long after the first edition of the present book, is a perfect example of petty-bourgeois distortion of Marxism and base renunciation of it *in deeds*, while hypocritically recognising it *in words* (see my pamphlet, *The Proletarian Revolution and the Renegade Kautsky*, Petrograd and Moscow, 1918)*.

Opportunism today, as represented by its principal spokesman, the ex-Marxist Karl Kautsky, fits in completely with Marx's characterisation of the *bourgeois* position quoted above, for this opportunism limits recognition of the class struggle to the sphere of bourgeois relations. (Within this sphere, within its framework, not a single educated liberal will refuse to recognise the class struggle "in principle"!) Opportunism *does not extend* recognition of the class struggle to the cardinal point, to the period of *transition* from

* See *Collected Works*, Vol. 28, pp. 227-319.—*Ed.*

capitalism to communism, of the *overthrow* and the complete *abolition* of the bourgeoisie. In reality, this period inevitably is a period of an unprecedentedly violent class struggle in unprecedentedly acute forms, and, consequently, during this period the state must inevitably be a state that is democratic *in a new way* (for the proletariat and the propertyless in general) and dictatorial *in a new way* (against the bourgeoisie).

Further. The essence of Marx's theory of the state has been mastered only by those who realise that the dictatorship of a *single* class is necessary not only for every class society in general, not only for the *proletariat* which has overthrown the bourgeoisie, but also for the entire *historical period* which separates capitalism from "classless society", from communism. Bourgeois states are most varied in form, but their essence is the same: all these states, whatever their form, in the final analysis are inevitably the *dictatorship of the bourgeoisie*. The transition from capitalism to communism is certainly bound to yield a tremendous abundance and variety of political forms, but the essence will inevitably be the same: *the dictatorship of the proletariat*.

CHAPTER III

THE STATE AND REVOLUTION. EXPERIENCE OF THE PARIS COMMUNE OF 1871. MARX'S ANALYSIS

1. WHAT MADE THE COMMUNARDS' ATTEMPT HEROIC?

It is well known that in the autumn of 1870, a few months before the Commune, Marx warned the Paris workers that any attempt to overthrow the government would be the folly of despair. But when, in March 1871, a decisive battle was *forced* upon the workers and they accepted it, when the uprising had become a fact, Marx greeted the proletarian revolution with the greatest enthusiasm, in spite of unfavourable auguries. Marx did not persist in the pedantic attitude of condemning an "untimely" movement as did the ill-famed Russian renegade from Marxism, Plekhanov, who in November 1905 wrote encouragingly about the workers' and peasants' struggle, but after December 1905 cried, liberal fashion: "They should not have taken up arms."

Marx, however, was not only enthusiastic about the heroism of the Communards, who, as he expressed it, "stormed heaven". Although the mass revolutionary movement did not achieve its aim, he regarded it as a historic experience of enormous importance, as a certain advance of the world proletarian revolution, as a practical step that was more important than hundreds of programmes and arguments. Marx endeavoured to analyse this experiment, to draw tactical lessons from it and re-examine his theory in the light of it.

The only "correction" Marx thought it necessary to make to the *Communist Manifesto* he made on the basis of the revolutionary experience of the Paris Communards.

The last preface to the new German edition of the *Communist Manifesto*, signed by both its authors, is dated June 24, 1872. In this preface the authors, Karl Marx and Frederick Engels, say that the programme of the *Communist Manifesto* "has in some details become out-of-date", and they go on to say:

"...*One thing especially was proved by the Commune, viz., that 'the working class cannot simply lay hold of the ready-made state machinery and wield it for its own purposes'*...."[147]

The authors took the words that are in single quotation marks in this passage from Marx's book, *The Civil War in France*.

Thus, Marx and Engels regarded one principal and fundamental lesson of the Paris Commune as being of such enormous impor-tance that they introduced it as an important correction into the *Communist Manifesto*.

Most characteristically, it is this important correction that has been distorted by the opportunists, and its meaning probably is not known to nine-tenths, if not ninety-nine-hundredths, of the readers of the *Communist Manifesto*. We shall deal with this distortion more fully farther on, in a chapter devoted specially to distortions. Here it will be sufficient to note that the current, vulgar "inter-pretation" of Marx's famous statement just quoted is that Marx here allegedly emphasises the idea of slow development in contra-distinction to the seizure of power, and so on.

As a matter of fact, *the exact opposite is the case*. Marx's idea is that the working class must *break up*, *smash* the "ready-made state machinery", and not confine itself merely to laying hold of it.

On April 12, 1871, i.e., just at the time of the Commune, Marx wrote to Kugelmann:

"...If you look up the last chapter of my *Eighteenth Bru-maire*, you will find that I declare that the next attempt of the French Revolution will be no longer, as before, to transfer the bureaucratic-military machine from one hand to another, but to *smash* it [Marx's italics—the original is *zerbrechen*], and this is the precondition for every real people's revolution on the Continent. And this is what our heroic Party comrades in Paris are attempting." (*Neue Zeit*, Vol. XX, 1, 1901-02, p. 709.)[148] (The letters of Marx to Kugelmann have appeared in Russian in no less than two editions, one of which I edited and supplied with a preface.)*

* See *Collected Works*, Vol. 12, pp. 104-12.—*Ed.*

The words, "to smash the bureaucratic-military machine", briefly express the principal lesson of Marxism regarding the tasks of the proletariat during a revolution in relation to the state. And it is this lesson that has been not only completely ignored, but positively distorted by the prevailing, Kautskyite, "interpretation" of Marxism!

As for Marx's reference to *The Eighteenth Brumaire*, we have quoted the relevant passage in full above.

It is interesting to note, in particular, two points in the above-quoted argument of Marx. First, he restricts his conclusion to the Continent. This was understandable in 1871, when Britain was still the model of a purely capitalist country, but without a militarist clique and, to a considerable degree, without a bureaucracy. Marx therefore excluded Britain, where a revolution, even a people's revolution, then seemed possible, and indeed was possible, *without* the precondition of destroying the "ready-made state machinery".

Today, in 1917, at the time of the first great imperialist war, this restriction made by Marx is no longer valid. Both Britain and America, the biggest and the last representatives—in the whole world—of Anglo-Saxon "liberty", in the sense that they had no militarist cliques and bureaucracy, have completely sunk into the all-European filthy, bloody morass of bureaucratic-military institutions which subordinate everything to themselves, and suppress everything. Today, in Britain and America, too, "the precondition for every real people's revolution" is the *smashing*, the *destruction* of the "ready-made state machinery" (made and brought up to "European", general imperialist, perfection in those countries in the years 1914-17).

Secondly, particular attention should be paid to Marx's extremely profound remark that the destruction of the bureaucratic-military state machine is "the precondition for every real *people's* revolution". This idea of a "people's" revolution seems strange coming from Marx, so that the Russian Plekhanovites and Mensheviks, those followers of Struve who wish to be regarded as Marxists, might possibly declare such an expression to be a "slip of the pen" on Marx's part. They have reduced Marxism to such a state of wretchedly liberal distortion that nothing exists for them beyond the antithesis between bourgeois revolution and proletarian revolution, and even this antithesis they interpret in an utterly lifeless way.

If we take the revolutions of the twentieth century as examples we shall, of course, have to admit that the Portuguese and the Turkish revolutions are both bourgeois revolutions. Neither of them, however, is a "people's" revolution, since in neither does the mass of the people, their vast majority, come out actively, independently, with their own economic and political demands to any noticeable degree. By contrast, although the Russian bourgeois revolution of 1905-07 displayed no such "brilliant" successes as at times fell to the Portuguese[149] and Turkish revolutions, it was undoubtedly a "real people's" revolution, since the mass of the people, their majority, the very lowest social groups, crushed by oppression and exploitation, rose independently and stamped on the entire course of the revolution the imprint of *their* own demands, *their* attempts to build in their own way a new society in place of the old society that was being destroyed.

In Europe, in 1871, the proletariat did not constitute the majority of the people in any country on the Continent. A "people's" revolution, one actually sweeping the majority into its stream, could be such only if it embraced both the proletariat and the peasants. These two classes then constituted the "people". These two classes are united by the fact that the "bureaucratic-military state machine" oppresses, crushes, exploits them. To *smash* this machine, *to break it up*, is truly in the interest of the "people", of their majority, of the workers and most of the peasants, is "the precondition" for a free alliance of the poor peasants and the proletarians, whereas without such an alliance democracy is unstable and socialist transformation is impossible.

As is well known, the Paris Commune was actually working its way toward such an alliance, although it did not reach its goal owing to a number of circumstances, internal and external.

Consequently, in speaking of a "real people's revolution", Marx, without in the least discounting the special features of the petty bourgeoisie (he spoke a great deal about them and often), took strict account of the actual balance of class forces in most of the continental countries of Europe in 1871. On the other hand, he stated that the "smashing" of the state machine was required by the interests of both the workers and the peasants, that it united them, that it placed before them the common task of removing the "parasite" and of replacing it by something new.

By what exactly?

2. WHAT IS TO REPLACE THE SMASHED STATE MACHINE?

In 1847, in the *Communist Manifesto*, Marx's answer to this question was as yet a purely abstract one; to be exact, it was an answer that indicated the tasks, but not the ways of accomplishing them. The answer given in the *Communist Manifesto* was that this machine was to be replaced by "the proletariat organised as the ruling class", by the "winning of the battle of democracy".

Marx did not indulge in utopias; he expected the *experience* of the mass movement to provide the reply to the question as to the

specific forms this organisation of the proletariat as the ruling
class would assume and as to the exact manner in which this
organisation would be combined with the most complete, most
consistent "winning of the battle of democracy".

Marx subjected the experience of the Commune, meagre as it
was, to the most careful analysis in *The Civil War in France.* Let
us quote the most important passages of this work.

> Originating from the Middle Ages, there developed in the
> nineteenth century "the centralised state power, with its ubiq-
> uitous organs of standing army, police, bureaucracy, clergy,
> and judicature". With the development of class antagonisms
> between capital and labour, "state power assumed more and
> more the character of a public force for the suppression of the
> working class, of a machine of class rule. After every revolution,
> which marks an advance in the class struggle, the purely
> coercive character of the state power stands out in bolder and
> bolder relief". After the revolution of 1848-49, state power
> became "the national war instrument of capital against labour".
> The Second Empire consolidated this.
>
> "The direct antithesis to the empire was the Commune." It
> was the "specific form" of "a republic that was not only to
> remove the monarchical form of class rule, but class rule
> itself. . . ."

What was this "specific" form of the proletarian, socialist
republic? What was the state it began to create?

> ". . .The first decree of the Commune . . . was the suppression
> of the standing army, and its replacement by the armed
> people. . . ."

This demand now figures in the programme of every party calling
itself socialist. The real worth of their programmes, however, is
best shown by the behaviour of our Socialist-Revolutionaries and
Mensheviks, who, right after the revolution of February 27, actually refused to carry out this demand!

> "The Commune was formed of the municipal councillors,
> chosen by universal suffrage in the various wards of Paris,
> responsible and revocable at any time. The majority of its
> members were naturally working men, or acknowledged
> representatives of the working class. . . .
>
> The police, which until then had been the instrument of the
> Government, was at once stripped of its political attributes,
> and turned into the responsible and at all times revocable in-
> strument of the Commune. So were the officials of all other
> branches of the administration. From the members of the

Commune downwards, public service had to be done at *workmen's wages*. The privileges and the representation allowances of the high dignitaries of state disappeared along with the dignitaries themselves.... Having once got rid of the standing army and the police, the instruments of the physical force of the old Government, the Commune proceeded at once to break the instrument of spiritual suppression, the power of the priests.... The judicial functionaries lost that sham independence... they were thenceforward to be elective, responsible, and revocable...."[150]

The Commune, therefore, appears to have replaced the smashed state machine "only" by fuller democracy: abolition of the standing army; all officials to be elected and subject to recall. But as a matter of fact this "only" signifies a gigantic replacement of certain institutions by other institutions of a fundamentally different type. This is exactly a case of "quantity being transformed into quality": democracy, introduced as fully and consistently as is at all conceivable, is transformed from bourgeois into proletarian democracy; from the state (=a special force for the suppression of a particular class) into something which is no longer the state proper.

It is still necessary to suppress the bourgeoisie and crush their resistance. This was particularly necessary for the Commune; and one of the reasons for its defeat was that it did not do this with sufficient determination. The organ of suppression, however, is here the majority of the population, and not a minority, as was always the case under slavery, serfdom and wage slavery. And since the majority of the people *itself* suppresses its oppressors, a "special force" for suppression *is no longer necessary*! In this sense, the state *begins to wither away*. Instead of the special institutions of a privileged minority (privileged officialdom, the chiefs of the standing army), the majority itself can directly fulfil all these functions, and the more the functions of state power are performed by the people as a whole, the less need there is for the existence of this power.

In this connection, the following measures of the Commune, emphasised by Marx, are particularly noteworthy: the abolition of all representation allowances, and of all monetary privileges to officials, the reduction of the remuneration of *all* servants of the state to the level of *"workmen's wages"*. This shows more clearly than anything else the *turn* from bourgeois to proletarian democracy, from the democracy of the oppressors to that of the oppressed classes, from the state as a *"special force"* for the suppression of a particular class to the suppression of the oppressors by the *general force* of the majority of the people—the workers and the peasants. And it is on this particularly striking point, perhaps the most important as far as the problem of the state is concerned, that the ideas of Marx have been most completely ignored! In popular commentaries, the number of which is legion, this is not mentioned. The thing done is to keep silent about it as if it were a piece of old-fashioned "naïveté", just as Christians, after their religion had been given the status of a state religion, "forgot" the "naïveté" of primitive Christianity with its democratic revolutionary spirit.

The reduction of the remuneration of high state officials seems to be "simply" a demand of naïve, primitive democracy. One of the "founders" of modern opportunism, the ex-Social-Democrat Eduard Bernstein, has more than once repeated the vulgar bourgeois jeers at "primitive" democracy. Like all opportunists, and like the present Kautskyites, he did not understand at all that, first of all, the transition from capitalism to socialism is *impossible* without a certain "reversion" to "primitive" democracy (for how else can the majority, and then the whole population without exception, proceed to discharge state functions?); and that, secondly, "primitive democracy" based on capitalism and capitalist culture is not the same as primitive democracy in prehistoric or pre-capitalist times. Capitalist culture has *created* large-scale production, factories, railways, the postal service, telephones, etc., and *on this basis* the great majority of the functions of the old "state power" have become so simplified and can be reduced to such exceedingly simple operations of registration, filing and checking that they can be easily performed by every literate person, can quite easily be performed for ordinary "workmen's wages", and that these functions can (and must) be stripped of every shadow of privilege, of every semblance of "official grandeur".

All officials, without exception, elected and subject to recall *at any time,* their salaries reduced to the level of ordinary "workmen's wages"—these simple and "self-evident" democratic measures, while completely uniting the interests of the workers and the majority of the peasants, at the same time serve as a bridge leading from capitalism to socialism. These measures concern the reorganisation of the state, the purely political reorganisation of society; but, of course, they acquire their full meaning and significance only in connection with the "expropriation of the expropriators" either being accomplished or in preparation, i.e., with the transformation of capitalist private ownership of the means of production into social ownership.

"The Commune," Marx wrote, "made that catchword of all bourgeois revolutions, cheap government, a reality, by abolishing the two greatest sources of expenditure—the army and the officialdom."

From the peasants, as from other sections of the petty bourgeoisie, only an insignificant few "rise to the top", "get on in the world" in the bourgeois sense, i.e., become either well-to-do, bourgeois, or officials in secure and privileged positions. In every capitalist country where there are peasants (as there are in most capitalist countries), the vast majority of them are oppressed by the government and long for its overthrow, long for "cheap" government. This can be achieved *only* by the proletariat; and by achieving it, the proletariat at the same time takes a step towards the socialist reorganisation of the state.

3. ABOLITION OF PARLIAMENTARISM

"The Commune," Marx wrote, "was to be a working, not a parliamentary, body, executive and legislative at the same time. . . .

"Instead of deciding once in three or six years which member of the ruling class was to represent and repress [ver- und zertreten] the people in parliament, universal suffrage was to serve the people constituted in communes, as individual suffrage serves every other employer in the search for workers, foremen and accountants for his business."

Owing to the prevalence of social-chauvinism and opportunism, this remarkable criticism of parliamentarism, made in 1871, also belongs now to the "forgotten words" of Marxism. The professional Cabinet Ministers and parliamentarians, the traitors to the proletariat and the "practical" socialists of our day, have left all criticism of parliamentarism to the anarchists, and, on this wonderfully reasonable ground, they denounce *all* criticism of parliamentarism as "anarchism"!! It is not surprising that the proletariat of the "advanced" parliamentary countries, disgusted with such "socialists" as the Scheidemanns, Davids, Legiens, Sembats, Renaudels, Hendersons, Vanderveldes, Staunings, Brantings, Bissolatis and Co., has been with increasing frequency giving its sympathies to anarcho-syndicalism, in spite of the fact that the latter is merely the twin brother of opportunism.

For Marx, however, revolutionary dialectics was never the empty fashionable phrase, the toy rattle, which Plekhanov, Kautsky and others have made of it. Marx knew how to break with anarchism ruthlessly for its inability to make use even of the "pigsty" of bourgeois parliamentarism, especially when the situation was obviously not revolutionary; but at the same time he knew how to subject parliamentarism to genuinely revolutionary proletarian criticism.

To decide once every few years which member of the ruling class is to repress and crush the people through parliament—this is the real essence of bourgeois parliamentarism, not only in parliamentary-constitutional monarchies, but also in the most democratic republics.

But if we deal with the question of the state, and if we consider parliamentarism as one of the institutions of the state, from the point of view of the tasks of the proletariat in *this* field, what is the way out of parliamentarism? How can it be dispensed with?

Once again we must say: the lessons of Marx, based on the study of the Commune, have been so completely forgotten that the present-day "Social-Democrat" (i.e., present-day traitor to socialism) really cannot understand any criticism of parliamentarism other than anarchist or reactionary criticism.

The way out of parliamentarism is not, of course, the abolition of representative institutions and the elective principle, but the conversion of the representative institutions from talking shops into "working" bodies. "The Commune was to be a working, not a parliamentary, body, executive and legislative at the same time."

"A working, not a parliamentary, body"—this is a blow straight from the shoulder at the present-day parliamentarians and parliamentary "lap dogs" of Social-Democracy! Take any parliamentary country, from America to Switzerland, from France to Britain, Norway and so forth—in these countries the real business of "state" is performed behind the scenes and is carried on by the departments, chancelleries and General Staffs. Parliament is given up to talk for the special purpose of fooling the "common people". This is so true that even in the Russian republic, a bourgeois-democratic republic, all these sins of parliamentarism came out at once, even before it managed to set up a real parliament. The heroes of rotten philistinism, such as the Skobelevs and Tseretelis, the Chernovs and Avksentyevs, have even succeeded in polluting the Soviets after the fashion of the most disgusting bourgeois parliamentarism, in converting them into mere talking shops. In the Soviets, the "socialist" Ministers are fooling the credulous rustics with phrase-mongering and resolutions. In the government itself a sort of permanent shuffle is going on in order that, on the one hand, as many Socialist-Revolutionaries and Mensheviks as possible may in turn get near the "pie", the lucrative and honourable posts, and that, on the other hand, the "attention" of the people may be "engaged". Meanwhile the chancelleries and army staffs "do" the business of "state".

Dyelo Naroda,[151] the organ of the ruling Socialist-Revolutionary Party, recently admitted in a leading article—with the matchless frankness of people of "good society", in which "all" are engaged in political prostitution—that even in the ministries headed by the "socialists" (save the mark!), the whole bureaucratic apparatus is in fact unchanged, is working in the old way and quite "freely" sabotaging revolutionary measures! Even without this admission does not the actual history of the participation of the Socialist-Revolutionaries and Mensheviks in the government prove this? It is noteworthy, however, that in the ministerial company of the Cadets, the Chernovs, Rusanovs, Zenzinovs and the other editors of *Dyelo Naroda* have so completely lost all sense of shame as to brazenly assert, as if it were a mere bagatelle, that in "their" ministries everything is unchanged!! Revolutionary-democratic phrases to gull the rural Simple Simons, and bureaucracy and red tape to "gladden the hearts" of the capitalists—that is the *essence* of the "honest" coalition.

The Commune substitutes for the venal and rotten parliamentarism of bourgeois society institutions in which freedom of opinion and discussion does not degenerate into deception, for the parliamentarians themselves have to work, have to execute their own laws, have themselves to test the results achieved in reality, and to account directly to their constituents. Representative institutions remain, but there is *no* parliamentarism here as a special system, as the division of labour between the legislative and the executive, as a privileged position for the deputies. We cannot imagine democracy, even proletarian democracy, without representative institutions, but we can and *must* imagine democracy without parliamentarism, if criticism of bourgeois society is not mere words for us, if the desire to overthrow the rule of the bourgeoisie is our earnest and sincere desire, and not a mere "election" cry for catching workers' votes, as it is with the Mensheviks and Socialist-Revolutionaries, and also the Scheidemanns and Legiens, the Sembats and Vanderveldes.

It is extremely instructive to note that, in speaking of the functions of *those* officials who are necessary for the Commune and for proletarian democracy, Marx compares them to the workers of "every other employer", that is, of the ordinary capitalist enterprise, with its "workers, foremen and accountants".

There is no trace of utopianism in Marx, in the sense that he made up or invented a "new" society. No, he studied the *birth* of the new society *out of* the old, and the forms of transition from the latter to the former, as a natural-historical process. He examined the actual experience of a mass proletarian movement and tried to draw practical lessons from it. He "learned" from the Commune, just as all the great revolutionary thinkers learned unhesitatingly from the experience of great movements of the oppressed classes, and never addressed them with pedantic "homilies" (such as Plekhanov's: "They should not have taken up arms" or Tsereteli's: "A class must limit itself").

Abolishing the bureaucracy at once, everywhere and completely, is out of the question. It is a utopia. But to *smash* the old bureaucratic machine at once and to begin immediately to construct a

new one that will make possible the gradual abolition of all
bureaucracy—this is *not* a utopia, it is the experience of the
Commune, the direct and immediate task of the revolutionary
proletariat.

Capitalism simplifies the functions of "state" administration; it
makes it possible to cast "bossing" aside and to confine the whole
matter to the organisation of the proletarians (as the ruling class),
which will hire "workers, foremen and accountants" in the name
of the whole of society.

We are not utopians, we do not "dream" of dispensing *at once*
with all administration, with all subordination. These anarchist
dreams, based upon incomprehension of the tasks of the proletarian
dictatorship, are totally alien to Marxism, and, as a matter of fact,
serve only to postpone the socialist revolution until people are different. No, we want the socialist revolution with people as they are
now, with people who cannot dispense with subordination, control
and "foremen and accountants".

The subordination, however, must be to the armed vanguard of
all the exploited and working people, i.e., to the proletariat. A beginning can and must be made at once, overnight, to replace the
specific "bossing" of state officials by the simple functions of "foremen and accountants", functions which are already fully within the
ability of the average town dweller and can well be performed for
"workmen's wages".

We, the workers, shall organise large-scale production on the
basis of what capitalism has already created, relying on our own
experience as workers, establishing strict, iron discipline backed
up by the state power of the armed workers. We shall reduce the
role of state officials to that of simply carrying out our instructions
as responsible, revocable, modestly paid "foremen and accountants"
(of course, with the aid of technicians of all sorts, types and
degrees). This is *our* proletarian task, this is what we can and must
start with in accomplishing the proletarian revolution. Such a beginning, on the basis of large-scale production, will of itself lead
to the gradual "withering away" of all bureaucracy, to the gradual
creation of an order—an order without inverted commas, an order
bearing no similarity to wage slavery—an order under which the
functions of control and accounting, becoming more and more simple, will be performed by each in turn, will then become a habit and
will finally die out as the *special* functions of a special section of
the population.

A witty German Social-Democrat of the seventies of the last century called the *postal service* an example of the socialist economic
system. This is very true. At present the postal service is a business
organised on the lines of a state-*capitalist* monopoly. Imperialism
is gradually transforming all trusts into organisations of a similar

type, in which, standing over the "common" people, who are over-worked and starved, one has the same bourgeois bureaucracy. But the mechanism of social management is here already to hand. Once we have overthrown the capitalist, crushed the resistance of these exploiters with the iron hand of the armed workers, and smashed the bureaucratic machine of the modern state, we shall have a splendidly equipped mechanism, freed from the "parasite", a mechanism which can very well be set going by the united workers themselves, who will hire technicians, foremen and accountants, and pay them *all,* as indeed *all* "state" officials in general, workmen's wages. Here is a concrete, practical task which can immediately be fulfilled in relation to all trusts, a task whose fulfilment will rid the working people of exploitation, a task which takes account of what the Commune had already begun to practise (particularly in building up the state).

To organise the *whole* economy on the lines of the postal service so that the technicians, foremen and accountants, as well as *all* officials, shall receive salaries no higher than "a workman's wage", all under the control and leadership of the armed proletariat—this is our immediate aim. This is the state and this is the economic foundation we need. This is what will bring about the abolition of parliamentarism and the preservation of representative institutions. This is what will rid the labouring classes of the bourgeoisie's prostitution of these institutions.

4. ORGANISATION OF NATIONAL UNITY

"In a brief sketch of national organisation which the Commune had no time to develop, it states explicitly that the Commune was to be the political form of even the smallest village...." The communes were to elect the "National Delegation" in Paris.

"...The few but important functions which would still remain for a central government were not to be suppressed, as has been deliberately mis-stated, but were to be transferred to communal, i.e., strictly responsible, officials.

"...National unity was not to be broken, but, on the contrary, organised by the communal constitution; it was to become a reality by the destruction of state power which posed as the embodiment of that unity yet wanted to be independent of, and superior to, the nation, on whose body it was but a parasitic excrescence. While the merely repressive organs of the old governmental power were to be amputated, its legitimate functions were to be wrested from an authority claiming the right to stand above society, and restored to the responsible servants of society."

The extent to which the opportunists of present-day Social-Democracy have failed—perhaps it would be more true to say, have refused—to understand these observations of Marx is best shown by that book of Herostratean fame of the renegade Bernstein, *The Premises of Socialism and the Tasks of the Social-Democrats.* It is in connection with the above passage from Marx that Bernstein wrote that "as far as its political content is concerned", this programme "displays, in all its essential features, the greatest similarity to the federalism of Proudhon.... In spite of all the other points of difference between Marx and the 'petty-bourgeois' Proudhon [Bernstein places the word "petty-bourgeois" in inverted commas to make it sound ironical] on these points, their lines of reasoning run as close as could be". Of course, Bernstein continues, the importance of the municipalities is growing, but "it seems doubtful to me whether the first job of democracy would be such a dissolution [Auflösung] of the modern states and such a complete transformation [Umwandlung] of their organisation as is visualised by Marx and Proudhon (the formation of a National Assembly from delegates of the provincial or district assemblies, which, in their turn, would consist of delegates from the communes), so that consequently the previous mode of national representation would disappear." (Bernstein, *Premises,* German edition, 1899, pp. 134 and 136.)

To confuse Marx's views on the "destruction of state power, a parasitic excrescence", with Proudhon's federalism is positively monstrous! But it is no accident, for it never occurs to the opportunist that Marx does not speak here at all about federalism as opposed to centralism, but about smashing the old, bourgeois state machine which exists in all bourgeois countries.

The only thing that does occur to the opportunist is what he sees around him, in an environment of petty-bourgeois philistinism and "reformist" stagnation, namely, only "municipalities"! The opportunist has even grown out of the habit of thinking about proletarian revolution.

It is ridiculous. But the remarkable thing is that nobody argued with Bernstein on this point. Bernstein has been refuted by many, especially by Plekhanov in Russian literature and by Kautsky in European literature, but neither of them has said *anything* about *this* distortion of Marx by Bernstein.

The opportunist has so much forgotten how to think in a revolutionary way and to dwell on revolution that he attributes "federalism" to Marx, whom he confuses with the founder of anarchism, Proudhon. As for Kautsky and Plekhanov, who claim to be orthodox Marxists and defenders of the theory of revolutionary Marxism, they are silent on this point! Here is one of the roots of the extreme vulgarisation of the views on the difference between Marxism and anarchism, which is characteristic of both the Kautskyites and the opportunists, and which we shall discuss again later.

There is not a trace of federalism in Marx's above-quoted observations on the experience of the Commune. Marx agreed with Proudhon on the very point that the opportunist Bernstein did not see. Marx disagreed with Proudhon on the very point on which Bernstein found a similarity between them.

Marx agreed with Proudhon in that they both stood for the "smashing" of the modern state machine. Neither the opportunists nor the Kautskyites wish to see the similarity of views on this point between Marxism and anarchism (both Proudhon and Bakunin) because this is where they have departed from Marxism.

Marx disagreed both with Proudhon and Bakunin precisely on the question of federalism (not to mention the dictatorship of the proletariat). Federalism as a principle follows logically from the petty-bourgeois views of anarchism. Marx was a centralist. There is no departure whatever from centralism in his observations just quoted. Only those who are imbued with the philistine "superstitious belief" in the state can mistake the destruction of the bourgeois state machine for the destruction of centralism!

Now if the proletariat and the poor peasants take state power into their own hands, organise themselves quite freely in communes, and *unite* the action of all the communes in striking at capital, in crushing the resistance of the capitalists, and in transferring the privately-owned railways, factories, land and so on to the *entire* nation, to the whole of society, won't that be centralism? Won't that be the most consistent democratic centralism and, moreover, proletarian centralism?

Bernstein simply cannot conceive of the possibility of voluntary centralism, of the voluntary amalgamation of the communes into a nation, of the voluntary fusion of the proletarian communes, for the purpose of destroying bourgeois rule and the bourgeois state machine. Like all philistines, Bernstein pictures centralism as something which can be imposed and maintained solely from above, and solely by the bureaucracy and the military clique.

As though foreseeing that his views might be distorted, Marx expressly emphasised that the charge that the Commune had wanted to destroy national unity, to abolish the central authority, was a deliberate fraud. Marx purposely used the words: "National unity was ... to be organised", so as to oppose conscious, democratic, proletarian centralism to bourgeois, military, bureaucratic centralism.

But there are none so deaf as those who will not hear. And the very thing the opportunists of present-day Social-Democracy do not want to hear about is the destruction of state power, the amputation of the parasitic excrescence.

5. ABOLITION OF THE PARASITE STATE

We have already quoted Marx's words on this subject, and we must now supplement them.

"...It is generally the fate of new historical creations," he wrote, "to be mistaken for the counterpart of older and even defunct forms of social life, to which they may bear a certain likeness. Thus, this new Commune, which breaks [bricht, smashes] the modern state power, has been regarded as a revival of the medieval communes ... as a federation of small states (as Montesquieu and the Girondins visualised it) ... as an exaggerated form of the old struggle against over-centralisation. ...

"...The Communal Constitution would have restored to the social body all the forces hitherto absorbed by that parasitic excrescence, the 'state', feeding upon and hampering the free movement of society. By this one act it would have initiated the regeneration of France. ...

"...The Communal Constitution would have brought the rural producers under the intellectual lead of the central towns of their districts, and there secured to them, in the town working men, the natural trustees of their interests. The very existence of the Commune involved, as a matter of course, local self-government, but no longer as a counterpoise to state power, now become superfluous."

"Breaking state power", which was a "parasitic excrescence"; its "amputation", its "smashing"; "state power, now become superfluous"—these are the expressions Marx used in regard to the state when appraising and analysing the experience of the Commune.

All this was written a little less than half a century ago; and now one has to engage in excavations, as it were, in order to bring undistorted Marxism to the knowledge of the mass of the people. The conclusions drawn from the observation of the last great revolution which Marx lived through were forgotten just when the time for the next great proletarian revolutions had arrived.

"...The multiplicity of interpretations to which the Commune has been subjected, and the multiplicity of interests which expressed themselves in it show that it was a thoroughly flexible political form, while all previous forms of gòvernment had been essentially repressive. Its true secret was this: it was essentially *a working-class government,* the result of the struggle of the producing against the appropriating class, the political form at last discovered under which the economic emancipation of labour could be accomplished. ...

"Except on this last condition, the Communal Constitution would have been an impossibility and a delusion...."

The utopians busied themselves with "discovering" political forms under which the socialist transformation of society was to take place. The anarchists dismissed the question of political forms altogether. The opportunists of present-day Social-Democracy accepted the bourgeois political forms of the parliamentary democratic state as the limit which should not be overstepped; they battered their foreheads praying before this "model", and denounced as anarchism every desire to *break* these forms.

Marx deduced from the whole history of socialism and the political struggle that the state was bound to disappear, and that the transitional form of its disappearance (the transition from state to non-state) would be the "proletariat organised as the ruling class". Marx, however, did not set out to *discover* the political *forms* of this future stage. He limited himself to carefully observing French history, to analysing it, and to drawing the conclusion to which the year 1851 had led, namely, that matters were moving towards the *destruction* of the bourgeois state machine.

And when the mass revolutionary movement of the proletariat burst forth, Marx, in spite of its failure, in spite of its short life and patent weakness, began to study the forms it had *discovered*.

The Commune is the form "at last discovered" by the proletarian revolution, under which the economic emancipation of labour can take place.

The Commune is the first attempt by a proletarian revolution to *smash* the bourgeois state machine; and it is the political form "at last discovered", by which the smashed state machine can and must be *replaced*.

We shall see further on that the Russian revolutions of 1905 and 1917, in different circumstances and under different conditions, continue the work of the Commune and confirm Marx's brilliant historical analysis.

CHAPTER IV

CONTINUATION. SUPPLEMENTARY EXPLANATIONS BY ENGELS

Marx gave the fundamentals concerning the significance of the experience of the Commune. Engels returned to the same subject time and again, and explained Marx's analysis and conclusions, sometimes elucidating *other* aspects of the question with such power and vividness that it is necessary to deal with his explanations specially.

1. THE HOUSING QUESTION

In his work, *The Housing Question* (1872),[152] Engels already took into account the experience of the Commune, and dealt several times with the tasks of the revolution in relation to the state. It is interesting to note that the treatment of this specific subject clearly revealed, on the one hand, points of similarity between the proletarian state and the present state—points that warrant speaking of the state in both cases—and, on the other hand, points of difference between them, or the transition to the destruction of the state.

"How is the housing question to be settled, then? In present-day society, it is settled just as any other social question: by the gradual economic levelling of demand and supply, a settlement which reproduces the question itself again and again and therefore is no settlement. How a social revolution would settle this question not only depends on the circumstances in each particular case, but is also connected with much more far-reaching questions, one of the most fundamental of which is the abolition of the antithesis between town and country. As it is not our task to create utopian systems for the organisation of the future society, it would be more than idle to go into the question here. But one thing is certain: there is already a sufficient quantity of houses in the big cities to remedy immediately all real 'housing *shortage*', provided they are used judiciously. This can naturally only occur through the expropriation of the present owners and by quartering in their houses homeless workers or workers overcrowded in their present homes. As soon as the proletariat has won political power, such a measure prompted by concern for the common good will be just as easy to carry out as are other expropriations and billetings by the present-day state." (German edition, 1887, p. 22.)

The change in the form of state power is not examined here, but only the content of its activity. Expropriations and billetings take place by order even of the present state. From the formal point of view, the proletarian state will also "order" the occupation of dwellings and expropriation of houses. But it is clear that the old executive apparatus, the bureaucracy, which is connected with the bourgeoisie, would simply be unfit to carry out the orders of the proletarian state.

"...It must be pointed out that the 'actual seizure' of all the instruments of labour, the taking possession of industry as a whole by the working people, is the exact opposite of the Proudhonist 'redemption'. In the latter case the individual worker becomes the owner of the dwelling, the peasant farm, the instruments of labour; in the former case, the 'working people' remain the collective owners of the houses, factories and instruments of labour, and will hardly permit their use, at least during a transitional period, by individuals or associations without compensation for the cost. In the same way, the abolition of property in land is not the abolition of ground rent but its transfer, if in a modified form, to society. The actual seizure of all the instruments of labour by the working people, therefore, does not at all preclude the retention of rent relations." (P. 68).

We shall examine the question touched upon in this passage, namely, the economic basis for the withering away of the state, in the next chapter. Engels expresses himself most cautiously, saying that the proletarian state would "hardly" permit the use of houses without payment, "at least during a transitional period". The letting of houses owned by the whole people to individual families presupposes the collection of rent, a certain amount of control, and the employment of some standard in allotting the housing. All this calls for a certain form of state, but it does not at all call for a special military and bureaucratic apparatus, with officials occupying especially privileged positions. The transition to a situation in which it will be possible to supply dwellings rent-free depends on the complete "withering away" of the state.

Speaking of the Blanquists' adoption of the fundamental position of Marxism after the Commune and under the influence of its experience, Engels, in passing, formulates this position as follows:

"...Necessity of political action by the proletariat and of its dictatorship as the transition to the abolition of classes and, with them, of the state...." (P. 55.)

Addicts to hair-splitting criticism, or bourgeois "exterminators of Marxism", will perhaps see a contradiction between this *recognition* of the "abolition of the state" and repudiation of this formula as an anarchist one in the above passage from *Anti-Dühring*. It would not be surprising if the opportunists classed Engels, too, as an "anarchist", for it is becoming increasingly common with the social-chauvinists to accuse the internationalists of anarchism.

Marxism has always taught that with the abolition of classes the state will also be abolished. The well-known passage on the "withering away of the state" in *Anti-Dühring* accuses the anarchists not simply of favouring the abolition of the state, but of preaching that the state can be abolished "overnight".

As the now prevailing "Social-Democratic" doctrine completely distorts the relation of Marxism to anarchism on the question of the abolition of the state, it will be particularly useful to recall a certain controversy in which Marx and Engels came out against the anarchists.

2. CONTROVERSY WITH THE ANARCHISTS

This controversy took place in 1873. Marx and Engels contributed articles against the Proudhonists, "autonomists" or "anti-authoritarians", to an Italian socialist annual, and it was not until 1913 that these articles appeared in German in *Neue Zeit*.[153]

> "...If the political struggle of the working class assumes revolutionary forms," wrote Marx, ridiculing the anarchists for their repudiation of politics, "and if the workers set up their revolutionary dictatorship in place of the dictatorship of the bourgeoisie, they commit the terrible crime of violating principles, for in order to satisfy their wretched, vulgar everyday needs and to crush the resistance of the bourgeoisie, they give the state a revolutionary and transient form, instead of laying down their arms and abolishing the state...." (*Neue Zeit*, Vol. XXXII, 1, 1913-14, p. 40.[154])

It was solely against this kind of "abolition" of the state that Marx fought in refuting the anarchists! He did not at all oppose the view that the state would disappear when classes disappeared, or that it would be abolished when classes were abolished. What he did oppose was the proposition that the workers should renounce the use of arms, organised violence, *that is, the state*, which is to serve to "crush the resistance of the bourgeoisie".

To prevent the true meaning of his struggle against anarchism from being distorted, Marx expressly emphasised the "revolutionary and *transient* form" of the state which the proletariat needs. The proletariat needs the state only temporarily. We do not at all differ with the anarchists on the question of the abolition of the state as the *aim*. We maintain that, to achieve this aim, we must temporarily make use of the instruments, resources and methods of state power *against* the exploiters, just as the temporary dictatorship of the oppressed class is necessary for the abolition of classes. Marx chooses the sharpest and clearest way of stating his case against the anarchists: After overthrowing the yoke of the capitalists, should the workers "lay down their arms", or use them against the capitalists in order to crush their resistance? But what is the systematic use of arms by one class against another if not a "transient form" of state?

Let every Social-Democrat ask himself: Is *that* how he has been posing the question of the state in controversy with the anarchists?

Is *that* how it has been posed by the vast majority of the official socialist parties of the Second International?

Engels expounds the same ideas in much greater detail and still more popularly. First of all he ridicules the muddled ideas of the Proudhonists, who called themselves "anti-authoritarians", i.e., repudiated all authority, all subordination, all power. Take a factory, a railway, a ship on the high seas, said Engels: is it not clear that not one of these complex technical establishments, based on the use of machinery and the systematic co-operation of many people, could function without a certain amount of subordination and, consequently, without a certain amount of authority or power?

> "...When I counter the most rabid anti-authoritarians with these arguments, the only answer they can give me is the following: Oh, that's true, except that here it is not a question of authority with which we vest our delegates, *but of a commission!* These people imagine they can change a thing by changing its name...."[155]

Having thus shown that authority and autonomy are relative terms, that the sphere of their application varies with the various phases of social development, that it is absurd to take them as absolutes, and adding that the sphere of application of machinery and large-scale production is steadily expanding, Engels passes from the general discussion of authority to the question of the state.

> "...Had the autonomists," he wrote, "contented themselves with saying that the social organisation of the future would allow authority only within the bounds which the conditions of production make inevitable, one could have come to terms with them. But they are blind to all facts that make authority necessary and they passionately fight the word.
>
> "Why do the anti-authoritarians not confine themselves to crying out against political authority, the state? All socialists are agreed that the state, and with it political authority, will disappear as a result of the coming social revolution, that is, that public functions will lose their political character and become mere administrative functions of watching over social interests. But the anti-authoritarians demand that the political state be abolished at one stroke, even before the social relations that gave birth to it have been destroyed. They demand that the first act of the social revolution shall be the abolition of authority.
>
> "Have these gentlemen ever seen a revolution? A revolution is certainly the most authoritarian thing there is; it is an act

whereby one part of the population imposes its will upon the other part by means of rifles, bayonets and cannon, all of which are highly authoritarian means. And the victorious party must maintain its rule by means of the terror which its arms inspire in the reactionaries. Would the Paris Commune have lasted more than a day if it had not used the authority of the armed people against the bourgeoisie? Cannot we, on the contrary, blame it for having made too little use of that authority? Therefore, one of two things: either the anti-authoritarians don't know what they are talking about, in which case they are creating nothing but confusion. Or they do know, and in that case they are betraying the cause of the proletariat. In either case they serve only reaction." (P. 39.[156])

This argument touches upon questions which should be examined in connection with the relationship between politics and economics during the withering away of the state (the next chapter is devoted to this). These questions are: the transformation of public functions from political into simple functions of administration, and the "political state". This last term, one particularly liable to cause misunderstanding, indicates the process of the withering away of the state: at a certain stage of this process, the state which is withering away may be called a non-political state.

Again, the most remarkable thing in this argument of Engels is the way he states his case against the anarchists. Social-Democrats, claiming to be disciples of Engels, have argued on this subject against the anarchists millions of times since 1873, but they have *not* argued as Marxists could and should. The anarchist idea of the abolition of the state is muddled and *non-revolutionary*—that is how Engels put it. It is precisely the revolution in its rise and development, with its specific tasks in relation to violence, authority, power, the state, that the anarchists refuse to see.

The usual criticism of anarchism by present-day Social-Democrats has boiled down to the purest philistine banality: "We recognise the state, whereas the anarchists do not!" Naturally, such banality cannot but repel workers who are at all capable of thinking and revolutionary-minded. What Engels says is different. He stresses that all socialists recognise that the state will disappear as a result of the socialist revolution. He then deals specifically with the question of the revolution—the very question which, as a rule, the Social-Democrats evade out of opportunism, leaving it, so to speak, exclusively for the anarchists "to work out". And when dealing with this question, Engels takes the bull by the horns; he asks: should not the Commune have made *more* use of the *revolutionary* power of the *state*, that is, of the proletariat armed and organised as the ruling class?

Prevailing official Social-Democracy usually dismissed the question of the concrete tasks of the proletariat in the revolution either with a philistine sneer, or, at best, with the sophistic evasion: "The future will show." And the anarchists were justified in saying about such Social-Democrats that they were failing in their task of giving the workers a revolutionary education. Engels draws upon the experience of the last proletarian revolution precisely for the purpose of making a most concrete study of what should be done by the proletariat, and in what manner, in relation to both the banks and the state.

3. LETTER TO BEBEL

One of the most, if not *the* most, remarkable observation on the state in the works of Marx and Engels is contained in the following passage in Engels's letter to Bebel dated March 18-28, 1875. This letter, we may observe in parenthesis, was, as far as we know, first published by Bebel in the second volume of his memoirs (*Aus meinem Leben*), which appeared in 1911, i.e., thirty-six years after the letter had been written and sent.

Engels wrote to Bebel criticising that same draft of the Gotha Programme which Marx criticised in his famous letter to Bracke.[157] Referring specially to the question of the state, Engels said:

"The free people's state has been transformed into the free state. Taken in its grammatical sense, a free state is one where the state is free in relation to its citizens, hence a state with a despotic government. The whole talk about the state should be dropped, especially since the Commune, which was no longer a state in the proper sense of the word. The 'people's state' has been thrown in our faces by the anarchists to the point of disgust, although already Marx's book against Proudhon and later the *Communist Manifesto* say plainly that with the introduction of the socialist order of society the state dissolves of itself [sich auflöst] and disappears. As the state is only a transitional institution which is used in the struggle, in the revolution, to hold down one's adversaries by force, it is sheer nonsense to talk of a 'free people's state'; so long as the proletariat still *needs* the state, it does not need it in the interests of freedom but in order to hold down its adversaries, and as soon as it becomes possible to speak of freedom the state as such ceases to exist. We would therefore propose replacing *state* everywhere by *Gemeinwesen*, a good old German word which can very well take the place of the French word *commune*." (Pp. 321-22 of the German original.)[158]

It should be borne in mind that this letter refers to the party programme which Marx criticised in a letter dated only a few weeks later than the above (Marx's letter is dated May 5, 1875), and that at the time Engels was living with Marx in London. Consequently, when he says "we" in the last sentence, Engels undoubtedly, in his own as well as in Marx's name, suggests to the leader of the German workers' party that the word "state" *be struck out of the programme* and replaced by the word "*community*".

What a howl about "anarchism" would be raised by the leading lights of present-day "Marxism", which has been falsified for the convenience of the opportunists, if such an amendment of the programme were suggested to them!

Let them howl. This will earn them the praises of the bourgeoisie.

And we shall go on with our work. In revising the programme of our Party, we must by all means take the advice of Engels and Marx into consideration in order to come nearer the truth, to restore Marxism by ridding it of distortions, to guide the struggle of the working class for its emancipation more correctly. Certainly no one opposed to the advice of Engels and Marx will be found among the Bolsheviks. The only difficulty that may perhaps arise will be in regard to the term. In German there are two words meaning "community", of which Engels used the one which does *not* denote a single community, but their totality, a system of communities. In Russian there is no such word, and we may have to choose the French word "commune", although this also has its drawbacks.

"The Commune was no longer a state in the proper sense of the word"—this is the most theoretically important statement Engels makes. After what has been said above, this statement is perfectly clear. The Commune *was ceasing* to be a state since it had to suppress, not the majority of the population, but a minority (the exploiters). It had smashed the bourgeois state machine. In place of a *special* coercive force the population itself came on the scene. All this was a departure from the state in the proper sense of the word. And had the Commune become firmly established, all traces of the state in it would have "withered away" of themselves; it would not have had to "abolish" the institutions of the state—they would have ceased to function as they ceased to have anything to do.

"The 'people's state' has been thrown in our faces by the anarchists." In saying this, Engels above all has in mind Bakunin and his attacks on the German Social-Democrats. Engels admits that these attacks were justified *insofar* as the "people's state" was as much an absurdity and as much a departure from socialism as the "free people's state". Engels tried to put the struggle of the German

Social-Democrats against the anarchists on the right lines, to make this struggle correct in principle, to rid it of opportunist prejudices concerning the "state". Unfortunately, Engels's letter was pigeon-holed for thirty-six years. We shall see farther on that, even after this letter was published, Kautsky persisted in virtually the same mistakes against which Engels had warned.

Bebel replied to Engels in a letter dated September 21, 1875, in which he wrote, among other things, that he "fully agreed" with Engels's opinion of the draft programme, and that he had reproached Liebknecht with readiness to make concessions (p. 334 of the German edition of Bebel's memoirs, Vol. II). But if we take Bebel's pamphlet, *Our Aims*, we find there views on the state that are absolutely wrong.

"The state must ... be transformed from one based on *class rule* into a *people's state*." (*Unsere Ziele*, German edition, 1886, p. 14.)

This was printed in the *ninth* (the ninth!) edition of Bebel's pamphlet! It is not surprising that opportunist views on the state, so persistently repeated, were absorbed by the German Social-Democrats, especially as Engels's revolutionary interpretations had been safely pigeon-holed, and all the conditions of life were such as to "wean" them from revolution for a long time.

4. CRITICISM OF THE DRAFT OF THE ERFURT PROGRAMME

In analysing Marxist teachings on the state, the criticism of the draft of the Erfurt Programme,[159] sent by Engels to Kautsky on June 29, 1891, and published only ten years later in *Neue Zeit*, cannot be ignored; for it is with the *opportunist* views of the Social-Democrats on questions of *state* organisation that this criticism is mainly concerned.

We shall note in passing that Engels also makes an exceedingly valuable observation on economic questions, which shows how attentively and thoughtfully he watched the various changes occurring in modern capitalism, and how for this reason he was able to foresee to a certain extent the tasks of our present, the imperialist, epoch. Here is that observation: referring to the word "planlessness" (Planlosigkeit), used in the draft programme, as characteristic of capitalism, Engels wrote:

"When we pass from joint-stock companies to trusts which assume control over, and monopolise, whole industries, it is not only private production that ceases, but also planlessness." (*Neue Zeit*, Vol. XX, 1, 1901-02, p. 8.)

Here we have what is most essential in the theoretical appraisal of the latest phase of capitalism, i.e., imperialism, namely, that capitalism becomes monopoly *capitalism*. The latter must be emphasised because the erroneous bourgeois reformist assertion that monopoly capitalism or state-monopoly capitalism is *no longer* capitalism, but can now be called "state socialism" and so on, is very common. The trusts, of course, never provided, do not now provide, and cannot provide complete planning. But however much they do plan, however much the capitalist magnates calculate in advance the volume of production on a national and even on an international scale, and however much they systematically regulate it, we still remain under *capitalism*—at its new stage, it is true, but still capitalism, without a doubt. The "proximity" of *such* capitalism to socialism should serve genuine representatives of the proletariat as an argument proving the proximity, facility, feasibility and urgency of the socialist revolution, and not at all as an argument for tolerating the repudiation of such a revolution and the efforts to make capitalism look more attractive, something which all reformists are trying to do.

But to return to the question of the state. In his letter Engels makes three particularly valuable suggestions: first, in regard to the republic; second, in regard to the connection between the national question and state organisation, and, third, in regard to local self-government.

In regard to the republic, Engels made this the focal point of his criticism of the draft of the Erfurt Programme. And when we recall the importance which the Erfurt Programme acquired for all the Social-Democrats of the world, and that it became the model for the whole Second International, we may say without exaggeration that Engels thereby criticised the opportunism of the whole Second International.

"The political demands of the draft," Engels wrote, "have one great fault. *It lacks* [Engels's italics] precisely what should have been said."

And, later on, he makes it clear that the German Constitution is, strictly speaking, a copy of the extremely reactionary Constitution of 1850, that the Reichstag is only, as Wilhelm Liebknecht put it, "the fig leaf of absolutism" and that to wish "to transform all the instruments of labour into common property" on the basis of a constitution which legalises the existence of petty states and the federation of petty German states is an "obvious absurdity".

"To touch on that is dangerous, however," Engels added, knowing only too well that it was impossible legally to include in the programme the demand for a republic in Germany. But he refused to merely accept this obvious consideration which satisfied "everybody". He continued: "Nevertheless, somehow or other, the thing has to be attacked. How necessary this is is shown precisely at the present time by opportunism, which is gaining ground [einreissende] in a large section of the Social-Democratic press. Fearing a renewal of the Anti-Socialist Law,[160] or recalling all manner of overhasty pronouncements made during the reign of that law, they now want the Party to find the present legal order in Germany adequate for putting through all Party demands by peaceful means...."

Engels particularly stressed the fundamental fact that the German Social-Democrats were prompted by fear of a renewal of the Anti-Socialist Law, and explicitly described it as opportunism; he declared that precisely because there was no republic and no freedom in Germany, the dreams of a "peaceful" path were perfectly absurd. Engels was careful not to tie his hands. He admitted that in republican or very free countries "one can conceive" (only "conceive"!) of a peaceful development towards socialism, but in Germany, he repeated,

"...in Germany, where the government is almost omnipotent and the Reichstag and all other representative bodies have no real power, to advocate such a thing in Germany, where, moreover, there is no need to do so, means removing the fig leaf from absolutism and becoming oneself a screen for its nakedness."

The great majority of the official leaders of the German Social-Democratic Party, which pigeon-holed this advice, have really proved to be a screen for absolutism.

"...In the long run such a policy can only lead one's own party astray. They push general, abstract political questions into the foreground, thereby concealing the immediate concrete questions, which at the moment of the first great events, the first political crisis, automatically pose themselves. What can result from this except that at the decisive moment the party suddenly proves helpless and that uncertainty and discord on the most decisive issues reign in it because these issues have never been discussed?...

"This forgetting of the great, the principal considerations for the momentary interests of the day, this struggling and striving for the success of the moment regardless of later consequences, this sacrifice of the future of the movement for its present may be 'honestly' meant, but it is and remains opportunism, and 'honest' opportunism is perhaps the most dangerous of all....

"If one thing is certain it is that our party and the working class can only come to power in the form of the democratic republic. This is even the specific form for the dictatorship of the proletariat, as the Great French Revolution has already shown...."

Engels repeated here in a particularly striking form the fundamental idea which runs through all of Marx's works, namely, that the democratic republic is the nearest approach to the dictatorship of the proletariat. For such a republic, without in the least abolishing the rule of capital, and, therefore, the oppression of the masses and the class struggle, inevitably leads to such an extension, development, unfolding and intensification of this struggle that, as soon as it becomes possible to meet the fundamental interests of the oppressed masses, this possibility is realised inevitably and solely through the dictatorship of the proletariat, through the leadership of those masses by the proletariat. These, too, are "forgotten words" of Marxism for the whole of the Second International, and the fact that they have been forgotten was demonstrated with particular vividness by the history of the Menshevik Party during the first six months of the Russian revolution of 1917.

On the subject of a federal republic, in connection with the national composition of the population, Engels wrote:

"...What should take the place of present-day Germany [with its reactionary monarchical Constitution and its equally reactionary division into petty states, a division which perpetuates all the specific features of "Prussianism" instead of dissolving them in Germany as a whole]? In my view, the proletariat can only use the form of the one and indivisible republic. In the gigantic territory of the United States, a federal republic is still, on the whole, a necessity, although in the Eastern states it is already becoming a hindrance. It would be a step forward in Britain where the two islands are peopled by four nations and in spite of a single Parliament three different systems of legislation already exist side by side. In little Switzerland, it has long been a hindrance, tolerable only because Switzerland is content to be a purely passive member of the European state system. For Germany, federalisation on the Swiss model would be an enormous step backward. Two points distinguish a union state from a completely unified state: first, that each member state, each canton, has its own civil and criminal legislative and judicial system, and, second, that alongside a popular chamber there is also a federal chamber in which each canton, whether large or small, votes as such." In Germany, the union state is the transition to the completely unified state, and the "revolution from above" of

1866 and 1870[161] must not be reversed but supplemented by a "movement from below".

Far from being indifferent to the forms of state, Engels, on the contrary, tried to analyse the transitional forms with the utmost thoroughness in order to establish, in accordance with the concrete historical peculiarities of each particular case, *from what and to what* the given transitional form is passing.

Approaching the matter from the standpoint of the proletariat and the proletarian revolution, Engels, like Marx, upheld democratic centralism, the republic—one and indivisible. He regarded the federal republic either as an exception and a hindrance to development, or as a transition from a monarchy to a centralised republic, as a "step forward" under certain special conditions. And among these special conditions, he puts the national question to the fore.

Although mercilessly criticising the reactionary nature of small states, and the screening of this by the national question in certain concrete cases, Engels, like Marx, never betrayed the slightest desire to brush aside the national question—a desire of which the Dutch and Polish Marxists, who proceed from their perfectly justified opposition to the narrow philistine nationalism of "their" little states, are often guilty.

Even in regard to Britain, where geographical conditions, a common language and the history of many centuries would seem to have "put an end" to the national question in the various small divisions of the country—even in regard to that country, Engels reckoned with the plain fact that the national question was not yet a thing of the past, and recognised in consequence that the establishment of a federal republic would be a "step forward". Of course, there is not the slightest hint here of Engels abandoning the criticism of the shortcomings of a federal republic or renouncing the most determined advocacy of, and struggle for, a unified and centralised democratic republic.

But Engels did not at all mean democratic centralism in the bureaucratic sense in which this term is used by bourgeois and petty-bourgeois ideologists, the anarchists among the latter. His idea of centralism did not in the least preclude such broad local self-government as would combine the voluntary defence of the unity of the state by the "communes" and districts, and the complete elimination of all bureaucratic practices and all "ordering" from above. Carrying forward the programme views of Marxism on the state, Engels wrote:

"...So, then, a unified republic—but not in the sense of the present French Republic, which is nothing but the Empire established in 1798 without the Emperor. From 1792 to 1798 each French department, each commune [Gemeindc], enjoyed complete self-government on the American model, and this is what we too must have. How self-government is to be organised and how we can manage without a bureaucracy has been shown to us by America and the first French Republic, and is being shown even today by Australia, Canada and the other English colonies. And a provincial [regional] and communal self-government of this type is far freer than, for instance, Swiss federalism, under which, it is true, the canton is very independent in relation to the Bund [i.e., the federated state as a whole], but is also independent in relation to the district [Bezirk] and the commune. The cantonal governments appoint the district governors [Bezirksstatthalter] and prefects —which is unknown in English-speaking countries and which we want to abolish here as resolutely in the future as the Prussian Landräte and Regierungsräte" (commissioners, district police chiefs, governors, and in general all officials appointed from above). Accordingly, Engels proposes the following wording for the self-government clause in the programme: "Complete self-government for the provinces [gubernias or regions], districts and communes through officials elected by universal suffrage. The abolition of all local and provincial authorities appointed by the state."

I have already had occasion to point out—in *Pravda*[162] (No. 68, May 28, 1917),* which was suppressed by the government of Kerensky and other "socialist" Ministers—how on this point (of course, not on this point alone by any means) our pseudo-socialist representatives of pseudo-revolutionary pseudo-democracy have made glaring departures *from democracy*. Naturally, people who have bound themselves by a "coalition" to the imperialist bourgeoisie have remained deaf to this criticism.

It is extremely important to note that Engels, armed with facts, disproved by a most precise example the prejudice which is very widespread, particularly among petty-bourgeois democrats, that a federal republic necessarily means a greater amount of freedom than a centralised republic. This is wrong. It is disproved by the facts cited by Engels regarding the centralised French Republic of 1792-98 and the federal Swiss Republic. The really democratic centralised republic gave *more* freedom than the federal republic. In other words, the *greatest* amount of local, regional and other freedom known in history was accorded by a *centralised* and not by a federal republic.

---

* See *Collected Works*, Vol. 24, pp. 536-38.—*Ed.*

Insufficient attention has been and is being paid in our Party propaganda and agitation to this fact, as, indeed, to the whole question of the federal and the centralised republic and local self-government.

5. THE 1891 PREFACE TO MARX'S *THE CIVIL WAR IN FRANCE*

In his preface to the third edition of *The Civil War in France* (this preface is dated March 18, 1891, and was originally published in *Neue Zeit*), Engels, in addition to some interesting incidental remarks on questions concerning the attitude towards the state, gave a remarkably vivid summary of the lessons of the Commune.[163] This summary, made more profound by the entire experience of the twenty years that separated the author from the Commune, and directed expressly against the "superstitious belief in the state" so widespread in Germany, may justly be called the *last word* of Marxism on the question under consideration.

> In France, Engels observed, the workers emerged with arms from every revolution; "therefore the disarming of the workers was the first commandment for the bourgeois, who were at the helm of the state. Hence, after every revolution won by the workers, a new struggle, ending with the defeat of the workers".

This summary of the experience of bourgeois revolutions is as concise as it is expressive. The essence of the matter—among other things, on the question of the state (*has the oppressed class arms?*) —is here remarkably well grasped. It is precisely this essence that is most often evaded both by professors influenced by bourgeois ideology, and by petty-bourgeois democrats. In the Russian revolution of 1917, the honour (Cavaignac honour) of blabbing this secret of bourgeois revolutions fell to the Menshevik, would-be Marxist, Tsereteli. In his "historic" speech of June 11, Tsereteli blurted out that the bourgeoisie were determined to disarm the Petrograd workers—presenting, of course, this decision as his own, and as a necessity for the "state" in general!

Tsereteli's historic speech of June 11 will, of course, serve every historian of the revolution of 1917 as a graphic illustration of how the Socialist-Revolutionary and Menshevik bloc, led by Mr. Tsereteli, deserted to the bourgeoisie *against* the revolutionary proletariat.

Another incidental remark of Engels's, also connected with the question of the state, deals with religion. It is well known that the German Social-Democrats, as they degenerated and became increasingly opportunist, slipped more and more frequently into the philistine misinterpretation of the celebrated formula: "Religion is to be declared a private matter." That is, this formula was twisted to mean that religion was a private matter *even for the party* of the revolutionary proletariat!! It was against this complete betrayal of the revolutionary programme of the proletariat that Engels vigorously protested. In 1891 he saw only the *very feeble* beginnings of opportunism in his party, and, therefore, he expressed himself with extreme caution:

> "As almost only workers, or recognised representatives of the workers, sat in the Commune, its decisions bore a decidedly proletarian character. Either they decreed reforms which the republican bourgeoisie had failed to pass solely out of cowardice, but which provided a necessary basis for the free activity of the working class—such as the realisation of the principle that *in relation to the state* religion is a purely private matter—or the Commune promulgated decrees which were in the direct interest of the working class and in part cut deeply into the old order of society."

Engels deliberately emphasised the words "in relation to the state", as a straight thrust at German opportunism, which had declared religion to be a private matter *in relation to the party*, thus degrading the party of the revolutionary proletariat to the level of the most vulgar "freethinking" philistinism, which is prepared to allow a non-denominational status, but which renounces the *party* struggle against the opium of religion which stupefies the people.

The future historian of the German Social-Democrats, in tracing the roots of their shameful bankruptcy in 1914, will find a fair amount of interesting material on this question, beginning with the evasive declarations in the articles of the party's ideological leader, Kautsky, which throw the door wide open to opportunism, and ending with the attitude of the party towards the "Los-von-Kirche-Bewegung" (the "Leave-the-Church" movement) in 1913.[164]

But let us see how, twenty years after the Commune, Engels summed up its lessons for the fighting proletariat.

Here are the lessons to which Engels attached prime importance:

> "...It was precisely the oppressing power of the former centralised government, army, political police, bureaucracy, which Napoleon had created in 1798 and which every new government had since then taken over as a welcome instrument and used against its opponents—it was this power which was to fall everywhere, just as it had fallen in Paris.
>
> "From the very outset the Commune had to recognise that the working class, once in power, could not go on managing

with the old state machine; that in order not to lose again its only just gained supremacy, this working class must, on the one hand, do away with all the old machinery of oppression previously used against it itself, and, on the other, safe-guard itself against its own deputies and officials, by declaring them all, without exception, subject to recall at any time...."

Engels emphasised once again that not only under a monarchy, but *also in a democratic republic* the state remains a state, i.e., it retains its fundamental distinguishing feature of transforming the officials, the "servants of society", its organs, into the *masters* of society.

"...Against this transformation of the state and the organs of the state from servants of society into masters of society— an inevitable transformation in all previous states—the Com-mune used two infallible means. In the first place, it filled all posts—administrative, judicial and educational—by election on the basis of universal suffrage of all concerned, subject to recall at any time by the electors. And, in the second place, it paid all officials, high or low, only the wages received by other workers. The highest salary paid by the Commune to anyone was 6,000 francs.* In this way a dependable barrier to place-hunting and careerism was set up, even apart from the binding mandates to delegates to representative bodies, which were added besides...."

Engels here approached the interesting boundary line at which consistent democracy, on the one hand, is *transformed* into social-ism and, on the other, *demands* socialism. For, in order to abolish the state, it is necessary to convert the functions of the civil serv-ice into the simple operations of control and accounting that are within the scope and ability of the vast majority of the population, and, subsequently, of every single individual. And if careerism is to be abolished completely, it must be made *impossible* for "hon-ourable" though profitless posts in the Civil Service to be used as a springboard to highly lucrative posts in banks or joint-stock companies, as *constantly* happens in all the freest capitalist coun-tries.

Engels, however, did not make the mistake some Marxists make in dealing, for example, with the question of the right of nations to self-determination, when they argue that it is impossible under capitalism and will be superfluous under socialism. This seemingly

---

* Nominally about 2,400 rubles or, according to the present rate of exchange, about 6,000 rubles. The action of those Bolsheviks who propose that a salary of 9,000 rubles be paid to members of municipal councils, for instance, instead of a maximum salary of 6,000 rubles—quite an adequate sum—*throughout the state,* is inexcusable[465].

clever but actually incorrect statement might be made in regard to *any* democratic institution, including moderate salaries for officials, because fully consistent democracy is impossible under capitalism, and under socialism all democracy *will wither away.* This is a sophism like the old joke about a man becoming bald by losing one more hair.

To develop democracy *to the utmost*, to find the *forms* for this development, to test them *by practice*, and so forth—all this is one of the component tasks of the struggle for the social revolution. Taken separately, no kind of democracy will bring socialism. But in actual life democracy will never be "taken separately"; it will be "taken together" with other things, it will exert its influence on economic life as well, will stimulate *its* transformation; and in its turn it will be influenced by economic development, and so on. This is the dialectics of living history.

Engels continued:

"...This shattering [Sprengung] of the former state power and its replacement by a new and truly democratic one is described in detail in the third section of *The Civil War.* But it was necessary to touch briefly here once more on some of its features, because in Germany particularly the superstitious belief in the state has passed from philosophy into the general consciousness of the bourgeoisie and even of many workers. According to the philosophical conception, the state is the 'realisation of the idea', or the Kingdom of God on earth, translated into philosophical terms, the sphere in which eternal truth and justice are, or should be, realised. And from this follows a superstitious reverence for the state and everything connected with it, which takes root the more readily since people are accustomed from childhood to imagine that the affairs and interests common to the whole of society could not be looked after other than as they have been looked after in the past, that is, through the state and its lucratively positioned officials. And people think they have taken quite an extraordinarily bold step forward when they have rid themselves of belief in hereditary monarchy and swear by the democratic republic. In reality, however, the state is nothing but a machine for the oppression of one class by another, and indeed in the democratic republic no less than in the monarchy. And at best it is an evil inherited by the proletariat after its victorious struggle for class supremacy, whose worst sides the victorious proletariat will have to lop off as speedily as possible, just as the Commune had to, until a generation reared in new, free social conditions is able to discard the entire lumber of the state."

Engels warned the Germans not to forget the principles of socialism with regard to the state in general in connection with the substitution of a republic for the monarchy. His warnings now read like a veritable lesson to the Tseretelis and Chernovs, who in their "coalition" practice have revealed a superstitious belief in, and a superstitious reverence for, the state!

Two more remarks. 1. Engels's statement that in a democratic republic, "no less" than in a monarchy, the state remains a "machine for the oppression of one class by another" by no means signifies that the *form* of oppression makes no difference to the proletariat, as some anarchists "teach". A wider, freer and more open *form* of the class struggle and of class oppression vastly assists the proletariat in its struggle for the abolition of classes in general.

2. Why will only a new generation be able to discard the entire lumber of the state? This question is bound up with that of overcoming democracy, with which we shall deal now.

6. ENGELS ON THE OVERCOMING OF DEMOCRACY

Engels came to express his views on this subject when establishing that the term "Social-Democrat" was *scientifically* wrong.

In a preface to an edition of his articles of the seventies on various subjects, mostly on "international" questions (*Internationales aus dem Volksstaat*[166*]), dated January 3, 1894, i.e., written a year and a half before his death, Engels wrote that in all his articles he used the word "Communist", and *not* "Social-Democrat", because at that time the Proudhonists in France and the Lassalleans in Germany called themselves Social-Democrats.[167]

> "...For Marx and myself," continued Engels, "it was therefore absolutely impossible to use such a loose term to characterise our special point of view. Today things are different, and the word ["Social-Democrat"] may perhaps pass muster [mag passieren], inexact [*unpassend,* unsuitable] though it still is for a party whose economic programme is not merely socialist in general, but downright communist, and whose ultimate political aim is to overcome the whole state and, consequently, democracy as well. The names of *real* [Engels's italics] political parties, however, are never wholly appropriate; the party develops while the name stays."[168]

The dialectician Engels remained true to dialectics to the end of his days. Marx and I, he said, had a splendid, scientifically exact

---

* *On International Topics from "The People's State".—Ed.*

name for the party, but there was no real party, i.e., no mass proletarian party. Now (at the end of the nineteenth century) there
was a real party, but its name was scientifically wrong. Never mind,
it would "pass muster", so long as the party *developed*, so long as
the scientific inaccuracy of its name was not hidden from it and
did not hinder its development in the right direction!

Perhaps some wit would console us Bolsheviks in the manner
of Engels: we have a real party, it is developing splendidly; even
such a meaningless and ugly term as "Bolshevik" will "pass muster", although it expresses nothing whatever but the purely acci-
dental fact that at the Brussels-London Congress of 1903 we were
in the majority.[169] Perhaps now that the persecution of our Party
by republicans and "revolutionary" petty-bourgeois democrats in
July and August has earned the name "Bolshevik" such universal
respect, now that, in addition, this persecution marks the tremendous historical progress our Party has made in its *real* development—perhaps now even I might hesitate to insist on the suggestion I made in April to change the name of our Party.* Perhaps I
would propose a "compromise" to my comrades, namely, to call
ourselves the Communist Party, but to retain the word "Bolsheviks" in brackets.

But the question of the name of the Party is incomparably less
important than the question of the attitude of the revolutionary
proletariat to the state.

In the usual arguments about the state, the mistake is constantly
made against which Engels warned and which we have in passing
indicated above, namely, it is constantly forgotten that the abolition
of the state means also the abolition of democracy: that the withering away of the state means the withering away of democracy.

At first sight this assertion seems exceedingly strange and
incomprehensible; indeed, someone may even suspect us of
expecting the advent of a system of society in which the principle of subordination of the minority to the majority will not
be observed—for democracy means the recognition of this very
principle.

No, democracy is *not* identical with the subordination of the
minority to the majority. Democracy is a *state* which recognises
the subordination of the minority to the majority, i.e., an organisation for the systematic use of *force* by one class against another,
by one section of the population against another.

We set ourselves the ultimate aim of abolishing the state, i.e.,
all organised and systematic violence, all use of violence against
people in general. We do not expect the advent of a system of
society in which the principle of subordination of the minority to

---

* See *Collected Works*, Vol. 24, p. 24; Vol. 36, pp. 432, 442.—*Ed.*

the majority will not be observed. In striving for socialism, however, we are convinced that it will develop into communism and, therefore, that the need for violence against people in general, for the *subordination* of one man to another, and of one section of the population to another, will vanish altogether since people will *become accustomed* to observing the elementary conditions of social life *without violence* and *without subordination*.

In order to emphasise this element of habit, Engels speaks of a new *generation,* "reared in new, free social conditions", which will "be able to discard the entire lumber of the state"—of any state, including the democratic-republican state.

In order to explain this, it is necessary to analyse the economic basis of the withering away of the state.

CHAPTER V

THE ECONOMIC BASIS OF THE WITHERING AWAY OF THE STATE

Marx explains this question most thoroughly in his *Critique of the Gotha Programme* (letter to Bracke, May 5, 1875, which was not published until 1891 when it was printed in *Neue Zeit*, Vol. IX, 1, and which has appeared in Russian in a special edition). The polemical part of this remarkable work, which contains a criticism of Lassalleanism, has, so to speak, overshadowed its positive part, namely, the analysis of the connection between the development of communism and the withering away of the state.

1. PRESENTATION OF THE QUESTION BY MARX

From a superficial comparison of Marx's letter to Bracke of May 5, 1875, with Engels's letter to Bebel of March 28, 1875, which we examined above, it might appear that Marx was much more of a "champion of the state" than Engels, and that the difference of opinion between the two writers on the question of the state was very considerable.

Engels suggested to Bebel that all chatter about the state be dropped altogether, that the word "state" be eliminated from the programme altogether and the word "community" substituted for it. Engels even declared that the Commune was no longer a state in the proper sense of the word. Yet Marx even spoke of the "future state in communist society", i.e., he would seem to recognise the need for the state even under communism.

But such a view would be fundamentally wrong. A closer examination shows that Marx's and Engels's views on the state and its withering away were completely identical, and that Marx's expression quoted above refers to the state in the process of *withering away*.

Clearly there can be no question of specifying the moment of the *future* "withering away", the more so since it will obviously be a lengthy process. The apparent difference between Marx and Engels is due to the fact that they dealt with different subjects and pursued different aims. Engels set out to show Bebel graphically, sharply and in broad outline the utter absurdity of the current prejudices concerning the state (shared to no small degree by Lassalle). Marx only touched upon *this* question in passing, being interested in another subject, namely, the *development* of communist society.

The whole theory of Marx is the application of the theory of development—in its most consistent, complete, considered and pithy form—to modern capitalism. Naturally, Marx was faced with the problem of applying this theory both to the *forthcoming* collapse of capitalism and to the *future* development of *future* communism.

On the basis of what *facts*, then, can the question of the future development of future communism be dealt with?

On the basis of the fact that it *has its origin* in capitalism, that it develops historically from capitalism, that it is the result of the action of a social force to which capitalism *gave birth*. There is no trace of an attempt on Marx's part to make up a utopia, to indulge in idle guess-work about what cannot be known. Marx treated the question of communism in the same way as a naturalist would treat the question of the development of, say, a new biological variety, once he knew that it had originated in such and such a way and was changing in such and such a definite direction.

To begin with, Marx brushed aside the confusion the Gotha Programme brought into the question of the relationship between state and society. He wrote:

"...'Present-day society' is capitalist society, which exists in all civilised countries, being more or less free from medieval admixture, more or less modified by the particular historical development of each country, more or less developed. On the other hand, the 'present-day state' changes with a country's frontier. It is different in the Prusso-German Empire from what it is in Switzerland, and different in England from what it is in the United States. '*The* present-day state' is, therefore, a fiction.

"Nevertheless, the different states of the different civilised countries, in spite of their motley diversity of form, all have this in common, that they are based on modern bourgeois society, only one more or less capitalistically developed. They have, therefore, also certain essential characteristics in common. In this sense it is possible to speak of the 'present-day state', in contrast with the future, in which its present root, bourgeois society, will have died off.

"The question then arises: what transformation will the state undergo in communist society? In other words, what social functions will remain in existence there that are analogous to present state functions? This question can only be answered scientifically, and one does not get a flea-hop nearer to the problem by a thousandfold combination of the word people with the word state."[170]

After thus ridiculing all talk about a "people's state", Marx formulated the question and gave warning, as it were, that those seeking a scientific answer to it should use only firmly-established scientific data.

The first fact that has been established most accurately by the whole theory of development, by science as a whole—a fact that was ignored by the utopians, and is ignored by the present-day opportunists, who are afraid of the socialist revolution—is that, historically, there must undoubtedly be a special stage, or a special phase, of *transition* from capitalism to communism.

2. THE TRANSITION FROM CAPITALISM TO COMMUNISM

Marx continued:

"...Between capitalist and communist society lies the period of the revolutionary transformation of the one into the other. Corresponding to this is also a political transition period in which the state can be nothing but *the revolutionary dictatorship of the proletariat*."

Marx bases this conclusion on an analysis of the role played by the proletariat in modern capitalist society, on the data concerning the development of this society, and on the irreconcilability of the antagonistic interests of the proletariat and the bourgeoisie.

Previously the question was put as follows: to achieve its emancipation, the proletariat must overthrow the bourgeoisie, win political power and establish its revolutionary dictatorship.

Now the question is put somewhat differently: the transition from capitalist society—which is developing towards communism—to communist society is impossible without a "political transition period", and the state in this period can only be the revolutionary dictatorship of the proletariat.

What, then, is the relation of this dictatorship to democracy?

We have seen that the *Communist Manifesto* simply places side by side the two concepts: "to raise the proletariat to the position of the ruling class" and "to win the battle of democracy".[171] On the basis of all that has been said above, it is possible to determine more precisely how democracy changes in the transition from capitalism to communism.

In capitalist society, providing it develops under the most favourable conditions, we have a more or less complete democracy in the democratic republic. But this democracy is always hemmed in by the narrow limits set by capitalist exploitation, and consequently always remains, in effect, a democracy for the minority, only for the propertied classes, only for the rich. Freedom in capitalist society always remains about the same as it was in the ancient Greek republics: freedom for the slave-owners. Owing to the conditions of capitalist exploitation, the modern wage slaves are so crushed by want and poverty that "they cannot be bothered with democracy", "cannot be bothered with politics"; in the ordinary, peaceful course of events, the majority of the population is debarred from participation in public and political life.

The correctness of this statement is perhaps most clearly confirmed by Germany, because constitutional legality steadily endured there for a remarkably long time—nearly half a century (1871-1914)—and during this period the Social-Democrats were able to achieve far more than in other countries in the way of "utilising legality", and organised a larger proportion of the workers into a political party than anywhere else in the world.

What is this largest proportion of politically conscious and active wage slaves that has so far been recorded in capitalist society? One million members of the Social-Democratic Party—out of fifteen million wage-workers! Three million organised in trade unions—out of fifteen million!

Democracy for an insignificant minority, democracy for the rich—that is the democracy of capitalist society. If we look more closely into the machinery of capitalist democracy, we see everywhere, in the "petty"—supposedly petty—details of the suffrage (residential qualification, exclusion of women, etc.), in the technique of the representative institutions, in the actual obstacles to the right of assembly (public buildings are not for "paupers"!), in the purely capitalist organisation of the daily press, etc., etc.—we see restriction after restriction upon democracy. These restrictions, exceptions, exclusions, obstacles for the poor seem slight, especially in the eyes of one who has never known want himself and has never been in close contact with the oppressed classes in their mass life (and nine out of ten, if not ninety-nine out of a hundred, bourgeois publicists and politicians come under this category); but in their sum total these restrictions exclude and squeeze out the poor from politics, from active participation in democracy.

Marx grasped this *essence* of capitalist democracy splendidly when, in analysing the experience of the Commune, he said that the oppressed are allowed once every few years to decide which particular representatives of the oppressing class shall represent and repress them in parliament!

But from this capitalist democracy—that is inevitably narrow and stealthily pushes aside the poor, and is therefore hypocritical and false through and through—forward development does not proceed simply, directly and smoothly, towards "greater and greater democracy", as the liberal professors and petty-bourgeois opportunists would have us believe. No, forward development, i.e., development towards communism, proceeds through the dictatorship of the proletariat, and cannot do otherwise, for the *resistance* of the capitalist exploiters cannot be *broken* by anyone else or in any other way.

And the dictatorship of the proletariat, i.e., the organisation of the vanguard of the oppressed as the ruling class for the purpose of suppressing the oppressors, cannot result merely in an expansion of democracy. *Simultaneously* with an immense expansion of democracy, which *for the first time* becomes democracy for the poor, democracy for the people, and not democracy for the moneybags, the dictatorship of the proletariat imposes a series of restrictions on the freedom of the oppressors, the exploiters, the capitalists. We must suppress them in order to free humanity from wage slavery, their resistance must be crushed by force; it is clear that there is no freedom and no democracy where there is suppression and where there is violence.

Engels expressed this splendidly in his letter to Bebel when he said, as the reader will remember, that "the proletariat needs the state, not in the interests of freedom but in order to hold down its adversaries, and as soon as it becomes possible to speak of freedom the state as such ceases to exist."[172]

Democracy for the vast majority of the people, and suppression by force, i.e., exclusion from democracy, of the exploiters and oppressors of the people—this is the change democracy undergoes during the *transition* from capitalism to communism.

Only in communist society, when the resistance of the capitalists has been completely crushed, when the capitalists have disappeared when there are no classes (i.e., when there is no distinctions between the members of society as regards their relation to the social means of production), *only* then "the state ... ceases to exist", and "*it becomes possible to speak of freedom*". Only then will a truly complete democracy become possible and be realised, a democracy without any exceptions whatever. And only then will democracy begin to *wither away*, owing to the simple fact that, freed from capitalist slavery, from the untold horrors, savagery, absurdities and infamies of capitalist exploitation, people will gradually *become accustomed* to observing the elementary rules of social intercourse that have been known for centuries and repeated for thousands of years in all copy-book maxims. They will become accustomed to observing them without force, without coercion, without subordination, *without the special apparatus* for coercion called the state.

The expression "the state *withers away*" is very well chosen, for it indicates both the gradual and the spontaneous nature of the process. Only habit can, and undoubtedly will, have such an effect; for we see around us on millions of occasions how readily people become accustomed to observing the necessary rules of social intercourse when there is no exploitation, when there is nothing that arouses indignation, evokes protest and revolt, and creates the need for *suppression*.

And so in capitalist society we have a democracy that is curtailed, wretched, false, a democracy only for the rich, for the minority. The dictatorship of the proletariat, the period of transition to communism, will for the first time create democracy for the people, for the majority, along with the necessary suppression of the exploiters, of the minority. Communism alone is capable of providing really complete democracy, and the more complete it is, the sooner it will become unnecessary and wither away of its own accord.

In other words, under capitalism we have the state in the proper sense of the word, that is, a special machine for the suppression of one class by another, and, what is more, of the majority by the minority. Naturally, to be successful, such an undertaking as the systematic suppression of the exploited majority by the exploiting minority calls for the utmost ferocity and savagery in the matter of suppressing, it calls for seas of blood, through which mankind is actually wading its way in slavery, serfdom and wage labour.

Furthermore, during the *transition* from capitalism to communism suppression is *still* necessary, but it is now the suppression of the exploiting minority by the exploited majority. A special apparatus, a special machine for suppression, the "state", is *still* necessary, but this is now a transitional state. It is no longer a state in the proper sense of the word; for the suppression of the minority of exploiters by the majority of the wage slaves of *yesterday* is comparatively so easy, simple and natural a task that it will entail far less bloodshed than the suppression of the risings of slaves, serfs or wage-labourers, and it will cost mankind far less. And it is compatible with the extension of democracy to such an overwhelming majority of the population that the need for a *special machine* of suppression will begin to disappear. Naturally, the exploiters are unable to suppress the people without a highly complex machine for performing this task, but *the people* can suppress the exploiters even with a very simple "machine", almost without a "machine", without a special apparatus, by the simple *organisation of the armed people* (such as the Soviets of Workers' and Soldiers' Deputies, we would remark, running ahead).

Lastly, only communism makes the state absolutely unnecessary, for there is *nobody* to be suppressed—"nobody" in the sense of a *class*, of a systematic struggle against a definite section of the population. We are not utopians, and do not in the least deny the possibility and inevitability of excesses on the part of *individual persons*, or the need to stop *such* excesses. In the first place, however, no special machine, no special apparatus of suppression, is needed for this; this will be done by the armed people themselves, as simply and as readily as any crowd of civilised people, even in modern society, interferes to put a stop to a scuffle or to prevent a woman from being assaulted. And, secondly, we know that the fundamental social cause of excesses, which consist in the violation of the rules of social intercourse, is the exploitation of the people, their want and their poverty. With the removal of this chief cause, excesses will inevitably begin to *"wither away"*. We do not know how quickly and in what succession, but we do know they will wither away. With their withering away the state will also *wither away*.

Without building utopias, Marx defined more fully what can be defined *now* regarding this future, namely, the difference between the lower and higher phases (levels, stages) of communist society.

3. THE FIRST PHASE OF COMMUNIST SOCIETY

In the *Critique of the Gotha Programme*, Marx goes into detail to disprove Lassalle's idea that under socialism the worker will receive the "undiminished" or "full product of his labour". Marx shows that from the whole of the social labour of society there must be deducted a reserve fund, a fund for the expansion of production, a fund for the replacement of the "wear and tear" of machinery, and so on. Then, from the means of consumption must be deducted a fund for administrative expenses, for schools, hospitals, old people's homes, and so on.

Instead of Lassalle's hazy, obscure, general phrase ("the full product of his labour to the worker"), Marx makes a sober estimate of exactly how socialist society will have to manage its affairs. Marx proceeds to make a *concrete* analysis of the conditions of life of a society in which there will be no capitalism, and says:

"What we have to deal with here [in analysing the programme of the workers' party] is a communist society, not as
it has *developed* on its own foundations, but, on the contrary,
just as it *emerges* from capitalist society; which is, therefore,
in every respect, economically, morally and intellectually, still
stamped with the birthmarks of the old society from whose
womb it comes."

It is this communist society, which has just emerged into the
light of day out of the womb of capitalism and which is in every
respect stamped with the birthmarks of the old society, that Marx
terms the "first", or lower, phase of communist society.

The means of production are no longer the private property of
individuals. The means of production belong to the whole of society. Every member of society, performing a certain part of the
socially necessary work, receives a certificate from society to the
effect that he has done a certain amount of work. And with this
certificate he receives from the public store of consumer goods a
corresponding quantity of products. After a deduction is made of
the amount of labour which goes to the public fund, every worker,
therefore, receives from society as much as he has given to it.

"Equality" apparently reigns supreme.

But when Lassalle, having in view such a social order (usually
called socialism, but termed by Marx the first phase of communism), says that this is "equitable distribution", that this is "the
equal right of all to an equal product of labour", Lassalle is
mistaken and Marx exposes the mistake.

"Equal right," says Marx, we certainly do have here; but it is
still a "bourgeois right", which, like every right, *implies inequality.*
Every right is an application of an *equal* measure to *different*
people who in fact are not alike, are not equal to one another. That
is why "equal right" is a violation of equality and an injustice. In
fact, everyone, having performed as much social labour as another,
receives an equal share of the social product (after the above-
mentioned deductions).

But people are not alike: one is strong, another is weak; one is
married, another is not; one has more children, another has less,
and so on. And the conclusion Marx draws is:

"...With an equal performance of labour, and hence an
equal share in the social consumption fund, one will in fact
receive more than another, one will be richer than another,
and so on. To avoid all these defects, right would have to be
unequal rather than equal."

The first phase of communism, therefore, cannot yet provide
justice and equality: differences, and unjust differences, in wealth

will still persist, but the *exploitation of* man by man will have become impossible because it will be impossible to seize the *means of production*—the factories, machines, land, etc.—and make them private property. In smashing Lassalle's petty-bourgeois, vague phrases about "equality" and "justice" *in general*, Marx shows the *course of development* of communist society, which is *compelled* to abolish at first *only* the "injustice" of the means of production seized by individuals, and which is *unable* at once to eliminate the other injustice, which consists in the distribution of consumer goods "according to the amount of labour performed" (and not according to needs).

The vulgar economists, including the bourgeois professors and "our" Tugan, constantly reproach the socialists with forgetting the inequality of people and with "dreaming" of eliminating this inequality. Such a reproach, as we see, only proves the extreme ignorance of the bourgeois ideologists.

Marx not only most scrupulously takes account of the inevitable inequality of men, but he also takes into account the fact that the mere conversion of the means of production into the common property of the whole of society (commonly called "socialism") *does not remove* the defects of distribution and the inequality of "bourgeois right", which *continues to prevail* so long as products are divided "according to the amount of labour performed". Continuing, Marx says:

> "...But these defects are inevitable in the first phase of communist society as it is when it has just emerged, after prolonged birth pangs, from capitalist society. Right can never be higher than the economic structure of society and its cultural development conditioned thereby."

And so, in the first phase of communist society (usually called socialism) "bourgeois right" is *not* abolished in its entirety, but only in part, only in proportion to the economic revolution so far attained, i.e., only in respect of the means of production. "Bourgeois right" recognises them as the private property of individuals. Socialism converts them into *common property*. *To that extent*—and to that extent alone—"bourgeois right" disappears.

However, it persists as far as its other part is concerned; it persists in the capacity of regulator (determining factor) in the distribution of products and the allotment of labour among the members of society. The socialist principle, "He who does not work shall not eat", is *already* realised; the other socialist principle, "An equal amount of products for an equal amount of labour", is also *already* realised. But this is not yet communism, and it does not yet abolish "bourgeois right", which gives unequal individuals, in return for unequal (really unequal) amounts of labour, equal amounts of products.

This is a "defect", says Marx, but it is unavoidable in the first phase of communism; for if we are not to indulge in utopianism, we must not think that having overthrown capitalism people will at once learn to work for society *without any standard of right*. Besides, the abolition of capitalism *does not immediately create* the economic prerequisites for *such a* change.

Now, there is no other standard than that of "bourgeois right". To this extent, therefore, there still remains the need for a state, which, while safeguarding the common ownership of the means of production, would safeguard equality in labour and in the distribution of products.

The state withers away insofar as there are no longer any capitalists, any classes, and, consequently, no *class* can be *suppressed*.

But the state has not yet completely withered away, since there still remains the safeguarding of "bourgeois right", which sanctifies actual inequality. For the state to wither away completely, complete communism is necessary.

4. THE HIGHER PHASE OF COMMUNIST SOCIETY

Marx continues:

> "...In a higher phase of communist society, after the enslaving subordination of the individual to the division of labour and with it also the antithesis between mental and physical labour has vanished, after labour has become not only a livelihood but life's prime want, after the productive forces have increased with the all-round development of the individual, and all the springs of co-operative wealth flow more abundantly—only then can the narrow horizon of bourgeois right be crossed in its entirety and society inscribe on its banners: From each according to his ability, to each according to his needs!"

Only now can we fully appreciate the correctness of Engels's remarks mercilessly ridiculing the absurdity of combining the words "freedom" and "state". So long as the state exists there is no freedom. When there is freedom, there will be no state.

The economic basis for the complete withering away of the state is such a high stage of development of communism at which the antithesis between mental and physical labour disappears, at which there consequently disappears one of the principal sources of modern *social* inequality—a source, moreover, which cannot on any account be removed immediately by the mere conversion of the means of production into public property, by the mere expropriation of the capitalists.

This expropriation will make it *possible* for the productive forces to develop to a tremendous extent. And when we see how incredibly capitalism is already *retarding* this development, when we see how much progress could be achieved on the basis of the level of technique already attained, we are entitled to say with the fullest confidence that the expropriation of the capitalists will inevitably result in an enormous development of the productive forces of human society. But how rapidly this development will proceed, how soon it will reach the point of breaking away from the division of labour, of doing away with the antithesis between mental and physical labour, of transforming labour into "life's prime want"—we do not and *cannot* know.

That is why we are entitled to speak only of the inevitable withering away of the state, emphasising the protracted nature of this process and its dependence upon the rapidity of development of the *higher phase* of communism, and leaving the question of the time required for, or the concrete forms of, the withering away quite open, because there is *no* material for answering these questions.

The state will be able to wither away completely when society adopts the rule: "From each according to his ability, to each according to his needs", i.e., when people have become so accustomed to observing the fundamental rules of social intercourse and when their labour has become so productive that they will voluntarily work *according to their ability*. "The narrow horizon of bourgeois right", which compels one to calculate with the heartlessness of a Shylock[173] whether one has not worked half an hour more than somebody else, whether one is not getting less pay than somebody else—this narrow horizon will then be crossed. There will then be no need for society, in distributing products, to regulate the quantity to be received by each; each will take freely "according to his needs".

From the bourgeois point of view, it is easy to declare that such a social order is "sheer utopia" and to sneer at the socialists for promising everyone the right to receive from society, without any control over the labour of the individual citizen, any quantity of truffles, cars, pianos, etc. Even to this day, most bourgeois "savants" confine themselves to sneering in this way, thereby betraying both their ignorance and their selfish defence of capitalism.

Ignorance—for it has never entered the head of any socialist to "promise" that the higher phase of the development of communism will arrive; as for the great socialists' *forecast* that it will arrive, it presupposes not the present productivity of labour and *not the present* ordinary run of people, who, like the seminary students in Pomyalovsky's stories,[174] are capable of damaging the stocks of public wealth "just for fun", and of demanding the impossible. Until the "higher" phase of communism arrives, the socialists demand the *strictest* control by society *and by the state* over the measure of labour and the measure of consumption; but this control must *start with* the expropriation of the capitalists, with the establishment of workers' control over the capitalists, and must be exercised not by a state of bureaucrats, but by a state of *armed workers*.

The selfish defence of capitalism by the bourgeois ideologists (and their hangers-on, like the Tseretelis, Chernovs and Co.) consists in that they *substitute* arguing and talk about the distant future for the vital and burning question of *present-day* politics, namely, the expropriation of the capitalists, the conversion of *all* citizens into workers and other employees of *one* huge "syndicate" —the whole state—and the complete subordination of the entire work of this syndicate to a genuinely democratic state, *the state of the Soviets of Workers' and Soldiers' Deputies.*

In fact, when a learned professor, followed by the philistine, followed in turn by the Tseretelis and Chernovs, talks of wild utopias, of the demagogic promises of the Bolsheviks, of the impossibility of "introducing" socialism, it is the higher stage, or phase, of communism he has in mind, which no one has ever promised or even thought to "introduce", because, generally speaking, it cannot be "introduced".

And this brings us to the question of the scientific distinction between socialism and communism which Engels touched on in his above-quoted argument about the incorrectness of the name "Social-Democrat". Politically, the distinction between the first, or lower, and the higher phase of communism will in time, probably, be tremendous. But it would be ridiculous to recognise this distinction now, under capitalism, and only individual anarchists, perhaps, could invest it with primary importance (if there still are people among the anarchists who have learned nothing from the "Plekhanov" conversion of the Kropotkins, of Grave, Cornelissen and other stars" of anarchism into social-chauvinists or "anarchotrenchists", as Ghe, one of the few anarchists who have still preserved a sense of honour and a conscience, has put it).

But the scientific distinction between socialism and communism is clear. What is usually called socialism was termed by Marx the "first", or lower, phase of communist society. Insofar as the means of production become *common* property, the word "communism" is also applicable here, providing we do not forget that this is *not* complete communism. The great significance of Marx's explanations is that here, too, he consistently applies materialist dialectics, the theory of development, and regards communism as something which develops *out of* capitalism. Instead of scholastically invented, "concocted" definitions and fruitless disputes over words (What is socialism? What is communism?), Marx gives an analysis of what might be called the stages of the economic maturity of communism.

In its first phase, or first stage, communism *cannot* as yet be fully mature economically and entirely free from traditions or vestiges of capitalism. Hence the interesting phenomenon that communism in its first phase retains "the narrow horizon of *bourgeois* right". Of course, bourgeois right in regard to the distribution of *consumer* goods inevitably presupposes the existence of the *bourgeois state*, for right is nothing without an apparatus capable of *enforcing* the observance of the standards of right.

It follows that under communism there remains for a time not only bourgeois right, but even the bourgeois state, without the bourgeoisie!

This may sound like a paradox or simply a dialectical conundrum, of which Marxism is often accused by people who have not taken the slightest trouble to study its extraordinarily profound content.

But in fact, remnants of the old, surviving in the new, confront us in life at every step, both in nature and in society. And Marx did not arbitrarily insert a scrap of "bourgeois" right into communism, but indicated what is economically and politically inevitable in a society emerging *out of the womb* of capitalism.

Democracy is of enormous importance to the working class in its struggle against the capitalists for its emancipation. But democracy is by no means a boundary not to be overstepped; it is only one of the stages on the road from feudalism to capitalism, and from capitalism to communism.

Democracy means equality. The great significance of the proletariat's struggle for equality and of equality as a slogan will be clear if we correctly interpret it as meaning the abolition of *classes*. But democracy means only *formal* equality. And as soon as equality is achieved for all members of society *in relation* to ownership of the means of production, that is, equality of labour and wages, humanity will inevitably be confronted with the question of advancing farther, from formal equality to actual equality, i.e., to the operation of the rule "from each according to his ability, to each according to his needs". By what stages, by means of what practical measures humanity will proceed to this supreme aim we do not and cannot know. But it is important to realise how infinitely mendacious is the ordinary bourgeois conception of socialism as something lifeless, rigid, fixed once and for all, whereas in reality *only* socialism will be the beginning of a rapid, genuine, truly mass forward movement, embracing first the *majority* and then the whole of the population, in all spheres of public and private life.

Democracy is a form of the state, one of its varieties. Consequently, it, like every state, represents, on the one hand, the organised, systematic use of force against persons; but, on the other hand, it signifies the formal recognition of equality of citizens, the equal right of all to determine the structure of, and to administer, the state. This, in turn, results in the fact that, at a certain stage in the development of democracy, it first welds together the class that wages a revolutionary struggle against capitalism—the proletariat, and enables it to crush, smash to atoms, wipe off the face of the earth the bourgeois, even the republican-bourgeois, state machine, the standing army, the police and the bureaucracy and to substitute for them a *more* democratic state machine, but a state machine nevertheless, in the shape of armed workers who proceed to form a militia involving the entire population.

Here "quantity turns into quality": *such* a degree of democracy implies overstepping the boundaries of bourgeois society and beginning its socialist reorganisation. If really *all* take part in the administration of the state, capitalism cannot retain its hold. The development of capitalism, in turn, creates the *preconditions* that *enable* really "all" to take part in the administration of the state. Some of these preconditions are: universal literacy, which has already been achieved in a number of the most advanced capitalist countries, then the "training and disciplining" of millions of workers by the huge, complex, socialised apparatus of the postal service, railways, big factories, large-scale commerce, banking, etc., etc.

Given these *economic* preconditions, it is quite possible, after the overthrow of the capitalists and the bureaucrats, to proceed immediately, overnight, to replace them in the *control* over production and distribution, in the work of *keeping account* of labour and products, by the armed workers, by the whole of the armed population. (The question of control and accounting should not be confused with the question of the scientifically trained staff of engineers, agronomists and so on. These gentlemen are working today in obedience to the wishes of the capitalists, and will work even better tomorrow in obedience to the wishes of the armed workers.)

Accounting and control—that is *mainly* what is needed for the "smooth working", for the proper functioning, of the *first phase* of communist society. *All* citizens are transformed into hired employees of the state, which consists of the armed workers. *All* citizens become employees and workers of a *single* country-wide state "syndicate". All that is required is that they should work equally, do their proper share of work, and get equal pay. The accounting and control necessary for this have been *simplified* by capitalism to the utmost and reduced to the extraordinarily simple operations—which any literate person can perform—of supervising and recording, knowledge of the four rules of arithmetic, and issuing appropriate receipts.*

When the *majority* of the people begin independently and everywhere to keep such accounts and exercise such control over the capitalists (now converted into employees) and over the intellectual gentry who preserve their capitalist habits, this control will really become universal, general and popular; and there will be no getting away from it, there will be "nowhere to go".

The whole of society will have become a single office and a single factory, with equality of labour and pay.

But this "factory" discipline, which the proletariat, after defeating the capitalists, after overthrowing the exploiters, will extend to the whole of society, is by no means our ideal, or our ultimate goal. It is only a necessary *step* for thoroughly cleaning society of all the infamies and abominations of capitalist exploitation, *and for further* progress.

From the moment all members of society, or at least the vast majority, have learned to administer the state *themselves,* have taken this work into their own hands, have organised control over the insignificant capitalist minority, over the gentry who wish to preserve their capitalist habits and over the workers who have been thoroughly corrupted by capitalism—from this moment the need for government of any kind begins to disappear altogether. The more complete the democracy, the nearer the moment when it becomes unnecessary. The more democratic the "state" which consists of the armed workers, and which is "no longer a state in the proper sense of the word", the more rapidly *every form* of state begins to wither away.

For when *all* have learned to administer and actually do independently administer social production, independently keep accounts and exercise control over the parasites, the sons of the wealthy, the swindlers and other "guardians of capitalist traditions", the escape from this popular accounting and control will inevitably become so incredibly difficult, such a rare exception, and will probably be accompanied by such swift and severe punishment (for the armed workers are practical men and not sentimental intellectuals, and they will scarcely allow anyone to trifle with them), that the *necessity* of observing the simple, fundamental rules of the community will very soon become a *habit*.

Then the door will be thrown wide open for the transition from the first phase of communist society to its higher phase, and with it to the complete withering away of the state.

---

* When the more important functions of the state are reduced to such accounting and control by the workers themselves, it will cease to be a "political state" and "public functions will lose their political character and become mere administrative functions" (cf. above, Chapter IV, 2, Engels's controversy with the anarchists).

CHAPTER VI

THE VULGARISATION OF MARXISM BY THE OPPORTUNISTS

The question of the relation of the state to the social revolution, and of the social revolution to the state, like the question of revolution generally, was given very little attention by the leading theoreticians and publicists of the Second International (1889-1914). But the most characteristic thing about the process of the gradual growth of opportunism that led to the collapse of the Second International in 1914 is the fact that even when these people were squarely faced with this question they *tried to evade* it or ignored it.

In general, it may be said that *evasiveness* over the question of the relation of the proletarian revolution to the state—an evasiveness which benefited and fostered opportunism—resulted in the *distortion* of Marxism and in its complete vulgarisation.

To characterise this lamentable process, if only briefly, we shall take the most prominent theoreticians of Marxism: Plekhanov and Kautsky.

1. PLEKHANOV'S CONTROVERSY WITH THE ANARCHISTS

Plekhanov wrote a special pamphlet on the relation of anarchism to socialism, entitled *Anarchism and Socialism*, which was published in German in 1894.

In treating this subject, Plekhanov contrived completely to evade the most urgent, burning, and most politically essential issue in the struggle against anarchism, namely, the relation of the revolution to the state, and the question of the state in general! His pamphlet falls into two distinct parts: one of them is historical and literary, and contains valuable material on the history of the ideas of Stirner, Proudhon and others; the other is philistine, and contains a clumsy dissertation on the theme that an anarchist cannot be distinguished from a bandit.

It is a most amusing combination of subjects and most characteristic of Plekhanov's whole activity on the eve of the revolution and during the revolutionary period in Russia. In fact, in the years 1905 to 1917, Plekhanov revealed himself as a semi-doctrinaire and semi-philistine who, in politics, trailed in the wake of the bourgeoisie.

We have seen how, in their controversy with the anarchists, Marx and Engels with the utmost thoroughness explained their views on the relation of revolution to the state. In 1891, in his foreword to Marx's *Critique of the Gotha Programme*, Engels wrote that "we" —that is, Engels and Marx—"were at that time, hardly two years[175] after The Hague Congress of the [First] International,[176] engaged in the most violent struggle against Bakunin and his anarchists".

The anarchists had tried to claim the Paris Commune as their "own", so to say, as a corroboration of their doctrine; and they completely misunderstood its lessons and Marx's analysis of these lessons. Anarchism has given nothing even approximating true answers to the concrete political questions: Must the old state machine be *smashed*? And *what* should be put in its place?

But to speak of "anarchism and socialism" while completely evading the question of the state, and *disregarding* the whole development of Marxism before and after the Commune, meant inevitably slipping into opportunism. For what opportunism needs most of all is that the two questions just mentioned should *not* be raised at all. That *in itself* is a victory for opportunism.

2. KAUTSKY'S CONTROVERSY WITH THE OPPORTUNISTS

Undoubtedly, an immeasurably larger number of Kautsky's works have been translated into Russian than into any other language. It is not without reason that some German Social-Democrats say in jest that Kautsky is read more in Russia than in Germany (let us say, in parenthesis, that this jest has a far deeper historical meaning than those who first made it suspect. The Russian workers, by making in 1905 an unusually great and unprecedented demand for the best works of the best Social-Democratic literature in the world, and by receiving translations and editions of these works in quantities unheard of in other countries, rapidly transplanted, so to speak, the enormous experience of a neighbouring, more advanced country to the young soil of our proletarian movement).

Besides his popularisation of Marxism, Kautsky is particularly known in our country for his controversy with the opportunists, with Bernstein at their head. One fact, however, is almost unknown, one which cannot be ignored if we set out to investigate how Kautsky drifted into the morass of unbelievably disgraceful confusion and defence of social-chauvinism during the supreme crisis of 1914-15. This fact is as follows: shortly before he came out against the most prominent representatives of opportunism in France (Millerand and Jaurès) and in Germany (Bernstein), Kautsky betrayed very considerable vacillation. The Marxist *Zarya*, which was published in Stuttgart in 1901-02, and advocated revolutionary proletarian views, was forced to *enter into controversy* with Kautsky and describe as "elastic" the half-hearted, evasive resolution, conciliatory towards the opportunists, that he proposed at the International Socialist Congress in Paris in 1900.[177] Kautsky's letters published in Germany reveal no less hesitancy on his part before he took the field against Bernstein.

Of immeasurably greater significance, however, is the fact that, in his very controversy with the opportunists, in his formulation of the question and his manner of treating it, we can now see, as we study the *history* of Kautsky's latest betrayal of Marxism, his systematic deviation towards opportunism precisely on the question of the state.

Let us take Kautsky's first important work against opportunism, *Bernstein and the Social-Democratic Programme*. Kautsky refutes Bernstein in detail, but here is a characteristic thing:

Bernstein, in his *Premises of Socialism*, of Herostratean fame, accuses Marxism of "*Blanquism*" (an accusation since repeated thousands of times by the opportunists and liberal bourgeoisie in Russia against the revolutionary Marxists, the Bolsheviks). In this connection Bernstein dwells particularly on Marx's *The Civil War in France*, and tries, quite unsuccessfully, as we have seen, to identify Marx's views on the lessons of the Commune with those of Proudhon. Bernstein pays particular attention to the conclusion which Marx emphasised in his 1872 preface to the *Communist Manifesto*, namely, that "the working class cannot simply lay hold of the ready-made state machinery and wield it for its own purposes".This statement "pleased" Bernstein so much that he used it no less than three times in his book, interpreting it in the most distorted, opportunist way.

As we have seen, Marx meant that the working class must *smash, break, shatter* (*Sprengung*, explosion—the expression used by Engels) the whole state machine. But according to Bernstein it would appear as though Marx in these words warned the working class *against* excessive revolutionary zeal when seizing power.

A cruder and more hideous distortion of Marx's idea cannot be imagined.

How, then, did Kautsky proceed in his most detailed refutation of Bernsteinism?

He refrained from analysing the utter distortion of Marxism by opportunism on this point. He cited the above-quoted passage from Engels's preface to Marx's *Civil War* and said that according to Marx the working class cannot *simply* take over the *ready-made* state machinery, but that, generally speaking, it *can* take it over— and that was all. Kautsky did not say a word about the fact that Bernstein attributed to Marx the *very opposite* of Marx's real idea, that since 1852 Marx had formulated the task of the proletarian revolution as being to "smash" the state machine.

The result was that the most essential distinction between Marxism and opportunism on the subject of the tasks of the proletarian revolution was slurred over by Kautsky!

"We can quite safely leave the solution of the problem of the proletarian dictatorship to the future," said Kautsky, writing "*against*" Bernstein. (P. 172, German edition.)

This is not a polemic *against* Bernstein, but, in essence, a *concession* to him, a surrender to opportunism; for at present the opportunists ask nothing better than to "quite safely leave to the future" all fundamental questions of the tasks of the proletarian revolution.

From 1852 to 1891, or for forty years, Marx and Engels taught the proletariat that it must smash the state machine. Yet, in 1899, Kautsky, confronted with the complete betrayal of Marxism by the opportunists on this point, fraudulently *substituted* for the question whether it is necessary to smash this machine the question of the concrete forms in which it is to be smashed, and then sought refuge behind the "indisputable" (and barren) philistine truth that concrete forms cannot be known in advance!!

A gulf separates Marx and Kautsky over their attitudes towards the proletarian party's task of training the working class for revolution.

Let us take the next, more mature, work by Kautsky, which was also largely devoted to a refutation of opportunist errors. It is his pamphlet, *The Social Revolution*. In this pamphlet, the author chose as his special theme the question of "the proletarian revolution" and "the proletarian regime". He gave much that was exceedingly valuable, but he *avoided* the question of the state. Throughout the pamphlet the author speaks of the winning of state power—and no more; that is, he has chosen a formula which makes a concession to the opportunists, inasmuch as it *admits* the possibility of seizing power *without* destroying the state machine. The very thing which Marx in 1872 declared to be "obsolete" in the programme of the *Communist Manifesto, is revived* by Kautsky in 1902.

A special section in the pamphlet is devoted to the "forms and weapons of the social revolution". Here Kautsky speaks of the mass political strike, of civil war, and of the "instruments of the might of the modern large state, its bureaucracy and the army"; but he does not say a word about what the Commune has already taught the workers. Evidently, it was not without reason that Engels issued a warning, particularly to the German socialists, against "superstitious reverence" for the state.

Kautsky treats the matter as follows: the victorious proletariat "will carry out the democratic programme", and he goes on to formulate its clauses. But he does not say a word about the new material provided by 1871 on the subject of the replacement of bourgeois democracy by proletarian democracy. Kautsky disposes of the question by using such "impressive-sounding" banalities as:

"Still, it goes without saying that we shall not achieve supremacy under the present conditions. Revolution itself presupposes long and deep-going struggles, which, in themselves, will change our present political and social structure."

Undoubtedly, this "goes without saying", just as the fact that horses eat oats or the Volga flows into the Caspian. Only it is a pity that an empty and bombastic phrase about "deep-going" struggles is used to *avoid* a question of vital importance to the revolutionary proletariat, namely, *what* makes *its* revolution "deep-going" in relation to the state, to democracy, as distinct from previous, non-proletarian revolutions.

By avoiding this question, Kautsky *in practice* makes a concession to opportunism on this most essential point, although *in words* he declares stern war against it and stresses the importance of the "idea of revolution" (how much is this "idea" worth when one is afraid to teach the workers the concrete lessons of revolution?), or says, "revolutionary idealism before everything else", or announces that the English workers are now "hardly more than petty bourgeois".

"The most varied forms of enterprises—bureaucratic [??], trade unionist, co-operative, private ... can exist side by side in socialist society," Kautsky writes. "... There are, for example enterprises which cannot do without a bureaucratic [??] organisation, such as the railways. Here the democratic organisation may take the following shape: the workers elect delegates who form a sort of parliament, which establishes the working regulations and supervises the management of the bureaucratic apparatus. The management of other enterprises may be transferred to the trade unions, and still others may become co-operative enterprises."

This argument is erroneous; it is a step backward compared with the explanations Marx and Engels gave in the seventies, using the lessons of the Commune as an example.

As far as the supposedly necessary "bureaucratic" organisation is concerned, there is no difference whatever between a railway and any other enterprise in large-scale machine industry, any factory, large shop, or large-scale capitalist agricultural enterprise. The technique of all these enterprises makes absolutely imperative the strictest discipline, the utmost precision on the part of everyone in carrying out his allotted task, for otherwise the whole enterprise may come to a stop, or machinery or the finished product may be damaged. In all these enterprises the workers will, of course, "elect delegates who will form *a sort of parliament*".

The whole point, however, is that this "sort of parliament" will *not* be a parliament in the sense of a bourgeois parliamentary institution. The whole point is that this "sort of parliament" will *not* merely "establish the working regulations and supervise the management of the bureaucratic apparatus", as Kautsky, whose thinking does not go beyond the bounds of bourgeois parliamentarism, imagines. In socialist society, the "sort of parliament" consisting

of workers' deputies will, of course, "establish the working regulations and supervise the management" of the "apparatus", *but* this
apparatus will *not* be "bureaucratic". The workers, after winning
political power, will smash the old bureaucratic apparatus, shatter
it to its very foundations, and raze it to the ground; they will replace it by a new one, consisting of the very same workers and
other employees, *against* whose transformation into bureaucrats
the measures will at once be taken which were specified in detail
by Marx and Engels: 1) not only election, but also recall at any
time; 2) pay not to exceed that of a workman; 3) immediate introduction of control and supervision by *all*, so that *all* may become
"bureaucrats" for a time and that, therefore, *nobody* may be able
to become a "bureaucrat".

Kautsky has not reflected at all on Marx's words: "The Commune was a working, not a parliamentary, body, executive and
legislative at the same time."[178]

Kautsky has not understood at all the difference between bourgeois parliamentarism, which combines democracy (*not for the
people*) with bureaucracy (*against the people*), and proletarian
democracy, which will take immediate steps to cut bureaucracy
down to the roots, and which will be able to carry these measures
through to the end, to the complete abolition of bureaucracy, to
the introduction of complete democracy for the people.

Kautsky here displays the same old "superstitious reverence" for
the state, and "superstitious belief" in bureaucracy.

Let us now pass to the last and best of Kautsky's works against
the opportunists, his pamphlet *The Road to Power* (which, I believe, has not been published in Russian, for it appeared in 1909,
when reaction was at its height in our country). This pamphlet is
a big step forward, since it does not deal with the revolutionary
programme in general, as the pamphlet of 1899 against Bernstein,
or with the tasks of the social revolution irrespective of the time
of its occurrence, as the 1902 pamphlet, *The Social Revolution*; it
deals with the concrete conditions which compel us to recognise
that the "era of revolutions" is *setting in.*

The author explicitly points to the aggravation of class antagonisms in general and to imperialism, which plays a particularly important part in this respect. After the "revolutionary period of
1789-1871" in Western Europe, he says, a similar period began in
the East in 1905. A world war is approaching with menacing rapidity. "It [the proletariat] can no longer talk of premature revolution." "We have entered a revolutionary period." The "revolutionary
era is beginning".

These statements are perfectly clear. This pamphlet of Kautsky's
should serve as a measure of comparison of what the German
Social-Democrats *promised to be* before the imperialist war and the

depth of degradation to which they, including Kautsky himself, sank when the war broke out. "The present situation," Kautsky wrote in the pamphlet under survey, "is fraught with the danger that we [i.e., the German Social-Democrats] may easily appear to be more 'moderate' than we really are." It turned out that in reality the German Social-Democratic Party was much more moderate and opportunist than it appeared to be!

It is all the more characteristic, therefore, that although Kautsky so explicitly declared that the era of revolutions had already begun, in the pamphlet which he himself said was devoted to an analysis of the "*political* revolution", he again completely avoided the question of the state.

These evasions of the question, these omissions and equivocations, inevitably added up to that complete swing-over to opportunism with which we shall now have to deal.

Kautsky, the German Social-Democrats' spokesman, seems to have declared: I abide by revolutionary views (1899), I recognise, above all, the inevitability of the social revolution of the proletariat (1902), I recognise the advent of a new era of revolutions (1909). Still, I am going back on what Marx said as early as 1852, since the question of the tasks of the proletarian revolution in relation to the state is being raised (1912).

It was in this point-blank form that the question was put in Kautsky's controversy with Pannekoek.

3. KAUTSKY'S CONTROVERSY WITH PANNEKOEK

In opposing Kautsky, Pannekoek came out as one of the representatives of the "Left radical" trend which included Rosa Luxemburg, Karl Radek and others. Advocating revolutionary tactics, they were united in the conviction that Kautsky was going over to the "Centre", which wavered in an unprincipled manner between Marxism and opportunism. This view was proved perfectly correct by the war, when this "Centrist" (wrongly called Marxist) trend, or Kautskyism, revealed itself in all its repulsive wretchedness.

In an article touching on the question of the state, entitled "Mass Action and Revolution" (*Neue Zeit*, 1912, Vol. XXX, 2), Pannekoek described Kautsky's attitude as one of "passive radicalism", as "a theory of inactive expectancy". "Kautsky refuses to see the process of revolution," wrote Pannekoek (p. 616). In presenting the matter in this way, Pannekoek approached the subject which interests us, namely, the tasks of the proletarian revolution in relation to the state.

"The struggle of the proletariat," he wrote, "is not merely a struggle against the bourgeoisie *for* state power, but a struggle *against* state power.... The content of this [the proletarian] revolution is the destruction and dissolution [Auflösung] of the instruments of power of the state with the aid of the instruments of power of the proletariat (p. 544). The struggle will cease only when, as the result of it, the state organisation is completely destroyed. The organisation of the majority will then have demonstrated its superiority by destroying the organisation of the ruling minority." (P. 548.)

The formulation in which Pannekoek presented his ideas suffers from serious defects. But its meaning is clear nonetheless, and it is interesting to note *how* Kautsky combated it.

"Up to now," he wrote, "the antithesis between the Social-Democrats and the anarchists has been that the former wished to win state power while the latter wished to destroy it. Pannekoek wants to do both." (P. 724.)

Although Pannekoek's exposition lacks precision and concreteness—not to speak of other shortcomings of his article which have no bearing on the present subject—Kautsky seized precisely on the point of *principle* raised by Pannekoek; and *on this fundamental* point of *principle* Kautsky completely abandoned the Marxist position and went over wholly to opportunism. His definition of the distinction between the Social-Democrats and the anarchists is absolutely wrong; he completely vulgarises and distorts Marxism.

The distinction between the Marxists and the anarchists is this: (1) The former, while aiming at the complete abolition of the state, recognise that this aim can only be achieved after classes have been abolished by the socialist revolution, as the result of the establishment of socialism, which leads to the withering away of the state. The latter want to abolish the state completely overnight, not understanding the conditions under which the state can be abolished. (2) The former recognise that after the proletariat has won political power it must completely destroy the old state machine and replace it by a new one consisting of an organisation of the armed workers, after the type of the Commune. The latter, while insisting on the destruction of the state machine, have a very vague idea of *what* the proletariat will put in its place and *how* it will use its revolutionary power. The anarchists even deny that the revolutionary proletariat should use the state power, they reject its revolutionary dictatorship. (3) The former demand that the proletariat be trained for revolution by utilising the present state. The anarchists reject this.

In this controversy, it is not Kautsky but Pannekoek who represents Marxism, for it was Marx who taught that the proletariat cannot simply win state power in the sense that the old state apparatus passes into new hands, but must smash this apparatus, must break it and replace it by a new one.

Kautsky abandons Marxism for the opportunist camp, for this destruction of the state machine, which is utterly unacceptable to the opportunists, completely disappears from his argument, and he leaves a loophole for them in that "conquest" may be interpreted as the simple acquisition of a majority.

To cover up his distortion of Marxism, Kautsky behaves like a doctrinaire: he puts forward a "quotation" from Marx himself. In 1850 Marx wrote that a "resolute centralisation of power in the hands of the state authority"[179] was necessary, and Kautsky triumphantly asks: does Pannekoek want to destroy "Centralism"?

This is simply a trick, like Bernstein's identification of the views of Marxism and Proudhonism on the subject of federalism as against centralism.

Kautsky's "quotation" is neither here nor there. Centralism is possible with both the old and the new state machine. If the workers voluntarily unite their armed forces, this will be centralism, but it will be based on the "complete destruction" of the centralised state apparatus—the standing army, the police and the bureaucracy. Kautsky acts like an outright swindler by evading the perfectly well-known arguments of Marx and Engels on the Commune and plucking out a quotation which has nothing to do with the point at issue.

"... Perhaps he [Pannekoek]," Kautsky continues, "wants to abolish the state functions of the officials? But we cannot do without officials even in the party and the trade unions, let alone in the state administration. And our programme does not demand the abolition of state officials, but that they be elected by the people.... We are discussing here not the form the administrative apparatus of the 'future state' will assume, but whether our political struggle abolishes [literally dissolves—auflöst] the state power before we have captured it [Kautsky's italics]. Which ministry with its officials could be abolished?" Then follows an enumeration of the ministries of education, justice, finance and war. "No, not one of the present ministries will be removed by our political struggle against the government.... I repeat, in order to prevent misunderstanding: we are not discussing here the form the 'future state' will be given by the victorious Social-Democrats, but how the present state is changed by our opposition." (P. 725.)

This is an obvious trick. Pannekoek raised the question of *revolution*. Both the title of his article and the passages quoted above clearly indicate this. By skipping to the question of "opposition", Kautsky substitutes the opportunist for the revolutionary point of view. What he says means: at present we are an opposition; what we shall be *after* we have captured power, that we shall see. *Revolution has vanished!* And that is exactly what the opportunists wanted.

The point at issue is neither opposition nor political struggle in general, but *revolution*. Revolution consists in the proletariat *destroying* the "administrative apparatus" and the *whole* state machine, replacing it by a new one, made up of the armed workers. Kautsky displays a "superstitious reverence" for "ministries"; but why can they not be replaced, say, by committees of specialists working under sovereign, all-powerful Soviets of Workers' and Soldiers' Deputies?

The point is not at all whether the "ministries" will remain, or whether "committees of specialists" or some other bodies will be set up; that is quite immaterial. The point is whether the old state machine (bound by thousands of threads to the bourgeoisie and permeated through and through with routine and inertia) shall remain, or be *destroyed* and replaced by a *new* one. Revolution consists not in the new class commanding, governing with the aid of the *old* state machine, but in this class smashing this machine and commanding, governing with the aid of a *new* machine. Kautsky slurs over this *basic* idea of Marxism, or he does not understand it at all.

His question about officials clearly shows that he does not understand the lessons of the Commune or the teachings of Marx. "We cannot do without officials even in the party and the trade unions. ..."

We cannot do without officials *under capitalism, under the rule of the bourgeoisie*. The proletariat is oppressed, the working people are enslaved by capitalism. Under capitalism, democracy is restricted, cramped, curtailed, mutilated by all the conditions of wage slavery, and the poverty and misery of the people. This and this alone is the reason why the functionaries of our political organisations and trade unions are corrupted—or rather tend to be corrupted—by the conditions of capitalism and betray a tendency to become bureaucrats, i.e., privileged persons divorced from the people and standing *above* the people.

That is the *essence* of bureaucracy; and until the capitalists have been expropriated and the bourgeoisie overthrown, *even* proletarian functionaries will inevitably be "bureaucratised" to a certain extent.

According to Kautsky, since elected functionaries will remain under socialism, so will officials, so will the bureaucracy! This is exactly where he is wrong. Marx, referring to the example of the Commune, showed that under socialism functionaries will cease to be "bureaucrats", to be "officials", they will cease to be so *in proportion as*—in addition to the principle of election of officials—the principle of recall at any time is *also* introduced, as salaries are reduced to the level of the wages of the average workman, *and* as parliamentary institutions are replaced by "working bodies, executive and legislative at the same time".[180]

As a matter of fact, the whole of Kautsky's argument against Pannekoek, and particularly the former's wonderful point that we cannot do without officials even in our party and trade union organisations, is merely a repetition of Bernstein's old "arguments" against Marxism in general. In his renegade book, *The Premises of Socialism*, Bernstein combats the ideas of "primitive" democracy, combats what he calls "doctrinaire democracy": binding mandates, unpaid officials, impotent central representative bodies, etc. To prove that this "primitive" democracy is unsound, Bernstein refers to the experience of the British trade unions, as interpreted by the Webbs. Seventy years of development "in absolute freedom", he says (p. 137, German edition), convinced the trade unions that primitive democracy was useless, and they replaced it by ordinary democracy, i.e., parliamentarism combined with bureaucracy.

In reality, the trade unions did not develop "in absolute freedom" *but in absolute capitalist slavery*, under which, it goes without saying, a number of concessions to the prevailing evil, violence, falsehood, exclusion of the poor from the affairs of "higher" administration, "cannot be done without". Under socialism much of "primitive" democracy will inevitably be revived, since, for the first time in the history of civilised society, the *mass* of the population will rise to taking an *independent* part, not only in voting and elections, *but also in the everyday administration of the state*. Under socialism *all* will govern in turn and will soon become accustomed to no one governing.

Marx's critico-analytical genius saw in the practical measures of the Commune the *turning-point* which the opportunists fear and do not want to recognise because of their cowardice, because they do not want to break irrevocably with the bourgeoisie, and which the anarchists do not want to see, either because they are in a hurry or because they do not understand at all the conditions of great social changes. "We must not even think of destroying the old state machine; how can we do without ministries and officials?" argues the opportunist, who is completely saturated with philistinism and who, at bottom, not only does not believe in revolution, in the creative power of revolution, but lives in mortal dread of it (like our Mensheviks and Socialist-Revolutionaries).

"We must think *only* of destroying the old state machine; it is no use probing into the *concrete* lessons of earlier proletarian revolutions and analysing *what* to put in the place of what has been destroyed, and *how*," argues the anarchist (the best of the anarchists, of course, and not those who, following the Kropotkins and Co., trail behind the bourgeoisie). Consequently, the tactics of the anarchist become the tactics of *despair* instead of a ruthlessly bold revolutionary effort to solve concrete problems while taking into account the practical conditions of the mass movement.

Marx teaches us to avoid both errors; he teaches us to act with supreme boldness in destroying the entire old state machine, and at the same time he teaches us to put the question concretely: the Commune was able in the space of a few weeks to *start* building a *new*, proletarian state machine by introducing such-and-such measures to provide wider democracy and to uproot bureaucracy. Let us learn revolutionary boldness from the Communards; let us see in their practical measures the *outline* of really urgent and immediately possible measures, and then, *following this road,* we shall achieve the complete destruction of bureaucracy.

The possibility of this destruction is guaranteed by the fact that socialism will shorten the working day, will raise the *people* to a new life, will create such conditions for the *majority* of the population as will enable *everybody*, without exception, to perform "state functions", and this will lead to the *complete withering away* of every form of state in general.

"... Its object [the object of the mass strike]," Kautsky continues, "cannot be to *destroy* the state power; its only object can be to make the government compliant on some specific question, or to replace a government hostile to the proletariat by one willing to meet it half-way [entgegenkommende].... But never, under no circumstances, can it [that is, the proletarian victory over a hostile government] lead to the *destruction* of the state power; it can lead only to a certain *shifting* [verschiebung] of the balance of forces *within the state power....* The aim of our political struggle remains, as in the past, the conquest of state power by winning a majority in parliament and by raising parliament to the rank of master of the government." (Pp. 726, 727, 732.)

This is nothing but the purest and most vulgar opportunism: repudiating revolution in deeds, while accepting it in words. Kautsky's thoughts go no further than a "government ... willing to meet the proletariat half-way"—a step backward to philistinism compared with 1847, when the *Communist Manifesto* proclaimed "the organisation of the proletariat as the ruling class".[181]

Kautsky will have to achieve his beloved "unity" with the Scheidemanns, Plekhanovs and Vanderveldes, all of whom agree to fight for a government "willing to meet the proletariat half-way".

We, however, shall break with these traitors to socialism, and we shall fight for the complete destruction of the old state machine, in order that the armed proletariat itself *may become the government*. These are two vastly different things.

Kautsky will have to enjoy the pleasant company of the Legiens and Davids, Plekhanovs, Potresovs, Tseretelis and Chernovs, who are quite willing to work for the "shifting of the balance of forces within the state power", for "winning a majority in parliament", and "raising parliament to the rank of master of the government". A most worthy object, which is wholly acceptable to the opportunists and which keeps everything within the bounds of the bourgeois parliamentary republic.

We, however, shall break with the opportunists; and the entire class-conscious proletariat will be with us in the fight—not to "shift the balance of forces", but to *overthrow the bourgeoisie, to destroy* bourgeois parliamentarism, for a democratic republic after the type of the Commune, or a republic of Soviets of Workers' and Soldiers' Deputies, for the revolutionary dictatorship of the proletariat.

* * *

To the right of Kautsky in international socialism there are trends such as *Socialist Monthly*[182] in Germany (Legien, David, Kolb and many others, including the Scandinavians Stauning and Branting); Jaurès's followers and Vandervelde in France and Belgium; Turati, Trèves and other Right-wingers of the Italian Party; the Fabians and "Independents" (the Independent Labour Party, which, in fact, has always been dependent on the Liberals) in Britain; and the like. All these gentry, who play a tremendous, very often a predominant role in the parliamentary work and the press of their parties, repudiate outright the dictatorship of the proletariat and pursue a policy of undisguised opportunism. In the eyes of these gentry, the "dictatorship" of the proletariat "contradicts" democracy!! There is really no essential distinction between them and the petty-bourgeois democrats.

Taking this circumstance into consideration, we are justified in drawing the conclusion that the Second International, that is, the overwhelming majority of its official representatives, has completely sunk into opportunism. The experience of the Commune has been not only ignored, but distorted. Far from inculcating in the workers' minds the idea that the time is nearing when they must act to smash the old state machine, replace it by a new one, and in this way make their political rule the foundation for the socialist reorganisation of society, they have actually preached to the masses the very opposite and have depicted the "conquest of power" in a way that has left thousands of loopholes for opportunism.

The distortion and hushing up of the question of the relation of the proletarian revolution to the state could not but play an immense role at a time when states, which possess a military apparatus expanded as a consequence of imperialist rivalry, have become military monsters which are exterminating millions of people in order to settle the issue as to whether Britain or Germany—this or that finance capital—is to rule the world.*

---

* The MS. continues as follows:

"C H A P T E R   VII
"THE EXPERIENCE OF THE RUSSIAN REVOLUTIONS
OF 1905 AND 1917

"The subject indicated in the title of this chapter is so vast that volumes could and should be written about it. In the present pamphlet we shall have to confine ourselves, naturally, to the most important lessons provided by experience, those bearing directly upon the tasks of the proletariat in the revolution with regard to state power." (Here the manuscript breaks off.)—*Ed.*

POSTSCRIPT TO THE FIRST EDITION

This pamphlet was written in August and September 1917. I had already drawn up the plan for the next, the seventh, chapter, "The Experience of the Russian Revolutions of 1905 and 1917". Apart from the title, however, I had no time to write a single line of the chapter; I was "interrupted" by a political crisis—the eve of the October Revolution of 1917. Such an "interruption" can only be welcomed; but the writing of the second part of the pamphlet ("The Experience of the Russian Revolutions of 1905 and 1917") will probably have to be put off for a long time. It is more pleasant and useful to go through the "experience of the revolution" than to write about it.

The Author

Petrograd
November 30, 1917

Written August-September 1917
Postscript to the First Edition—
    November 30, 1917
§3 of Chapter II—earlier than
    December 17, 1918

Published in 1918
in pamphlet form
in Petrograd
by the Publishing House
Zhizn i Znaniye

Collected Works, Vol. 25

ON COMPROMISES

The term compromise in politics implies the surrender of certain demands, the renunciation of part of one's demands, by agreement with another party.

The usual idea the man in the street has about the Bolsheviks, an idea encouraged by a press which slanders them, is that the Bolsheviks will never agree to a compromise with anybody.

The idea is flattering to us as the party of the revolutionary proletariat, for it proves that even our enemies are compelled to admit our loyalty to the fundamental principles of socialism and revolution. Nevertheless, we must say that this idea is wrong. Engels was right when, in his criticism of the Manifesto of the Blanquist Communists (1873), he ridiculed their declaration: "No compromises!"[183] This, he said, was an empty phrase, for compromises are often unavoidably forced upon a fighting party by circumstances, and it is absurd to refuse once and for all to accept "payments on account". The task of a truly revolutionary party is not to declare that it is impossible to renounce all compromises, but to be able, *through all compromises,* when they are unavoidable, to remain true to its principles, to its class, to its revolutionary purpose, to its task of paving the way for revolution and educating the mass of the people for victory in the revolution.

To agree, for instance, to participate in the Third and Fourth Dumas[184] was a compromise, a temporary renunciation of revolutionary demands. But this was a compromise absolutely forced upon us, for the balance of forces made it impossible for us for the time being to conduct a mass revolutionary struggle, and in order to prepare this struggle over a long period we *had* to be able to work even from *inside* such a "pigsty". History has proved that this approach to the question by the Bolsheviks as a party was perfectly correct.

Now the question is not of a forced, but of a voluntary compromise.

Our Party, like any other political party, is striving after political domination *for itself*. Our aim is the dictatorship of the revolutionary proletariat. Six months of revolution have proved very clearly, forcefully and convincingly that this demand is correct and inevitable in the interests of *this particular* revolution, for otherwise the people will never obtain a democratic peace, land for the peasants, or complete freedom (a fully democratic republic). This has been shown and proved by the course of events during the six months of our revolution, by the struggle of the classes and parties and by the development of the crises of April 20-21, June 9-10 and 18-19, July 3-5 and August 27-31.[185]

The Russian revolution is experiencing so abrupt and original a turn that we, as a party, may offer a voluntary compromise— true, not to our direct and main class enemy, the bourgeoisie, but to our nearest adversaries, the "ruling" petty-bourgeois-democratic parties, the Socialist-Revolutionaries and Mensheviks.

We may offer a compromise to these parties only by way of exception, and only by virtue of the particular situation, which will obviously last only a very short time. And I think we should do so.

The compromise on our part is our return to the pre-July demand of all power to the Soviets and a government of S.R.s and Mensheviks responsible to the Soviets.

Now, and only now, perhaps *during only a few days* or a week or two, such a government could be set up and consolidated in a perfectly peaceful way. In all probability it could secure the peaceful *advance* of the whole Russian revolution, and provide exceptionally good chances for great strides in the world movement towards peace and the victory of socialism.

In my opinion, the Bolsheviks, who are partisans of world revolution and revolutionary methods, may and should consent to this compromise only for the sake of the revolution's peaceful development—an opportunity that is *extremely* rare in history and *extremely* valuable, an opportunity that only occurs once in a while.

The compromise would amount to the following: the Bolsheviks, without making any claim to participate in the government (which is impossible for the internationalists unless a dictatorship of the proletariat and the poor peasants has been realised), would refrain from demanding the immediate transfer of power to the proletariat and the poor peasants and from employing revolutionary methods of fighting for this demand. A condition that is self-evident and not new to the S.R.s and Mensheviks would be complete freedom of propaganda and the convocation of the Constituent Assembly without further delays or even at an earlier date.

The Mensheviks and S.R.s, being the government bloc, would then agree (assuming that the compromise had been reached) to form a government wholly and exclusively responsible to the Soviets, the latter taking over all power locally as well. This would constitute the "new" condition. I think the Bolsheviks would advance no other conditions, trusting that the revolution would proceed peacefully and party strife in the Soviets would be *peacefully overcome* thanks to really complete freedom of propaganda and to the immediate establishment of a new democracy in the composition of the Soviets (new elections) and in their functioning.

Perhaps this is *already* impossible? Perhaps. But if there is even one chance in a hundred, the attempt at realising this opportunity is still worth while.

What would both "contracting" parties gain by this "compromise", i.e., the Bolsheviks, on the one hand, and the S.R. and Menshevik bloc, on the other? If *neither* side gains anything, then the compromise must be recognised as impossible, and nothing more is to be said. No matter how difficult this compromise may be at present (after July and August, two months equivalent to two decades in "peaceful", somnolent times), I think it stands a small chance of being realised. This chance has been created by the decision of the S.R.s and Mensheviks not to participate in a government together with the Cadets.

The Bolsheviks would gain the opportunity of quite freely advocating their views and of trying to win influence in the Soviets under a really complete democracy. In words, "everybody" now concedes the Bolsheviks this freedom. In reality, this freedom is *impossible* under a bourgeois government or a government in which the bourgeoisie participate, or under any government, in fact, other than the Soviets. Under a Soviet government, such freedom would be *possible* (we do not say it would be a certainty, but still it would be possible). For the sake of such a possibility at such a difficult time, it would be worth compromising with the present majority in the Soviets. *We* have nothing to fear from real democracy, for reality is on our side, and even the course of development of trends within the S.R. and Menshevik parties, which are hostile to us, proves us right.

The Mensheviks and S.R.s would gain in that they would at once obtain every opportunity to carry out *their* bloc's programme with the support of the obviously overwhelming majority of the people and in that they would secure for themselves the "peaceful" use of their majority in the Soviets.

Of course, there would probably be two voices heard from this bloc, which is heterogeneous both because it is a bloc and because petty-bourgeois democracy is *always* less homogeneous than the bourgeoisie and the proletariat.

One voice would say: we cannot follow the same road as the Bolsheviks and the revolutionary proletariat. It will demand too much anyway and will entice the peasant poor by demagogy. It will demand peace and a break with the Allies. That is impossible. We are better off and safer with the bourgeoisie; after all, we have not parted ways with them but only had a temporary *quarrel*, and only over the Kornilov incident. We have quarrelled, but we shall make it up. Moreover, the Bolsheviks are not "ceding" us anything, for their attempts at insurrection are as doomed to defeat as was the Commune of 1871.

The other voice would say: the allusion to the Commune is very superficial and even foolish. For, in the first place, the Bolsheviks have learnt something since 1871; they would not fail to seize the banks, and would not refuse to advance on Versailles. Under such conditions even the Commune might have been victorious. Furthermore, the Commune could not immediately offer the people what the Bolsheviks will be able to offer if they come to power, namely, land to the peasants, an immediate offer of peace, real control over production, an honest peace with the Ukrainians, Finns, etc. The Bolsheviks, to put it bluntly, hold ten times more "trumps" than the Commune did. In the second place, the Commune, after all, means a strenuous civil war, a setback to peaceful cultural development for a long time to come, an opportunity for all sorts of MacMahons and Kornilovs to operate and plot with greater ease— and such operations are a menace to our whole bourgeois society. Is it wise to risk a Commune?

Now a Commune is inevitable in Russia if we do not take power into our own hands, if things remain in as grave a state as they were between May 6 and August 31. Every revolutionary worker and soldier will inevitably think about the Commune and believe in it; he will inevitably attempt to bring it about, for he will argue: "The people are perishing; war, famine and ruin are spreading. Only the Commune can save us. So let us all perish, let us die, but let us set up the Commune." Such thoughts are inevitable with the workers, and it will not be as easy to crush the Commune now as it was in 1871. The Russian Commune will have allies throughout the world, allies a hundred times stronger than those the Commune had in 1871.... Is it wise for us to risk a Commune? I cannot agree, either, that the Bolsheviks virtually cede us nothing by their compromise. For, in all civilised countries, civilised ministers value highly every agreement with the proletariat in war-time, however small. They value it very, very highly. And these are men of action, real ministers. The Bolsheviks are rapidly becoming stronger, in spite of repression, and the weakness of their press.... Is it wise for us to risk a Commune?

We have a safe majority; the peasant poor will not wake up for some time to come; we are safe for our lifetime. I do not believe that in a peasant country the majority will follow the extremists.

And against an obvious majority, no insurrection is possible in a really democratic republic. This is what the second voice would say.

There may also be a third voice coming from among the supporters of Martov or Spiridonova, which would say: I am indignant, "comrades", that both of you, speaking about the Commune and its likelihood, unhesitatingly side with its opponents. In one form or another, both of you side with those who suppressed the Commune. I will not undertake to campaign for the Commune and I cannot promise beforehand to fight in its ranks as every Bolshevik will do, but I must say that *if* the Commune does start *in spite of* my efforts, I shall rather help its defenders than its opponents.

The medley of voices in the "bloc" is great and inevitable, for a host of shades is represented among the petty-bourgeois democrats—from that of the completely ministerial bourgeois down to the semi-pauper who is not yet capable of taking up the proletarian position. Nobody knows what will be the result of this medley of voices at any given moment.

* * *

The above lines were written on Friday, September 1, but due to unforeseen circumstances (under Kerensky, as history will tell, not all Bolsheviks were free to choose their domicile) they did not reach the editorial office that day. After reading Saturday's and today's (Sunday's) papers, I say to myself: perhaps it is already too late to offer a compromise. Perhaps the few days in which a peaceful development was *still* possible have passed *too*. Yes, to all appearances, they have already passed.[186] In one way or another, Kerensky will abandon both the S.R. Party and the S.R.s themselves, and will consolidate his position with the aid of the bourgeoisie *without* the S.R.s, and thanks to their inaction.... Yes, to all appearances, the days when by chance the path of peaceful development became possible have *already* passed. All that remains is to send these notes to the editor with the request to have them entitled: "Belated Thoughts". Perhaps even belated thoughts are some times not without interest.

September 3, 1917

Written September 1-3 (14-16), 1917

Published in *Rabochy Put* No. 3 September 19 (6), 1917 Signed: *N. Lenin*

Collected Works, Vol. 25

MARXISM AND INSURRECTION

A LETTER TO THE CENTRAL COMMITTEE OF THE R.S.D.L.P.(B.)

One of the most vicious and probably most widespread distortions of Marxism resorted to by the dominant "socialist" parties is the opportunist lie that preparation for insurrection, and generally the treatment of insurrection as an art, is "Blanquism".

Bernstein, the leader of opportunism, has already earned himself unfortunate fame by accusing Marxism of Blanquism, and when our present-day opportunists cry Blanquism they do not improve on or "enrich" the meagre "ideas" of Bernstein one little bit.

Marxists are accused of Blanquism for treating insurrection as an art! Can there be a more flagrant perversion of the truth, when not a single Marxist will deny that it was Marx who expressed himself on this score in the most definite, precise and categorical manner, referring to insurrection specifically as an *art*, saying that it must be treated as an art, that you must *win* the first success and then proceed from success to success, never ceasing the *offensive* against the enemy, taking advantage of his confusion, etc., etc.?

To be successful, insurrection must rely not upon conspiracy and not upon a party, but upon the advanced class. That is the first point. Insurrection must rely upon a *revolutionary upsurge of the people*. That is the second point. Insurrection must rely upon that *turning-point* in the history of the growing revolution when the activity of the advanced ranks of the people is at its height, and when the *vacillations* in the ranks of the enemy and *in the ranks of the weak, half-hearted and irresolute friends of the revolution* are strongest. That is the third point. And these three conditions for raising the question of insurrection distinguish *Marxism from Blanquism*.

Once these conditions exist, however, to refuse to treat insurrection as an *art* is a betrayal of Marxism and a betrayal of the revolution.

To show that it is precisely the present moment that the Party *must* recognise as the one in which the entire course of events has objectively placed *insurrection* on the order of the day and that insurrection must be treated as an art, it will perhaps be best to use the method of comparison, and to draw a parallel between July 3-4 and the September days.

On July 3-4 it could have been argued, without violating the truth, that the correct thing to do was to take power, for our enemies would in any case have accused us of insurrection and ruthlessly treated us as rebels. However, to have decided on this account in favour of taking power at that time would have been wrong, because the objective conditions for the victory of the insurrection did not exist.

1) We still lacked the support of the class which is the vanguard of the revolution.

We still did not have a majority among the workers and soldiers of Petrograd and Moscow. Now we have a majority in both Soviets. It was created *solely* by the history of July and August, by the experience of the "ruthless treatment" meted out to the Bolsheviks, and by the experience of the Kornilov revolt.

2) There was no country-wide revolutionary upsurge at the time. There is now, after the Kornilov revolt; the situation in the provinces and assumption of power by the Soviets in many localities prove this.

3) At that time there was no *vacillation* on any serious political scale among our enemies and among the irresolute petty bourgeoisie. Now the vacillation is enormous. Our main enemy, Allied and world imperialism (for world imperialism is headed by the "Allies"), *has begun to waver* between a war to a victorious finish and a separate peace directed against Russia. Our petty-bourgeois democrats, having clearly lost their majority among the people, have begun to vacillate enormously, and have rejected a bloc, i.e., a coalition, with the Cadets.

4) Therefore, an insurrection on July 3-4 would have been a mistake; we could not have retained power either physically or politically. We could not have retained it physically even though Petrograd was at times in our hands, because at that time our workers and soldiers would not have *fought and died* for Petrograd. There was not at the time that "savageness", or fierce hatred *both of* the Kerenskys *and of* the Tseretelis and Chernovs. Our people had still not been tempered by the experience of the persecution of the Bolsheviks in which the Socialist-Revolutionaries and Mensheviks participated.

We could not have retained power politically on July 3-4 because, *before the Kornilov revolt,* the army and the provinces could and would have marched against Petrograd.

Now the picture is entirely different.

We have the following of the majority of a *class*, the vanguard of the revolution, the vanguard of the people, which is capable of carrying the masses with it.

We have the following of the *majority* of the people, because Chernov's resignation, while by no means the only symptom, is the most striking and obvious symptom that the peasants *will not receive land* from the Socialist-Revolutionaries' bloc (or from the Socialist-Revolutionaries themselves). And that is the chief reason for the popular character of the revolution.

We are in the advantageous position of a party that knows for certain which way to go at a time when *imperialism as a whole* and the Menshevik and Socialist-Revolutionary bloc as a whole are vacillating in an incredible fashion.

Our victory is assured, for the people are close to desperation, and we are showing the entire people a sure way out; we demonstrated to the entire people during the "Kornilov days" the value of our leadership, and then *proposed* to the politicians of the bloc a compromise, *which they rejected,* although there is no let-up in their vacillations.

It would be a great mistake to think that our offer of a compromise had not *yet* been rejected, and that the Democratic Conference[187] may *still* accept it. The compromise was proposed *by a party to parties*; it could not have been proposed in any other way. It was rejected by *parties*. The Democratic Conference is a *conference*, and nothing more. One thing must not be forgotten, namely, that the *majority* of the revolutionary people, the poor, embittered peasants, are not represented in it. It is a conference of *a minority of the people*—this obvious truth must not be forgotten. It would be a big mistake, sheer parliamentary cretinism on our part, if we were to regard the Democratic Conference as a parliament; for even *if it were* to proclaim itself a permanent and sovereign parliament of the revolution, it would nevertheless *decide nothing*. The power of decision lies *outside it* in the working-class quarters of Petrograd and Moscow.

All the objective conditions exist for a successful insurrection. We have the exceptional advantage of a situation in which *only* our victory in the insurrection can put an end to that most painful thing on earth, vacillation, which has worn the people out; in which only our victory in the insurrection will give the peasants land immediately; a situation in which *only our* victory in the insurrection can *foil* the game of a separate peace directed against the revolution—foil it by publicly proposing a fuller, juster and earlier peace, a peace that will *benefit* the revolution.

Finally, our Party alone *can*, by a victorious insurrection, save Petrograd; for if our proposal for peace is rejected, if we do not secure even an armistice, then *we* shall become "defencists", we shall place ourselves *at the head of the war parties*, we shall be the *war party par excellence*, and we shall conduct the war in a truly revolutionary manner. We shall take away all the bread and boots

from the capitalists. We shall leave them only crusts and dress
them in bast shoes. We shall send all the bread and footwear to
the front.

And then we shall save Petrograd.

The resources, both material and spiritual, for a truly revolutionary war in Russia are still immense; the chances are a hundred to
one that the Germans will grant us at least an armistice. And to
secure an armistice now would in itself mean to win the *whole
world*.

* * *

Having recognised the absolute necessity for an insurrection of
the workers of Petrograd and Moscow in order to save the revolution and to save Russia from a "separate" partition by the imperialists of both groups, we must first adapt our political tactics at
the conference to the conditions of the growing insurrection;
secondly, we must show that it is not only in words that we accept
Marx's idea that insurrection must be treated as an art.

At the conference we must immediately cement the Bolshevik
group, without striving after numbers, and without fearing to leave
the waverers in the waverers' camp. They are more useful to the
cause of the revolution *there* than in the camp of the resolute and
devoted fighters.

We must draw up a brief declaration from the Bolsheviks, emphasising in no uncertain manner the irrelevance of long speeches
and of "speeches" in general, the necessity for immediate action
to save the revolution, the absolute necessity for a complete break
with the bourgeoisie, for the removal of the present government,
in its entirety, for a complete rupture with the Anglo-French
imperialists, who are preparing a "separate" partition of Russia,
and for the immediate transfer of all power to *revolutionary
democrats, headed by the revolutionary proletariat*.

Our declaration must give the briefest and most trenchant formulation of *this* conclusion in connection with the programme
proposals of peace for the peoples, land for the peasants, confiscation of scandalous profits, and a check on the scandalous sabotage
of production by the capitalists.

The briefer and more trenchant the declaration, the better. Only
two other highly important points must be clearly indicated in it,
namely, that the people are worn out by the vacillations, that they
are fed up with the irresolution of the Socialist-Revolutionaries
and Mensheviks; and that we are definitely breaking with these
parties because they have betrayed the revolution.

And another thing. By immediately proposing a peace without
annexations, by immediately breaking with the Allied imperialists
and with all imperialists, either we shall at once obtain an armis-

tice, or the entire revolutionary proletariat will rally to the defence of the country, and a really just, really revolutionary war will then be waged by revolutionary democrats under the leadership of the proletariat.

Having read this declaration, and having appealed for *decisions* and not talk, for *action* and not resolution-writing, we must *dispatch* our entire group to the *factories and the barracks*. Their place is there, the pulse of life is there, there is the source of salvation for our revolution, and there is the motive force of the Democratic Conference.

There, in ardent and impassioned speeches, we must explain our programme and put the alternative: either the conference adopts it *in its entirety*, or else insurrection. There is no middle course. Delay is impossible. The revolution is dying.

By putting the question in this way, by concentrating our entire group in the factories and barracks, *we shall be able to determine the right moment to start the insurrection*.

In order to treat insurrection in a Marxist way, i.e., as an art, we must at the same time, without losing a single moment, organise a *headquarters* of the insurgent detachments, distribute our forces, move the reliable regiments to the most important points, surround the Alexandrinsky Theatre, occupy the Peter and Paul Fortress,[188] arrest the General Staff and the government, and move against the officer cadets[189] and the Savage Division[190] those detachments which would rather die than allow the enemy to approach the strategic points of the city. We must mobilise the armed workers and call them to fight the last desperate fight, occupy the telegraph and the telephone exchange at once, move *our* insurrection headquarters to the central telephone exchange and connect it by telephone with all the factories, all the regiments, all the points of armed fighting, etc.

Of course, this is all by way of example, only to *illustrate* the fact that at the present moment it is impossible to remain loyal to Marxism, to remain loyal to the revolution *unless insurrection is treated as an art*.

N. Lenin

Written September 13-14 (26-27), 1917   *Collected Works*, Vol. 26

First published in 1921
in the magazine
Proletarskaya Revolutsia No. 2

CAN THE BOLSHEVIKS RETAIN STATE POWER?

FOREWORD TO THE SECOND EDITION

The present pamphlet, as is evident from the text, was written at the end of September and was finished on October 1, 1917.

The October 25 Revolution has transferred the question raised in this pamphlet from the sphere of theory to the sphere of practice.

This question must now be answered by deeds, not words. The theoretical arguments advanced against the Bolsheviks taking power were feeble in the extreme. These arguments have been shot to pieces.

The task now is for the advanced class—the proletariat—to prove *in practice* the viability of the workers' and peasants' government. All class-conscious workers, all the active and honest peasants, all working and exploited people, will do everything they can to solve the immense historic question in practice.

To work, everybody to work, the cause of the world socialist revolution must and will triumph.

St. Petersburg, November 9, 1917

N. Lenin

First published in 1918
in the pamphlet by N. Lenin,
*Can the Bolsheviks Retain State
Power?*, "Soldiers' and Peasants'
Library" Series, St. Petersburg

On what are all trends agreed, from *Rech* to *Novaya Zhizn*[191] inclusively, from the Kornilovite Cadets to the semi-Bolsheviks, *all,* except the Bolsheviks?

They all agree that the Bolsheviks will either never dare take over full state power alone, or, if they do dare, and do take power, they will not be able to retain it even for the shortest while.

If anybody asserts that the question of the Bolsheviks alone taking over full state power is a totally unfeasible political question, that only a swelled-headed "fanatic" of the worst kind can regard it as feasible, we refute this assertion by quoting the exact statements of the most responsible and most influential political parties and trends of various "hues".

But let me begin with a word or two about the first of the questions mentioned—will the Bolsheviks dare take over full state power alone? I have already had occasion, at the All-Russia Congress of Soviets, to answer this question in the affirmative in no uncertain manner by a remark that I shouted from my seat during one of Tsereteli's[192] ministerial speeches. And I have not met in the press, or heard, any statements by Bolsheviks to the effect that we ought not to take power alone. I still maintain that a political party—and the party of the advanced class in particular—would have no right to exist, would be unworthy of the name of party, would be a nonentity in any sense, if it refused to take power when opportunity offers.

We shall now quote statements by the Cadets, Socialist-Revolutionaries and semi-Bolsheviks (I would prefer to say quarter-Bolsheviks) on the question that interests us.

The leading article in *Rech* of September 16:

"... Discord and confusion reigned in the Alexandrinsky Theatre, and the socialist press reflects the same picture. Only the views of the Bolsheviks are definite and straightforward. At the Conference, they are the views of the minority. In the Soviets, they represent a constantly growing trend. But in spite of all their verbal pugnacity, their boastful phrases and display of self-confidence, the Bolsheviks, except for a few fanatics, are brave only in words. They would not attempt to take 'full power' on their own accord. Disorganisers and disrupters *par excellence*, they are really cowards who in their heart of hearts are fully aware of both their own intrinsic ignorance and the ephemeral nature of their present successes. They know as well as we all do that the first day of their ultimate triumph would also be the first day of their precipitous fall. Irresponsible by their very nature, anarchists in method and practice, they should be regarded only as a trend of political thought, or rather, as one of its aberrations. The best way to get rid of Bolshevism for many a year, to banish it, would be to place the country's fate in the hands of its leaders. And if it were not for the awareness that experiments of this kind are impermissible and fatal, one might in desperation decide on even this heroic measure. Happily, we repeat, these dismal heroes of the day are not by any means actually out to seize full power. Not under any circumstances are they capable of constructive work. Thus, all their definite and straightforward views are confined to the political rostrum, to soapbox oratory. For practical purposes their position cannot be taken into consideration from any point of view. In one respect, however, it has some practical consequence: it unites all other shades of 'socialist thought' opposed to it...."

This is the way the Cadets reason. Here, however, is the view of the biggest, "ruling and governing", party in Russia, the Socialist-Revolutionaries, also expressed in an unsigned, i.e., editorial, leading article in their official organ *Dyelo Naroda* of September 21:

"... If the bourgeoisie refuse, pending the convocation of the Constituent Assembly, to work with the democracy on the basis of the platform that was endorsed by the conference, then the *coalition must arise from within the conference itself.* This would be a serious sacrifice on the part of the supporters of the coalition, but *even those campaigning for the idea of a 'pure line' of power will have to agree to it.* We are afraid, however, that agreement may not be reached here. In that case a third and final combination remains, namely: the government *must* be organised by that half of the conference which on *principle* advocated the idea of a homogeneous government.

"Let us put it definitely: *the Bolsheviks will be obliged to form a Cabinet.* With the greatest energy, they imbued the revolutionary democrats with hatred of the coalition, promising them all sorts of benefits as soon as 'compromise' was abandoned, and attributing to the latter all the country's misfortunes.

"If they were aware of what they were doing by their *agitation*, if they were *not deceiving the people, it is their duty* to redeem the promissory notes they have been handing out right and left.

"The question is clear.

"Let them not make futile attempts to hide behind hastily concocted theory that it is impossible for them to take power.

"The democracy will not accept these theories.

"At the same time, the advocates of coalition must guarantee them full support. These are the three combinations, the three ways, open to us—there are no others!" (The italics are those of *Dyelo Naroda.*)

This is the way the Socialist-Revolutionaries reason. And here, finally, is the "position" (if attempts to sit between two stools can be called a position) of the *Novaya Zhizn* "quarter-Bolsheviks", taken from the editorial in *Novaya Zhizn* of September 23.

"... If a coalition with Konovalov and Kishkin is formed again, it will mean nothing but a new capitulation by the democracy and the abrogation of the conference resolution on the formation of a responsible government on the platform of August 14....

"... A homogeneous ministry of Mensheviks and Socialist-Revolutionaries will be able to feel its responsibility as little as the responsible socialist ministers felt it in the coalition cabinet.... This government would not only be incapable of rallying the 'live forces' of the revolution around itself, but would not even be able to count on any active support from its vanguard—the proletariat.

"But the formation of another type of homogeneous cabinet, a government of the 'proletariat and poor peasants', would be, not a better, but an even worse way out of the situation, in fact it would not be a way out at all, but sheer bankruptcy. True, nobody is advancing such a slogan except in casual, timid and later systematically 'explained away' comments in *Rabochy Put*[193]."

(This glaring untruth is "boldly" written by responsible journalists who have forgotten even the *Dyelo Naroda* editorial of September 21.)

"Formally, the Bolsheviks have now revived the slogan 'All Power to the Soviets'. It was withdrawn after the July days, when the Soviets, represented by the Central Executive Committee, definitely adopted an active anti-Bolshevik policy. Now, however, not only can the 'Soviet line' be regarded as straightened out, but there is every ground to assume that at the proposed Congress of Soviets the Bolsheviks will have a majority. Under such circumstances, the slogan 'All Power to the Soviets', resurrected by the Bolsheviks, is a 'tactical line' for achieving precisely the dictatorship of the proletariat and the 'poor peasants'. True, the Soviets also imply the Soviets of Peasants' Deputies; the Bolshevik slogan therefore implies a power resting on the overwhelmingly greater part of the entire democracy of Russia. In that case, however, the slogan 'All Power to the Soviets' loses all independent significance, for it makes the Soviets almost identical in composition to the Pre-parliament set up by the Conference...."

(*Novaya Zhizn*'s assertion is a brazen lie, equivalent to declaring that spurious and fraudulent democracy is "almost identical" to democracy: the Pre-parliament is a *sham* which passes off the will of the minority of the people, particularly of Kuskova, Berkenheim, Chaikovsky and Co., as the will of the majority. This is the first point. The second point is that at the Conference even the Peasants' Soviets that had been packed by the Avksentyevs and Chaikovskys gave such a high percentage opposed to the coalition that taken together with the Soviets of Workers' and Soldiers' Deputies, they would have brought about the *absolute collapse of the coalition*. And the third point is that "Power to the Soviets" means that the power of the Peasants' Soviets would embrace mainly the rural districts, and in the rural districts the predominance of the *poor* peasants is assured.)

"If it is one and the same thing, then the Bolshevik slogan should be immediately withdrawn. If, however, 'Power to the Soviets' is only a disguise for the dictatorship of the proletariat, then such a power would mean precisely the failure and collapse of the revolution.

"Does it need proof that the proletariat, isolated not only from the other classes in the country, but also from the real live forces of the democracy, will not be able either technically to lay hold of the state apparatus and set it in motion in an exceptionally complicated situation, or politically to resist all the pressure by hostile forces that will sweep away not only the proletarian dictatorship, but the entire revolution into the bargain?

"The only power that will answer the requirements of the present situation is a really honest coalition within the democracy."

* * *

We apologise to the reader for quoting these lengthy extracts, but they are absolutely necessary. It is necessary to present a precise picture of the positions taken by the different parties hostile to the Bolsheviks. It is necessary to prove in a definite manner the extremely important fact that *all* these parties have admitted that the question of the Bolsheviks taking full state power alone is not only feasible, but also urgent.

Let us now proceed to examine the arguments which convince "everybody", from the Cadets to the *Novaya Zhizn* people, that the Bolsheviks will not be able to retain power.

The respectable *Rech* advances no arguments whatsoever. It merely pours out upon the Bolsheviks a flood of the choicest and most irate abuse. The extract we quoted shows, among other things, how utterly wrong it would be to say, "Watch out, comrades, for what the enemy advises must certainly be bad", thinking that *Rech* is "provoking" the Bolsheviks to take power. If, instead of weighing up the general and concrete considerations in a practical way, we allow ourselves to be "persuaded" by the plea that the bourgeoisie are "provoking" us to take power, we shall be fooled by the bourgeoisie, for the latter will of course always maliciously prophesy millions of disasters that will result from the Bolsheviks taking power and will always maliciously shout, "It would be better to get rid of the Bolsheviks at one blow and 'for many a year' by allowing them to take power and then crushing them." These cries are also "provocation", if you will, but from a different angle. The Cadets and the bourgeoisie do not by any means "advise", and have never "advised", us to take power; they are only trying to *frighten* us with the allegedly insoluble problems of government.

No. We must not allow ourselves to be frightened by the screams of the frightened bourgeoisie. We must bear firmly in mind that we have never set ourselves "insoluble" social problems, and as for the *perfectly* soluble problem of taking immediate steps towards socialism, which is the only way out of the exceedingly difficult situation, that will be *solved only* by the dictatorship of the proletariat and poor peasants. Victory, and lasting victory, is now more than ever, more than anywhere else, assured for the proletariat in Russia if it takes power.

We shall in a purely practical manner discuss the *concrete* circumstances that make a certain moment unfavourable; but we shall not for a moment allow ourselves to be scared by the savage howls of the bourgeoisie; and we shall not forget that the question of the Bolsheviks taking full power is becoming really *urgent*. Our Party will now be threatened with an immeasurably greater danger if we forget this than if we were to admit that taking power is "premature". In this respect, there can be *nothing* "premature" now: there is every chance in a million, except one or two perhaps, in favour of this.

Concerning the irate abuse poured out by *Rech,* we can, and must, say:

> In savage cries of irritation
> We hear the voice of approbation,
> Not in dulcet sounds of praise.[194]

That the bourgeoisie hate us so passionately is one of the most striking proofs that we are showing the people the *right* ways and means of overthrowing the rule of the bourgeoisie.

* * *

This time, by way of rare exception, *Dyelo Naroda* did not deign to honour us with its abuse nor did it advance a ghost of an argument. It merely tried, by indirect hints, to *frighten* us with the prospect that "the Bolsheviks will be obliged to form a cabinet". I can quite believe that while trying to frighten us, the Socialist-Revolutionaries are themselves sincerely scared to death by the phantom of the frightened liberal. I can equally believe that the Socialist-Revolutionaries do succeed in certain exceptionally high and exceptionally rotten institutions, such as the Central Executive Committee and similar "contact" (i.e., contact with the Cadets, in plain language, hobnobbing with the Cadets) commissions, in scaring some Bolsheviks because, first, the atmosphere in all those Central Executives, Pre-parliaments, etc., is abominable, putrid to the point of nausea, and harmful for *any* man to breathe for any length of time; and secondly, sincerity is contagious, and a sincerely frightened philistine is capable of converting even an individual revolutionary into a philistine for a time.

But however much we may, "humanly" speaking, understand the sincere fright of a Socialist-Revolutionary who has had the misfortune to be a minister in the company of the Cadets, or who is eligible as a minister in the eyes of the Cadets, we would be committing a political error that might only too easily border on treachery to the proletariat if we allowed ourselves to be scared. Let us have your practical arguments, gentlemen! Cherish no hope that we shall allow ourselves to be scared by your fright!

* * *

This time we find practical arguments only in *Novaya Zhizn.* On this occasion the paper comes out in the role of counsel for the bourgeoisie, a role that suits it far better than that of counsel for the defence of the Bolsheviks, which so obviously "shocks" this lady with many good points.[195]

The counsel has advanced *six* pleas:

1) the proletariat is "isolated from the other classes in the country";

2) it is "isolated from the real live forces of the democracy";

3) it "will not be able technically to lay hold of the state apparatus";

4) it "will not be able to set this apparatus in motion";

5) "the situation is exceptionally complicated";

6) it "will be incapable of resisting all the pressure by hostile forces that will sweep away not only the proletarian dictatorship, but the entire revolution into the bargain".

Novaya Zhizn formulates the first plea in a ridiculously clumsy fashion, for in capitalist and semi-capitalist society we know of only three classes: the bourgeoisie, the petty bourgeoisie (which consists mainly of the peasantry), and the proletariat. What sense is there in talking about the proletariat being isolated from the other classes when the point at issue is the proletariat's struggle against the bourgeoisie, revolution against the bourgeoisie?

Evidently, *Novaya Zhizn* wanted to say that the proletariat is isolated from the peasants, for it could not possibly have meant the landowners. It could not, however, say clearly and definitely that the proletariat is now isolated from the peasants, for the utter incorrectness of this assertion would be too obvious.

It is difficult to imagine that in a capitalist country the proletariat should be so little isolated from the petty bourgeoisie—and, mark you, in a revolution *against the bourgeoisie*—as the proletariat now is in Russia. The latest returns of the voting by "curias" *for* and *against* coalition with the bourgeoisie in Tsereteli's "Bulygin Duma", i.e., in the notorious "Democratic" Conference, constitute one of the objective and incontrovertible proofs of this. If we take the Soviets' curias we get:

	For coalition	Against
Soviets of Workers' aud Soldiers' Deputies	83	192
Soviets of Peasants' Deputies	102	70
All Soviets	185	262

So, the majority as a whole is on the side of the proletarian slogan: *against* coalition with the bourgeoisie. We have seen above that even the Cadets are obliged to admit the growth of Bolshevik influence in the Soviets. And here we have the conference convened by *yesterday*'s leaders in the Soviets, Socialist-Revolutionaries and Mensheviks, who have an assured majority in the central institutions! Obviously, the *actual* degree to which the Bolsheviks predominate in the Soviets is here *understated*.

Both on the question of coalition with the bourgeoisie and on the question of immediately transferring the landed estates to peasant committees, the Bolsheviks already have a *majority* in the Soviets of Workers', Soldiers' and Peasants' Deputies, a *majority of the people*, a majority of the petty bourgeoisie. *Rabochy Put* No. 19, of September 24 quotes from No. 25 of the organ of the Socialist-Revolutionaries *Znamya Truda*[196] a report on a conference of local Soviets of Peasants' Deputies held in Petrograd on September 18. At this conference the Executive Committees of four Peasants' Soviets (Kostroma, Moscow, Samara and Taurida gubernias) voted for an unrestricted coalition. The Executive Committees of *three* gubernias and *two* armies (Vladimir, Ryazan and the Black Sea gubernias) voted in favour of a coalition without the Cadets. The Executive Committees of *twenty-three* gubernias and *four* armies voted against a coalition.

So, the majority of the peasants are against a coalition!

So much for the "isolation of the proletariat".

We should note, by the way, that the supporters of a coalition were three outlying gubernias, Samara, Taurida and the Black Sea, where there is a relatively very large number of rich peasants and big landowners who employ hired labour, and also four industrial gubernias (Vladimir, Ryazan, Kostroma and Moscow) in which the peasant bourgeoisie are also stronger than in the majority of the gubernias in Russia. It would be interesting to collect more detailed figures on this question and to ascertain whether information is available concerning the *poor* peasants in the gubernias where there are larger numbers of "*rich*" peasants.

It is interesting, moreover, that the "non-Russian groups" revealed a considerable predominance of opponents of a coalition, namely, 40 votes against 15. The policy of annexation and open violence pursued by the Bonapartist Kerensky and Co. towards the non-sovereign nations of Russia has borne fruit. Wide sections of the people of the oppressed nations (i.e., including the mass of the petty bourgeoisie) trust the proletariat of Russia more than they do the bourgeoisie, for here history has brought to the fore the struggle for liberation of the oppressed nations against the oppressing nations. The bourgeoisie has despicably betrayed the cause of freedom of the oppressed nations; the proletariat is faithful to the cause of freedom.

At the present time the national and agrarian questions are fundamental questions for the petty-bourgeois sections of the population of Russia. This is indisputable. And on both these questions the proletariat is "*not* isolated"—farther from it than ever. It has the majority of the people behind it. It *alone* is capable of pursuing such a determined, genuinely "revolutionary-democratic" policy on both questions which would immediately ensure the proletarian state power not only the support of the majority of the population, but also a real outburst of revolutionary enthusiasm among the people. This is because, for the first time, the people would not see the ruthless oppression of peasants by landowners and of Ukrainians by Great Russians on the part of the government, as was the case under tsarism, nor the effort to continue the same policy camouflaged in pompous phrases under the republic, nor nagging, insult, chicanery, procrastination, underhand dealing and evasions (all that with which Kerensky rewards the peasants and the oppressed nations), but would receive warm sympathy proved by deeds, immediate and revolutionary measures against the landowners, immediate restitution of *full* freedom for Finland, the Ukraine, Byelorussia, for the Moslems, and so on.

The Socialist-Revolutionary and Menshevik gentlemen know this perfectly well, and are therefore dragging in the semi-Cadet bosses of the co-operative societies to help them pursue their *reactionary*-democratic policy *against* the people. That is why they will never dare canvass popular opinion, take a popular referendum, or at least a vote of all the local Soviets, of all the local organisations, concerning definite points of practical policy, for example, whether all the landed estates should at once be handed over to peasant committees, whether certain demands of the Finns or the Ukrainians should be conceded, etc.

Take the question of peace, the crucial issue of today. The proletariat "is isolated from the other classes".... On this issue the proletariat truly represents the *whole* nation, all live and honest people *in all* classes, the vast majority of the petty bourgeoisie; because only the proletariat, on achieving power, will *immediately* offer a just peace to all the belligerent nations, because only the proletariat will dare take genuinely *revolutionary* measures (publication of the secret treaties, and so forth) to achieve the speediest and most just peace possible.

The proletariat is not isolated. The gentlemen of *Novaya Zhizn* who are shouting about the proletariat being isolated are only betraying their subjective fear of the bourgeoisie. The objective state of affairs in Russia is undoubtedly such that the proletariat, *precisely at the present time*, is not "isolated" from the majority of the petty bourgeoisie. Precisely now, after the sad experience with the "coalition", the proletariat enjoys the sympathy of the *majority* of the people. *This* condition for the retention of power by the Bolsheviks *does exist*.

*   *   *

The second plea is that the proletariat "is isolated from the real live forces of the democracy". What this means is incomprehensible. It is probably "Greek", as the French say in such cases.

The writers of *Novaya Zhizn* would make good ministers. They would be quite suitable as ministers in a Cadet cabinet because all these ministers need is the ability to spout plausible, polished, but utterly meaningless phrases with which to cover up the dirtiest work and which are therefore sure of winning the applause of the imperialists and social-imperialists. The *Novaya Zhizn* writers are sure to earn the applause of the Cadets, Breshkovskaya, Plekhanov and Co. for asserting that the proletariat is isolated from the real live forces of the democracy, because *indirectly* they imply— or will be understood to imply—that the Cadets, Breshkovskaya, Plekhanov, Kerensky and Co. are the "live forces of democracy".

This is not true. They are dead forces. The history of the coalition has proved this.

Overawed by the bourgeoisie and by their bourgeois-intellectual environment, the *Novaya Zhizn* people regard as "live" the *Right* wing of the Socialist-Revolutionaries and Mensheviks like *Volya Naroda, Yedinstvo,*[197] and others who in essentials do not differ from the Cadets. We, however, regard as live only those who are connected with the people and not with the kulaks, only those whom the lessons of the coalition have repelled. The "active live forces" of the petty-bourgeois democracy are represented by the Left wing of the Socialist-Revolutionaries and Mensheviks. That this wing has gained strength, particularly since the July counter-revolution, is one of the surest objective signs that the proletariat is *not* isolated.

This has been made even more strikingly evident by the very recent swing to the left of the Socialist-Revolutionary Centrists, as is proved by Chernov's statement on September 24 that his group cannot support the new coalition with Kishkin and Co. This swing to the left of the Socialist-Revolutionary Centre, which up to now had constituted the overwhelming majority of the members of the Socialist-Revolutionary Party, the leading and dominant party from the point of view of the number of votes it obtained in the urban and particularly in the rural districts, proves that the statements we quoted from *Dyelo Naroda* that the democracy must, under certain circumstances, "guarantee full support" for a purely Bolshevik government are at any rate not mere empty phrases.

Facts like the refusal of the Socialist-Revolutionary Centre to support the new coalition with Kishkin, or the predominance of the *opponents* of the coalition among the *Menshevik-defencists* in the provinces (Jordania in the Caucasus, etc.), are objective proof that a certain section of the *people* which has up to now followed the Mensheviks and Socialist-Revolutionaries *will support* a purely Bolshevik government.

It is precisely from the *live* forces of the democracy that the proletariat of Russia is now not isolated.

* * *

The third plea, that the proletariat "will not be able technically to lay hold of the state apparatus" is, perhaps, the most common and most frequent. It deserves most attention for this reason, and also because it indicates one of the most *serious* and *difficult* tasks that will confront the victorious proletariat. There is no doubt that these tasks will be very difficult, but if we, who call ourselves socialists, indicate this difficulty only to *shirk* these tasks, in practice the distinction between us and the lackeys of the bourgeoisie will be reduced to nought. The difficulty of the tasks of the proletarian revolution should prompt the proletariat's supporters to make a closer and more definite study of the means of carrying out these tasks.

The state apparatus is primarily the standing army, the police and the bureaucracy. By saying that the proletariat will not be able technically to lay hold of this apparatus, the writers of *Novaya Zhizn* reveal their utter ignorance and their reluctance to take into account either facts or the arguments long ago cited in Bolshevik literature.

All the *Novaya Zhizn* writers regard themselves, if not as Marxists, then at least as being familiar with Marxism, as educated socialists. But Marx, basing himself on the experience of the Paris Commune, taught that the proletariat *cannot* simply lay hold of the ready-made state machine and use it for its own purposes, that the proletariat must *smash* this machine and substitute a new one for it (I deal with this in greater detail in a pamphlet, the first part of which is now finished and will soon appear under the title *The State and Revolution. A Marxist Theory of the State and the Tasks of the Proletariat in the Revolution**). This new type of state machinery was created by the Paris Commune, and the Russian Soviets of Workers', Soldiers' and Peasants' Deputies are a "state apparatus" of the *same type*. I have indicated this many times since April 4, 1917[198]; it is dealt with in the resolutions of Bolshevik conferences and also in Bolshevik literature. *Novaya Zhizn* could, of course, have expressed its utter disagreement with Marx and with the Bolsheviks, but for a paper that has so often, and so haughtily, scolded the Bolsheviks for their allegedly frivolous attitude to difficult problems to evade this question completely is tantamount to issuing itself a certificate of mental poverty.

The proletariat *cannot* "lay hold of" the "state apparatus" and "set it in motion". But it can *smash* everything that is oppressive, routine, incorrigibly bourgeois in the old state apparatus and sub-

---

* See pp. 264-351 of the present volume.—*Ed.*

stitute its *own*, new apparatus. The Soviets of Workers', Soldiers' and Peasants' Deputies are exactly this apparatus.

That *Novaya Zhizn* has completely forgotten about this "state apparatus" can be called nothing but monstrous. Behaving in this way in their theoretical reasoning, the *Novaya Zhizn* people are, in essence, doing in the sphere of political theory what the Cadets are doing in political practice. Because, if the proletariat and the revolutionary democrats *do not* in fact *need* a new state apparatus, then the Soviets lose their *raison d'être*, lose their right to existence, and the Kornilovite Cadets are *right* in trying to reduce the Soviets to nought!

This monstrous theoretical blunder and political blindness on the part of *Novaya Zhizn* is all the more monstrous because even the internationalist Mensheviks[199] (with whom *Novaya Zhizn* formed a bloc during the last City Council elections in Petrograd) have on this question shown some proximity to the Bolsheviks. So, in the declaration of the Soviet majority made by Comrade Martov at the Democratic Conference, we read:

"The Soviets of Workers', Soldiers' and Peasants' Deputies, set up in the first days of the revolution by a mighty burst of creative enthusiasm that stems from the people themselves, constitute the new fabric of the revolutionary state that has replaced the outworn state fabric of the old regime...."

This is a little too flowery; that is to say, rhetoric here covers up lack of clear political thinking. The Soviets have *not yet* replaced the old "fabric", and this old "fabric" is *not* the state fabric of the old regime, but the state fabric of *both* tsarism *and* of the bourgeois republic. But at any rate, Martov here stands head and shoulders above *Novaya Zhizn*.

The Soviets are a new state apparatus which, in the first place, provides an armed force of workers and peasants; and this force is not divorced from the people, as was the old standing army, but is very closely bound up with the people. From the military point of view this force is incomparably more powerful than previous forces; from the revolutionary point of view, it cannot be replaced by anything else. Secondly, this apparatus provides a bond with the people, with the majority of the people, so intimate, so indissoluble, so easily verifiable and renewable, that nothing even remotely like it existed in the previous state apparatus. Thirdly, this apparatus, by virtue of the fact that its personnel is elected and subject to recall at the people's will without any bureaucratic formalities, is far more democratic than any previous apparatus. Fourthly, it provides a close contact with the most varied professions, thereby facilitating the adoption of the most varied and most radical reforms without red tape. Fifthly, it provides an organisational form for the vanguard, i.e., for the most class-conscious, most energetic and most progressive section of the *oppressed* classes, the workers and peasants, and so constitutes an apparatus by means of which the vanguard of the oppressed classes can elevate, train, educate, and lead *the entire vast mass* of these classes, which has up to now stood completely outside of political life and history. Sixthly, it makes it possible to combine the advantages of the parliamentary system with those of immediate and direct democracy, i.e., to vest in the people's elected representatives both legislative *and executive functions.* Compared with the bourgeois parliamentary system, this is an advance in democracy's development which is of world-wide, historic significance.

In 1905, our Soviets existed only in embryo, so to speak, as they lived altogether only a few weeks. Clearly, under the conditions of that time, their comprehensive development was out of the question. It is still out of the question in the 1917 Revolution, for a few months is an extremely short period and—this is most important—the Socialist-Revolutionary and Menshevik leaders have *prostituted* the Soviets, have reduced their role to that of a talking-shop, of an accomplice in the compromising policy of the leaders. The Soviets have been rotting and decaying alive under the leadership of the Liebers, Dans, Tseretelis and Chernovs. The Soviets will be able to develop properly, to display their potentialities and capabilities to the full only by taking over *full* state power; for otherwise they have *nothing to do,* otherwise they are either simply embryos (and to remain an embryo too long is fatal), or playthings. "Dual power" means paralysis for the Soviets.

If the creative enthusiasm of the revolutionary classes had not given rise to the Soviets, the proletarian revolution in Russia would have been a hopeless cause, for the proletariat could certainly not retain power with the old state apparatus, and it is impossible to create a new apparatus immediately. The sad history of the prostitution of the Soviets by the Tseretelis and Chernovs, the history of the "coalition", is also the history of the liberation of the Soviets from petty-bourgeois illusions, of their passage through the "purgatory" of the practical experience of the utter abomination and filth of *all* and *sundry* bourgeois coalitions. Let us hope that this "purgatory" has steeled rather than weakened the Soviets.

* * *

The chief difficulty facing the proletarian revolution is the establishment on a country-wide scale of the most precise and most conscientious accounting and control, of *workers' control* of the production and distribution of goods.

When the writers of *Novaya Zhizn* argued that in advancing the slogan "workers' control" we were slipping into syndicalism, this argument was an example of the stupid schoolboy method of applying "Marxism" without studying it, just *learning it by rote* in the Struve manner. Syndicalism either repudiates the revolutionary dictatorship of the proletariat, or else relegates it, as it does political power in general, to a back seat. We, however, put it in the forefront. If we simply say in unison with the *Novaya Zhizn* writers: *not* workers' control *but* state control, it is simply a bourgeois-reformist phrase, it is, in essence, a purely Cadet formula, because the Cadets have no objection to the workers *participating* in "state" control. The Kornilovite Cadets know perfectly well that such participation offers the bourgeoisie the best way of fooling the workers, the most subtle way of politically *bribing* all the Gvozdyovs, Nikitins, Prokopoviches, Tseretelis and the rest of that gang.

When we say: "workers' control", always *juxtaposing* this slogan to dictatorship of the proletariat, always putting it *immediately after* the latter, we thereby explain what kind of state we mean. The state is the organ of *class* domination. Of which class? If of the bourgeoisie, then it is the Cadet-Kornilov-"Kerensky" state which has been "Kornilovising" and "Kerenskyising" the working people of Russia for more than six months. If it is of the proletariat, if we are speaking of a proletarian state, *that is*, of the proletarian dictatorship, then workers' control *can* become the country-wide, all-embracing, omnipresent, most precise and most conscientious *accounting* of the production and distribution of goods.

This is the chief difficulty, the chief task that faces the proletarian, i.e., socialist, revolution. Without the Soviets, this task would be impracticable, at least in Russia. The Soviets *indicate* to the proletariat the organisational work which *can* solve this historically important problem.

This brings us to another aspect of the question of the state apparatus. In addition to the chiefly "oppressive" apparatus—the standing army, the police and the bureaucracy—the modern state possesses an apparatus which has extremely close connections with the banks and syndicates, an apparatus which performs an enormous amount of accounting and registration work, if it may be expressed this way. This apparatus must not, and should not, be smashed. It must be wrested from the control of the capitalists; the capitalists and the wires they pull must be *cut off, lopped off, chopped away from* this apparatus; it must be *subordinated* to the proletarian Soviets; it must be expanded, made more comprehensive, and nation-wide. And this *can* be done by utilising the achievements already made by large-scale capitalism (in the same way as the proletarian revolution can, in general, reach its goal only by utilising these achievements).

Capitalism has created an accounting *apparatus* in the shape of the banks, syndicates, postal service, consumers' societies, and office employees' unions. *Without big banks socialism would be impossible.*

The big banks *are* the "state apparatus" which we *need* to bring about socialism, and which we *take ready-made* from capitalism; our task here is merely to *lop off* what *capitalistically mutilates* this excellent apparatus, to make it *even bigger,* even more democratic, even more comprehensive. Quantity will be transformed into quality. A single State Bank, the biggest of the big, with branches in every rural district, in every factory, will constitute as much as nine-tenths of the *socialist* apparatus. This will be country-wide *book-keeping,* country-wide *accounting* of the production and distribution of goods, this will be, so to speak, something in the nature of the *skeleton* of socialist society.

We can "lay hold of" and "set in motion" this "state apparatus" (which is not fully a state apparatus under capitalism, but which will be so with us, under socialism) at one stroke, by a single decree, because the actual work of book-keeping, control, registering, accounting and counting is performed by *employees,* the majority of whom themselves lead a proletarian or semi-proletarian existence.

By a single decree of the proletarian government these employees can and must be transferred to the status of state employees, in the same way as the watchdogs of capitalism like Briand and other bourgeois ministers, by a single decree, transfer railwaymen on strike to the status of state employees. We shall need many more state employees of this kind, and more *can* be obtained, because capitalism has simplified the work of accounting and control, has reduced it to a comparatively simple system of *book-keeping,* which any literate person can do.

The conversion of the bank, syndicate, commercial, etc., etc., rank-and-file employees into state employees is quite feasible both technically (thanks to the preliminary work performed for us by capitalism, including finance capitalism) and politically, provided the *Soviets* exercise control and supervision.

As for the higher officials, of whom there are very few, but who gravitate towards the capitalists, they will have to be dealt with in the same way as the capitalists, i.e., "severely". Like the capitalists, they will offer *resistance.* This resistance will have to be *broken,* and if the immortally naïve Peshekhonov, as early as June 1917, lisped like the infant that he was in state affairs, that "the resistance of the capitalists has been broken", this childish phrase, this childish boast, this childish swagger, *will be converted by the proletariat into reality.*

We can do this, for it is merely a question of breaking the resistance of an insignificant minority of the population, literally a handful of people, over each of whom the employees' unions, the trade unions, the consumers' societies and the Soviets will institute such *supervision* that every Tit Titych[200] will be *surrounded* as the French were at Sedan.[201] We know these Tit Tityches by name: we only have to consult the lists of directors, board members, large shareholders, etc. There are several hundred, at most several thousand of them in the *whole* of Russia, and the proletarian state, with the apparatus of the Soviets, of the employees' unions, etc., will be able to appoint ten or even a hundred supervisors to each of them, so that instead of "breaking resistance" it may even be possible, by means of *workers' control* (over the capitalists), to make all resistance *impossible*.

The important thing will not be even the confiscation of the capitalists' property, but country-wide, all-embracing workers' control over the capitalists and their possible supporters. Confiscation alone leads nowhere, as it does not contain the element of organisation, of accounting for proper distribution. Instead of confiscation, we could easily impose a *fair* tax (even on the Shingaryov scale, for instance), taking care, of course, to preclude the possibility of anyone evading assessment, concealing the truth, evading the law. And this possibility can be *eliminated only* by the workers' control of the *workers' state*.

Compulsory syndication, i.e., compulsory amalgamation in associations under state control—this is what capitalism has prepared the way for, this is what has been carried out in Germany by the Junkers' state, this is what can be easily carried out in Russia by the Soviets, by the proletarian dictatorship, and this is what will *provide us with a state apparatus* that will be universal, up-to-date, and non-bureaucratic.*

* * *

The fourth plea of the counsels for the bourgeoisie is that the proletariat will not be able "to set the state apparatus in motion" There is nothing new in this plea compared with the preceding one. We could not, of course, either lay hold of or set in motion the old apparatus. The new apparatus, the Soviets, *has already* been set in motion by "a mighty burst of creative enthusiasm that stems from the people themselves". We only have to free it from the *shackles* put on it by the domination of the Socialist-Revolutionary and Menshevik leaders. This apparatus *is already* in motion; we only have to free it from the monstrous, petty-bourgeois impediments preventing it from going full speed ahead.

Two circumstances must be considered here to supplement what has already been said. In the first place, the new means of control

---

* For further details of the meaning of compulsory syndication see my pamphlet: *The Impending Catastrophe and How to Combat It.* (See *Collected Works,* Vol. 25, pp. 342-45.—*Ed.*)

have been created *not* by us, but by capitalism in its military-imperialist stage; and in the second place, it is important to introduce more democracy into the *administration* of a proletarian state.

The grain monopoly and bread rationing were introduced not by us, but by the capitalist state in war-time. It had already introduced universal labour conscription within the framework of capitalism, which is war-time penal servitude for the workers. But here too, as in all its history-making activities, the proletariat takes its weapons from capitalism and does not "invent" or "create them out of nothing".

The grain monopoly, bread rationing and labour conscription in the hands of the proletarian state, in the hands of sovereign Soviets, will be the most powerful means of accounting and control, means which, applied to the capitalists, and to *the rich in general,* applied to them by the *workers,* will provide a force unprecedented in history for "setting the state apparatus in motion", for overcoming the resistance of the capitalists, for subordinating them to the proletarian state. These means of control and of *compelling people to work* will be more potent than the laws of the Convention and its guillotine. The guillotine *only* terrorised, only broke *active* resistance. *For us, this is not enough.*

For us, this is not enough. We must not only "terrorise" the capitalists, i.e., make them feel the omnipotence of the proletarian state and give up all idea of actively resisting it. We must also break *passive* resistance, which is undoubtedly more dangerous and harmful. We must not only break resistance of every kind. We must also *compel the capitalists to work* within the framework of the new state organisation. It is not enough to "remove" the capitalists; we must (after removing the undesirable and incorrigible "resisters") employ them *in the service of the new state.* This applies both to the capitalists and to the upper section of the bourgeois intellectuals, office employees, etc.

And we have the means to do this. The means and instruments for this have been placed in our hands by the capitalist state in the war. These means are the grain monopoly, bread rationing and labour conscription. "He who does not work, neither shall he eat" —this is the fundamental, the first and most important rule the Soviets of Workers' Deputies can and will introduce when they become the ruling power.

Every worker has a work-book. This book does not degrade him, although *at present* it is undoubtedly a document of capitalist wage-slavery, certifying that the workman belongs to some parasite.

The Soviets will introduce work-books *for the rich* and *then* gradually for the whole population (in a peasant country work-books will probably not be needed for a long time for the overwhelming majority of the peasants). The work-book will cease to be the badge of the "common herd", a document of the "lower" orders, a certificate of wage-slavery. It will become a document certifying that in the new society there are no longer any "workmen", nor, on the other hand, are there any longer men *who do not work.*

The rich will be obliged to get a work-book from the workers' or office employees' union with which their occupation is most closely connected, and every week, or other definite fixed period, they will have to get from that union a certificate to the effect that they are performing their work conscientiously; without this they will not be able to receive bread ration cards or provisions in general. The proletarian state will say: we need good organisers of banking and the amalgamation of enterprises (in this matter the capitalists have more experience, and it is easier to work with experienced people), and we need far, far more engineers, agronomists, technicians and scientifically trained specialists of every kind than were needed before. We shall give all these specialists work to which they are accustomed and which they can cope with; in all probability we shall introduce complete wage equality only gradually and shall pay these specialists higher salaries during the transition period. We shall place them, however, under comprehensive workers' control and we shall achieve the complete and absolute operation of the rule "He who does not work, neither shall he eat." We shall not invent the organisational form of the work, but take it ready-made from capitalism—we shall take over the banks, syndicates, the best factories, experimental stations, academies, and so forth; all that we shall have to do is to borrow the best models furnished by the advanced countries.

Of course, we shall not in the least descend to a utopia, we are not deserting the soil of most sober, practical reason when we say that the entire capitalist class will offer the most stubborn resistance, but this resistance will be broken by the organisation of the entire population in Soviets. Those capitalists who are exceptionally stubborn and recalcitrant will, of course, have to be punished by the confiscation of their whole property and by imprisonment. On the other hand, however, the victory of the proletariat will bring about *an increase* in the number of cases of the kind that I read about in today's *Izvestia*,[202] for example:

"On September 26, two engineers came to the Central Council of Factory Committees to report that a group of engineers had decided to form a union of socialist engineers. The Union believes that the present times is actually the beginning of the social revolution and places itself at the disposal of the working people, desiring, in defence of the workers' interests, to work in complete unity with the workers' organisations. The representatives of the Central Council of Factory

Committees answered that the Council will gladly set up in its organisation an Engineers' Section which will embody in its programme the main theses of the First Conference of Factory Committees on workers' control over production. A joint meeting of delegates of the Central Council of Factory Committees and of the initiative group of socialist engineers will be held within the next few days." (*Izvestia*, September 27, 1917.)

* * *

The proletariat, we are told, will not be able to set the state apparatus in motion.

Since the 1905 revolution, Russia has been governed by 130,000 landowners, who have perpetrated endless violence against 150,000,000 people, heaped unconstrained abuse upon them, and condemned the vast majority to inhuman toil and semi-starvation.

Yet we are told that the 240,000 members of the Bolshevik Party will not be able to govern Russia, govern her in the interests of the poor and against the rich. These 240,000 are already backed by no less than a million votes of the adult population, for this is precisely the proportion between the number of Party members and the number of votes cast for the Party that has been established by the experience of Europe and the experience of Russia as shown, for example, by the elections to the Petrograd City Council last August. We therefore already have a "state apparatus" of *one million* people devoted to the socialist state for the sake of high ideals and not for the sake of a fat sum received on the 20th of every month.

In addition to that we have a "magic way" to enlarge our state apparatus *tenfold* at once, at one stroke, a way which no capitalist state ever possessed or could possess. This magic way is to draw the working people, to draw the poor, into the daily work of state administration.

To explain how easy it will be to employ this magic way and how faultlessly it will operate, let us take the simplest and most striking example possible.

The state is to forcibly evict a certain family from a flat and move another in. This often happens in the capitalist state, and it will also happen in our proletarian or socialist state.

The capitalist state evicts a working-class family which has lost its breadwinner and cannot pay the rent. The bailiff appears with police, or militia, a whole squad of them. To effect an eviction in a working-class district a whole detachment of Cossacks is required. Why? Because the bailiff and the militiaman refuse to go without a very strong military guard. They know that the scene of an eviction arouses such fury among the neighbours, among thousands and thousands of people who have been driven to the verge of desperation, arouses such hatred towards the capitalists and the capitalist state, that the bailiff and the squad of militiamen run the risk of being torn to pieces at any minute. Large military forces are required, several regiments must be brought into a big city, and the troops must come from some distant, outlying region so that the soldiers will not be familiar with the life of the urban poor, so that the soldiers will not be "infected" with socialism.

The proletarian state has to forcibly move a very poor family into a rich man's flat. Let us suppose that our squad of workers' militia is fifteen strong; two sailors, two soldiers, two class-conscious workers (of whom, let us suppose, only one is a member of our Party, or a sympathiser), one intellectual, and eight from the poor working people, of whom at least five must be women, domestic servants, unskilled labourers, and so forth. The squad arrives at the rich man's flat, inspects it and finds that it consists of five rooms occupied by two men and two women—"You must squeeze up a bit into two rooms this winter, citizens, and prepare two rooms for two families now living in cellars. Until the time, with the aid of engineers (you are an engineer, aren't you?), we have built good dwellings for everybody, you will have to squeeze up a little. Your telephone will serve ten families. This will save a hundred hours of work wasted on shopping, and so forth. Now in your family there are two unemployed persons who can perform light work: a citizeness fifty-five years of age and a citizen fourteen years of age. They will be on duty for three hours a day supervising the proper distribution of provisions for ten families and keeping the necessary account of this. The student citizen in our squad will now write out this state order in two copies and you will be kind enough to give us a signed declaration that you will faithfully carry it out."

This, in my opinion, can illustrate how the distinction between the old bourgeois and the new socialist state apparatus and state administration could be illustrated.

We are not utopians. We know that an unskilled labourer or a cook cannot immediately get on with the job of state administration. In this we agree with the Cadets, with Breshkovskaya, and with Tsereteli. We differ, however, from these citizens in that we demand an immediate break with the prejudiced view that only the rich, or officials chosen from rich families, are capable of *administering* the state, of performing the ordinary, everyday work of administration. We demand that *training* in the work of state administration be conducted by class-conscious workers and soldiers and that this training be begun at once, i.e., that a *beginning* be made at once in training all the working people, all the poor, for this work.

We know that the Cadets are also willing to teach the people democracy. Cadet ladies are willing to deliver lectures to domestic servants on equal rights for women in accordance with the best

English and French sources. And also, at the very next concert-meeting, before an audience of thousands, an exchange of kisses will be arranged on the platform: the Cadet lady lecturer will kiss Breshkovskaya, Breshkovskaya will kiss ex-Minister Tsereteli, and the grateful people will therefore receive an object-lesson in republican equality, liberty and fraternity. . . .

Yes, we agree that the Cadets, Breshkovskaya and Tsereteli are in their own way devoted to democracy and are propagating it among the people. But what is to be done if our conception of democracy is somewhat different from theirs?

In our opinion, to ease the incredible burdens and miseries of the war and also to heal the terrible wounds the war has inflicted on the people, *revolutionary* democracy is needed, *revolutionary* measures of the kind described in the example of the distribution of housing accommodation in the interests of the poor. *Exactly the same* procedure must be adopted in both town and country for the distribution of provisions, clothing, footwear, etc., in respect of the land in the rural districts, and so forth. For the administration of the state in *this* spirit we can *at once set in motion a state* apparatus consisting of ten if not twenty million people, an apparatus such as no capitalist state has ever known. We alone can create such an apparatus, for we are sure of the fullest and devoted sympathy of the vast majority of the population. We alone can create such an apparatus, because we have class-conscious workers disciplined by long capitalist "schooling" (it was not for nothing that we went to learn in the school of capitalism), workers who are *capable* of forming a workers' militia and of *gradually* expanding it (beginning to expand it at once) into a militia *embracing the whole people*. The class-conscious workers must lead, but for the work of administration they can enlist the vast mass of the working and oppressed people.

It goes without saying that this new apparatus is bound to make mistakes in taking its first steps. But did not the peasants make mistakes when they emerged from serfdom and began to manage their own affairs? Is there any way other than practice by which the people can learn to govern themselves and to avoid mistakes? Is there any way other than by proceeding immediately to genuine self-government by the people? The chief thing now is to abandon the prejudiced bourgeois-intellectualist view that only special officials, who by their very social position are entirely dependent upon capital, can administer the state. The chief thing is to put an end to the state of affairs in which bourgeois officials and "socialist" ministers are trying to govern in the old way, but are incapable of doing so and, after seven months, are faced with a peasant revolt in a peasant country! The chief thing is to imbue the oppressed and the working people with confidence in their own strength, to prove to them in practice that they can and must themselves ensure the *proper*, most strictly regulated and organised distribution of bread, all kinds of food, milk, clothing, housing, etc., *in the interests of the poor*. Unless this is done, Russia *cannot* be saved from collapse and ruin. The conscientious, bold, universal move to hand over administrative work to proletarians and semi-proletarians, will, however, rouse such unprecedented revolutionary enthusiasm among the people, will so multiply the people's forces in combating distress, that much that seemed impossible to our narrow, old, bureaucratic forces will become possible for the millions, who will *begin to work for themselves* and not for the capitalists, the gentry, the bureaucrats, and not out of fear of punishment.

* * *

Pertinent to the question of the state apparatus is also the question of centralism raised with unusual vehemence and ineptitude by Comrade Bazarov in *Novaya Zhizn* No. 138, of September 27, in an article entitled: "The Bolsheviks and the Problem of Power".

Comrade Bazarov reasons as follows: "The Soviets are not an apparatus suitable for all spheres of state life", for, he says, seven months' experience has shown, and "scores and hundreds of documents in the possession of the Economic Department of the St. Petersburg Executive Committee" have confirmed, that the Soviets, although actually enjoying "full power" in many places, "have not been able to achieve anything like satisfactory results in combating economic ruin". What is needed is an apparatus "divided up according to branches of production, with strict centralisation within each branch, and subordinated to one, country-wide centre". "It is a matter", if you please, "not of replacing the old apparatus, but merely of reforming it ... no matter how much the Bolsheviks may jeer at people with a plan...."

All these arguments of Comrade Bazarov's are positively amazing for their helplessness, they echo the arguments of the bourgeoisie and reflect their class point of view.

In fact, to say that the Soviets have anywhere in Russia ever enjoyed "full power" is simply ridiculous (if it is not a repetition of the selfish class lie of the capitalists). Full power means power over all the land, over all the banks, over all the factories; a man who is at all familiar with the facts of history and science on the connection between politics and economics could not have "forgotten" this "trifling" circumstance.

The bourgeoisie's device is to *withhold* power from the Soviets, *sabotage* every important step they take, while at the same time retaining government in their own hands, retaining power over the land, the banks, etc., and then throwing the blame for the ruin upon the Soviets! This is exactly what the whole sad experience of the coalition amounts to.

The Soviets have never had full power, and the measures they have taken could not result in anything but palliatives that added to the confusion.

The effort to prove the necessity for centralism to the Bolsheviks who are centralists by conviction, by their programme and by the entire tactics of their Party, is really like forcing an open door. The writers of *Novaya Zhizn* are wasting their time only because they have totally failed to understand the meaning and significance of our jeers at their "country-wide" point of view. And the *Novaya Zhizn* people have failed to understand this because they merely pay *lip-service* to the doctrine of the class struggle, but do not accept it seriously. Repeating the words about the class struggle they have learned by rote, they are constantly slipping into the "above-class point of view", amusing in theory and reactionary in practice, and are calling this fawning upon the bourgeoisie a "country-wide" plan.

The state, dear people, is a class concept. The state is an organ or instrument of violence exercised by one class against another. So long as it is an instrument of violence exercised by the bourgeoisie against the proletariat, the proletariat can have only one slogan: *destruction* of this state. But when the state will be a proletarian state, when it will be an instrument of violence exercised by the proletariat against the bourgeoisie, we shall be fully and unreservedly in favour of a strong state power and of centralism.

To put it in more popular language, we do not jeer at "plans", but at Bazarov and Co.'s failure to understand that by repudiating "workers' control", by repudiating the "dictatorship of the proletariat" they *are for* the dictatorship of the bourgeoisie. There is no middle course; a middle course is the futile dream of the petty-bourgeois democrat.

Not a single central body, not a single Bolshevik has ever argued against *centralisation* of the Soviets, against their amalgamation. None of us objects to having factory committees in each branch of production, or to their centralisation. Bazarov is *wide of the mark*.

We laugh, have laughed, and will laugh not at "centralism", and not at "plans", but at *reformism*, because, after the experience of the coalition, your reformism is utterly ridiculous. And to say "not replace the apparatus but reform it" means to be a reformist, means to become not a revolutionary but a reformist democrat. Reformism means nothing more than concessions on the part of the ruling class, but *not* its overthrow; it makes concessions, but power remains in *its hands*.

This is precisely what has been tried during six months of the coalition.

This is what we laugh at. Having failed to obtain a thorough grasp of the doctrine of the class struggle, Bazarov allows himself to be caught by the bourgeoisie who sing in chorus "Just so, just so, we are by no means opposed to reform, we are in favour of the workers participating in country-wide control, we fully agree with that", and good Bazarov *objectively* sings the descant for the capitalists.

This has always been and always will be the case with people who in the thick of intense class struggle want to take up a "middle" position. And it is because the writers of *Novaya Zhizn* are incapable of understanding the class struggle that their policy is such a ridiculous and eternal oscillation between the bourgeoisie and the proletariat.

Get busy on "plans", dear citizens, that is not politics, that is not the class struggle; here you may be of use to the people. You have many economists on your paper. Unite with those engineers and others who are willing to work on problems of regulating production and distribution; devote the centre page of your big "apparatus" (your paper) to a practical study of precise facts on the production and distribution of goods in Russia, on banks, syndicates, etc., etc.—that is how you will be of use to the people; that is how your sitting between two stools will not be particularly harmful; such work on "plans" will earn not the ridicule, but the gratitude of the workers.

When the proletariat is victorious it will do the following, it will set economists, engineers, agronomists, and so forth, to work *under the control* of the workers' organisations on drawing up a "plan", on verifying it, on devising labour-saving methods of centralisation, on devising the simplest, cheapest, most convenient and universal measures and methods of control. For this we shall pay the economists, statisticians and technicians good money... but we shall not give them anything to eat if they do not perform this work conscientiously and entirely *in the interests of the working people*.

We are in favour of centralism and of a "plan", but of the centralism and plan of the *proletarian* state, of proletarian regulation of production and distribution in the interests of the poor, the working people, the exploited, *against* the exploiters. We can agree to only one meaning of the term "country-wide", namely, that which breaks the resistance of the capitalists, which gives all power to the majority of the people, i.e., the proletarians and semi-proletarians, the workers and the poor peasants.

* * *

The fifth plea is that the Bolsheviks will not be able to retain power because "the situation is exceptionally complicated"....

O wise men! They, perhaps, would be willing to reconcile themselves to revolution if only the "situation" were not "exceptionally complicated".

Such revolutions never occur, and sighs for such a revolution amount to nothing more than the reactionary wails of a bourgeois intellectual. Even if a revolution has started in a situation that seemed to be not very complicated, the development of the revolution itself *always* creates an *exceptionally* complicated situation. A revolution, a real, profound, a "people's" revolution, to use Marx's expression, is the incredibly complicated and painful process of the death of the old and birth of the new social order, of the mode of life of tens of millions of people. Revolution is a most intense, furious, desperate class struggle and civil war. Not a single great revolution in history has taken place without civil war. And only a "man in a muffler" can think that civil war is conceivable without an "exceptionally complicated situation".

If the situation were not exceptionally complicated there would be no revolution. If you are afraid of wolves don't go into the forest.

There is nothing to discuss in the fifth plea, because there is no economic, political, or any other meaning whatever in it. It contains only the yearning of people who are distressed and frightened by the revolution. To characterise this yearning I shall take the liberty of mentioning two little things from my personal experience.

I had a conversation with a wealthy engineer shortly before the July days. This engineer had once been a revolutionary, had been in the Social-Democratic movement and even a member of the Bolshevik Party. Now he was full of fear and rage at the turbulent and indomitable workers. "If they were at least like the German workers," he said (he is an educated man and has been abroad), "of course, I understand that the social revolution is, in general, inevitable, but here, when the workers' level has been so reduced by the war ... it is not a revolution, it is an abyss."

He was willing to accept the social revolution if history were to lead to it in the peaceful, calm, smooth and precise manner of a German express train pulling into a station. A sedate conductor would open the carriage door and announce: "Social Revolution Station! *Alle aussteigen!* (All change!)" In that case he would have no objection to changing his position of engineer under the Tit Tityches to that of engineer under the workers' organisations.

That man has seen strikes. He knows what a storm of passion the most ordinary strike arouses even in the most peaceful times. He, of course, understands how many million times more furious this storm must be when the class struggle has aroused *all* the working people of a vast country, when war and exploitation have driven almost to desperation millions of people who for centuries have been tormented by the landowners, for decades have been robbed and downtrodden by the capitalists and the tsar's officials. He understands all this "theoretically", he only pays *lip service* to this, he is simply terrified by the "exceptionally complicated situation".

After the July days, thanks to the extremely solicitous attention with which the Kerensky government honoured me, I was obliged to go underground. Of course, it was the workers who sheltered people like us. In a small working-class house in a remote working-class suburb of Petrograd, dinner is being served. The hostess puts bread on the table. The host says: "Look what fine bread. 'They' dare not give us bad bread now. And we had almost given up even thinking that we'd ever get good bread in Petrograd again."

I was amazed at this class appraisal of the July days. My thoughts had been revolving around the political significance of those events, weighing the role they played in the general course of events, analysing the situation that caused this zigzag in history and the situation it would create, and how we ought to change our slogans and alter our Party apparatus to adapt it to the changed situation. As for bread, I, who had not known want, did not give it a thought. I took bread for granted, as a by-product of the writer's work, as it were. The mind approaches the foundation of everything, the class struggle for bread, through political analysis that follows an extremely complicated and devious path.

This member of the oppressed class, however, even though one of the well-paid and quite intelligent workers, takes the bull by the horns with that astonishing simplicity and straightforwardness, with that firm determination and amazing clarity of outlook from which we intellectuals are as remote as the stars in the sky. The whole world is divided into two camps: "us", the working people, and "them", the exploiters. Not a shadow of embarrassment over what had taken place; it was just one of the battles in the long struggle between labour and capital. When you fell trees, chips fly.

"What a painful thing is this 'exceptionally complicated situation' created by the revolution," that's how the bourgeois intellectual thinks and feels.

"We squeezed 'them' a bit; 'they' won't dare to lord it over us as they did before. We'll squeeze again—and chuck them out altogether," that's how the worker thinks and feels.

* * *

The sixth and last plea: the proletariat "will be incapable of resisting all the pressure by hostile forces that will sweep away not only the proletarian dictatorship, but the entire revolution into the bargain".

Don't try to scare us, gentlemen, you won't succeed. We saw these hostile forces and their pressure in Kornilovism (from which the Kerensky regime in no way differs). Everybody saw, and the people remember, how the proletariat and the poor peasants swept away the Kornilov gang, and how pitiful and helpless proved to be the position of the supporters of the bourgeoisie and of the few exceptionally well-to-do local small landowners who were exceptionally "hostile" to the revolution. *Dyelo Naroda* of September 30 urges the workers to "be patient and put up with" Kerensky (i.e., Kornilov) and the fake Tsereteli Bulygin Duma until the convocation of the Constituent Assembly (convened under the protection of "military measures" against insurgent peasants!) and, with great gusto, it repeats precisely *Novaya Zhizn*'s sixth plea and shouts until it is hoarse: "The Kerensky government will under no circumstances submit" (to the rule of the Soviets, the rule of the workers and peasants, which *Dyelo Naroda*, not wishing to lag behind the pogrom-mongers and anti-Semites, monarchists and Cadets, calls the rule of "Trotsky and Lenin": these are the lengths to which the Socialist-Revolutionaries go!).

But neither *Novaya Zhizn* nor *Dyelo Naroda* can scare the class-conscious workers. "The Kerensky government," you say, "will under no circumstances submit", i.e., it will repeat the Kornilov revolt, to put it more simply, bluntly and clearly. And the gentlemen of *Dyelo Naroda* dare to say that this will be "civil war", that this is a "horrible prospect"!

No, gentlemen, you will not fool the workers. It will not be civil war but a hopeless revolt of a handful of Kornilovites. If they want to "refuse to submit" to the people and at all costs provoke a repetition on a wide scale of what happened to the Kornilov men in Vyborg—*if* that is what the Socialist-Revolutionaries *want*, if that is what the member of the Socialist-Revolutionary Party Kerensky wants, he may drive the people to desperation. But you will not scare the workers and soldiers with this, gentlemen.

What boundless insolence. They faked up a new Bulygin Duma; by means of fraud they recruited a crowd of reactionary co-operators and village kulaks to help them, added to these the capitalists and landowners (the so-called property-owning classes) and with the aid of this gang of Kornilovites they want *to thwart the will of the people*, the will of the workers and peasants.

They have brought affairs in a peasant country to such a pass that peasant revolt is spreading everywhere like a river in flood! Think of it! In a democratic republic in which 80 per cent of the population are peasants, the peasants have been driven to revolt.... This same *Dyelo Naroda*, Chernov's newspaper, the organ of the "Socialist-Revolutionary" Party, which on September 30 has the effrontery to advise the workers and peasants to "be patient", was obliged to admit in a leading article on September 29:

> "*So far practically nothing* has been done to put an end to those relations of *bondage* that still *prevail* in the villages of Central Russia."

This same *Dyelo Naroda*, in the same leading article of September 29, says that "the dead hand of Stolypin is still making itself strongly felt" in the methods employed by the "revolutionary ministers"; in other words, putting it more clearly and simply, it brands Kerensky, Nikitin, Kishkin and Co. as *Stolypins*.

The "'Stolypins" Kerensky and Co. have driven the peasants to revolt, are now taking "military measures" against the peasants, are trying to soothe the people with the convocation of the Constituent Assembly (although Kerensky and Tsereteli **have** already *deceived* the people once by solemnly proclaiming on July 8 that the Constituent Assembly would be convened on the appointed date, September 17; they then *broke their promise* and postponed the Constituent Assembly even against the advice of the *Menshevik Dan,* postponed the Constituent Assembly not to the end of October as the Menshevik 'Central Executive Committee of that time wished, but to the end of November). The "Stolypins" Kerensky and Co. are trying to soothe the people with the imminent convocation of the Constituent Assembly, as if the people can believe those who have already lied in this matter, as if the people can believe that the Constituent Assembly will be *properly* convened by a government which has taken *military measures* in remote villages, that is to say, is openly *conniving* at the arbitrary arrest of class-conscious peasants and the *rigging* of the elections.

The government has driven the peasants to revolt and now has the effrontery to say to them: "You must 'be patient', you must wait, trust the government which is pacifying insurgent peasants by 'military measures'!"

To bring matters to such a pitch that hundreds of thousands of Russian soldiers perish in the offensive after June 19, the war is being protracted, German sailors have mutinied and are throwing their officers overboard, to bring matters to such a pitch, all the time uttering phrases about peace but *not offering* a just peace to *all* the belligerents, and yet to have the effrontery to tell the workers and peasants, to tell the dying soldiers, "you must be patient", trust the government of the "Stolypin man" Kerensky, trust the Kornilov generals for another month, perhaps in that month they will send several tens of thousands more soldiers to the slaughter.... "You must be patient"....

Isn't that shameless?

But you won't fool the soldiers, gentlemen of the Socialist-Revolutionaries, Kerensky's fellow party members.

The workers and soldiers will not endure the Kerensky government for a single day, for an *extra* hour, for they know that the *Soviet* Government will *immediately* offer all the belligerents a just peace and therefore will *in all probability* achieve an immediate armistice and a speedy peace.

Not for a single day, not for an *extra* hour will the soldiers of our peasant army allow the Kerensky government—the government which is employing *military measures* to suppress the peasant revolt—to remain in power against the will of the Soviets.

No, gentlemen of the Socialist-Revolutionaries, Kerensky's fellow party members, you won't fool the workers and peasants any more.

* * *

On the question of the pressure by hostile forces which the mortally frightened *Novaya Zhizn* assures us will sweep away the proletarian dictatorship, still another monstrous logical and political mistake is made, which only people who have allowed themselves to be frightened out of their wits can fail to see.

"Pressure by hostile forces will sweep away the proletarian dictatorship," you say. Very well. But you are all economists and educated people, dear fellow-citizens. You all know that to contrast democracy to the bourgeoisie is senseless and a sign of ignorance; it is the same as contrasting pounds to yards, for there is a democratic bourgeoisie and undemocratic groups of the petty bourgeoisie (capable of raising a Vendée[203]).

"Hostile forces" is merely an empty phrase. The class term is *bourgeoisie* (backed by the landowners).

The bourgeoisie and the landowners, the proletariat, and the petty bourgeoisie, the small proprietors, primarily the peasants—these are the three main "forces" into which Russia, like *every* capitalist country, is divided. These are the three main "forces" that have long been revealed in every capitalist country (including Russia) not only by scientific economic analysis, but also by the *political experience* of the modern history of *all* countries, by the experience of *all* European revolutions since the eighteenth century, by the experience of the *two* Russian revolutions of 1905 and 1917.

So, you threaten the proletariat with the prospect that its rule will be swept away by the pressure of the bourgeoisie? That, and that alone, is what your threat amounts to, it has no other meaning.

Very well. If, for example, the bourgeoisie can sweep away the rule of the workers and poor peasants, then the only alternative is a "coalition", i.e., an alliance, or agreement, between the petty bourgeoisie and the bourgeoisie. Nothing else can be contemplated!

But coalition has been tried for about six months and it has led to bankruptcy, and you yourselves, my dear but dense citizens of *Novaya Zhizn*, have *renounced* coalition.

So what do we get?

You have become so muddled, citizens of *Novaya Zhizn*, you have allowed yourselves to be so scared, that you cannot think straight in the extremely simple matter of *counting even up to three, let alone up to five*.

Either all power to the bourgeoisie—the slogan you have long ceased to advocate, and which the bourgeoisie themselves dare not even hint at, for they know that the people overthrew this power with one hitch of the shoulder at the time of the April 20-21 events, and would overthrow it now with thrice that determination and ruthlessness; or power to the petty bourgeoisie, i.e., a coalition (alliance, agreement) between them and the bourgeoisie, for the petty bourgeoisie do not wish to and *cannot* take power alone and independently, as has been proved by the experience of all revolutions, and as is proved by economics, which explains that in a capitalist country it is possible to stand for capital and it is possible to stand for labour, but it is impossible to stand for long in between. In Russia this coalition has for six months tried scores of ways and failed.

Or, finally, all power to the proletarians and the poor peasants against the bourgeoisie in order to break their resistance. This has not yet been tried, and you, gentlemen of *Novaya Zhizn*, are *dissuading* the people from this, you are trying to frighten them with your own fear of the bourgeoisie.

No fourth way can be invented.

If *Novaya Zhizn*, therefore, is afraid of the proletarian dictatorship and rejects it because, as it claims, the proletarian power may be defeated by the bourgeoisie, it is tantamount to its *surreptitiously reverting* to the position of *compromise* with the capitalists! It is as clear as daylight, that whoever is afraid of resistance, whoever does not believe that it is possible to break this resistance, whoever warns the people: "beware of the resistance of the capitalists, you will not be able to cope with it", is *thereby* again calling for compromise with the capitalists.

Novaya Zhizn is hopelessly and pitifully muddled, as are all the petty-bourgeois democrats who now realise that the coalition is bankrupt, dare not defend it openly and, at the same time, protected by the bourgeoisie, fear the transfer of all power to the proletarians and poor peasants.

* * *

To fear the resistance of the capitalists and yet to call oneself a revolutionary, to wish to be regarded as a socialist—isn't that disgraceful? How low must international socialism, corrupted by opportunism, have fallen ideologically if such voices *could* be raised?

We have already seen the strength of the capitalists' resistance; the entire people have seen it, for the capitalists are more class-conscious than the other classes and at once realised the significance of the Soviets, at once exerted *all their efforts* to the utmost, resorted to everything, went to all lengths, resorted to the most incredible lies and slander, to military plots *in order to frustrate the Soviets*, to reduce them to nought, to prostitute them (with the aid of the Mensheviks and Socialist-Revolutionaries), to transform them into talking-shops, to wear down the peasants and workers by months and months of empty talk and playing at revolution.

We have not yet seen, however, the strength of resistance of the proletarians and poor peasants, for this strength will become fully apparent only when power is in the hands of the proletariat, when tens of millions of people who have been crushed by want and capitalist slavery see from experience and *feel* that state power has passed into the hands of the oppressed classes, that the state is helping the poor to fight the landowners and capitalists, is *breaking* their resistance. *Only* then shall we see what untapped forces of resistance to the capitalists are latent among the people; only then will what Engels called "latent socialism" manifest itself. Only then, for every *ten thousand* overt and concealed enemies of working-class rule, manifesting themselves actively or by passive resistance, there will arise *a million* new fighters who had been politically dormant, writhing in the torments of poverty and despair, having ceased to believe that they were human, that they had the right to live, that they too could be served by the entire might of the modern centralised state, that contingents of the proletarian militia could, with the fullest confidence, also call upon *them* to take a direct, immediate, daily part in state administration.

The capitalists and landowners, with the kind help of Plekhanov, Breshkovskaya, Tsereteli, Chernov and Co., have done *everything* in their power to *defile* the democratic republic, to defile it by servility to wealth to such a degree that the people are being overcome by apathy, indifference; *it is all the same to them*, because the hungry man cannot see the difference between the republic and the monarchy; the freezing, barefooted, worn-out soldier sacrificing his life for alien interests is not inclined to love the republic.

But when every labourer, every unemployed worker, every cook, every ruined peasant sees, not from the newspapers, but with his own eyes, that the proletarian state is not cringing to wealth but is helping the poor, that this state does not hesitate to adopt revolutionary measures, that it confiscates surplus stocks of provisions from the parasites and distributes them to the hungry, that it forcibly installs the homeless in the houses of the rich, that it compels the rich to pay for milk but does not give them a drop until the children of *all* poor families are sufficiently supplied, that the land is being transferred to the working people and the factories and banks are being placed under the control of the workers, and that immediate and severe punishment is meted out to the millionaires who conceal their wealth—when the poor see and feel this, no capitalist or kulak forces, no forces of world finance capital which manipulates thousands of millions, will vanquish the people's revolution; on the contrary, *the socialist revolution* will triumph all over the world for it is maturing in all countries.

Our revolution will be invincible if it is not afraid of itself, if it transfers all power to the proletariat, for behind us stand the immeasurably larger, more developed, more organised world forces of the proletariat which are temporarily held down by the war but not destroyed; on the contrary, the war has multiplied them.

* * *

How can one be afraid that the Bolshevik government, that is to say, the proletarian government, which is assured of the devoted support of the poor peasants, will be "swept away" by the capitalist gentlemen! What short-sightedness! What disgraceful fear of the people! What hypocrisy! Those who show this fear belong to that "high" (by capitalist standards, but actually *rotten*) "society" which utters the word "justice" without believing in it, from habit, as a trite phrase, attaching no meaning to it.

Here is an example.

Mr. Peshekhonov is a well-known semi-Cadet. A more moderate Trudovik,[204] one of the same mind as the Breshkovskayas and Plekhanovs, will not be found. There has never been a minister more servile to the bourgeoisie. The world had never seen a more ardent advocate of "coalition", of compromise with the capitalists.

Here are the admissions this gentleman was *forced* to make in his speech at the "Democratic" (read: Bulygin) Conference as reported by the defencist *Izvestia*:

"There are two programmes. One is the programme of group claims, class and national claims. This programme is most frankly advocated by the Bolsheviks. It is not easy, however, for the other sections of the democracy to reject this programme. They are the claims of the working people, the claims of the cheated and oppressed nationalities. It is not so easy, therefore, for the democracy to break with the Bolsheviks, to reject these class demands, primarily because in essence these demands are just. But this programme, for which we fought before the revolution, for the sake of which we made the revolution, and which we would all unanimously support under other circumstances, constitutes a very grave danger under present conditions. The danger is all the greater now because these demands have to be presented at a time when it is impossible for the state to comply with them. We must first defend the whole—the state, to save it from doom, and there is only one way to do that; not the satisfaction of demands, however just and cogent they may be, but, on the contrary, restriction and sacrifice, which must be contributed from all quarters." (*Izvestia*, September 17.)

Mr. Peshekhonov fails to understand that as long as the capitalists are in power he is defending *not* the whole, but the selfish interests of Russian and "Allied" imperialist capital. Mr. Peshekhonov fails to understand that the war would cease to be an imperialist, predatory war of annexation only after a rupture with the capitalists, with *their* secret treaties, with *their* annexations (seizure of alien territory), with *their* banking and financial swindles. Mr. Peshekhonov fails to understand that only *after* this would the war become—if the enemy rejected the formal offer of a just peace—a defensive war, a just war. Mr. Peshekhonov fails to understand that the defence potential of a country that has thrown off the yoke of capital, that has given the peasants land and has placed the banks and factories under workers' control, would be *many times* greater than the defence potential of a capitalist country.

The main thing that Mr. Peshekhonov *fails* to understand is that he *surrenders* his entire position, the entire position of the entire petty-bourgeois democracy when he is forced to admit the justice of Bolshevism, to admit that its demands are the demands of the "*working people*", i.e., of the majority of the people.

This is where our strength lies. This is why our government will be invincible; because even our opponents are forced to admit that the Bolshevik programme is that of the "working people" and the "oppressed nationalities".

After all, Mr. Peshekhonov is the political friend of the Cadets, of the *Yedinstvo* and *Dyelo Naroda* people, of the Breshkovskayas and Plekhanovs, he is the representative of the kulaks[205] and of the gentlemen whose wives and sisters would come tomorrow to gouge out with their umbrellas the eyes of wounded Bolsheviks if they were to be defeated by Kornilov's or (which is the same thing) Kerensky's troops.

A gentleman like that is *forced* to admit the "justice" of the Bolshevik demands.

For him "justice" is merely an empty phrase. For the mass of semi-proletarians, however, and for the majority of the urban and rural petty bourgeoisie who have been ruined, tortured and worn out by the war, it is not an empty phrase, but a most acute, most burning and immense question of death from starvation, of a crust of bread. That is why *no* policy can be based on a "coalition", on a "compromise" between the interests of the starving and ruined and the interests of the exploiters. That is why the Bolshevik government is *assured* of the support of the overwhelming majority of *these* people.

Justice is an empty word, say the intellectuals and those rascals who are inclined to proclaim themselves Marxists on the lofty grounds that they have "contemplated the *hind parts*" of economic materialism.

Ideas become a power when they grip the people. And precisely at the present time the Bolsheviks, i.e., the representatives of revolutionary proletarian internationalism, have embodied in their policy the idea that is motivating countless working people all over the world.

Justice alone, the mere anger of the people against exploitation, would never have brought them on to the true path of socialism. But now that, thanks to capitalism, the material apparatus of the big banks, syndicates, railways, and so forth, has grown, now that the immense experience of the advanced countries has accumulated a stock of engineering marvels, the employment of which is being *hindered* by capitalism, now that the class-conscious workers have built up a party of a quarter of a million members to systematically lay hold of this apparatus and set it in motion with the support of all the working and exploited people—now that these conditions *exist*, no power on earth can prevent the Bolsheviks, *if they do not allow themselves to be scared* and if they succeed in taking power, from retaining it until the triumph of the world socialist revolution.

AFTERWORD

The foregoing lines were already written when the leading article in *Novaya Zhizn* of October 1 produced another gem of stupidity which is all the more dangerous because it professes sympathy with the Bolsheviks and offers most sagacious philistine admonitions "not to allow yourselves to be provoked" (not to allow ourselves to be caught in the trap of screams about provocation, the object of which is to frighten the Bolsheviks and cause them to *refrain* from taking power).

Here is this gem:

"The lessons of movements, like that of July 3-5, on the one hand, and of the Kornilov days, on the other, have shown quite clearly that the democracy, having at its command organs that exercise immense influence among the population, is invincible when it takes a defensive position in civil war, and that it suffers defeat, loses all the middle vacillating groups when it takes the initiative and launches an offensive."

If the Bolsheviks were to yield in any form and in the slightest degree to the philistine stupidity of this argument they would ruin their Party and the revolution.

For the author of this argument, taking it upon himself to talk about civil war (just the subject for a lady with many good points), has distorted *the lessons of history* on this question in an incredibly comical manner.

This is how *these* lessons, the lessons of history on *this* question, were treated by the representative and founder of proletarian revolutionary tactics, Karl Marx:

"Now, insurrection is an art quite as much as war or any other art, and is subject to certain procedural rules which. when neglected, will bring about the downfall of the party neglecting them. These rules, logical deductions from the nature of the parties and the circumstances you have to deal with in such a case, are so plain and simple that the brief experience of 1848 made the Germans fairly well acquainted with them. Firstly, never play with insurrection unless you are fully prepared to go the whole way [literally: face the consequences of your game].* "Insurrection is an equation with very indefinite magnitudes, the value of which may change every day; the forces opposed to you have all the advantage of organisation, discipline and habitual authority [Marx has in mind the most "difficult" case of insurrection: against the "firmly established" old authority, against the army not yet disintegrated by the influence of the revolution and the vacillation of the government]; unless you bring strong odds against them you are defeated and ruined. Secondly, once you have entered upon the insurrectionary career, act with the greatest determination, and on the offensive. The defensive is the death of every armed rising; it is lost before it measures itself with its enemies. Surprise your antagonists while their forces are scattered, prepare the way for new successes, however small, but prepare daily; keep up the moral superiority which the first successful rising has given to you; rally in this way those vacillating elements to your side which always follow the strongest impulse and which always look out for the safer side; force your enemies to retreat before they can collect their strength against you; in the words of Danton, the greatest master of revolutionary tactics yet known: *de l'audace, de l'audace, encore de l'audace!*" (*Revolution and Counter-revolution in Germany*, German edition, 1907, p. 118.)

We have changed all that, the "would-be Marxists" of *Novaya Zhizn* may say about themselves; instead of triple audacity they have two virtues: "We have two, sir: moderation and accuracy." For "us", the experience of world history, the experience of the Great French Revolution, is nothing. The important thing for "us" is the experience of the two movements in 1917, distorted by Molchalin spectacles.[206]

Let us examine this experience without these charming spectacles.

You compare July 3-5 with "civil war", because you believed Alexinsky, Pereverzev and Co. It is typical of the gentlemen of *Novaya Zhizn* that they believe *such* people (and do absolutely nothing themselves to *collect information* about July 3-5, although they have the huge apparatus of a big daily newspaper at their disposal).

Let us assume for a moment, however, that July 3-5 was not the rudiment of civil war that was kept within the rudimentary stage by the Bolsheviks, but actual civil war. Let us assume this.

In that case, then, what does this lesson prove?

First, the Bolsheviks did *not* take the offensive, for it is indisputable that on the night of July 3-4, and even on July 4, they

---

* Interpolations in square brackets (within passages quoted by Lenin) have been introduced by Lenin unless otherwise indicated.—*Ed.*

would have gained a great deal if they had taken the offensive. Their defensive position was their weakness, if we are to speak of civil war (as *Novaya Zhizn* does, and not of converting a spontaneous outburst into a demonstration of the type of April 20-21, as the *facts* show).

The "lesson" therefore proves that the wise men of *Novaya Zhizn* are *wrong*.

Secondly, if the Bolsheviks did not even set out to start an insurrection on July 3 or 4, if *not a single* Bolshevik *body* even raised such a question, the reason for it lies *beyond* the scope of our controversy with *Novaya Zhizn*. For we are arguing about the *lessons* of "civil war", i.e., of insurrection, and not about the point that obvious lack of a majority to support it restrains the revolutionary party from thinking of insurrection.

Since everybody knows that the Bolsheviks received a majority in the metropolitan Soviets and in the country (over 49 per cent of the Moscow votes) *much later* than July 1917, it again follows that the "lessons" are far, far from what *Novaya Zhizn*, that lady with many good points, would like them to be.

No, no, you had better not meddle with politics, citizens of *Novaya Zhizn*!

If the revolutionary party has no majority in the advanced contingents of the revolutionary classes and in the country, insurrection is out of the question. Moreover, insurrection requires: 1) growth of the revolution on a country-wide scale; 2) the complete moral and political bankruptcy of the old government, for example, the "coalition" government; 3) extreme vacillation in the camp of all middle groups, i.e., those who do *not* fully support the government, although they did fully support it yesterday.

Why did *Novaya Zhizn*, when speaking of the "lessons" of July 3-5, fail even to note this very important lesson? Because a political question was not dealt with by politicians but by a circle of intellectuals who had been terrified by the bourgeoisie.

To proceed. Thirdly, the facts show that it was *after* July 3-4 that the *rot* set in among the Socialist-Revolutionaries and Mensheviks, precisely because the Tseretelis had *exposed* themselves by their *July* policy, precisely because the mass of the *people* realised that the Bolsheviks were *their own* front-rank fighters and that the "social-bloc" advocates were traitors. *Even before* the Kornilov revolt this rot was fully revealed by the Petrograd elections on August 20, which resulted in a victory of the Bolsheviks and the rout of the "social-bloc" advocates (*Dyelo Naroda* recently tried to refute this *by concealing* the returns for *all* parties, but this was both self-deception and deception of its readers; according to the figures published in *Dyen* of August 24, covering only the city, the Cadets' share of the total vote increased from 22 to 23 per cent, but the absolute number of votes cast for the Cadets dropped 40 per cent; the Bolsheviks' share of the total vote increased from 20 to 33 per cent, while the absolute number of votes cast for the Bolsheviks dropped only 10 per cent; the share of all "middle groups" dropped from 58 to 44 per cent, but the absolute number of votes cast for them dropped 60 per cent!).

That a rot had set in among the Socialist-Revolutionaries and Mensheviks after the July days and before the Kornilov days is also proved by the growth of the Left wings in both parties, reaching almost 40 per cent: this is "retribution" for the persecution of the Bolsheviks by the Kerenskys.

In spite of the "loss" of a few hundred members, the proletarian party *gained* enormously from July 3-4, for it was precisely during those stern days that the *people* realised and saw its devotion and the *treachery* of the Socialist-Revolutionaries and Mensheviks. So, the "lesson" is far, very far from being of the *Novaya Zhizn* sort, it is one entirely different, namely: don't desert the seething masses for the "Molchalins of democracy"; and if you launch an insurrection, go over to the offensive while the enemy forces are scattered, catch the enemy unawares.

Is that not so, gentlemen "would-be Marxists" of *Novaya Zhizn*?

Or does "Marxism" mean *not* basing tactics on an exact appraisal of the *objective* situation but senselessly and uncritically lumping together "civil war" and "a Congress of Soviets and the convocation of the Constituent Assembly"?

But this is simply ridiculous, gentlemen, this is a sheer mockery of Marxism and of logic in general!

If there is *nothing* in the *objective* situation that warrants the intensification of the class struggle to the point of "civil war", why did you speak of "civil war" *in connection* with "a Congress of Soviets and the Constituent Assembly"? (For this is the title of the leading article in *Novaya Zhizn* here under discussion.) In that case you should clearly have told the reader and proved to him that there is *no* ground in the objective situation for civil war and that, therefore, peaceful, constitutionally-legal, juridically and parliamentarily "simple" things like a Congress of Soviets and a Constituent Assembly can and should be the cornerstone of tactics. In that case it is *possible* to hold the opinion that such a congress and such an assembly are really capable *of making decisions*.

If, however, the present objective conditions harbour the inevitability or even only the probability of civil war, if you did not "idly" speak about it, but did so clearly seeing, feeling, sensing the existence of a situation of civil war, how could you make a Congress of Soviets or a Constituent Assembly the cornerstone? This is a sheer mockery of the starving and tormented people! Do you think the starving will consent to "wait" two months? Or that the ruin, about the increase of which you yourselves write every day, will consent to "wait" for the Congress of Soviets or for the Constituent Assembly? Or that the German offensive, in the absence of serious steps on our part towards peace (i.e., in the absence of a formal offer of a just peace to all belligerents), will consent to "wait" for the Congress of Soviets or for the Constituent Assembly? Or are you in possession of facts which permit you to conclude that the history of the Russian revolution, which from February 28 to September 30 had proceeded with extraordinary turbulence and unprecedented rapidity, will, from October 1 to November 29,[207] proceed at a super-tranquil, peaceful, legally balanced pace that will preclude upheavals, spurts, military defeats and economic crises? Or will the army at the front, concerning which the non-Bolshevik officer Dubasov said officially, in the name of the front, "it will not fight", quietly starve and freeze until the "appointed" date? Or will the peasant revolt cease to be a factor of civil war because you call it "anarchy" and "pogrom", or because Kerensky will send "military" forces *against the peasants*? Or is it possible, *conceivable*, that the government can work calmly, honestly, and *without* deception to convene the Constituent Assembly in a *peasant* country when that same government is *suppressing* the peasant revolt?

Don't laugh at the "confusion in the Smolny Institute",[208] gentlemen! There is no less confusion in your own ranks. You answer the formidable questions of civil war with confused phrases and pitiful constitutional illusions. That is why I say that if the Bolsheviks were to give into these moods they would ruin both their Party and their revolution.

N. Lenin

October 1, 1917

Written in late September-October 1(14), 1917   *Collected Works*, Vol. 26

Published in October 1917
in the magazine
Prosveshcheniye No. 1-2

THE IMMEDIATE TASKS
OF THE SOVIET GOVERNMENT[209]

THE INTERNATIONAL POSITION OF THE RUSSIAN SOVIET REPUBLIC AND THE FUNDAMENTAL TASKS OF THE SOCIALIST REVOLUTION

Thanks to the peace which has been achieved[210]—despite its extremely onerous character and extreme instability—the Russian Soviet Republic has gained an opportunity to concentrate its efforts for a while on the most important and most difficult aspect of the socialist revolution, namely, the task of organisation.

This task was clearly and definitely set before all the working and oppressed people in the fourth paragraph (Part 4) of the resolution adopted at the Extraordinary Congress of Soviets in Moscow on March 15, 1918, in that paragraph (or part) which speaks of the self-discipline of the working people and of the ruthless struggle against chaos and disorganisation.*

Of course, the peace achieved by the Russian Soviet Republic is unstable not because she is now thinking of resuming military operations; apart from bourgeois counter-revolutionaries and their henchmen (the Mensheviks and others), no sane politician thinks of doing that. The instability of the peace is due to the fact that in the imperialist states bordering on Russia to the West and the East, which command enormous military forces, the military party, tempted by Russia's momentary weakness and egged on by capitalists, who hate socialism and are eager for plunder, may gain the upper hand at any moment.

Under these circumstances the only real, not paper, guarantee of peace we have is the antagonism among the imperialist powers, which has reached extreme limits, and which is apparent on the one hand in the resumption of the imperialist butchery of the peoples in the West, and on the other hand in the extreme intensification of imperialist rivalry between Japan and America for supremacy in the Pacific and on the Pacific coast.

It goes without saying that with such an unreliable guard for protection, our Soviet Socialist Republic is in an extremely

---

* See Collected Works, Vol. 27, p. 200.—Ed.

unstable and certainly critical international position. All our efforts must be exerted to the very utmost to make use of the respite given us by the combination of circumstances so that we can heal the very severe wounds inflicted by the war upon the entire social organism of Russia and bring about an economic revival, without which a real increase in our country's defence potential is inconceivable.

It also goes without saying that we shall be able to render effective assistance to the socialist revolution in the West, which has been delayed for a number of reasons, only to the extent that we are able to fulfil the task of organisation confronting us.

A fundamental condition for the successful accomplishment of the primary task of organisation confronting us is that the people's political leaders, i.e., the members of the Russian Communist Party (Bolsheviks), and following them all the class-conscious representatives of the mass of the working people, shall fully appreciate the radical distinction in this respect between previous bourgeois revolutions and the present socialist revolution.

In bourgeois revolutions, the principal task of the mass of working people was to fulfil the negative or destructive work of abolishing feudalism, monarchy and medievalism. The positive or constructive work of organising the new society was carried out by the property-owning bourgeois minority of the population. And the latter carried out this task with relative ease, despite the resistance of the workers and the poor peasants, not only because the resistance of the people exploited by capital was then extremely weak, since they were scattered and uneducated, but also because the chief organising force of anarchically built capitalist society is the spontaneously growing and expanding national and international market.

In every socialist revolution, however—and consequently in the socialist revolution in Russia which we began on October 25, 1917—the principal task of the proletariat, and of the poor peasants which it leads, is the positive or constructive work of setting up an extremely intricate and delicate system of new organisational relationships extending to the planned production and distribution of the goods required for the existence of tens of millions of people. Such a revolution can be successfully carried out only if the majority of the population, and primarily the majority of the working people, engage in independent creative work as makers of history. Only if the proletariat and the poor peasants display sufficient class-consciousness, devotion to principle, self-sacrifice and perseverance, will the victory of the socialist revolution be assured. By creating a new, Soviet type of state, which gives the working and oppressed people the chance to take an active part in the independent building up of a new society, we solved only a small part of this difficult problem. The principal difficulty lies in the economic sphere, namely, the introduction of the strictest and universal accounting and control of the production and distribution of goods, raising the productivity of labour and *socialising* production *in practice*.

———

The development of the Bolshevik Party, which today is the governing party in Russia, very strikingly indicates the nature of the turning-point in history we have now reached, which is the peculiar feature of the present political situation, and which calls for a new orientation of Soviet power, i.e., for a new presentation of new tasks.

The first task of every party of the future is to convince the majority of the people that its programme and tactics are correct. This task stood in the forefront both in tsarist times and in the period of the Chernovs' and Tseretelis' policy of compromise with the Kerenskys and Kishkins. This task has now been fulfilled in the main, for, as the recent Congress of Soviets in Moscow incontrovertibly proved, the majority of the workers and peasants of Russia are obviously on the side of the Bolsheviks; but of course, it is far from being completely fulfilled (and it can never be completely fulfilled).

The second task that confronted our Party was to capture political power and to suppress the resistance of the exploiters. This task has not been completely fulfilled either, and it cannot be ignored because the monarchists and Constitutional-Democrats on the one hand, and their henchmen and hangers-on, the Mensheviks and Right Socialist-Revolutionaries, on the other, are continuing their efforts to unite for the purpose of overthrowing Soviet power. In the main, however, the task of suppressing the resistance of the exploiters was fulfilled in the period from October 25, 1917 to (approximately) February 1918, or to the surrender of Bogayevsky.

A third task is now coming to the fore as the immediate task and one which constitutes the peculiar feature of the present situation, namely, the task of organising administration of Russia. Of course, we advanced and tackled this task on the very day following October 25, 1917. Up to now, however, since the resistance of the exploiters still took the form of open civil war, up to now the task of administration *could not* become the *main*, the *central* task.

Now it has become the main and central task. We, the Bolshevik Party, have *convinced* Russia. We have *won* Russia from the rich for the poor, from the exploiters for the working people. Now we must *administer* Russia. And the whole peculiarity of the present situation, the whole difficulty, lies in understanding *the specific features of the transition* from the principal task of convincing the people and of suppressing the exploiters by armed force to the principal task of *administration.*

For the first time in human history a socialist party has managed to complete in the main the conquest of power and the suppression of the exploiters, and has managed to *approach directly* the task of *administration.* We must prove worthy executors of this most difficult (and most gratifying) task of the socialist revolution. We must *fully realise* that in order to administer successfully, *besides* being able to convince people, besides being able to win a civil war, we must be able to do *practical organisational work.* This is the most difficult task, because it is a matter of organising in a new way the most deep-rooted, the economic, foundations of life of scores of millions of people. And it is the most gratifying task, because only *after* it has been fulfilled (in the principal and main outlines) will it be possible to say that Russia *has become* not only a Soviet, but also a socialist, republic.

THE GENERAL SLOGAN OF THE MOMENT

The objective situation reviewed above, which has been created by the extremely onerous and unstable peace, the terrible state of ruin, the unemployment and famine we inherited from the war and the rule of the bourgeoisie (represented by Kerensky and the Mensheviks and Right Socialist-Revolutionaries who supported him), all this has inevitably caused extreme weariness and even exhaustion of wide sections of the working people. These people insistently demand—and cannot but demand—a respite. The task of the day is to restore the productive forces destroyed by the war and by bourgeois rule; to heal the wounds inflicted by the war, by the defeat in the war, by profiteering and the attempts of the bourgeoisie to restore the overthrown rule of the exploiters; to achieve economic revival; to provide reliable protection of elementary order. It may sound paradoxical, but in fact, considering the objective conditions indicated above, it is absolutely certain that at the present moment the Soviet system can secure Russia's transition to socialism only if these very elementary, extremely elementary problems of maintaining public life are practically solved in spite of the resistance of the bourgeoisie, the Mensheviks and the Right Socialist-Revolutionaries. In view of the specific features of the present situation, and in view of the existence of Soviet power with its land socialisation[211] law, workers' control law, etc., the practical solution of these extremely elementary problems and the overcoming of the organisational difficulties of the first stages of progress toward socialism are now two aspects of the same picture.

Keep regular and honest accounts of money, manage economically, do not be lazy, do not steal, observe the strictest labour discipline—it is these slogans, justly scorned by the revolutionary proletariat when the bourgeoisie used them to conceal its rule as an exploiting class, that are now, since the overthrow of the bourgeoisie, becoming the immediate and the principal slogans of the moment. On the one hand, the practical application of these slogans by *the mass* of working people is the *sole* condition for the salvation of a country which has been tortured almost to death by the imperialist war and by the imperialist robbers (headed by Kerensky); on the other hand, the practical application of these slogans by the *Soviet* state, by *its* methods, on the basis of *its* laws, is a necessary and *sufficient* condition for the final victory of socialism. This is precisely what those who contemptuously brush aside the idea of putting such "hackneyed" and "trivial" slogans in the forefront fail to understand. In a small-peasant country, which overthrew tsarism only a year ago, and which liberated itself from the Kerenskys less than six months ago, there has naturally remained not a little of spontaneous anarchy, intensified by the brutality and savagery that accompany every protracted and reactionary war, and there has arisen a good deal of despair and aimless bitterness. And if we add to this the provocative policy of the lackeys of the bourgeoisie (the Mensheviks, the Right Socialist-Revolutionaries, etc.) it will become perfectly clear what prolonged and persistent efforts must be exerted by the best and the most class-conscious workers and peasants in order to bring about a complete change in the mood of the people and to bring them on to the proper path of steady and disciplined labour. Only such a transition brought about by the mass of the poor (the proletarians and semi-proletarians) can consummate the victory over the bourgeoisie and particularly over the peasant bourgeoisie, more stubborn and numerous.

THE NEW PHASE OF THE STRUGGLE AGAINST THE BOURGEOISIE

The bourgeoisie in our country has been conquered, but it has not yet been uprooted, not yet destroyed, and not even utterly broken. That is why we are faced with a new and higher form of struggle against the bourgeoisie, the transition from the very simple task of further expropriating the capitalists to the much more complicated and difficult task of creating conditions in which it will be impossible for the bourgeoisie to exist, or for a new bourgeoisie to arise. Clearly, this task is immeasurably more significant than the previous one; and until it is fulfilled there will be no socialism.

If we measure our revolution by the scale of West-European revolutions we shall find that at the present moment we are approximately at the level reached in 1793 and 1871.[212] We can be legitimately proud of having risen to this level, and of having certainly, in one respect, advanced somewhat further, namely: we have decreed and introduced throughout Russia the highest *type* of state—Soviet power. Under no circumstances, however, can we rest content with what we have achieved, because we have only just started the transition to socialism, we have *not yet* done the decisive thing in *this* respect.

The decisive thing is the organisation of the strictest and country-wide accounting and control of production and distribution of goods. And yet, we have *not yet* introduced accounting and control in those enterprises and in those branches and fields of economy which we have taken away from the bourgeoisie; and without this there can be no thought of achieving the second and equally essential material condition for introducing socialism, namely, raising the productivity of labour on a national scale.

That is why the present task could not be defined by the simple formula: continue the offensive against capital. Although we have certainly not finished off capital and although it is certainly necessary to continue the offensive against this enemy of the working people, such a formula would be inexact, would not be concrete, would not take into account the *peculiarity* of the present situation in which, in order to go on advancing successfully *in the future*, we must "suspend" our offensive *now*.

This can be explained by comparing our position in the war against capital with the position of a victorious army that has captured, say, a half or two-thirds of the enemy's territory and is compelled to halt in order to muster its forces, to replenish its supplies of munitions, repair and reinforce the lines of communication, build new storehouses, bring up new reserves, etc. To suspend the offensive of a victorious army under such conditions is necessary precisely in order to gain the rest of the enemy's territory, i.e., in order to achieve complete victory. Those who have failed to understand that the objective state of affairs at the present moment dictates to us precisely such a "suspension" of the offensive against capital have failed to understand anything at all about the present political situation.

It goes without saying that we can speak about the "suspension" of the offensive against capital only in quotation marks, i.e., only metaphorically. In ordinary war, a general order can be issued to stop the offensive, the advance can actually be stopped. In the war against capital, however, the advance cannot be stopped, and there can be no thought of our abandoning the further expropriation of capital. What we are discussing is the shifting of the *centre of gravity* of our economic and political work. Up to now measures for the direct expropriation of the expropriators were *in the forefront*. Now the organisation of accounting and control in those enterprises in which the capitalists have already been expropriated, and in all other enterprises, advances *to the forefront*.

If we decided to continue to expropriate capital at the same rate at which we have been doing it up to now, we should certainly suffer defeat, because our work of organising proletarian accounting and control has obviously—obviously to every thinking person—*fallen behind* the work of *directly* "expropriating the expropriators". If we now concentrate all our efforts on the organisation of accounting and control, we shall be able to solve this problem, we shall be able to make up for lost time, we shall *completely* win our "campaign" against capital.

But is not the admission that we must make up for lost time tantamount to admission of some kind of an error? Not in the least. Take another military example. If it is possible to defeat and push back the enemy merely with detachments of light cavalry, it should be done. But if this can be done successfully only up to a certain point, then it is quite conceivable that when this point has been reached, it will be necessary to bring up heavy artillery. By admitting that it is now necessary to make up for lost time in bringing up heavy artillery, we do not admit that the successful cavalry attack was a mistake.

Frequently, the lackeys of the bourgeoisie reproached us for having launched a "Red Guard" attack on capital. The reproach is absurd and is worthy only of the lackeys of the money-bags, because *at one time* the "Red Guard" attack on capital was absolutely dictated by circumstances. Firstly, *at that time* capital put up military resistance through the medium of Kerensky and Krasnov, Savinkov and Gotz (Gegechkori is putting up such resistance even now), Dutov and Bogayevsky. Military resistance cannot be broken except by military means, and the Red Guards fought in the noble and supreme historical cause of liberating the working and exploited people from the yoke of the exploiters.

Secondly, we could not at that time put methods of administration in the forefront in place of methods of suppression, because the art of administration is not innate, but is acquired by experience. At that time we lacked this experience; now we have it. Thirdly, at that time we could not have specialists in the various fields of knowledge and technology at our disposal because those specialists were either fighting in the ranks of the Bogayevskys, or were still able to put up systematic and stubborn passive resistance

by way of *sabotage*. Now we have broken the sabotage. The "Red
Guard" attack on capital was successful, was victorious, because
we broke capital's military resistance and its resistance by
sabotage.

Does that mean that a "Red Guard" attack on capital is *always*
appropriate, under *all* circumstances, that we have *no* other means
of fighting capital? It would be childish to think so. We achieved
victory with the aid of light cavalry, but we also have heavy artillery. We achieved victory by methods of suppression; we shall
be able to achieve victory also by methods of administration. We
must know how to change our methods of fighting the enemy to
suit changes in the situation. We shall not for a moment renounce
"Red Guard" suppression of the Savinkovs and Gegechkoris and
all other landowner and bourgeois counter-revolutionaries. We shall
not be so foolish, however, as to put "Red Guard" methods in the
forefront at a time when the period in which Red Guard attacks
were necessary has, in the main, drawn to a close (and to a
victorious close), and when the period of utilising bourgeois
specialists by the proletarian state power for the purpose of re-
ploughing the soil in order to prevent the growth of any bourgeoisie
whatever is knocking at the door.

This is a peculiar epoch, or rather stage of development, and
in order to defeat capital completely, we must be able to adapt the
forms of our struggle to the peculiar conditions of this stage.

Without the guidance of experts in the various fields of knowledge, technology and experience, the transition to socialism will be
impossible, because socialism calls for a conscious mass advance
to greater productivity of labour compared with capitalism, and
on the basis achieved by capitalism. Socialism must achieve this
advance *in its own way*, by its own methods—or, to put it more
concretely, by *Soviet* methods. And the specialists, because of the
whole social environment which made them specialists, are, in
the main, inevitably bourgeois. Had our proletariat, after capturing
power, quickly solved the problem of accounting, control and
organisation on a national scale (which was impossible owing to
the war and Russia's backwardness), then we, after breaking the
sabotage, would also have completely subordinated these bourgeois
experts to ourselves by means of universal accounting and control.
Owing to the considerable "delay" in introducing accounting and
control generally, we, although we have managed to conquer
sabotage, have *not yet* created the conditions which would place
the bourgeois specialists at our disposal. The mass of saboteurs are
"going to work", but the best organisers and the top experts can
be utilised by the state either in the old way, in the bourgeois way
(i.e., for high salaries), or in the new way, in the proletarian way
(i.e., creating the conditions of national accounting and control

from below, which would inevitably and of itself subordinate the experts and enlist them for our work).

Now we have to resort to the old bourgeois method and to agree to pay a very high price for the "services" of the top bourgeois experts. All those who are familiar with the subject appreciate this, but not all ponder over the significance of this measure being adopted by the proletarian state. Clearly, this measure is a compromise, a departure from the principles of the Paris Commune and of every proletarian power, which call for the reduction of all salaries to the level of the wages of the average worker, which urge that careerism be fought not merely in words, but in deeds.

Moreover, it is clear that this measure not only implies the cessation—in a certain field and to a certain degree—of the offensive against capital (for capital is not a sum of money, but a definite social relation); it is also *a step backward* on the part of our socialist Soviet state power, which from the very outset proclaimed and pursued the policy of reducing high salaries to the level of the wages of the average worker.[213]

Of course, the lackeys of the bourgeoisie, particularly the small fry, such as the Mensheviks, the *Novaya Zhizn* people and the Right Socialist-Revolutionaries, will giggle over our confession that we are taking a step backward. But we need not mind their giggling. We must study the specific features of the extremely difficult and new path to socialism without concealing our mistakes and weaknesses, and try to be prompt in doing what has been left undone. To conceal from the people the fact that the enlistment of bourgeois experts by means of extremely high salaries is a retreat from the principles of the Paris Commune would be sinking to the level of bourgeois politicians and deceiving the people. Frankly explaining how and why we took this step backward, and then publicly discussing what means are available for making up for lost time, means educating the people and learning from experience, learning together with the people how to build socialism. There is hardly a single victorious military campaign in history, in which the victor did not commit certain mistakes, suffer partial reverses, temporarily yield something and in some places retreat. The "campaign" which we have undertaken against capitalism is a million times more difficult than the most difficult military campaign, and it would be silly and disgraceful to give way to despondency because of a particular and partial retreat.

We shall now discuss the question from the practical point of view. Let us assume that the Russian Soviet Republic requires one thousand first-class scientists and experts in various fields of knowledge, technology and practical experience to direct the labour of the people towards securing the speediest possible economic revival. Let us assume also that we shall have to pay these "stars of the first magnitude"—of course the majority of those who shout loudest about the corruption of the workers are themselves utterly corrupted by bourgeois morals—25,000 rubles per annum each. Let us assume that this sum (25,000,000 rubles) will have to be doubled (assuming that we have to pay bonuses for particularly successful and rapid fulfilment of the most important organisational and technical tasks), or even quadrupled (assuming that we have to enlist several hundred foreign specialists, who are more demanding). The question is, would the annual expenditure of fifty or a hundred million rubles by the Soviet Republic for the purpose of reorganising the labour of the people on modern scientific and technological lines be excessive or too heavy? Of course not. The overwhelming majority of the class-conscious workers and peasants will approve of this expenditure because they know from practical experience that our backwardness causes us to lose thousands of millions, and that we have *not yet* reached that degree of organisation, accounting and control which would induce all the "stars" of the bourgeois intelligentsia to participate voluntarily in *our* work.

It goes without saying that this question has another side to it. The corrupting influence of high salaries—both upon the Soviet authorities (especially since the revolution occurred so rapidly that it was impossible to prevent a certain number of adventurers and rogues from getting into positions of authority, and they, together with a number of inept or dishonest commissars, would not be averse to becoming "star" embezzlers of state funds) and upon the mass of the workers—is indisputable. Every thinking and honest worker and poor peasant, however, will agree with us, will admit, that we cannot immediately rid ourselves of the evil legacy of capitalism, and that we can liberate the Soviet Republic from the duty of paying an annual "tribute" of fifty million or one hundred million rubles (a tribute for our own backwardness in organising *country-wide* accounting and control *from below*) only by organising ourselves, by tightening up discipline in our own ranks, by purging our ranks of all those who are "preserving the legacy of capitalism", who "follow the traditions of capitalism", i.e., of idlers, parasites and embezzlers of state funds (now all the land, all the factories and all the railways are the "state funds" of the Soviet Republic). If the class-conscious advanced workers and poor peasants manage with the aid of the Soviet institutions to organise, become disciplined, pull themselves together, create powerful labour discipline in the course of one year, then in a year's time we shall throw off this "tribute", which can be reduced even before that ... in exact proportion to the successes we achieve in our workers' and peasants' labour discipline and organisation. The sooner we ourselves, workers and peasants, learn the best labour discipline and the most modern technique of labour, using the bourgeois experts to teach us, the sooner we shall liberate ourselves from any "tribute" to these specialists.

Our work of organising country-wide accounting and control of production and distribution under the supervision of the proletariat has lagged very much behind our work of directly expropriating the expropriators. This proposition is of fundamental importance for understanding the specific features of the present situation and the tasks of the Soviet government that follow from it. The centre of gravity of our struggle against the bourgeoisie is shifting to the organisation of such accounting and control. Only with this as our starting-point will it be possible to determine correctly the immediate tasks of economic and financial policy in the sphere of nationalisation of the banks, monopolisation of foreign trade, the state control of money circulation, the introduction of a property and income tax satisfactory from the proletarian point of view, and the introduction of compulsory labour service.

We have been lagging very far behind in introducing socialist reforms in these spheres (very, very important spheres), and this is because accounting and control are insufficiently organised in general. It goes without saying that this is one of the most difficult tasks, and in view of the ruin caused by the war, it can be fulfilled only over a long period of time; but we must not forget that it is precisely here that the bourgeoisie—and particularly the numerous petty and peasant bourgeoisie—are putting up the most serious fight, disrupting the control that is already being organised, disrupting the grain monopoly, for example, and gaining positions for profiteering and speculative trade. We have far from adequately carried out the things we have decreed, and the principal task of the moment is to concentrate all efforts on the businesslike, practical *realisation* of the principles of the reforms which have already become law (but not yet reality).

In order to proceed with the nationalisation of the banks and to go on steadfastly towards transforming the banks into nodal points of public accounting under socialism, we must first of all, and above all, achieve real success in increasing the number of branches of the People's Bank, in attracting deposits, in simplifying the paying in and withdrawal of deposits by the public, in abolishing queues, in catching and *shooting* bribe-takers and rogues, etc. At first we must really carry out the simplest things, properly organise what is available, and then prepare for the more intricate things.

Consolidate and improve the state monopolies (in grain, leather, etc.) which have already been introduced, and by doing so prepare for the state monopoly of foreign trade. Without this monopoly we shall not be able to "free ourselves" from foreign capital by paying "tribute". And the possibility of building up socialism depends entirely upon whether we shall be able, by paying a certain tribute to foreign capital during a certain transitional period, to safeguard our internal economic independence.

We are also lagging very far behind in regard to the collection of taxes generally, and of the property and income tax in particular. The imposing of indemnities upon the bourgeoisie—a measure which in principle is absolutely permissible and deserves proletarian approval—shows that in this respect we are still nearer to the methods of warfare (to win Russia from the rich for the poor) than to the methods of administration. In order to become stronger, however, and in order to be able to stand firmer on our feet, we must adopt the latter methods, we must substitute for the indemnities imposed upon the bourgeoisie the constant and regular collection of a property and income tax, which will bring a *greater* return to the proletarian state, and which calls for better organisation on our part and better accounting and control.

The fact that we are late in introducing compulsory labour service also shows that the work that is coming to the fore at the present time is precisely the preparatory organisational work that, on the one hand, will finally consolidate our gains and that, on the other, is necessary in order to prepare for the operation of "surrounding" capital and compelling it to "surrender". We ought to begin introducing compulsory labour service immediately, but we must do so very gradually and circumspectly, testing every step by practical experience, and, of course, taking the first step by introducing compulsory labour service *for the rich*. The introduction of work and consumers' budget books for every bourgeois, including every rural bourgeois, would be an important step towards completely "surrounding" the enemy and towards the creation of a truly popular accounting and control of the production and distribution of goods.

THE SIGNIFICANCE OF THE STRUGGLE
FOR COUNTRY-WIDE ACCOUNTING AND CONTROL

The state, which for centuries has been an organ for oppression and robbery of the people, has left us a legacy of the people's supreme hatred and suspicion of everything that is connected with the state. It is very difficult to overcome this, and only a Soviet government can do it. Even a Soviet government, however, will require plenty of time and enormous perseverance to accomplish it. This "legacy" is especially apparent in the problem of accounting and control—the fundamental problem facing the socialist revolution on the morrow of the overthrow of the bourgeoisie. A certain amount of time will inevitably pass before the people, who feel free for the first time now that the landowners and the bourgeoisie have been overthrown, will understand—not from books, but from their own, *Soviet* experience—will understand and *feel* that without comprehensive state accounting and control of the production and distribution of goods, the power of the working people, the freedom of the working people, *cannot* be maintained, and that a return to the yoke of capitalism is *inevitable*.

All the habits and traditions of the bourgeoisie, and of the petty bourgeoisie in particular, also oppose *state* control, and uphold the inviolability of "sacred private property", of "sacred" private enterprise. It is now particularly clear to us how correct is the Marxist thesis that anarchism and anarcho-syndicalism are *bourgeois* trends, how irreconcilably opposed they are to socialism, proletarian dictatorship and communism. The fight to instil into the people's minds the idea of *Soviet* state control and accounting, and to carry out this idea in practice; the fight to break with the rotten past, which taught the people to regard the procurement of bread and clothes as a "private" affair, and buying and selling as a transaction "which concerns only myself"—is a great fight of world-historic significance, a fight between socialist consciousness and bourgeois-anarchist spontaneity.

We have introduced workers' control as a law, but this law is only just beginning to operate and is only just beginning to penetrate the minds of broad sections of the proletariat. In our agitation we do not sufficiently explain that lack of accounting and control in the production and distribution of goods means the death of the rudiments of socialism, means the embezzlement of state funds (for all property belongs to the state and the state is the Soviet state in which power belongs to the majority of the working people). We do not sufficiently explain that carelessness in accounting and control is downright aiding and abetting the German and the Russian Kornilovs, who can overthrow the power of the working people *only* if we fail to cope with the task of accounting and control, and who, with the aid of the whole of the rural bourgeoisie, with the aid of the Constitutional-Democrats, the Mensheviks and the Right Socialist-Revolutionaries, are "watching" us and waiting for an opportune moment to attack us. And the advanced workers and peasants do not think and speak about this sufficiently. Until workers' control has become a fact, until the advanced workers have organised and carried out a victorious and ruthless crusade against the violators of this control, or against those who are careless in matters of control, it will be impossible to pass from the first step (from workers' control) to the second step towards socialism, i.e., to pass on to workers' regulation of production.

The socialist state can arise only as a network of producers' and consumers' communes, which conscientiously keep account of their production and consumption, economise on labour, and steadily raise the productivity of labour, thus making it possible to reduce the working day to seven, six and even fewer hours. Nothing will be achieved unless the strictest, country-wide, comprehensive accounting and control of *grain* and the *production of grain* (and later of all other essential goods) are set going. Capitalism left us a legacy of mass organisations which can facilitate our transition to the mass accounting and control of the distribution of goods, namely, the consumers' co-operative societies. In Russia these societies are not so well developed as in the advanced countries, nevertheless, they have over ten million members. The Decree on Consumers' Co-operative Societies, issued the other day, is an extremely significant phenomenon, which strikingly illustrates the peculiar position and the specific tasks of the Soviet Socialist Republic at the present moment.

The decree is an agreement with the bourgeois co-operative societies and the workers' co-operative societies which still adhere to the bourgeois point of view. It is an agreement, or compromise, firstly because the representatives of the above-mentioned institutions not only took part in discussing the decree, but actually had a decisive say in the matter, for the parts of the decree which were strongly opposed by these institutions were dropped. Secondly, the essence of the compromise is that the Soviet government has abandoned the principle of admission of new members to co-operative societies without entrance fees (which is the only consistently proletarian principle); it has also abandoned the idea of uniting the whole population of a given locality in a *single* co-operative society. Contrary to this principle, which is the only socialist principle and which corresponds to the task of abolishing classes, the "working-class co-operative societies" (which in this case call themselves "class" societies only because they subordinate themselves to the class interests of the bourgeoisie) were given the right to continue to exist. Finally, the Soviet government's proposal to expel the bourgeoisie entirely from the boards of the co-operative societies was also considerably modified, and only owners of private capitalist trading and industrial enterprises were forbidden to serve on the boards.

Had the proletariat, acting through the Soviet government, managed to organise accounting and control on a national scale, or at least laid the foundation for such control, it would not have been necessary to make such compromises. Through the food departments of the Soviets, through the supply organisations under the Soviets we should have organised the population into a single co-operative society under proletarian management. We should have done this without the assistance of the bourgeois co-operative societies, without making any concession to the purely bourgeois principle which prompts the workers' co-operative societies to remain workers' societies *side by side* with bourgeois societies, *instead of* subordinating these bourgeois co-operative societies entirely to themselves, merging the two together and taking the *entire* management of the society and the supervision of the consumption of the rich *in their own* hands.

In concluding such an agreement with the bourgeois co-operative societies, the Soviet government concretely defined its tactical aims and its peculiar methods of action in the present stage of development as follows: by directing the bourgeois elements, utilising them, making certain partial concessions to them, we create the conditions for further progress that will be slower than we at first anticipated, but surer, with the base and lines of communication better secured and with the positions which have been won better consolidated. The Soviets can (*and should*) now gauge their successes in the field of socialist construction, among other things, by extremely clear, simple and practical standards, namely, in how many communities (communes or villages, or blocks of houses, etc.) co-operative societies have been organised, and to what extent their development has reached the point of embracing the whole population.

RAISING THE PRODUCTIVITY OF LABOUR

In every socialist revolution, after the proletariat has solved the problem of capturing power, and to the extent that the task of expropriating the expropriators and suppressing their resistance has been carried out in the main, there necessarily comes to the forefront the fundamental task of creating a social system superior to capitalism, namely, raising the productivity of labour, and in this connection (and for this purpose) securing better organisation of labour. Our Soviet state is precisely in the position where, thanks to the victories over the exploiters—from Kerensky to Kornilov—it is able to approach this task directly, to tackle it in earnest. And here it becomes immediately clear that while it is possible to take over the central government in a few days, while it is possible to suppress the military resistance (and sabotage) of the exploiters even in different parts of a great country in a few weeks, the capital solution of the problem of raising the productivity of labour requires, at all events (particularly after a most terrible and devastating war), several years. The protracted nature of the work is certainly dictated by objective circumstances.

The raising of the productivity of labour first of all requires that the material basis of large-scale industry shall be assured, namely, the development of the production of fuel, iron, the engineering and chemical industries. The Russian Soviet Republic enjoys the favourable position of having at its command, even after the Brest peace, enormous reserves of ore (in the Urals), fuel in Western Siberia (coal), in the Caucasus and the South-East (oil), in Central Russia (peat), enormous timber reserves, water power, raw materials for the chemical industry (Karabugaz), etc. The development of these natural resources by methods of modern technology will provide the basis for the unprecedented progress of the productive forces.

Another condition for raising the productivity of labour is, firstly, the raising of the educational and cultural level of the mass of the population. This is now taking place extremely rapidly, a fact which those who are blinded by bourgeois routine are unable to see; they are unable to understand what an urge towards enlightenment and initiative is now developing among the "lower ranks" of the people thanks to the Soviet form of organisation. Secondly, a condition for economic revival is the raising of the working people's discipline, their skill, the effectiveness, the intensity of labour and its better organisation.

In this respect the situation is particularly bad and even hopeless if we are to believe those who have allowed themselves to be intimidated by the bourgeoisie or by those who are serving the bourgeoisie for their own ends. These people do not understand that there has not been, nor could there be, a revolution in which the supporters of the old system did not raise a howl about chaos, anarchy, etc. Naturally, among the people who have only just thrown off an unprecedentedly savage yoke there is deep and widespread seething and ferment; the working out of new principles of labour discipline by the people is a very protracted process, and this process could not even start until complete victory had been achieved over the landowners and the bourgeoisie.

We, however, without in the least yielding to the despair (it is often false despair) which is spread by the bourgeoisie and the bourgeois intellectuals (who have despaired of retaining their old privileges), must under no circumstances conceal an obvious evil. On the contrary, we shall expose it and intensify the Soviet methods of combating it, because the victory of socialism is inconceivable without the victory of proletarian conscious discipline over spontaneous petty-bourgeois anarchy, this real guarantee of a possible restoration of Kerenskyism and Kornilovism.

The more class-conscious vanguard of the Russian proletariat has already set itself the task of raising labour discipline. For example, both the Central Committee of the Metalworkers' Union and the Central Council of Trade Unions have begun to draft the necessary measures and decrees.[214] This work must be supported and pushed ahead with all speed. We must raise the question of piece-work and apply and test it in practice; we must raise the question of applying much of what is scientific and progressive in the Taylor system; we must make wages correspond to the total amount of goods turned out, or to the amount of work done by the railways, the water transport system, etc., etc.

The Russian is a bad worker compared with people in advanced countries. It could not be otherwise under the tsarist regime and in view of the persistence of the hangover from serfdom. The task that the Soviet government must set the people in all its scope is—learn to work. The Taylor system, the last word of capitalism in this respect, like all capitalist progress, is a combination of the refined brutality of bourgeois exploitation and a number of the greatest scientific achievements in the field of analysing mechanical motions during work, the elimination of superfluous and awkward motions, the elaboration of correct methods of work, the introduction of the best system of accounting and control, etc. The Soviet Republic must at all costs adopt all that is valuable in the achievements of science and technology in this field. The possibility of building socialism depends exactly upon our success in combining the Soviet power and the Soviet organisation of administration with the up-to-date achievements of capitalism. We must organise in Russia the study and teaching of the Taylor system and systematically try it out and adapt it to our own ends. At the same time, in working to raise the productivity of labour, we must take into account the specific features of the transition period from capitalism to socialism, which, on the one hand, require that the foundations be laid of the socialist organisation of competition, and, on the other hand, require the use of compulsion, so that the slogan of the dictatorship of the proletariat shall not be desecrated by the practice of a lily-livered proletarian government.

THE ORGANISATION OF COMPETITION

Among the absurdities which the bourgeoisie are fond of spreading about socialism is the allegation that socialists deny the importance of competition. In fact, it is only socialism which, by abolishing classes, and, consequently, by abolishing the enslavement of the people, for the first time opens the way for competition on a really mass scale. And it is precisely the Soviet form of organisation, by ensuring transition from the formal democracy of the bourgeois republic to real participation of the mass of working people in *administration*, that for the first time puts competition on a broad basis. It is much easier to organise this in the political field than in the economic field; but for the success of socialism, it is the economic field that matters.

Take, for example, a means of organising competition such as publicity. The bourgeois republic ensures publicity only formally; in practice, it subordinates the press to capital, entertains the "mob" with sensationalist political trash and conceals what takes place in the workshops, in commercial transactions, contracts, etc., behind a veil of "trade secrets", which protect "the sacred right of property". The Soviet government has abolished trade secrets; it has taken a new path; but we have done hardly anything to utilise publicity for the purpose of encouraging economic competition. While ruthlessly suppressing the thoroughly mendacious and insolently slanderous bourgeois press, we must set to work systematically to create a press that will not entertain and fool the people with political sensation and trivialities, but which will submit the questions of everyday economic life to the people's judgement and assist in the serious study of these questions. Every factory, every village is a producers' and consumers' commune, whose right and duty it is to apply the general Soviet laws in their own way ("in their own way", not in the sense of violating them, but in the sense that they can apply them in various forms) and in their own way to solve the problem of accounting in the production and distribution of goods. Under capitalism, this was the "private affair" of the individual capitalist, landowner or kulak. Under the Soviet system, it is not a private affair, but a most important affair of state.

We have scarcely yet started on the enormous, difficult but rewarding task of organising competition between communes, of introducing accounting and publicity in the process of the production of grain, clothes and other things, of transforming dry, dead, bureaucratic accounts into living examples, some repulsive, others attractive. Under the capitalist mode of production, the significance of individual example, say the example of a co-operative workshop, was inevitably very much restricted, and only those imbued with petty-bourgeois illusions could dream of "correcting" capitalism through the example of virtuous institutions. After political power has passed to the proletariat, after the expropriators have been expropriated, the situation radically changes and—as prominent socialists have repeatedly pointed out—force of example for the first time is able to influence the people. Model communes must and will serve as educators, teachers, helping to raise the backward communes. The press must serve as an instrument of socialist construction, give publicity to the successes achieved by the model communes in all their details, must study the causes of these successes, the methods of management these communes employ, and, on the other hand, must put on the "black list" those communes which persist in the "traditions of capitalism", i.e., anarchy, laziness, disorder and profiteering. In capitalist society, statistics were entirely a matter for "government servants", or for narrow specialists; we must carry statistics to the people and make them popular so that the working people themselves may gradually learn to understand and see how long and in what way it is necessary to work, how much time and in what way one may rest, so that *the comparison of the business results* of the various communes may become a matter of general interest and study, and that the most outstanding communes may be rewarded immediately (by reducing the working day, raising remuneration, placing a larger amount of cultural or aesthetic facilities or values at their disposal, etc.).

When a new class comes on to the historical scene as the leader and guide of society, a period of violent "rocking", shocks, struggle and storm, on the one hand, and a period of uncertain steps, experiments, wavering, hesitation in regard to the selection of new methods corresponding to new objective circumstances, on the other, are inevitable. The moribund feudal nobility avenged themselves on the bourgeoisie which vanquished them and took their place, not only by conspiracies and attempts at rebellion and restoration, but also by pouring ridicule over the lack of skill, the clumsiness and the mistakes of the "upstarts" and the "insolent" who dared to take over the "sacred helm" of state without the centuries of training which the princes, barons, nobles and dignitaries had had; in exactly the same way the Kornilovs and Kerenskys, the Gotzes and Martovs, the whole of that fraternity of heroes of bourgeois swindling or bourgeois scepticism, avenge themselves on the working class of Russia for having had the "audacity" to take power.

Of course, not weeks, but long months and years are required for a new social class, especially a class which up to now has been oppressed and crushed by poverty and ignorance, to get used to its new position, look around, organise its work and promote its *own* organisers. It is understandable that the Party which leads the revolutionary proletariat has not been able to acquire the experience and habits of large organisational undertakings embracing millions and tens of millions of citizens; the remoulding of the old, almost exclusively agitators' habits is a very lengthy process. But there is nothing impossible in this, and as soon as the necessity for a change is clearly appreciated, as soon as there is firm determination to effect the change and perseverance in pursuing a great and difficult aim, we shall achieve it. There is an enormous amount of organising talent among the "people", i.e., among the workers and the peasants who do not exploit the labour of others. Capital crushed these talented people in thousands; it killed their talent and threw them on to the scrap-heap. We are not yet able to find them, encourage them, put them on their feet, promote them. But we shall learn to do so if we set about it with all-out revolutionary enthusiasm, without which there can be no victorious revolutions.

No profound and mighty popular movement has ever occurred in history without dirty scum rising to the top, without adventurers and rogues, boasters and ranters attaching themselves to the inexperienced innovators, without absurd muddle and fuss, without individual "leaders" trying to deal with twenty matters at once and not finishing any of them. Let the lap-dogs of bourgeois society, from Belorussov to Martov, squeal and yelp about every extra chip that is sent flying in cutting down the big, old wood. What else are lap-dogs for if not to yelp at the proletarian elephant? Let them yelp. We shall go our way and try as carefully and as patiently as possible to test and discover real organisers, people with sober and practical minds, people who combine loyalty to socialism with ability without fuss (and in spite of muddle and fuss) to get a large number of people working together steadily and concertedly within the framework of Soviet organisation. *Only* such people, after they have been tested a dozen times, by being transferred from the simplest to the more difficult tasks, should be promoted to the responsible posts of leaders of the people's labour, leaders of administration. We have not yet learned to do this, but we shall learn.

"HARMONIOUS ORGANISATION" AND DICTATORSHIP

The resolution adopted by the recent Moscow Congress of Soviets advanced as the primary task of the moment the establishment of a "harmonious organisation", and the tightening of discipline.* Everyone now readily "votes for" and "subscribes to" resolutions of this kind; but usually people do not think over the fact that the application of such resolutions calls for coercion—coercion precisely in the form of dictatorship. And yet it would be extremely stupid and absurdly utopian to assume that the transition from capitalism to socialism is possible without coercion and without dictatorship. Marx's theory very definitely opposed this petty-bourgeois-democratic and anarchist absurdity long ago. And Russia of 1917-18 confirms the correctness of Marx's theory in this respect so strikingly, palpably and imposingly that only those who are hopelessly dull or who have obstinately decided to turn their backs on the truth can be under any misapprehension concerning this. Either the dictatorship of Kornilov (if we take him as the Russian type of bourgeois Cavaignac), or the dictatorship of the proletariat—any other choice is *out of the question* for a country which is developing at an extremely rapid rate with extremely sharp turns and amidst desperate ruin created by one of the most horrible wars in history. Every solution that offers a middle path is either a deception of the people by the bourgeoisie—for the bourgeoisie dare not tell the truth, dare not

---

* See *Collected Works*, Vol. 27, p. 200.—*Ed.*

say that they need Kornilov—or an expression of the dull-wittedness of the petty-bourgeois democrats, of the Chernovs, Tseretelis and Martovs, who chatter about the unity of democracy, the dictatorship of democracy, the general democratic front, and similar nonsense. Those whom even the progress of the Russian revolution of 1917-18 has not taught that a middle course is impossible, must be given up for lost.

On the other hand, it is not difficult to see that during every transition from capitalism to socialism, dictatorship is necessary for two main reasons, or along two main channels. Firstly, capitalism cannot be defeated and eradicated without the ruthless suppression of the resistance of the exploiters, who cannot at once be deprived of their wealth, of their advantages of organisation and knowledge, and consequently for a fairly long period will inevitably try to overthrow the hated rule of the poor; secondly, every great revolution, and a socialist revolution in particular, even if there is no external war, is inconceivable without internal war, i.e., civil war, which is even more devastating than external war, and involves thousands and millions of cases of wavering and desertion from one side to another, implies a state of extreme indefiniteness, lack of equilibrium and chaos. And of course, all the elements of disintegration of the old society, which are inevitably very numerous and connected mainly with the petty bourgeoisie (because it is the petty bourgeoisie that every war and every crisis ruins and destroys first), are bound to "reveal themselves" during such a profound revolution. And these elements of disintegration *cannot* "reveal themselves" otherwise than in an increase of crime, hooliganism, corruption, profiteering and outrages of every kind. To put these down requires time and *requires an iron hand*.

There has not been a single great revolution in history in which the people did not instinctively realise this and did not show salutary firmness by shooting thieves on the spot. The misfortune of previous revolutions was that the revolutionary enthusiasm of the people, which sustained them in their state of tension and gave them the strength to suppress ruthlessly the elements of disintegration, did not last long. The social, i.e., the class, reason for this instability of the revolutionary enthusiasm of the people was the weakness of the proletariat, which *alone* is able (if it is sufficiently numerous, class-conscious and disciplined) to win over to its side *the majority* of the working and exploited people (the majority of the poor, to speak more simply and popularly) and retain power sufficiently long to suppress completely all the exploiters as well as all the elements of disintegration.

It was this historical experience of all revolutions, it was this world-historic—economic and political—lesson that Marx summed up when he gave his short, sharp, concise and expressive formula:

dictatorship of the proletariat. And the fact that the Russian revolution has been correct in its approach to this world-historic task *has been proved* by the victorious progress of the Soviet form of organisation among all the peoples and tongues of Russia. For Soviet power is nothing but an organisational form of the dictatorship of the proletariat, the dictatorship of the advanced class, which raises to a new democracy and to independent participation in the administration of the state tens upon tens of millions of working and exploited people, who by their own experience learn to regard the disciplined and class-conscious vanguard of the proletariat as their most reliable leader.

Dictatorship, however, is a big word, and big words should not be thrown about carelessly. Dictatorship is iron rule, government that is revolutionarily bold, swift and ruthless in suppressing both exploiters and hooligans. But our government is excessively mild, very often it resembles jelly more than iron. We must not forget for a moment that the bourgeois and petty-bourgeois element is fighting against the Soviet system in two ways; on the one hand, it is operating from without, by the methods of the Savinkovs, Gotzes, Gegechkoris and Kornilovs, by conspiracies and rebellions, and by their filthy "ideological" reflection, the flood of lies and slander in the Constitutional-Democratic, Right Socialist-Revolutionary and Menshevik press; on the other hand, this element operates from within and takes advantage of every manifestation of disintegration, of every weakness, in order to bribe, to increase indiscipline, laxity and chaos. The nearer we approach the complete military suppression of the bourgeoisie, the more dangerous does the element of petty-bourgeois anarchy become. And the fight against this element cannot be waged solely with the aid of propaganda and agitation, solely by organising competition and by selecting organisers. The struggle must also be waged by means of coercion.

As the fundamental task of the government becomes, not military suppression, but administration, the typical manifestation of suppression and compulsion will be, not shooting on the spot, but trial by court. In this respect also the revolutionary people after October 25, 1917 took the right path and demonstrated the viability of the revolution by setting up their own workers' and peasants' courts, even before the decrees dissolving the bourgeois bureaucratic judiciary were passed. But our revolutionary and people's courts are extremely, incredibly weak. One feels that we have not yet done away with the people's attitude towards the courts as towards something official and alien, an attitude inherited from the yoke of the landowners and of the bourgeoisie. It is not yet sufficiently realised that the courts are an organ which enlists precisely the poor, every one of them, in the work of state administration (for the work of the courts is one of the functions of state administration), that the courts are an *organ of the power* of the proletariat and of the poor peasants, that the courts are an instrument *for inculcating discipline*. There is not yet sufficient appreciation of the simple and obvious fact that if the principal misfortunes of Russia at the present time are hunger and unemployment, these misfortunes cannot be overcome by spurts, but only by comprehensive, all-embracing, country-wide organisation and discipline in order to increase the output of bread for the people and bread for industry (fuel), to transport these in good time to the places where they are required, and to distribute them properly; and it is not fully appreciated that, consequently, it is *those* who violate labour discipline at any factory, in any undertaking, in any matter, who are *responsible* for the sufferings caused by the famine and unemployment, that we must know how to find the guilty ones, to bring them to trial and ruthlessly punish them. Where the petty-bourgeois anarchy against which we must now wage a most persistent struggle makes itself felt is in the failure to appreciate the economic and political connection between famine and unemployment, on the one hand, and general laxity in matters of organisation and discipline, on the other—in the tenacity of the *small proprietor* outlook, namely, I'll grab all I can for myself; the rest can go hang.

In the rail transport service, which perhaps most strikingly embodies the economic ties of an organism created by large-scale capitalism, the struggle between the element of petty-bourgeois laxity and proletarian organisation is particularly evident. The "administrative" elements provide a host of saboteurs and bribe-takers; the best part of the proletarian elements fight for discipline; but among both elements there are, of course, many waverers and "weak" characters who are unable to withstand the "temptation" of profiteering, bribery, personal gain obtained by spoiling the whole apparatus, upon the proper working of which the victory over famine and unemployment depends.

The struggle that has been developing around the recent decree on the management of the railways, the decree which grants individual executives dictatorial powers (or "unlimited" powers), is characteristic. The conscious (and to a large extent, probably, unconscious) representatives of petty-bourgeois laxity would like to see in this granting of "unlimited" (i.e., dictatorial) powers to individuals a departure from the collegiate principle, from democracy and from the principles of Soviet government. Here and there, among Left Socialist-Revolutionaries,[215] a positively hooligan agitation, i.e., agitation appealing to the base instincts and to the small proprietor's urge to "grab all he can", has been developed against the dictatorship decree. The question has become one of really enormous significance. Firstly, the question of principle, namely, is the appointment of individuals, dictators with unlimited powers, in general compatible with the fundamental principles of Soviet government? Secondly, what relation has this case—this precedent, if you will—to the special tasks of government in the present concrete situation? We must deal very thoroughly with both these questions.

That in the history of revolutionary movements the dictatorship of individuals was very often the expression, the vehicle, the channel of the dictatorship of the revolutionary classes has been shown by the irrefutable experience of history. Undoubtedly, the dictatorship of individuals was compatible with bourgeois democracy. On this point, however, the bourgeois denigrators of the Soviet system, as well as their petty-bourgeois henchmen, always display sleight of hand: on the one hand, they declare the Soviet system to be something absurd, anarchistic and savage, and carefully pass over in silence all our historical examples and theoretical arguments which prove that the Soviets are a higher form of democracy, and what is more, the beginning of a *socialist* form of democracy; on the other hand, they demand of us a higher democracy than bourgeois democracy and say: personal dictatorship is absolutely incompatible with your, Bolshevik (i.e., not bourgeois, *but socialist*), Soviet democracy.

These are exceedingly poor arguments. If we are not anarchists, we must admit that the state, *that is, coercion*, is necessary for the transition from capitalism to socialism. The form of coercion is determined by the degree of development of the given revolutionary class, and also by special circumstances, such as, for example, the legacy of a long and reactionary war and the forms of resistance put up by the bourgeoisie and the petty bourgeoisie. There is, therefore, absolutely *no* contradiction in principle between Soviet (*that is*, socialist) democracy and the exercise of dictatorial powers by individuals. The difference between proletarian dictatorship and bourgeois dictatorship is that the former strikes at the exploiting minority in the interests of the exploited majority, and that it is exercised—*also through individuals*—not only by the working and exploited people, but also by organisations which are built in such a way as to rouse these people to history-making activity. (The Soviet organisations are organisations of this kind.)

In regard to the second question, concerning the significance of individual dictatorial powers from the point of view of the specific tasks of the present moment, it must be said that large-scale machine industry—which is precisely the material source, the productive source, the foundation of socialism—calls for absolute and strict *unity of will,* which directs the joint labours of hundreds, thousands and tens of thousands of people. The technical, economic and historical necessity of this is obvious, and all those who have thought about socialism have always regarded it as one of the conditions of socialism. But how can strict unity of will be ensured? By thousands subordinating their will to the will of one.

Given ideal class-consciousness and discipline on the part of those participating in the common work, this subordination would be something like the mild leadership of a conductor of an orchestra. It may assume the sharp forms of a dictatorship if ideal discipline and class-consciousness are lacking. But be that as it may, *unquestioning subordination* to a single will is absolutely necessary for the success of processes organised on the pattern of large-scale machine industry. On the railways it is twice and three times as necessary. In this transition from one political task to another, which *on the surface* is totally dissimilar to the first, lies the whole originality of the present situation. The revolution has only just smashed the oldest, strongest and heaviest of fetters, to which the people submitted under duress. That was yesterday. Today, however, the same revolution demands—precisely in the interests of its development and consolidation, precisely in the interests of socialism—that the people *unquestioningly obey the single will* of the leaders of labour. Of course, such a transition cannot be made at one step. Clearly, it can be achieved only as a result of tremendous jolts, shocks, reversions to old ways, the enormous exertion of effort on the part of the proletarian vanguard, which is leading the people to the new ways. Those who drop into the philistine hysterics of *Novaya Zhizn* or *Vperyod*,[216] *Dyelo Naroda* or *Nash Vek*[217] do not stop to think about this.

Take the psychology of the average, ordinary representative of the toiling and exploited masses, compare it with the objective, material conditions of his life in society. Before the October Revolution he did *not* see a single instance of the propertied, exploiting classes making any real sacrifice for him, giving up anything for his benefit. He did *not* see them giving him the land and liberty that had been repeatedly promised him, giving him peace, sacrificing "Great Power" interests and the interests of Great Power secret treaties, sacrificing capital and profits. He saw this only *after* October 25, 1917, when he took it himself by force, and had to defend by force what he had taken, against the Kerenskys, Gotzes, Gegechkoris, Dutovs and Kornilovs. Naturally, for a certain time, all his attention, all his thoughts, all his spiritual strength, were concentrated on taking a breath, on unbending his back, on straightening his shoulders, on taking the blessings of life that were there for the taking, and that had always been denied him by the now overthrown exploiters. Of course, a certain amount of time is required to enable the ordinary working man not only to see for himself, not only to become convinced, but also to feel that he cannot simply "take", snatch, grab things, that this leads to increased disruption, to ruin, to the return of the Kornilovs. The corresponding change in the conditions of life (and consequently in the psychology) of the ordinary working men is only just beginning. And our whole task, the task of the Communist Party (Bolsheviks), which is the class-conscious spokesman for the strivings of the exploited for emancipation, is to appreciate this change, to understand that it is necessary, to stand at the head of the exhausted people who are wearily seeking a way out and lead them along the true path, along the path of labour discipline, along the path of co-ordinating the task of arguing at mass meetings *about* the conditions of work with the task of unquestioningly obeying the will of the Soviet leader, of the dictator, *during* the work.

The "mania for meetings" is an object of the ridicule, and still more often of the spiteful hissing of the bourgeoisie, the Mensheviks, the *Novaya Zhizn* people, who see only the chaos, the confusion and the outbursts of small-proprietor egoism. But without the discussions at public meetings the mass of the oppressed could never have changed from the discipline forced upon them by the exploiters to conscious, voluntary discipline. The airing of questions at public meetings is the genuine democracy of the working people, their way of unbending their backs, their awakening to a new life, their first steps along the road which they themselves have cleared of vipers (the exploiters, the imperialists, the landowners and capitalists) and which they want to learn to build themselves, in their own way, for themselves, on the principles of their own *Soviet*, and not alien, not aristocratic, not bourgeois rule. It required precisely the October victory of the working people over the exploiters, it required a whole historical period in which the working people themselves could first of all discuss the new conditions of life and the new tasks, in order to make possible the durable transition to superior forms of labour discipline, to the conscious appreciation of the necessity for the dictatorship of the proletariat, to unquestioning obedience to the orders of individual representatives of the Soviet government during the work.

This transition has now begun.

We have successfully fulfilled the first task of the revolution; we have seen how the mass of working people evolved in themselves the fundamental condition for its success: they united their efforts against the exploiters in order to overthrow them. Stages like that of October 1905, February and October 1917 are of world-historic significance.

We have successfully fulfilled the second task of the revolution: to awaken, to raise those very "lower ranks" of society whom the exploiters had pushed down, and who only after October 25, 1917 obtained complete freedom to overthrow the exploiters and to begin to take stock of things and arrange life in their own way. The airing of questions at public meetings by the most oppressed and downtrodden, by the least educated mass of working people, their coming over to the side of the Bolsheviks, their setting up everywhere of their own Soviet organisations—this was the second great stage of the revolution.

The third stage is now beginning. We must consolidate what we ourselves have won, what we ourselves have decreed, made law, discussed, planned—consolidate all this in stable forms of *everyday labour discipline*. This is the most difficult, but the most gratifying task, because only its fulfilment will give us a socialist system. We must learn to combine the "public meeting" democracy of the working people—turbulent, surging, overflowing its banks like a spring flood—with *iron* discipline while at work, with *unquestioning obedience* to the will of a single person, the Soviet leader, while at work.

We have not yet learned to do this.

We shall learn it.

Yesterday we were menaced by the restoration of bourgeois exploitation, personified by the Kornilovs, Gotzes, Dutovs, Gegechkoris and Bogayevskys. We conquered them. This restoration, this very same restoration menaces us today in another form, in the form of the element of petty-bourgeois laxity and anarchism, or small-proprietor "it's not my business" psychology, in the form of the daily, petty, but numerous sorties and attacks of this element against proletarian discipline. We must, and we shall, vanquish this element of petty-bourgeois anarchy.

THE DEVELOPMENT OF SOVIET ORGANISATION

The socialist character of Soviet, i.e., proletarian, democracy, as concretely applied today, lies first in the fact that the electors are the working and exploited people; the bourgeoisie is excluded. Secondly, it lies in the fact that all bureaucratic formalities and restrictions of elections are abolished; the people themselves determine the order and time of elections, and are completely free to recall any elected person. Thirdly, it lies in the creation of the best mass organisation of the vanguard of the working people, i.e., the proletariat engaged in large-scale industry, which enables it to lead the vast mass of the exploited, to draw them into independent political life, to educate them politically by their own experience; therefore for the first time a start is made by the *entire* population in learning the art of administration, and in beginning to administer.

These are the principal distinguishing features of the democracy now applied in Russia, which is a higher *type* of democracy, a break with the bourgeois distortion of democracy, transition to socialist democracy and to the conditions in which the state can begin to wither away.

It goes without saying that the element of petty-bourgeois disorganisation (which must *inevitably* be apparent to some extent in *every* proletarian revolution, and which is especially apparent in our revolution, owing to the petty-bourgeois character of our country, its backwardness and the consequences of a reactionary war) cannot but leave its impress upon the Soviets as well.

We must work unremittingly to develop the organisation of the Soviets and of the Soviet government. There is a petty-bourgeois tendency to transform the members of the Soviets into "parliamentarians", or else into bureaucrats. We must combat this by drawing *all* the members of the Soviets into the practical work of administration. In many places the departments of the Soviets are gradually merging with the Commissariats. Our aim is to draw *the whole of the poor* into the practical work of administration, and all steps that are taken in this direction—the more varied they are, the better—should be carefully recorded, studied, systematised, tested by wider experience and embodied in law. Our aim is to ensure that *every* toiler, having finished his eight hours' "task" in productive labour, shall perform state duties *without pay*; the transition to this is particularly difficult, but this transition alone can guarantee the final consolidation of socialism. Naturally, the novelty and difficulty of the change lead to an abundance of steps being taken, as it were, gropingly, to an abundance of mistakes, vacillation—without this, any marked progress is impossible. The reason why the present position seems peculiar to many of those who would like to be regarded as socialists is that they have been accustomed to contrasting capitalism with socialism abstractly, and that they profoundly put between the two the word "leap" (some of them, recalling fragments of what they have read of Engels's writings, still more profoundly add the phrase "leap from the realm of necessity into the realm of freedom"[218]). The majority of these so-called socialists, who have "read in books" about socialism but who have never seriously thought over the matter, are unable to consider that by "leap" the teachers of socialism meant turning-points on a world-historical scale, and that leaps of this kind extend over decades and even longer periods. Naturally, in such times, the notorious "intelligentsia" provides an infinite number of mourners of the dead. Some mourn over the Constituent Assembly, others mourn over bourgeois discipline, others again mourn over the capitalist system, still others mourn over the cultured landowner, and still others again mourn over imperialist Great Power policy, etc., etc.

The real interest of the epoch of great leaps lies in the fact that the abundance of fragments of the old, which sometimes accumulate more rapidly than the rudiments (not always immediately discernible) of the new, calls for the ability to discern what is most important in the line or chain of development. History knows moments when the most important thing for the success of the revolution is to heap up as large a quantity of the fragments as possible, i.e., to blow up as many of the old institutions as possible; moments arise when enough has been blown up and the next task is to perform the "prosaic" (for the petty-bourgeois revolutionary, the "boring") task of clearing away the fragments; and moments arise when the careful nursing of the rudiments of the new system, which are growing amidst the wreckage on a soil which as yet has been badly cleared of rubble, is the most important thing.

It is not enough to be a revolutionary and an adherent of socialism or a Communist in general. You must be able at each particular moment to find the particular link in the chain which you must grasp with all your might in order to hold the whole chain and to prepare firmly for the transition to the next link; the order of the links, their form, the manner in which they are linked together, the way they differ from each other in the historical chain of events, are not as simple and not as meaningless as those in an ordinary chain made by a smith.

The fight against the bureaucratic distortion of the Soviet form of organisation is assured by the firmness of the connection between the Soviets and the "people", meaning by that the working and exploited people, and by the flexibility and elasticity of this connection. Even in the most democratic capitalist republics in the world, the poor never regard the bourgeois parliament as "their" institution. But the Soviets are "theirs" and not alien institutions to the mass of workers and peasants. The modern "Social-Democrats" of the Scheidemann or, what is almost the same thing, of the Martov type are repelled by the Soviets, and they are drawn towards the respectable bourgeois parliament, or to the Constituent Assembly, in the same way as Turgenev, sixty years ago, was drawn towards a moderate monarchist and noblemen's Constitution and was repelled by the peasant democracy of Dobrolyubov and Chernyshevsky.

It is the closeness of the Soviets to the "people", to the working people, that creates the special forms of recall and other means of control from below which must be most zealously developed now. For example, the Councils of Public Education, as periodical conferences of Soviet electors and their delegates called to discuss and control the activities of the Soviet authorities in this field, deserve full sympathy and support. Nothing could be sillier than to transform the Soviets into something congealed and self-contained. The more resolutely we now have to stand for a ruthlessly firm government, for the dictatorship of individuals in *definite processes of work*, in definite aspects of *purely executive* functions, the more varied must be the forms and methods of control from below in order to counteract every shadow of a possibility of distorting the principles of Soviet government, in order repeatedly and tirelessly to weed out bureaucracy.

CONCLUSION

An extraordinarily difficult, complex and dangerous situation in international affairs; the necessity of manoeuvring and retreating; a period of waiting for new outbreaks of the revolution which is maturing in the West at a painfully slow pace; within the country a period of slow construction and ruthless "tightening up", of prolonged and persistent struggle waged by stern, proletarian discipline against the menacing element of petty-bourgeois laxity and anarchy —these in brief are the distinguishing features of the special stage of the socialist revolution in which we are now living. This is the link in the historical chain of events which we must at present grasp with all our might in order to prove equal to the tasks that confront us before passing to the next link to which we are drawn by a special brightness, the brightness of the victories of the international proletarian revolution.

Try to compare with the ordinary everyday concept "revolutionary" the slogans that follow from the specific conditions of the present stage, namely, manoeuvre, retreat, wait, build slowly, ruthlessly tighten up, rigorously discipline, smash laxity.... Is it surprising that when certain "revolutionaries" hear this they are seized with noble indignation and begin to "thunder" abuse at us for forgetting the traditions of the October Revolution, for compromising with the bourgeois experts, for compromising with the bourgeoisie, for being petty bourgeois, reformists, and so on and so forth?

The misfortune of these sorry "revolutionaries" is that even those of them who are prompted by the best motives in the world and are absolutely loyal to the cause of socialism fail to understand the particular, and particularly "unpleasant". condition that a backward country, which has been lacerated by a reactionary and disastrous war and which began the socialist revolution long before the more advanced countries, inevitably has to pass through; they lack stamina in the difficult moments of a difficult transition. Naturally, it is the "Left Socialist-Revolutionaries" who are acting as an "official" opposition of *this* kind against our Party. Of course, there are and always will be individual exceptions from group and class types. But social types remain. In the land in which the small-proprietor population greatly predominates over the purely proletarian population, the difference between the proletarian revolutionary and petty-bourgeois revolutionary will inevitably make itself felt, and from time to time will make itself felt very sharply. The petty-bourgeois revolutionary wavers and vacillates at every turn of events; he is an ardent revolutionary in March 1917 and praises "coalition" in May, hates the Bolsheviks (or laments over their "adventurism") in July and apprehensively turns away from them at the end of October, supports them in December, and, finally, in March and April 1918 such types, more often than not, turn up their noses contemptuously and say: "I am not one of those who sing hymns to 'organic' work, to practicalness and gradualism."

The social origin of such types is the small proprietor, who has been driven to frenzy by the horrors of war, by sudden ruin, by unprecedented torments of famine and devastation, who hysterically rushes about seeking a way out, seeking salvation, places his confidence in the proletariat and supports it one moment and the next gives way to fits of despair. We must clearly understand and firmly remember the fact that socialism cannot be built on such a social basis. The only class that can lead the working and exploited people is the class that unswervingly follows its path without losing courage and without giving way to despair even at the most difficult, arduous and dangerous stages. Hysterical impulses are of no use to us. What we need is the steady advance of the iron battalions of the proletariat.

Written between
April 13 and 26, 1918

Published April 28, 1918
in *Pravda* No. 83
and in the Supplement
to *Izvestia VTsIK* No. 85
Signed: *N. Lenin*

Collected Works, Vol. 27

"LEFT-WING" CHILDISHNESS
AND THE PETTY-BOURGEOIS MENTALITY

The publication by a small group of "Left Communists" of their journal, *Kommunist*[219] (No. 1, April 20, 1918), and of their "theses", strikingly confirms my views expressed in the pamphlet *The Immediate Tasks of the Soviet Government*.* There could not be better confirmation, in political literature, of the utter naïveté of the defence of petty-bourgeois sloppiness that is sometimes concealed by "Left" slogans. It is useful and necessary to deal with the arguments of "Left Communists" because they are characteristic of the period we are passing through. They show up with exceptional clarity the negative side of the "core" of this period. They are instructive, because the people we are dealing with are the best of those who have failed to understand the present period, people who by their knowledge and loyalty stand far, far above the *ordinary* representatives of the same mistaken views, namely, the Left Socialist-Revolutionaries.

I

As a political magnitude, or as a group claiming to play a political role, the "Left Communist" group has presented its "Theses on the Present Situation". It is a good Marxist custom to give a coherent and complete exposition of the principles underlying one's views and tactics. And this good Marxist custom has helped to reveal the mistake committed by our "Lefts", because the mere attempt to argue and not to declaim exposes the unsoundness of their argument.

The first thing that strikes one is the abundance of allusions, hints and evasions with regard to the old question of whether it was right to conclude the Brest Treaty. The "Lefts" dare not put the question in a straightforward manner. They flounder about in a comical fashion, pile argument on argument, fish for reasons,

* See pp. 401-31 of the present volume.—*Ed.*

plead that "on the one hand" it may be so, but "on the other hand" it may not, their thoughts wander over all and sundry subjects, they try all the time not to see that they are defeating themselves. The "Lefts" are very careful to quote the figures: twelve votes at the Party Congress against peace, twenty-eight votes in favour,[220] but they discreetly refrain from mentioning that of the hundreds of votes cast at the meeting of the Bolshevik group of the Congress of Soviets they obtained less than one-tenth.[221] They have invented a "theory" that the peace was carried by "the exhausted and de-classed elements", while it was opposed by "the workers and peasants of the southern regions, where there was greater vitality in economic life and the supply of bread was more assured".... Can one do anything but laugh at this? There is not a word about the voting at the All-Ukraine Congress of Soviets in favour of peace, nor about the social and class character of the typically petty-bourgeois and declassed political conglomeration in Russia who were opposed to peace (the Left Socialist-Revolutionary party). In an utterly childish manner, by means of amusing "scientific" ex-planations, they try to conceal their own bankruptcy, to conceal the facts, the mere review of which would show that it was precisely the declassed, intellectual "cream" of the party, the élite, who op-posed the peace with slogans couched in revolutionary petty-bour-geois phrases, that it was precisely the *mass* of workers and ex-ploited peasants who carried the peace.

Nevertheless, in spite of all the above-mentioned declarations and evasions of the "Lefts" on the question of war and peace, the plain and obvious truth manages to come to light. The authors of the theses are compelled to admit that "the conclusion of peace has for the time being weakened the imperialists' attempts to make a deal on a world scale" (this is inaccurately formulated by the "Lefts", but this is not the place to deal with inaccuracies). "The conclusion of peace has already caused the conflict between the imperialist powers to become more acute."

Now this is a fact. Here is something that has *decisive* signif-icance. That is why those who opposed the conclusion of peace were unwittingly playthings in the hands of the imperialists and fell into the trap laid for them by the imperialists. For, until the world socialist revolution breaks out, until it embraces several countries and is strong enough to overcome *international imperial-ism*, it is the direct duty of the socialists who have conquered in one country (especially a backward one) *not* to accept battle against the giants of imperialism. Their duty is to try to avoid battle, to wait until the conflicts between the imperialists weaken them *even more*, and bring the revolution in other countries even nearer. Our "Lefts" did not understand this simple truth in January, February and March. Even now they are afraid of admitting it openly. But it comes to light through all their confused reasoning like "on the one hand it must be confessed, on the other hand one must admit".

"During the coming spring and summer," the "Lefts" write in their theses, "the collapse of the imperialist system must begin. In the event of a victory for German imperialism in the present phase of the war this collapse can only be postponed, but it will then express itself in even more acute forms."

This formulation is even more childishly inaccurate despite its playing at science. It is natural for children to "understand" science to mean something that can determine in what year, spring, summer, autumn or winter the "collapse must begin".

These are ridiculous, vain attempts to ascertain what cannot be ascertained. No serious politician will ever say *when* this or that collapse of a "system" "must begin" (the more so that the collapse of the *system* has already begun, and it is now a question of the moment when the outbreak of revolution in *particular* countries will begin). But an indisputable truth forces its way through this childishly helpless formulation, namely, the outbreaks of revolution in other, more advanced, countries are *nearer* now, a month since the beginning of the "respite" which followed the conclusion of peace, than they were a month or six weeks ago.

What follows?

It follows that the peace supporters were absolutely right, and their stand has been justified by the course of events. They were right in having drummed into the minds of the lovers of ostentation that one must be able to calculate the balance of forces and *not help* the imperialists by making the battle against socialism easier for them, when socialism is still weak, and when the chances of the battle are manifestly *against* socialism.

Our "Left" Communists, however, who are also fond of calling themselves "proletarian" Communists, because there is very little that is proletarian about them and very much that is petty-bourgeois, are incapable of giving thought to the balance of forces, to calculating it. This is the core of Marxism and Marxist tactics, but they disdainfully brush aside the "core" with "proud" phrases such as:

"...That the masses have become firmly imbued with an inactive 'peace mentality' is an objective fact of the political situation...."

What a gem! After three years of the most agonising and reactionary war, the people, thanks to Soviet power and its correct tactics, which never lapsed into mere phrase-making, have obtained a very, very brief, insecure and far from sufficient respite. The "Left" intellectual striplings, however, with the magnificence of a self-infatuated Narcissus, profoundly declare "that the masses [???] have become firmly imbued [!!!] with an inactive [!!!???] peace mentality". Was I not right when I said at the Party Congress that the paper or journal of the "Lefts" ought to have been called not *Kommunist* but *Szlachcic*?[222]

Can a Communist with the slightest understanding of the mentality and the conditions of life of the toiling and exploited people descend to the point of view of the typical declassed petty-bourgeois intellectual with the mental outlook of a noble or *szlachcic*, which declares that a "peace mentality" is "inactive" and believes that the brandishing of a cardboard sword is "activity"? For our "Lefts" merely brandish a cardboard sword when they ignore the universally known fact, of which the war in the Ukraine has served as an additional proof, that peoples utterly exhausted by three years of butchery cannot go on fighting without a respite; and that war, if it cannot be organised on a national scale, very often creates a mentality of disintegration peculiar to petty proprietors, instead of the iron discipline of the proletariat. Every page of *Kommunist* shows that our "Lefts" have no idea of iron proletarian discipline and how it is achieved, that they are thoroughly imbued with the mentality of the declassed petty-bourgeois intellectual.

II

Perhaps all these phrases of the "Lefts" about war can be put down to mere childish exuberance, which, moreover, concerns the past, and therefore has not a shadow of political significance? This is the argument some people put up in defence of our "Lefts". But this is wrong. Anyone aspiring to political leadership must be able to *think out* political problems, and lack of this ability converts the "Lefts" into spineless preachers of a policy of vacillation, which objectively can have only one result, namely, by their vacillation the "Lefts" *are helping* the imperialists to provoke the Russian Soviet Republic into a battle that will obviously be to its disadvantage, they *are helping* the imperialists to draw us into a snare. Listen to this:

"... The Russian workers' revolution cannot 'save itself' by abandoning the path of world revolution, by continually avoiding battle and yielding to the pressure of international capital, by making concessions to 'home capital'.

"From this point of view it is necessary to adopt a determined class international policy which will unite international revolutionary propaganda by word and deed, and to strengthen the organic connection with international socialism (and not with the international bourgeoisie)...."

I shall deal separately with the thrusts at home policy contained in this passage. But examine this riot of phrase-making—and timidity in deeds—in the sphere of foreign policy. What tactics *are binding* at the *present* time on all who do not wish to be tools of imperialist provocation, and who do not wish to walk into the snare? Every politician must give a clear, straightforward reply to this question. Our Party's reply is well known. At the *present* moment we must *retreat* and avoid battle. Our "Lefts" dare not contradict this and shoot into the air: "A determined class international policy"!!

This is deceiving the people. If you want to fight now, say so openly. If you don't wish to *retreat* now, say so openly. Otherwise, in your objective role, you are a tool of imperialist provocation. And your subjective "mentality" is that of a frenzied petty bourgeois who swaggers and blusters but senses perfectly well that the proletarian is *right* in retreating and in trying to retreat in an organised way. He senses that the proletarian is right in arguing that because we lack strength we must retreat (before Western and Eastern imperialism) even as far as the Urals, for in this lies the *only* chance of playing for time while the revolution in the West matures, the revolution which is not "bound" (despite the twaddle of the "Lefts") to begin in "spring or summer", but which is coming nearer and becoming more probable *every month*.

The "Lefts" have no policy of their "own". They *dare not* declare that retreat at the *present moment* is unnecessary. They twist and turn, play with words, substitute the question of "continuously" avoiding battle for the question of avoiding battle at the *present moment*. They blow soap bubbles such as "international revolutionary propaganda by deed"!! What does this mean?

It can only mean one of two things: either it is mere Nozdryovism,[223] or it means an offensive war to overthrow international imperialism. Such nonsense cannot be uttered openly, and that is why the "Left" Communists are obliged to take refuge from the derision of every politically conscious proletarian behind high-sounding and empty phrases. They hope the inattentive reader will not notice the real meaning of the phrase "international revolutionary propaganda by deed".

The flaunting of high-sounding phrases is characteristic of the declassed petty-bourgeois intellectuals. The organised proletarian Communists will certainly punish this "habit" with nothing less than derision and expulsion from all responsible posts. The people must be told the bitter truth simply, clearly and in a straightforward manner: it is possible, and even probable, that the war party will again get the upper hand in Germany (that is, an offensive against us will commence at once), and that Germany together with Japan, by official agreement or by tacit understanding, will partition and strangle us. Our tactics, if we do not want to listen to the ranters, must be to wait, procrastinate, avoid battle and retreat. If we shake off the ranters and "brace ourselves" by creating genuinely iron, genuinely proletarian, genuinely communist discipline, we shall have a good chance of gaining many months. And then by retreating even, if the worst comes to the worst, to the Urals, we shall *make it easier* for our ally (the international proletariat) to come to our aid, to "catch up" (to use the language of sport) the distance between the beginning of revolutionary outbreaks and revolution.

These, and these alone, are the tactics which can in fact strengthen the connection between one temporarily isolated section of international socialism and the other sections. But to tell the truth, all that your arguments lead to, dear "Left Communists", is the "strengthening of the organic connection" between one high-sounding phrase and another. A bad sort of "organic connection", this!

I shall enlighten you, my amiable friends, as to why such disaster overtook you. It is because you devote more effort to learning by heart and committing to memory revolutionary slogans than to thinking them out. This leads you to write "the defence of the socialist fatherland" in quotation marks, which are probably meant to signify your attempts at being ironical, but which really prove that you are muddle-heads. You are accustomed to regard "defencism" as something base and despicable; you have learned this and committed it to memory. You have learned this by heart so thoroughly that some of you have begun talking nonsense to the effect that defence of the fatherland in an imperialist *epoch* is impermissible (as a matter of fact, it is impermissible only in an imperialist, reactionary war, waged by the bourgeoisie). But you have not thought out why and when "defencism" is abominable.

To recognise defence of the fatherland means recognising the legitimacy and justice of war. Legitimacy and justice from what point of view? Only from the point of view of the socialist proletariat and its struggle for its emancipation. We do not recognise any other point of view. If war is waged by the exploiting class with the object of strengthening its rule as a class, such a war is a criminal war, and "defencism" in *such* a war is a base betrayal of socialism. If war is waged by the proletariat after it has conquered the bourgeoisie in its own country, and is waged with the object of strengthening and developing socialism, such a war is legitimate and "holy".

We have been "defencists" since October 25, 1917. I have said this more than once very definitely, and you dare not deny this. It is precisely in the interests of "strengthening the connection" with international socialism that we *are in duty bound* to defend our *socialist* fatherland. Those who treat frivolously the defence of the country in which the proletariat has already achieved victory are the ones who destroy the connection with international socialism. When we were the representatives of an oppressed class we did not adopt a frivolous attitude towards defence of the fatherland in an imperialist war. We opposed such defence on principle. Now that we have become representatives of the ruling class, which has begun to organise socialism, we demand that everybody adopt a *serious* attitude towards defence of the country. And adopting a serious attitude towards defence of the country means thoroughly preparing for it, and strictly calculating the balance of forces. If our forces are obviously small, the best means of defence is *retreat into the interior of the country* (anyone who regards this as an artificial formula, made up to suit the needs of the moment, should read old Clausewitz, one of the greatest authorities on military matters, concerning the lessons of history to be learned in this connection). The "Left Communists", however, do not give the slightest indication that they understand the significance of the question of the balance of forces.

When we were opposed to defencism on principle we were justified in holding up to ridicule those who wanted to "save" their fatherland, ostensibly in the interests of socialism. When we gained the right to be proletarian defencists the whole question was radically altered. It has become our duty to calculate with the utmost accuracy the different forces involved, to weigh with the utmost care the chances of our ally (the international proletariat) being able to come to our aid in time. It is in the interest of capital to destroy its enemy (the revolutionary proletariat) bit by bit, before the workers in all countries have united (actually united, i.e., by beginning the revolution). It is in our interest to do all that is possible, to take advantage of the slightest opportunity to postpone the decisive battle until the moment (or *until after* the moment) the revolutionary workers' contingents have united in a single great international army.

III

We shall pass on to the misfortunes of our "Left" Communists in the sphere of home policy. It is difficult to read the following phrases in the theses on the *present* situation without smiling.

"... The systematic use of the remaining means of production is conceivable only if a most determined policy of socialisation is pursued" ... "not to capitulate to the bourgeoisie and its petty-bourgeois intellectualist servitors, but to rout the bourgeoisie and to put down sabotage completely...."

Dear "Left Communists", how determined they are, but how little thinking they display. What do they mean by pursuing "a most determined policy of socialisation"?

One may or may not be determined on the question of nationalisation or confiscation, but the whole point is that even the greatest possible "determination" in the world is not enough to pass *from* nationalisation and confiscation *to* socialisation. The misfortune of our "Lefts" is that by their naïve, childish combination of the words "most determined policy of socialisation" they reveal their utter failure to understand the crux of the question, the crux of the "present" situation. The misfortune of our "Lefts" is that they have missed the very essence of the "present situation", the transition from confiscation (the carrying out of which requires above all determination in a politician) to socialisation (the carrying out of which requires a *different* quality in the revolutionary).

Yesterday, the main task of the moment was, as determinedly as possible, to nationalise, confiscate, beat down and crush the bourgeoisie, and put down sabotage. Today, only a blind man could fail to see that we have nationalised, confiscated, beaten down and put down more *than we have had time to count*. The difference between socialisation and simple confiscation is that confiscation can be carried out by "determination" alone, without the ability to calculate and distribute properly, *whereas socialisation cannot be brought about without this ability*.

The historical service we have rendered is that yesterday we were determined (and we shall be tomorrow) in confiscating, in beating down the bourgeoisie, in putting down sabotage. To write about this today in "theses on the present situation" is to fix one's eyes on the past and to fail to understand the transition to the future.

"... To put down sabotage completely...." What a task they have found! Our saboteurs are quite sufficiently "put down". What we lack is something quite different. We lack the proper *calculation* of which saboteurs to set to work and where to place them. We lack the organisation of *our own* forces that is needed for, say, one Bolshevik leader or controller to be able to supervise a hundred saboteurs who are now coming into our service. When that is how matters stand, to flaunt such phrases as "a most determined policy of socialisation", "routing", and "completely putting down" is just missing the mark. It is typical of the petty-bourgeois revolutionary not to notice that routing, putting down, etc., is not enough for socialism. It is sufficient for a small proprietor enraged against a big proprietor. But no proletarian revolutionary would ever fall into such error.

If the words we have quoted provoke a smile, the following discovery made by the "Left Communists" will provoke nothing short of Homeric laughter. According to them, under the "Bolshevik deviation to the right" the Soviet Republic is threatened with "evolution towards state capitalism". They have really frightened us this time! And with what gusto these "Left Communists" repeat this threatening revelation in their theses and articles....

It has not occurred to them that state capitalism would be a *step forward* as compared with the present state of affairs in our Soviet Republic. If in approximately six months' time state capitalism became established in our Republic, this would be a great success and a sure guarantee that within a year socialism will have gained a permanently firm hold and will have become invincible in our country.

I can imagine with what noble indignation a "Left Communist" will recoil from these words, and what "devastating criticism" he will make to the workers against the "Bolshevik deviation to the right". What! Transition to state *capitalism* in the Soviet *Socialist* Republic would be a step forward?... Isn't this the betrayal of socialism?

Here we come to the root of the *economic* mistake of the "Left Communists". And that is why we must deal with this point in greater detail.

Firstly, the "Left Communists" do not understand what kind of *transition* it is from capitalism to socialism that gives us the right and the grounds to call our country the Socialist Republic of Soviets.

Secondly, they reveal their petty-bourgeois mentality precisely by *not recognising* the petty-bourgeois element as the *principal* enemy of socialism in our country.

Thirdly, in making a bugbear of "state capitalism", they betray their failure to understand that the Soviet state differs from the bourgeois state economically.

Let us examine these three points.

No one, I think, in studying the question of the economic system of Russia, has denied its transitional character. Nor, I think, has any Communist denied that the term Socialist Soviet Republic implies the determination of Soviet power to achieve the transition to socialism, and not that the new economic system is recognised as a socialist order.

But what does the word "transition" mean? Does it not mean, as applied to an economy, that the present system contains elements, particles, fragments of *both* capitalism and socialism? Everyone will admit that it does. But not all who admit this take the trouble to consider what elements actually constitute the various socio-economic structures that exist in Russia at the present time. And this is the crux of the question.

Let us enumerate these elements:

1) patriarchal, i.e., to a considerable extent natural, peasant farming;

2) small commodity production (this includes the majority of those peasants who sell their grain);

3) private capitalism;

4) state capitalism;

5) socialism.

Russia is so vast and so varied that all these different types of socio-economic structures are intermingled. This is what constitutes the specific feature of the situation.

The question arises: what elements predominate? Clearly, in a small-peasant country, the petty-bourgeois element predominates and it must predominate, for the great majority of those working the land are small commodity producers. The shell of our state capitalism (grain monopoly, state controlled entrepreneurs and traders, bourgeois co-operators) is pierced now in one place, now in another by *profiteers*, the chief object of profiteering being *grain*.

It is in this field that the main struggle is being waged. Between what elements is this struggle being waged if we are to speak in terms of economic categories such as "state capitalism"? Between the fourth and the fifth in the order in which I have just enumerated them? Of course not. It is not state capitalism that is at war with socialism, but the petty bourgeoisie plus private capitalism fighting together against both state capitalism and socialism. The petty bourgeoisie oppose *every* kind of state interference, accounting and control, whether it be state capitalist or state socialist. This is an absolutely unquestionable fact of reality, and the root of the economic mistake of the "Left Communists" is that they have failed to understand it. The profiteer, the commercial racketeer, the disrupter of monopoly—these are our principal "internal" enemies, the enemies of the economic measures of Soviet power. A hundred and twenty-five years ago it might have been excusable for the French petty bourgeoisie, the most ardent and sincere revolutionaries, to try to crush the profiteer by executing a few of the "chosen" and by making thunderous declamations. Today, however, the purely rhetorical attitude to this question assumed by some Left Socialist-Revolutionaries can rouse nothing but disgust and revulsion in every politically conscious revolutionary. We know perfectly well that the economic basis of profiteering is both the small proprietors, who are exceptionally widespread in Russia, and private capitalism, of which *every* petty bourgeois is an agent. We know that the million tentacles of this petty-bourgeois hydra now and again encircle various sections of the workers, that, *instead of state monopoly*, profiteering forces its way into every pore of our social and economic organism.

Those who fail to see this show by their blindness that they are slaves of petty-bourgeois prejudices. This is precisely the case with our "Left Communists", who in words (and of course in their deepest convictions) are merciless enemies of the petty bourgeoisie, while in deeds they help only the petty bourgeoisie, serve only this section of the population and express only its point of view by fighting—*in April 1918!!*—against ... "state capitalism". They are wide of the mark!

The petty bourgeoisie have money put away, the few thousand that they made during the war by "honest" and especially by dishonest means. They are the characteristic economic type that serves as the basis of profiteering and private capitalism. Money is a certificate entitling the possessor to receive social wealth; and a vast section of small proprietors, numbering millions, cling to this certificate and conceal it from the "state". They do not believe in socialism or communism, and "mark time" until the proletarian storm blows over. Either we subordinate the petty bourgeoisie to *our* control and accounting (we can do this if we organise the poor, that is, the majority of the population or semi-proletarians, around the politically conscious proletarian vanguard), or they will overthrow our workers' power as surely and as inevitably as the revolution was overthrown by the Napoleons and Cavaignacs who sprang from this very soil of petty proprietorship. This is how the question stands. Only the Left Socialist-Revolutionaries fail to see this plain and evident truth through their mist of empty phrases about the "toiling" peasants. But who takes these phrase-mongering Left Socialist-Revolutionaries seriously?

The petty bourgeois who hoards his thousands is an enemy of state capitalism. He wants to employ his thousands just for himself, against the poor, in opposition to any kind of state control. And the sum total of these thousands, amounting to many thousands of millions, forms the base for profiteering, which undermines our socialist construction. Let us assume that a certain number of workers produce in a few days values equal to 1,000. Let us then assume that 200 of this total vanishes owing to petty profiteering, various kinds of embezzlement and the "evasion" by the small proprietors of Soviet decrees and regulations. Every politically conscious worker will say that if better order and organisation could be obtained at the price of 300 out of the 1,000 he would willingly give 300 instead of 200, for it will be quite easy under Soviet power to reduce this "tribute" later on to, say, 100 or 50, once order and organisation are established and once the petty-bourgeois disruption of state monopoly is completely overcome.

This simple illustration in figures, which I have deliberately simplified to the utmost in order to make it absolutely clear, explains the present *correlation* of state capitalism and socialism. The workers hold state power and have every legal opportunity of "taking" the whole thousand, without giving up a single kopek, except for socialist purposes. This legal opportunity, which rests upon the actual transition of power to the workers, is an element of socialism.

But in many ways, the small proprietary and private capitalist element undermines this legal position, drags in profiteering, hinders the execution of Soviet decrees. State capitalism would be a gigantic step forward *even if* we paid *more* than we are paying at present (I took a numerical example deliberately to bring this out more sharply), because it is worth while paying for "tuition", because it is useful for the workers, because victory over disorder, economic ruin and laxity is the most important thing; because the continuation of the anarchy of small ownership is the greatest, the most serious danger, and it will *certainly* be our ruin (unless we overcome it), whereas not only will the payment of a heavier tribute to state capitalism not ruin us, it will lead us to socialism by the surest road. When the working class has learned how to defend the state system against the anarchy of small ownership, when it has learned to organise large-scale production on a national scale, along state capitalist lines, it will hold, if I may use the expression, all the trump cards, and the consolidation of socialism will be assured.

In the first place, *economically*, state capitalism is immeasurably superior to our present economic system.

In the second place, there is nothing terrible in it for Soviet power, for the Soviet state is a state in which the power of the workers and the poor is assured. The "Left Communists" failed to understand these unquestionable truths, which, of course, a "Left Socialist-Revolutionary", who cannot connect any ideas on political economy in his head in general, will never understand, but which every Marxist *must* admit. It is not even worth while arguing with a Left Socialist-Revolutionary. It is enough to point to him as a "repulsive example" of a windbag. But the "Left Communists" *must* be argued with because it is Marxists who are making a mistake, and an analysis of their mistake will help the *working class* to find the true road.

IV

To make things even clearer, let us first of all take the most concrete example of state capitalism. Everybody knows what this example is. It is Germany. Here we have "the last word" in modern large-scale capitalist engineering and planned organisation, *subordinated to Junker-bourgeois imperialism*. Cross out the words in italics, and in place of the militarist, Junker, bourgeois, imperialist *state* put *also a state*, but of a different social type, of a different class content—a *Soviet* state, that is, a proletarian state, and you will have the *sum total* of the conditions necessary for socialism.

Socialism is inconceivable without large-scale capitalist engineering based on the latest discoveries of modern science. It is inconceivable without planned state organisation, which keeps tens of millions of people to the strictest observance of a unified standard in production and distribution. We Marxists have always spoken of this, and it is not worth while wasting two seconds talking to people who do not understand *even* this (anarchists and a good half of the Left Socialist-Revolutionaries).

At the same time socialism is inconceivable unless the proletariat is the ruler of the state. This also is ABC. And history (which nobody, except Menshevik blockheads of the first order, ever expected to bring about "complete" socialism smoothly, gently, easily and simply) has taken such a peculiar course that it *has given birth* in 1918 to two unconnected halves of socialism existing side by side like two future chickens in the single shell of international imperialism. In 1918 Germany and Russia have become the most striking embodiment of the material realisation of the economic, the productive and the socio-economic conditions for socialism. on the one hand, and the political conditions, on the other.

A successful proletarian revolution in Germany would immediately and very easily smash any shell of imperialism (which unfortunately is made of the best steel, and hence cannot be broken by the efforts of *any* ... chicken) and would bring about the victory of world socialism for certain, without any difficulty, or with slight difficulty —if, of course, by "difficulty" we mean difficult on a world-historical scale, and not in the parochial philistine sense.

While the revolution in Germany is still slow in "coming forth", our task is to study the state capitalism of the Germans, to spare *no effort* in copying it and not shrink from adopting *dictatorial* methods to hasten the copying of it. Our task is to hasten this copying even more than Peter hastened the copying of Western culture by barbarian Russia, and we must not hesitate to use barbarous methods in fighting barbarism. If there are anarchists and Left Socialist-Revolutionaries (I recall off-hand the speeches of Karelin and Ghe at the meeting of the Central Executive Committee) who indulge in Narcissus-like reflections and say that it is unbecoming for us revolutionaries to "take lessons" from German imperialism, there is only one thing we can say in reply: the revolution that took these people seriously would perish irrevocably (and deservedly).

At present, petty-bourgeois capitalism prevails in Russia, and it is *one and the same road* that leads from it to *both* large-scale state capitalism and to socialism, *through one and the same* intermediary station called "national accounting and control of production and distribution". Those who fail to understand this are committing an unpardonable mistake in economics. Either they do not know the facts of life, do not see what actually exists and are unable to look the truth in the face, or they confine themselves to abstractly comparing "capitalism" with "socialism" and fail to study the concrete forms and stages of the transition that is taking place in our country. Let it be said in parentheses that this is the very theoretical mistake which misled the best people in the *Novaya Zhizn* and *Vperyod* camp. The worst and the mediocre of these, owing to their stupidity and spinelessness, tag along behind the bourgeoisie, of whom they stand in awe. The best of them have failed to understand that it was not without reason that the teachers of socialism spoke of a whole period of transition from capitalism to socialism and emphasised the "prolonged birthpangs" of the new society. And this new society is again an abstraction which can come into being only by passing through a series of varied, imperfect concrete attempts to create this or that socialist state.

It is because Russia cannot advance from the economic situation now existing here without traversing the ground which *is common* to state capitalism and to socialism (national accounting and control) that the attempt to frighten others as well as themselves with "evolution *towards* state capitalism" (*Kommunist* No. 1, p. 8, col. 1) is utter theoretical nonsense. This is letting one's thoughts wander away from the true road of "evolution", and failing to understand what this road is. In practice, it is equivalent to pulling us back to small proprietary capitalism.

In order to convince the reader that this is not the first time I have given this "high" appreciation of state capitalism and that I gave it *before* the Bolsheviks seized power I take the liberty of quoting the following passage from my pamphlet *The Impending Catastrophe and How to Combat It*, written in September 1917.

"...Try to substitute *for* the Junker-capitalist state, for the landowner-capitalist state, a *revolutionary-democratic* state, i.e., a state which in a revolutionary way abolishes *all* privileges and does not fear to introduce the fullest democracy in a revolutionary way. You will find that, given a really revolutionary-democratic state, state-monopoly capitalism inevitably and unavoidably implies a step, and more than one step, towards socialism!

"...For socialism is merely the next step forward from state-capitalist monopoly.

"...State-monopoly capitalism is a complete *material* preparation for socialism, the *threshold* of socialism, a rung on the ladder of history between which and the rung called socialism *there are no intermediate rungs*" (pp. 27 and 28).*

Please note that this was written when Kerensky was in power, that we are discussing *not* the dictatorship of the proletariat, *not* the socialist state, but the "revolutionary-democratic" state. Is it not clear that the *higher* we stand on this political ladder, *the more completely* we incorporate the socialist state and the dictatorship of the proletariat in the Soviets, *the less* ought we to fear "state capitalism"? Is it not clear that from the *material*, economic and productive point of view, we are not yet on "the threshold" of

---

* See *Collected Works*, Vol. 25, pp. 357, 358, 359.—*Ed.*

socialism? Is it not clear that we cannot pass through the door of socialism without crossing "the threshold" we have not yet reached?

From whatever side we approach the question, only one conclusion can be drawn: the argument of the "Left Communists" about the "state capitalism" which is alleged to be threatening us is an utter mistake in economics and is evident proof that they are complete slaves of petty-bourgeois ideology.

V

The following is also extremely instructive.

When we argued with Comrade Bukharin* in the Central Executive Committee, he declared, among other things, that on the question of high salaries for specialists "we" (evidently meaning the "Left Communists") were "more to the right than Lenin", for in this case "we" saw no deviation from principle, bearing in mind Marx's words that under certain conditions it is more expedient for the working class to "buy out the whole lot of them"[224] (namely, the whole lot of capitalists, i.e., *to buy* from the bourgeoisie the land, factories, works and other means of production).

This extremely interesting statement shows, in the first place, that Bukharin is head and shoulders above the Left Socialist-Revolutionaries and anarchists, that he is by no means hopelessly stuck in the mud of phrase-making, but on the contrary is making efforts to think out the *concrete* difficulties of the transition—the painful and difficult transition—from capitalism to socialism.

In the second place, this statement makes Bukharin's mistake still more glaring.

Let us consider Marx's idea carefully.

Marx was talking about the Britain of the seventies of the last century, about the culminating point in the development of pre-monopoly capitalism. At that time Britain was a country in which militarism and bureaucracy were less pronounced than in any other, a country in which there was the greatest possibility of a "peaceful" victory for socialism in the sense of the workers "buying out" the bourgeoisie. And Marx said that under certain conditions the workers would certainly not refuse to buy out the bourgeoisie. Marx did not commit himself, or the future leaders of the socialist revolution, to matters of form, to ways and means of bringing about the revolution. He understood perfectly well that a vast number of new problems would arise, that the whole situation would change in the course of the revolution, and that the situation would change *radically* and *often* in the course of revolution.

---

* Ibid., Vol. 27, pp. 310-12.—*Ed.*

Well, and what about Soviet Russia? Is it not clear that *after* the seizure of power by the proletariat and *after* the crushing of the exploiters' armed resistance and sabotage, *certain* conditions prevail which correspond to those which might have existed in Britain half a century ago had a peaceful transition to socialism begun there? The subordination of the capitalists to the workers in Britain would have been assured at that time owing to the following circumstances: 1) the absolute preponderance of workers, of proletarians, in the population owing to the absence of a peasantry (in Britain in the seventies there was hope of an extremely rapid spread of socialism among agricultural labourers); 2) the excellent organisation of the proletariat in trade unions (Britain was at that time the leading country in the world in this respect); 3) the comparatively high level of culture of the proletariat, which had been trained by centuries of development of political liberty; 4) the old habit of the well-organised British capitalists of settling political and economic questions by compromise—at that time the British capitalists were better organised than the capitalists of any country in the world (this superiority has now passed to Germany). These were the circumstances which at that time gave rise to the idea that the *peaceful* subjugation of the British capitalists by the workers was possible.

In our country, at the present time, this subjugation is assured by certain premises of fundamental significance (the victory in October and the suppression, from October to February, of the capitalists' armed resistance and sabotage). But *instead of* the absolute preponderance of workers, of proletarians, in the population, and *instead of* a high degree of organisation among them, the important factor of victory in Russia was the support the proletarians received from the poor peasants and those who had experienced sudden ruin. Finally, we have neither a high degree of culture nor the habit of compromise. If these concrete conditions are carefully considered, it will become clear that we can and ought to employ two methods *simultaneously*. On the one hand we must ruthlessly suppress* the uncultured capitalists who refuse to have anything to do with "state capitalism" or to consider any form of compromise, and who continue by means of profiteering, by bribing the poor peasants, etc.,

---

* In this case also we must look truth in the face. We still have too little of that ruthlessness which is indispensable for the success of socialism, and we have too little not because we lack determination. We have sufficient determination. What we do lack is the ability to *catch* quickly enough a sufficient number of profiteers, racketeers and capitalists—the people who infringe the measures passed by the Soviets. The "ability" to do this can only be acquired by establishing accounting and control! Another thing is that the courts are not sufficiently firm. Instead of sentencing people who take bribes to be shot, they sentence them to six months' imprisonment. These two defects have the same social root: the influence of the petty-bourgeois element, its flabbiness.

to hinder the realisation of the measures taken by the Soviets. On the other hand, we must use the *method of compromise*, or of buying off the cultured capitalists who agree to "state capitalism", who are capable of putting it into practice and who are useful to the proletariat as intelligent and experienced organisers of the *largest* types of enterprises, which actually supply products to tens of millions of people.

Bukharin is an extremely well-read Marxist economist. He therefore remembered that Marx was profoundly right when he taught the workers the importance of preserving the organisation of large-scale production, precisely for the purpose of facilitating the transition to socialism. Marx taught that (as an exception, and Britain was then an exception) the idea was conceivable of *paying the capitalists well*, of buying them off, *if* the circumstances were such as to compel the capitalists to submit peacefully and to come over to socialism in a cultured and organised fashion, provided they were paid.

But Bukharin went astray because he did not go deep enough into the specific features of the situation in Russia at the present time—an exceptional situation when we, the Russian proletariat, are in *advance* of any Britain or any Germany as regards our political order, as regards the strength of the workers' political power, but are *behind* the most backward West-European country as regards organising a good state capitalism, as regards our level of culture and the degree of material and productive preparedness for the "introduction" of socialism. Is it not clear that the specific nature of the present situation creates the need for a specific type of "buying out" which the workers must offer to the most cultured, the most skilled, the most capable organisers among the capitalists who are ready to enter the service of Soviet power and to help honestly in organising "state" production on the largest possible scale? Is it not clear that in this specific situation we must make every effort to avoid two mistakes, both of which are of a petty-bourgeois nature? On the one hand, it would be a fatal mistake to declare that since there is a discrepancy between our economic "forces" and our political strength, it "follows" that we should not have seized power. Such an argument can be advanced only by a "man in a muffler", who forgets that there will always be such a "discrepancy", that it always exists in the development of nature as well as in the development of society, that only by a series of attempts—each of which, taken by itself, will be one-sided and will suffer from certain inconsistencies—will complete socialism be created by the revolutionary co-operation of the proletarians of *all* countries.

On the other hand, it would be an obvious mistake to give free rein to ranters and phrase-mongers who allow themselves to be carried away by the "dazzling" revolutionary spirit, but who are incapable of sustained, thoughtful and deliberate revolutionary work which takes into account the most difficult stages of transition.

Fortunately, the history of the development of the revolutionary parties and of the struggle that Bolshevism waged against them has left us a heritage of sharply defined types, of which the Left Socialist-Revolutionaries and anarchists are striking examples of bad revolutionaries. They are now shouting hysterically, choking and shouting themselves hoarse, against the "compromise" of the "Right Bolsheviks". But they are incapable of thinking *what* is bad in "compromise", and *why* "compromise" has been justly condemned by history and the course of the revolution.

Compromise in Kerensky's time meant the surrender of power to the imperialist bourgeoisie, and the question of power is the fundamental question of every revolution. Compromise by a section of the Bolsheviks in October-November 1917 either meant that they feared the proletariat seizing power or wished to *share* power equally, not only with "unreliable fellow-travellers" like the Left Socialist-Revolutionaries, but also with the enemies, with the Chernovists and the Mensheviks. The latter would inevitably have hindered us in fundamental matters, such as the dissolution of the Constituent Assembly, the ruthless suppression of the Bogayevskys, the universal setting up of the Soviet institutions, and in every act of confiscation.

Now power has been seized, retained and consolidated in the hands of a single party, the party of the proletariat, even without the "unreliable fellow-travellers". To speak of compromise at the present time when there is no question, and can be none, of sharing *power*, of renouncing the dictatorship of the proletariat over the bourgeoisie, is merely to repeat, parrot-fashion, words which have been learned by heart but not understood. To describe as "compromise" the fact that, having arrived at a situation when we can and must rule the country, we try to win over to our side, not grudging the cost, the most skilled people capitalism has trained and to take them into our service against small proprietary disintegration, reveals a total incapacity to think out the economic tasks of socialist construction.

Therefore, while it is to Comrade Bukharin's credit that on the Central Executive Committee he "felt ashamed" of the "service" he had been rendered by Karelin and Ghe, nevertheless, as far as the "Left Communist" *trend* is concerned, the reference to their political comrades-in-arms still remains a serious warning.

Take, for example, *Znamya Truda*, the organ of the Left Socialist-Revolutionaries, of April 25, 1918, which proudly declares, "The present position of our party coincides with that of another trend in Bolshevism (Bukharin, Pokrovsky and others)". Or take the

Menshevik *Vperyod* of the same date, which contains among other articles the following "thesis" by the notorious Menshevik Isuv:

"The policy of Soviet power, from the very outset devoid of a genuinely proletarian character, has lately pursued more and more openly a course of compromise with the bourgeoisie and has assumed an obviously anti-working-class character. On the pretext of nationalising industry, they are pursuing a policy of establishing industrial trusts, and on the pretext of restoring the pro-ductive forces of the country, they are attempting to abolish the eight-hour day, to introduce piece-work and the Taylor system, black lists and victimisation. This policy threatens to deprive the proletariat of its most important economic gains and to make it a victim of unrestricted exploitation by the bourgeoisie."

Isn't it marvellous?

Kerensky's friends, who, together with him, conducted an im-perialist war for the sake of the secret treaties, which promised an-nexations to the Russian capitalists, the colleagues of Tsereteli, who, on June 11, threatened to disarm the workers, the Lieber-dans,[225] who screened the rule of the bourgeoisie with high-sounding phrases—these are the very people who accuse Soviet power of "compromising with the bourgeoisie", of "establishing trusts" (that is, of establishing "state capitalism"!), of introducing the Taylor system.

Indeed, the Bolsheviks ought to present Isuv with a medal, and his thesis ought to be exhibited in every workers' club and union as an example of the *provocative speeches of the bourgeoisie*. The workers know these Lieberdans, Tseretelis and Isuvs very well now. They know them from experience, and it would be extremely useful indeed for the workers to think over the reason why *such lackeys of the bourgeoisie* should incite the workers to resist the Taylor system and the "establishment of trusts".

Class-conscious workers will carefully compare the "thesis" of Isuv, a friend of the Lieberdans and the Tseretelis, with the follow-ing thesis of the "Left Communists".

"The introduction of labour discipline in connection with the restoration of capitalist management of industry cannot considerably increase the productivity of labour, but it will diminish the class initiative, activity and organisation of the proletariat. It threatens to enslave the working class; it will rouse discontent among the backward elements as well as among the vanguard of the proletariat. In order to implement this system in the face of the hatred prevailing among the proletariat against the 'capitalist saboteurs', the Com-munist Party would have to rely on the petty bourgeoisie, as against the workers, and in this way would ruin itself as the party of the proletariat" (*Kommunist* No. 1, p. 8, col. 2).

This is most striking proof that the "Lefts" have fallen into the trap, have allowed themselves to be provoked by the Isuvs and the other Judases of capitalism. It serves as a good lesson for the

workers, who know that it is precisely the vanguard of the proletariat which stands for the introduction of labour discipline, and
that it is precisely the petty bourgeoisie which is doing its utmost to
disrupt this discipline. Speeches such as the thesis of the "Lefts"
quoted above are a terrible disgrace and imply the complete
renunciation of communism in practice and complete desertion
to the camp of the petty bourgeoisie.

"In connection with the restoration of capitalist management"—
these are the words with which the "Left Communists" hope to
"defend themselves". A perfectly useless defence, because, in the
first place, when putting "management" in the hands of capitalists
Soviet power appoints workers' Commissars or workers' committees
who watch the manager's every step, who learn from his management experience and who not only have the right to appeal against
his orders, but can secure his removal through the organs of Soviet
power. In the second place, "management" is entrusted to capitalists
only for executive functions while at work, the conditions of which
are determined by the Soviet power, by which they may be abolished
or revised. In the third place, "management" is entrusted by the
Soviet power to capitalists not as capitalists, but as technicians or
organisers for higher salaries. And the workers know very well
that ninety-nine per cent of the organisers and first-class technicians of really large-scale and giant enterprises, trusts or other
establishments belong to the capitalist class. But it is precisely these
people whom we, the proletarian party, must appoint to "manage"
the labour process and the organisation of production, for there are
no other people who have practical experience in this matter. The
workers, having grown out of the infancy when they could have
been misled by "Left" phrases or petty-bourgeois loose thinking,
are advancing towards socialism precisely through the capitalist
management of trusts, through gigantic machine industry, through
enterprises which have a turnover of several millions per year—only
through such a system of production and such enterprises. The
workers are not petty bourgeois. They are not afraid of large-scale
"state capitalism", they prize it as their *proletarian* weapon which
their Soviet power will use against small proprietary disintegration
and disorganisation.

This is incomprehensible only to the declassed and consequently
thoroughly petty-bourgeois intelligentsia, typified among the "Left
Communists" by Osinsky, when he writes in their journal:

"... The whole initiative in the organisation and management of any enterprise will belong to the 'organisers of the trusts'. We are not going to *teach* them,
or make rank-and-file workers out of them, we are going to *learn* from them"
(*Kommunist* No. 1, p. 14, col. 2).

The attempted irony in this passage is aimed at my words "learn
socialism from the organisers of the trusts".

Osinsky thinks this is funny. He wants to make "rank-and-file workers" out of the organisers of the trusts. If this had been written by a man of the age of which the poet wrote "But fifteen years, not more? ..."[226] there would have been nothing surprising about it. But it is somewhat strange to hear such things from a Marxist who has learned that socialism is impossible unless it makes use of the achievements of the engineering and culture created by large-scale capitalism. There is no trace of Marxism in this.

No. Only those are worthy of the name of Communists who understand that it is *impossible* to create or introduce socialism *without learning* from the organisers of the trusts. For socialism is not a figment of the imagination, but the assimilation and application by the proletarian vanguard, which has seized power, of what has been created by the trusts. We, the party of the proletariat, have *no other way* of acquiring the ability to organise large-scale production on trust lines, as trusts are organised, except by acquiring it from first-class capitalist experts.

We have nothing to teach them, unless we undertake the childish task of "teaching" the bourgeois intelligentsia socialism. We must not teach them, but expropriate them (as is being done in Russia "determinedly" enough), *put a stop* to their sabotage, *subordinate* them as a section or group to Soviet power. We, on the other hand, if we are not Communists of infantile age and infantile understanding, must learn from them, and there is something to learn, for the party of the proletariat and its vanguard have *no experience* of independent work in organising giant enterprises which serve the needs of scores of millions of people.

The best workers in Russia have realised this. They have begun to learn from the capitalist organisers, the managing engineers and the technicians. They have begun to learn steadily and cautiously with easy things, gradually passing on to the more difficult things. If things are going more slowly in the iron and steel and engineering industries, it is because they present greater difficulties. But the textile and tobacco workers and tanners are not afraid of "state capitalism" or of "learning from the organisers of the trusts", as the declassed petty-bourgeois intelligentsia are. These workers in the central leading institutions like Chief Leather Committee and Central Textile Committee take their place by the side of the capitalists, *learn from them*, establish trusts, establish "state capitalism", which under Soviet power represents the threshold of socialism, the condition of its firm victory.

This work of the advanced workers of Russia, together with their work of introducing labour discipline, has begun and is proceeding quietly, unobtrusively, without the noise and fuss so necessary to some "Lefts". It is proceeding very cautiously and gradually, taking into account the lessons of practical experience. This hard work, the work of *learning* practically how to build up large-scale production, is the guarantee that we are on the right road, the guarantee that the class-conscious workers in Russia are carrying on the struggle against small proprietary disintegration and disorganisation, against petty-bourgeois indiscipline*—the guarantee of the victory of communism.

VI

Two remarks in conclusion.

In arguing with the "Left Communists" on April 4, 1918 (see *Kommunist* No. 1, p. 4, footnote), I put it to them bluntly: "Explain what you are dissatisfied with in the railway decree; submit *your* amendments to it. It is your duty as Soviet leaders of the proletariat to do so, otherwise what you say is nothing but empty phrases."

The first issue of *Kommunist* appeared on April 20, 1918, but did not contain a *single word* about how, according to the "Left Communists", the railway decree should be altered or amended.

The "Left Communists" stand condemned by their own silence. They did nothing but *attack* the railway decree with all sorts of insinuations (pp. 8 and 16 of No. 1), they *gave no* articulate answer to the question, "How should the decree be amended if it is wrong?"

No comment is needed. The class-conscious workers will call *such* "criticism" of the railway decree (which is a typical example of our line of action, the line of firmness, the line of dictatorship, the line of proletarian discipline) either "Isuvian" criticism or empty phrase-making.

Second remark. The first issue of *Kommunist* contained a very flattering review by Comrade Bukharin of my pamphlet *The State and Revolution*. But however much I value the opinion of people like Bukharin, my conscience compels me to say that the *character* of the review reveals a sad and significant fact. Bukharin regards the tasks of the proletarian dictatorship from the point of view of the *past* and not of the future. Bukharin noted and emphasised what the proletarian revolutionary and the petty-bourgeois revolutionary may have in common on the question of the state. But Bukharin "overlooked" the very thing that distinguishes the one from the other.

---

* It is extremely characteristic that the authors of the theses do not say a single word about the significance of the *dictatorship* of the proletariat in the *economic* sphere. They talk only of the "organisation" and so on. But that is accepted also by the petty bourgeoisie, who shun *dictatorship* by the workers in economic relations. A proletarian revolutionary could never at such a moment "forget" this core of the proletarian revolution, which is directed against the economic foundations of capitalism.

Bukharin noted and emphasised that the old state machinery must be "smashed" and "blown up", that the bourgeoisie must be "finally and completely strangled" and so on. The frenzied petty bourgeoisie may also want this. And this, in the main, is what our revolution has *already* done between October 1917 and February 1918.

In my pamphlet I also mention what even the most revolutionary petty bourgeois cannot want, what the class-conscious proletarian does want, what our revolution has *not yet* accomplished. On this task, the task of tomorrow, Bukharin said nothing.

And I have all the more reason not to be silent on this point, because, in the first place, a Communist is expected to devote greater attention to the tasks of tomorrow, and not of yesterday, and, in the second place, my pamphlet was written *before* the Bolsheviks seized power, when it was impossible to treat the Bolsheviks to vulgar petty-bourgeois arguments such as: "Yes, *of course, after* seizing power, you begin to talk about discipline."

"...Socialism will develop into communism ... since people will become accustomed to observing the elementary conditions of social life without violence and without subordination." (*The State and Revolution*, pp. 77-78*; thus, "elementary conditions" were discussed *before* the seizure of power.)

"...Only then will democracy begin to wither away ..." when "people gradually become accustomed to observing the elementary rules of social intercourse that have been known for centuries and repeated for thousands of years in all copy-book maxims; they will become accustomed to observing them without force, without coercion, without the special apparatus for coercion called the state" (ibid., p. 84**; thus mention was made of "copy-book maxims" *before* the seizure of power).

"...The higher phase of the development of communism" (from each according to his ability, to each according to his needs) "... presupposes not the present productivity of labour and not the present ordinary run of people, who, like the seminary students in Pomyalovsky's stories, are capable of damaging the stocks of public wealth just for fun, and of demanding the impossible" (ibid., p. 91).***

"Until the higher phase of communism arrives, the socialists demand the strictest control by society and by the state over the measure of labour and the measure of consumption ..." (ibid.).

"Accounting and control—that is mainly what is needed for the smooth working, for the proper functioning of the first phase of

---

* See pp. 322-23 of the present volume.—*Ed.*
** Ibid., pp. 327-28.—*Ed.*
*** Ibid., pp. 333-34.—*Ed.*

communist society" (ibid., p. 95).* And this control must be established not only over "the insignificant capitalist minority, over the gentry who wish to preserve their capitalist habits", but also over the workers who "have been thoroughly corrupted by capitalism" (ibid., p. 96)** and over the "parasites, the sons of the wealthy, the swindlers and other guardians of capitalist traditions" (ibid.).***

It is significant that Bukharin did *not* emphasise *this*.

May 5, 1918

Published May 9, 10 and 11, 1918   *Collected Works*, Vol. 27
in *Pravda* Nos. 88, 89 and 90
    Signed: *N. Lenin*

---

* Ibid., p. 336.—*Ed.*
** Ibid., p. 337.—*Ed.*
*** *Ibid.*, p. 337.—*Ed.*

LETTER TO AMERICAN WORKERS[227]

Comrades! A Russian Bolshevik who took part in the 1905 Revolution, and who lived in your country for many years afterwards, has offered to convey my letter to you. I have accepted his proposal all the more gladly because just at the present time the American revolutionary workers have to play an exceptionally important role as uncompromising enemies of American imperialism—the freshest, strongest and latest in joining in the world-wide slaughter of nations for the division of capitalist profits. At this very moment, the American multimillionaires, these modern slave-owners, have turned an exceptionally tragic page in the bloody history of bloody imperialism by giving their approval—whether direct or indirect, open or hypocritically concealed, makes no difference—to the armed expedition launched by the brutal Anglo-Japanese imperialists for the purpose of throttling the first socialist republic.

The history of modern, civilised America opened with one of those great, really liberating, really revolutionary wars of which there have been so few compared to the vast number of wars of conquest which, like the present imperialist war, were caused by squabbles among kings, landowners or capitalists over the division of usurped lands or ill-gotten gains. That was the war the American people waged against the British robbers who oppressed America and held her in colonial slavery, in the same way as these "civilised" bloodsuckers are still oppressing and holding in colonial slavery hundreds of millions of people in India, Egypt, and all parts of the world.

About 150 years have passed since then. Bourgeois civilisation has borne all its luxurious fruits. America has taken first place among the free and educated nations in level of development of the productive forces of collective human endeavour, in the utilisation of machinery and of all the wonders of modern engineering. At the same time, America has become one of the foremost countries in regard to the depth of the abyss which lies between the handful of arrogant multimillionaires who wallow in filth and luxury, and the millions of working people who constantly live on the verge of pauperism. The American people, who set the world an example in waging a revolutionary war against feudal slavery, now find themselves in the latest, capitalist stage of wage-slavery to a handful of multimillionaires, and find themselves playing the role of hired thugs who, for the benefit of wealthy scoundrels, throttled the Philippines in 1898 on the pretext of "liberating"[228] them, and are throttling the Russian Socialist Republic in 1918 on the pretext of "protecting" it from the Germans.

The four years of the imperialist slaughter of nations, however, have not passed in vain. The deception of the people by the scoundrels of both robber groups, the British and the German, has been utterly exposed by indisputable and obvious facts. The results of the four years of war have revealed the general law of capitalism as applied to war between robbers for the division of spoils: the richest and strongest profited and grabbed most, while the weakest were utterly robbed, tormented, crushed and strangled.

The British imperialist robbers were the strongest in number of "colonial slaves". The British capitalists have not lost an inch of "their" territory (i.e., territory they have grabbed over the centuries), but they have grabbed all the German colonies in Africa, they have grabbed Mesopotamia and Palestine, they have throttled Greece, and have begun to plunder Russia.

The German imperialist robbers were the strongest in organisation and discipline of "their" armies, but weaker in regard to colonies. They have lost all their colonies, but plundered half of Europe and throttled the largest number of small countries and weak nations. What a great war of "liberation" on both sides! How well the robbers of both groups, the Anglo-French and the German capitalists, together with their lackeys, the social-chauvinists, i.e., the socialists who went over to the side of "*their own*" bourgeoisie, have "defended their country"!

The American multimillionaires were, perhaps, richest of all, and geographically the most secure. They have profited more than all the rest. They have converted all, even the richest, countries into their tributaries. They have grabbed hundreds of billions of dollars. And every dollar is sullied with filth: the filth of the secret treaties between Britain and her "allies", between Germany and her vassals, treaties for the division of the spoils, treaties of mutual "aid" for oppressing the workers and persecuting the internationalist socialists. Every dollar is sullied with the filth of "profitable" war contracts, which in every country made the rich richer and the poor poorer. And every dollar is stained with blood—from that ocean of blood that has been shed by the ten million killed and twenty million maimed in the great, noble, liberating and holy war to decide whether the British or the German robbers are to get most of the spoils, whether the British or the German thugs are to be *foremost* in throttling the weak nations all over the world.

While the German robbers broke all records in war atrocities, the British have broken all records not only in the number of colonies they have grabbed, but also in the subtlety of their disgusting hypocrisy. This very day, the Anglo-French and American bourgeois newspapers are spreading, in millions and millions of copies, lies and slander about Russia, and are hypocritically justifying their predatory expedition against her on the plea that they want to "protect" Russia from the Germans!

It does not require many words to refute this despicable and hideous lie; it is sufficient to point to one well-known fact. In October 1917, after the Russian workers had overthrown their imperialist government, the Soviet government, the government of the revolutionary workers and peasants, openly proposed a just peace, a peace without annexations or indemnities, a peace that fully guaranteed equal rights to all nations—and it proposed such a peace to *all* the belligerent countries.

It was the Anglo-French and the American bourgeoisie who refused to accept our proposal; it was they who even refused to talk to us about a general peace! It was *they* who betrayed the interests of all nations; it was they who prolonged the imperialist slaughter!

It was they who, banking on the possibility of dragging Russia back into the imperialist war, refused to take part in the peace negotiations and thereby gave a free hand to the no less predatory German capitalists who imposed the annexationist and harsh Brest Peace upon Russia!

It is difficult to imagine anything more disgusting than the hypocrisy with which the Anglo-French and American bourgeoisie are now "blaming" us *for* the Brest Peace Treaty. The very capitalists of those countries which could have turned the Brest negotiations into general negotiations for a general peace are now our "accusers"! The Anglo-French imperialist vultures, who have profited from the plunder of colonies and the slaughter of nations, have prolonged the war for nearly a whole year after Brest, and yet they "accuse" *us*, the Bolsheviks, who proposed a just peace to all countries, they accuse *us*, who tore up, published and exposed to public disgrace the secret, criminal treaties concluded between the ex-tsar and the Anglo-French capitalists.[229]

The workers of the whole world, no matter in what country they live, greet us, sympathise with us, applaud us for breaking the iron ring of imperialist ties, of sordid imperialist treaties, of imperialist chains—for breaking through to freedom, and making the heaviest sacrifices in doing so—for, as a socialist republic, although torn and plundered by the imperialists, keeping *out* of the imperialist war and raising the banner of peace, the banner of socialism for the whole world to see.

Small wonder that the international imperialist gang hates us for this, that it "accuses" us, that all the lackeys of the imperialists, including our Right Socialist-Revolutionaries and Mensheviks, also "accuse" us. The hatred these watchdogs of imperialism express for the Bolsheviks, and the sympathy of the class-conscious workers of the world, convince us more than ever of the justice of our cause.

A real socialist would not fail to understand that for the sake of achieving victory over the bourgeoisie, for the sake of power passing to the workers, for the sake of *starting* the world proletarian revolution, we *cannot* and must *not* hesitate to make the heaviest sacrifices, including the sacrifice of part of our territory, the sacrifice of heavy defeats at the hands of imperialism. A real socialist would have proved by *deeds* his willingness for "his" country to make the greatest sacrifice to give a real push forward to the cause of the socialist revolution.

For the sake of "their" cause, that is, for the sake of winning world hegemony, the imperialists of Britain and Germany have not hesitated to utterly ruin and throttle a whole number of countries, from Belgium and Serbia to Palestine and Mesopotamia. But must socialists wait with "their" cause, the cause of liberating the working people of the whole world from the yoke of capital, of winning universal and lasting peace, until a path without sacrifice is found? Must they fear to open the battle until an easy victory is "guaranteed"? Must they place the integrity and security of "their" bourgeois-created "fatherland" above the interests of the world socialist revolution? The scoundrels in the international socialist movement who think this way, those lackeys who grovel to bourgeois morality, thrice stand condemned.

The Anglo-French and American imperialist vultures "accuse" us of concluding an "agreement" with German imperialism. What hypocrites, what scoundrels they are to slander the workers' government while trembling because of the sympathy displayed towards us by the workers of "their own" countries! But their hypocrisy will be exposed. They pretend not to see the difference between an agreement entered into by "socialists" with the bourgeoisie (their own or foreign) *against the workers*, against the working people, and an agreement entered into *for the protection* of the workers who have defeated their bourgeoisie, with the bourgeoisie of one national colour *against the bourgeoisie* of another colour in order that the proletariat may take advantage of the antagonisms between the different groups of bourgeoisie.

In actual fact, every European sees this difference very well, and, as I shall show in a moment, the American people have had a par-

ticularly striking "illustration" of it in their own history. There are
agreements and agreements, there are *fagots et fagots*, as the French
say.

When in February 1918 the German imperialist vultures hurled
their forces against unarmed, demobilised Russia, who had relied
on the international solidarity of the proletariat before the world
revolution had fully matured, I did not hesitate for a moment to
enter into an "agreement" with the French monarchists. Captain
Sadoul, a French army officer who, in words, sympathised with the
Bolsheviks, but was in deeds a loyal and faithful servant of French
imperialism, brought the French officer de Lubersac to see me. "I
am a monarchist. My only aim is to secure the defeat of Germany,"
de Lubersac declared to me. "That goes without saying (*cela va sans
dire*)," I replied. But this did not in the least prevent me from entering into an "agreement" with de Lubersac concerning certain services that French army officers, experts in explosives, were ready to
render us by blowing up railway lines in order to hinder the German invasion. This is an example of an "agreement" of which every
class-conscious worker will approve, an agreement in the interests
of socialism. The French monarchist and I shook hands, although
we knew that each of us would willingly hang his "partner". But
for a time our interests coincided. Against the advancing rapacious
Germans, *we*, in the interests of the Russian and the world socialist
revolution, utilised the equally rapacious counter-interests of *other*
imperialists. In this way we served the interests of the working class
of Russia and of other countries, we strengthened the proletariat
and weakened the bourgeoisie of the whole world, we resorted to
the methods, most legitimate and essential in *every* war, of
manoeuvre, stratagem, retreat, in anticipation of the moment
when the rapidly maturing proletarian revolution in a number of
advanced countries *completely matured*.

However much the Anglo-French and American imperialist sharks
fume with rage, however much they slander us, no matter how many
millions they spend on bribing the Right Socialist-Revolutionary,
Menshevik and other social-patriotic newspapers, *I shall not hesitate
one second* to enter into a *similar* "agreement" with the German
imperialist vultures if an attack upon Russia by Anglo-French troops
calls for it. And I know perfectly well that my tactics will be approved by the class-conscious proletariat of Russia, Germany,
France, Britain, America—in short, of the whole civilised world.
Such tactics will ease the task of the socialist revolution, will hasten
it, will weaken the international bourgeoisie, will strengthen the
position of the working class which is defeating the bourgeoisie.

The American people resorted to these tactics long ago to the
advantage of their revolution. When they waged their great war of
liberation against the British oppressors, they had also against them

the French and the Spanish oppressors who owned a part of what is now the United States of North America. In their arduous war for freedom, the American people also entered into "agreements" with some oppressors against others for the purpose of weakening the oppressors and strengthening those who were fighting in a revolutionary manner against oppression, for the purpose of serving the interests of the oppressed *people*. The American people took advantage of the strife between the French, the Spanish and the British; sometimes they even fought side by side with the forces of the French and Spanish oppressors against the British oppressors; first they defeated the British and then freed themselves (partly by ransom) from the French and the Spanish.

Historical action is not the pavement of Nevsky Prospekt, said the great Russian revolutionary Chernyshevsky. A revolutionary would not "agree" to a proletarian revolution only "on the condition" that it proceeds easily and smoothly, that there is, from the outset, combined action on the part of the proletarians of different countries, that there are guarantees against defeats, that the road of the revolution is broad, free and straight, that it will not be necessary during the march to victory to sustain the heaviest casualties, to "bide one's time in a besieged fortress", or to make one's way along extremely narrow, impassable, winding and dangerous mountain tracks. Such a person is no revolutionary, he has not freed himself from the pedantry of the bourgeois intellectuals; such a person will be found constantly slipping into the camp of the counter-revolutionary bourgeoisie, like our Right Socialist-Revolutionaries, Mensheviks and even (although more rarely) Left Socialist-Revolutionaries.

Echoing the bourgeoisie, these gentlemen like to blame us for the "chaos" of the revolution, for the "destruction" of industry, for the unemployment and the food shortage. How hypocritical these accusations are, coming from those who welcomed and supported the imperialist war, or who entered into an "agreement" with Kerensky who continued this war! It is this imperialist war that is the cause of all these misfortunes. The revolution engendered by the war cannot avoid the terrible difficulties and suffering bequeathed it by the prolonged, ruinous, reactionary slaughter of the nations. To blame us for the "destruction" of industry, or for the "terror", is either hypocrisy or dull-witted pedantry; it reveals an inability to understand the basic conditions of the fierce class struggle, raised to the highest degree of intensity that is called revolution.

Even when "accusers" of this type do "recognise" the class struggle, they limit themselves to verbal recognition; actually, they constantly slip into the philistine utopia of class "agreement" and "collaboration"; for in revolutionary epochs the class struggle has always, inevitably, and in every country, assumed the form of *civil war*, and civil war is inconceivable without the severest destruction, terror and the restriction of formal democracy in the interests of this war. Only unctuous parsons—whether Christian or "secular" in the persons of parlour, parliamentary socialists—cannot see, understand and feel this necessity. Only a lifeless "man in the muffler" can shun the revolution for this reason instead of plunging into battle with the utmost ardour and determination at a time when history demands that the greatest problems of humanity be solved by struggle and war.

The American people have a revolutionary tradition which has been adopted by the best representatives of the American proletariat, who have repeatedly expressed their complete solidarity with us Bolsheviks. That tradition is the war of liberation against the British in the eighteenth century and the Civil War in the nineteenth century. In some respects, if we only take into consideration the "destruction" of some branches of industry and of the national economy, America in 1870 was *behind* 1860. But what a pedant, what an idiot would anyone be to deny on *these* grounds the immense, world-historic, progressive and revolutionary significance of the American Civil War of 1863-65![230]

The representatives of the bourgeoisie understand that for the sake of overthrowing Negro slavery, of overthrowing the rule of the slave-owners, it was worth letting the country go through long years of civil war, through the abysmal ruin, destruction and terror that accompany every war. But now, when we are confronted with the vastly greater task of overthrowing capitalist *wage*-slavery, of overthrowing the rule of the bourgeoisie—now, the representatives and defenders of the bourgeoisie, and also the reformist socialists who have been frightened by the bourgeoisie and are shunning the revolution, cannot and do not want to understand that civil war is necessary and legitimate.

The American workers will not follow the bourgeoisie. They will be with us, for civil war against the bourgeoisie. The whole history of the world and of the American labour movement strengthens my conviction that this is so. I also recall the words of one of the most beloved leaders of the American proletariat, Eugene Debs, who wrote in the *Appeal to Reason*,[231] I believe towards the end of 1915, in the article "What Shall I Fight For" (I quoted this article at the beginning of 1916 at a public meeting of workers in Berne, Switzerland)*—that he, Debs, would rather be shot than vote credits for the present criminal and reactionary war; that he, Debs, knows of only one holy and, from the proletarian standpoint, legitimate war, namely: the war against the capitalists, the war to liberate mankind from wage-slavery.

---

* See *Collected Works*, Vol. 22, p. 125.—*Ed.*

I am not surprised that Wilson, the head of the American multi-millionaires and servant of the capitalist sharks, has thrown Debs into prison. Let the bourgeoisie be brutal to the true international-ists, to the true representatives of the revolutionary proletariat! The more fierce and brutal they are, the nearer the day of the victorious proletarian revolution.

We are blamed for the destruction caused by our revolution.... Who are the accusers? The hangers-on of the bourgeoisie, of that very bourgeoisie who, during the four years of the imperialist war, have destroyed almost the whole of European culture and have reduced Europe to barbarism, brutality and starvation. These bour-geoisie now demand we should not make a revolution on these ruins, amidst this wreckage of culture, amidst the wreckage and ruins created by the war, nor with the people who have been brutalised by the war. How humane and righteous the bourgeoisie are!

Their servants accuse us of resorting to terror.... The British bourgeoisie have forgotten their 1649, the French bourgeoisie have forgotten their 1793.[232] Terror was just and legitimate when the bourgeoisie resorted to it for their own benefit against feudalism. Terror became monstrous and criminal when the workers and poor peasants dared to use it against the bourgeoisie! Terror was just and legitimate when used for the purpose of substituting one exploiting minority for another exploiting minority. Terror became monstrous and criminal when it began to be used for the purpose of overthrow-ing *every* exploiting minority, to be used in the interests of the vast actual majority, in the interests of the proletariat and semi-proletariat, the working class and the poor peasants!

The international imperialist bourgeoisie have slaughtered ten million men and maimed twenty million in "their" war, the war to decide whether the British or the German vultures are to rule the world.

If *our* war, the war of the oppressed and exploited against the the oppressors and the exploiters, results in half a million or a million casualties in all countries, the bourgeoisie will say that the former casualties are justified, while the latter are criminal.

The proletariat will have something entirely different to say.

Now, amidst the horrors of the imperialist war, the proletariat is receiving a most vivid and striking illustration of the great truth taught by all revolutions and bequeathed to the workers by their best teachers, the founders of modern socialism. This truth is that no revolution can be successful unless *the resistance of the exploit-ers is crushed*. When we, the workers and toiling peasants, captured state power, it became our duty to crush the resistance of the exploiters. We are proud we have been doing this. We regret we are not doing it with sufficient firmness and determination.

We know that fierce resistance to the socialist revolution on the part of the bourgeoisie is inevitable in all countries, and that this resistance will *grow* with the growth of this revolution. The proletariat will crush this resistance; during the struggle against the resisting bourgeoisie it will finally mature for victory and for power.

Let the corrupt bourgeois press shout to the whole world about every mistake our revolution makes. We are not daunted by our mistakes. People have not become saints because the revolution has begun. The toiling classes who for centuries have been oppressed, downtrodden and forcibly held in the vice of poverty, brutality and ignorance cannot avoid mistakes when making a revolution. And, as I pointed out once before, the corpse of bourgeois society cannot be nailed in a coffin and buried.* The corpse of capitalism is decaying and disintegrating in our midst, polluting the air and poisoning our lives, enmeshing that which is new, fresh, young and virile in thousands of threads and bonds of that which is old, moribund and decaying.

For every hundred mistakes we commit, and which the bourgeoisie and their lackeys (including our own Mensheviks and Right Socialist-Revolutionaries) shout about to the whole world, 10,000 great and heroic deeds are performed, greater and more heroic because they are simple and inconspicuous amidst the everyday life of a factory district or a remote village, performed by people who are not accustomed (and have no opportunity) to shout to the whole world about their successes.

But even if the contrary were true—although I know such an assumption is wrong—even if we committed 10,000 mistakes for every 100 correct actions we performed, even in that case our revolution would be great and invincible, and *so it will be in the eyes of world history*, because, *for the first time*, not the minority, not the rich alone, not the educated alone, but the real people, the vast majority of the working people, are *themselves* building a new life, are *by their own experience* solving the most difficult problems of socialist organisation.

Every mistake committed in the course of such work, in the course of this most conscientious and earnest work of tens of millions of simple workers and peasants in reorganising their whole life, every such mistake is worth thousands and millions of "flawless" successes achieved by the exploiting minority—successes in swindling and duping the working people. For only *through* such mistakes will the workers and peasants *learn* to build the new life, learn to do *without* capitalists; only in this way will they hack a path for them-selves—through thousands of obstacles—to victorious socialism.

---

* See *Collected Works*, Vol. 27, p. 434.—*Ed.*

Mistakes are being committed in the course of their revolutionary work by our peasants, who at one stroke, in one night, October 25-26 (old style), 1917, entirely abolished the private ownership of land,[233] and are now, month after month, overcoming tremendous difficulties and correcting their mistakes themselves, solving in a practical way the most difficult tasks of organising new conditions of economic life, of fighting the kulaks, providing land for the *working people* (and not for the rich), and of changing to *communist* large-scale agriculture.

Mistakes are being committed in the course of their revolutionary work by our workers, who have already, after a few months, nationalised almost all the biggest factories and plants, and are learning by hard, everyday work the new task of managing whole branches of industry, are setting the nationalised enterprises going, overcoming the powerful resistance of inertia, petty-bourgeois mentality and selfishness, and, brick by brick, are laying the foundation of *new* social ties, of a *new* labour discipline, of a *new* influence of the workers' trade unions over their members.

Mistakes are committed in the course of their revolutionary work by our Soviets, which were created as far back as 1905 by a mighty upsurge of the people. The Soviets of Workers and Peasants are a new *type* of state, a new and higher *type* of democracy, a form of the proletarian dictatorship, a means of administering the state *without* the bourgeoisie and *against* the bourgeoisie. For the first time democracy is here serving the people, the working people, and has ceased to be democracy for the rich as it still is in all bourgeois republics, even the most democratic. For the first time, the people are grappling, on a scale involving one hundred million, with the problem of implementing the dictatorship of the proletariat and semi-proletariat—a problem which, if not solved, makes socialism *out of the question*.

Let the pedants, or the people whose minds are incurably stuffed with bourgeois-democratic or parliamentary prejudices, shake their heads in perplexity about our Soviets, about the absence of direct elections, for example. These people have forgotten nothing and have learned nothing during the period of the great upheavals of 1914-18. The combination of the proletarian dictatorship with the new democracy for the working people—of civil war with the widest participation of the people in politics—such a combination cannot be brought about at one stroke, nor does it fit in with the outworn modes of routine parliamentary democracy. The contours of a new world, the world of socialism, are rising before us in the shape of the Soviet Republic. It is not surprising that this world does not come into being ready-made, does not spring forth like Minerva from the head of Jupiter.[234]

The old bourgeois-democratic constitutions waxed eloquent about formal equality and right of assembly; but our proletarian and peasant Soviet Constitution casts aside the hypocrisy of formal equality. When the bourgeois republicans overturned thrones they did not worry about formal equality between monarchists and republicans. When it is a matter of overthrowing the bourgeoisie, only traitors or idiots can demand formal equality of rights for the bourgeoisie. "Freedom of assembly" for workers and peasants is not worth a farthing when the best buildings belong to the bourgeoisie. Our Soviets have *confiscated* all the good buildings in town and country from the rich and have *transferred all* of them to the workers and peasants for *their* unions and meetings. This is *our* freedom of assembly—for the working people! This is the meaning and content of our Soviet, our socialist Constitution![235]

That is why we are all so firmly convinced that no matter what misfortunes may still be in store for it, our Republic of Soviets is *invincible*.

It is invincible because every blow struck by frenzied imperialism, every defeat the international bourgeoisie inflict on us, rouses more and more sections of the workers and peasants to the struggle, teaches them at the cost of enormous sacrifice, steels them and engenders new heroism on a mass scale.

We know that help from you will probably not come soon, comrade American workers, for the revolution is developing in different countries in different forms and at different tempos (and it cannot be otherwise). We know that although the European proletarian revolution has been maturing very rapidly lately, it may, after all, not flare up within the next few weeks. We are banking on the inevitability of the world revolution, but this does not mean that we are such fools as to bank on the revolution inevitably coming on a *definite* and early date. We have seen two great revolutions in our country, 1905 and 1917, and we know revolutions are not made to order, or by agreement. We know that circumstances brought *our* Russian detachment of the socialist proletariat to the fore not because of our merits, but because of the exceptional backwardness of Russia, and that *before* the world revolution breaks out a number of separate revolutions may be defeated.

In spite of this, we are firmly convinced that we are invincible, because the spirit of mankind will not be broken by the imperialist slaughter. Mankind will vanquish it. And the first country to *break* the convict chains of the imperialist war was *our* country. We sustained enormously heavy casualties in the struggle to break these chains, but we *broke* them. We are *free from* imperialist dependence, we have raised the banner of struggle for the complete overthrow of imperialism for the whole world to see.

We are now, as it were, in a besieged fortress, waiting for the other detachments of the world socialist revolution to come to our relief. These detachments *exist*, they are *more numerous* than ours, they are maturing, growing, gaining more strength the longer the brutalities of imperialism continue. The workers are breaking away from their social-traitors—the Gomperses, Hendersons, Renaudels, Scheidemanns and Renners. Slowly but surely the workers are adopting communist, Bolshevik tactics and are marching towards the proletarian revolution, which alone is capable of saving dying culture and dying mankind.

In short, we are invincible, because the world proletarian revolution is invincible.

N. Lenin

August 20, 1918

Pravda No. 178,
August 22, 1918

Collected Works, Vol. 28

THE PROLETARIAN REVOLUTION
AND THE RENEGADE KAUTSKY

This is the title of a pamphlet[236] I have begun to write in criticism of Kautsky's pamphlet, *The Dictatorship of the Proletariat*, which has just appeared in Vienna. But as this work is taking longer than I had anticipated, I have decided to ask *Pravda* to find space for a short article on the subject.

Over four years of a most exhausting and reactionary war have done their work. One can feel the impending proletarian revolution in Europe—in Austria, Italy, Germany, France and even in Britain (very significant, for example, is the article "Confessions of a Capitalist" in the July number of the arch-opportunist *Socialist Review*,[237] edited by the semi-liberal Ramsay MacDonald).

And at a time like this, Mr. Kautsky, leader of the Second International, comes out with a book on the dictatorship of the proletariat—in other words, on the proletarian revolution—that is a hundred times more disgraceful, outrageous and renegade than Berstein's notorious *Premises of Socialism*. Nearly twenty years have elapsed since the appearance of that renegade book, and now Kautsky repeats this renegacy in an even grosser form!

Only a very small part of the book deals with the Russian Bolshevik revolution as such. Kautsky repeats every one of the Mensheviks' pearls of wisdom in a way that would make the Russian worker split his sides laughing. Just imagine, for example, what goes by the name of "Marxism": the argument—peppered with quotations from the semi-liberal works by the semi-liberal Maslov—that the rich peasants are trying to appropriate the land (novel!), that they find high grain prices profitable, and so on. Then our "Marxist" makes the following contemptuous, and utterly liberal, statement: "The poor peasant is recognised here [that is, by the Bolsheviks in the Soviet Republic] to be a permanent and wholesale product of the socialist agrarian reform under the dictatorship of the proletariat'." (P. 48 of Kautsky's pamphlet.)

Fine. Here is a socialist, a Marxist, who tries to prove to *us* the *bourgeois* nature of the revolution, and who at the same time scoffs at the organisation of the poor peasants, quite in the spirit of Maslov, Potresov *and the Cadets*.

"The expropriation of the rich peasants only introduces a new element of unrest and civil war into the production process, which urgently needs peace and security for its recovery." (P. 49.)

Incredible, but there we are. These are the very words, not of Savinkov or Milyukov, but of Kautsky!

Kautsky does not surprise us since we in Russia have seen so many cases of "Marxism" being used as a screen by defenders of the kulaks. For the benefit of the European reader, I should perhaps dwell in greater detail on this despicable kowtowing to the bourgeoisie and the liberal fear of civil war. But for the Russian worker and peasant it is enough to point one's finger at Kautsky's renegacy—and pass on.

* * *

Nearly nine-tenths of Kautsky's book is devoted to a general theoretical question of the utmost importance, the question of the relation between the dictatorship of the proletariat and "democracy". And it is here that Kautsky's complete break with Marxism is particularly evident.

Kautsky assures his reader—in a perfectly serious and extremely "learned" tone—that what Marx meant by "revolutionary dictatorship of the proletariat" was not a "*form of governing*" that precludes democracy, but a *state, namely*, "a state of rule". And the rule of the proletariat, as the majority of the population, is possible with the strictest observance of democracy, and, for instance, the Paris Commune, which was in fact a dictatorship of the proletariat, was elected by universal suffrage. "The fact that Marx thought that in England and America the transition [to communism] might take place peacefully, i.e., in a democratic way, proves" that when he spoke of the dictatorship of the proletariat Marx did not have in mind a "form of governing" (or a form of government, *Regierungsform*) (pp. 20-21).

Incredible, but there we are! That is exactly the way Kautsky argues and he angrily accuses the Bolsheviks of violating "democracy" in their Constitution and throughout their policy; and he takes every opportunity to energetically preach "the democratic instead of the dictatorial method".

This is a complete desertion to the opportunists (those like David, Kolb and other pillars of German social-chauvinism, or the English Fabians and Independents, or the French and Italian reformists), who have declared more frankly and honestly that they do not accept Marx's doctrine of the dictatorship of the proletariat on the ground that it runs counter to democracy.

It is a complete reversion to the views of the pre-Marxist German socialists, who used to claim they wanted a "free people's state", to the views of the petty-bourgeois democrats, who did not understand that *every* state is a machine for the suppression of one class by another.

It is a complete renunciation of the proletarian revolution, which is replaced by the liberal theory of "winning a majority" and "utilising democracy"! Kautsky the renegade has completely forgotten, distorted and thrown overboard everything Marx and Engels taught for forty years, from 1852 to 1891, demonstrating the need for the proletariat to "smash" the bourgeois state machine.

To analyse Kautsky's theoretical mistakes in detail would mean repeating what I have said in *The State and Revolution.** There is no need for that. I shall only say briefly:

Kautsky has renounced Marxism by forgetting that *every* state is a machine for the suppression of one class by another, and that the most *democratic* bourgeois republic is a machine for the oppression of the proletariat by the bourgeoisie.

The dictatorship of the proletariat, the proletarian state, which is a machine for the suppression *of the bourgeoisie by the proletariat*, is not a "form of governing", but a *state of a different type*. Suppression is necessary because the bourgeoisie will always furiously resist being expropriated.

(The argument that Marx in the seventies allowed for the possibility of a peaceful transition to socialism in England and America is completely fallacious, or, to put it bluntly, dishonest in that it is juggling with quotations and references. Firstly, Marx regarded it as an exception even then. Secondly, in those days monopoly capitalism, i.e., imperialism, did not exist. Thirdly, in England and America there was no militarist clique then—*as there is now*—serving as the chief apparatus of the bourgeois state machine.)

You cannot have liberty, equality and so on where there is suppression. That is why Engels said: "So long as the proletariat still needs the state, it does not need it in the interests of freedom but in order to hold down its adversaries, and as soon as it becomes possible to speak of freedom the state as such ceases to exist."

Bourgeois democracy, which is invaluable in educating the proletariat and training it for the struggle, is always narrow, hypocritical, spurious and false; it always remains democracy for the rich and a swindle for the poor.

---

* See pp. 264-351 of the present volume.—*Ed.*

Proletarian democracy suppresses the exploiters, the bourgeoisie—and is therefore not hypocritical, *does not promise them* freedom and democracy—and gives the working people *genuine democracy*. Only Soviet Russia has given the proletariat and the whole vast labouring majority of Russia a *freedom and democracy* unprecedented, impossible and inconceivable in any bourgeois democratic republic, by, for example, taking the palaces and mansions away from the bourgeoisie (without which freedom of assembly is sheer hypocrisy), by taking the print-shops and stocks of paper away from the capitalists (without which freedom of the press for the nation's labouring majority is a lie), and by replacing bourgeois parliamentarism by the democratic organisation of the *Soviets, which are a thousand times* nearer to the people and more democratic than the most democratic bourgeois parliament. *And so on.*

Kautsky has thrown overboard ... the "class struggle" as applied to democracy! Kautsky has become a downright renegade and a lackey of the bourgeoisie.

* * *

I must mention, in passing, a few gems of his renegacy.

Kautsky has to admit that the Soviet form of organisation is of world-wide, and not only of Russian significance, that it is one of the "most important phenomena of our times", and that it promises to acquire "decisive significance" in the future great "battles between capital and labour". But, imitating the wisdom of the Mensheviks, who have happily sided with the bourgeoisie against the proletariat, Kautsky "deduces" that the Soviets are all right as "battle organisations", but not as "state organisations".

Marvellous! Form up in Soviets, you proletarians and poor peasants! But, for God's sake, don't you dare win! Don't even think of winning! The moment you win and vanquish the bourgeoisie, that will be the end of you; for you must not be "state" organisations in a proletarian state. In fact, as soon as you have won you must break up!

What a marvellous Marxist this man Kautsky is! What an inimitable "theoretician" of renegacy!

Gem No. 2. Civil war is the "mortal enemy" of "social revolution", for, as we have already heard, the latter "needs peace [for the rich?] and security" (for the capitalist?).

Workers of Europe, don't think of revolution until you have found a bourgeoisie who *will not hire* Savinkov and Dan, Dutov and Krasnov, Czechs[238] and kulaks to wage civil war on you!

Marx wrote in 1870 that the chief hope lay in the practice in arms that the war had given the French workers. What Kautsky the /

"Marxist" expects of four years of war is not the use of arms by the workers against the bourgeoisie (Heaven forbid, that wouldn't really be "democratic"!), but ... the conclusion of a nice little peace by the nice little capitalists!

Gem No. 3. Civil war has another unpleasant side to it: whereas "democracy" provides for the "protection of the minority" (as—we might note in parenthesis—those in France who stood up for Dreyfus, and people like Liebknecht, Maclean or Debs in more recent times, have learned so well from their own experience), civil war (mark that!) "threatens the vanquished with complete annihilation".

Well, isn't this man Kautsky a real revolutionary? He is heart and soul for revolution ... provided there is no serious struggle threatening annihilation! He has completely "overcome" the old errors of old Engels, who so enthusiastically lauded the educational value of violent revolutions. Like the "serious" historian he is, he has completely renounced the delusions of those who said that civil war steels the exploited and teaches them to build a new society *without* exploiters.

Gem No. 4. Viewed historically, was the dictatorship of the workers and petty bourgeoisie in the 1789 Revolution great and beneficial? Certainly not. For along came Napoleon. "The dictatorship of the lower sections of the population paves the way for the dictatorship of the sword" (p. 26). Like all liberals, to whose camp he has deserted, our "serious" historian is firmly convinced that in countries which have not known the "dictatorship of the lower sections"—Germany, for example—there has never been a dictatorship of the sword. Germany has never been distinguished from France by a grosser and viler dictatorship of the sword—that is all slander thought up by Marx and Engels, who brazenly lied when they said that there have so far been a greater love of freedom and a greater pride of the oppressed among the "people" in France than in England or Germany, and that it was precisely her revolutions that France has to thank for this.

...But enough! One would have to write a whole pamphlet to enumerate all the gems of renegacy of that despicable renegade Kautsky.

* * *

I must say a word or two about Mr. Kautsky's "internationalism". He inadvertently cast light upon it himself by his most sympathetic way of portraying the internationalism of the Mensheviks, who, dear Mr. Kautsky assures us, were also Zimmerwaldists and, if you please, are "brothers" of the Bolsheviks!

Here is his lovely little picture of the "Zimmerwaldism" of the Mensheviks:

"The Mensheviks wanted universal peace. They wanted all those in the war to accept the slogan: no annexations or indemnities. Until this would have been achieved, the Russian army, in their opinion, should have maintained itself in a state of fighting readiness...." But the wretched Bolsheviks "disorganised" the army and concluded the wretched Brest-Litovsk Peace Treaty.... And Kautsky says as clear as clear can be that the Constituent Assembly should have been preserved, and the Bolsheviks should not have taken power.

So internationalism means *supporting one's "own"* imperialist government, as the Mensheviks and Socialist-Revolutionaries supported Kerensky, it means concealing its secret treaties, hoodwinking the people with fancy phrases, such as that we "demand" the savage beasts be tame, we "demand" the imperialist governments "accept the slogan of no annexations or indemnities".

That, in Kautsky's opinion, is internationalism.

In our opinion it is sheer renegacy.

Internationalism means breaking with *one's own* social-chauvinists (i.e., defence advocates) and with *one's own* imperialist government; it means waging a revolutionary struggle against that government and overthrowing it, and being ready to make the greatest national sacrifices (even down to a Brest-Litovsk Peace Treaty), if it should benefit the development of the *world* worker's revolution.

We all know very well that Kautsky and his friends (Ströbel, Bernstein, and the rest) were greatly "put out" by the Brest-Litovsk Peace; they would have liked us to have made a "gesture" ... that would at once have turned over power in Russia to the bourgeoisie! These dim-witted but all too nice and kind German petty bourgeois were not interested in the proletarian Soviet Republic—the first country in the world to overthrow its imperialism by revolutionary means—maintaining itself until the revolution took place in Europe, fanning the flames of the conflagration in other countries (the petty bourgeoisie *dread* a conflagration in Europe, they *dread* civil war, which would disturb "peace and security"). No, what interested them was to maintain in *all* countries the *petty-bourgeois* nationalism which calls itself "internationalism" because of its "moderation and propriety".[239] If only the Russian Republic had remained bourgeois and ... had waited ... then everybody on earth would have been a good, moderate, non-predatory, petty-bourgeois nationalist—and that, in fact, would have been internationalism!

That is the line of thought of the Kautskyites in Germany, the Longuetists[240] in France, the Independents (I.L.P.) in England, Turati and his "comrades" in renegacy in Italy, and the rest of the crowd.

By now only an utter idiot can fail to see that we were not only right in overthrowing our bourgeoisie (and their lackeys, the Mensheviks and Socialist-Revolutionaries), but also in concluding the Brest-Litovsk Peace Treaty *after* our open appeal for universal peace, backed by the publication and annulment of the secret treaties, had been rejected by the bourgeoisie of the Entente.[241] In the first place, if we had not concluded the Brest-Litovsk Peace Treaty, we would at once have surrendered power to the Russian bourgeoisie and thus have done untold damage to the world socialist revolution. In the second place, at the cost of *national* sacrifices, we preserved such an *international* revolutionary influence that today we have Bulgaria directly imitating us, Austria and Germany in a state of ferment, *both* imperialist systems weakened, while we have grown stronger and *begun* to create a real proletarian army.

From the tactics of Kautsky the renegade it follows that the German workers should now defend their homeland together with the bourgeoisie and dread a German revolution most of all, for the British might impose a new edition of the Brest-Litovsk Peace on it. There's renegacy for you. There's petty-bourgeois nationalism.

We, however, say that while the loss of the Ukraine was a grave national sacrifice, it helped to steel and *strengthen* the workers and poor peasants of the Ukraine as revolutionary fighters for the world workers' revolution. The Ukraine's suffering was the world revolution's gain, for the German troops were corrupted, German imperialism was weakened, and the German, Ukrainian and Russian revolutionary workers were *drawn closer together*.

It would of course be "nicer" if we could overthrow both Wilhelm and Wilson simply by war. But that is utter nonsense. We cannot overthrow them by a war from without. But we can speed up their *internal* disintegration. We have achieved that on an *immense* scale by the Soviet, proletarian revolution.

The German workers would do it even more successfully if they began a revolution *disregarding* national sacrifices (that alone is internationalism), if they said (and backed their word *by actions*) that they prize the interests of the world workers' revolution *higher* than the integrity, security and peace of any national state, *and of their own in particular*.

*   *   *

Europe's greatest misfortune and danger is that it has *no* revolutionary party. It has parties of traitors like the Scheidemanns, Renaudels, Hendersons, Webbs and Co., and of servile souls like Kautsky. But it has no revolutionary party.

Of course, a mighty, popular revolutionary movement may rectify this deficiency, but it is nevertheless a serious misfortune and a grave danger.

That is why we must do our utmost to expose renegades like Kautsky, thereby supporting the revolutionary *groups* of genuine internationalist workers, who are to be found in *all* countries. The proletariat will very soon turn away from the traitors and renegades and follow these groups, drawing and training leaders from their midst. No wonder the bourgeoisie of all countries are howling about "world Bolshevism".

World Bolshevism will conquer the world bourgeoisie.

9.X.1918

Pravda No. 219,   *Collected Works*, Vol. 28
October 11, 1918
Signed: *N. Lenin*

WHAT IS SOVIET POWER?[242]

What is Soviet power? What is the essence of this new power. which people in most countries still will not, or cannot, understand? The nature of this power, which is attracting larger and larger numbers of workers in every country, is the following: in the past the country was, in one way or another, governed by the rich, or by the capitalists, but now, for the first time, the country is being governed by the classes, and moreover, by the masses of those classes, which capitalism formerly oppressed. Even in the most democratic and freest republics, as long as capital rules and the land remains private property, the government will always be in the hands of a small minority, nine-tenths of which consist of capitalists, or rich men.

In this country, in Russia, for the first time in the world history, the government of the country is so organised that only the workers and the working peasants, to the exclusion of the exploiters, constitute those mass organisations known as Soviets, and these Soviets wield all state power. That is why, in spite of the slander that the representatives of the bourgeoisie in all countries spread about Russia, the word "Soviet" has now become not only intelligible but popular all over the world, has become the favourite word of the workers, and of all working people. And that is why, notwithstanding all the persecution to which the adherents of communism in the different countries are subjected, Soviet power must necessarily, inevitably, and in the not distant future, triumph all over the world.

We know very well that there are still many defects in the organisation of Soviet power in this country. Soviet power is not a miracle-working talisman. It does not, overnight, heal all the evils of the past—illiteracy, lack of culture, the consequences of a barbarous war, the aftermath of predatory capitalism. But it does pave the way to socialism. It gives those who were formerly oppressed the chance to straighten their backs and to an ever-increasing degree to take the whole government of the country, the whole administration of the economy, the whole management of production, into their own hands.

Soviet power is the road to socialism that was discovered by the masses of the working people, and that is why it is the true road, that is why it is invincible.

The speech was made
at the end of March 1919

Collected Works, Vol. 29

Published January 21, 1928
in *Pravda* No. 18

A GREAT BEGINNING
HEROISM OF THE WORKERS IN THE REAR.
"COMMUNIST SUBBOTNIKS"

The press reports many instances of the heroism of the Red Army men. In the fight against Kolchak, Denikin and other forces of the landowners and capitalists, the workers and peasants very often display miracles of bravery and endurance, defending the gains of the socialist revolution. The guerrilla spirit, weariness and indiscipline are being overcome; it is a slow and difficult process, but it is making headway in spite of everything. The heroism of the working people making voluntary sacrifices for the victory of socialism—this is the foundation of the new, comradely discipline in the Red Army, the foundation on which that army is regenerating, gaining strength and growing.

The heroism of the workers in the rear is no less worthy of attention. In this connection, the *communist subbotniks* organised by the workers on their own initiative are really of enormous significance. Evidently, this is only a beginning, but it is a beginning of exceptionally great importance. It is the beginning of a revolution that is more difficult, more tangible, more radical and more decisive than the overthrow of the bourgeoisie, for it is a victory over our own conservatism, indiscipline, petty-bourgeois egoism, a victory over the habits left as a heritage to the worker and peasant by accursed capitalism. Only when *this* victory is consolidated will the new social discipline, socialist discipline, be created; then and only then will a reversion to capitalism become impossible, will communism become really invincible.

Pravda in its issue of May 17 published an article by A. J. entitled: "Work in a Revolutionary Way. *A Communist Saturday*". This article is so important that we reproduce it here in full.

"WORK IN A REVOLUTIONARY WAY
"A COMMUNIST SATURDAY

"The letter of the Russian Communist Party's Central Committee on working in a *revolutionary way* was a powerful stimulus to communist organisations and to Communists. The general wave of enthusiasm carried many communist railway workers to the front, but the majority of them could not leave their responsible posts or find new forms of working in a revolutionary way. Reports from the localities about the tardiness with which the work of mobilisation was proceeding and the prevalence of red tape compelled the Moscow-Kazan Railway district to turn its attention to the way the railway was functioning. It turned out that, owing to the shortage of labour and low productivity of labour, urgent orders and repairs to locomotives were being held up. At a general meeting of Communists and sympathisers of the Moscow-Kazan Railway district held on May 7, the question was raised of passing from words to deeds in helping to achieve victory over Kolchak. The following resolution was moved:

"'In view of the grave domestic and foreign situation, Communists and sympathisers, in order to gain the upper hand over the class enemy, must spur themselves on again and deduct an extra hour from their rest, i.e., lengthen their working day by one hour, accumulate these extra hours and put in six extra hours of manual labour on Saturday for the purpose of creating real values of immediate worth. Since Communists must not grudge their health and life for the gains of the revolution, this work should be performed without pay. *Communist Saturdays* are to be introduced throughout the district and to continue until complete victory over Kolchak has been achieved.'

"After some hesitation, the resolution was adopted unanimously.

"On Saturday, May 10, at 6 p. m., the Communists and sympathisers turned up to work like soldiers, formed ranks, and without fuss or bustle were taken by the foremen to the various jobs.

"The results of working *in a revolutionary way are evident.* The accompanying table gives the places of work and the character of the work performed (See Table on p. 480).

"The total value of the work performed at ordinary rates of pay is five million rubles; calculated at overtime rates it would be fifty per cent higher.

"The productivity of labour in loading waggons was 270 per cent higher than that of regular workers. The productivity of labour on other jobs was approximately the same.

"Jobs (urgent) were done which had been held up for periods ranging from seven days to three months owing to the shortage of labour and to red tape.

"The work was done in spite of the state of disrepair (easily remedied) of implements, as a result of which certain groups were held up from thirty to forty minutes.

"The administration left in charge of the work could hardly keep pace with the men in finding new jobs for them, and perhaps it was only a slight exaggeration when on old foreman said that as much work was done at this *communist Saturday* as would have been done in a week by non-class-conscious and slack workers.

"In view of the fact that many non-Communists, sincere supporters of the Soviet government, took part in the work, and that many more are expected on future Saturdays, and also in view of the fact that many other districts desire to follow the example of the communist railway workers of the Moscow-Kazan Railway, I shall deal in greater detail with the organisational side of the matter as seen from reports received from the localities.

"Of those taking part in the work, some ten per cent were Communists permanently employed in the localities. The rest were persons occupying responsible and elective posts, from the commissar of the railway to commissars of individual enterprises, representatives of the trade union, and employees of the head office and of the Commissariat of Railways.

"The enthusiasm and team spirit displayed during work were extraordinary. When the workers, clerks and head office employees, without even an oath or argument, caught hold of the forty-pood wheel tire of a passenger locomotive and, like industrious ants, rolled it into place, one's heart was filled with fervent joy at the sight of this collective effort, and one's conviction was strengthened

Place of work	Character of work	Number employed	Hours worked		Work performed
			per person	Total	
Moscow. Main locomotive shops	Loading materials for the line, devices for repairing locomotives and carriage parts for Perovo, Murom, Alatyr and Syzran	48 21 5	5 3 4	240 63 20	Loaded 7,500 poods Unloaded 1,800 poods
Moscow. Passenger depot	Complex current repairs to locomotives	26	5	130	Repairs done on $1\frac{1}{2}$ locomotives
Moscow. Shunting yards	Current repairs to locomotives	24	6	144	2 locomotives completed and parts to be repaired dismantled on 4
Moscow. Carriage department	Current repairs to passenger carriages	12	6	72	2 third-class carriages
Perovo. Main carriage workshops	Carriage repairs and minor repairs on Saturday and Sunday	46 23	5 5	230 115	12 box carriage and two flat carriages
	Total	205	—	1,014	4 locomotives and 16 carriages turned out and 9,300 poods unloaded and loaded

that the victory of the working class was unshakable. The international bandits will not crush the victorious workers; the internal saboteurs will not live to see Kolchak.

"When the work was finished those present witnessed an unprecedented scene: a hundred Communists, weary, but with the light of joy in their eyes, greeted their success with the solemn strains of the *Internationale*. And it seemed as if the triumphant strains of the triumphant anthem would sweep over the walls through the whole of working-class Moscow and that like the waves caused by a stone thrown into a pool they would spread through the whole of working-class Russia and shake up the weary and the slack.

"A. J."

Appraising this remarkable "example worthy of emulation", Comrade N. R. in an article in *Pravda* of May 20, under that heading, wrote:

"Cases of Communists working like this are not rare. I know of similar cases at an electric power station, and on various railways. On the Nikolayevskaya Railway, the Communists worked overtime several nights to lift a locomotive that had fallen into the turn-table pit. In the winter, all the Communists and sympathisers on the Northern Railway worked several Sundays clearing the track of snow; and the communist cells at many goods stations patrol the stations at night to prevent stealing. But all this work was casual and unsystematic. The comrades on the Moscow-Kazan line are making this work systematic and permanent, and this is new. They say in their resolution, 'until complete victory over Kolchak has been achieved', and therein lies the significance of their work. They are lengthening the working day of every Communist and sympathiser by one hour for the duration of the state of war; simultaneously, their productivity of labour is exemplary.

"This example has called forth, and *is bound* to call forth, further emulation. A general meeting of the Communists and sympathisers on the Alexandrovskaya Railway, after discussing the military situation and the resolution adopted by the comrades on the Moscow-Kazan Railway, resolved: (1) to introduce 'subbotniks' for the Communists and sympathisers on the Alexandrovskaya Railway, the first subbotnik to take place on May 17; (2) to organise the Communists and sympathisers in exemplary, model teams which must show the workers how to work and what can really be done with the present materials and tools, and in the present food situation.

"The Moscow-Kazan comrades say that their example has made a great impression and that they expect a large number of *non-Party* workers to turn up next Saturday. At the time these lines are being written, the Communists have not yet started working overtime in the Alexandrovskaya Railway workshops, but as soon as the rumour spread that they were to do so the mass of non-Party workers stirred themselves. 'We did not know yesterday, otherwise we would have worked as well!' 'I will certainly come next Saturday,' can be heard on all sides. The impression created by work of this sort is very great.

"The example set by the Moscow-Kazan comrades should be emulated by all the communist cells in the rear; not only the communist cells at Moscow Junction, but the whole Party organisation in Russia. In the rural districts too, the communist cells should in the first place set to work to till the fields of Red Army men and thus help their families.

"The comrades on the Moscow-Kazan line finished their first communist subbotnik by singing the *Internationale*. If the communist organisations throughout Russia follow this example and consistently apply it, the Russian Soviet Republic will successfully weather the coming severe months to the mighty strains of the *Internationale* sung by all the working people of the Republic....

"To work, communist comrades!"

On May 23, 1919, *Pravda* reported the following:

"The first communist 'subbotnik' on the Alexandrovskaya Railway took place on May 17. In accordance with the resolution adopted by their general meeting, ninety-eight Communists and sympathisers worked five hours overtime without pay, receiving in return only the right to purchase a second dinner, and, as manual labourers, half a pound of bread to go with their dinner."

Although the work was poorly prepared and organised the *productivity of labour was* nevertheless *from two to three times higher than usual.*

Here are a few examples.

Five turners turned eighty spindles in four hours. The productivity is 213 per cent of the usual level.

Twenty unskilled workers in four hours collected scrap materials of a total weight of 600 poods, and seventy laminated carriage springs, each weighing $3^1/_2$ poods, making a total of 850 poods. Productivity, 300 per cent of the usual level.

"The comrades explain this by the fact that ordinarily their work is boring and tiresome, whereas here they worked with a will and with enthusiasm. Now, however, they will be ashamed to turn out less in regular working hours than they did at the communist subbotnik."

"Now many non-Party workers say that they would like to take part in the subbotniks. The locomotive crews volunteer to take locomotives from the 'cemetery', during the subbotnik, repair them and set them going.

"It is reported that similar subbotniks are to be organised on the Vyazma line".

How the work is done at these communist subbotniks is described by Comrade A. Dyachenko in an article in *Pravda* of June 7, entitled "Notes of a Subbotnik Worker". We quote the main passages from this article.

"A comrade and I were very pleased to go and do our 'bit' in the subbotnik arranged by a decision of the railway district committee of the Party; for a time, for a few hours, I would give my head a rest and my muscles a bit of exercise.... We were detailed off to the railway carpentry shop. We got there, found a number of our people, exchanged greetings, engaged in banter for a bit, counted up our forces and found that there were thirty of us.... And in front of us lay a 'monster', a steam boiler weighing no less than six or seven hundred poods; our job was to 'shift' it, i.e., move it over a distance of a quarter or a third of a verst, to its base. We began to have our doubts.... However, we started on the job. Some comrades placed wooden rollers under the boiler, attached two ropes to it, and we began to tug away.... The boiler gave way reluctantly, but at length it budged. We were delighted. After all, there were so few of us.... For nearly two weeks this boiler had resisted the efforts of thrice our number of non-communist workers and nothing could make it budge until we tackled it.... We worked for an hour, strenuously, rhythmically, to the command of our 'foreman'—'one, two, three', and the boiler kept on rolling. Suddenly there was confusion, and a number of our comrades went tumbling on to the ground in the funniest fashion. The rope 'let them down'.... A moment's delay, and a thicker rope was made fast.... Evening. It was getting dark, but we had yet to negotiate a small hillock, and then our job would soon be done. Our arms ached, our palms burned, we were hot and pulled for all we were worth—and were making headway. The 'management' stood round and somewhat shamed by our success, clutched at a rope. 'Lend a hand, it's time you did!' A Red Army man was watching our labours; in his hands he held an accordion. What was he thinking? Who were these people? Why should they work on Saturday when everybody was at home? I solved his riddle and said to him: 'Comrade, play us a jolly tune. We are not raw hands, we are real Communists. Don't you see how fast the work is going under our hands? We are not lazy, we are pulling for all we are worth!' In response, the Red Army man carefully put his accordion on the ground and hastened to grab at a rope end....

"Suddenly Comrade U. struck up the workers' song 'Dublnushka', '*unglichanin mudrets*', he sang, in an excellent tenor voice and we all joined in the refrain of this labour shanty: '*Eh, dubinushka, ukhnem, podyornem, podyornem....*'

"We were unaccustomed to the work, our muscles were weary, our shoulders, our backs ached ... but the next day would be a free day, our day of rest, and we would be able to get all the sleep we wanted. The goal was near, and after a little hesitation our 'monster' rolled almost right up to the base. 'Put some boards under, raise it on the base, and let the boiler do the work that has long been expected of it.' We went off in a crowd to the 'Club room' of the local Party cell. The room was brightly lit; the walls decorated with posters; rifles stacked around the room. After lustily singing the *Internationale* we enjoyed a glass of tea and 'rum', and even bread. This treat, given us by the local comrades, was very welcome after our arduous toil. We took a brotherly farewell of our comrades and lined up. The strains of revolutionary songs echoed through the slumbering streets in the silence of the night and our measured tread kept time with the music. We sang 'Comrades, the Bugles Are Sounding', 'Arise Ye Starvelings from Your Slumbers', songs of the International and of labour.

"A week passed. Our arms and shoulders were back to normal and we were going to another 'subbotnik', nine versts away this time, to repair railway waggons. Our destination was Perovo. The comrades climbed on the roof of an 'American' box waggon and sang the *Internationale* well and with gusto. The people on the train listened to the singing, evidently in surprise. The wheels knocked a measured beat, and those of us who failed to get on to the roof clung to the steps, pretending to be 'devil-may-care' passengers. The train pulled in. We had reached our destination. We passed through a long yard and were warmly greeted by the commissar, Comrade G.

"'There is plenty of work, but few to do it! Only thirty of us, and in six hours we have to do average repairs to a baker's dozen of waggons! Here are twin-wheels already marked. We have not only empty waggons, but also a filled cistern.... But that's nothing, we'll "make a job of it", comrades!'

"Work went with a swing. Five comrades and I were working with hoists. Under pressure of our shoulders and two hoists, and directed by our 'foreman', these twin-wheels, weighing from sixty to seventy poods apiece, skipped from one track to another in the liveliest possible manner. One pair disappeared, another rolled into place. At last all were in their assigned places, and swiftly we shifted the old worn-out junk into a shed.... One, two, three—and, raised by a revolving iron hoist, they were dislodged from the rails in a trice. Over there, in the dark, we heard the rapid strokes of hammers; the comrades, like worker bees, were busy on their 'sick' cars. Some were carpentering, others painting, still others were covering roofs, to the joy of the comrade commissar and our own. The smiths also asked for our aid. In a portable smithy a rod with a coupling hook was gleaming white-hot; it had been bent by careless shunting. It was laid on the anvil, scattering white sparks, and, under the experienced direction of the smith, our trusty hammers beat it back into its proper shape. Still red-hot and spitting sparks, we rushed it on our shoulders to where it had to go. We pushed it into its socket. A few hammer strokes and it was fixed. We crawled under the waggon. The coupling system is not as simple as it looks; there are all sorts of contraptions with rivets and springs....

"Work was in full swing. Night was falling. The torches seemed to burn brighter than before. Soon it would be time to knock off. Some of the comrades were taking a 'rest' against some tires and 'sipping' hot tea. The May night was cool, and the new moon shone beautifully like a gleaming sickle in the sky. People were laughing and joking.

" 'Knock off, Comrade G., thirteen waggons are enough!'

"But Comrade G. was not satisfied.

"We finished our tea, broke into our songs of triumph, and marched to the door...."

The movement of "communist subbotniks" is not confined to Moscow. *Pravda* of June 6 reported the following:

"The first communist subbotnik in Tver took place on May 31. One hundred and twenty-eight Communists worked on the railway. In three and a half hours they loaded and unloaded fourteen waggons, repaired three locomotives, cut up ten sagenes of firewood and performed other work. The productivity of labour of the skilled communist workers was thirteen times above normal."

Again, on June 8 we read in *Pravda*:

"COMMUNIST SUBBOTNIKS

"*Saratov*, June 5. In response to the appeal of their Moscow comrades, the communist railway workers here at a general Party meeting resolved: to work five hours overtime on Saturdays without pay in order to support the national economy."

* * *

I have given the fullest and most detailed information about the communist subbotniks because in this we undoubtedly observe one of the most important aspects of communist construction, to which our press pays insufficient attention, and which all of us have as yet failed properly to appreciate.

Less political fireworks and more attention of the simplest but living facts of communist construction, taken from and tested by actual life—this is the slogan which all of us, our writers, agitators, propagandists, organisers, etc., should repeat unceasingly.

It was natural and inevitable in the first period after the proletarian revolution that we should be engaged primarily on the main and fundamental task of overcoming the resistance of the bourgeoisie, of vanquishing the exploiters, of crushing their conspiracy (like the "slave-owners' conspiracy" to surrender Petrograd,[243] in which all from the Black Hundreds and Cadets to the Mensheviks and Socialist-Revolutionaries were involved). But simultaneously with this task, another task comes to the forefront just as inevitably and ever more imperatively as time goes on, namely, the more important task of positive communist construction, the creation of new economic relations, of a new society.

As I have had occasion to point out more than once, among other occasions in the speech I delivered at a session of the Petrograd Soviet on March 12, the dictatorship of the proletariat is not only the use of force against the exploiters, and not even mainly the use of force. The economic foundation of this use of revolutionary force, the guarantee of its effectiveness and success is the fact that the proletariat represents and creates a higher type of social organisation of labour compared with capitalism. This is what is important, this is the source of the strength and the guarantee that the final triumph of communism is inevitable.

The feudal organisation of social labour rested on the discipline of the bludgeon, while the working people, robbed and tyrannised by a handful of landowners, were utterly ignorant and downtrodden. The capitalist organisation of social labour rested on the discipline of hunger, and, notwithstanding all the progress of bourgeois culture and bourgeois democracy, the vast mass of the working people in the most advanced, civilised and democratic republics remained an ignorant and downtrodden mass of wage slaves or oppressed peasants, robbed and tyrannised by a handful of capitalists. The communist organisation of social labour, the first step towards which is socialism, rests, and will do so more and more as time goes on, on the free and conscious discipline of the working people themselves who have thrown off the yoke both of the landowners and capitalists.

This new discipline does not drop from the skies, nor is it born from pious wishes; it grows out of the material conditions of large-scale capitalist production, and out of them alone. Without them it is impossible. And the repository, or the vehicle, of these material conditions is a definite historical class, created, organised, united, trained, educated and hardened by large-scale capitalism. This class is the proletariat.

If we translate the Latin, scientific, historico-philosophical term "dictatorship of the proletariat" into simpler language, it means just the following:

Only a definite class, namely, the urban workers and the factory, industrial workers in general, is able to lead the whole mass of the working and exploited people in the struggle to throw off the yoke of capital, in actually carrying it out, in the struggle to maintain and consolidate the victory, in the work of creating the new, socialist social system and in the entire struggle for the complete abolition of classes. (Let us observe in parenthesis that the only scientific distinction between socialism and communism is that the first term implies the first stage of the new society arising out of capitalism, while the second implies the next and higher stage.)

The mistake the "Berne" yellow International makes is that its leaders accept the class struggle and the leading role of the proletariat only in word and are afraid to think it out to its logical conclusion. They are afraid of that inevitable conclusion which particularly terrifies the bourgeoisie, and which is absolutely unacceptable to them. They are afraid to admit that the dictatorship of the proletariat is *also* a period of class struggle, which is inevitable as long as classes have not been abolished, and which changes in form, being particularly fierce and particularly peculiar in the period immediately following the overthrow of capital. The proletariat does not cease the class struggle after it has captured political power, but continues it until classes are abolished— of course, under different circumstances, in different form and by different means.

And what does the "abolition of classes" mean? All those who call themselves socialists recognise this as the ultimate goal of socialism, but by no means all give thought to its significance. Classes are large groups of people differing from each other by the place they occupy in a historically determined system of social production, by their relation (in most cases fixed and formulated in law) to the means of production, by their role in the social organisation of labour, and, consequently, by the dimensions of the share of social wealth of which they dispose and the mode of acquiring it. Classes are groups of people one of which can appropriate the labour of another owing to the different places they occupy in a definite system of social economy.

Clearly, in order to abolish classes completely, it is not enough to overthrow the exploiters, the landowners and capitalists, not enough to abolish *their* rights of ownership; it is necessary also to abolish *all* private ownership of the means of production, it is necessary to abolish the distinction between town and country, as well as the distinction between manual workers and brain workers. This requires a very long period of time. In order to achieve this an enormous step forward must be taken in developing the productive forces; it is necessary to overcome the resistance (frequently passive, which is particularly stubborn and particularly difficult to overcome) of the numerous survivals of small-scale production; it is necessary to overcome the enormous force of habit and conservatism which are connected with these survivals.

The assumption that all "working people" are equally capable of doing this work would be an empty phrase, or the illusion of an antediluvian, pre-Marxist socialist; for this ability does not come of itself, but grows historically, and grows *only* out of the material conditions of large-scale capitalist production. This ability, at the beginning of the road from capitalism to socialism, is possessed by the proletariat *alone*. It is capable of fulfilling the gigantic task that confronts it, first, because it is the strongest and most advanced class in civilised society; secondly, because in the most developed countries it constitutes the majority of the population, and thirdly, because in backward capitalist countries, like Russia, the majority of the population consists of semi-proletarians, i.e., of people who regularly live in a proletarian way part of the year, who regularly earn a part of their means of subsistence as wage-workers in capitalist enterprises.

Those who try to solve the problems involved in the transition from capitalism to socialism on the basis of general talk about liberty, equality, democracy in general, equality of labour democracy, etc. (as Kautsky, Martov and other heroes of the Berne yellow International do), thereby only reveal their petty-bourgeois, philistine nature and ideologically slavishly follow in the wake of the bourgeoisie. The correct solution of this problem can be found only in a concrete study of the specific relations between the specific class which has conquered political power, namely, the proletariat, and the whole non-proletarian, and also semi-proletarian, mass of the working population—relations which do not take shape in fantastically harmonious, "ideal" conditions, but in the real conditions of the frantic resistance of the bourgeoisie which assumes many and diverse forms.

The vast majority of the population—and all the more so of the working population—of any capitalist country, including Russia, have thousands of times experienced, themselves and through their kith and kin, the oppression of capital, the plunder and every sort of tyranny it perpetrates. The imperialist war, i.e., the slaughter of ten million people in order to decide whether British or German capital was to have supremacy in plundering the whole world, has greatly intensified these ordeals, has increased and deepened them, and has made the people realise their meaning. Hence the inevitable sympathy displayed by the vast majority of the population, particularly the working people, for the proletariat, because it is with heroic courage and revolutionary ruthlessness throwing off the yoke of capital, overthrowing the exploiters, suppressing their resistance, and shedding its blood to pave the road for the creation of the new society, in which there will be no room for exploiters.

Great and inevitable as may be their petty-bourgeois vacillations and their tendency to go back to bourgeois "order", under the "wing" of the bourgeoisie, the non-proletarian and semi-proletarian mass of the working population cannot but recognise the moral and political authority of the proletariat, who are not only overthrowing the exploiters and suppressing their resistance, but are building a new and higher social bond, a social discipline, the discipline of class-conscious and united working people, who know no yoke and no authority except the authority of their own unity, of their own, more class-conscious, bold, solid, revolutionary and steadfast vanguard.

In order to achieve victory, in order to build and consolidate socialism, the·proletariat must fulfil a twofold or dual task: first, it must, by its supreme heroism in the revolutionary struggle against capital, win over the entire mass of the working and exploited people; it must win them over, organise them and lead them in the struggle to overthrow the bourgeoisie and utterly suppress their resistance. Secondly, it must lead the whole mass of the working and exploited people, as well as all the petty-bourgeois groups, on to the road of new economic development, towards the creation of a new social bond, a new labour discipline, a new organisation of labour, which will combine the last word in science and capitalist technology with the mass association of class-conscious workers creating large-scale socialist industry.

The second task is more difficult than the first, for it cannot possibly be fulfilled by single acts of heroic fervour; it requires the most prolonged, most persistent and most difficult mass heroism in *plain, everyday* work. But this task is more essential than the first, because, in the last analysis, the deepest source of strength for victories over the bourgeoisie and the sole guarantee of the durability and permanence of these victories can only be a new and higher mode of social production, the substitution of large-scale socialist production for capitalist and petty-bourgeois production.

* * *

"Communist subbotniks" are of such enormous historical significance precisely because they demonstrate the conscious and voluntary initiative of the workers in developing the productivity of labour, in adopting a new labour discipline, in creating socialist conditions of economy and life.

J. Jacoby, one of the few, in fact it would be more correct to say one of the exceptionally rare, German bourgeois democrats who, after the lessons of 1870-71, went over not to chauvinism or national-liberalism, but to socialism, once said that the formation of a single trade union was of greater historical importance than the battle of Sadowa.[244] This is true. The battle of Sadowa decided the supremacy of one of two bourgeois monarchies, the Austrian or the Prussian, in creating a German national capitalist state. The formation of one trade union was a small step towards the world victory of the proletariat over the bourgeoisie. And we may similarly say that the first communist subbotnik, organised by the workers of the Moscow-Kazan Railway in Moscow on May 10, 1919, was of greater historical significance than any of the victories of Hindenburg, or of Foch and the British, in the 1914-18 imperialist war. The victories of the imperialists mean the slaughter of millions of workers for the sake of the profits of the Anglo-American and French multimillionaires, they are the atrocities of doomed capitalism, bloated with over-eating and rotting alive. The communist subbotnik organised by the workers of the Moscow-Kazan Railway is one of the cells of the new, socialist society, which brings to all the peoples of the earth emancipation from the yoke of capital and from wars.

The bourgeois gentlemen and their hangers-on, including the Mensheviks and Socialist-Revolutionaries, who are wont to regard themselves as the representatives of "public opinion", naturally jeer at the hopes of the Communists, call those hopes "a baobab tree in a mignonette pot", sneer at the insignificance of the number of subbotniks compared with the vast number of cases of thieving, idleness, lower productivity, spoilage of raw materials and finished goods, etc. Our reply to these gentlemen is that if the bourgeois intellectuals had dedicated their knowledge to assisting the working people instead of giving it to the Russian and foreign capitalists in order to restore their power, the revolution would have proceeded more rapidly and more peacefully. But this is utopian, for the issue is decided by the class struggle, and the majority of the intellectuals gravitate towards the bourgeoisie. Not with the assistance of the intellectuals will the proletariat achieve victory, but in spite of their opposition (at least in the majority of cases), removing those of them who are incorrigibly bourgeois, reforming, re-educating and subordinating the waverers, and gradually winning ever larger sections of them to its side. Gloating over the difficulties and setbacks of the revolution, sowing panic, preaching a return to the past—these are all weapons and methods of class struggle of the bourgeois intellectuals. The proletariat will not allow itself to be deceived by them.

If we get down to brass tacks, however, has it ever happened in history that a new mode of production has taken root immediately, without a long succession of setbacks, blunders and relapses? Half a century after the abolition of serfdom[245] there were still quite a number of survivals of serfdom in the Russian countryside. Half a century after the abolition of slavery in America the position of the Negroes was still very often one of semi-slavery. The bourgeois intellectuals, including the Mensheviks and Socialist-Revolutionaries, are true to themselves in serving capital and in continuing to use absolutely false arguments—before the proletarian revolution they accused us of being utopian; after the revolution they demand that we wipe out all traces of the past with fantastic rapidity!

We are not utopians, however, and we know the real value of bourgeois "arguments"; we also know that for some time after the revolution traces of the old ethics will inevitably predominate over the young shoots of the new. When the new has just been born the old always remains stronger than it for some time; this is always the case in nature and in social life. Jeering at the feebleness of the young shoots of the new order, cheap scepticism of the intellectuals and the like—these are, essentially, methods of bourgeois class struggle against the proletariat, a defence of capitalism against socialism. We must carefully study the feeble new shoots, we must devote the greatest attention to them, do everything to promote their growth and "nurse" them. Some of them will inevitably perish. We cannot vouch that precisely the "communist subbotniks" will play a particularly important role. But that is not the point. The point is to foster each and every shoot of the new; and life will select the most viable. If the Japanese scientist, in order to help mankind vanquish syphilis, had the patience to test six hundred and five preparations before he developed a six hundred and sixth which met definite requirements, then those who want to solve a more difficult problem, namely, to vanquish capitalism, must have the perseverance to try hundreds and thousands of new methods, means and weapons of struggle in order to elaborate the most suitable of them.

The "communist subbotniks" are so important because they were initiated by workers who were by no means placed in exceptionally good conditions, by workers of various specialities, and some with no speciality at all, just unskilled labourers, who are living under *ordinary*, i.e., *exceedingly hard*, conditions. We all know very well the main cause of the decline in the productivity of labour that is to be observed not only in Russia, but all over the world; it is ruin and impoverishment, embitterment and weariness caused by the imperialist war, sickness and malnutrition. The latter is first in importance. Starvation—that is the cause. And in order to do away with starvation, productivity of labour must be raised in agriculture, in transport and in industry. So, we get a sort of vicious circle: in order to raise productivity of labour we must save ourselves from starvation, and in order to save ourselves from starvation we must raise productivity of labour.

We know that in practice such contradictions are solved by breaking the vicious circle, by bringing about a radical change in the temper of the people, by the heroic initiative of the individual groups which often plays a decisive role against the background of such a radical change. The unskilled labourers and railway workers of Moscow (of course, we have in mind the majority of them, and not a handful of profiteers, officials and other whiteguards) are working people who are living in desperately hard conditions. They are constantly underfed, and now, before the new harvest is gathered, with the general worsening of the food situation, they are actually starving. And yet these starving workers, surrounded by the malicious counter-revolutionary agitation of the bourgeoisie, the Mensheviks and the Socialist-Revolutionaries, are organising "communist subbotniks", working overtime *without any pay,* and achieving *an enormous increase in the productivity of labour* in spite of the fact that they are weary, tormented, and exhausted by malnutrition. Is this not supreme heroism? Is this not the beginning of a change of momentous significance?

In the last analysis, productivity of labour is the most important, the principal thing for the victory of the new social system. Capitalism created a productivity of labour unknown under serfdom. Capitalism can be utterly vanquished, and will be utterly vanquished by socialism creating a new and much higher productivity of labour. This is a very difficult matter and must take a long time; but *it has been started,* and that is the main thing. If in starving Moscow, in the summer of 1919, the starving workers who had gone through four trying years of imperialist war and another year and a half of still more trying civil war could start this great work, how will things develop later when we triumph in the civil war and win peace?

Communism is the higher productivity of labour—compared with that existing under capitalism—of voluntary, class-conscious and united workers employing advanced techniques. Communist subbotniks are extraordinarily valuable as the *actual* beginning of *communism*; and this is a very rare thing, because we are in a stage when "only the *first steps* in the transition from capitalism to communism are being taken" (as our Party Programme[246] quite rightly says).

Communism begins when the *rank-and-file workers* display an enthusiastic concern that is undaunted by arduous toil to increase the productivity of labour, husband *every pood of grain, coal, iron* and other products, which do not accrue to the workers personally or to their "close" kith and kin, but to their "distant" kith and kin, i.e., to society as a whole, to tens and hundreds of millions of people united first in one socialist state, and then in a union of Soviet republics.

In *Capital,* Karl Marx ridicules the pompous and grandiloquent bourgeois-democratic great charter of liberty and the rights of man, ridicules all this phrase-mongering about liberty, equality and fraternity *in general,* which dazzles the petty bourgeois and philistines of all countries, including the present despicable heroes of the despicable Berne International. Marx contrasts these pompous declarations of rights to the plain, modest, practical, simple manner in which the question is presented by the proletariat—the legislative enactment of a shorter working day is a typical example of such treatment. The aptness and profundity of Marx's observation become the clearer and more obvious to us the more the content of the proletarian revolution unfolds. The "formulas" of genuine communism differ from the pompous, intricate, and solemn phraseology of the Kautskys, the Mensheviks and the

Socialist-Revolutionaries and their beloved "brethren" of Berne in that they reduce everything to the *conditions of labour*. Less chatter about "labour democracy", about "liberty, equality and fraternity", about "government by the people", and all such stuff; the class-conscious workers and peasants of our day see through these pompous phrases of the bourgeois intellectual and discern the trickery as easily as a person of ordinary common sense and experience, when glancing at the irreproachably "polished" features and immaculate appearance of the "fain fellow, dontcher know", immediately and unerringly puts him down as "in all probability, a scoundrel!"

Fewer pompous phrases, more plain, *everyday* work, concern for the pood of grain and the pood of coal! More concern about providing this pood of grain and pood of coal needed by the hungry workers and ragged and barefoot peasants *not by haggling*, not in a capitalist manner, but by the conscious, voluntary, boundlessly heroic labour of plain working men like the unskilled labourers and railwaymen of the Moscow-Kazan line.

We must all admit that vestiges of the bourgeois-intellectual phrase-mongering approach to questions of the revolution are in evidence at every step, everywhere, even in our own ranks. Our press, for example, does little to fight these rotten survivals of the rotten, bourgeois-democratic past; it does little to foster the simple, modest, ordinary but viable shoots of genuine communism.

Take the position of women. In this field, not a single democratic party in the world, not even in the most advanced bourgeois republic, has done in decades so much as a hundredth part of what we did in our very first year in power. We really razed to the ground the infamous laws placing women in a position of inequality, restricting divorce and surrounding it with disgusting formalities, denying recognition to children born out of wedlock, enforcing a search for their fathers, etc., laws numerous survivals of which, to the shame of the bourgeoisie and of capitalism, are to be found in all civilised countries. We have a thousand times the right to be proud of what we have done in this field. But the more *thoroughly* we have cleared the ground of the lumber of the old, bourgeois laws and institutions, the clearer it is to us that we have only cleared the ground to build on but are not yet building.

Notwithstanding all the laws emancipating woman, she continues to be a *domestic slave*, because *petty housework* crushes, strangles, stultifies and degrades her, chains her to the kitchen and the nursery, and she wastes her labour on barbarously unproductive, petty, nerve-racking, stultifying and crushing drudgery. The real *emancipation of women,* real communism, will begin only where and when an all-out struggle begins (led by the proletariat wielding the state power) against this petty housekeeping, or rather when its *wholesale transformation* into a large-scale socialist economy begins.

Do we in practice pay sufficient attention to this question, which in theory every Communist considers indisputable? Of course not. Do we take proper care of the *shoots* of communism which already exist in this sphere? Again the answer is *no*. Public catering establishments, nurseries, kindergartens—here we have examples of these shoots, here we have the simple, everyday means, involving nothing pompous, grandiloquent or ceremonial, which can *really emancipate women*, really lessen and abolish their inequality with men as regards their role in social production and public life. These means are not new, they (like all the material prerequisites for socialism) were created by large-scale capitalism. But under capitalism they remained, first, a rarity, and secondly—which is particularly important—either *profit-making* enterprises, with all the worst features of speculation, profiteering, cheating and fraud, or "acrobatics of bourgeois charity", which the best workers rightly hated and despised.

There is no doubt that the number of these institutions in our country has increased enormously and that they are *beginning* to change in character. There is no doubt that we have far more *organising talent* among the working and peasant women than we are aware of, that we have far more people than we know of who can organise practical work, with the co-operation of large numbers of workers and of still larger numbers of consumers, without that abundance of talk, fuss, squabbling and chatter about plans, systems, etc., with which our big-headed "intellectuals" or half-baked "Communists" are "affected". But we *do not nurse* these shoots of the new as we should.

Look at the bourgeoisie. How very well they know how to advertise what *they* need! See how millions of copies of *their* newspapers extol what the capitalists regard as "model" enterprises, and how "model" bourgeois institutions are made an object of national pride! Our press does not take the trouble, or hardly ever, to describe the best catering establishments or nurseries, in order, by daily insistence, to get some of them turned into models of their kind. It does not give them enough publicity, does not describe in detail the saving in human labour, the conveniences for the consumer, the economy of products, the emancipation of women from domestic slavery, the improvement in sanitary conditions, that can be achieved with *exemplary communist work* and extended to the whole of society, to all working people.

Exemplary production, exemplary communist subbotniks, exemplary care and conscientiousness in procuring and distributing every pood of grain, exemplary catering establishments, exemplary cleanliness in such-and-such a workers' house, in such-and-such a block, should all receive ten times more attention and care from our press, as well as from *every* workers' and peasants' organisation, than they receive now. All these are shoots of communism, and it is our common and primary duty to nurse them. Difficult as our food and production situation is, in the year and a half of Bolshevik rule there has been undoubted progress *all along the line*: grain procurements have increased from 30 million poods (from August 1, 1917 to August 1, 1918) to 100 million poods (from August 1, 1918 to May 1, 1919); vegetable gardening has expanded, the margin of unsown land has diminished, railway transport has begun to improve despite the enormous fuel difficulties, and so on. Against this general background, and with the support of the proletarian state power, the shoots of communism will not wither; they will grow and blossom into complete communism.

* * *

We must give very great thought to the significance of the "communist subbotniks", in order that we may draw all the very important practical lessons that follow from this great beginning.

The first and main lesson is that this beginning must be given every assistance. The word "commune" is being handled much too freely. Any kind of enterprise started by Communists or with their participation is very often at once declared to be a "commune", it being not infrequently forgotten that this *very honourable title* must be *won* by prolonged and persistent effort, by *practical* achievement in genuine communist development.

That is why, in my opinion, the decision that has matured in the minds of the majority of the members of the Central Executive Committee to *repeal* the decree of the Council of People's Commissars, as far as it pertains to the title "consumers' communes",[247] is quite right. Let the title be simpler—and, incidentally, the defects and shortcomings of the *initial* stages of the new organisational work will not be blamed on the "communes", but (as in all fairness they should be) on *bad* Communists. It would be a good thing to eliminate the word "commune" from *common* use, to prohibit every Tom, Dick and Harry from grabbing at it, or to *allow this title to be borne only* by genuine communes, which have really demonstrated in practice (and have proved by the unanimous recognition of the whole of the surrounding population) that they are capable of organising their work in a communist manner. First show that you are capable of working without remuneration in the interests of society, in the interests of all the working people, show that you are capable of "working in a revolutionary way", that you are capable of raising productivity of labour, of organising the work in exemplary manner, and then hold out your hand for the honourable title "commune"!

In this respect, the "communist subbotniks" are a most valuable exception; for the unskilled labourers and railwaymen of the Moscow-Kazan Railway *first* demonstrated *by deeds* that they are capable of working like *Communists*, and then adopted the title of "communist subbotniks" for their undertaking. We must see to it and make sure that in future anyone who calls his enterprise, institution or undertaking a commune *without having proved* this by hard work and practical *success in prolonged effort*, by exemplary and truly communist organisation, is mercilessly ridiculed and pilloried as a charlatan or a windbag.

That great beginning, the "communist subbotniks", must also be utilised for another purpose, namely, to *purge* the Party. In the early period following the revolution, when the mass of "honest" and philistine-minded people was particularly timorous, and when the bourgeois intellectuals to a man, including, of course, the Mensheviks and Socialist-Revolutionaries, played the lackey to the bourgeoisie and carried on sabotage, it was absolutely inevitable that adventurers and other pernicious elements should hitch themselves to the ruling party. There never has been, and there never can be, a revolution without that. The whole point is that the ruling party should be able, relying on a sound and strong advanced class, to purge its ranks.

We started this work long ago. It must be continued steadily and untiringly. The mobilisation of Communists for the war helped us in this respect: the cowards and scoundrels fled from the Party's ranks. Good riddance! *Such* a reduction in the Party's membership means an *enormous increase* in its strength and weight. We must continue the purge, and that new beginning, the "communist subbotniks", must be utilised for this purpose: members should be accepted into the Party only after six months', say, "trial", or "probation", at "working in a revolutionary way". A similar test should be demanded of *all* members of the Party who joined after October 25, 1917, and who have not proved by some special work or service that they are absolutely reliable, loyal and capable of being Communists.

The purging of the Party, through the steadily *increasing demands* it makes in regard to working in a genuinely communist way, will improve the state *apparatus* and will bring much nearer the *final transition* of the peasants to the side of the revolutionary proletariat.

Incidentally, the "communist subbotniks" have thrown a remarkably strong light on the class character of the state apparatus under the dictatorship of the proletariat. The Central Committee of the Party drafts a letter on "working in a revolutionary way".* The

---

* See *Collected Works*, Vol. 29, pp. 276-79.—*Ed.*

idea is suggested by the Central Committee of a party with from 100,000 to 200,000 members (I assume that that is the number that will remain after a thorough purging; at present the membership is larger).

The idea is taken up by the workers organised in trade unions. In Russia and the Ukraine they number about four million. The overwhelming majority of them are for the state power of the proletariat, for proletarian dictatorship. Two hundred thousand and four million—such is the ratio of the "gear-wheels", if one may so express it. Then follow the *tens of millions* of peasants, who are divided into three main groups: the most numerous and the one standing closest to the proletariat is that of the semi-proletarians or poor peasants; then come the middle peasants, and lastly the numerically very small group of kulaks or rural bourgeoisie.

As long as it is possible to trade in grain and to make profit out of famine, the peasant will remain (and this will for some time be inevitable under the dictatorship of the proletariat) a semi-working man, a semi-profiteer. As a profiteer he is hostile to us, hostile to the proletarian state; he is inclined to agree with the bourgeoisie and their faithful lackeys, up to and including the Menshevik Sher or the Socialist-Revolutionary B. Chernenkov, who stand for freedom to trade in grain. But *as a working man*, the peasant is a friend of the proletarian state, a most loyal ally of the worker in the struggle against the landowner and against the capitalist. As working men, the peasants, the vast mass of them, the peasant millions, support the state "machine" which is headed by the one or two hundred thousand Communists of the proletarian vanguard, and which consists of millions of organised proletarians.

A state more democratic, in the true sense of the word, one more closely connected with the working and exploited people, has *never yet existed*.

It is precisely proletarian work such as that put into "communist subbotniks" that will win the complete respect and love of peasants for the proletarian state. Such work and such work alone will completely convince the peasant that we are right, that communism is right, and make him our devoted ally, and, hence, will lead to the complete elimination of our food difficulties, to the complete victory of communism over capitalism in the matter of the production and distribution of grain, to the unqualified consolidation of communism.

June 28, 1919

Published July 1919 in pamphlet form by the State Publishing House, Moscow
Signed: *N. Lenin*

Collected Works, Vol. 29

ECONOMICS AND POLITICS IN THE ERA
OF THE DICTATORSHIP OF THE PROLETARIAT

I had intended to write a short pamphlet on the subject indicated in the title on the occasion of the second anniversary of Soviet power. But owing to the rush of everyday work I have so far been unable to get beyond preliminary preparations for some of the sections.* I have therefore decided to essay a brief, summarised exposition of what, in my opinion, are the most essential ideas on the subject. A summarised exposition, of course, possesses many disadvantages and shortcomings. Nevertheless, a short magazine article may perhaps achieve the modest aim in view, which is to present the problem and the groundwork for its discussion by the Communists of various countries.

1

Theoretically, there can be no doubt that between capitalism and communism there lies a definite transition period which must combine the features and properties of both these forms of social economy. This transition period has to be a period of struggle between dying capitalism and nascent communism—or, in other words, between capitalism which has been defeated but not destroyed and communism which has been born but is still very feeble.

The necessity for a whole historical era distinguished by these transitional features should be obvious not only to Marxists, but to any educated person who is in any degree acquainted with the theory of development. Yet all the talk on the subject of the transition to socialism which we hear from present-day petty-bourgeois democrats (and such, in spite of their spurious socialist label, are all the leaders of the Second International, including such individuals as MacDonald, Jean Longuet, Kautsky and Friedrich Adler) is marked by complete disregard of this obvious truth. Petty-bourgeois democrats are distinguished by an aversion to

---

* See *Collected Works*, Vol. 30, pp. 93-104.—*Ed.*

class struggle, by their dreams of avoiding it, by their efforts to smooth over, to reconcile, to remove sharp corners. Such democrats, therefore, either avoid recognising any necessity for a whole historical period of transition from capitalism to communism or regard it as their duty to concoct schemes for reconciling the two contending forces instead of leading the struggle of one of these forces.

2

In Russia, the dictatorship of the proletariat must inevitably differ in certain particulars from what it would be in the advanced countries, owing to the very great backwardness and petty-bourgeois character of our country. But the basic forces—and the basic forms of social economy—are the same in Russia as in any capitalist country, so that the peculiarities can apply only to what is of lesser importance.

The basic forms of social economy are capitalism, petty commodity production, and communism. The basic forces are the bourgeoisie, the petty bourgeoisie (the peasantry in particular) and the proletariat.

The economic system of Russia in the era of the dictatorship of the proletariat represents the struggle of labour, united on communist principles on the scale of a vast state and making its first steps—the struggle against petty commodity production and against the capitalism which still persists and against that which is newly arising on the basis of petty commodity production.

In Russia, labour is united communistically insofar as, first, private ownership of the means of production has been abolished, and, secondly, the proletarian state power is organising large-scale production on state-owned land and in state-owned enterprises on a national scale, is distributing labour-power among the various branches of production and the various enterprises, and is distributing among the working people large quantities of articles of consumption belonging to the state.

We speak of "the first steps" of communism in Russia (it is also put that way in our Party Programme adopted in March 1919), because all these things have been only partially effected in our country, or, to put it differently, their achievement is only in its early stages. We accomplished instantly, at one revolutionary blow, all that can, in general, be accomplished instantly; on the first day of the dictatorship of the proletariat, for instance, on October 26 (November 8), 1917, the private ownership of land was abolished without compensation for the big landowners—the big landowners were expropriated. Within the space of a few months practically all the big capitalists, owners of factories, joint-stock companies, banks, railways, and so forth, were also expropriated without compensation. The state organisation of large-scale production in industry and the transition from "workers' control" to "workers' management" of factories and railways—this has, by and large, already been accomplished; but in relation to agriculture it has only just begun ("state farms", i.e., large farms organised by the workers' state on state-owned land). Similarly, we have only just begun the organisation of various forms of co-operative societies of small farmers as a transition from petty commodity agriculture to communist agriculture.* The same must be said of the state-organised distribution of products in place of private trade, i.e., the state procurement and delivery of grain to the cities and of industrial products to the countryside. Available statistical data on this subject will be given below.

Peasant farming continues to be petty commodity production. Here we have an extremely broad and very sound, deep-rooted basis for capitalism, a basis on which capitalism persists or arises anew in a bitter struggle against communism. The forms of this struggle are private speculation and profiteering versus state procurement of grain (and other products) and state distribution of products in general.

3

To illustrate these abstract theoretical propositions, let us quote actual figures.

According to the figures of the People's Commissariat of Food, state procurements of grain in Russia between August 1, 1917, and August 1, 1918, amounted to about 30,000,000 poods, and in the following year to about 110,000,000 poods. During the first three months of the next campaign (1919-20) procurements will presumably total about 45,000,000 poods, as against 37,000,000 poods for the same period (August-October) in 1918.

These figures speak clearly of a slow but steady improvement in the state of affairs from the point of view of the victory of communism over capitalism. This improvement is being achieved in spite of difficulties without world parallel, difficulties due to the Civil War organised by Russian and foreign capitalists who are harnessing all the forces of the world's strongest powers.

Therefore, in spite of the lies and slanders of the bourgeoisie

---

* The number of "state farms" and "agricultural communes" in Soviet Russia is, as far as is known, 3,536 and 1,961 respectively, and the number of agricultural artels is 3,696. Our Central Statistical Board is at present taking an exact census of all state farms and communes. The results will begin coming in in November 1919.

of all countries and of their open or masked henchmen (the "socialists" of the Second International), one thing remains beyond dispute—as far as the basic economic problem of the dictatorship of the proletariat is concerned, the victory of communism over capitalism in our country is assured. Throughout the world the bourgeoisie is raging and fuming against Bolshevism and is organising military expeditions, plots, etc., against the Bolsheviks, because it realises full well that our success in reconstructing the social economy is inevitable, provided we are not crushed by military force. And its attempts to crush us in this way are not succeeding.

The extent to which we have already vanquished capitalism in the short time we have had at our disposal, and despite the incredible difficulties under which we have had to work, will be seen from the following, summarised figures. The Central Statistical Board has just prepared for the press data on the production and consumption of grain—not for the whole of Soviet Russia, but only for twenty-six gubernias.

The results are as follows:

26 gubernias of Soviet Russia	Population in millions		Production of grain (excluding seed and fodder), million poods	Grain delivered, million poods		Total amount of grain at disposal of population, million poods	Grain consumption, poods per capita
				Commissariat of food	Profiteers		
Producing gubernias	Urban	4.4	—	20.9	20.6	41.5	9.5
	Rural	28.6	625.4	—	—	481.8	16.9
Consuming gubernias	Urban	5.9	—	20.0	20.0	40.0	6.8
	Rural	13.8	114.0	12.1	27.8	151.4	11.0
Total (26 gubernias)		52.7	739.4	53.0	68.4	714.7	13.6

Thus, approximately half the amount of grain supplied to the cities is provided by the Commissariat of Food and the other half by profiteers. This same proportion is revealed by a careful survey. made in 1918, of the food consumed by city workers. It should be borne in mind that for bread supplied by the state the worker pays *one-ninth* of what he pays the profiteer. The profiteering price for bread is *ten times* greater than the state price; this is revealed by a detailed study of workers' budgets.

4

A careful study of the figures quoted shows that they present an exact picture of the fundamental features of Russia's present-day economy.

The working people have been emancipated from their age-old oppressors and exploiters, the landowners and capitalists. This step in the direction of real freedom and real equality, a step which for its extent, dimensions and rapidity is without parallel in the world, is ignored by the supporters of the bourgeoisie (including the petty-bourgeois democrats), who, when they talk of freedom and equality, mean parliamentary bourgeois democracy, which they falsely declare to be "democracy" in general, or "pure democracy" (Kautsky).

But the working people are concerned only with real equality and real freedom (freedom from the landowners and capitalists), and that is why they give the Soviet government such solid support.

In this peasant country it was the peasantry as a whole who were the first to gain, who gained most, and gained immediately from the dictatorship of the proletariat. The peasant in Russia starved under the landowners and capitalists. Throughout the long centuries of our history, the peasant never had an opportunity to work for himself: he starved while handing over hundreds of millions of poods of grain to the capitalists, for the cities and for export. Under the dictatorship of the proletariat the peasant *for the first time* has been working for himself and *feeding better than the city dweller*. For the first time the peasant has seen real freedom—freedom to eat his bread, freedom from starvation. In the distribution of the land, as we know, the maximum equality has been established; in the vast majority of cases the peasants are dividing the land according to the number of "mouths to feed".

Socialism means the abolition of classes.

In order to abolish classes it is necessary, first, to overthrow the landowners and capitalists. This part of our task has been accomplished, but it is only a part, and moreover, *not* the most difficult part. In order to abolish classes it is necessary, secondly, to abolish the difference between factory worker and peasant, to make *workers of all of them*. This cannot be done all at once. This task is incomparably more difficult and will of necessity take a long time. It is not a problem that can be solved by overthrowing a class. It can be solved only by the organisational reconstruction of the whole social economy, by a transition from individual, dis-united, petty commodity production to large-scale social production. This transition must of necessity be extremely protracted. It may only be delayed and complicated by hasty and incautious administrative and legislative measures. It can be accelerated only by affording such assistance to the peasant as will enable him to effect an immense improvement in his whole farming technique, to reform it radically.

In order to solve the second and most difficult part of the problem, the proletariat, after having defeated the bourgeoisie, must unswervingly conduct its policy towards the peasantry along the following fundamental lines. The proletariat must separate, demarcate the working peasant from the peasant owner, the peasant worker from the peasant huckster, the peasant who labours from the peasant who profiteers.

In this demarcation lies the *whole essence* of socialism.

And it is not surprising that the socialists who are socialists in word but petty-bourgeois democrats in deed (the Martovs, the Chernovs, the Kautskys and others) do not understand this essence of socialism.

The demarcation we here refer to is an extremely difficult one, because in real life all the features of the "peasant", however diverse they may be, however contradictory they may be, are fused into one whole. Nevertheless, demarcation is possible; and not only is it possible, it inevitably follows from the conditions of peasant farming and peasant life. The working peasant has for ages been oppressed by the landowners, the capitalists, the hucksters and profiteers and by *their* state, including even the most democratic bourgeois republics. Throughout the ages the working peasant has trained himself to hate and loathe these oppressors and exploiters, and this "training", engendered by the conditions of life, *compels* the peasant to seek an alliance with the worker against the capitalist and against the profiteer and huckster. Yet at the same time, economic conditions, the conditions of commodity production, inevitably turn the peasant (not always, but in the vast majority of cases) into a huckster and profiteer.

The statistics quoted above reveal a striking difference between the working peasant and the peasant profiteer. That peasant who during 1918-19 delivered to the hungry workers of the cities 40,000,000 poods of grain at fixed state prices, who delivered this grain to the state agencies despite all the shortcomings of the latter, shortcomings fully realised by the workers' government, but which were unavoidable in the first period of the transition to socialism—that peasant is a working peasant, the comrade and equal of the socialist worker, his most faithful ally, his blood brother in the fight against the yoke of capital. Whereas that peasant who clandestinely sold 40,000,000 poods of grain at ten times the state price, taking advantage of the need and hunger of the city worker, deceiving the state, and everywhere increasing and creating deceit, robbery and fraud—that peasant is a profiteer, an ally of the capitalist, a class enemy of the worker, an exploiter. For whoever possesses surplus grain gathered from land belonging to the whole state with the help of implements in which in one way or another is embodied the labour not only of the peasant but also of the worker and so on—whoever possesses a surplus of grain and profiteers in that grain is an exploiter of the hungry worker.

You are violators of freedom, equality, and democracy—they shout at us on all sides, pointing to the inequality of the worker and the peasant under our Constitution,[248] to the dissolution of the Constituent Assembly, to the forcible confiscation of surplus grain, and so forth. We reply—never in the world has there been a state which has done so much to remove the actual inequality, the actual lack of freedom from which the working peasant has been suffering for centuries. But we shall never recognise equality with the peasant profiteer, just as we do not recognise "equality" between the exploiter and the exploited, between the sated and the hungry, nor the "freedom" for the former to rob the latter. And those educated people who refuse to recognise this difference we shall treat as whiteguards, even though they may call themselves democrats, socialists, internationalists, Kautskys, Chernovs, or Martovs.

5

Socialism means the abolition of classes. The dictatorship of the proletariat has done all it could to abolish classes. But classes cannot be abolished at one stroke.

And classes still *remain* and *will remain* in the era of the dictatorship of the proletariat. The dictatorship will become unnecessary when classes disappear. Without the dictatorship of the proletariat they will not disappear.

Classes have remained, but in the era of the dictatorship of the proletariat *every* class has undergone a change, and the relations between the classes have also changed. The class struggle does not disappear under the dictatorship of the proletariat; it merely assumes different forms.

Under capitalism the proletariat was an oppressed class, a class which had been deprived of the means of production, the only class which stood directly and completely opposed to the bourgeoisie, and therefore the only one capable of being revolutionary to the very end. Having overthrown the bourgeoisie and conquered political power, the proletariat has become the *ruling* class; it wields state power, it exercises control over means of production already socialised; it guides the wavering and intermediary elements and classes; it crushes the increasingly stubborn resistance of the exploiters. All these are *specific* tasks of the class struggle, tasks which the proletariat formerly did not and could not have set itself.

The class of exploiters, the landowners and capitalists, has not disappeared and cannot disappear all at once under the dictatorship of the proletariat. The exploiters have been smashed, but not destroyed. They still have an international base in the form of international capital, of which they are a branch. They still retain certain means of production in part, they still have money, they still have vast social connections. Because they have been defeated, the energy of their resistance has increased a hundred- and a thousandfold. The "art" of state, military and economic administration gives them a superiority, and a very great superiority, so that their importance is incomparably greater than their numerical proportion of the population. The class struggle waged by the overthrown exploiters against the victorious vanguard of the exploited, i.e., the proletariat, has become incomparably more bitter. And it cannot be otherwise in the case of a revolution, unless this concept is replaced (as it is by all the heroes of the Second International) by reformist illusions.

Lastly, the peasants, like the petty bourgeoisie in general, occupy a half-way, intermediate position *even* under the dictatorship of the proletariat: on the one hand, they are a fairly large (and in backward Russia, a vast) mass of working people, united by the common interest of all working people to emancipate themselves from the landowner and the capitalist; on the other hand, they are disunited small proprietors, property-owners and traders. Such an economic position inevitably causes them to vacillate between the proletariat and the bourgeoisie. In view of the acute form which the struggle between these two classes has assumed, in view of the incredibly severe break-up of all social relations, and in view of the great attachment of the peasants and the petty bourgeoisie generally to the old, the routine, and the unchanging, it is only natural that we should inevitably find them swinging from one side to the other, that we should find them wavering, changeable, uncertain, and so on.

In relation to this class—or to these social elements—the proletariat must strive to establish its influence over it, to guide it. To give leadership to the vacillating and unstable—such is the task of the proletariat.

If we compare all the basic forces or classes and their interrelations, as modified by the dictatorship of the proletariat, we shall realise how unutterably nonsensical and theoretically stupid is the common petty-bourgeois idea shared by all representatives of the Second International, that the transition to socialism is possible "by means of democracy" in general. The fundamental source of this error lies in the prejudice inherited from the bourgeoisie that "democracy" is something absolute and above classes. As a matter of fact, democracy itself passes into an entirely new phase under the dictatorship of the proletariat, and the class struggle rises to a higher level, dominating over each and every form.

General talk about freedom, equality and democracy is in fact but a blind repetition of concepts shaped by the relations of commodity production. To attempt to solve the concrete problems of the dictatorship of the proletariat by such generalities is tantamount to accepting the theories and principles of the bourgeoisie in their entirety. From the point of view of the proletariat, the question can be put only in the following way: freedom from oppression by which class? equality of which class with which? democracy based on private property, or on a struggle for the abolition of private property?—and so forth.

Long ago Engels in his *Anti-Dühring* explained that the concept "equality" is moulded from the relations of commodity production; equality becomes a prejudice if it is not understood to mean the *abolition of classes.* This elementary truth regarding the distinction between the bourgeois-democratic and the socialist conception of equality is constantly being forgotten. But if it is not forgotten, it becomes obvious that by overthrowing the bourgeoisie the proletariat takes the most decisive step towards the abolition of classes, and that in order to complete the process the proletariat must continue its class struggle, making use of the apparatus of state power and employing various methods of combating, influencing and bringing pressure to bear on the overthrown bourgeoisie and the vacillating petty bourgeoisie.

(*To be continued*[249])

October 30, 1919

Pravda No. 250,
November 7, 1919
Signed: *N. Lenin*

Collected Works, Vol. 30

ADDRESS TO THE SECOND ALL-RUSSIA CONGRESS OF COMMUNIST ORGANISATIONS OF THE PEOPLES OF THE EAST[250]
NOVEMBER 22, 1919

Comrades, I am very glad of the opportunity to greet this congress of Communist comrades representing Moslem organisations of the East, and to say a few words about the situation now obtaining in Russia and throughout the world. The subject of my address is current affairs, and it seems to me that the most essential aspects of this question at present are the attitude of the peoples of the East to imperialism, and the revolutionary movement among those peoples. It is self-evident that this revolutionary movement of the peoples of the East can now develop effectively, can reach a successful issue, only in direct association with the revolutionary struggle of our Soviet Republic against international imperialism. Owing to a number of circumstances, among them the backwardness of Russia and her vast area, and the fact that she constitutes a frontier between Europe and Asia, between the West and the East, we had to bear the whole brunt—and we regard that as a great honour—of being the pioneers of the world struggle against imperialism. Consequently, the whole course of development in the immediate future presages a still broader and more strenuous struggle against international imperialism, and will inevitably be linked with the struggle of the Soviet Republic against the forces of united imperialism —of Germany, France, Britain and the U.S.A.

As regards the military aspect of the matter, you know how favourable our situation now is on all the fronts. I shall not dwell in detail on this question; I shall only say that the Civil War which was forced upon us by international imperialism has in two years inflicted incalculable hardship upon the Russian Socialist Federative Soviet Republic, and imposed upon the peasants and workers a burden so intolerable that it often seemed they would not be able to endure it. But at the same time, because of its brute violence, because of the ruthlessly brutal onslaught of our so-called allies, turned wild beasts, who robbed us even before the socialist revolution, this war has performed a miracle and turned people weary of fighting and seemingly incapable of bearing another war into warriors who have not only withstood the war for two years but are bringing it to a victorious end. The victories we are now gaining over Kolchak, Yudenich and Denikin signify the advent of a new phase in the history of the struggle of world imperialism against the countries and nations which have risen up to fight for their emancipation. In this respect, the two years of our Civil War have fully confirmed what has long been known to history—that the character of a war and its success depend chiefly upon the internal regime of the country that goes to war, that war is a reflection of the internal policy conducted by the given country before the war. All this is inevitably reflected in the prosecution of a war.

Which class waged the war, and is continuing to wage it, is a very important question. Only due to our Civil War being waged by workers and peasants who have emancipated themselves, and to its being a continuation of the political struggle for the emancipation of the working people from the capitalists of their own country and of the whole world—only thanks to this were people to be found in such a backward country as Russia, worn out as she was by four years of imperialist war, who were strong-willed enough to carry on that war during two years of incredible and unparalleled hardship and difficulty.

This was very strikingly illustrated in the history of the Civil War in the case of Kolchak. Kolchak was an enemy who had the assistance of all the world's strongest powers; he had a railway which was protected by some hundred thousand foreign troops, including the finest troops of the world imperialists, such as the Japanese, for example, who had been trained for the imperialist war, but took practically no part in it and therefore suffered little; Kolchak had the backing of the Siberian peasants, who were the most prosperous and had never known serfdom, and therefore, naturally, were farthest of all from communism. It seemed that Kolchak was an invincible force, because his troops were the advance guard of international imperialism. To this day, Japanese and Czechoslovak troops and the troops of a number of other imperialist nations are operating in Siberia. Nevertheless, the more than a year's experience of Kolchak's rule over Siberia and her vast natural resources, which was at first supported by the socialist parties of the Second International, by the Mensheviks and the Socialist-Revolutionaries, who set up the Constituent Assembly Committee front,[251] and which therefore, under these conditions, from the standpoint of the man in the street and of the ordinary course of history, appeared to be firm and invincible—that experience actually revealed the following. The farther Kolchak advanced into the heart of Russia, the more he wore himself out, and in the end we have witnessed Soviet Russia's complete triumph over Kolchak. Here we undoubtedly have practical proof that the united forces of workers and peasants who have been emancipated from the capitalist yoke can perform real miracles. Here we have practical proof that when a revolutionary war really does attract and interest the working and oppressed people, when it makes them conscious that they are fighting the exploiters—such a revolutionary war engenders the strength and ability to perform miracles.

I think that what the Red Army has accomplished, its struggle, and the history of its victory, will be of colossal, epochal significance for all the peoples of the East. It will show them that, weak as they may be, and invincible as may seem the power of the European oppressors, who in the struggle employ all the marvels of technology and of the military art—nevertheless, a revolutionary war waged by oppressed peoples, if it really succeeds in arousing the millions of working and exploited people, harbours such potentialities, such miracles, that the emancipation of the peoples of the East is now quite practicable, from the standpoint not only of the prospects of the international revolution, but also of the direct military experience acquired in Asia, in Siberia, the experience of the Soviet Republic, which has suffered the armed invasion of all the powerful imperialist countries.

Furthermore, the experience of the Civil War in Russia has shown us and the Communists of all countries that, in the crucible of civil war, the development of revolutionary enthusiasm is accompanied by a powerful inner cohesion. War tests all the economic and organisational forces of a nation. In the final analysis, infinitely hard as the war has been for the workers and peasants, who are suffering famine and cold, it may be said on the basis of these two years' experience that we are winning and will continue to win, because we have a hinterland, and a strong one, because, despite famine and cold, the peasants and workers stand together, have grown strong, and answer every heavy blow with a greater cohesion of their forces and increased economic might. And it is this alone that has made possible the victories over Kolchak, Yudenich and their allies, the strongest powers in the world. The past two years have shown, on the one hand, that a revolutionary war can be developed, and, on the other, that the Soviet system is growing stronger under the heavy blows of the foreign invasion, the aim of which is to destroy quickly the revolutionary centre, the republic of workers and peasants who have dared to declare war on international imperialism. But instead of destroying the workers and peasants of Russia, these heavy blows have served to harden them.

That is the chief lesson, the chief content of the present period. We are on the eve of decisive victories over Denikin, the last enemy left on our soil. We feel strong and may reiterate a thousand times over that we are not mistaken when we say that internally the Republic has become consolidated, and that we shall emerge from the war against Denikin very much stronger and better prepared for the task of erecting the socialist edifice—to which we have been able to devote all too little time and energy during the Civil War, but to which, now that we are setting foot on a free road, we shall undoubtedly be able to devote ourselves entirely.

In Western Europe we see the decay of imperialism. You know that a year ago it seemed even to the German socialists, and to the vast majority of socialists—who did not understand the state of affairs—that what was in progress was a struggle of two world imperialist groups, and they believed that this struggle constituted the whole of history, that there was no force capable of producing anything else. It seemed to them that even socialists had no alternative but to join sides with one of the groups of powerful world predators. That is how it seemed at the close of October 1918. But we find that in the year that has since elapsed world history has witnessed unparalleled events, profound and far-reaching events, and these have opened the eyes of many socialists who during the imperialist war were patriots and justified their conduct on the plea that they were faced with an enemy; they justified their alliance with the British and French imperialists on the grounds that these were supposedly bringing delivery from German imperialism. See how many illusions were shattered by that war! We are witnessing the decay of German imperialism, a decay which has led not only to a republican, but even to a socialist revolution. You know that in Germany today the class struggle has become still more acute and that civil war is drawing nearer and nearer—a war of the German proletariat against the German imperialists, who have adopted republican colours, but who remain imperialists.

Everyone knows that the social revolution is maturing in Western Europe by leaps and bounds, and that the same thing is happening in America and in Britain, the countries ostensibly representing culture and civilisation, victors over the Huns, the German imperialists. Yet when it came to the Treaty of Versailles, everyone saw that it was a hundred times more rapacious than the Treaty of Brest which the German robbers forced upon us, and that it was the heaviest blow the capitalists and imperialists of those luckless victor countries could possibly have struck at themselves. The Treaty of Versailles opened the eyes of the people of the victor nations, and showed that in the case of Britain and France, even though they are democratic states, we have before us not representatives of culture and civilisation, but countries ruled by imperialist predators. The internal struggle among these predators is developing so swiftly that we may rejoice in the knowledge that the Treaty of Versailles is only a seeming victory for the jubilant imperialists, and that in reality it signifies the bankruptcy of the entire imperialist world and the resolute abandonment by the working people of those socialists who during the war allied themselves with the representatives of decaying imperialism and defended one of the groups of belligerent predators. The eyes of the working people have been opened because the Treaty of Versailles was a rapacious peace and showed that France and Britain had actually fought Germany in order to strengthen their rule over the colonies and to enhance their imperialist might. That internal struggle grows broader as time goes on. Today I saw a wireless message from London dated November 21, in which American journalists—men who cannot be suspected of sympathising with revolutionaries—say that in France an unprecedented outburst of hatred towards the Americans is to be observed, because the Americans refuse to ratify the Treaty of Versailles.

Britain and France are victors, but they are up to their ears in debt to America, who has decided that the French and the British may consider themselves victors as much as they like, but that she is going to skim the cream and exact usurious interest for her assistance during the war; and the guarantee of this is to be the American Navy which is now being built and is overtaking the British Navy in size. And the crudeness of the Americans' rapacious imperialism may be seen from the fact that American agents are buying white slaves, women and girls, and shipping them to America for the development of prostitution. Just think, free, cultured America supplying white slaves for brothels! Conflicts with American agents are occurring in Poland and Belgium. That is a tiny illustration of what is taking place on a vast scale in every little country which received assistance from the Entente. Take Poland, for instance. You find American agents and profiteers going there and buying up all the wealth of Poland, who boasts that she is now an independent power. Poland is being bought up by American agents. There is not a factory or branch of industry which is not in the pockets of the Americans. The Americans have become so brazen that they are beginning to enslave that "great and free victor", France, who was formerly a country of usurers, but is now deep in debt to America, because she has lost her economic strength, and has not enough grain or coal of her own and cannot develop her material resources on a large scale, while America insists that the tribute be paid unreservedly and in full. It is thus becoming increasingly apparent that France, Britain and other powerful countries are economically bankrupt. In the French elections the Clericals have gained the upper hand. The French people, who were deceived into devoting all their strength supposedly to the defence of freedom and democracy against Germany, have now been rewarded with an interminable debt, with the sneers of the rapacious American imperialists and, on top of it, with a Clerical majority consisting of representatives of the most savage reaction.

The situation all over the world has become immeasurably more complicated. Our victory over Kolchak and Yudenich, those lackeys of international capital, is a big one; but far bigger, though not so evident, is the victory we are gaining on an international scale. That victory consists in the internal decay of imperialism, which is unable to send its troops against us. The Entente tried it, but to no purpose, because its troops become demoralised when they contact our troops and acquaint themselves with our Russian Soviet Constitution, translated into their languages. Despite the influence of the leaders of putrid socialism, our Constitution will always win the sympathy of the working people. The word "Soviet" is now understood by everybody, and the Soviet Constitution has been translated into all languages and is known to every worker. He knows that it is the constitution of working people, the political system of working people who are calling for victory over international capital, that it is a triumph we have achieved over the international imperialists. This victory of ours has had its repercussions in all imperialist countries, since we have deprived them of their own troops, won them over, deprived them of the possibility of using those troops against Soviet Russia.

They tried to wage war with the troops of other countries—Finland, Poland, and Latvia—but nothing came of it. British Minister Churchill, speaking in the House of Commons several weeks ago, boasted—and it was cabled all over the world—that a campaign of fourteen nations against Soviet Russia had been organised, and that this would result in victory over Russia by the New Year. And it is true that many nations participated in it—Finland, the Ukraine, Poland, Georgia, as well as the Czechoslovaks, the Japanese, the French, the British, and the Germans. But we know what came of it! We know that the Estonians left Yudenich's forces in the lurch; and now a fierce controversy is going on in the press because the Estonians do not want to help him, while Finland, much as her bourgeoisie wanted it, has not assisted Yudenich either. Thus the second attempt to attack us has likewise failed. The first stage was the dispatch by the Entente of its own troops, equipped according to all the rules of military technique, so that it seemed they would defeat the Soviet Republic. They have already withdrawn from the Caucasus, Archangel and the Crimea; they still remain in Murmansk, as the Czechoslovaks do in Siberia, but only as isolated groups. The first attempt of the Entente to defeat us with its own forces ended in victory for us. The second attempt consisted in launching against us nations which are our neighbours, and which are entirely dependent financially on the Entente, and in trying to force them to crush us, as a nest of socialism. But that attempt, too, ended in failure: it turned out that not one of these little countries is capable of waging such a war. What is more, hatred of the Entente has taken firm root in every little country. If Finland did not set out to capture Petrograd when Yudenich had already captured Krasnoye Selo, it was because she hesitated, realising that she could live independently side by side with Soviet Russia, but could not live in peace with the Entente. All little nations have felt that. It is felt in Finland, Lithuania, Estonia, and Poland, where chauvinism is rampant, but where there is hatred of the Entente, which is expanding its exploitation in those countries. And now, accurately assessing the course of developments, we may say without exaggeration that not only the first, but also the second stage of the international war against the Soviet Republic has failed. All that remains for us to do now is to defeat Denikin's forces, and they are already half-defeated.

Such is the present Russian and international situation, which I have summarised briefly in my address. Permit me, in conclusion, to say something about the situation that is developing in respect of the nationalities of the East. You are representatives of the communist organisations and Communist Parties of various Eastern peoples. I must say that the Russian Bolsheviks have succeeded in forcing a breach in the old imperialism, in undertaking the exceedingly difficult, but also exceedingly noble task of blazing new paths of revolution, whereas you, the representatives of the working people of the East, have before you a task that is still greater and newer. It is becoming quite clear that the socialist revolution which is impending for the whole world will not be merely the victory of the proletariat of each country over its own bourgeoisie. That would be possible if revolutions came easily and swiftly. We know that the imperialists will not allow this, that all countries are armed against their domestic Bolshevism and that their one thought is how to defeat Bolshevism at home. That is why in every country a civil war is brewing in which the old socialist compromisers are enlisted on the side of the bourgeoisie. Hence, the socialist revolution will not be solely, or chiefly, a struggle of the revolutionary proletarians in each country against their bourgeoisie—no, it will be a struggle of all the imperialist-oppressed colonies and countries, of all dependent countries, against international imperialism. Characterising the approach of the world social revolution in the Party Programme we adopted last March, we said that the civil war of the working people against the imperialists and exploiters in all the advanced countries is beginning to be combined with national wars against international imperialism. That is confirmed by the course of the revolution, and will be more and more confirmed as time goes on. It will be the same in the East.

We know that in the East the masses will rise as independent participants, as builders of a new life, because hundreds of millions of the people belong to dependent, underprivileged nations, which until now have been objects of international imperialist policy, and have only existed as material to fertilise capitalist culture and civilisation. And when they talk of handing out mandates for colonies, we know very well that it means handing out mandates for spoliation and plunder—handing out to an insignificant section of the world's population the right to exploit the majority of the population of the globe. That majority, which up till then had been completely outside the orbit of historical progress, because it could not constitute an independent revolutionary force, ceased, as we know, to play such a passive role at the beginning of the twentieth century. We know that 1905 was followed by revolutions in Turkey, Persia and China, and that a revolutionary movement developed in India. The imperialist war likewise contributed to the growth of the revolutionary movement, because the European imperialists had to enlist whole colonial regiments in their struggle. The imperialist war aroused the East also and drew its peoples into international politics. Britain and France armed colonial peoples and helped them to familiarise themselves with military technique and up-to-date machines. That knowledge they will use against the imperialist gentry. The period of the awakening of the East in the contemporary revolution is being succeeded by a period in which all the Eastern peoples will participate in deciding the destiny of the whole world, so as not to be simply objects of the enrichment of others. The peoples of the East are becoming alive to the need for practical action, the need for every nation to take part in shaping the destiny of all mankind.

That is why I think that in the history of the development of the world revolution—which, judging by its beginning, will continue for many years and will demand much effort—that in the revolutionary struggle, in the revolutionary movement you will be called upon to play a big part and to merge with our struggle against international imperialism. Your participation in the international revolution will confront you with a complicated and difficult task, the accomplishment of which will serve as the foundation for our common success, because here the majority of the people for the first time begin to act independently and will be an active factor in the fight to overthrow international imperialism.

Most of the Eastern peoples are in a worse position than the most backward country in Europe—Russia. But in our struggle against feudal survivals and capitalism, we succeeded in uniting the peasants and workers of Russia; and it was because the peasants and workers united against capitalism and feudalism that our victory was so easy. Here contact with the peoples of the East is particularly important, because the majority of the Eastern peoples are typical representatives of the working people—not workers who have passed through the school of capitalist factories, but typical representatives of the working and exploited peasant masses who are victims of medieval oppression. The Russian revolution showed how the proletarians, after defeating capitalism and uniting with the vast diffuse mass of working peasants, rose up victoriously against medieval oppression. Our Soviet Republic must now muster all the awakening peoples of the East and, together with them, wage a struggle against international imperialism.

In this respect you are confronted with a task which has not previously confronted the Communists of the world: relying upon the general theory and practice of communism, you must adapt yourselves to specific conditions such as do not exist in the European countries; you must be able to apply that theory and practice to conditions in which the bulk of the population are peasants, and in which the task is to wage a struggle against medieval survivals and not against capitalism. That is a difficult and specific task, but a very thankful one, because masses that have taken no part in the struggle up to now are being drawn into it, and also because the organisation of communist cells in the East gives you an opportunity to maintain the closest contact with the Third International. You must find specific forms for this alliance of the foremost proletarians of the world with the labouring and exploited masses of the East whose conditions are in many cases medieval. We have accomplished on a small scale in our country what you will do on a big scale and in big countries. And that latter task you will, I hope, perform with success. Thanks to the communist organisations in the East, of which you here are the representatives, you have contact with the advanced revolutionary proletariat. Your task is to continue to ensure that communist propaganda is carried on in every country in a language the people understand.

It is self-evident that final victory can be won only by the proletariat of all the advanced countries of the world, and we, the Russians, are beginning the work which the British, French or German proletariat will consolidate. But we see that they will not be victorious without the aid of the working people of all the oppressed colonial nations, first and foremost, of Eastern nations. We must realise that the transition to communism cannot be accomplished by the vanguard alone. The task is to arouse the working masses to revolutionary activity, to independent action and to organisation, regardless of the level they have reached; to translate the true communist doctrine, which was intended for the

Communists of the more advanced countries, into the language of every people; to carry out those practical tasks which must be carried out immediately, and to join the proletarians of other countries in a common struggle.

Such are the problems whose solution you will not find in any communist book, but will find in the common struggle begun by Russia. You will have to tackle that problem and solve it through your own independent experience. In that you will be assisted, on the one hand, by close alliance with the vanguard of the working people of other countries, and, on the other, by ability to find the right approach to the peoples of the East whom you here represent. You will have to base yourselves on the bourgeois nationalism which is awakening, and must awaken, among those peoples, and which has its historical justification. At the same time, you must find your way to the working and exploited masses of every country and tell them in a language they understand that their only hope of emancipation lies in the victory of the international revolution, and that the international proletariat is the only ally of all the hundreds of millions of the working and exploited peoples of the East.

Such is the immense task which confronts you, and which, thanks to the era of revolution and the growth of the revolutionary movement—of that there can be no doubt—will, by the joint efforts of the communist organisations of the East, be successfully accomplished and crowned by complete victory over international imperialism.

Bulletin
of the C.C., R.C.P.(B.)
No. 9, December 20, 1919

Collected Works, Vol. 30

"LEFT-WING" COMMUNISM—AN INFANTILE DISORDER[252]

I

IN WHAT SENSE WE CAN SPEAK OF THE INTERNATIONAL SIGNIFICANCE OF THE RUSSIAN REVOLUTION

In the first months after the proletariat in Russia had won political power (October 25 [November 7], 1917), it might have seemed that the enormous difference between backward Russia and the advanced countries of Western Europe would lead to the proletarian revolution in the latter countries bearing very little resemblance to ours. We now possess quite considerable international experience, which shows very definitely that certain fundamental features of our revolution have a significance that is not local, or peculiarly national, or Russian alone, but international. I am not speaking here of international significance in the broad sense of the term: not merely several but all the primary features of our revolution, and many of its secondary features, are of international significance in the meaning of its effect on all countries. I am speaking of it in the narrowest sense of the word, taking international significance to mean the international validity or the historical inevitability of a repetition, on an international scale, of what has taken place in our country. It must be admitted that certain fundamental features of our revolution do possess that significance.

It would, of course, be grossly erroneous to exaggerate this truth and to extend it beyond certain fundamental features of our revolution. It would also be erroneous to lose sight of the fact that, soon after the victory of the proletarian revolution in at least one of the advanced countries, a sharp change will probably come about: Russia will cease to be the model and will once again become a backward country (in the "Soviet" and the socialist sense).

At the present moment in history, however, it is the Russian model that reveals to *all* countries something—and something highly significant—of their near and inevitable future. Advanced workers in all lands have long realised this; more often than not, they have grasped it with their revolutionary class instinct rather than realised it. Herein lies the international "significance" (in the narrow sense of the word) of Soviet power, and of the fundamentals of Bolshevik theory and tactics. The "revolutionary" leaders of the Second International, such as Kautsky in Germany and Otto Bauer and Friedrich Adler in Austria, have failed to understand this, which is why they have proved to be reactionaries and advocates of the worst kind of opportunism and social treachery. Incidentally, the anonymous pamphlet entitled *The World Revolution (Weltrevolution)*,[253] which appeared in Vienna in 1919 (*Sozialistische Bücherei*, Heft 11; Ignaz Brand*) very clearly reveals their entire thinking and their entire range of ideas, or, rather, the full extent of their stupidity, pedantry, baseness and betrayal of working-class interests—and that, moreover, under the guise of "defending" the idea of "world revolution".

We shall, however, deal with this pamphlet in greater detail some other time. We shall here note only one more point: in bygone days, when he was still a Marxist and not a renegade, Kautsky, dealing with the question as an historian, foresaw the possibility of a situation arising in which the revolutionary spirit of the Russian proletariat would provide a model to Western Europe. This was in 1902, when Kautsky wrote an article for the revolutionary *Iskra*, entitled "The Slavs and Revolution". Here is what he wrote in the article:

"At the present time [in contrast with 1848] it would seem that not only have the slavs entered the ranks of the revolutionary nations, but that the centre of revolutionary thought and revolutionary action is shifting more and more to the Slavs. The revolutionary centre is shifting from the West to the East. In the first half of the nineteenth century it was located in France, at times in England. In 1848 Germany too joined the ranks of the revolutionary nations.... The new century has begun with events which suggest the idea that we are approaching a further shift of the revolutionary centre, namely, to Russia.... Russia, which has borrowed so much revolutionary initiative from the West, is now perhaps herself ready to serve the West as a source of revolutionary energy. The Russian revolutionary movement that is now flaring up will perhaps prove to be the most potent means of exorcising the spirit of flabby philistinism and coldly calculating politics that is beginning to spread in our midst, and it may cause the fighting spirit and the passionate devotion to our great ideals to flare up again. To Western Europe, Russia has long ceased to be a bulwark of reaction and absolutism. I think the reverse is true today. Western Europe is becoming Russia's bulwark of reaction and absolutism.... The Russian revolutionaries might perhaps have coped with the tsar long ago had they not been compelled at the same time to fight his ally—European capital. Let us hope that this time they will succeed in coping with both enemies, and that the new 'Holy Alliance' will collapse more rapidly than its predecessors did. However the present struggle in Russia may end, the blood and suffering of the martyrs whom, unfortunately, it will produce in too great numbers, will not have been in vain. They will nourish the shoots of social revolution throughout the civilised world and make them grow more luxuriantly and rapidly. In 1848 the Slavs were a killing frost which blighted the flowers of the people's spring. Perhaps

---

* Ignaz Brand, *Socialist Library*, Vol. 11.—*Ed.*

they are now destined to be the storm that will break the ice of reaction and irresistibly bring with it a new and happy spring for the nations" (Karl Kautsky, "The Slavs and Revolution", *Iskra*, Russian Social-Democratic revolutionary newspaper, No. 18, March 10, 1902).

How well Karl Kautsky wrote eighteen years ago!

II

AN ESSENTIAL CONDITION OF THE BOLSHEVIKS' SUCCESS

It is, I think, almost universally realised at present that the Bolsheviks could not have retained power for two and a half months, let alone two and a half years, without the most rigorous and truly iron discipline in our Party, or without the fullest and unreserved support from the entire mass of the working class, that is, from all thinking, honest, devoted and influential elements in it, capable of leading the backward strata or carrying the latter along with them.

The dictatorship of the proletariat means a most determined and most ruthless war waged by the new class against a *more powerful* enemy, the bourgeoisie, whose resistance is increased *tenfold* by their overthrow (even if only in a single country), and whose power lies, not only in the strength of international capital, the strength and durability of their international connections, but also in the *force of habit*, in the strength of *small-scale production*. Unfortunately, small-scale production is still widespread in the world, and small-scale production *engenders* capitalism and the bourgeoisie continuously, daily, hourly, spontaneously, and on a mass scale. All these reasons make the dictatorship of the proletariat necessary, and victory over the bourgeoisie is impossible without a long, stubborn and desperate life-and-death struggle which calls for tenacity, discipline, and a single and inflexible will.

I repeat: the experience of the victorious dictatorship of the proletariat in Russia has clearly shown even to those who are incapable of thinking or have had no occasion to give thought to the matter that absolute centralisation and rigorous discipline in the proletariat are an essential condition of victory over the bourgeoisie.

This is often dwelt on. However, not nearly enough thought is given to what it means, and under what conditions it is possible. Would it not be better if the salutations addressed to the Soviets and the Bolsheviks were *more frequently* accompanied by a *profound analysis* of the reasons *why* the Bolsheviks have been able to build up the discipline needed by the revolutionary proletariat?

As a current of political thought and as a political party, Bolshevism has existed since 1903. Only the history of Bolshevism during the *entire* period of its existence can satisfactorily explain why it has been able to build up and maintain, under most difficult conditions, the iron discipline needed for the victory of the proletariat.

The first questions to arise are: how is the discipline of the proletariat's revolutionary party maintained? How is it tested? How is it reinforced? First, by the class-consciousness of the proletarian vanguard and by its devotion to the revolution, by its tenacity, self-sacrifice and heroism. Second, by its ability to link up, maintain the closest contact, and—if you wish—merge, in certain measure, with the broadest masses of the working people—primarily with the proletariat, but also with the non-proletarian masses of working people. Third, by the correctness of the political leadership exercised by this vanguard, by the correctness of its political strategy and tactics, provided the broad masses have seen, *from their own experience*, that they are correct. Without these conditions, discipline in a revolutionary party really capable of being the party of the advanced class, whose mission it is to overthrow the bourgeoisie and transform the whole of society, cannot be achieved. Without these conditions, all attempts to establish discipline inevitably fall flat and end up in phrasemongering and clowning. On the other hand, these conditions cannot emerge at once. They are created only by prolonged effort and hard-won experience. Their creation is facilitated by a correct revolutionary theory, which, in its turn, is not a dogma, but assumes final shape only in close connection with the practical activity of a truly mass and truly revolutionary movement.

The fact that, in 1917-20, Bolshevism was able, under unprecedentedly difficult conditions, to build up and successfully maintain the strictest centralisation and iron discipline was due simply to a number of historical peculiarities of Russia.

On the one hand, Bolshevism arose in 1903 on a very firm foundation of Marxist theory. The correctness of this revolutionary theory, and of it alone, has been proved, not only by world experience throughout the nineteenth century, but especially by the experience of the seekings and vacillations, the errors and disappointments of revolutionary thought in Russia. For about half a century—approximately from the forties to the nineties of the last century—progressive thought in Russia, oppressed by a most brutal and reactionary tsarism, sought eagerly for a correct revolutionary theory, and followed with the utmost diligence and thoroughness each and every "last word" in this sphere in Europe and America. Russia achieved Marxism—the only correct revolutionary theory—through the *agony* she experienced in the course of half a century of unparalleled torment and sacrifice, of unparalleled revolutionary heroism, incredible energy, devoted searching, study, practical trial, disappointment, verification, and comparison with European experience. Thanks to the political emigration caused by tsarism, revolutionary Russia, in the second half of the nineteenth century, acquired a wealth of international links and excellent information on the forms and theories of the world revolutionary movement, such as no other country possessed.

On the other hand, Bolshevism, which had arisen on this granite foundation of theory, went through fifteen years of practical history (1903-17) unequalled anywhere in the world in its wealth of experience. During those fifteen years, no other country knew anything even approximating to that revolutionary experience, that rapid and varied succession of different forms of the movement—legal and illegal, peaceful and stormy, underground and open, local circles and mass movements, and parliamentary and terrorist forms. In no other country has there been concentrated, in so brief a period, such a wealth of forms, shades, and methods of struggle of *all* classes of modern society, a struggle which, owing to the backwardness of the country and the severity of the tsarist yoke, matured with exceptional rapidity, and assimilated most eagerly and successfully the appropriate "last world" of American and European political experience.

III

THE PRINCIPAL STAGES IN THE HISTORY OF BOLSHEVISM

The years of preparation for revolution (1903-05). The approach of a great storm was sensed everywhere. All classes were in a state of ferment and preparation. Abroad, the press of the political exiles discussed the theoretical aspects of *all* the fundamental problems of the revolution. Representatives of the three main classes, of the three principal political trends—the liberal-bourgeois, the petty-bourgeois-democratic (concealed behind "social-democratic" and "social-revolutionary" labels[254]), and the proletarian-revolutionary—anticipated and prepared the impending open class struggle by waging a most bitter struggle on issues of programme and tactics. *All* the issues on which the masses waged an armed struggle in 1905-07 and 1917-20 can (and should) be studied, in their embryonic form, in the press of the period. Among these three main trends there were, of course, a host of intermediate, transitional or half-hearted forms. It would be more correct to say that those political and ideological trends which were genuinely of a class nature crystallised in the struggle of press organs, parties, factions and groups; the classes were forging the requisite political and ideological weapons for the impending battles.

The years of revolution (1905-07). All classes came out into the open. All programmatical and tactical views were tested by the action of the masses. In its extent and acuteness, the strike struggle had no parallel anywhere in the world. The economic strike developed into a political strike, and the latter into insurrection. The relations between the proletariat, as the leader, and the vacillating and unstable peasantry, as the led, were tested in practice. The Soviet form of organisation came into being in the spontaneous development of the struggle. The controversies of that period over the significance of the Soviets anticipated the great struggle of 1917-20. The alternation of parliamentary and non-parliamentary forms of struggle, of the tactics of boycotting parliament and that of participating in parliament, of legal and illegal forms of struggle, and likewise their interrelations and connections—all this was marked by an extraordinary wealth of content. As for teaching the fundamentals of political science to masses and leaders, to classes and parties alike, each month of this period was equivalent to an entire year of "peaceful" and "constitutional" development. Without the "dress rehearsal" of 1905, the victory of the October Revolution in 1917 would have been impossible.

The years of reaction (1907-10). Tsarism was victorious. All the revolutionary and opposition parties were smashed. Depression, demoralisation, splits, discord, defection, and pornography took the place of politics. There was an ever greater drift towards philosophical idealism; mysticism became the garb of counter-revolutionary sentiments. At the same time, however, it was this great defeat that taught the revolutionary parties and the revolutionary class a real and very useful lesson, a lesson in historical dialectics, a lesson in an understanding of the political struggle, and in the art and science of waging that struggle. It is at moments of need that one learns who one's friends are. Defeated armies learn their lesson.

Victorious tsarism was compelled to speed up the destruction of the remnants of the pre-bourgeois, patriarchal mode of life in Russia. The country's development along bourgeois lines proceeded apace. Illusions that stood outside and above class distinctions, illusions concerning the possibility of avoiding capitalism, were scattered to the winds. The class struggle manifested itself in a quite new and more distinct way.

The revolutionary parties had to complete their education. They were learning how to attack. Now they had to realise that such knowledge must be supplemented with the knowledge of how to retreat in good order. They had to realise—and it is from bitter

experience that the revolutionary class learns to realise this—that
victory is impossible unless one has learned how to attack and
retreat properly. Of all the defeated opposition and revolutionary
parties, the Bolsheviks effected the most orderly retreat, with the
least loss to their "army", with its core best preserved, with the
least significant splits (in point of depth and incurability), with
the least demoralisation, and in the best condition to resume work
on the broadest scale and in the most correct and energetic manner. The Bolsheviks achieved this only because they ruthlessly
exposed and expelled the revolutionary phrase-mongers, those
who did not wish to understand that one had to retreat, that one
had to know how to retreat, and that one had absolutely to learn
how to work legally in the most reactionary of parliaments, in
the most reactionary of trade unions, co-operative and insurance
societies and similar organisations.

The years of revival (1910-14). At first progress was incredibly
slow, then, following the Lena events of 1912,[255] it became somewhat more rapid. Overcoming unprecedented difficulties, the Bolsheviks thrust back the Mensheviks, whose role as bourgeois agents
in the working-class movement was clearly realised by the entire
bourgeoisie after 1905, and whom the bourgeoisie therefore supported in a thousand ways against the Bolsheviks. But the Bolsheviks would never have succeeded in doing this had they not followed the correct tactics of combining illegal work with the utilisation of "legal opportunities", which they made a point of doing.
In the elections to the arch-reactionary Duma, the Bolsheviks won
the full support of the worker curia.

The First Imperialist World War (1914-17). Legal parliamentarianism, with an extremely reactionary "parliament", rendered
most useful service to the Bolsheviks, the party of the revolutionary
proletariat. The Bolshevik deputies were exiled to Siberia.[256] All
shades of social-imperialism, social-chauvinism, social-patriotism,
inconsistent and consistent internationalism, pacifism, and the
revolutionary repudiation of pacifist illusions found full expression
in the Russian émigré press. The learned fools and the old women
of the Second International, who had arrogantly and contemptuously turned up their noses at the abundance of "factions" in the
Russian socialist movement and at the bitter struggle they were
waging among themselves, were unable—when the war deprived
them of their vaunted "legality" in all the advanced countries—to
organise anything even approximating such a free (illegal) inter-
change of views and such a free (illegal) evolution of correct views
as the Russian revolutionaries did in Switzerland and in a number
of other countries. That was why both the avowed social-patriots
and the "Kautskyites" of all countries proved to be the worst
traitors to the proletariat. One of the principal reasons why Bolshe-

vism was able to achieve victory in 1917-20 was that, since the end of 1914, it has been ruthlessly exposing the baseness and vileness of social-chauvinism and "Kautskyism" (to which Longuetism in France, the views of the Fabians and the leaders of the Independent Labour Party in Britain, of Turati in Italy, etc., correspond), the masses later becoming more and more convinced, from their own experience, of the correctness of the Bolshevik views.

The second revolution in Russia (February to October 1917). Tsarism's senility and obsoleteness had (with the aid of the blows and hardships of a most agonising war) created an incredibly destructive force directed against it. Within a few days Russia was transformed into a democratic bourgeois republic, freer—in war conditions—than any other country in the world. The leaders of the opposition and revolutionary parties began to set up a government, just as is done in the most "strictly parliamentary" republics, the fact that a man had been a leader of an opposition party in parliament—even in a most reactionary parliament—*facilitated* his subsequent role in the revolution.

In a few weeks the Mensheviks and Socialist-Revolutionaries thoroughly assimilated all the methods and manners, the arguments and sophistries of the European heroes of the Second International, of the ministerialists and other opportunist riff-raff. Everything we now read about the Scheidemanns and Noskes, about Kautsky and Hilferding, Renner and Austerlitz, Otto Bauer and Fritz Adler, Turati and Longuet, about the Fabians and the leaders of the Independent Labour Party of Britain—all this seems to us (and indeed is) a dreary repetition, a reiteration, of an old and familiar refrain. We have already witnessed all this in the instance of the Mensheviks. As history would have it, the opportunists of a backward country became the forerunners of the opportunists in a number of advanced countries.

If the heroes of the Second International have all gone bankrupt and have disgraced themselves over the question of the significance and role of the Soviets and Soviet rule; if the leaders of the three very important parties which have now left the Second International (namely, the German Independent Social-Democratic Party, the French Longuetists and the British Independent Labour Party) have disgraced themselves and become entangled in this question in a most "telling" fashion; if they have all shown themselves slaves to the prejudices of petty-bourgeois democracy (fully in the spirit of the petty-bourgeois of 1848 who called themselves "Social-Democrats")—then we can only say that we have *already* witnessed *all this* in the instance of the Mensheviks. As history would have it, the Soviets came into being in Russia in 1905; from February to October 1917 they were turned to a false use by the Mensheviks, who went bankrupt because of their inability to understand the role and significance of the Soviets; today the idea of Soviet power has emerged *throughout the world* and is spreading among the proletariat of all countries with extraordinary speed. Like our Mensheviks, the old heroes of the Second International are *everywhere* going bankrupt, because they are incapable of understanding the role and significance of the Soviets. Experience has proved that, on certain very important questions of the proletarian revolution, *all* countries will inevitably have to do what Russia has done.

Despite views that are today often to be met with in Europe and America, the Bolsheviks began their victorious struggle against the parliamentary and (in fact) bourgeois republic and against the Mensheviks in a very cautious manner, and the preparations they made for it were by no means simple. At the beginning of the period mentioned, we did *not* call for the overthrow of the government but explained that it was impossible to overthrow it *without* first changing the composition and the temper of the Soviets. We did not proclaim a boycott of the bourgeois parliament, the Constituent Assembly, but said—and following the April (1917) Conference of our Party began to state officially in the name of the Party—that a bourgeois republic with a Constituent Assembly would be better than a bourgeois republic without a Constituent Assembly, but that a "workers' and peasants' " republic, a Soviet republic, would be better than any bourgeois-democratic, parliamentary republic. Without such thorough, circumspect and long preparations, we could not have achieved victory in October 1917, or have consolidated that victory.

IV

THE STRUGGLE AGAINST WHICH ENEMIES WITHIN THE WORKING-CLASS MOVEMENT HELPED BOLSHEVISM DEVELOP, GAIN STRENGTH, AND BECOME STEELED

First and foremost, the struggle against opportunism, which in 1914 definitely developed into social-chauvinism and definitely sided with the bourgeoisie, against the proletariat. Naturally, this was Bolshevism's principal enemy within the working-class movement. It still remains the principal enemy on an international scale. The Bolsheviks have been devoting the greatest attention to this enemy. This aspect of Bolshevik activities is now fairly well known abroad too.

It was, however, different with Bolshevism's other enemy within the working-class movement. Little is known in other countries of the fact that Bolshevism took shape, developed and became steeled in the long years of struggle against *petty-bourgeois revolutionism*, which smacks of anarchism, or borrows something from the latter and, in all essential matters, does not measure up to the conditions and requirements of a consistently proletarian class struggle. Marxist theory has established—and the experience of all European revolutions and revolutionary movements has fully confirmed—that the petty proprietor, the small master (a social type existing on a very extensive and even mass scale in many European countries), who, under capitalism, always suffers oppression and very frequently a most acute and rapid deterioration in his conditions of life, and even ruin, easily goes to revolutionary extremes, but is incapable of perseverance, organisation, discipline and steadfastness. A petty bourgeois driven to frenzy by the horrors of capitalism is a social phenomenon which, like anarchism, is characteristic of all capitalist countries. The instability of such revolutionism, its barrenness, and its tendency to turn rapidly into submission, apathy, phantasms, and even a frenzied infatuation with one bourgeois fad or another—all this is common knowledge. However, a theoretical or abstract recognition of these truths does not at all rid revolutionary parties of old errors, which always crop up at unexpected occasions, in somewhat new forms, in a hitherto unfamiliar garb or surroundings, in an unusual—a more or less unusual—situation.

Anarchism was not infrequently a kind of penalty for the opportunist sins of the working-class movement. The two monstrosities complemented each other. And if in Russia—despite the more petty-bourgeois composition of her population as compared with the other European countries—anarchism's influence was negligible during the two revolutions (of 1905 and 1917) and the preparations for them, this should no doubt stand partly to the credit of Bolshevism, which has always waged a most ruthless and uncompromising struggle against opportunism. I say "partly", since of still greater importance in weakening anarchism's influence in Russia was the circumstance that in the past (the seventies of the nineteenth century) it was able to develop inordinately and to reveal its absolute erroneousness, its unfitness to serve the revolutionary class as a guiding theory.

When it came into being in 1903, Bolshevism took over the tradition of a ruthless struggle against petty-bourgeois, semi-anarchist (or dilettante-anarchist) revolutionism, a tradition which had always existed in revolutionary Social-Democracy and had become particularly strong in our country during the years 1900-03, when the foundations for a mass party of the revolutionary proletariat were being laid in Russia. Bolshevism took over and carried on the struggle against a party which, more than any other, expressed the tendencies of petty-bourgeois revolutionism, namely, the

"Socialist-Revolutionary" Party, and waged that struggle on three main issues. First, that party, which rejected Marxism, stubbornly refused (or, it might be more correct to say: was unable) to understand the need for a strictly objective appraisal of the class forces and their alignment, before taking any political action. Second, this party considered itself particularly "revolutionary", or "Left", because of its recognition of individual terrorism, assassination—something that we Marxists emphatically rejected. It was, of course, only on grounds of expediency that we rejected individual terrorism, whereas people who were capable of condemning "on principle" the terror of the Great French Revolution, or, in general, the terror employed by victorious revolutionary party which is besieged by the bourgeoisie of the whole world, were ridiculed and laughed to scorn by Plekhanov in 1900-03, when he was a Marxist and a revolutionary. Third, the "Socialist-Revolutionaries" thought it very "Left" to sneer at the comparatively insignificant opportunist sins of the German Social-Democratic Party, while they themselves imitated the extreme opportunists of that party, for example, on the agrarian question, or on the question of the dictatorship of the proletariat.

History, incidentally, has now confirmed on a vast and worldwide scale the opinion we have always advocated, namely, that German *revolutionary* Social-Democracy (note that as far back as 1900-03 Plekhanov demanded Bernstein's expulsion from the Party, and in 1913 the Bolsheviks, always continuing this tradition, exposed Legien's baseness, vileness and treachery) *came closest* to being the party the revolutionary proletariat needs in order to achieve victory. Today, in 1920, after all the ignominious failures and crises of the war period and the early post-war years, it can be plainly seen that, of all the Western parties, the German revolutionary Social-Democrats produced the finest leaders, and recovered and gained new strength more rapidly than the others did. This may be seen in the instances both of the Spartacists and the Left, proletarian wing of the Independent Social-Democratic Party of Germany, which is waging an incessant struggle against the opportunism and spinelessness of the Kautskys, Hilferdings, Ledebours and Crispiens. If we now cast a glance to take in a complete historical period, namely, from the Paris Commune to the first Socialist Soviet Republic, we shall find that Marxism's attitude to anarchism in general stands out most definitely and unmistakably. In the final analysis, Marxism proved to be correct, and although the anarchists rightly pointed to the opportunist views on the state prevalent among most of the socialist parties, it must be said, first, that this opportunism was connected with the distortion, and even deliberate suppression, of Marx's views on the state (in my book, *The State and Revolution*, I pointed out that for thirty-six years, from 1875 to 1911, Bebel withheld a letter by Engels, which very clearly, vividly, bluntly and definitively exposed the opportunism of the current Social-Democratic views on the state*); second, that the rectification of these opportunist views, and the recognition of Soviet power and its superiority to bourgeois parliamentary democracy proceeded most rapidly and extensively among those trends in the socialist parties of Europe and America that were most Marxist.

The struggle that Bolshevism waged against "Left" deviations within its own Party assumed particularly large proportions on two occasions: in 1908, on the question of whether or not to participate in a most reactionary "parliament" and in the legal workers' societies, which were being restricted by most reactionary laws; and again in 1918 (the Treaty of Brest-Litovsk), on the question of whether one "compromise" or another was permissible.

In 1908 the "Left" Bolsheviks were expelled from our Party for stubbornly refusing to understand the necessity of participating in a most reactionary "parliament".[257] The "Lefts"—among whom there were many splendid revolutionaries who subsequently were (and still are) commendable members of the Communist Party—based themselves particularly on the successful experience of the 1905 boycott. When, in August 1905, the tsar proclaimed the convocation of a consultative "parliament",[258] the Bolsheviks called for its boycott, in the teeth of all the opposition parties and the Mensheviks, and the "parliament" was in fact swept away by the revolution of October 1905.[259] The boycott proved correct at the time, not because non-participation in reactionary parliaments is correct in general, but because we accurately appraised the objective situation, which was leading to the rapid development of the mass strikes first into a political strike, then into a revolutionary strike, and finally into an uprising. Moreover, the struggle centred at that time on the question of whether the convocation of the first representative assembly should be left to the tsar, or an attempt should be made to wrest its convocation from the old regime. When there was not, and could not be, any certainty that the objective situation was of a similar kind, and when there was no certainty of a similar trend and the same rate of development, the boycott was no longer correct.

The Bolsheviks' boycott of "parliament" in 1905 enriched the revolutionary proletariat with highly valuable political experience and showed that, when legal and illegal, parliamentary and non-parliamentary forms of struggle are combined, it is sometimes useful and even essential to reject parliamentary forms. It would, however, be highly erroneous to apply this experience blindly, imita-

---

* See pp. 309-11 of the present volume.—*Ed.*

tively and uncritically to *other* conditions and *other* situations. The Bolsheviks' boycott of the Duma in 1906 was a mistake, although a minor and easily remediable one.* The boycott of the Duma in 1907, 1908 and subsequent years was a most serious error and difficult to remedy, because, on the one hand, a very rapid rise of the revolutionary tide and its conversion into an uprising was not to be expected, and, on the other hand, the entire historical situation attendant upon the renovation of the bourgeois monarchy called for legal and illegal activities being combined. Today, when we look back at this fully completed historical period, whose connection with subsequent periods has now become quite clear, it becomes most obvious that in 1908-14 the Bolsheviks *could not have* preserved (let alone strengthened and developed) the core of the revolutionary party of the proletariat, had they not upheld, in a most strenuous struggle, the viewpoint that it was *obligatory* to combine legal and illegal forms of struggle, and that it was *obligatory* to participate even in a most reactionary parliament and in a number of other institutions hemmed in by reactionary laws (sick benefit societies, etc.).

In 1918 things did not reach a split. At that time the "Left" Communists formed only a separate group or "faction" within our Party, and that not for long. In the same year, 1918, the most prominent representatives of "Left Communism", for example, Comrades Radek and Bukharin, openly acknowledged their error. It had seemed to them that the Treaty of Brest-Litovsk was a compromise with the imperialists, which was inexcusable on principle and harmful to the party of the revolutionary proletariat. It was indeed a compromise with the imperialists, but it was a compromise which, under the circumstances, *had to be made*.

Today, when I hear our tactics in signing the Brest-Litovsk Treaty being attacked by the Socialist-Revolutionaries, for instance, or when I hear Comrade Lansbury say, in a conversation with me, "Our British trade union leaders say that if it was permissible for the Bolsheviks to compromise, it is permissible for them to compromise too", I usually reply by first of all giving a simple and "popular" example:

Imagine that your car is held up by armed bandits. You hand them over your money, passport, revolver and car. In return you are rid of the pleasant company of the bandits. That is unquestionably a compromise. "*Do ut des*" (I "give" you money, fire-arms and a car "so that you give" me the opportunity to get away from you with a whole skin). It would, however, be difficult to find a sane

---

* What applies to individuals also applies—with necessary modifications—to politics and parties. It is not he who makes no mistakes that is intelligent. There are no such men, nor can there be. It is he whose errors are not very grave and who is able to rectify them easily and quickly that is intelligent.

man who would declare such a compromise to be "inadmissible on principle", or who would call the compromiser an accomplice of the bandits (even though the bandits might use the car and the fire-arms for further robberies). Our compromise with the bandits of German imperialism was just that kind of compromise.

But when, in 1914-18 and then in 1918-20, the Mensheviks and Socialist-Revolutionaries in Russia, the Scheidemannites (and to a large extent the Kautskyites) in Germany, Otto Bauer and Friedrich Adler (to say nothing of the Renners and Co.) in Austria, the Renaudels and Longuets and Co. in France, the Fabians, the Independents and the Labourites[260] in Britain entered into *compromises* with the bandits of their own bourgeoisie, and sometimes of the "Allied" bourgeoisie, and *against* the revolutionary proletariat of their own countries, all these gentlemen were actually acting as *accomplices in banditry*.

The conclusion is clear: to reject compromises "on principle", to reject the permissibility of compromises in general, no matter of what kind, is childishness, which it is difficult even to consider seriously. A political leader who desires to be useful to the revolutionary proletariat must be able to distinguish *concrete* cases of compromises that are inexcusable and are an expression of opportunism and *treachery*; he must direct all the force of criticism, the full intensity of merciless exposure and relentless war, against *these concrete* compromises, and not allow the past masters of "practical" socialism and the parliamentary Jesuits to dodge and wriggle out of responsibility by means of disquisitions on "compromises in general". It is in this way that the "leaders" of the British trade unions, as well as of the Fabian society and the "Independent" Labour Party, dodge responsibility *for the treachery they have perpetrated,* for having made *a compromise* that is really tantamount to the worst kind of opportunism, treachery and betrayal.

There are different kinds of compromises. One must be able to analyse the situation and the concrete conditions of each compromise, or of each variety of compromise. One must learn to distinguish between a man who has given up his money and fire-arms to bandits so as to lessen the evil they can do and to facilitate their capture and execution, and a man who gives his money and fire-arms to bandits so as to share in the loot. In politics this is by no means always as elementary as it is in this childishly simple example. However, anyone who is out to think up for the workers some kind of recipe that will provide them with cut-and-dried solutions for all contingencies, or promises that the policy of the revolutionary proletariat will never come up against difficult or complex situations, is simply a charlatan.

To leave no room for misinterpretation, I shall attempt to outline, if only very briefly, several fundamental rules for the analysis of concrete compromises.

The party which entered into a compromise with the German imperialists by signing the Treaty of Brest-Litovsk had been evolving its internationalism in practice ever since the end of 1914. It was not afraid to call for the defeat of the tsarist monarchy and to condemn "defence of country" in a war between two imperialist robbers. The parliamentary representatives of this party preferred exile in Siberia to taking a road leading to ministerial portfolios in a bourgeois government. The revolution that overthrew tsarism and established a democratic republic put this party to a new and tremendous test—it did not enter into any agreements with its "own" imperialists, but prepared and brought about their overthrow. When it had assumed political power, this party did not leave a vestige of either landed or capitalist ownership. After making public and repudiating the imperialists' secret treaties, this party proposed peace to *all* nations, and yielded to the violence of the Brest-Litovsk robbers only after the Anglo-French imperialists had torpedoed the conclusion of a peace, and after the Bolsheviks had done everything humanly possible to hasten the revolution in Germany and other countries. The absolute correctness of this compromise, entered into by such a party in such a situation, is becoming ever clearer and more obvious with every day.

The Mensheviks and the Socialist-Revolutionaries in Russia (like all the leaders of the Second International throughout the world, in 1914-20) began with treachery—by directly or indirectly justifying "defence of country", i.e., the defence of *their own* predatory bourgeoisie. They continued their treachery by entering into a coalition with the bourgeoisie of *their own* country, and fighting, together with *their own* bourgeoisie, against the revolutionary proletariat of their own country. Their bloc, first with Kerensky and the Cadets, and then with Kolchak and Denikin in Russia— like the bloc of the *confrères* abroad with the bourgeoisie of *their* respective countries—was in fact desertion to the side of the bourgeoisie, against the proletariat. From beginning to end, *their* compromise with the bandits of imperialism meant their becoming *accomplices* in imperialist banditry.

V

"LEFT-WING" COMMUNISM IN GERMANY. THE LEADERS, THE PARTY, THE CLASS, THE MASSES

The German Communists we must now speak of call themselves, not "Left-wingers" but, if I am not mistaken, an "opposition on principle". From what follows below it will, however, be seen that they reveal all the symptoms of the "infantile disorder of Leftism".

Published by the "local group in Frankfurt am Main", a pamphlet reflecting the point of view of this opposition, and entitled *The Split in the Communist Party of Germany (The Spartacus League)* sets forth the substance of this opposition's views most saliently, and with the utmost clarity and concision. A few quotations will suffice to acquaint the reader with that substance:

"... The Communist Party is the party of the most determined class struggle...."

"... Politically, the transitional period [between capitalism and socialism]: is one of the proletarian dictatorship...."

"... The question arises: who is to exercise this dictatorship: *the Communist Party or the proletarian class?* ...*Fundamentally,* should we strive for a dictatorship of the Communist Party, or for a dictatorship of the proletarian class? ..."

(All italics as in the original.)

The author of the pamphlet goes on to accuse the Central Committee of the Communist Party of Germany of seeking ways of achieving a *coalition with the Independent Social-Democratic Party of Germany,* and of raising *"the question of recognising, in principle, all political means"* of struggle, including parliamentarianism, with the sole purpose of concealing its actual and main efforts to form a coalition with the Independents. The pamphlet goes on to say:

"The opposition have chosen another road. They are of the opinion that the question of the rule of the Communist Party and of the dictatorship of the Party is merely one of tactics. In any case, rule by the Communist Party is the ultimate form of any party rule. *Fundamentally,* we must work for the dictatorship of the proletarian class. And all the measures of the Party, its organisations, methods of struggle, strategy and tactics should be directed to that end. Accordingly, all compromise with other parties, all reversion to parliamentary forms of struggle, which have become historically and politically obsolete, and any policy of manoeuvring and compromise must be emphatically rejected." "Specifically proletarian methods of revolutionary struggle must be strongly emphasised. New forms of organisation must be created on the widest basis and with the widest scope in order to enlist the most extensive proletarian circles and strata to take part in the revolutionary struggle under the leadership of the Communist Party. A *Workers' Union,* based on factory organisations, should be the rallying point for all revolutionary elements. This should unite all workers who follow the slogan: 'Get out of the trade unions!' It is here that the militant proletariat musters its ranks for battle. Recognition of the class struggle, of the Soviet system and of the dictatorship should be sufficient for enrolment. All subsequent political education of the fighting masses and their political orientation in the struggle are the task of the Communist Party, which stands outside the Workers' Union....

"... Consequently, two Communist parties are now arrayed against each other:

"*One is a party of leaders,* which is out to organise the revolutionary struggle and to direct it from *above,* accepting compromises and parliamentarianism so as to create a situation enabling it to join a coalition government exercising a dictatorship.

"*The other is a mass party*, which expects an upsurge of the revolutionary struggle from *below*, which knows and applies a single method in this struggle —a method which clearly leads to the goal—and rejects all parliamentary and opportunist methods. That single method is the unconditional *overthrow of the bourgeoisie*, so as then to set up the proletarian class dictatorship for the accomplishment of socialism....

"... There—the dictatorship of leaders; here—the dictatorship of the masses! That is our slogan."

Such are the main features characterising the views of the opposition in the German Communist Party.

Any Bolshevik who has consciously participated in the development of Bolshevism since 1903 or has closely observed that development will at once say, after reading these arguments, "What old and familiar rubbish! What 'Left-wing' childishness!"

But let us examine these arguments a little more closely.

The mere presentation of the question—"dictatorship of the party *or* dictatorship of the class; dictatorship (party) of the leaders, *or* dictatorship (party) of the masses?"—testifies to most incredibly and hopelessly muddled thinking. These people want to *invent* something quite out of the ordinary, and, in their effort to be clever, make themselves ridiculous. It is common knowledge that the masses are divided into classes; that the masses can be contrasted with classes only by contrasting the vast majority in general, regardless of division according to status in the social system of production, with categories holding a definite status in the social system of production; that as a rule and in most cases—at least in present-day civilised countries—classes are led by political parties; that political parties, as a general rule, are run by more or less stable groups composed of the most authoritative, influential and experienced members, who are elected to the most responsible positions, and are called leaders. All this is elementary. All this is clear and simple. Why replace this with some kind of rigmarole, some new Volapük? On the one hand, these people seem to have got muddled when they found themselves in a predicament, when the party's abrupt transition from legality to illegality upset the customary, normal and simple relations between leaders, parties and classes. In Germany, as in other European countries, people had become too accustomed to legality, to the free and proper election of "leaders" at regular party congresses, to the convenient method of testing the class composition of parties through parliamentary elections, mass meetings, the press, the sentiments of the trade unions and other associations, etc. When, instead of this customary procedure, it became necessary, because of the stormy development of the revolution and the development of the civil war, to go over rapidly from legality to illegality, to combine the two, and to adopt the "inconvenient" and "undemocratic" methods of selecting, or forming, or preserving "groups of leaders"—people lost their bearings and began to think up some unmitigated nonsense. Certain members of the Communist Party of Holland, who were unlucky enough to be born in a small country with traditions and conditions of highly privileged and highly stable legality, and who had never seen a transition from legality to illegality, probably fell into confusion, lost their heads, and helped create these absurd inventions.

On the other hand, one can see simply a thoughtless and incoherent use of the now "fashionable" terms: "masses" and "leaders". These people have heard and memorised a great many attacks on "leaders" , in which the latter have been contrasted with the "masses"; however, they have proved unable to think matters out and gain a clear understanding of what it was all about.

The divergence between "leaders" and "masses" was brought out with particular clarity and sharpness in all countries at the end of the imperialist war and following it. The principal reason for this was explained many times by Marx and Engels between the years 1852 and 1892, from the example of Britain. That country's exclusive position led to the emergence, from the "masses", of a semi-petty-bourgeois, opportunist "labour aristocracy". The leaders of this labour aristocracy were constantly going over to the bourgeoisie, and were directly or indirectly on its pay roll. Marx earned the honour of incurring the hatred of these disreputable persons by openly branding them as traitors. Present-day (twentieth-century) imperialism has given a few advanced countries an exceptionally privileged position, which, everywhere in the Second International, has produced a certain type of traitor, opportunist, and social-chauvinist leaders, who champion the interests of their own craft, their own section of the labour aristocracy. The opportunist parties have become separated from the "masses", i.e., from the broadest strata of the working people, their majority, the lowest-paid workers. The revolutionary proletariat cannot be victorious unless this evil is combated, unless the opportunist, social-traitor leaders are exposed, discredited and expelled. That is the policy the Third International has embarked on.

To go so far, in this connection, as to contrast, *in general,* the dictatorship of the masses with a dictatorship of the leaders is ridiculously absurd, and stupid. What is particularly amusing is that, in fact, instead of the old leaders, who hold generally accepted views on simple matters, *new leaders* are brought forth (under cover of the slogan "Down with the leaders!"), who talk rank stuff and nonsense. Such are Laufenberg, Wolffheim, Horner, Karl

Schröder, Friedrich Wendel and Karl Erler,* in Germany. Erler's attempts to give the question more "profundity" and to proclaim that in general political parties are unnecessary and "bourgeois" are so supremely absurd that one can only shrug one's shoulders. It all goes to drive home the truth that a minor error can always assume monstrous proportions if it is persisted in, if profound justifications are sought for it, and if it is carried to its logical conclusion.

Repudiation of the Party principle and of Party discipline—that is what the opposition has *arrived at*. And this is tantamount to completely disarming the proletariat *in the interests of the bourgeoisie*. It all adds up to that petty-bourgeois diffuseness and instability, that incapacity for sustained effort, unity and organised action, which, if encouraged, must inevitably destroy any proletarian revolutionary movement. From the standpoint of communism, repudiation of the Party principle means attempting to leap from the eve of capitalism's collapse (in Germany), not to the lower or the intermediate phase of communism, but to the higher. We in Russia (in the third year since the overthrow of the bourgeoisie) are making the first steps in the transition from capitalism to socialism or the lower stage of communism. Classes still remain, and will remain everywhere *for years after* the proletariat's conquest of power. Perhaps in Britain, where there is no peasantry (but where petty proprietors exist), this period may be shorter. The abolition of classes means, not merely ousting the landowners and the capitalists—that is something we accomplished with comparative ease; it also means *abolishing the small commodity producers*, and they *cannot be ousted,* òr crushed; we *must learn to live* with them. They can (and must) be transformed and re-educated only by means of very prolonged, slow, and cautious organisational work. They surround the proletariat on every side with a petty-bourgeois atmosphere, which permeates and corrupts the proletariat, and constantly causes among the proletariat relapses into petty-bourgeois spinelessness, disunity, individualism, and alternating moods

---

* Karl Erler, "The Dissolution of the Party", *Kommunistische Arbeiterzeitung*,[261] Hamburg, February 7, 1920, No. 32: "The working class cannot destroy the bourgeois state without destroying bourgeois democracy, and it cannot destroy bourgeois democracy without destroying parties."

The more muddle-headed of the syndicalists and anarchists in the Latin countries may derive "satisfaction" from the fact that solid Germans, who evidently consider themselves Marxists (by their articles in the above-mentioned paper K. Erler and K. Horner have shown most plainly that they consider themselves sound Marxists, but talk incredible nonsense in a most ridiculous manner and reveal their failure to understand the ABC of Marxism), go to the length of making utterly inept statements. Mere acceptance of Marxism does not save one from errors. We Russians know this especially well, because Marxism has been very often the "fashion" in our country.

of exaltation and dejection. The strictest centralisation and discipline are required within the political party of the proletariat in order to counteract this, in order that the *organisational* role of the proletariat (and that is its *principal* role) may be exercised correctly, successfully and victoriously. The dictatorship of the proletariat means a persistent struggle—bloody and bloodless, violent and peaceful, military and economic, educational and administrative—against the forces and traditions of the old society. The force of habit in millions and tens of millions is a most formidable force. Without a party of iron that has been tempered in the struggle, a party enjoying the confidence of all honest people in the class in question, a party capable of watching and influencing the mood of the masses, such a struggle cannot be waged successfully. It is a thousand times easier to vanquish the centralised big bourgeoisie than to "vanquish" the millions upon millions of petty proprietors; however, through their ordinary, everyday, imperceptible, elusive and demoralising activities, they produce the *very* results which the bourgeoisie need and which tend to *restore* the bourgeoisie. Whoever brings about even the slightest weakening of the iron discipline of the party of the proletariat (especially during its dictatorship), is actually aiding the bourgeoisie against the proletariat.

Parallel with the question of the leaders—the party—the class—the masses, we must pose the question of the "reactionary" trade unions. But first I shall take the liberty of making a few concluding remarks based on the experience of our Party. There *have always been* attacks on the "dictatorship of leaders" in our Party. The first time I heard such attacks, I recall, was in 1895, when, officially, no party yet existed, but a central group was taking shape in St. Petersburg, which was to assume the leadership of the district groups.[262] At the Ninth Congress of our Party (April 1920) there was a small opposition, which also spoke against the "dictatorship of leaders", against the "oligarchy", and so on.[263] There is therefore nothing surprising, new, or terrible in the "infantile disorder" of "Left-wing communism" among the Germans. The ailment involves no danger, and after it the organism even becomes more robust. In our case, on the other hand, the rapid alternation of legal and illegal work, which made it necessary to keep the general staff—the leaders—under cover and cloak them in the greatest secrecy, sometimes gave rise to extremely dangerous consequences. The worst of these was that in 1912 the *agent provocateur* Malinovsky got into the Bolshevik Central Committee. He betrayed scores and scores of the best and most loyal comrades, caused them to be sentenced to penal servitude, and hastened the death of many of them. That he did not cause still greater harm was due to the correct balance between legal and illegal work. As member of the Party's Central Committee and Duma deputy, Malinovsky was forced, in order to gain our confidence, to help us establish legal daily papers, which even under tsarism were able to wage a struggle against the Menshevik opportunism and to spread the fundamentals of Bolshevism in a suitably disguised form. While, with one hand, Malinovsky sent scores and scores of the finest Bolsheviks to penal servitude and death, he was obliged, with the other, to assist in the education of scores and scores of thousands of new Bolsheviks through the medium of the legal press. Those German (and also British, American, French and Italian) comrades who are faced with the task of learning how to conduct revolutionary work within the reactionary trade unions would do well to give serious thought to this fact.*

In many countries, including the most advanced, the bourgeoisie are undoubtedly sending *agents provocateurs* into the Communist parties and will continue to do so. A skilful combining of illegal and legal work is one of the ways to combat this danger.

VI

SHOULD REVOLUTIONARIES WORK IN REACTIONARY TRADE UNIONS?

The German "Lefts" consider that, as far as they are concerned, the reply to this question is an unqualified negative. In their opinion, declamations and angry outcries (such as uttered by K. Horner in a particularly "solid" and particularly stupid manner) against "reactionary" and "counter-revolutionary" trade unions are sufficient "proof" that it is unnecessary and even inexcusable for revolutionaries and Communists to work in yellow, social-chauvinist, compromising and counter-revolutionary trade unions of the Legien type.

However firmly the German "Lefts" may be convinced of the revolutionism of such tactics, the latter are in fact fundamentally wrong, and contain nothing but empty phrases.

To make this clear, I shall begin with our own experience, in keeping with the general plan of the present pamphlet, which is aimed at applying to Western Europe whatever is universally prac-

---

* Malinovsky was a prisoner of war in Germany. On his return to Russia when the Bolsheviks were in power he was instantly put on trial and shot by our workers. The Mensheviks attacked us most bitterly for our mistake—the fact that an *agent provocateur* had become a member of the Central Committee of our Party. But when, under Kerensky, we demanded the arrest and trial of Rodzyanko, the Chairman of the Duma, because he had known, even before the war, that Malinovsky was an *agent provocateur* and *had not informed* the Trudoviks and the workers in the Duma, neither the Mensheviks nor the Socialist-Revolutionaries in the Kerensky government supported our demand, and Rodzyanko remained at large and made off unhindered to join Denikin.

ticable, significant and relevant in the history and the present-day tactics of Bolshevism.

In Russia today, the connection between leaders, party, class and masses, as well as the attitude of the dictatorship of the proletariat and its party to the trade unions, are concretely as follows: the dictatorship is exercised by the proletariat organised in the Soviets; the proletariat is guided by the Communist Party of Bolsheviks, which, according to the figures of the latest Party Congress (April 1920), has a membership of 611,000. The membership varied greatly both before and after the October Revolution, and used to be much smaller, even in 1918 and 1919. We are apprehensive of an excessive growth of the Party, because careerists and charlatans, who deserve only to be shot, inevitably do all they can to insinuate themselves into the ranks of the ruling party. The last time we opened wide the doors of the Party—to workers and peasants only—was when (in the winter of 1919) Yudenich was within a few versts of Petrograd, and Denikin was in Orel (about 350 versts from Moscow), i.e., when the Soviet Republic was in mortal danger, and when adventurers, careerists, charlatans and unreliable persons generally could not possibly count on making a profitable career (and had more reason to expect the gallows and torture) by joining the Communists. The Party, which holds annual congresses (the most recent on the basis of one delegate per 1,000 members), is directed by a Central Committee of nineteen elected at the Congress, while the current work in Moscow has to be carried on by still smaller bodies, known as the Organising Bureau and the Political Bureau, which are elected at plenary meetings of the Central Committee, five members of the Central Committee to each bureau. This, it would appear, is a full-fledged "oligarchy". No important political or organisational question is decided by any state institution in our republic without the guidance of the Party's Central Committee.

In its work, the Party relies directly on the *trade unions,* which, according to the data of the last congress (April 1920), now have a membership of over four million and are formally *non-Party.* Actually, all the directing bodies of the vast majority of the unions, and primarily, of course, of the all-Russia general trade union centre or bureau (the All-Russia Central Council of Trade Unions), are made up of Communists and carry out all the directives of the Party. Thus, on the whole, we have a formally non-communist, flexible and relatively wide and very powerful proletarian apparatus, by means of which the Party is closely linked up with the *class* and the *masses,* and by means of which, under the leadership of the Party, the *class dictatorship* is exercised. Without close contacts with the trade unions, and without their energetic support and devoted efforts, not only in economic, *but also in military* affairs, it would of course have been impossible for us to govern the country and to maintain the dictatorship for two and a half months, let alone two and a half years. In practice, these very close contacts naturally call for highly complex and diversified work in the form of propaganda, agitation, timely and frequent conferences, not only with the leading trade union workers, but with influential trade union workers generally; they call for a determined struggle against the Mensheviks, who still have a certain though very small following to whom they teach all kinds of counter-revolutionary machinations, ranging from an ideological defence of (*bourgeois*) democracy and the preaching that the trade unions should be "independent" (independent of proletarian state power!) to sabotage of proletarian discipline, etc., etc.

We consider that contacts with the "masses" through the trade unions are not enough. In the course of our revolution, practical activities have given rise to such institutions as *non-Party workers' and peasants' conferences*, and we strive by every means to support, develop and extend this institution in order to be able to observe the temper of the masses, come closer to them, meet their requirements, promote the best among them to state posts, etc. Under a recent decree on the transformation of the People's Commissariat of State Control into the Workers' and Peasants' Inspection, non-Party conferences of this kind have been empowered to select members of the State Control to carry out various kinds of investigations, etc.

Then, of course, all the work of the Party is carried on through the Soviets, which embrace the working masses, irrespective of occupation. The district congresses of Soviets are *democratic* institutions, the like of which even the best of the democratic republics of the bourgeois world have never known; through these congresses (whose proceedings the Party endeavours to follow with the closest attention), as well as by continually appointing class-conscious workers to various posts in the rural districts, the proletariat exercises its role of leader of the peasantry, gives effect to the dictatorship of the urban proletariat, wages a systematic struggle against the rich, bourgeois, exploiting and profiteering peasantry, etc.

Such is the general mechanism of the proletarian state power viewed "from above", from the standpoint of the practical implementation of the dictatorship. We hope that the reader will understand why the Russian Bolshevik, who has known this mechanism for twenty-five years and has seen it develop out of small, illegal and underground circles, cannot help regarding all this talk about "from above" or "from below", about the dictatorship of leaders or the dictatorship of the masses, etc., as ridiculous and childish nonsense, something like discussing whether a man's left leg or right arm is of greater use to him.

We cannot but regard as equally ridiculous and childish nonsense the pompous, very learned, and frightfully revolutionary disquisitions of the German Lefts to the effect that Communists cannot and should not work in reactionary trade unions, that it is permissible to turn down such work, that it is necessary to withdraw from the trade unions and create a brand-new and immaculate "Workers' Union" invented by very pleasant (and, probably, for the most part very youthful) Communists, etc., etc.

Capitalism inevitably leaves socialism the legacy, on the one hand, of the old trade and craft distinctions among the workers, distinctions evolved in the course of centuries; on the other hand, trade unions, which only very slowly, in the course of years and years, can and will develop into broader industrial unions with less of the craft union about them (embracing entire industries, and not only crafts, trades and occupations), and later proceed, through these industrial unions, to eliminate the division of labour among people, to educate and school people, give them *all-round development and an all-round* training, so that they *are able to do everything*. Communism is advancing and must advance towards that goal, and *will reach* it, but only after very many years. To attempt in practice, today, to anticipate this future result of a fully developed, fully stabilised and constituted, fully comprehensive and mature communism would be like trying to teach higher mathematics to a child of four.

We can (and must) begin to build socialism, not with abstract human material, or with human material specially prepared by us, but with the human material bequeathed to us by capitalism. True, that is no easy matter, but no other approach to this task is serious enough to warrant discussion.

The trade unions were a tremendous step forward for the working class in the early days of capitalist development, inasmuch as they marked a transition from the workers' disunity and helplessness to the *rudiments* of class organisation. When the *revolutionary party of the proletariat, the highest* form of proletarian class organisation, began to take shape (and the Party will not merit the name until it learns to weld the leaders into one indivisible whole with the class and the masses) the trade unions inevitably began to reveal *certain* reactionary features, a certain craft narrow-mindedness, a certain tendency to be non-political, a certain inertness, etc. However, the development of the proletariat did not, and could not, proceed anywhere in the world otherwise than through the trade unions, through reciprocal action between them and the party of the working class. The proletariat's conquest of political power is a gigantic step forward for the proletariat as a class, and the Party must more than ever and in a new way, not only in the old, educate and guide the trade unions, at the same time bearing in mind that they are and will long remain an indispensable "school of communism" and a preparatory school that trains proletarians to exercise their dictatorship, an indispensable organisation of the workers for the gradual transfer of the management of the whole economic life of the country to the working *class* (and not to the separate trades), and later to all the working people.

In the sense mentioned above, a *certain* "reactionism" in the trade unions is *inevitable* under the dictatorship of the proletariat. Not to understand this means a complete failure to understand the fundamental conditions of the *transition* from capitalism to socialism. It would be egregious folly to fear *this* "reactionism" or to try to *evade* or leap over it, for it would mean fearing that function of the proletarian vanguard which consists in training, educating, enlightening and drawing into the new life the most backward strata and masses of the working class and the peasantry. On the other hand, it would be a still graver error to postpone the achievement of the dictatorship of the proletariat until a time when there will not be a single worker with a narrow-minded craft outlook, or with craft and craft-union prejudices. The art of politics (and the Communist's correct understanding of his tasks) consists in correctly gauging the conditions and the moment when the vanguard of the proletariat can successfully assume power, when it is able—during and after the seizure of power—to win adequate support from sufficiently broad strata of the working class and of the non-proletarian working masses, and when it is able thereafter to maintain, consolidate and extend its rule by educating, training and attracting ever broader masses of the working people.

Further. In countries more advanced than Russia, a certain reactionism in the trade unions has been and was bound to be manifested in a far greater measure than in our country. Our Mensheviks found support in the trade unions (and to some extent still do so in a small number of unions), as a result of the latter's craft narrow-mindedness, craft selfishness and opportunism. The Mensheviks of the West have acquired a much firmer footing in the trade unions; there the *craft-union, narrow-minded, selfish, case-hardened, covetous, and petty-bourgeois "labour aristocracy", imperialist-minded, and imperialist-corrupted*, has developed into a much stronger section than in our country. That is incontestable. The struggle against the Gomperses, and against the Jouhaux, Hendersons, Merrheims, Legiens and Co. in Western Europe is much more difficult than the struggle against our Mensheviks, who are an *absolutely homogeneous* social and political type. This struggle must be waged ruthlessly, and it must unfailingly be brought—as we brought it—to a point when all the incorrigible leaders of opportunism and social-chauvinism are completely discredited and driven out of the trade unions. Political power cannot be captured (and the attempt to capture it should not be made) until the struggle has reached a *certain* stage. This "certain stage" will be *different* in different countries and in different circumstances; it can be correctly gauged only by thoughtful, experienced and knowledgeable political leaders of the proletariat in each particular country. (In Russia the elections to the Constituent Assembly in November 1917, a few days after the proletarian revolution of October 25, 1917, were one of the criteria of the success of this struggle. In these elections the Mensheviks were utterly defeated; they received 700,000 votes—1,400,000 if the vote in Transcaucasia is added—as against 9,000,000 votes polled by the Bolsheviks. See my article, "The Constituent Assembly Elections and the Dictatorship of the Proletariat",* in the *Communist International*264 No. 7-8.)

We are waging a struggle against the "labour aristocracy" in the name of the masses of the workers and in order to win them over to our side; we are waging the struggle against the opportunist and social-chauvinist leaders in order to win the working class over to our side. It would be absurd to forget this most elementary and most self-evident truth. Yet it is this very absurdity that the German "Left" Communists perpetrate when, *because* of the reactionary and counter-revolutionary character of the trade union *top leadership*, they jump to the conclusion that ... we must withdraw from the trade unions, refuse to work in them, and create new and *artificial* forms of labour organisation! This is so unpardonable a blunder that it is tantamount to the greatest service Communists could render the bourgeoisie. Like all the opportunist, social-chauvinist, and Kautskyite trade union leaders, our Mensheviks are nothing but "agents of the bourgeoisie in the working-class movement" (as we have always said the Mensheviks are), or "labour lieutenants of the capitalist class", to use the splendid and profoundly true expression of the followers of Daniel De Leon in America. To refuse to work in the reactionary trade unions means leaving the insufficiently developed or backward masses of workers under the influence of the reactionary leaders, the agents of the bourgeoisie, the labour aristocrats, or "workers who have become completely bourgeois" (cf. Engels's letter to Marx in 1858 about the British workers).

This ridiculous "theory" that Communists should not work in reactionary trade unions reveals with the utmost clarity the frivolous attitude of the "Left" Communists towards the question of influencing the "masses", and their misuse of clamour about the "masses". If you want to help the "masses" and win the sympathy and support of the "masses", you should not fear difficulties, or pinpricks, chicanery, insults and persecution from the "leaders" (who

---

* See *Collected Works*, Vol. 30, pp. 253-75.—*Ed.*

being opportunists and social-chauvinists, are in most cases directly or indirectly connected with the bourgeoisie and the police), but must absolutely *work wherever the masses are to be found*. You must be capable of any sacrifice, of overcoming the greatest obstacles, in order to carry on agitation and propaganda systematically, perseveringly, persistently and patiently in those institutions, societies and associations—even the most reactionary—in which proletarian or semi-proletarian masses are to be found. The trade unions and the workers' co-operatives (the latter sometimes, at least) are the very organisations in which the masses are to be found. According to figures quoted in the Swedish paper *Folkets Dagblad Politiken*[265] of March 10, 1920, the trade union membership in Great Britain increased from 5,500,000 at the end of 1917 to 6,600,000 at the end of 1918, an increase of 19 per cent. Towards the close of 1919, the membership was estimated at 7,500,000. I have not got the corresponding figures for France and Germany to hand, but absolutely incontestable and generally known facts testify to a rapid rise in the trade union membership in these countries too.

These facts make crystal clear something that is confirmed by thousands of other symptoms, namely, that class-consciousness and the desire for organisation are growing among the proletarian masses, among the rank and file, among the backward elements. Millions of workers in Great Britain, France and Germany are *for the first time* passing from a complete lack of organisation to the elementary, lowest, simplest, and (to those still thoroughly imbued with bourgeois-democratic prejudices) most easily comprehensible form of organisation, namely, the trade unions; yet the revolutionary but imprudent Left Communists stand by, crying out "the masses", "the masses!" but *refusing to work within the trade unions*, on the pretext that they are "reactionary", and invent a brand-new, immaculate little "Workers' Union", which is guiltless of bourgeois-democratic prejudices and innocent of craft or narrow-minded craft-union sins, a union which, they claim, will be(!) a broad organisation. "Recognition of the Soviet system and the dictatorship" will be the *only* (!) condition of membership. (See the passage quoted above.)

It would be hard to imagine any greater ineptitude or greater harm to the revolution than that caused by the "Left" revolutionaries! Why, if we in Russia today, after two and a half years of unprecedented victories over the bourgeoisie of Russia and the Entente, were to make "recognition of the dictatorship" a condition of trade union membership, we would be doing a very foolish thing, damaging our influence among the masses, and helping the Mensheviks. The task devolving on Communists is to *convince* the backward elements, to work *among* them, and not to *fence themselves off* from them with artificial and childishly "Left" slogans.

There can be no doubt that the Gomperses, the Hendersons, the Jouhaux and the Legiens are very grateful to those "Left" revolutionaries who, like the German opposition "on principle" (heaven preserve us from such "principles"!), or like some of the revolutionaries in the American Industrial Workers of the World[266] advocate quitting the reactionary trade unions and refusing to work in them. These men, the "leaders" of opportunism, will no doubt resort to every device of bourgeois diplomacy and to the aid of bourgeois governments, the clergy, the police and the courts, to keep Communists out of the trade unions, oust them by every means, make their work in the trade unions as unpleasant as possible, and insult, bait and persecute them. We must be able to stand up to all this, agree to make any sacrifice, and even—if need be—to resort to various stratagems, artifices and illegal methods, to evasions and subterfuges, as long as we get into the trade unions, remain in them, and carry on communist work within them at all costs. Under tsarism we had no "legal opportunities" whatsoever until 1905. However, when Zubatov, agent of the secret police, organised Black-Hundred workers' assemblies and workingmen's societies for the purpose of trapping revolutionaries and combating them, we sent members of our Party to these assemblies and into these societies (I personally remember one of them, Comrade Babushkin, a leading St. Petersburg factory worker, shot by order of the tsar's generals in 1906). They established contacts with the masses, were able to carry on their agitation, and succeeded in wresting workers from the influence of Zubatov's agents.* Of course, in Western Europe, which is imbued with most deep-rooted legalistic, constitutionalist and bourgeois-democratic prejudices, this is more difficult of achievement. However, it can and must be carried out, and systematically at that.

The Executive Committee of the Third International must, in my opinion, positively condemn, and call upon the next congress of the Communist International to condemn both the policy of refusing to work in reactionary trade unions in general (explaining in detail why such refusal is unwise, and what extreme harm it does to the cause of the proletarian revolution) and, in particular, the line of conduct of some members of the Communist Party of Holland, who—whether directly or indirectly, overtly or covertly, wholly or partly, it does not matter—have supported this erroneous policy. The Third International must break with the tactics of the Second International; it must not evade or play down points at issue, but must pose them in a straightforward fashion. The whole truth has been put

---

* The Gomperses, Hendersons, Jouhaux and Legiens are nothing but Zubatovs, differing from our Zubatov only in their European garb and polish, and the civilised, refined and democratically suave manner of conducting their despicable policy.

squarely to the "Independents" (the Independent Social-Democratic Party of Germany)*; the whole truth must likewise be put squarely to the "Left" Communists.

VII

SHOULD WE PARTICIPATE IN BOURGEOIS PARLIAMENTS?

It is with the utmost contempt—and the utmost levity—that the German "Left" Communists reply to this question in the negative. Their arguments? In the passage quoted above we read:

"... All reversion to parliamentary forms of struggle, which have become historically and politically obsolete, must be emphatically rejected...."

This is said with ridiculous pretentiousness, and is patently wrong. "Reversion" to parliamentarianism, forsooth! Perhaps there is already a Soviet republic in Germany? It does not look like it! How, then, can one speak of "reversion"? Is this not an empty phrase?

Parliamentarianism has become "historically obsolete". That is true in the propaganda sense. However, everybody knows that this is still a far cry from overcoming it in *practice*. Capitalism could have been declared—and with full justice—to be "historically obsolete" many decades ago, but that does not at all remove the need for a very long and very persistent struggle *on the basis* of capitalism. Parliamentarianism is "historically obsolete" from the standpoint of *world history*, i.e., the *era* of bourgeois parliamentarianism is over, and the *era* of the proletarian dictatorship has *begun*. That is incontestable. But world history is counted in decades. Ten or twenty years earlier or later makes no difference when measured with the yardstick of world history; from the standpoint of world history it is a trifle that cannot be considered even approximately. But for that very reason, it is a glaring theoretical error to apply the yardstick of world history to practical politics.

Is parliamentarianism "politically obsolete"? That is quite a different matter. If that were true, the position of the "Lefts" would be a strong one. But it has to be proved by a most searching analysis, and the "Lefts" do not even know how to approach the matter. In the "Theses on Parliamentarianism", published in the *Bulletin of the Provisional Bureau in Amsterdam of the Communist International* No. 1, February 1920, and obviously expressing the Dutch-Left or Left-Dutch strivings, the analysis, as we shall see, is also hopelessly poor.

In the first place, contrary to the opinion of such outstanding political leaders as Rosa Luxemburg and Karl Liebknecht, the German "Lefts", as we know, considered parliamentarianism "politically

---

* See *Collected Works*, Vol. 30, pp. 337-44.—*Ed.*

obsolete" even in January 1919. We know that the "Lefts" were mistaken. This fact alone utterly destroys, at a single stroke, the proposition that parliamentarianism is "politically obsolete". It is for the "Lefts" to prove why their error, indisputable at that time, is no longer an error. They do not and cannot produce even a shred of proof. A political party's attitude towards its own mistakes is one of the most important and surest ways of judging how earnest the party is and how it fulfils *in practice* its obligations towards its *class* and the *working people*. Frankly acknowledging a mistake, ascertaining the reasons for it, analysing the conditions that have led up to it, and thrashing out the means of its rectification—that is the hallmark of a serious party; that is how it should perform its duties, and how it should educate and train its *class*, and then the *masses*. By failing to fulfil this duty and give the utmost attention and consideration to the study of their patent error, the "Lefts" in Germany (and in Holland) have proved that they are not a *party of a class*, but a circle, not a *party of the masses*, but a group of intellectualists and of a few workers who ape the worst features of intellectualism.

Second, in the same pamphlet of the Frankfurt group of "Lefts", which we have already cited in detail, we read:

"... The millions of workers who still follow the policy of the Centre [the Catholic "Centre" Party] are counter-revolutionary. The rural proletarians provide the legions of counter-revolutionary troops." (Page 3 of the pamphlet.)

Everything goes to show that this statement is far too sweeping and exaggerated. But the basic fact set forth here is incontrovertible, and its acknowledgement by the "Lefts" is particularly clear evidence of their mistake. How can one say that "parliamentarianism is politically obsolete", when "millions" and "legions" of *proletarians* are not only still in favour of parliamentarianism in general, but are downright "counter-revolutionary"!? It is obvious that parliamentarianism in Germany is *not yet* politically obsolete. It is obvious that the "Lefts" in Germany have mistaken *their desire*, their politico-ideological attitude, for objective reality. That is a most dangerous mistake for revolutionaries to make. In Russia—where, over a particularly long period and in particularly varied forms, the most brutal and savage yoke of tsarism produced revolutionaries of diverse shades, revolutionaries who displayed amazing devotion, enthusiasm, heroism and will-power—in Russia we have observed this mistake of the revolutionaries at very close quarters; we have studied it very attentively and have a first-hand knowledge of it; that is why we can also see it especially clearly in others. Parliamentarianism is of course "politically obsolete" to the Communists in Germany; but— and that is the whole point—we must *not* regard what is obsolete *to us* as something obsolete *to a class, to the masses*. Here again we find that the "Lefts" do not know how to reason, do not know how to act as the party of a *class*, as the party of the *masses*. You must

not sink to the level of the masses, to the level of the backward strata
of the class. That is incontestable. You must tell them the bitter
truth. You are in duty bound to call their bourgeois-democratic and
parliamentary prejudices what they are—prejudices. But at the same
time you must *soberly* follow the *actual* state of the class-consciousness and preparedness of the entire class (not only of its communist
vanguard), and of all the *working people* (not only of their advanced
elements).

Even if only a fairly large *minority* of the industrial workers, and
not "millions" and "legions", follow the lead of the Catholic clergy—
and a similar minority of rural workers follow the landowners and
kulaks (Grossbauern)—it *undoubtedly* signifies that parliamentarianism in Germany has *not yet* politically outlived itself, that participation in parliamentary elections and in the struggle on the parliamentary rostrum is *obligatory* on the party of the revolutionary
proletariat *specifically* for the purpose of educating the backward
strata of *its own class*, and for the purpose of awakening and
enlightening the undeveloped, downtrodden and ignorant rural
masses. Whilst you lack the strength to do away with bourgeois
parliaments and every other type of reactionary institution, you *must*
work within them because *it is there* that you will still find workers
who are duped by the priests and stultified by the conditions of
rural life; otherwise you risk turning into nothing but windbags.

Third, the "Left" Communists have a great deal to say in praise
of us Bolsheviks. One sometimes feels like telling them to praise
us less and to try to get a better knowledge of the Bolsheviks'
tactics. We took part in the elections to the Constituent Assembly,
the Russian bourgeois parliament, in September-November 1917.
Were our tactics correct or not? If not, then this should be clearly
stated and proved, for it is necessary in evolving the correct tactics
for international communism. If they were correct, then certain
conclusions must be drawn. Of course, there can be no question of
placing conditions in Russia on a par with conditions in Western
Europe. But as regards the particular question of the meaning of
the concept that "parliamentarianism has become politically
obsolete", due account should be taken of our experience, for unless
concrete experience is taken into account such concepts very easily
turn into empty phrases. In September-November 1917, did we, the
Russian Bolsheviks, not have *more* right than any Western Communists to consider that parliamentarianism was politically obsolete
in Russia? Of course we did, for the point is not whether bourgeois
parliaments have existed for a long time or a short time, but how
far the masses of the working people are *prepared* (ideologically,
politically and practically) to accept the Soviet system and to dissolve
the bourgeois-democratic parliament (or allow it to be dissolved).
It is an absolutely incontestable and fully established historical fact

that, in September-November 1917, the urban working class and the soldiers and peasants of Russia were, because of a number of special conditions, exceptionally well prepared to accept the Soviet system and to disband the most democratic of bourgeois parliaments. Nevertheless, the Bolsheviks did *not* boycott the Constituent Assembly, but took part in the elections both before *and after* the proletariat conquered political power. That these elections yielded exceedingly valuable (and to the proletariat, highly useful) political results has, I make bold to hope, been proved by me in the above-mentioned article, which analyses in detail the returns of the elections to the Constituent Assembly in Russia.*

The conclusion which follows from this is absolutely incontrovertible: it has been proved that, far from causing harm to the revolutionary proletariat, participation in a bourgeois-democratic parliament, even a few weeks before the victory of a Soviet republic and even *after* such a victory, actually helps that proletariat to *prove to* the backward masses why such parliaments deserve to be done away with; it *facilitates* their successful dissolution, and *helps* to make bourgeois parliamentarianism "politically obsolete". To ignore this experience, while at the same time claiming affiliation to the Communist *International*, which must work out its tactics internationally (not as narrow or exclusively national tactics, but as international tactics), means committing a gross error and actually abandoning internationalism in deed, while recognising it in word.

Now let us examine the "Dutch-Left" arguments in favour of non-participation in parliaments. The following is the text of Thesis No. 4, the most important of the above-mentioned "Dutch" theses:

"When the capitalist system of production has broken down, and society is in a state of revolution, parliamentary action gradually loses importance as compared with the action of the masses themselves. When, in these conditions, parliament becomes the centre and organ of the counter-revolution, whilst, on the other hand, the labouring class builds up the instruments of its power in the Soviets, it may even prove necessary to abstain from all and any participation in parliamentary action."

The first sentence is obviously wrong, since action by the masses, a big strike, for instance, is more important than parliamentary activity at *all* times, and not only during a revolution or in a revolutionary situation. This obviously untenable and historically and politically incorrect argument merely shows very clearly that the authors completely ignore both the general European experience (the French experience before the revolutions of 1848 and 1870; the German experience of 1878-90, etc.) and the Russian experience (see above) of the importance of *combining* legal and illegal struggle. This question is of immense importance both in general and in partic-

---

* See *Collected Works*, Vol. 30, pp. 253-75.—*Ed.*

ular, because in *all* civilised and advanced countries the time is
rapidly approaching when such a combination will more and more
become—and has already partly become—mandatory on the party
of the revolutionary proletariat, inasmuch as civil war between the
proletariat and the bourgeoisie is maturing and is imminent, and
because of savage persecution of the Communists by republican
governments and bourgeois governments generally, which resort to
any violation of legality (the example of America is edifying
enough), etc. The Dutch, and the Lefts in general, have utterly failed
to understand this highly important question.

The second sentence is, in the first place, historically wrong. We
Bolsheviks participated in the most counter-revolutionary parliaments, and experience has shown that this participation was not only
useful but indispensable to the party of the revolutionary proletariat,
after the first bourgeois revolution in Russia (1905), so as to pave
the way for the second bourgeois revolution (February 1917), and
then for the socialist revolution (October 1917). In the second place,
this sentence is amazingly illogical. If a parliament becomes an organ and a "centre" (in reality it never has been and never can be
a "centre", but that is by the way) of counter-revolution, while the
workers are building up the instruments of their power in the form
of the Soviets, then it follows that the workers must prepare—ideologically, politically and technically—for the struggle of the Soviets
against parliament, for the dispersal of parliament by the Soviets.
But it does not at all follow that this dispersal is hindered, or is not
facilitated, by the presence of a Soviet opposition *within* the counter-revolutionary parliament. In the course of our victorious struggle
against Denikin and Kolchak, we never found that the existence of
a Soviet and proletarian opposition in their camp was immaterial to
our victories. We know perfectly well that the dispersal of the Constituent Assembly on January 5, 1918 was not hampered but was
actually facilitated by the fact that, within the counter-revolutionary
Constituent Assembly which was about to be dispersed, there was a
consistent Bolshevik, as well as an inconsistent, Left Socialist-Revolutionary Soviet opposition. The authors of the theses are engaged
in muddled thinking; they have forgotten the experience of many,
if not all, revolutions, which shows the great usefulness, during a
revolution, of a *combination* of mass action outside a reactionary
parliament with an opposition sympathetic to (or, better still, directly supporting) the revolution within it. The Dutch, and the "Lefts"
in general, argue in this respect like doctrinaires of the revolution,
who have never taken part in a real revolution, have never given
thought to the history of revolutions, or have naïvely mistaken
subjective "rejection" of a reactionary institution for its actual destruction by the combined operation of a number of objective factors.
The surest way of discrediting and damaging a new political (and

not only political) idea is to reduce it to absurdity on the plea of defending it. For any truth, if "overdone" (as Dietzgen Senior put it), if exaggerated, or if carried beyond the limits of its actual applicability, can be reduced to an absurdity, and is even bound to become an absurdity under these conditions. That is just the kind of disservice the Dutch and German Lefts are rendering to the new truth of the Soviet form of government being superior to bourgeois-democratic parliaments. Of course, anyone would be in error who voiced the outmoded viewpoint or in general considered it impermissible, in all and any circumstances, to reject participation in bourgeois parliaments. I cannot attempt here to formulate the conditions under which a boycott is useful, since the object of this pamphlet is far more modest, namely, to study Russian experience in connection with certain topical questions of international communist tactics. Russian experience has provided us with one successful and correct instance (1905), and another that was incorrect (1906), of the use of a boycott by the Bolsheviks. Analysing the first case, we see that we succeeded in *preventing* a reactionary government from *convening* a reactionary parliament in a situation in which extra-parliamentary revolutionary mass action (strikes in particular) was developing at great speed, when not a single section of the proletariat and the peasantry could support the reactionary government in any way, and when the revolutionary proletariat was gaining influence over the backward masses through the strike struggle and through the agrarian movement. It is quite obvious that *this* experience is not applicable to present-day European conditions. It is likewise quite obvious—and the foregoing arguments bear this out—that the advocacy, even if with reservations, by the Dutch and the other "Lefts" of refusal to participate in parliaments is fundamentally wrong and detrimental to the cause of the revolutionary proletariat.

In Western Europe and America, parliament has become most odious to the revolutionary vanguard of the working class. That cannot be denied. It can readily be understood, for it is difficult to imagine anything more infamous, vile or treacherous than the behaviour of the vast majority of socialist and Social-Democratic parliamentary deputies during and after the war. It would, however, be not only unreasonable but actually criminal to yield to this mood when deciding *how* this generally recognised evil should be fought. In many countries of Western Europe, the revolutionary mood, we might say, is at present a "novelty", or a "rarity", which has all too long been vainly and impatiently awaited; perhaps that is why people so easily yield to that mood. Certainly, without a revolutionary mood among the masses, and without conditions facilitating the growth of this mood, revolutionary tactics will never develop into action. In Russia, however, lengthy, painful and sanguinary experience has taught us the truth that revolutionary tactics cannot be built on a revolutionary mood alone. Tactics must be based on a sober and strictly objective appraisal of *all* the class forces in a particular state (and of the states that surround it, and of all states the world over) as well as of the experience of revolutionary movements. It is very easy to show one's "revolutionary" temper merely by hurling abuse at parliamentary opportunism, or merely by repudiating participation in parliaments; its very ease, however, cannot turn this into a solution of a difficult, a very difficult, problem. It is far more difficult to create a really revolutionary parliamentary group in a European parliament than it was in Russia. That stands to reason. But it is only a particular expression of the general truth that it was easy for Russia, in the specific and historically unique situation of 1917, to *start* the socialist revolution, but it will be more difficult for Russia than for the European countries to *continue* the revolution and bring it to its consummation. I had occasion to point this out already at the beginning of 1918, and our experience of the past two years has entirely confirmed the correctness of this view. Certain specific conditions, viz., 1) the possibility of linking up the Soviet revolution with the ending, as a consequence of this revolution, of the imperialist war, which had exhausted the workers and peasants to an incredible degree; 2) the possibility of taking temporary advantage of the mortal conflict between the world's two most powerful groups of imperialist robbers, who were unable to unite against their Soviet enemy; 3) the possibility of enduring a comparatively lengthy civil war, partly owing to the enormous size of the country and to the poor means of communication; 4) the existence of such a profound bourgeois-democratic revolutionary movement among the peasantry that the party of the proletariat was able to adopt the revolutionary demands of the peasant party[267] (the Socialist-Revolutionary Party, the majority of whose members were definitely hostile to Bolshevism) and realise them at once, thanks to the conquest of political power by the proletariat—all these specific conditions do not at present exist in Western Europe, and a repetition of such or similar conditions will not occur so easily. Incidentally, apart from a number of other causes, that is why it is more difficult for Western Europe to *start* a socialist revolution than it was for us. To attempt to "circumvent" this difficulty by "skipping" the arduous job of utilising reactionary parliaments for revolutionary purposes is absolutely childish. You want to create a new society, yet you fear the difficulties involved in forming a good parliamentary group made up of convinced, devoted and heroic Communists, in a reactionary parliament! Is that not childish? If Karl Liebknecht in Germany and Z. Höglund in Sweden were able, even without mass support from below, to set examples of the truly revolutionary utilisation of reactionary parliaments, why should a rapidly growing revolutionary mass party, in the midst of the post-war disillusionment and embitterment of the masses, be unable to *forge* a communist group in the worst of parliaments? It is because, in Western Europe, the backward masses of the workers and—to an even greater degree—of the small peasants are much more imbued with bourgeois-democratic and parliamentary prejudices than they were in Russia; because of that, it is *only* from within such institutions as bourgeois parliaments that Communists can (and must) wage a long and persistent struggle, undaunted by any difficulties, to expose, dispel and overcome these prejudices.

The German "Lefts" complain of bad "leaders" in their party, give way to despair, and even arrive at a ridiculous "negation" of "leaders". But in conditions in which it is often necessary to hide "leaders" underground, the *evolution* of good "leaders", reliable, tested and authoritative, is a very difficult matter; these difficulties *cannot* be successfully overcome without combining legal and illegal work, and *without testing the "leaders", among other ways*, in parliaments. Criticism—the most keen, ruthless and uncompromising criticism—should be directed, not against parliamentarianism or parliamentary activities, but against those leaders who are unable—and still more against those who are *unwilling*—to utilise parliamentary elections and the parliamentary rostrum in a revolutionary and communist manner. Only such criticism—combined, of course, with the dismissal of incapable leaders and their replacement by capable ones—will constitute useful and fruitful revolutionary work that will simultaneously train the "leaders" to be worthy of the working class and of all working people, and train the masses to be able properly to understand the political situation and the often very complicated and intricate tasks that spring from that situation.*

* I have had too little opportunity to acquaint myself with "Left-wing" communism in Italy. Comrade Bordiga and his faction of Abstentionist Communists (*Comunista astensionista*) are certainly wrong in advocating non-participation in parliament. But on one point, it seems to me, Comrade Bordiga is right—as far as can be judged from two issues of his paper, *Il Soviet*[268] (Nos. 3 and 4, January 18 and February 1, 1920), from four issues of Comrade Serrati's excellent periodical, *Comunismo*[269] (Nos. 1-4, October 1-November 30, 1919), and from separate issues of Italian bourgeois papers which I have seen. Comrade Bordiga and his group are right in attacking Turati and his partisans, who remain in a party which has recognised Soviet power and the dictatorship of the proletariat, and yet continue their former pernicious and opportunist policy as members of parliament. Of course, in tolerating this, Comrade Serrati and the entire Italian Socialist Party are making a mistake which threatens to do as much harm and give rise to the same dangers as it did in Hungary, where the Hungarian Turatis sabotaged both the party and the Soviet government[270] from within. Such a mistaken, inconsistent, or spineless attitude towards the opportunist parliamentarians gives rise to "Left-wing" communism, on the one hand, and *to a certain extent* justifies its existence, on the other. Comrade Serrati is obviously wrong when he accuses Deputy Turati of being "inconsistent" (*Communismo* No. 3), for it is the Italian Socialist Party itself that is inconsistent in tolerating such opportunist parliamentarians as Turati and Co.

VIII

NO COMPROMISES?

In the quotation from the Frankfurt pamphlet, we have seen how emphatically the "Lefts" have advanced this slogan. It is sad to see people who no doubt consider themselves Marxists, and want to be Marxists, forget the fundamental truths of Marxism. This is what Engels—who, like Marx, was one of those rarest of authors whose every sentence in every one of their fundamental works contains a remarkably profound content—wrote in 1874, against the manifesto of the thirty-three Blanquist Communards:

" 'We are Communists' [the Blanquist Communards wrote in their manifesto], 'because we want to attain our goal without stopping at intermediate stations, without any compromises, which only postpone the day of victory and prolong the period of slavery.'

"The German Communists are Communists because, through all the intermediate stations and all compromises created, not by them but by the course of historical development, they clearly perceive and constantly pursue the final aim—the abolition of classes and the creation of a society in which there will no longer be private ownership of land or of the means of production. The thirty-three Blanquists are Communists just because they imagine that, merely because *they* want to skip the intermediate stations and compromises, the matter is settled, and if 'it begins' in the next few days—which they take for granted—and they take over power, 'communism will be introduced' the day after tomorrow. If that is not immediately possible, they are not Communists.

"What childish innocence it is to present one's own impatience as a theoretically convincing argument!" (Frederick Engels, "Programme of the Blanquist Communards", from the German Social-Democratic newspaper *Volksstaat*, 1874, No. 73, given in the Russian translation of *Articles, 1871-1875*, Petrograd, 1919, pp. 52-53).

In the same article, Engels expresses his profound esteem for Vaillant, and speaks of the "unquestionable merit" of the latter (who, like Guesde, was one of the most prominent leaders of international socialism until their betrayal of socialism in August 1914). But Engels does not fail to give a detailed analysis of an obvious error. Of course, to very young and inexperienced revolutionaries, as well as to petty-bourgeois revolutionaries of even very respectable age and great experience, it seems extremely "dangerous", incomprehensible and wrong to "permit compromises". Many sophists (being unusually or excessively "experienced" politicians) reason exactly in the same way as the British leaders of opportunism mentioned by Comrade Lansbury: "If the Bolsheviks are permitted a certain compromise, why should we not be permitted any kind of compromise?" However, proletarians schooled in numerous strikes (to take only this manifestation of the class struggle) usually assimilate in admirable fashion the very profound truth (philosophical, historical, political and psychological) expounded by Engels. Every proletarian has been through strikes and has experienced "compromises" with the hated oppressors and exploiters, when the workers have had to return to work either without having achieved anything or else agreeing to only a partial satisfaction of their demands. Every proletarian—as a result of the conditions of the mass struggle and the acute intensification of class antagonisms he lives among—sees the difference between a compromise enforced by objective conditions (such as lack of strike funds, no outside support, starvation and exhaustion)—a compromise which in no way minimises the revolutionary devotion and readiness to carry on the struggle on the part of the workers who have agreed to such a compromise—and, on the other hand, a compromise by traitors who try to ascribe to objective causes their self-interest (strike-breakers also enter into "compromises"!), their cowardice, desire to toady to the capitalists, and readiness to yield to intimidation, sometimes to persuasion, sometimes to sops, and sometimes to flattery from the capitalists. (The history of the British labour movement provides a very large number of instances of such treacherous compromises by British trade union leaders, but, in one form or another, almost all workers in all countries have witnessed the same sort of thing.)

Naturally, there are individual cases of exceptional difficulty and complexity, when the greatest efforts are necessary for a proper assessment of the actual character of this or that "compromise", just as there are cases of homicide when it is by no means easy to establish whether the homicide was fully justified and even necessary (as, for example, legitimate self-defence), or due to unpardonable negligence, or even to a cunningly executed perfidious plan. Of course, in politics, where it is sometimes a matter of extremely complex relations—national and international—between classes and parties, very many cases will arise that will be much more difficult than the question of a legitimate "compromise" in a strike or a treacherous "compromise" by a strike-breaker, treachrous leader, etc. It would be absurd to formulate a recipe or general rule ("No compromises!") to suit all cases. One must use one's own brains and be able to find one's bearings in each particular instance. It is, in fact, one of the functions of a party organisation and of party leaders worthy of the name, to acquire, through the prolonged, persistent, variegated and comprehensive efforts of all thinking representatives of a given class,* the knowledge, experience and—in

---

* Within every class, even in the conditions prevailing in the most enlightened countries, even within the most advanced class, and even when the circumstances

addition to knowledge and experience—the political flair necessary for the speedy and correct solution of complex political problems.

Naïve and quite inexperienced people imagine that the permissibility of compromise *in general* is sufficient to obliterate any distinction between opportunism, against which we are waging, and must wage, an unremitting struggle, and revolutionary Marxism, or communism. But if such people do not yet know that in nature and in society *all* distinctions are fluid and up to a certain point conventional, nothing can help them but lengthy training, education, enlightenment, and political and everyday experience. In the practical questions that arise in the politics of any particular or specific historical moment, it is important to single out those which display the principal type of intolerable and treacherous compromises, such as embody an opportunism that is fatal to the revolutionary class, and to exert all efforts to explain them and combat them. During the 1914-18 imperialist war between two groups of equally predatory countries, social-chauvinism was the principal and fundamental type of opportunism, i.e., support of "defence of country", which in *such* a war was really equivalent to defence of the predatory interests of one's "own" bourgeoisie. After the war, defence of the robber League of Nations,[271] defence of direct or indirect alliances with the bourgeoisie of one's own country against the revolutionary proletariat and the "Soviet" movement, and defence of bourgeois democracy and bourgeois parliamentarianism against "Soviet power" became the principal manifestations of those intolerable and treacherous compromises, whose sum total constituted an opportunism fatal to the revolutionary proletariat and its cause.

"...All compromise with other parties ... any policy of manoeuvring and compromise must be emphatically rejected,"

the German Lefts write in the Frankfurt pamphlet.

It is surprising that, with such views, these Lefts do not emphatically condemn Bolshevism! After all, the German Lefts cannot but know that the entire history of Bolshevism, both before and after the October Revolution, is *full* of instances of changes of tack, conciliatory tactics and compromises with other parties, including bourgeois parties!

To carry on a war for the overthrow of the international bourgeoisie, a war which is a hundred times more difficult, protracted and complex than the most stubborn of ordinary wars between

of the moment have aroused all its spiritual forces to an exceptional degree, there always are—and inevitably *will be* as long as classes exist, as long as a classless society has not fully consolidated itself, and has not developed on its own foundations—representatives of the class who do *not* think, and are incapable of thinking, for themselves. Capitalism would not be the oppressor of the masses that it actually is, if things were otherwise.

states, and to renounce in advance any change of tack, or any utilisation of a conflict of interests (even if temporary) among one's enemies, or any conciliation or compromise with possible allies (even if they are temporary, unstable, vacillating or conditional allies)—is that not ridiculous in the extreme? Is it not like making a difficult ascent of an unexplored and hitherto inaccessible mountain and refusing in advance ever to move in zigzags, ever to retrace one's steps, or ever to abandon a course once selected, and to try others? And yet people so immature and inexperienced (if youth were the explanation, it would not be so bad; young people are preordained to talk such nonsense for a certain period) have met with support—whether direct or indirect, open or covert, whole or partial, it does not matter—from some members of the Communist Party of Holland.

After the first socialist revolution of the proletariat, and the overthrow of the bourgeoisie in some country, the proletariat of that country remains *for a long time weaker* than the bourgeoisie, simply because of the latter's extensive international links, and also because of the spontaneous and continuous restoration and regeneration of capitalism and the bourgeoisie by the small commodity producers of the country which has overthrown the bourgeoisie. The more powerful enemy can be vanquished only by exerting the utmost effort, and by the most thorough, careful, attentive, skilful and *obligatory* use of any, even the smallest, rift between the enemies, any conflict of interests among the bourgeoisie of the various countries and among the various groups or types of bourgeoisie within the various countries, and also by taking advantage of any, even the smallest, opportunity of winning a mass ally, even though this ally is temporary, vacillating, unstable, unreliable and conditional. Those who do not understand this reveal a failure to understand even the smallest grain of Marxism, of modern scientific socialism *in general*. Those who have not proved *in practice*, over a fairly considerable period of time and in fairly varied political situations, their ability to apply this truth in practice have not yet learned to help the revolutionary class in its struggle to emancipate all toiling humanity from the exploiters. And this applies equally to the period *before* and *after* the proletariat has won political power.

Our theory is not a dogma, but a *guide to action*, said Marx and Engels. The greatest blunder, the greatest crime, committed by such "out-and-out" Marxists as Karl Kautsky, Otto Bauer, etc., is that they have not understood this and have been unable to apply it at crucial moments of the proletarian revolution. "Political activity is not like the pavement of Nevsky Prospekt" (the well-kept, broad and level pavement of the perfectly straight principal thoroughfare of St. Petersburg), N. G. Chernyshevsky, the great Russian socialist of the pre-Marxist period, used to say. Since Chernyshevsky's time,

disregard of forgetfulness of this truth has cost Russian revolutionaries countless sacrifices. We must strive at all costs to *prevent* the
Left Communists and West-European and American revolutionaries
that are devoted to the working class from paying *as dearly* as the
backward Russians did to learn this truth.

Prior to the downfall of tsarism, the Russian revolutionary
Social-Democrats made repeated use of the services of the bourgeois
liberals, i.e., they concluded numerous practical compromises with
the latter. In 1901-02, even prior to the appearance of Bolshevism,
the old editorial board of *Iskra* (consisting of Plekhanov, Axelrod,
Zasulich, Martov, Potresov and myself) concluded (not for long,
it is true) a formal political alliance with Struve, the political leader
of bourgeois liberalism, while at the same time being able to wage
an unremitting and most merciless ideological and political struggle
against bourgeois liberalism and against the slightest manifestations of its influence in the working-class movement. The Bolsheviks
have always adhered to this policy. Since 1905 they have systematically advocated an alliance between the working class and the
peasantry, against the liberal bourgeoisie and tsarism, never, however, refusing to support the bourgeoisie against tsarism (for instance, during second rounds of elections, or during second ballots)
and never ceasing their relentless ideological and political struggle
against the Socialist-Revolutionaries, the bourgeois-revolutionary
peasant party, exposing them as petty-bourgeois democrats who
have falsely described themselves as socialists. During the Duma
elections of 1907, the Bolsheviks entered briefly into a formal
political bloc with the Socialist-Revolutionaries. Between 1903 and
1912, there were periods of several years in which we were formally
united with the Mensheviks in a single Social-Democratic Party, but
we *never stopped* our ideological and political struggle against them
as opportunists and vehicles of bourgeois influence on the proletariat. During the war, we concluded certain compromises with the
Kautskyites, with the Left Mensheviks (Martov), and with a section
of the Socialist-Revolutionaries (Chernov and Natanson); we were
together with them at Zimmerwald and Kienthal,[272] and issued joint
manifestos. However, we never ceased and never relaxed our ideological and political struggle against the Kautskyites, Martov and
Chernov (when Natanson died in 1919, a "Revolutionary-Commu-
nist" Narodnik,[273] he was very close to and almost in agreement with
us). At the very moment of the October Revolution, we entered into
an informal but very important (and very successful) political bloc
with the petty-bourgeois peasantry by adopting the *Socialist-Revolutionary* agrarian programme *in its entirety*, without a single altera-
tion—i.e., we effected an undeniable compromise in order to prove
to the peasants that we wanted, not to "steam-roller" them but to
reach agreement with them. At the same time we proposed (and

soon after effected) a formal political bloc, including participation in the government, with the Left Socialist-Revolutionaries, who dissolved this bloc after the conclusion of the Treaty of Brest-Litovsk and then, in July 1918, went to the length of armed rebellion, and subsequently of an armed struggle, against us.

It is therefore understandable why the attacks made by the German Lefts against the Central Committee of the Communist Party of Germany for entertaining the idea of a bloc with the Independents (the Independent Social-Democratic Party of Germany—the Kautskyites) are absolutely inane, in our opinion, and clear proof that the "Lefts" are in the *wrong*. In Russia, too, there were Right Mensheviks (participants in the Kerensky government), who corresponded to the German Scheidemanns, and Left Mensheviks (Martov), corresponding to the German Kautskyites and standing in opposition to the Right Mensheviks. A gradual shift of the worker masses from the Mensheviks over to the Bolsheviks was to be clearly seen in 1917. At the First All-Russia Congress of Soviets, held in June 1917, we had only 13 per cent of the votes; the Socialist-Revolutionaries and the Mensheviks had a majority. At the Second Congress of Soviets (October 25, 1917, old style) we had 51 per cent of the votes. Why is it that in Germany the *same* and absolutely *identical* shift of the workers from Right to Left did not immediately strengthen the Communists, but first strengthened the midway Independent Party, although the latter never had independent political ideas or an independent policy, but merely wavered between the Scheidemanns and the Communists?

One of the evident reasons was the *erroneous* tactics of the German Communists, who must fearlessly and honestly admit this error and learn to rectify it. The error consisted in their denial of the need to take part in the reactionary bourgeois parliaments and in the reactionary trade unions; the error consisted in numerous manifestations of that "Left-wing" infantile disorder which has now come to the surface and will consequently be cured the more thoroughly, the more rapidly and with greater advantage to the organism.

The German Independent Social-Democratic Party is obviously not a homogeneous body. Alongside the old opportunist leaders (Kautsky, Hilferding and apparently, to a considerable extent, Crispien, Ledebour and others)—these have revealed their inability to understand the significance of Soviet power and the dictatorship of the proletariat, and their inability to lead the proletariat's revolutionary struggle—there has emerged in this party a Left and proletarian wing, which is growing most rapidly. Hundreds of thousands of members of this party (which has, I think, a membership of some three-quarters of a million) are proletarians who are abandoning Scheidemann and are rapidly going over to communism.

This proletarian wing has already proposed—at the Leipzig Congress of the Independents (1919)—immediate and unconditional affiliation to the Third International. To fear a "compromise" with this wing of the party is positively ridiculous. On the contrary, it is the *duty* of Communists to seek *and find* a suitable form of compromise with them, a compromise which, on the one hand, will facilitate and accelerate the necessary complete fusion with this wing and, on the other, will in no way hamper the Communists in their ideological and political struggle against the opportunist Right wing of the Independents. It will probably be no easy matter to devise a suitable form of compromise—but only a charlatan could promise the German workers and the German Communists an "easy" road to victory.

Capitalism would not be capitalism if the proletariat *pur sang* were not surrounded by a large number of exceedingly motley types intermediate between the proletarian and the semi-proletarian (who earns his livelihood in part by the sale of his labour-power), between the semi-proletarian and the small peasant (and petty artisan, handicraft worker and small master in general), between the small peasant and the middle peasant, and so on, and if the proletariat itself were not divided into more developed and less developed strata, if it were not divided according to territorial origin, trade, sometimes according to religion, and so on. From all this follows the necessity, the absolute necessity, for the Communist Party, the vanguard of the proletariat, its class-conscious section, to resort to changes of tack, to conciliation and compromises with the various groups of proletarians, with the various parties of the workers and small masters. It is entirely a matter of *knowing how* to apply these tactics in order to *raise*—not lower—the *general* level of proletarian class-consciousness, revolutionary spirit, and ability to fight and win. Incidentally, it should be noted that the Bolsheviks' victory over the Mensheviks called for the application of tactics of changes of tack, conciliation and compromises, not only before *but also after* the October Revolution of 1917, but the changes of tack and compromises were, of course, such as assisted, boosted and consolidated the Bolsheviks at the expense of the Mensheviks. The petty-bourgeois democrats (including the Mensheviks) inevitably vacillate between the bourgeoisie and the proletariat, between bourgeois democracy and the Soviet system, between reformism and revolutionism, between love for the workers and fear of the proletarian dictatorship, etc. The Communists' proper tactics should consist in *utilising* these vacillations, not ignoring them; utilising them calls for concessions to elements that are turning towards the proletariat—whenever and in the measure that they turn towards the proletariat—in addition to fighting those who turn towards the bourgeoisie. As a result of the application of the correct tactics, Menshevism began to disintegrate, and has been disintegrating more and more in our country; the stubbornly opportunist leaders are being isolated, and the best of the workers and the best elements among the petty-bourgeois democrats are being brought into our camp. This is a lengthy process, and the hasty "decision"—"No compromises, no manoeuvres"—can only prejudice the strengthening of the revolutionary proletariat's influence and the enlargement of its forces.

Lastly, one of the undoubted errors of the German "Lefts" lies in their downright refusal to recognise the Treaty of Versailles. The more "weightily" and "pompously", the more "emphatically" and peremptorily this viewpoint is formulated (by K. Horner, for instance), the less sense it seems to make. It is not enough, under the present conditions of the international proletarian revolution, to repudiate the preposterous absurdities of "National Bolshevism" (Laufenberg and others), which has gone to the length of advocating a bloc with the German bourgeoisie for a war against the Entente. One must realise that it is utterly false tactics to refuse to admit that a Soviet Germany (if a German Soviet republic were soon to arise) would have to recognise the Treaty of Versailles for a time, and to submit to it. From this it does not follow that the Independents—at a time when the Scheidemanns were in the government, when the Soviet government in Hungary had not yet been overthrown, and when it was still possible that a Soviet revolution in Vienna would support Soviet Hungary—were right, *under the circumstances*, in putting forward the demand that the Treaty of Versailles should be signed. At that time the Independents tacked and manoeuvred very clumsily, for they more or less accepted responsibility for the Scheidemann traitors, and more or less backslid from advocacy of a ruthless (and most calmly conducted) class war against the Scheidemanns, to advocacy of a "classless" or "above-class" standpoint.

In the present situation, however, the German Communists should obviously not deprive themselves of freedom of action by giving a positive and categorical promise to repudiate the Treaty of Versailles in the event of communism's victory. That would be absurd. They should say: the Scheidemanns and the Kautskyites have committed a number of acts of treachery hindering (and in part quite ruining) the chances of an alliance with Soviet Russia and Soviet Hungary. We Communists will do all we can to *facilitate* and *pave the way* for such an alliance. However, we are in no way obligated to repudiate the Treaty of Versailles, come what may, or to do so at once. The possibility of its successful repudiation will depend, not only on the Germany, but also on the international successes of the Soviet movement. The Scheidemanns and the Kautskyites have hampered this movement; we are helping it. That is the gist of the matter; therein lies the fundamental difference. And if our class enemies, the exploiters and their Scheidemann and Kautskyite lackeys, have missed many an opportunity of strengthening both the German and the international Soviet movement, of strengthening both the German and the international Soviet revolution, the blame lies with them. The Soviet revolution in Germany will strengthen the international Soviet movement, which is the strongest bulwark (and the only reliable, invincible and world-wide bulwark) against the Treaty of Versailles and against international imperialism in general. To give absolute, categorical and immediate precedence to liberation from the Treaty of Versailles and to give it *precedence over the question* of liberating *other* countries oppressed by imperialism, from the yoke of imperialism, is philistine nationalism (worthy of the Kautskys, the Hilferdings, the Otto Bauers and Co.), not of revolutionary internationalism. The overthrow of the bourgeoisie in any of the large European countries, including Germany, would be such a gain for the international revolution that, for its sake, one can, and if necessary should, tolerate a *more prolonged existence of the Treaty of Versailles.* If Russia, standing alone, could endure the Treaty of Brest-Litovsk for several months, to the advantage of the revolution, there is nothing impossible in a Soviet Germany, allied with Soviet Russia, enduring the existence of the Treaty of Versailles for a longer period, to the advantage of the revolution.

The imperialists of France, Britain, etc., are trying to provoke and ensnare the German Communists: "Say that you will not sign the Treaty of Versailles!" they urge. Like babes, the Left Communists fall into the trap laid for them, instead of skilfully manoeuvring against the crafty and, *at present*, stronger enemy, and instead of telling him, "We shall sign the Treaty of Versailles now." It is folly, not revolutionism, to deprive ourselves in advance of any freedom of action, openly to inform an enemy who is at present better armed than we are whether we shall fight him, and when. To accept battle at a time when it is obviously advantageous to the enemy, but not to us, is criminal; political leaders of the revolutionary class are absolutely useless if they are incapable of "changing tack, or offering conciliation and compromise" in order to take evasive action in a patently disadvantageous battle.

IX

"LEFT-WING" COMMUNISM IN GREAT BRITAIN

There is no Communist Party in Great Britain as yet, but there is a fresh, broad, powerful and rapidly growing communist movement among the workers, which justifies the best hopes. There are several political parties and organisations (the British Socialist Party,[274] the

Socialist Labour Party, the South Wales Socialist Society, the Workers' Socialist Federation[275]), which desire to form a Communist Party and are already negotiating among themselves to this end. In its issue of February 21, 1920, Vol. VI, No. 48, *The Workers' Dreadnought*,[276] weekly organ of the last of the organisations mentioned, carried an article by the editor, Comrade Sylvia Pankhurst, entitled "Towards a Communist Party". The article outlines the progress of the negotiations between the four organisations mentioned, for the formation of a united Communist Party, on the basis of affiliation to the Third International, the recognition of the Soviet system instead of parliamentarianism, and the recognition of the dictatorship of the proletariat. It appears that one of the greatest obstacles to the immediate formation of a united Communist Party is presented by the disagreement on the questions of participation in Parliament and on whether the new Communist Party should affiliate to the old, trade-unionist, opportunist and social-chauvinist Labour Party, which is mostly made up of trade unions. The Workers' Socialist Federation and the Socialist Labour Party* are opposed to taking part in parliamentary elections and in Parliament, and they are opposed to affiliation to the Labour Party; in this they disagree with all or with most of the members of the British Socialist Party, which they regard as the "Right wing of the Communist parties" in Great Britain. (Page 5, Sylvia Pankhurst's article.)

Thus, the main division is the same as in Germany, notwithstanding the enormous difference in the forms in which the disagreements manifest themselves (in Germany the form is far closer to the "Russian" than it is in Great Britain), and in a number of other things. Let us examine the arguments of the "Lefts".

On the question of participation in Parliament, Comrade Sylvia Pankhurst refers to an article in the same issue, by Comrade Gallacher, who writes in the name of the Scottish Workers' Council in Glasgow.

"The above council," he writes, "is definitely anti-parliamentarian, and has behind it the Left wing of the various political bodies. We represent the revolutionary movement in Scotland, striving continually to build up a revolutionary organisation within the industries [in various branches of production], and a Communist Party, based on social committees, throughout the country. For a considerable time we have been sparring with the official parliamentarians. We have not considered it necessary to declare open warfare on them, and they are *afraid* to open an attack on us.

"But this state of affairs cannot long continue. We are winning all along the line.

"The rank and file of the I.L.P. in Scotland is becoming more and more disgusted with the thought of Parliament, and the Soviets [the Russian word transliterated into English is used] or Workers' Councils are being supported by

---

* I believe this party is opposed to affiliation to the Labour Party but not all its members are opposed to participation in Parliament.

almost every branch. This is very serious, of course, for the gentlemen who look to politics for a profession, and they are using any and every means to persuade their members to come back into the parliamentary fold. Revolutionary comrades *must not* [all italics are the author's] give any support to this gang. Our fight here is going to be a difficult one. One of the worst features of it will be the treachery of those whose personal ambition is a more impelling force than their regard for the revolution. Any support given to parliamentarism is simply assisting to put power into the hands of our British Scheidemanns and Noskes. Henderson, Clynes and Co. are hopelessly reactionary. The official I.L.P. is more and more coming under the control of middle-class liberals, who ... have found their 'spiritual home' in the camp of Messrs. MacDonald, Snowden and Co. The official I.L.P. is bitterly hostile to the Third International, the rank and file is for it. Any support to the parliamentary opportunists is simply playing into the hands of the former. The B.S.P. doesn't count at all here.... What is wanted here is a sound revolutionary industrial organisation, and a Communist Party working along clear, well-defined, scientific lines. If our comrades can assist us in building these, we will take their help gladly; if they cannot, for God's sake let them keep out altogether, lest they betray the revolution by lending their support to the reactionaries, who are so eagerly clamouring for parliamentary 'honours' (?) [the query mark is the author's] and who are so anxious to prove that they *can rule* as effectively as the 'boss' class politicians themselves."

In my opinion, this letter to the editor expresses excellently the temper and point of view of the young Communists, or of rank-and-file workers who are only just beginning to accept communism. This temper is highly gratifying and valuable; we must learn to appreciate and support it for, in its absence, it would be hopeless to expect the victory of the proletarian revolution in Great Britain, or in any other country for that matter. People who can give expression to this temper of the masses, and are able to evoke such a temper (which is very often dormant, unconscious and latent) among the masses, should be appreciated and given every assistance. At the same time, we must tell them openly and frankly that a state of mind is *by itself* insufficient for leadership of the masses in a great revolutionary struggle, and that the cause of the revolution may well be harmed by certain errors that people who are most devoted to the cause of the revolution are about to commit, or are committing. Comrade Gallacher's letter undoubtedly reveals the rudiments of *all* the mistakes that are being made by the German "Left" Communists and were made by the Russian "Left" Bolsheviks in 1908 and 1918.

The writer of the letter is full of a noble and working-class hatred for the bourgeois "class politicians" (a hatred understood and shared, however, not only by proletarians but by all working people, by all *Kleinen Leuten** to use the German expression). In a representative of the oppressed and exploited masses, this hatred is truly the "beginning of all wisdom", the basis of any socialist and communist movement and of its success. The writer, however, has apparently lost sight of the fact that politics is a science and an art

---

* "Small folk, little people" (Germ.).—*Ed.*

that does not fall from the skies or come gratis, and that, if it wants to overcome the bourgeoisie, the proletariat must train its *own* proletarian "class politicians", of a kind in no way inferior to bourgeois politicians.

The writer of the letter fully realises that only workers' Soviets, not parliament, can be the instrument enabling the proletariat to achieve its aims; those who have failed to understand this are, of course, out-and-out reactionaries, even if they are most highly educated people, most experienced politicians, most sincere socialists, most erudite Marxists, and most honest citizens and fathers of families. But the writer of the letter does not even ask—it does not occur to him to ask—whether it is possible to bring about the Soviets' victory over parliament without getting pro-Soviet politicians *into* parliament, without disintegrating parliamentarianism from *within*, without working within parliament for the success of the Soviets in their forthcoming task of dispersing parliament. Yet the writer of the letter expresses the absolutely correct idea that the Communist Party in Great Britain must act on *scientific* principles. Science demands, first, that the experience of other countries be taken into account, especially if these other countries, which are also capitalist, are undergoing, or have recently undergone, a very similar experience; second, it demands that account be taken of *all* the forces, groups, parties, classes and masses operating in a given country, and also that policy should not be determined only by the desires and views, by the degree of class-consciousness and the militancy of one group or party alone.

It is true that the Hendersons, the Clyneses, the MacDonalds and the Snowdens are hopelessly reactionary. It is equally true that they want to assume power (though they would prefer a coalition with the bourgeoisie), that they want to "rule" along the old bourgeois lines, and that when they are in power they will certainly behave like the Scheidemanns and Noskes. All that is true. But it does not at all follow that to support them means treachery to the revolution; what does follow is that, in the interests of the revolution, working-class revolutionaries should give these gentlemen a certain amount of parliamentary support. To explain this idea, I shall take two contemporary British political documents: 1) the speech delivered by Prime Minister Lloyd George on March 18, 1920 (as reported in *The Manchester Guardian*[277] of March 19, 1920), and 2) the arguments of a "Left" Communist, Comrade Sylvia Pankhurst, in the article mentioned above.

In his speech Lloyd George entered into a polemic with Asquith (who had been especially invited to this meeting but declined to attend) and with those Liberals who want, not a coalition with the Conservatives, but closer relations with the Labour Party. (In the above-quoted letter, Comrade Gallacher also points to the fact that

Liberals are joining the Independent Labour Party.) Lloyd George argued that a coalition—and a *close* coalition at that—between the Liberals and the Conservatives was essential, otherwise there might be a victory for the Labour Party, which Lloyd George prefers to call "Socialist" and which is working for the "common ownership" of the means of production. "It is ... known as communism in France," the leader of the British bourgeoisie said, putting it popularly for his audience, Liberal M.P.s who probably never knew it before. In Germany it was called socialism, and in Russia it is called Bolshevism, he went on to say. To Liberals this is unacceptable on principle, Lloyd George explained, because they stand in principle for private property. "Civilisation is in jeopardy," the speaker declared, and consequently Liberals and Conservatives must unite. . . .

"... If you go to the agricultural areas," said Lloyd George, "I agree you have the old party divisions as strong as ever. They are removed from the danger. It does not walk their lanes. But when they see it they will be as strong as some of these industrial constituencies are now. Four-fifths of this country is industrial and commercial; hardly one-fifth is agricultural. It is one of the things I have constantly in my mind when I think of the dangers of the future here. In France the population is agricultural, and you have a solid body of opinion which does not move very rapidly, and which is not very easily excited by revolutionary movements. That is not the case here. This country is more top-heavy than any country in the world, and if it begins to rock, the crash here, for that reason, will be greater than in any land."

From this the reader will see that Mr. Lloyd George is not only a very intelligent man, but one who has also learned a great deal from the Marxists. We too have something to learn from Lloyd George.

Of definite interest is the following episode, which occurred in the course of the discussion after Lloyd George's speech:

"*Mr. Wallace, M. P.*: I should like to ask what the Prime Minister considers the effect might be in the industrial constituencies upon the industrial workers, so many of whom are Liberals at the present time and from whom we get so much support. Would not a possible result be to cause an immediate overwhelming accession of strength to the Labour Party from men who at present are our cordial supporters?

"*The Prime Minister*: I take a totally different view. The fact that Liberals are fighting among themselves undoubtedly drives a very considerable number of Liberals in despair to the Labour Party, where you get a considerable body of Liberals, very able men, whose business it is to discredit the Government. The result is undoubtedly to bring a good accession of public sentiment to the Labour Party. It does not go to the Liberals who are outside, it goes to the Labour Party, the by-elections show that."

It may be said, in passing, that this argument shows in particular how muddled even the most intelligent members of the bourgeoisie have become and how they cannot help committing irreparable blunders. That, in fact, is what will bring about the downfall of the bourgeoisie. Our people, however, may commit blunders (provided, of course, that they are not too serious and are rectified in time) and yet, in the long run, will prove the victors.

The second political document is the following argument advanced by Comrade Sylvia Pankhurst, a "Left" Communist:

"... Comrade Inkpin [the General Secretary of the British Socialist Party] refers to the Labour Party as 'the main body of the working-class movement'. Another comrade of the British Socialist Party, at the Third International, just held, put the British Socialist Party position more strongly. He said: 'We regard the Labour Party as the organised working class.'

"We do not take this view of the Labour Party. The Labour Party is very large numerically though its membership is to a great extent quiescent and apathetic, consisting of men and women who have joined the trade unions because their workmates are trade unionists, and to share the friendly benefits.

"But we recognise that the great size of the Labour Party is also due to the fact that it is the creation of a school of thought beyond which the majority of the British working class has not yet emerged, though great changes are at work in the mind of the people which will presently alter this state of affairs....

"The British Labour Party, like the social-patriotic organisations of other countries, will, in the natural development of society, inevitably come into power. It is for the Communists to build up the forces that will overthrow the social patriots, and in this country we must not delay or falter in that work.

"We must not dissipate our energy in adding to the strength of the Labour Party; its rise to power is inevitable. We must concentrate on making a communist movement that will vanquish it. The Labour Party will soon be forming a government; the revolutionary opposition must make ready to attack it...."

Thus the liberal bourgeoisie are abandoning the historical system of "two parties" (of exploiters), which has been hallowed by centuries of experience and has been extremely advantageous to the exploiters, and consider it necessary for these two parties to join forces against the Labour Party. A number of Liberals are deserting to the Labour Party like rats from a sinking ship. The Left Communists believe that the transfer of power to the Labour Party is inevitable and admit that it now has the backing of most workers. From this they draw the strange conclusion which Comrade Sylvia Pankhurst formulates as follows:

"The Communist Party must not compromise.... The Communist Party must keep its doctrine pure, and its independence of reformism inviolate; its mission is to lead the way, without stopping or turning, by the direct road to the communist revolution."

On the contrary, the fact that most British workers still follow the lead of the British Kerenskys or Scheidemanns and have not yet had experience of a government composed of these people—an experience which was necessary in Russia and Germany so as to secure the mass transition of the workers to communism—undoubtedly indicates that the British Communists *should* participate in parliamentary action, that they should, from *within* parliament, help the masses of the workers see the results of a Henderson and Snowden government in practice, and that they should help the Hendersons and Snowdens defeat the united forces of Lloyd George and Churchill. To act otherwise would mean hampering the cause of the revolution, since revolution is impossible without a change in the views of the majority of the working class, a change brought about by the political experience of the masses, never by propaganda alone. "To lead the way without compromises, without turning"— this slogan is obviously wrong if it comes from a patently impotent minority of the workers who know (or at all events should know) that given a Henderson and Snowden victory over Lloyd George and Churchill, the majority will soon become disappointed in their leaders and will begin to support communism (or at all events will adopt an attitude of neutrality, and, in the main, of sympathetic neutrality, towards the Communists). It is as though 10,000 soldiers were to hurl themselves into battle against an enemy force of 50,000, when it would be proper to "halt", "take evasive action", or even effect a "compromise" so as to gain time until the arrival of the 100,000 reinforcements that are on their way but cannot go into action immediately. That is intellectualist childishness, not the serious tactics of a revolutionary class.

The fundamental law of revolution, which has been confirmed by all revolutions and especially by all three Russian revolutions in the twentieth century, is as follows: for a revolution to take place it is not enough for the exploited and oppressed masses to realise the impossibility of living in the old way, and demand changes; for a revolution to take place it is essential that the exploiters should not be able to live and rule in the old way. It is only when the *"lower classes" do not want* to live in the old way and the "upper classes" *cannot carry on in the old way* that the revolution can triumph. This truth can be expressed in other words: revolution is impossible without a nation-wide crisis (affecting both the exploited and the exploiters). It follows that, for a revolution to take place, it is essential, first, that a majority of the workers (or at least a majority of the class-conscious, thinking, and politically active workers) should fully realise that revolution is necessary, and that they should be prepared to die for it; second, that the ruling classes should be going through a governmental crisis, which draws even the most backward masses into politics (symptomatic of any genuine revolution is a rapid, tenfold and even hundredfold increase in the size of the working and oppressed masses—hitherto apathetic —who are capable of waging the political struggle), weakens the government, and makes it possible for the revolutionaries to rapidly overthrow it.

Incidentally, as can also be seen from Lloyd George's speech, both conditions for a successful proletarian revolution are clearly maturing in Great Britain. The errors of the Left Communists are particularly dangerous at present, because certain revolutionaries are not displaying a sufficiently thoughtful, sufficiently attentive, sufficiently intelligent and sufficiently shrewd attitude toward each of these conditions. If we are the party of the revolutionary *class*, and not merely a revolutionary group, and if we want the *masses* to follow us (and unless we achieve that, we stand the risk of remaining mere windbags), we must, first, help Henderson or Snowden to beat Lloyd George and Churchill (or, rather, compel the former to beat the latter, because the former *are afraid of their victory!*); second, we must help the majority of the working class to be convinced by their own experience that we are right, i.e., that the Hendersons and Snowdens are absolutely good for nothing, that they are petty-bourgeois and treacherous by nature, and that their bankruptcy is inevitable; third, we must bring nearer the moment when, *on the basis* of the disappointment of most of the workers in the Hendersons, it will be possible, with serious chances of success, to overthrow the government of the Hendersons at once; because if the most astute and solid Lloyd George, that big, not petty, bourgeois, is displaying consternation and is more and more weakening himself (and the bourgeoisie as a whole) by his "friction" with Churchill today and with Asquith tomorrow, how much greater will be the consternation of a Henderson government!

I will put it more concretely. In my opinion, the British Communists should unite their four parties and groups (all very weak, and some of them very, very weak) into a single Communist Party on the basis of the principles of the Third International and of *obligatory* participation in parliament. The Communist Party should propose the following "compromise" election agreement to the Hendersons and Snowdens: let us jointly fight against the alliance between Lloyd George and the Conservatives; let us share parliamentary seats in proportion to the number of workers' votes polled for the Labour Party and for the Communist Party (not in elections, but in a special ballot), and let us retain *complete freedom* of agitation, propaganda and political activity. Of course, without this latter condition, we cannot agree to a bloc, for that would be treachery; the British Communists must demand and get complete freedom to expose the Hendersons and the Snowdens in the same way as (*for fifteen years*—1903-17) the Russian Bolsheviks demanded and got it in respect of the Russian Hendersons and Snowdens, i.e., the Mensheviks.

If the Hendersons and the Snowdens accept a bloc on these terms, we shall be the gainers, because the number of parliamentary seats is of no importance to us; we are not out for seats. We shall yield on this point (whilst the Hendersons and especially their new friends —or new masters—the Liberals who have joined the Independent

Labour Party are most eager to get seats). We shall be the gainers, because we shall carry *our* agitation among the *masses* at a time when Lloyd George *himself* has "incensed" them, and we shall not only be helping the Labour Party to establish its government sooner, but shall also be helping the masses sooner to understand the communist propaganda that we shall carry on against the Hendersons, without any reticence or omission.

If the Hendersons and the Snowdens reject a bloc with us on these terms, we shall gain still more, for we shall at once have shown the *masses* (note that, even in the purely Menshevik and completely opportunist Independent Labour Party, the *rank and file* are in favour of Soviets) that the Hendersons prefer *their* close relations with the capitalists to the unity of all the workers. We shall immediately gain in the eyes of the *masses*, who, particularly after the brilliant, highly correct and highly useful (to communism) explanations given by Lloyd George, will be sympathetic to the idea of uniting all the workers against the Lloyd George-Conservative alliance. We shall gain immediately, because we shall have demonstrated to the masses that the Hendersons and the Snowdens are afraid to beat Lloyd George, afraid to assume power alone, and are striving to secure the *secret* support of Lloyd George, who is *openly* extending a hand to the Conservatives, against the Labour Party. It should be noted that in Russia, after the revolution of February 27, 1917 (old style), the Bolsheviks' propaganda against the Mensheviks and Socialist-Revolutionaries (i.e., the Russian Hendersons and Snowdens) derived benefit precisely from a circumstance of this kind. We said to the Mensheviks and the Socialist-Revolutionaries: assume full power without the bourgeoisie, because you have a majority in the Soviets (at the First All-Russia Congress of Soviets, in June 1917, the Bolsheviks had only 13 per cent of the votes). But the Russian Hendersons and Snowdens were afraid to assume power without the bourgeoisie, and when the bourgeoisie held up the elections to the Constituent Assembly, knowing full well that the elections would give a majority to the Socialist-Revolutionaries and the Mensheviks* (who formed a close political bloc and in fact represented *only* petty-bourgeois democracy), the Socialist-Revolutionaries and the Mensheviks were unable energetically and consistently to oppose these delays.

If the Hendersons and the Snowdens reject a bloc with the Communists, the latter will immediately gain by winning the sympathy

---

* The results of the November 1917 elections to the Constituent Assembly in Russia, based on returns embracing over 36,000,000 voters, were as follows: the Bolsheviks obtained 25 per cent of the votes; the various parties of the landowners and the bourgeoisie obtained 13 per cent, and the petty-bourgeois-democratic parties, i.e., the Socialist-Revolutionaries, Mensheviks and a number of similar small groups obtained 62 per cent.

of the masses and discrediting the Hendersons and Snowdens; if, as a result, we do lose a few parliamentary seats, it is a matter of no significance to us. We would put up our candidates in a very few but absolutely safe constituencies, namely, constituencies where our candidatures would not give any seats to the Liberals at the expense of the Labour candidates. We would take part in the election campaign, distribute leaflets agitating for communism, and, in *all* constituencies where we have no candidates, we would urge the electors *to vote for the Labour candidate and against the bourgeois candidate.* Comrades Sylvia Pankhurst and Gallacher are mistaken in thinking that this is a betrayal of communism, or a renunciation of the struggle against the social-traitors. On the contrary, the cause of communist revolution would undoubtedly gain thereby.

At present, British Communists very often find it hard even to approach the masses, and even to get a hearing from them. If I come out as a Communist and call upon them to vote for Henderson and against Lloyd George, they will certainly give me a hearing. And I shall be able to explain in a popular manner, not only why the Soviets are better than a parliament and why the dictatorship of the proletariat is better than the dictatorship of Churchill (disguised with the signboard of bourgeois "democracy"), but also that, with my vote, I want to support Henderson in the same way as the rope supports a hanged man—that the impending establishment of a government of the Hendersons will prove that I am right, will bring the masses over to my side, and will hasten the political death of the Hendersons and the Snowdens just as was the case with their kindred spirits in Russia and Germany.

If the objection is raised that these tactics are too "subtle" or too complex for the masses to understand, that these tactics will split and scatter our forces, will prevent us from concentrating them on Soviet revolution, etc., I will reply to the "Left" objectors: don't ascribe your doctrinairism to the masses! The masses in Russia are no doubt no better educated than the masses in Britain; if anything, they are less so. Yet the masses understood the Bolsheviks, and the fact that, in September 1917, *on the eve* of the Soviet revolution, the Bolsheviks put up their candidates for a bourgeois parliament (the Constituent Assembly) and *on the day after* the Soviet revolution, in November 1917, took part in the elections to this Constituent Assembly, which they got rid of on January 5, 1918—this did not hamper the Bolsheviks, but, on the contrary, helped them.

I cannot deal here with the second point of disagreement among the British Communists—the question of affiliation or non-affiliation to the Labour Party. I have too little material at my disposal on this question, which is highly complex because of the unique character of the British Labour Party, whose very structure is so unlike that of the political parties usual in the European continent.

It is beyond doubt, however, first, that in this question, too, those who try to deduce the tactics of the revolutionary proletariat from principles such as: "The Communist Party must keep its doctrine pure, and its independence of reformism inviolate; its mission is to lead the way, without stopping or turning, by the direct road to the communist revolution"—will inevitably fall into error. Such principles are merely a repetition of the mistake made by the French Blanquist Communards, who, in 1874, "repudiated" all compromises and all intermediate stages. Second, it is beyond doubt that, in this question too, as always, the task consists in learning to apply the general and basic principles of communism to the *specific relations* between classes and parties, to the *specific features* in the objective development towards communism, which are different in each country and which we must be able to discover, study, and predict.

This, however, should be discussed, not in connection with British communism alone, but in connection with the general conclusions concerning the development of communism in all capitalist countries. We shall now proceed to deal with this subject.

X

SEVERAL CONCLUSIONS

The Russian bourgeois revolution of 1905 revealed a highly original turn in world history: in one of the most backward capitalist countries, the strike movement attained a scope and power unprecedented anywhere in the world. In the *first month* of 1905 *alone*, the number of strikers was ten times the *annual* average for the previous decade (1895-1904); from January to October 1905, strikes grew all the time and reached enormous proportions. Under the influence of a number of unique historical conditions, backward Russia was the first to show the world, not only the growth, by leaps and bounds, of the independent activity of the oppressed masses in time of revolution (this had occurred in all great revolutions), but also that the significance of the proletariat is infinitely greater than its proportion in the total population; it showed a combination of the economic strike and the political strike, with the latter developing into an armed uprising, and the birth of the Soviets, a new form of mass struggle and mass organisation of the classes oppressed by capitalism.

The revolutions of February and October 1917 led to the all-round development of the Soviets on a nation-wide scale and to their victory in the proletarian socialist revolution. In less than two years, the international character of the Soviets, the spread of this form of struggle and organisation to the world working-class movement and the historical mission of the Soviets as the gravedigger, heir and successor of bourgeois parliamentarianism and of bourgeois democracy in general, all became clear.

But that is not all. The history of the working-class movement now shows that, in all countries, it is about to go through (and is already going through) a struggle waged by communism—emergent, gaining strength and advancing towards victory—against, primarily, Menshevism, i.e., opportunism and social-chauvinism (the home brand in each particular country), and then as a complement, so to say, Left-wing communism. The former struggle has developed in all countries, apparently without any exception, as a duel between the Second International (already virtually dead) and the Third International. The latter struggle is to be seen in Germany, Great Britain, Italy, America (at any rate, a certain *section* of the Industrial Workers of the World and of the anarcho-syndicalist trends uphold the errors of Left-wing communism alongside of an almost universal and almost unreserved acceptance of the Soviet system), and in France (the attitude of a section of the former syndicalists towards the political party and parliamentarianism, also alongside of the acceptance of the Soviet system); in other words, the struggle is undoubtedly being waged, not only on an international, but even on a world-wide scale.

But while the working-class movement is everywhere going through what is actually the same kind of preparatory school for victory over the bourgeoisie, it is achieving that development in its *own way* in each country. The big and advanced capitalist countries are travelling this road *far more rapidly* than did Bolshevism, to which history granted fifteen years to prepare itself for victory, as an organised political trend. In the brief space of a year, the Third International has already scored a decisive victory; it has defeated the yellow, social-chauvinist Second International, which only a few months ago was incomparably stronger than the Third International, seemed stable and powerful, and enjoyed every possible support— direct and indirect, material (Cabinet posts, passports, the press) and ideological—from the world bourgeoisie.

It is now essential that Communists of every country should quite consciously take into account both the fundamental objectives of the struggle against opportunism and "Left" doctrinairism, and the *concrete features* which this struggle assumes and must inevitably assume in each country, in conformity with the specific character of its economics, politics, culture, and national composition (Ireland, etc.), its colonies, religious divisions, and so on and so forth. Dissatisfaction with the Second International is felt everywhere and is spreading and growing, both because of its opportunism and because of its inability or incapacity to create a really centralised and really leading centre capable of directing the international tactics of the revolutionary proletariat in its struggle for a

world Soviet republic. It should be clearly realised that such a
leading centre can never be built up on stereotyped, mechanically
equated, and identical tactical rules of struggle. As long as national
and state distinctions exist among peoples and countries—and these
will continue to exist for a very long time to come, even after the
dictatorship of the proletariat has been established on a world-wide
scale—the unity of the international tactics of the communist working-class movement in all countries demands, not the elimination
of variety or the suppression of national distinctions (which is a pipe
dream at present), but an application of the *fundamental* principles
of communism (Soviet power and the dictatorship of the proletariat), which will *correctly modify* these principles in certain *particulars*, correctly adapt and apply them to national and national-
state distinctions. To seek out, investigate, predict, and grasp that
which is nationally specific and nationally distinctive, in the *concrete manner* in which each country should tackle a *single* international task: victory over opportunism and Left doctrinairism
within the working-class movement; the overthrow of the bourgeoisie; the establishment of a Soviet republic and a proletarian
dictatorship—such is the basic task in the historical period that all
the advanced countries (and not they alone) are going through. The
chief thing—though, of course, far from everything—the chief thing,
has already been achieved: the vanguard of the working class has
been won over, has ranged itself on the side of Soviet government
and against parliamentarianism, on the side of the dictatorship of
the proletariat and against bourgeois democracy. All efforts and all
attention should now be concentrated on the *next* step, which may
seem—and from a certain viewpoint actually is—less fundamental,
but, on the other hand, is actually closer to a practical accomplishment of the task. That step is: the search after forms of the *transition* or the *approach* to the proletarian revolution.

The proletarian vanguard has been won over ideologically. That
is the main thing. Without this, not even the first step towards
victory can be made. But that is still quite a long way from victory.
Victory cannot be won with a vanguard alone. To throw only the
vanguard into the decisive battle, before the entire class, the broad
masses, have taken up a position either of direct support for the
vanguard, or at least of sympathetic neutrality towards it and of
precluded support for the enemy, would be, not merely foolish but
criminal. Propaganda and agitation alone are not enough for an
entire class, the broad masses of the working people, those oppressed
by capital, to take up such a stand. For that, the masses must have
their own political experience. Such is the fundamental law of all
great revolutions, which has been confirmed with compelling force
and vividness, not only in Russia but in Germany as well. To turn
resolutely towards communism, it was necessary, not only for the

ignorant and often illiterate masses of Russia, but also for the literate and well-educated masses of Germany, to realise from their own bitter experience the absolute impotence and spinelessness, the absolute helplessness and servility to the bourgeoisie, and the utter vileness of the government of the paladins of the Second International; they had to realise that a dictatorship of the extreme reactionaries (Kornilov[278] in Russia; Kapp and Co. in Germany) is inevitably the only alternative to a dictatorship of the proletariat.

The immediate objective of the class-conscious vanguard of the international working-class movement, i.e., the Communist parties, groups and trends, is to be able to *lead* the broad masses (who are still, for the most part, apathetic, inert, dormant and convention-ridden) to their new position, or, rather, to be able to lead, *not only* their own party but also these masses in their advance and transition to the new position. While the first historical objective (that of winning over the class-conscious vanguard of the proletariat to the side of Soviet power and the dictatorship of the working class) could not have been reached without a complete ideological and political victory over opportunism and social-chauvinism, the second and immediate objective, which consists in being able to lead the *masses* to a new position ensuring the victory of the vanguard in the revolution, cannot be reached without the liquidation of Left doctrinairism, and without a full elimination of its errors.

As long as it was (and inasmuch as it still is) a question of winning the proletariat's vanguard over to the side of communism, priority went and still goes to propaganda work; even propaganda circles, with all their parochial limitations, are useful under these conditions, and produce good results. But when it is a question of practical action by the masses, of the disposition, if one may so put it, of vast armies, of the alignment of *all* the class forces in a given society *for the final and decisive battle*, then propagandist methods alone, the mere repetition of the truths of "pure" communism, are of no avail. In these circumstances, one must not count in thousands, like the propagandist belonging to a small group that has not yet given leadership to the masses; in these circumstances one must count in millions and tens of millions. In these circumstances, we must ask ourselves, not only whether we have convinced the vanguard of the revolutionary class, but also whether the historically effective forces of *all* classes—positively of all the classes in a given society, without exception—are arrayed in such a way that the decisive battle is at hand—in such a way that: (1) all the class forces hostile to us have become sufficiently entangled, are sufficiently at loggerheads with each other, have sufficiently weakened themselves in a struggle which is beyond their strength; (2) all the vacillating and unstable, intermediate elements—the petty bourgeoisie and the petty-bourgeois democrats, as distinct from the bourgeoisie—have sufficiently exposed themselves in the eyes of the people, have sufficiently disgraced themselves through their practical bankruptcy, and (3) among the proletariat, a mass sentiment favouring the most determined, bold and dedicated revolutionary action against the bourgeoisie has emerged and begun to grow vigorously. Then revolution is indeed ripe; then, indeed, if we have correctly gauged all the conditions indicated and summarised above, and if we have chosen the right moment, our victory is assured.

The differences between the Churchills and the Lloyd Georges—with insignificant national distinctions, these political types exist in *all* countries—on the one hand, and between the Hendersons and the Lloyd Georges on the other, are quite minor and unimportant from the standpoint of pure (i.e., abstract) communism, i.e., communism that has not yet matured to the stage of practical political action by the masses. However, from the standpoint of this practical action by the masses, these differences are most important. To take due account of these differences, and to determine the moment when the inevitable conflicts between these "friends", which weaken and enfeeble *all the "friends" taken together*, will have come to a head—that is the concern, the task, of a Communist who wants to be, not merely a class-conscious and convinced propagandist of ideas, but a practical leader of the *masses* in the revolution. It is necessary to link the strictest devotion to the ideas of communism with the ability to effect all the necessary practical compromises, tacks, conciliatory manoeuvres, zigzags, retreats and so on, in order to speed up the achievement and then loss of political power by the Hendersons (the heroes of the Second International, if we are not to name individual representatives of petty-bourgeois democracy who call themselves socialists); to accelerate their inevitable bankruptcy in practice, which will enlighten the masses in the spirit of our ideas, in the direction of communism; to accelerate the inevitable friction, quarrels, conflicts and complete disintegration among the Hendersons, the Lloyd Georges and the Churchills (the Mensheviks, the Socialist-Revolutionaries, the Constitutional-Democrats, the monarchists; the Scheidemanns, the bourgeoisie and the Kappists, etc.); to select the proper moment when the discord among these "pillars of sacrosanct private property" is at its height, so that, through a decisive offensive, the proletariat will defeat them all and capture political power.

History as a whole, and the history of revolutions in particular, is always richer in content, more varied, more multiform, more lively and ingenious than is imagined by even the best parties, the most class-conscious vanguards of the most advanced classes. This can readily be understood, because even the finest of vanguards express the class-consciousness, will, passion and imagination of tens of thousands, whereas at moments of great upsurge and the exertion of all human capacities, revolutions are made by the class-consciousness, will, passion and imagination of tens of millions, spurred on by a most acute struggle of classes. Two very important practical conclusions follow from this: first, that in order to accomplish its task the revolutionary class must be able to master *all* forms or aspects of social activity without exception (completing after the capture of political power—sometimes at great risk and with very great danger—what it did not complete before the capture of power); second, that the revolutionary class must be prepared for the most rapid and brusque replacement of one form by another.

One will readily agree that any army which does not train to use all the weapons, all the means and methods of warfare that the enemy possesses, or may possess, is behaving in an unwise or even criminal manner. This applies to politics even more than it does to the art of war. In politics it is even harder to know in advance which methods of struggle will be applicable and to our advantage in certain future conditions. Unless we learn to apply all the methods of struggle, we may suffer grave and sometimes even decisive defeat, if changes beyond our control in the position of the other classes bring to the forefront a form of activity in which we are especially weak. If, however, we learn to use all the methods of struggle, victory will be certain, because we represent the interests of the really foremost and really revolutionary class, even if circumstances do not permit us to make use of weapons that are most dangerous to the enemy, weapons that deal the swiftest mortal blows. Inexperienced revolutionaries often think that legal methods of struggle are opportunist because, in this field, the bourgeoisie has most frequently deceived and duped the workers (particularly in "peaceful" and non-revolutionary times), while illegal methods of struggle are revolutionary. That, however, is wrong. The truth is that those parties and leaders are opportunists and traitors to the working class that are unable or unwilling (do not say, "I can't"; say, "I shan't") to use illegal methods of struggle in conditions such as those which prevailed, for example, during the imperialist war of 1914-18, when the bourgeoisie of the freest democratic countries most brazenly and brutally deceived the workers, and smothered the truth about the predatory character of the war. But revolutionaries who are incapable of combining illegal forms of struggle with *every* form of legal struggle are poor revolutionaries indeed. It is not difficult to be a revolutionary when revolution has already broken out and is in spate, when all people are joining the revolution just because they are carried away, because it is the vogue, and sometimes even from careerist motives. After its victory, the proletariat has to make most strenuous efforts, even the most painful, so as to "liberate" itself from such pseudo-revolutionaries. It is far more difficult—and far more precious—to be a revolutionary when the conditions for direct, open, really mass and really revolutionary struggle *do not yet exist*, to be able to champion the interests of the revolution (by propaganda, agitation and organisation) in non-revolutionary bodies, and quite often in downright reactionary bodies, in a non-revolutionary situation, among the masses who are incapable of immediately appreciating the need for revolutionary methods of action. To be able to seek, find and correctly determine the specific path or the particular turn of events that will *lead* the masses to the real, decisive and final revolutionary struggle—such is the main objective of communism in Western Europe and in America today.

Britain is an example. We cannot tell—no one can tell in advance —how soon a real proletarian revolution will flare up there, and *what immediate cause* will most serve to rouse, kindle, and impel into the struggle the very wide masses, who are still dormant. Hence, it is our duty to carry on all our preparatory work in such a way as to be "well shod on all four feet" (as the late Plekhanov, when he was a Marxist and revolutionary, was fond of saying). It is possible that the breach will be forced, the ice broken, by a parliamentary crisis, or by a crisis arising from colonial and imperialist contradictions, which are hopelessly entangled and are becoming increasingly painful and acute, or perhaps by some third cause, etc. We are not discussing the kind of struggle that will *determine* the fate of the proletarian revolution in Great Britain (no Communist has any doubt on that score; for all of us this is a foregone conclusion): what we are discussing is the *immediate cause* that will bring into motion the now dormant proletarian masses, and lead them right up to revolution. Let us not forget that in the French bourgeois republic, for example, in a situation which, from both the international and the national viewpoints, was a hundred times less revolutionary than it is today, such an "unexpected" and "petty" cause as one of the many thousands of fraudulent machinations of the reactionary military caste (the Dreyfus case) was enough to bring the people to the brink of civil war!

In Great Britain the Communists should constantly, unremittingly and unswervingly utilise parliamentary elections and all the vicissitudes of the Irish, colonial and world-imperialist policy of the British Government, and all other fields, spheres and aspects of public life, and work in all of them in a new way, in a communist way, in the spirit of the Third, not the Second, International. I have neither the time nor the space here to describe the "Russian" "Bolshevik" methods of participation in parliamentary elections and in the parliamentary struggle; I can, however, assure foreign Communists that they were quite unlike the usual West-European parliamentary campaigns. From this the conclusion is often drawn: "Well, that was in Russia; in our country parliamentarianism is different." This is a false conclusion. Communists, adherents of the Third International in all countries, exist for the purpose of *changing*—all along the line, in all spheres of life—the old socialist, trade unionist, syndicalist, and parliamentary type of work into a *new* type of work, the communist. In Russia, too, there was always an abundance of opportunism, purely bourgeois sharp practices and capitalist rigging in the elections. In Western Europe and in America, the Communists must learn to create a new, uncustomary, non-opportunist, and non-careerist parliamentarianism; the Communist parties must issue their slogans; true proletarians, with the help of the unorganised and downtrodden poor, should distribute leaflets, canvass workers' houses and cottages of the rural proletarians and peasants in the remote villages (fortunately there are many times fewer remote villages in Europe than in Russia, and in Britain the number is very small); they should go into the public houses, penetrate into unions, societies and chance gatherings of the common people, and speak to the people, not in learned (or very parliamentary) language; they should not at all strive to "get seats" in parliament, but should everywhere try to get people to think, and draw the masses into the struggle, to take the bourgeoisie at its word and utilise the machinery it has set up, the elections it has appointed, and the appeals it has made to the people; they should try to explain to the people what Bolshevism is, in a way that was never possible (under bourgeois rule) outside of election times (exclusive, of course, of times of big strikes, when in Russia a *similar* apparatus for widespread popular agitation worked even more intensively). It is very difficult to do this in Western Europe and extremely difficult in America, but it can and must be done, for the objectives of communism cannot be achieved without effort. We must work to accomplish *practical* tasks, ever more varied and ever more closely connected with all branches of social life, *winning* branch after branch, and sphere after sphere *from the bourgeoisie*.

In Great Britain, further, the work of propaganda, agitation and organisation among the armed forces and among the oppressed and underprivileged nationalities in their *"own"* state (Ireland, the colonies) must also be tackled in a new fashion (one that is not socialist, but communist; not reformist, but revolutionary). That is because, in the era of imperialism in general and especially today after a war that was a sore trial to the peoples and has quickly opened their eyes to the truth (i.e., the fact that tens of millions were killed and maimed for the sole purpose of deciding whether the British or the German robbers should plunder the largest number of countries), all these spheres of social life are heavily charged with inflammable material and are creating numerous causes of conflicts, crises and an intensification of the class struggle. We do not and cannot know which spark—of the innumerable sparks that are flying about in all countries as a result of the world economic and political crisis—will kindle the conflagration, in the sense of raising up the masses; we must, therefore, with our new and communist principles, set to work to stir up all and sundry, even the oldest, mustiest and seemingly hopeless spheres, for otherwise we shall not be able to cope with our tasks, shall not be comprehensively prepared, shall not be in possession of all the weapons and shall not prepare ourselves either to gain victory over the bourgeoisie (which arranged all aspects of social life—and has now disarranged them— in its bourgeois fashion), or to bring about the impending communist reorganisation of every sphere of life, following that victory.

Since the proletarian revolution in Russia and its victories on an international scale, expected neither by the bourgeoisie nor the philistines, the entire world has become different, and the bourgeoisie everywhere has become different too. It is terrified of "Bolshevism", exasperated by it almost to the point of frenzy, and for that very reason it is, on the one hand, precipitating the progress of events and, on the other, concentrating on the forcible suppression of Bolshevism, thereby weakening its own position in a number of other fields. In their tactics the Communists in all the advanced countries must take both these circumstances into account.

When the Russian Cadets and Kerensky began furiously to hound the Bolsheviks—especially since April 1917, and more particularly in June and July 1917—they overdid things. Millions of copies of bourgeois papers, clamouring in every key against the Bolsheviks, helped the masses to make an appraisal of Bolshevism; apart from the newspapers, all public life was full of discussions about Bolshevism, as a result of the bourgeoisie's "zeal". Today the millionaires of all countries are behaving on an international scale in a way that deserves our heartiest thanks. They are hounding Bolshevism with the same zeal as Kerensky and Co. did; they, too, are overdoing things and *helping* us just as Kerensky did. When the French bourgeoisie makes Bolshevism the central issue in the elections, and accuses the comparatively moderate or vacillating socialists of being Bolsheviks; when the American bourgeoisie, which has completely lost its head, seizes thousands and thousands of people on suspicion of Bolshevism, creates an atmosphere of panic, and broadcasts stories of Bolshevik plots; when, despite all its wisdom and experience, the British bourgeoisie—the most "solid" in the world —makes incredible blunders, founds richly endowed "anti-Bolshevik societies", creates a special literature on Bolshevism, and recruits an extra number of scientists, agitators and clergymen to combat it, we must salute and thank the capitalists. They are working for us. They are helping us to get the masses interested in the essence and significance of Bolshevism, and they cannot do otherwise, for they have *already* failed to ignore Bolshevism and stifle it.

But at the same time, the bourgeoisie sees practically only one aspect of Bolshevism—insurrection, violence, and terror; it therefore strives to prepare itself for resistance and opposition primarily in *this* field. It is possible that, in certain instances, in certain countries, and for certain brief periods, it will succeed in this. We must reckon with such an eventuality, and we have absolutely nothing to fear if it does succeed. Communism is emerging in positively every sphere of public life; its beginnings are to be seen literally on all sides. The "contagion" (to use the favourite metaphor of the bourgeoisie and the bourgeois police, the one mostly to their liking) has very thoroughly penetrated the organism and has completely permeated it. If special efforts are made to block one of the channels, the "contagion" will find another one, sometimes very unexpectedly. Life will assert itself. Let the bourgeoisie rave, work itself into a frenzy, go to extremes, commit follies, take vengeance on the Bolsheviks in advance, and endeavour to kill off (as in India, Hungary, Germany, etc.) more hundreds, thousands, and hundreds of thousands of yesterday's and tomorrow's Bolsheviks. In acting thus, the bourgeoisie is acting as all historically doomed classes have done. Communists should know that, in any case, the future belongs to them; therefore, we can (and must) combine the most intense passion in the great revolutionary struggle, with the coolest and most sober appraisal of the frenzied ravings of the bourgeoisie. The Russian revolution was cruelly defeated in 1905; the Russian Bolsheviks were defeated in July 1917[279]; over 15,000 German Communists were killed as a result of the wily provocation and cunning manoeuvres of Scheidemann and Noske, who were working hand in glove with the bourgeoisie and the monarchist generals; White terror is raging in Finland and Hungary. But in all cases and in all countries, communism is becoming steeled and is growing; its roots are so deep that persecution does not weaken or debilitate it, but only strengthens it. Only one thing is lacking to enable us to march forward more confidently and firmly to victory, namely, the universal and thorough awareness of all Communists in all countries, of the necessity to display the utmost *flexibility* in their tactics. The communist movement, which is developing magnificently, now lacks, especially in the advanced countries, this awareness and the ability to apply it in practice.

That which happened to such leaders of the Second International, such highly erudite Marxists devoted to socialism as Kautsky, Otto Bauer and others, could (and should) provide a useful lesson. They fully appreciated the need for flexible tactics; they themselves learned Marxist dialectic and taught it to others (and much of what they have done in this field will always remain a valuable contribution to socialist literature); however, *in the application* of this dialectic they committed such an error, or proved to be so *un*dialectical in practice, so incapable of taking into account the rapid change of forms and the rapid acquisition of new content by the old forms, that their fate is not much more enviable than that of Hyndman, Guesde and Plekhanov. The principal reason for their bankruptcy was that they were hypnotised by a definite form of growth of the working-class movement and socialism, forgot all about the one-sidedness of that form, were afraid to see the breakup which objective conditions made inevitable, and continued to repeat simple and, at first glance, incontestable axioms that had been learned by rote, like: "three is more than two". But politics is more like algebra than arithmetic, and still more like higher than elementary mathematics. In reality, all the old forms of the socialist movement have acquired a new content, and, consequently, a new symbol, the "minus" sign, has appeared in front of all the figures; our wiseacres, however, have stubbornly continued (and still continue) to persuade themselves and others that "minus three" is more than "minus two".

We must see to it that Communists do not make a similar mistake, only in the opposite sense, or rather, we must see to it that a *similar mistake*, only made in the opposite sense by the "Left" Communists, is corrected as soon as possible and eliminated as rapidly and painlessly as possible. It is not only Right doctrinairism that is erroneous; Left doctrinairism is erroneous too. Of course, the mistake of Left doctrinairism in communism is at present a thousand times less dangerous and less significant than that of Right doctrinairism (i.e., social-chauvinism and Kautskyism); but, after all, that is only due to the fact that Left communism is a very young trend, is only just coming into being. It is only for this reason that, under certain conditions, the disease can be easily eradicated, and we must set to work with the utmost energy to eradicate it.

The old forms burst asunder, for it turned out that their new content—anti-proletarian and reactionary—had attained an inordinate development. From the standpoint of the development of international communism, our work today has such a durable and powerful content (for Soviet power and the dictatorship of the proletariat) that it can *and must* manifest itself in any form, both new and old; it can and must regenerate, conquer and subjugate all forms, not only the new, but also the old—not for the purpose of reconciling itself with the old, but for the purpose of making all and every form—new and old—a weapon for the complete and irrevocable victory of communism.

The Communists must exert every effort to direct the working-class movement and social development in general along the straightest and shortest road to the victory of Soviet power and the dictatorship of the proletariat on a world-wide scale. That is an incontestable truth. But it is enough to take one little step farther—a step that might seem to be in the same direction—and truth turns into error. We have only to say, as the German and British Left Communists do, that we recognise only one road, only the direct road, and that we will not permit tacking, conciliatory manoeuvres, or compromising—and it will be a mistake which may cause, and in part has already caused and is causing, very grave prejudice to communism. Right doctrinairism persisted in recognising only the old forms, and became utterly bankrupt, for it did not notice the new content. Left doctrinairism persists in the unconditional repudiation of certain old forms, failing to see that the new content is forcing its way through all and sundry forms, that it is our duty as Communists to master all forms, to learn how, with the maximum rapidity, to supplement one form with another, to substitute one for another, and to adapt our tactics to any such change that does not come from our class or from our efforts.

World revolution has been so powerfully stimulated and accelerated by the horrors, vileness and abominations of the world imperialist war and by the hopelessness of the situation created by it, this revolution is developing in scope and depth with such splendid rapidity, with such a wonderful variety of changing forms, with such an instructive practical refutation of all doctrinairism, that there is every reason to hope for a rapid and complete recovery of the international communist movement from the infantile disorder of "Left-wing" communism.

April 27, 1920

APPENDIX

Before publishing houses in our country—which has been plundered by the imperialists of the whole world in revenge for the proletarian revolution, and which is still being plundered and blockaded by them regardless of all promises they made to their workers—were able to bring out my pamphlet, additional material arrived from abroad. Without claiming to present in my pamphlet anything more than the cursory notes of a publicist, I shall dwell briefly upon a few points.

I

THE SPLIT AMONG THE GERMAN COMMUNISTS

The split among the Communists in Germany is an accomplished fact. The "Lefts", or the "opposition on principle", have formed a separate Communist Workers' Party,[280] as distinct from the Communist Party. A split also seems imminent in Italy—I say "seems", as I have only two additional issues (Nos. 7 and 8) of the Left newspaper, *Il Soviet*, in which the possibility of and necessity for a split is openly discussed, and mention is also made of a congress of the "Abstentionist" group (or the boycottists, i.e., opponents of participation in parliament), which group is still part of the Italian Socialist Party.

There is reason to fear that the split with the "Lefts", the antiparliamentarians (in part anti-politicals too, who are opposed to any political party and to work in the trade unions), will become an international phenomenon, like the split with the "Centrists" (i.e., Kautskyites, Longuetists, Independents, etc.). Let that be so. At all events, a split is better than confusion, which hampers the ideological, theoretical and revolutionary growth and maturing of the party, and its harmonious, really organised practical work which actually paves the way for the dictatorship of the proletariat.

Let the "Lefts" put themselves to a practical test on a national and international scale. Let them try to prepare for (and then implement) the dictatorship of the proletariat, without a rigorously centralised party with iron discipline, without the ability to become masters of every sphere, every branch, and every variety of political and cultural work. Practical experience will soon teach them.

Only, every effort should be made to prevent the split with the "Lefts" from impeding—or to see that it impedes as little as possible—the necessary amalgamation into a single party, inevitable in the near future, of all participants in the working-class movement who sincerely and conscientiously stand for Soviet government and the dictatorship of the proletariat. It was the exceptional good fortune of the Bolsheviks in Russia to have had fifteen years for a systematic and consummated struggle both against the Mensheviks (i.e., the opportunists and "Centrists") and against the "Lefts", long before the masses began direct action for the dictatorship of the proletariat. In Europe and America the same work has now to be done by forced marches, so to say. Certain individuals, especially among unsuccessful aspirants to leadership, may (if they lack proletarian discipline and are not honest towards themselves) persist in their mistakes for a long time; however, when the time is ripe, the masses of the workers will themselves unite easily and rapidly and unite all sincere Communists to form a single party capable of establishing the Soviet system and the dictatorship of the proletariat.*

II
THE COMMUNISTS AND THE INDEPENDENTS IN GERMANY

In this pamphlet I have expressed the opinion that a compromise between the Communists and the Left wing of the Independents is necessary and useful to communism, but will not be easy to bring

---

* With regard to the question of future amalgamation of the "Left" Communists, the anti-parliamentarians, with the Communists in general, I would make the following additional remarks. In the measure in which I have been able to familiarise myself with the newspapers of the "Left" Communists and the Communists in general in Germany, I find that the former have the advantage of being better able than the latter to carry on agitation among the masses. I have repeatedly observed something similar to this in the history of the Bolshevik Party, though on a smaller scale, in individual local organisations, and not on a national scale. For instance, in 1907-08 the "Left" Bolsheviks, on certain occasions and in certain places, carried on more successful agitation among the masses than we did. This may partly have been due to the fact that at a revolutionary moment, or at a time when revolutionary recollections are still fresh, it is easier to approach the masses with tactics of sheer negation. This, however, is not an argument to prove the correctness of such tactics. At all events, there is not the least doubt that a Communist *party* that wishes to be the real vanguard, the advanced detachment, of the revolutionary *class*, of the proletariat—and which, in addition wishes to learn to lead the *masses*, not only the proletarian, but also the *non*-proletarian masses of working and exploited people—must know how to conduct propaganda, how to organise, and how to carry on agitation in a manner most simple and comprehensible, most clear and vivid, both to the urban, factory masses and to the rural masses.

about. Newspapers which I have subsequently received have confirmed this opinion on both points. No. 32 of *The Red Flag*, organ of the Central Committee, the Communist Party of Germany (*Die Rote Fahne*,[281] Zentralorgan der Kommunistischen Partei Deutschlands, Spartakusbund,* of March 26, 1920) published a "statement" by this Central Committee regarding the Kapp-Lüttwitz military *putsch* and on the "socialist government". This statement is quite correct both in its basic premise and its practical conclusions. The basic premise is that at present there is no "objective basis" for the dictatorship of the proletariat because the "majority of the urban workers" support the Independents. The conclusion is: a promise to be a "loyal opposition" (i.e., renunciation of preparations for a "forcible overthrow") to a "socialist government if it excludes bourgeois-capitalist parties".

In the main, this tactic is undoubtedly correct. Yet, even if minor inaccuracies of formulation should not be dwelt on, it is impossible to pass over in silence the fact that a government consisting of social-traitors should not (in an official statement by the Communist Party) be called "socialist"; that one should not speak of the exclusion of "bourgeois-capitalist parties", when the parties both of the Scheidemanns and of the Kautskys and Crispiens are petty-bourgeois-democratic parties; that things should never be written that are contained in § 4 of the statement, which reads:

"... A state of affairs in which political freedom can be enjoyed without restriction, and bourgeois democracy cannot operate as the dictatorship of capital is, from the viewpoint of the development of the proletarian dictatorship, of the utmost importance in further winning the proletarian masses over to the side of communism...."

Such a state of affairs is impossible. Petty-bourgeois leaders, the German Hendersons (Scheidemanns) and Snowdens (Crispiens), do not and cannot go beyond the bounds of bourgeois democracy, which, in its turn, cannot but be a dictatorship of capital. To achieve the practical results that the Central Committee of the Communist Party had been quite rightly working for, there was no need to write such things, which are wrong in principle and politically harmful. It would have been sufficient to say (if one wished to observe parliamentary amenities): "As long as the majority of the urban workers follow the Independents, we Communists must do nothing to prevent those workers from getting rid of their last philistine-democratic (i.e., 'bourgeois-capitalist') illusions by going through the experience of having a government of their 'own'." That is sufficient ground for a compromise, which is really necessary and should consist in renouncing, for a certain period, all attempts at the forcible overthrow of a government which enjoys the confidence of a majority of the

* The Spartacus League.—*Ed.*

urban workers. But in everyday mass agitation, in which one is not bound by official parliamentary amenities, one might, of course, add: "Let scoundrels like the Scheidemanns, and philistines like the Kautskys and Crispiens reveal by their deeds how they have been fooled themselves and how they are fooling the workers; their 'clean' government will itself do the 'cleanest' job of all in 'cleansing' the Augean stables of socialism, Social-Democracy and other forms of social treachery."

The real nature of the present leaders of the Independent Social-Democratic Party of Germany (leaders of whom it has been wrongly said that they have already lost all influence, whereas in reality they are even more dangerous to the proletariat than the Hungarian Social-Democrats who styled themselves Communists and promised to "support" the dictatorship of the proletariat) was once again revealed during the German equivalent of the Kornilov revolt, i.e., the Kapp-Lüttwitz *putsch.** A small but striking illustration is provided by two brief articles—one by Karl Kautsky entitled "Decisive Hours" ("Entscheidende Stunden") in *Freiheit (Freedom)*,[283] organ of the Independents, of March 30, 1920, and the other by Arthur Crispien entitled "On the Political Situation" (in the same newspaper, issue of April 14, 1920). These gentlemen are absolutely incapable of thinking and reasoning like revolutionaries. They are snivelling philistine democrats, who become a thousand times more dangerous to the proletariat when they claim to be supporters of Soviet government and of the dictatorship of the proletariat because, in fact, whenever a difficult and dangerous situation arises they are sure to commit treachery ... while "sincerely" believing that they are helping the proletariat! Did not the Hungarian Social-Democrats, after rechristening themselves Communists, also want to "help" the proletariat when, because of their cowardice and spinelessness, they considered the position of Soviet power in Hungary hopeless and went snivelling to the agents of the Entente capitalists and the Entente hangmen?

III

TURATI AND CO. IN ITALY

The issues of the Italian newspaper *Il Soviet* referred to above fully confirm what I have said in the pamphlet about the Italian Socialist Party's error in tolerating such members and even such a

---

* Incidentally, this has been dealt with in an exceptionally clear, concise, precise and Marxist way in the excellent organ of the Austrian Communist Party, *The Red Banner*, of March 28 and 30, 1920. (*Die Rote Fahne*,[282] Wien, 1920, Nos. 266 and 267; L.L.: *"Ein neuer Abschnitt der deutschen Revolution"* ["A New Stage of the German Revolution."—*Ed.*]).

group of parliamentarians in their ranks. It is still further confirmed by an outside observer like the Rome correspondent of *The Manchester Guardian*, organ of the British liberal bourgeoisie, whose interview with Turati is published in its issue of March 12, 1920. The correspondent writes:

"... Signor Turati's opinion is that the revolutionary peril is not such as to cause undue anxiety in Italy. The Maximalists are fanning the fire of Soviet theories only to keep the masses awake and excited. These theories are, however, merely legendary notions, unripe programmes, incapable of being put to practical use. They are likely only to maintain the working classes in a state of expectation. The very men who use them as a lure to dazzle proletarian eyes find themselves compelled to fight a daily battle for the extortion of some often trifling economic advantages so as to delay the moment when the working classes will lose their illusions and faith in their cherished myths. Hence a long string of strikes of all sizes and with all pretexts up to the very latest ones in the mail and railway services—strikes which make the already hard conditions of the country still worse. The country is irritated owing to the difficulties connected with its Adriatic problem, is weighed down by its foreign debt and by its inflated paper circulation, and yet it is still far from realising the necessity of adopting that discipline of work which alone can restore order and prosperity...."

It is clear as daylight that this British correspondent has blurted out the truth, which is probably being concealed and glossed over both by Turati himself, and his bourgeois defenders, accomplices and inspirers in Italy. That truth is that the ideas and political activities of Turati, Trèves, Modigliani, Dugoni and Co. are really and precisely of the kind that the British correspondent has described. It is downright social treachery. Just look at this advocacy of order and discipline among the workers, who are wage slaves toiling to enrich the capitalists! And how familiar to us Russians are all these Menshevik speeches! What a valuable admission it is that the masses are *in favour of* Soviet government! How stupid and vulgarly bourgeois is the failure to understand the revolutionary role of strikes which are spreading spontaneously! Indeed, the correspondent of the British bourgeois-liberal newspaper has rendered Turati and Co. a disservice and has excellently confirmed the correctness of the demand by Comrade Bordiga and his friends on *Il Soviet*, who are insisting that the Italian Socialist Party, if it really wants to be *for* the Third International, should drum Turati and Co. out of its ranks and become a Communist Party both in name and in deed.

IV

FALSE CONCLUSIONS FROM CORRECT PREMISES

However, Comrade Bordiga and his "Left" friends draw from their correct criticism of Turati and Co. the wrong conclusion that any participation in parliament is harmful in principle. The Italian

"Lefts" cannot advance even a shadow of serious argument in support of this view. They simply do not know (or try to forget) the international examples of really revolutionary and communist utilisation of bourgeois parliaments, which has been of unquestionable value in preparing for the proletarian revolution. They simply cannot conceive of any "new" ways of that utilisation, and keep on repeatedly and endlessly vociferating about the "old" non-Bolshevik way.

Herein lies their fundamental error. In *all* fields of activity, and not in the parliamentary sphere alone, communism *must introduce* (and without long and persistent effort it will be *unable* to introduce) something new in principle that will represent a radical break with the traditions of the Second International (while retaining and developing what was good in the latter).

Let us take, say, journalistic work. Newspapers, pamphlets and leaflets perform the indispensable work of propaganda, agitation and organisation. No mass movement in any country at all civilised can get along without a journalistic apparatus. No outcries against "leaders" or solemn vows to keep the masses uncontaminated by the influence of leaders will relieve us of the necessity of using, for this work, people from a bourgeois-intellectual environment or will rid us of the bourgeois-democratic, "private property" atmosphere and environment in which this work is carried out under capitalism. Even two and a half years after the overthrow of the bourgeoisie, after the conquest of political power by the proletariat, we still have this atmosphere around us, this environment of mass (peasant, artisan) bourgeois-democratic private property relations.

Parliamentarianism is one form of activity; journalism is another. The content of both can and should be communist if those engaged in these two spheres are genuine Communists, really members of a proletarian mass party. Yet, in neither sphere—and *in no other sphere of activity* under capitalism and during the period of transition from capitalism to socialism—is it possible to avoid those difficulties which the proletariat must overcome, those special problems which the proletariat must solve so as to use, for its own purposes, the services of people from the ranks of the bourgeoisie, eradicate bourgeois-intellectualist prejudices and influences, and weaken the resistance of (and, ultimately, completely transform) the petty-bourgeois environment.

Did we not, before the war of 1914-18, witness in all countries innumerable cases of extreme "Left" anarchists, syndicalists and others fulminating against parliamentarianism, deriding bourgeois-vulgarised parliamentary socialists, castigating their careerism, and so on and so forth, and yet themselves pursuing the *same kind* of bourgeois career *through* journalism and *through* work in the syndicates (trade unions)? Is not the example of Jouhaux and Merrheim, to limit oneself to France, typical in this respect?

The childishness of those who "repudiate" participation in parliament consists in their thinking it possible to "*solve*" the difficult problem of combating bourgeois-democratic influences *within* the working-class movement in such a "simple", "easy", allegedly revolutionary manner, whereas they are actually merely running away from their own shadows, only closing their eyes to difficulties and trying to shrug them off with mere words. The most shameless careerism, the bourgeois utilisation of parliamentary seats, glaringly reformist perversion of parliamentary activity, and vulgar petty-bourgeois conservatism are all unquestionably common and prevalent features engendered everywhere by capitalism, not only outside but also within the working-class movement. But the selfsame capitalism and the bourgeois environment it creates (which disappears very slowly even after the overthrow of the bourgeoisie, since the peasantry constantly regenerates the bourgeoisie) give rise to what is essentially the same bourgeois careerism, national chauvinism, petty-bourgeois vulgarity, etc.—merely varying insignificantly in form—in positively every sphere of activity and life.

You think, my dear boycottists and anti-parliamentarians that you are "terribly revolutionary", but in reality *you are frightened* by the comparatively minor difficulties of the struggle against bourgeois influences within the working-class movement, whereas your victory—i.e., the overthrow of the bourgeoisie and the conquest of political power by the proletariat—will create *these very same* difficulties on a still larger, an infinitely larger scale. Like children, you are frightened by a minor difficulty which confronts you today, but you do not understand that tomorrow, and the day after, you will still have to learn, and learn thoroughly, to overcome the selfsame difficulties, only on an immeasurably greater scale.

Under Soviet rule, your proletarian party and ours will be invaded by a still larger number of bourgeois intellectuals. They will worm their way into the Soviets, the courts, and the administration, since communism cannot be built otherwise than with the aid of the human material created by capitalism, and the bourgeois intellectuals cannot be expelled and destroyed, but must be won over, remoulded, assimilated and re-educated, just as we must—in a protracted struggle waged on the basis of the dictatorship of the proletariat—re-educate the proletarians themselves, who do not abandon their petty-bourgeois prejudices at one stroke, by a miracle, at the behest of the Virgin Mary, at the behest of a slogan, resolution or decree, but only in the course of a long and difficult mass struggle against mass petty-bourgeois influences. Under Soviet rule, these same problems, which the anti-parliamentarians now so proudly, so haughtily, so lightly and so childishly brush aside with a wave of the hand—*these selfsame* problems are arising anew *within* the Soviets, within the Soviet administration, among the Soviet "pleaders" (in Russia we have abolished, and have rightly abolished, the bourgeois legal bar, but it is reviving again under the cover of the "Soviet pleaders"[284]). Among Soviet engineers, Soviet school-teachers and the privileged, i.e., the most highly skilled and best situated, *workers* at Soviet factories, we observe a constant revival of absolutely *all* the negative traits peculiar to bourgeois parliamentarianism, and we are conquering this evil—gradually—only by a tireless, prolonged and persistent struggle based on proletarian organisation and discipline.

Of course, under the rule of the bourgeoisie it is very "difficult" to eradicate bourgeois habits from our own, i.e., the workers', party; it is "difficult" to expel from the party the familiar parliamentary leaders who have been hopelessly corrupted by bourgeois prejudices; it is "difficult" to subject to proletarian discipline the absolutely essential (even if very limited) number of people coming from the ranks of the bourgeoisie; it is "difficult" to form, in a bourgeois parliament, a communist group fully worthy of the working class; it is "difficult" to ensure that the communist parliamentarians do not engage in bourgeois parliamentary inanities, but concern themselves with the very urgent work of propaganda, agitation and organisation among the masses. All this is "difficult", to be sure; it was difficult in Russia, and it is vastly more difficult in Western Europe and in America, where the bourgeoisie is far stronger, where bourgeois-democratic traditions are stronger, and so on.

Yet all these "difficulties" are mere child's play compared with the *same sort* of problems which, in any event, the proletariat will have most certainly to solve in order to achieve victory, both during the proletarian revolution and after the seizure of power by the proletariat. Compared with *these* truly gigantic problems of re-educating, under the proletarian dictatorship, millions of peasants and small proprietors, hundreds of thousands of office employees, officials and bourgeois intellectuals, of subordinating them all to the proletarian state and to proletarian leadership, of eradicating their bourgeois habits and traditions—compared with these gigantic problems it is childishly easy to create, under the rule of the bourgeoisie, and in a bourgeois parliament, a really communist group of a real proletarian party.

If our "Left" and anti-parliamentarian comrades do not learn to overcome even such a small difficulty now, we may safely assert that either they will prove incapable of achieving the dictatorship of the proletariat, and will be unable to subordinate and remould the bourgeois intellectuals and bourgeois institutions on a wide scale, or they will have to *hastily complete their education*, and, by that haste, will do a great deal of harm to the cause of the proletariat, will commit more errors than usual, will manifest more than average weakness and inefficiency, and so on and so forth.

Until the bourgeoisie has been overthrown and, after that, until small-scale economy and small commodity production have entirely disappeared, the bourgeois atmosphere, proprietary habits and petty-bourgeois traditions will hamper proletarian work both outside and within the working-class movement, not only in a single field of activity—the parliamentary—but, inevitably, in every field of social activity, in all cultural and political spheres without exception. The attempt to brush aside, to fence oneself off from *one* of the "unpleasant" problems or difficulties in some one sphere of activity is a profound mistake, which will later most certainly have to be paid for. We must learn how to master every sphere of work and activity without exception, to overcome all difficulties and eradicate all bourgeois habits, customs and traditions everywhere. Any other way of presenting the question is just trifling, mere childishness.

May 12, 1920

V

In the Russian edition of this book I somewhat incorrectly described the conduct of the Communist Party of Holland as a whole, in the sphere of international revolutionary policy. I therefore avail myself of the present opportunity to publish a letter from our Dutch comrades on this question and to correct the expression "Dutch Tribunists", which I used in the Russian text, and for which I now substitute the words "certain members of the Communist Party of Holland".[285]

N. Lenin

LETTER FROM WIJNKOOP

Moscow, June 30, 1920

Dear Comrade Lenin,

Thanks to your kindness, we members of the Dutch delegation to the Second Congress of the Communist International were able to read your *"Left-Wing" Communism—an Infantile Disorder* prior to its publication in the European languages. In several places in the book you emphasise your disapproval of the part played by some members of the Communist Party of Holland in international politics.

We feel, nevertheless, that we must protest against your laying the responsibility for their actions on the Communist Party. This is highly inaccurate. Moreover, it is unjust, because these members of the Communist Party of

Holland take little or no part in the Party's current activities and are endeavouring, directly or indirectly, to give effect, in the Communist Party of Holland, to opposition slogans against which the Party and all its organs have waged, and continue to wage to this day, a most energetic struggle.

Fraternally yours,
D. J. Wijnkoop
(On behalf of the Dutch delegation)

Written   April-May, 1920
Published June 1920
in pamphlet form
by the
State Publishing House,
Petrograd

Collected Works, Vol. 31

PRELIMINARY DRAFT THESES ON THE AGRARIAN QUESTION[286]

(FOR THE SECOND CONGRESS OF THE COMMUNIST INTERNATIONAL)

In his article,[287] Comrade Marchlewski gave an excellent explanation of the reasons why the Second International, which has now become the yellow International, failed, not only to define the revolutionary proletariat's tactics on the agrarian question, but even to pose that question properly. Comrade Marchlewski then went on to set forth the theoretical fundamentals of the Third International's communist agrarian programme.

These fundamentals can (and, I think, should) serve as the basis of the general resolution on the agrarian question for the Communist International Congress, which will meet on July 15, 1920.

The following is a preliminary draft of that resolution:

1) Only the urban and industrial proletariat, led by the Communist Party, can liberate the working masses of the countryside from the yoke of capital and landed proprietorship, from ruin and the imperialist wars which will inevitably break out again and again if the capitalist system remains. There is no salvation for the working masses of the countryside except in alliance with the communist proletariat, and unless they give the latter devoted support in its revolutionary struggle to throw off the yoke of the landowners (the big landed proprietors) and the bourgeoisie.

On the other hand, the industrial workers cannot accomplish their epoch-making mission of emancipating mankind from the yoke of capital and from wars if they confine themselves to their narrow craft, or trade interests, and smugly restrict themselves to attaining an improvement in their own conditions, which may sometimes be tolerable in the petty-bourgeois sense. This is exactly what happens to the "labour aristocracy" of many advanced countries, who constitute the core of the so-called socialist parties of the Second International; they are actually the bitter enemies and betrayers of socialism, petty-bourgeois chauvinists and agents of the bourgeoisie within the working-class movement. The proletariat is a really revolutionary class and acts in a really socialist manner only when it comes out and acts as the vanguard of all the working and exploited people, as their leader in the struggle for the overthrow of the exploiters; this, however, cannot be achieved unless the class struggle is carried into the countryside, unless the rural working masses are united about the Communist Party of the urban proletariat, and unless they are trained by the proletariat.

2) The working and exploited people of the countryside, whom the urban proletariat must lead into the struggle or, at all events, win over, are represented in all capitalist countries by the following classes:

first, the agricultural proletariat, wage-labourers (by the year, season, or day), who obtain their livelihood by working for hire at capitalist agricultural enterprises. The organisation of this class (political, military, trade union, co-operative, cultural, educational, etc.) independently and separately from other groups of the rural population, the conduct of intensive propaganda and agitation among this class, and the winning of its support for the Soviets and the dictatorship of the proletariat constitute the *fundamental* tasks of the Communist parties in all countries;

second, the semi-proletarians or peasants who till tiny plots of land, i.e., those who obtain their livelihood partly as wage-labourers at agricultural and industrial capitalist enterprises and partly by working their own or rented plots of land, which provide their families only with part of their means of subsistence. This group of the rural working population is very numerous in all capitalist countries; its existence and special position are played down by the representatives of the bourgeoisie and by the yellow "socialists" belonging to the Second International, partly by deliberately deceiving the workers and partly by blindly submitting to the routine of petty-bourgeois views and lumping together this group with the mass of the "peasantry". This bourgeois method of duping the workers is to be seen mostly in Germany and in France, but also in America and other countries. If the work of the Communist Party is properly organised, this group will become its assured supporter, for the lot of these semi-proletarians is a very hard one and they stand to gain enormously and immediately from Soviet government and the dictatorship of the proletariat;

third, the small peasantry, i.e., the small-scale tillers who, either as owners or as tenants, hold small plots of land which enable them to satisfy the needs of their families and their farms, and do not hire outside labour. This stratum, as such, undoubtedly stands to gain by the victory of the proletariat, which will fully and immediately bring it: (a) deliverance from the necessity of paying the big landowners rent or a share of the crop (for example, the *métayers* in France, also in Italy and other countries); (b) deliverance from mortgages; (c) deliverance from the numerous forms of oppression by and dependence on the big landowners (forest lands and their use, etc.):

(d) immediate aid for their farms from the proletarian state (the use of the agricultural implements and part of the buildings on the big capitalist farms confiscated by the proletariat and the immediate conversion, by the proletarian state, of the rural co-operative societies and agricultural associations from organisations which under capitalism served above all the rich and middle peasants, into organisations that will primarily assist the poor, i.e., proletarians, semi-proletarians, small peasants, etc.), and many other things.

At the same time the Communist Party must clearly realise that during the transitional period from capitalism to communism, i.e., during the dictatorship of the proletariat, this stratum, or at all events part of it, will inevitably vacillate towards unrestricted freedom of trade and the free enjoyment of the rights of private property. That is because this stratum, which, if only in a small way, is a seller of articles of consumption, has been corrupted by profiteering and by proprietary habits. However, if a firm proletarian policy is pursued, and if the victorious proletariat deals very resolutely with the big landowners and the big peasants, this stratum's vacillation cannot be considerable and cannot alter the fact that, on the whole, it will side with the proletarian revolution.

3) Taken together, the three groups enumerated above constitute the majority of the rural population in all capitalist countries. That is why the success of the proletarian revolution is fully assured, not only in the cities but in the countryside as well. The reverse view is widespread; however, it persists only, first, because of the deception systematically practised by bourgeois science and statistics, which do everything to gloss over both the gulf that separates the above-mentioned classes in the contryside from the exploiters, the landowners and capitalists, and that which separates the semi-proletarians and small peasants from the big peasants; second, it persists because of the inability and unwillingness of the heroes of the yellow Second International and of the "labour aristocracy" in the advanced countries, which has been corrupted by imperialist privileges, to conduct genuinely proletarian revolutionary work of propaganda, agitation and organisation among the rural poor; the attention of the opportunists has always been and still is wholly concentrated on inventing theoretical and practical compromises with the bourgeoisie, including the big and middle peasants (who are dealt with below), and not on the revolutionary overthrow of the bourgeois government and the bourgeoisie by the proletariat; it persists, third, because of the obstinate refusal to understand—so obstinate as to be equivalent to a prejudice (connected with all the other bourgeois-democratic and parliamentary prejudices)—a truth which has been fully proved by Marxist theory and fully corroborated by the experience of the proletarian revolution in Russia, namely, that although the three enumerated categories of the rural population—who are incredibly

downtrodden, disunited, crushed, and doomed to semi-barbarous conditions of existence in all countries, even the most advanced—are economically, socially, and culturally interested in the victory of socialism, they are capable of giving resolute support to the revolutionary proletariat only *after* the latter has won political power, only *after* it has resolutely dealt with the big landowners and capitalists, and only *after* these downtrodden people see *in practice* that they have an organised leader and champion, strong and firm enough to assist and lead them and to show them the right path.

4) In the economic sense, one should understand by "middle peasants" those small farmers who, (1) either as owners or tenants, hold plots of land that are also small but, under capitalism, are sufficient not only to provide, as a general rule, a meagre subsistence for the family and the bare minimum needed to maintain the farm, but also produce a certain surplus which may, in good years at least, be converted into capital; (2) quite frequently (for example, one farm out of two or three) resort to the employment of hired labour. A concrete example of the middle peasants in an advanced capitalist country is provided by the group of farms of five to ten hectares in Germany, in which, according to the census of 1907, the number of farms employing hired labourers is about one-third of the total number of farms in this group.* In France, where the cultivation of special crops is more developed—for example, grape-growing, which requires a very large amount of labour—this group probably employs outside hired labour to a somewhat greater extent.

The revolutionary proletariat cannot set itself the task—at least not in the immediate future or in the initial period of the dictatorship of the proletariat—of winning over this stratum, but must confine itself to the task of neutralising it, i.e., rendering it neutral in the struggle between the proletariat and the bourgeoisie. This stratum inevitably vacillates between these two forces; in the beginning of the new epoch and in the developed capitalist countries, it will, in the main, incline towards the bourgeoisie. That is because the world outlook and the sentiments of the property-owners are prevalent among this stratum, which has a direct interest in profiteering, in "freedom" of trade and in property, and stands in direct antagonism to the wage-workers. By abolishing rent and mortgages, the victorious proletariat will immediately improve the

---

* Here are the exact figures: the number of farms of five to ten hectares—652,798 (out of a total of 5,736,082); these employed 487,704 hired labourers of various kinds, while members of the farmers' families (*Familienangehörige*) working on the farms numbered 2,003,633. In Austria, according to the census of 1902, this group comprised 383,331 farms, of which 126,136 employed hired labour; the hired labourers working on these farms numbered 146,044 and the working members of the farmers' families 1,265,969. The total number of farms in Austria was 2,856,349.

position of this stratum. In most capitalist countries, however, the proletarian state should not at once completely abolish private property; at all events, it guarantees both the small and the middle peasantry, not only the preservation of their plots of land but also their enlargement to cover the total area they usually rented (the abolition of rent).

A combination of such measures with a ruthless struggle against the bourgeoisie fully guarantees the success of the policy of neutralisation. The proletarian state must effect the transition to collective farming with extreme caution and only very gradually, by the force of example, without any coercion of the middle peasant.

5) The big peasants (*Grossbauern*) are capitalist *entrepreneurs* in agriculture, who as a rule employ several hired labourers and are connected with the "peasantry" only in their low cultural level, habits of life, and the manual labour they themselves perform on their farms. These constitute the biggest of the bourgeois strata who are open and determined enemies of the revolutionary proletariat. In all their work in the countryside, the Communist parties must concentrate their attention mainly on the struggle against this stratum, on liberating the toiling and exploited majority of the rural population from the ideological and political influence of these exploiters, etc.

Following the victory of the proletariat in the cities, all sorts of manifestations of resistance and sabotage, as well as direct armed action of a counter-revolutionary character on the part of this stratum, are absolutely inevitable. The revolutionary proletariat must therefore immediately begin the ideological and organisational preparation of the forces necessary to completely disarm this stratum and, simultaneously with the overthrow of the capitalists in industry, to deal this stratum a most determined, ruthless and smashing blow at the very first signs of resistance; for this purpose, the rural proletariat must be armed and village Soviets organised, in which the exploiters must have no place, and in which proletarians and semi-proletarians must be ensured predominance.

However, the expropriation even of the big peasants can in no way be made an immediate task of the victorious proletariat, because the material and especially the technical conditions, as well as the social conditions, for the socialisation of such farms are still lacking. In individual and probably exceptional cases, those parts of their land which they rent out in small plots or which are particularly needed by the surrounding small-peasant population will be confiscated; the small peasants should also be guaranteed, on certain terms, the free use of part of the agricultural machinery belonging to the big peasants, etc. As a general rule, however, the proletarian state must allow the big peasants to retain their land, confiscating it only if they resist the power of the working and exploited people. The experience of the Russian proletarian revolution, in which the struggle against the big peasantry was complicated and protracted by a number of special conditions, showed nevertheless that, when taught a severe lesson for the slightest attempt at resistance, this stratum is capable of loyally fulfilling the tasks set by the proletarian state, and even begins to be imbued although very slowly with respect for the government which protects all who work and is ruthless towards the idle rich.

The special conditions which, in Russia, complicated and retarded the struggle of the proletariat against the big peasants after it had defeated the bourgeoisie were, in the main, the following: after October 25 (November 7), 1917, the Russian revolution passed through the stage of the "general democratic"—that is, basically the bourgeois-democratic—struggle of the peasantry as a whole against the landowners; the cultural and numerical weakness of the urban proletariat; and, lastly, the enormous distances and extremely poor means of communication. Inasmuch as these retarding conditions do not exist in the advanced countries, the revolutionary proletariat of Europe and America should prepare far more energetically, and achieve far more rapidly, resolutely, and successfully, complete victory over the resistance of the big peasantry, completely depriving it of the slightest possibility of offering resistance. This is imperative because, until such a complete and absolute victory is achieved, the masses of the rural proletarians, semi-proletarians, and small peasants cannot be brought to accept the proletarian state as a fully stable one.

6) The revolutionary proletariat must immediately and unreservedly confiscate all landed estates, those of the big landowners, who, in capitalist countries—directly or through their tenant farmers—systematically exploit wage-labour and the neighbouring small (and, not infrequently, part of the middle) peasantry, do not themselves engage in manual labour, and are in the main descended from feudal lords (the nobles in Russia, Germany, and Hungary, the restored seigneurs in France, the lords in Britain, and the former slave-owners in America), or are rich financial magnates, or else a mixture of both these categories of exploiters and parasites.

Under no circumstances is it permissible for Communist parties to advocate or practise compensating the big landowners for the confiscated lands, for under present-day conditions in Europe and America this would be tantamount to a betrayal of socialism and the imposition of new tribute upon the masses of working and exploited people, to whom the war has meant the greatest hardships, while it has increased the number of millionaires and enriched them.

As to the mode of cultivation of the land that the victorious proletariat confiscates from the big landowners, the distribution of that land among the peasantry for their use has been predominant in Russia, owing to her economic backwardness; it is only in relatively rare and exceptional cases that state farms have been organised on the former estates which the proletarian state runs at its own expense, converting the former wage-labourers into workers for the state and members of the Soviets, which administer the state. The Communist International is of the opinion that in the case of the advanced capitalist countries it would be correct to keep *most* of the big agricultural enterprises intact and to conduct them on the lines of the "state farms" in Russia.

It would, however, be grossly erroneous to exaggerate or to stereotype this rule and never to permit the free grant of *part* of the land that belonged to the expropriated expropriators to the neighbouring small and sometimes middle peasants.

First, the objection usually raised to this, namely, that large-scale farming is technically superior, often amounts to an indisputable theoretical truth being replaced by the worst kind of opportunism and betrayal of the revolution. To achieve the success of this revolution, the proletariat should not shrink from a temporary decline in production, any more than the bourgeois opponents of slavery in North America shrank from a temporary decline in cotton production as a consequence of the Civil War of 1863-65. What is most important to the bourgeois is production for the sake of production; what is most important to the working and exploited population is the overthrow of the exploiters and the creation of conditions that will permit the working people to work for themselves, and not for the capitalists. It is the primary and fundamental task of the proletariat to ensure the proletarian victory and its stability. There can, however, be no stable proletarian government unless the middle peasantry is neutralised and the support is secured of a very considerable section of the small peasantry, if not all of them.

Second, not merely an increase but even the preservation of large-scale production in agriculture presupposes the existence of a fully developed and revolutionarily conscious rural proletariat with considerable experience of trade union and political organisation behind it. Where this condition does not yet exist, or where this work cannot expediently be entrusted to class-conscious and competent industrial workers, hasty attempts to set up large state-conducted farms can only discredit the proletarian government. Under such conditions, the utmost caution must be exercised and the most thorough preparations made when state farms are set up.

Third, in all capitalist countries, even the most advanced, there still exist survivals of medieval, semi-feudal exploitation of the neighbouring small peasants by the big landowners as in the case of the *Instleute** in Germany, the *métayers* in France, and the

---

* Tenant farmers.—*Ed.*

sharecroppers in the United States (not only Negroes, who, in the Southern States, are mostly exploited in this way, but sometimes whites too). In such cases it is incumbent on the proletarian state to grant the small peasants free use of the lands they formerly rented, since no other economic or technical basis exists, and it cannot be created at one stroke.

The implements and stock of the big farms must be confiscated without fail and converted into state property, with the absolute condition that, *after* the requirements of the big state farms have been met, the neighbouring small peasants may have the use of these implements gratis, in compliance with conditions drawn up by the proletarian state.

In the period immediately following the proletarian revolution, it is absolutely necessary, not only to confiscate the estates of the big landowners at once, but also to deport or to intern them all as leaders of counter-revolution and ruthless oppressors of the entire rural population. However, with the consolidation of the proletarian power in the countryside as well as in the cities, systematic efforts should be made to employ (under the special control of highly reliable communist workers) those forces within this class that possess valuable experience, know-how, and organising skill, to build large-scale socialist agriculture.

7) The victory of socialism over capitalism and the consolidation of socialism may be regarded as ensured only when the proletarian state power, having completely suppressed all resistance by the exploiters and assured itself complete subordination and stability, has reorganised the whole of industry on the lines of large-scale collective production and on a modern technical basis (founded on the electrification of the entire economy). This alone will enable the cities to render such radical assistance, technical and social, to the backward and scattered rural population as will create the material basis necessary to boost the productivity of agricultural and of farm labour in general, thereby encouraging the small farmers by the force of example and in their own interests to adopt large-scale, collective and mechanised agriculture. Although nominally recognised by all socialists, this indisputable theoretical truth is in fact distorted by the opportunism prevalent in the yellow Second International and among the leaders of the German and the British "Independents", the French Longuetists, etc. This distortion consists in attention being directed towards the relatively remote, beautiful, and rosy future; attention is deflected from the immediate tasks of the difficult practical transition and approach to that future. In practice, it consists in preaching a compromise with the bourgeoisie and a "class truce", i.e., complete betrayal of the proletariat, which is now waging a struggle amidst the unprecedented ruin and impoverishment created everywhere by the war, and amidst the

unprecedented enrichment and arrogance of a handful of millionaires resulting from that war.

It is in the countryside that a genuine possibility of a successful struggle for socialism demands, first, that all Communist parties should inculcate in the industrial proletariat a realisation of the need to make sacrifices, and be prepared to make sacrifices so as to overthrow the bourgeoisie and consolidate proletarian power—since the dictatorship of the proletariat implies both the ability of the proletariat to organise and lead all the working and exploited people, and the vanguard's ability to make the utmost sacrifices and to display the utmost heroism to that end; second, success demands that, as a result of the workers' victory, the labouring and most exploited masses in the countryside achieve an immediate and considerable improvement in their conditions at the expense of the exploiters—for without that the industrial proletariat cannot get the support of the rural areas and, in particular, will be unable to ensure the supply of food for the cities.

8) The enormous difficulty of organising and training for the revolutionary struggle the masses of rural working people, whom capitalism has reduced to a state of great wretchedness, disunity and frequently semi-medieval dependence, makes it necessary for the Communist parties to devote special attention to the strike struggle in the rural districts, give greater support to mass strikes by the agricultural proletarians and semi-proletarians, and help develop the strike movement in every way. The experience of the Russian revolutions of 1905 and of 1917, now confirmed and extended by the experience of Germany and other advanced countries, shows that the growing mass strike struggle (into which, under certain conditions, the small peasants can and should also be drawn) is alone capable of rousing the countryside from its lethargy, awakening the class-consciousness of the exploited masses in the countryside, making them realise the need for class organisation, and revealing to them in a vivid and practical manner the importance of their alliance with the urban workers.

This Congress of the Communist International brands as traitors and renegades those socialists—to be found, unfortunately, not only in the yellow Second International, but also in the three very important European parties which have withdrawn from that International—who are not only capable of remaining indifferent to the strike struggle in the countryside, but even (like Karl Kautsky) of opposing it on the grounds that it threatens to reduce the output of articles of consumption. Neither programmes nor the most solemn declarations are of any value whatever unless it is proved in practice, in deed, that the Communists and workers' leaders are able to place above everything else in the world the development and the victory of the proletarian revolution, and to make the greatest sacrifices for it, for otherwise there is no way out, no salvation from starvation, ruin, and new imperialist wars.

In particular, it should be pointed out that the leaders of the old socialist movement and representatives of the "labour aristocracy" —who now often make verbal concessions to communism and even nominally side with it in order to preserve their prestige among the worker masses, which are rapidly becoming revolutionary—should be tested for their loyalty to the cause of the proletariat and their suitability for responsible positions in those spheres of work where the development of revolutionary consciousness and the revolutionary struggle is most marked, the resistance of the landowners and the bourgeoisie (the big peasants, the kulaks) most fierce, and the difference between the socialist compromiser and the communist revolutionary most striking.

9) The Communist parties must exert every effort to begin, as speedily as possible, to set up Soviets of Deputies in the countryside, and in the first place Soviets of hired labourers and semi-proletarians. Only if they are linked up with the mass strike struggle and with the most oppressed class can the Soviets perform their functions, and become consolidated enough to influence (and later to incorporate) the small peasants. If, however, the strike struggle has not yet developed, and the agricultural proletariat is as yet incapable of strong organisation owing both to the severe oppression by the landowners and the big peasants and to lack of support from the industrial workers and their unions, then the formation of Soviets of Deputies in the rural areas will require lengthy preparation by means of the organisation of communist cells, even if only small ones, intensified agitation—in which the demands of communism are enunciated in the simplest manner and illustrated by the most glaring examples of exploitation and oppression—and the arrangement of systematic visits of industrial workers to the rural districts, and so on.

Written at the beginning
of June 1920

Published July 20, 1920
in the magazine
Kommunisticheski Internatsional
No. 12

Collected Works, Vol. 31

THE SECOND CONGRESS OF THE COMMUNIST INTERNATIONAL
JULY 19-AUGUST 7, 1920

REPORT OF THE COMMISSION ON THE NATIONAL AND THE COLONIAL QUESTIONS
JULY 26[288]

Comrades, I shall confine myself to a brief introduction, after which Comrade Maring, who has been secretary to our commission, will give you a detailed account of the changes we have made in the theses. He will be followed by Comrade Roy, who has formulated the supplementary theses. Our commission have unanimously adopted both the preliminary theses,* as amended, and the supplementary theses. We have thus reached complete unanimity on all major issues. I shall now make a few brief remarks.

First, what is the cardinal idea underlying our theses? It is the distinction between oppressed and oppressor nations. Unlike the Second International and bourgeois democracy, we emphasise this distinction. In this age of imperialism, it is particularly important for the proletariat and the Communist International to establish the concrete economic facts and to proceed from concrete realities, not from abstract postulates, in all colonial and national problems.

The characteristic feature of imperialism consists in the whole world, as we now see, being divided into a large number of oppressed nations and an insignificant number of oppressor nations, the latter possessing colossal wealth and powerful armed forces. The vast majority of the world's population, over a thousand million, perhaps even 1,250 million people, if we take the total population of the world as 1,750 million, in other words, about 70 per cent of the world's population, belong to the oppressed nations, which are either in a state of direct colonial dependence or are semi-colonies, as, for example, Persia, Turkey and China, or else, conquered by some big imperialist power, have become greatly dependent on that power by virtue of peace treaties. This idea of distinction, of dividing the nations into oppressor and oppressed, runs through the theses, not only the first theses published earlier over my signature, but also those submitted by Comrade Roy. The latter were framed chiefly from the standpoint of the situation in India and other big Asian countries oppressed by Britain. Herein lies their great importance to us.

---

* See *Collected Works*, Vol. 31, pp. 144-51.—*Ed.*

The second basic idea in our theses is that, in the present world situation following the imperialist war, reciprocal relations between peoples and the world political system as a whole are determined by the struggle waged by a small group of imperialist nations against the Soviet movement and the Soviet states headed by Soviet Russia. Unless we bear that in mind, we shall not be able to pose a single national or colonial problem correctly, even if it concerns a most outlying part of the world. The Communist parties, in civilised and backward countries alike, can pose and solve political problems correctly only if they make this postulate their starting-point.

Third, I should like especially to emphasise the question of the bourgeois-democratic movement in backward countries. This is a question that has given rise to certain differences. We have discussed whether it would be right or wrong, in principle and in theory, to state that the Communist International and the Communist parties must support the bourgeois-democratic movement in backward countries. As a result of our discussion, we have arrived at the unanimous decision to speak of the national-revolutionary movement rather than of the "bourgeois-democratic" movement. It is beyond doubt that any national movement can only be a bourgeois-democratic movement, since the overwhelming mass of the population in the backward countries consist of peasants who represent bourgeois-capitalist relationships. It would be utopian to believe that proletarian parties in these backward countries, if indeed they can emerge in them, can pursue communist tactics and a communist policy, without establishing definite relations with the peasant movement and without giving it effective support. However, the objections have been raised that, if we speak of the bourgeois-democratic movement, we shall be obliterating all distinctions between the reformist and the revolutionary movements. Yet that distinction has been very clearly revealed of late in the backward and colonial countries, since the imperialist bourgeoisie is doing everything in its power to implant a reformist movement among the oppressed nations too. There has been a certain *rapprochement* between the bourgeoisie of the exploiting countries and that of the colonies, so that very often—perhaps even in most cases—the bourgeoisie of the oppressed countries, while it does support the national movement, is in full accord with the imperialist bourgeoisie, i.e., joins forces with it against all revolutionary movements and revolutionary classes. This was irrefutably proved in the commission, and we decided that the only correct attitude was to take this distinction into account and, in nearly all cases, substitute the term "national-revolutionary" for the term "bourgeois-democratic". The significance of this change is that we, as Communists, should and will support bourgeois-liberation movements in the colonies only when they are genuinely revolutionary, and when

their exponents do not hinder our work of educating and organising in a revolutionary spirit the peasantry and the masses of the
exploited. If these conditions do not exist, the Communists in these
countries must combat the reformist bourgeoisie, to whom the
heroes of the Second International also belong. Reformist parties
already exist in the colonial countries, and in some cases their
spokesmen call themselves Social-Democrats and socialists. The
distinction I have referred to has been made in all the theses with
the result, I think, that our view is now formulated much more
precisely.

Next, I would like to make a remark on the subject of peasants'
Soviets. The Russian Communists' practical activities in the former
tsarist colonies, in such backward countries as Turkestan, etc., have
confronted us with the question of how to apply the communist
tactics and policy in pre-capitalist conditions. The preponderance of
pre-capitalist relationships is still the main determining feature in
these countries, so that there can be no question of a purely proletarian movement in them. There is practically no industrial proletariat in these countries. Nevertheless, we have assumed, we
must assume, the role of leader even there. Experience has
shown us that tremendous difficulties have to be surmounted
in these countries. However, the practical results of our
work have also shown that despite these difficulties we are in a
position to inspire in the masses an urge for independent political
thinking and independent political action, even where a proletariat
is practically non-existent. This work has been more difficult for
us than it will be for comrades in the West-European countries, because in Russia the proletariat is engrossed in the work of state
administration. It will readily be understood that peasants living in
conditions of semi-feudal dependence can easily assimilate and give
effect to the idea of Soviet organisation. It is also clear that the oppressed masses, those who are exploited, not only by merchant
capital but also by the feudalists, and by a state based on feudalism,
can apply this weapon, this type of organisation, in their conditions
too. The idea of Soviet organisation is a simple one, and is applicable, not only to proletarian, but also to peasant feudal and semi-
feudal relations. Our experience in this respect is not as yet very
considerable. However, the debate in the commission, in which several representatives from colonial countries participated, demonstrated convincingly that the Communist International's theses
should point out that peasants' Soviets, Soviets of the exploited, are
a weapon which can be employed, not only in capitalist countries
but also in countries with pre-capitalist relations, and that it is the
absolute duty of Communist parties and of elements prepared to
form Communist parties, everywhere to conduct propaganda in
favour of peasants' Soviets or of working people's Soviets, this to in-

clude backward and colonial countries. Wherever conditions permit, they should at once make attempts to set up Soviets of the working people.

This opens up a very interesting and very important field for our practical work. So far our joint experience in this respect has not been extensive, but more and more data will gradually accumulate. It is unquestionable that the proletariat of the advanced countries can and should give help to the working masses of the backward countries, and that the backward countries can emerge from their present stage of development when the victorious proletariat of the Soviet Republics extends a helping hand to these masses and is in a position to give them support.

There was quite a lively debate on this question in the commission, not only in connection with the theses I signed, but still more in connection with Comrade Roy's theses, which he will defend here, and certain amendments to which were unanimously adopted.

The question was posed as follows: are we to consider as correct the assertion that the capitalist stage of economic development is inevitable for backward nations now on the road to emancipation and among whom a certain advance towards progress is to be seen since the war? We replied in the negative. If the victorious revolutionary proletariat conducts systematic propaganda among them, and the Soviet governments come to their aid with all the means at their disposal—in that event it will be mistaken to assume that the backward peoples must inevitably go through the capitalist stage of development. Not only should we create independent contingents of fighters and party organisations in the colonies and the backward countries, not only at once launch propaganda for the organisation of peasants' Soviets and strive to adapt them to the pre-capitalist conditions, but the Communist International should advance the proposition, with the appropriate theoretical grounding, that with the aid of the proletariat of the advanced countries, backward countries can go over to the Soviet system and, through certain stages of development, to communism, without having to pass through the capitalist stage.

The necessary means for this cannot be indicated in advance. These will be prompted by practical experience. It has, however, been definitely established that the idea of the Soviets is understood by the mass of the working people in even the most remote nations, that the Soviets should be adapted to the conditions of a pre-capitalist social system, and that the Communist parties should immediately begin work in this direction in all parts of the world.

I would also like to emphasise the importance of revolutionary work by the Communist parties. not only in their own, but also in the colonial countries, and particularly among the troops employed by the exploiting nations to keep the colonial peoples in subjection.

Comrade Quelch of the British Socialist Party spoke of this in our commission. He said that the rank-and-file British worker would consider it treasonable to help the enslaved nations in their uprisings against British rule. True, the jingoist[289] and chauvinist-minded labour aristocrats of Britain and America present a very great danger to socialism, and are a bulwark of the Second International. Here we are confronted with the greatest treachery on the part of leaders and workers belonging to this bourgeois International. The colonial question has been discussed in the Second International as well. The Basle Manifesto is quite clear on this point, too. The parties of the Second International have pledged themselves to revolutionary action, but they have given no sign of genuine revolutionary work or of assistance to the exploited and dependent nations in their revolt against the oppressor nations. This, I think, applies also to most of the parties that have withdrawn from the Second International and wish to join the Third International. We must proclaim this publicly for all to hear, and it is irrefutable. We shall see if any attempt is made to deny it.

All these considerations have formed the basis of our resolutions, which undoubtedly are too lengthy but will nevertheless, I am sure, prove of use and will promote the development and organisation of genuine revolutionary work in connection with the national and the colonial questions. And that is our principal task.

Vestnik Vtorogo kongressa   *Collected Works*, Vol. 31
Kommunisticheskogo Internatsionala
No. 6, August 7, 1920

THE TASKS OF THE YOUTH LEAGUES

SPEECH DELIVERED AT THE THIRD ALL-RUSSIA CONGRESS OF THE RUSSIAN YOUNG COMMUNIST LEAGUE OCTOBER 2, 1920[290]

(*The congress greets Lenin with a tremendous ovation.*) Comrades, today I would like to talk on the fundamental tasks of the Young Communist League and, in this connection, on what the youth organisations in a socialist republic should be like in general.

It is all the more necessary to dwell on this question because in a certain sense it may be said that it is the youth that will be faced with the actual task of creating a communist society. For it is clear that the generation of working people brought up in capitalist society can, at best, accomplish the task of destroying the foundations of the old, the capitalist way of life, which was built on exploitation. At best it will be able to accomplish the tasks of creating a social system that will help the proletariat and the working classes retain power and lay a firm foundation, which can be built on only by a generation that is starting to work under the new conditions, in a situation in which relations based on the exploitation of man by man no longer exist.

And so, in dealing from this angle with the tasks confronting the youth, I must say that the tasks of the youth in general, and of the Young Communist Leagues and all other organisations in particular, might be summed up in a single word: learn.

Of course, this is only a "single word". It does not reply to the principal and most essential questions: what to learn, and how to learn? And the whole point here is that, with the transformation of the old, capitalist society, the upbringing, training and education of the new generations that will create the communist society cannot be conducted on the old lines. The teaching, training and education of the youth must proceed from the material that has been left to us by the old society. We can build communism only on the basis of the totality of knowledge, organisations and institutions, only by using the stock of human forces and means that have been left to us by the old society. Only by radically remoulding the teaching, organisation and training of the youth shall we be able to ensure that the efforts of the younger generation will result in the creation of a society that will be unlike the old society, i.e., in the creation of a communist society. That is why we must deal in detail with the question of what we should teach the youth and how the youth should learn if it really wants to justify the name of communist youth, and how it should be trained so as to be able to complete and consummate what we have started.

I must say that the first and most natural reply would seem to be that the Youth League, and the youth in general, who want to advance to communism, should learn communism.

But this reply—"learn communism"—is too general. What do we need in order to learn communism? What must be singled out from the sum of general knowledge so as to acquire a knowledge of communism? Here a number of dangers arise, which very often manifest themselves whenever the task of learning communism is presented incorrectly, or when it is interpreted in too one-sided a manner.

Naturally, the first thought that enters one's mind is that learning communism means assimilating the sum of knowledge that is contained in communist manuals, pamphlets and books. But such a definition of the study of communism would be too crude and inadequate. If the study of communism consisted solely in assimilating what is contained in communist books and pamphlets, we might all too easily obtain communist text-jugglers or braggarts, and this would very often do us harm, because such people, after learning by rote what is set forth in communist books and pamphlets, would prove incapable of combining the various branches of knowledge, and would be unable to act in the way communism really demands.

One of the greatest evils and misfortunes left to us by the old, capitalist society is the complete rift between books and practical life; we have had books explaining everything in the best possible manner, yet in most cases these books contained the most pernicious and hypocritical lies, a false description of capitalist society.

That is why it would be most mistaken merely to assimilate book knowledge about communism. No longer do our speeches and articles merely reiterate what used to be said about communism, because our speeches and articles are connected with our daily work in all fields. Without work and without struggle book knowledge of communism obtained from communist pamphlets and works is absolutely worthless, for it would continue the old separation of theory and practice, the old rift which was the most pernicious feature of the old, bourgeois society.

It would be still more dangerous to set about assimilating only communist slogans. Had we not realised this danger in time, and had we not directed all our efforts to averting this danger, the half million or million young men and women who would have called themselves Communists after studying communism in this way would only greatly prejudice the cause of communism.

The question arises: how is all this to be blended for the study of communism? What must we take from the old schools, from the old kind of science? It was the declared aim of the old type of school to produce men with an all-round education, to teach the sciences in general. We know that this was utterly false, since the whole of society was based and maintained on the division of people into classes, into exploiters and oppressed. Since they were thoroughly imbued with the class spirit, the old schools naturally gave knowledge only to the children of the bourgeoisie. Every word was falsified in the interests of the bourgeoisie. In these schools the younger generation of workers and peasants were not so much educated as drilled in the interests of that bourgeoisie. They were trained in such a way as to be useful servants of the bourgeoisie, able to create profits for it without disturbing its peace and leisure. That is why, while rejecting the old type of schools, we have made it our task to take from it only what we require for genuine communist education.

This brings me to the reproaches and accusations which we constantly hear levelled at the old schools, and which often lead to wholly wrong conclusions. It is said that the old school was a school of purely book knowledge, of ceaseless drilling and grinding. That is true, but we must distinguish between what was bad in the old schools and what is useful to us, and we must be able to select from it what is necessary for communism.

The old schools provided purely book knowledge; they compelled their pupils to assimilate a mass of useless, superfluous and barren knowledge, which cluttered up the brain and turned the younger generation into bureaucrats regimented according to a single pattern. But it would mean falling into a grave error for you to try to draw the conclusion that one can become a Communist without assimilating the wealth of knowledge amassed by mankind. It would be mistaken to think it sufficient to learn communist slogans and the conclusions of communist science, without acquiring that sum of knowledge of which communism itself is a result. Marxism is an example which shows how communism arose out of the sum of human knowledge.

You have read and heard that communist theory—the science of communism created in the main by Marx, this doctrine of Marxism —has ceased to be the work of a single socialist of the nineteenth century, even though he was a genius, and that it has become the doctrine of millions and tens of millions of proletarians all over the world, who are applying it in their struggle against capitalism. If you were to ask why the teachings of Marx have been able to win the hearts and minds of millions and tens of millions of the most revolutionary class, you would receive only one answer: it was because Marx based his work on the firm foundation of the human knowledge acquired under capitalism. After making a study of the laws governing the development of human society, Marx realised the inevitability of capitalism developing towards communism. What is most important is that he proved this on the sole basis of a most precise, detailed and profound study of this capitalist society, by fully assimilating all that earlier science had produced. He critically reshaped everything that had been created by human society, without ignoring a single detail. He reconsidered, subjected to criticism, and verified on the working-class movement everything that human thinking had created, and therefrom formulated conclusions which people hemmed in by bourgeois limitations or bound by bourgeois prejudices could not draw.

We must bear this in mind when, for example, we talk about proletarian culture.[291] We shall be unable to solve this problem unless we clearly realise that only a precise knowledge and transformation of the culture created by the entire development of mankind will enable us to create a proletarian culture. The latter is not clutched out of thin air; it is not an invention of those who call themselves experts in proletarian culture. That is all nonsense. Proletarian culture must be the logical development of the store of knowledge mankind has accumulated under the yoke of capitalist, landowner and bureaucratic society. All these roads have been leading, and will continue to lead up to proletarian culture, in the same way as political economy, as reshaped by Marx, has shown us what human society must arrive at, shown us the passage to the class struggle, to the beginning of the proletarian revolution.

When we so often hear representatives of the youth, as well as certain advocates of a new system of education, attacking the old schools, claiming that they used the system of cramming, we say to them that we must take what was good in the old schools. We must not borrow the system of encumbering young people's minds with an immense amount of knowledge, nine-tenths of which was useless and one-tenth distorted. This, however, does not mean that we can restrict ourselves to communist conclusions and learn only communist slogans. You will not create communism that way. You can become a Communist only when you enrich your mind with a knowledge of all the treasures created by mankind.

We have no need of cramming, but we do need to develop and perfect the mind of every student with a knowledge of fundamental facts. Communism will become an empty word, a mere signboard, and a Communist a mere boaster, if all the knowledge he has acquired is not digested in his mind. You should not merely assimilate this knowledge, but assimilate it critically, so as not to cram your mind with useless lumber, but enrich it with all those facts that are indispensable to the well-educated man of today. If a Communist took it into his head to boast about his communism because of the cut-and-dried conclusions he had acquired, without putting in a great deal of serious and hard work and without understanding facts he should examine critically, he would be a deplorable Communist indeed. Such superficiality would be decidedly fatal. If I know that I know little, I shall strive to learn more; but if a man says that he is a Communist and that he need not know anything thoroughly, he will never become anything like a Communist.

The old schools produced servants needed by the capitalists; the old schools turned men of science into men who had to write and say whatever pleased the capitalists. We must therefore abolish them. But does the fact that we must abolish them, destroy them, mean that we should not take from them everything mankind has accumulated that is essential to man? Does it mean that we do not have to distinguish between what was necessary to capitalism and what is necessary to communism?

We are replacing the old drill-sergeant methods practised in bourgeois society, against the will of the majority, with the class-conscious discipline of the workers and peasants, who combine hatred of the old society with a determination, ability and readiness to unite and organise their forces for this struggle so as to forge the wills of millions and hundreds of millions of people—disunited, and scattered over the territory of a huge country—into a single will, without which defeat is inevitable. Without this solidarity, without this conscious discipline of the workers and peasants, our cause is hopeless. Without this, we shall be unable to vanquish the capitalists and landowners of the whole world. We shall not even consolidate the foundation, let alone build a new, communist society on that foundation. Likewise, while condemning the old schools, while harbouring an absolutely justified and necessary hatred for the old schools, and appreciating the readiness to destroy them, we must realise that we must replace the old system of instruction, the old cramming and the old drill, with an ability to acquire the sum total of human knowledge, and to acquire it in such a way that communism shall not be something to be learned by rote, but something that you yourselves have thought over, something that will embody conclusions inevitable from the standpoint of present-day education.

That is the way the main tasks should be presented when we speak of the aim: learn communism.

I shall take a practical example to make this clear to you, and to demonstrate the approach to the problem of how you must learn. You all know that, following the military problems, those of defending the republic, we are now confronted with economic tasks. Communist society, as we know, cannot be built unless we restore industry and agriculture, and that, not in the old way. They must be re-established on a modern basis, in accordance with the last word in science. You know that electricity is that basis, and that only after electrification of the entire country, of all branches of industry and agriculture, only when you have achieved that aim, will you be able to build for yourselves the communist society which the older generation will not be able to build. Confronting you is the task of economically reviving the whole country, of reorganising and restoring both agriculture and industry on modern technical lines, based on modern science and technology, on electricity. You realise perfectly well that illiterate people cannot tackle electrification, and that elementary literacy is not enough either. It is insufficient to understand what electricity is; what is needed is the knowledge of how to apply it technically in industry and agriculture, and in the individual branches of industry and agriculture. This has to be learnt for oneself, and it must be taught to the entire rising generation of working people. That is the task confronting every class-conscious Communist, every young person who regards himself a Communist and who clearly understands that, by joining the Young Communist League, he has pledged himself to help the Party build communism and to help the whole younger generation create a communist society. He must realise that he can create it only on the basis of modern education, and if he does not acquire this education communism will remain merely a pious wish.

It was the task of the older generation to overthrow the bourgeoisie. The main task then was to criticise the bourgeoisie, arouse hatred of the bourgeoisie among the masses, and foster class-consciousness and the ability to unite their forces. The new generation is confronted with a far more complex task. Your duty does not lie only in assembling your forces so as to uphold the workers' and peasants' government against an invasion instigated by the capitalists. Of course, you must do that; that is something you clearly realise, and is distinctly seen by the Communist. However, that is not enough. You have to build up a communist society. In many respects half of the work has been done. The old order has been destroyed, just as it deserved, it has been turned into a heap of ruins, just as it deserved. The ground has been cleared, and on this ground the younger communist generation must build a communist society. You are faced with the task of construction, and you can accomplish that task only by assimilating all modern knowledge, only if you are able to transform communism from cut-and-dried and memorised formulas, counsels, recipes, prescriptions and programmes into that living reality which gives unity to your immediate work, and only if you are able to make communism a guide in all your practical work.

That is the task you should pursue in educating, training and rousing the entire younger generation. You must be foremost among the millions of builders of a communist society in whose ranks every young man and young woman should be. You will not build a communist society unless you enlist the mass of young workers and peasants in the work of building communism.

This naturally brings me to the question of how we should teach communism and what the specific features of our methods should be.

I first of all shall deal here with the question of communist ethics.

You must train yourselves to be Communists. It is the task of the Youth League to organise its practical activities in such a way that, by learning, organising, uniting and fighting, its members shall train both themselves and all those who look to it for leadership; it should train Communists. The entire purpose of training, educating and teaching the youth of today should be to imbue them with communist ethics.

But is there such a thing as communist ethics? Is there such a thing as communist morality? Of course, there is. It is often suggested that we have no ethics of our own; very often the bourgeoisie accuse us Communists of rejecting all morality. This is a method of confusing the issue, of throwing dust in the eyes of the workers and peasants.

In what sense do we reject ethics, reject morality?

In the sense given to it by the bourgeoisie, who based ethics on God's commandments. On this point we, of course, say that we do not believe in God, and that we know perfectly well that the clergy, the landowners and the bourgeoisie invoked the name of God so as to further their own interests as exploiters. Or, instead of basing ethics on the commandments of morality, on the commandments of God, they based it on idealist or semi-idealist phrases, which always amounted to something very similar to God's commandments.

We reject any morality based on extra-human and extra-class concepts. We say that this is deception, dupery, stultification of the workers and peasants in the interests of the landowners and capitalists.

We say that our morality is entirely subordinated to the interests of the proletariat's class struggle. Our morality stems from the interests of the class struggle of the proletariat.

The old society was based on the oppression of all the workers and peasants by the landowners and capitalists. We had to destroy all that, and overthrow them but to do that we had to create unity. That is something that God cannot create.

This unity could be provided only by the factories, only by a proletariat trained and roused from its long slumber. Only when that class was formed did a mass movement arise which has led to what we have now—the victory of the proletarian revolution in one of the weakest of countries, which for three years has been repelling the onslaught of the bourgeoisie of the whole world. We can see how the proletarian revolution is developing all over the world. On the basis of experience, we now say that only the proletariat could have created the solid force which the disunited and scattered peasantry are following and which has withstood all onslaughts by the exploiters. Only this class can help the working masses unite, rally their ranks and conclusively defend, conclusively consolidate and conclusively build up a communist society.

That is why we say that to us there is no such thing as a morality that stands outside human society; that is a fraud. To us morality is subordinated to the interests of the proletariat's class struggle.

What does that class struggle consist in? It consists in overthrowing the tsar, overthrowing the capitalists, and abolishing the capitalist class.

What are classes in general? Classes are that which permits one section of society to appropriate the labour of another section. If one section of society appropriates all the land, we have a landowner class and a peasant class. If one section of society owns the factories, shares and capital, while another section works in these factories, we have a capitalist class and a proletarian class.

It was not difficult to drive out the tsar—that required only a few days. It was not very difficult to drive out the landowners—that was done in a few months. Nor was it very difficult to drive out the capitalists. But it is incomparably more difficult to abolish classes; we still have the division into workers and peasants. If the peasant is installed on his plot of land and appropriates his surplus grain, that is, grain that he does not need for himself or for his cattle, while the rest of the people have to go without bread, then the peasant becomes an exploiter. The more grain he clings to, the more profitable he finds it; as for the rest, let them starve: "The more they starve, the dearer I can sell this grain." All should work according to a single common plan, on common land, in common factories and in accordance with a common system. Is that easy to attain? You see that it is not as easy as driving out the tsar, the landowners and the capitalists. What is required is that the proletariat re-educate a section of the peasantry; it must win over the working peasants in order to crush the resistance of those peasants who are rich and are profiting from the poverty and want of the rest. Hence the task of the proletarian struggle is not quite completed after we have overthrown the tsar and driven out the landowners and capitalists; to accomplish that is the task of the system we call the dictatorship of the proletariat.

The class struggle is continuing; it has merely changed its forms. It is the class struggle of the proletariat to prevent the return of the old exploiters, to unite in a single union the scattered masses of unenlightened peasants. The class struggle is continuing and it is our task to subordinate all interests to that struggle. Our communist morality is also subordinated to that task. We say: morality is what serves to destroy the old exploiting society and to unite all the working people around the proletariat, which is building up a new, a communist society.

Communist morality is that which serves this struggle and unites the working people against all exploitation, against all petty private property; for petty property puts into the hands of one person that which has been created by the labour of the whole of society. In our country the land is common property.

But suppose I take a piece of this common property and grow on it twice as much grain as I need, and profiteer on the surplus? Suppose I argue that the more starving people there are, the more they will pay? Would I then be behaving like a Communist? No, I would be behaving like an exploiter, like a proprietor. That must be combated. If that is allowed to go on, things will revert to the rule of the capitalists, to the rule of the bourgeoisie, as has more than once happened in previous revolutions. To prevent the restoration of the rule of the capitalists and the bourgeoisie, we must not allow profiteering; we must not allow individuals to enrich themselves at the expense of the rest; the working people must unite with the proletariat and form a communist society. This is the principal feature of the fundamental task of the League and the organisation of the communist youth.

The old society was based on the principle: rob or be robbed; work for others or make others work for you; be a slave-owner or a slave. Naturally, people brought up in such a society assimilate with their mother's milk, one might say, the psychology, the habit, the concept which says: you are either a slave-owner or a slave, or else, a small owner, a petty employee, a petty official, or an intellectual—in short, a man who is concerned only with himself, and does not care a rap for anybody else.

If I work this plot of land, I do not care a rap for anybody else; if others starve, all the better, I shall get the more for my grain. If I have a job as a doctor, engineer, teacher, or clerk, I do not care a rap for anybody else. If I toady to and please the powers that be, I may be able to keep my job, and even get on in life and become a bourgeois. A Communist cannot harbour such a psychology and such sentiments. When the workers and peasants proved that they were able, by their own efforts, to defend themselves and create a new society—that was the beginning of the new and communist education, education in the struggle against the exploiters, education in alliance with the proletariat against the self-seekers and petty proprietors, against the psychology and habits which say: I seek my own profit and don't care a rap for anything else.

That is the reply to the question of how the young and rising generation should learn communism.

It can learn communism only by linking up every step in its studies, training and education with the continuous struggle the proletarians and the working people are waging against the old society of exploiters. When people tell us about morality, we say: to a Communist all morality lies in this united discipline and conscious mass struggle against the exploiters. We do not believe in an eternal morality, and we expose the falseness of all the fables about morality. Morality serves the purpose of helping human society rise to a higher level and rid itself of the exploitation of labour.

To achieve this we need that generation of young people who began to reach political maturity in the midst of a disciplined and desperate struggle against the bourgeoisie. In this struggle that generation is training genuine Communists; it must subordinate to this struggle, and link up with it, each step in its studies, education and training. The education of the communist youth must consist, not in giving them suave talks and moral precepts. This is not what education consists in. When people have seen the way in which their fathers and mothers lived under the yoke of the landowners and capitalists; when they have themselves experienced the sufferings of those who began the struggle against the exploiters; when they have seen the sacrifices made to keep what has been won, and seen what deadly enemies the landowners and capitalists are—they are taught by these conditions to become Communists. Communist morality is based on the struggle for the consolidation and completion of communism. That is also the basis of communist training, education, and teaching. That is the reply to the question of how communism should be learnt.

We could not believe in teaching, training and education if they were restricted only to the schoolroom and divorced from the ferment of life. As long as the workers and peasants are oppressed by the landowners and capitalists, and as long as the schools are controlled by the landowners and capitalists, the young generation will remain blind and ignorant. Our schools must provide the youth with the fundamentals of knowledge, the ability to evolve communist views independently; they must make educated people of the youth. While they are attending school, they must learn to become participants in the struggle for emancipation from the exploiters. The Young Communist League will justify its name as the League of the young communist generation only when every step in its teaching, training and education is linked up with participation in the common struggle of all working people against the exploiters. You are well aware that, as long as Russia remains the only workers' republic and the old, bourgeois system exists in the rest of the world, we shall be weaker than they are, and be constantly threatened with a new attack; and that only if we learn to be solidly united shall we win in the further struggle and—having gained strength—become really invincible. Thus, to be a Communist means that you must organise and unite the entire young generation and set an example of training and discipline in this struggle. Then you will be able to start building the edifice of communist society and bring it to completion.

To make this clearer to you, I shall quote an example. We call ourselves Communists. What is a Communist? Communist is a Latin word. *Communis* is the Latin for "common". Communist society is a society in which all things—the land, the factories—are owned in common and the people work in common. That is communism.

Is it possible to work in common if each one works separately on his own plot of land? Work in common cannot be brought about all at once. That is impossible. It does not drop from the skies. It comes through toil and suffering; it is created in the course of struggle. The old books are of no use here; no one will believe them. One's own experience of life is needed. When Kolchak and Denikin were advancing from Siberia and the South, the peasants were on their side. They did not like Bolshevism because the Bolsheviks took their grain at a fixed price. But when the peasants in Siberia and the Ukraine experienced the rule of Kolchak and Denikin, they realised that they had only one alternative: either to go to the capitalists, who would at once hand them over into slavery under the landowners; or to follow the workers, who, it is true, did not promise a land flowing with milk and honey, and demanded iron discipline and firmness in an arduous struggle, but would lead them out of enslavement by the capitalists and landowners. When even the ignorant peasants saw and realised this from their own experience, they became conscious adherents of communism, who had gone through a severe school. It is such experience that must form the basis of all the activities of the Young Communist League.

I have replied to the questions of what we must learn, what we must take from the old schools and from the old science. I shall now try to answer the question of how this must be learnt. The answer is: only by inseparably linking each step in the activities of the schools, each step in training, education and teaching, with the struggle of all the working people against the exploiters.

I shall quote a few examples from the experience of the work of some of the youth organisations so as to illustrate how this training in communism should proceed. Everybody is talking about abolishing illiteracy. You know that a communist society cannot be built in an illiterate country. It is not enough for the Soviet government to issue an order, or for the Party to issue a particular slogan, or to assign a certain number of the best workers to this task. The young generation itself must take up this work. Communism means that the youth, the young men and women who belong to the Youth League, should say: this is our job; we shall unite and go into the rural districts to abolish illiteracy, so that there shall be no illiterates among our young people. We are trying to get the rising generation to devote their activities to this work. You know that we cannot rapidly transform an ignorant and illiterate Russia into a literate country. But if the Youth League sets to work on the job, and if all young people work for the benefit of all, the League, with a membership of 400,000 young men and women, will be entitled to call itself a Young Communist League. It is also a task of the League, not only to acquire knowledge itself, but to help those young people who are unable to extricate themselves by their own efforts from the toils of illiteracy. Being a member of the Youth League means devoting one's labour and efforts to the common cause. That is what a communist education means. Only in the course of such work do young men and women become real Communists. Only if they achieve practical results in this work will they become Communists.

Take, for example, work in the suburban vegetable gardens. Is that not a real job of work? It is one of the tasks of the Young Communist League. People are starving; there is hunger in the factories. To save ourselves from starvation, vegetable gardens must be developed. But farming is being carried on in the old way. Therefore, more class-conscious elements should engage in this work, and then you will find that the number of vegetable gardens will increase, their acreage will grow, and the results will improve. The Young Communist League must take an active part in this work. Every League and League branch should regard this as its duty.

The Young Communist League must be a shock force, helping in every job and displaying initiative and enterprise. The League should be an organisation enabling any worker to see that it consists of people whose teachings he perhaps does not understand, and whose teachings he may not immediately believe, but from whose practical work and activity he can see that they are really people who are showing him the right road.

If the Young Communist League fails to organise its work in this way in all fields, it will mean that it is reverting to the old bourgeois path. We must combine our education with the struggle of the working people against the exploiters, so as to help the former accomplish the tasks set by the teachings of communism.

The members of the League should use every spare hour to improve the vegetable gardens, or to organise the education of young people at some factory, and so on. We want to transform Russia from a poverty-stricken and wretched country into one that is wealthy. The Young Communist League must combine its education, learning and training with the labour of the workers and peasants, so as not to confine itself to schools or to reading communist books and pamphlets. Only by working side by side with the workers and peasants can one become a genuine Communist. It has to be generally realised that all members of the Youth League are literate people and at the same time are keen at their jobs. When everyone sees that we have ousted the old drill-ground methods from the old schools and have replaced them with conscious discipline, that all young men and women take part in subbotniks, and utilise every suburban farm to help the population—people will cease to regard labour in the old way.

It is the task of the Young Communist League to organise assistance everywhere, in village or city block, in such matters as—and I shall take a small example—public hygiene or the distribution of food. How was this done in the old, capitalist society? Everybody worked only for himself and nobody cared a straw for the aged and the sick, or whether housework was the concern only of the women, who, in consequence, were in a condition of oppression and servitude. Whose business is it to combat this? It is the business of the Youth Leagues, which must say: we shall change all this; we shall organise detachments of young people who will help to assure public hygiene or distribute food, who will conduct systematic house-to-house inspections, and work in an organised way for the benefit of the whole of society, distributing their forces properly and demonstrating that labour must be organised.

The generation of people who are now at the age of fifty cannot expect to see a communist society. This generation will be gone before then. But the generation of those who are now fifteen will see a communist society, and will itself build this society. This generation should know that the entire purpose of their lives is to build a communist society. In the old society, each family worked separately and labour was not organised by anybody except the landowners and capitalists, who oppressed the masses of the people. We must organise all labour, no matter how toilsome or messy it may be, in such a way that every worker and peasant will be able to say: I am part of the great army of free labour, and shall be able to build up my life without the landowners and capitalists, able to help establish a communist system. The Young Communist League should teach all young people to engage in conscious and disciplined labour from an early age.* In this way we can be confident that the problems now confronting us will be solved. We must assume that no less than ten years will be required for the electrification of the country, so that our impoverished land may profit from the latest achievements of technology. And so, the generation of those who are now fifteen years old, and will be living

---

* In *Pravda* No. 223, October 7, 1920 instead of the words "from an early age" it was given "from the age of 12".—*Ed.*

in a communist society in ten or twenty years' time, should tackle
all its educational tasks in such a way that every day, in every
village and city, the young people shall engage in the practical
solution of some problem of labour in common, even though the
smallest or the simplest. The success of communist construction will
be assured when this is done in every village, as communist emulation develops, and the youth prove that they can unite their
labour. Only by regarding your every step from the standpoint of
the success of that construction, and only by asking ourselves
whether we have done all we can to be united and politically
conscious working people will the Young Communist League succeed in uniting its half a million members into a single army of
labour and win universal respect. (*Stormy applause.*)

Pravda Nos. 221, 222 and 223   *Collected Works*, Vol. 31
    October 5, 6 and 7, 1920

ON PROLETARIAN CULTURE[292]

We see from *Izvestia* of October 8 that, in his address to the Proletcult Congress, Comrade Lunacharsky said things that were *diametrically opposite* to what he and I had agreed upon yesterday. It is necessary that a draft resolution (of the Proletcult Congress) should be drawn up with the utmost urgency, and that it should be endorsed by the Central Committee, in time to have it put to the vote *at this very* session of the Proletcult. On behalf of the Central Committee it should be submitted not later than today, for endorsement both by the Collegium of the People's Commissariat of Education and by the Proletcult Congress, because the congress is closing today.

DRAFT RESOLUTION

1) All educational work in the Soviet Republic of workers and peasants, in the field of political education in general and in the field of art in particular, should be imbued with the spirit of the class struggle being waged by the proletariat for the successful achievement of the aims of its dictatorship, i.e., the overthrow of the bourgeoisie, the abolition of classes, and the elimination of all forms of exploitation of man by man.

2) Hence, the proletariat, both through its vanguard—the Communist Party—and through the many types of proletarian organisations in general, should display the utmost activity and play the leading part in all the work of public education.

3) All the experience of modern history and, particularly, the more than half-century-old revolutionary struggle of the proletariat of all countries since the appearance of the *Communist Manifesto* has unquestionably demonstrated that the Marxist world outlook is the only true expression of the interests, the viewpoint, and the culture of the revolutionary proletariat.

4) Marxism has won its historic significance as the ideology of the revolutionary proletariat because, far from rejecting the most valuable achievements of the bourgeois epoch, it has, on the contrary, assimilated and refashioned everything of value in the more than two thousand years of the development of human thought and culture. Only further work on this basis and in this direction, inspired by the practical experience of the proletarian dictatorship as the final stage in the struggle against every form of exploitation, can be recognised as the development of a genuine proletarian culture.

5) Adhering unswervingly to this stand of principle, the All-Russia Proletcult Congress rejects in the most resolute manner, as theoretically unsound and practically harmful, all attempts to invent one's own particular brand of culture, to remain isolated in self-contained organisations, to draw a line dividing the field of work of the People's Commissariat of Education and the Proletcult, or to set up a Proletcult "autonomy" within establishments under the People's Commissariat of Education and so forth. On the contrary, the congress enjoins all Proletcult organisations to fully consider themselves in duty bound to act as auxiliary bodies of the network of establishments under the People's Commissariat of Education, and to accomplish their tasks under the general guidance of the Soviet authorities (specifically, of the People's Commissariat of Education) and of the Russian Communist Party, as part of the tasks of the proletarian dictatorship.

* * *

Comrade Lunacharsky says that his words have been distorted. In that case this resolution is needed *all the more* urgently.

Written October 8, 1920   *Collected Works*, Vol. 31
First published in 1926
   in the magazine
Krasnaya Nov No. 3

SPEECH
DELIVERED AT AN ALL-RUSSIA CONFERENCE OF POLITICAL EDUCATION WORKERS OF GUBERNIA AND UYEZD EDUCATION DEPARTMENTS
NOVEMBER[293]

Comrades, allow me to speak on several ideas, some of which were dealt with by the Central Committee of the Communist Party and by the Council of People's Commissars in connection with the formation of the Chief Committee for Political Education, while others came to me in connection with the draft submitted to the Council of People's Commissars. This draft was adopted yesterday as a basis; its details have still to be discussed.

I shall permit myself only to say, for my part, that at first I was highly averse to any change in the name of your institution. In my opinion, the function of the People's Commissariat of Education is to help people learn and teach others. My Soviet experience has taught me to regard titles as childish jokes; after all, any title is a joke in its way. Another name has now been endorsed: the Chief Committee for Political Education.

As this matter has already been decided, you must take this as nothing more than a personal remark. If the matter is not limited merely to a change of label, it is only to be welcomed.

If we succeed in drawing new people into cultural and educational work, it will not be just a change of title, and then we can reconcile ourselves to the "Soviet" weakness of sticking a label on every new undertaking and every new institution. If we succeed, we shall have achieved something more than ever before.

The link between education and our policy should be the chief inducement in making people join us in our cultural and educational work. A title may express something if there is a need for it, for along the whole line of our educational work we have to abandon the old standpoint that education should be non-political; we cannot conduct educational work in isolation from politics.

That idea has always predominated in bourgeois society. The very term "apolitical" or "non-political" education is a piece of bourgeois hypocrisy, nothing but humbuggery practised on the masses, 99 per cent of whom are humiliated and degraded by the rule of the church, private property and the like. That, in fact, is the way the bourgeoisie, still in the saddle in all bourgeois countries, is deceiving the masses.

The greater the importance of a political apparatus in such countries, the less its independence of capital and its policy.

In all bourgeois states the connection between the political apparatus and education is very strong, although bourgeois society cannot frankly acknowledge it. Nevertheless, this society indoctrinates the masses through the church and the institution of private property.

It is one of our basic tasks to contrapose our own truth to bourgeois "truth", and win its recognition.

The transition from bourgeois society to the policy of the proletariat is a very difficult one, all the more so for the bourgeoisie incessantly slandering us through its entire apparatus of propaganda and agitation. It bends every effort to play down an even more important mission of the dictatorship of the proletariat, its educational mission, which is particularly important in Russia, where the proletariat constitutes a minority of the population. Yet in Russia this mission must be given priority, for we must prepare the masses to build up socialism. The dictatorship of the proletariat would have been out of the question if, in the struggle against the bourgeoisie, the proletariat had not developed a keen class-consciousness, strict discipline and profound devotion, in other words, all the qualities required to assure the proletariat's complete victory over its old enemy.

We do not hold the utopian view that the working masses are ready for a socialist society. From precise facts provided by the entire history of working-class socialism we know that this is not the case, and that preparedness for socialism is created only by large-scale industry, by the strike struggle and by political organisation. To win the victory and accomplish the socialist revolution, the proletariat must be capable of concerted action, of overthrowing the exploiters. We now see that it has acquired all the necessary qualities, and that it translated them into action when it won power.

Education workers, and the Communist Party as the vanguard in the struggle, should consider it their fundamental task to help enlighten and instruct the working masses, in order to cast off the old ways and habituated routine we have inherited from the old system, the private property habits the masses are thoroughly imbued with. This fundamental task of the entire socialist revolution should never be neglected during consideration of the particular problems that have demanded so much attention from the Party's Central Committee and the Council of People's Commissars. What kind of structure should the Chief Committee for Political Education have? How should it be linked up with other institutions? How should it be linked up, not only with the centre but with local bodies? These questions will be answered by comrades who are more competent in the matter, have already gained considerable experience, and have made a special study of the matter. I would like merely to stress the main principles involved. We must put the matter frankly and openly affirm, despite all the old untruths, that education cannot but be linked up with politics.

We are living in an historic period of struggle against the world bourgeoisie, which is far stronger than we are. At this stage of the struggle, we have to safeguard the development of the revolution and combat the bourgeoisie in the military sense and still more by means of our ideology through education, so that the habits, usages and convictions acquired by the working class in the course of many decades of struggle for political liberty—the sum total of these habits, usages and ideas—should serve as an instrument for the education of all working people. It is for the proletariat to decide how the latter are to be educated. We must inculcate in the working people the realisation that it is impossible and inexcusable to stand aside in the proletariat's struggle, which is now spreading more and more to all capitalist countries in the world, and to stand aside in international politics. An alliance of all the world's powerful capitalist countries against Soviet Russia—such is the real basis of international politics today. And it must, after all, be realised that on this will depend the fate of hundreds of millions of working people in the capitalist countries. We know that, at the present moment, there is not a corner of the earth which is not under the control of a small group of capitalist countries. Thus the situation is shaping in such a way that one is faced with the alternative of standing aloof from the present struggle and thereby proving one's utter lack of political consciousness, just like those benighted people who have held aloof from the revolution and the war and do not see the bourgeoisie's gross deception of the masses, the deliberate way in which the bourgeoisie is keeping the masses in ignorance; or else of joining the struggle for the dictatorship of the proletariat.

It is with absolute frankness that we speak of this struggle of the proletariat; each man must choose between joining our side or the other side. Any attempt to avoid taking sides in this issue must end in fiasco.

Observation of the many remnants of the Kerensky gang, the Socialist-Revolutionaries and the Social-Democrats, as represented by the Yudeniches, Kolchaks, Petlyuras, Makhnos and others, has shown us such a variety of forms and shades of counter-revolution in various parts of Russia that we have every reason to consider ourselves far more steeled in the struggle than anybody else is. A glance at Western Europe shows the same thing happening there as in our country—a repetition of our own history. Almost everywhere elements similar to the Kerensky gang are to be met alongside the bourgeoisie. They predominate in a number of countries, especially Germany. One can see the same thing everywhere—the impossibility of taking an intermediate position, and a clear realisation that there must be either a whiteguard dictatorship (for which the bourgeoisie of all the countries of Western Europe are preparing by arming against us), or the dictatorship of the proletariat. We have experienced this so acutely and profoundly that there is no need for me to talk at length about the Russian Communists. Hence there can be only a single conclusion, one that should be the corner-stone of all arguments and theories about the Chief Committee for Political Education: the primacy of the Communist Party's policy must be frankly recognised in the work of that body. We know of no other form of guidance; and no other has been evolved in any country. Parties may represent the interests of their class in one degree or another; they may undergo changes or modifications, but we do not yet know of any better form. The entire course of the struggle waged by Soviet Russia, which for three years has withstood the onslaught of world imperialism, is bound up with the fact that the Party has consciously set out to help the proletariat perform its function of educator, organiser and leader, without which the collapse of capitalism is impossible. The working masses, the masses of peasants and workers, must oust the old intellectualist habits and re-educate themselves for the work of building communism. Otherwise the work of construction cannot be undertaken. Our entire experience shows that this is a very serious matter, and we must therefore give prominence to Party primacy and never lose sight of it when discussing our activities and our organisational development. How this is to be done will still have to be discussed at length; it will have to be discussed in the Party's Central Committee and in the Council of People's Commissars. The decree which was endorsed yesterday laid down the fundamentals in respect of the Chief Committee for Political Education, but it has not yet gone through all the stages in the Council of People's Commissars. The decree will be published within the next few days, and you will see that its final form makes no direct mention of relations with the Party.

We must, however, know and remember that, in law and in practice, the Constitution of the Soviet Republic is based on the tenet that the Party rectifies, prescribes and builds according to a single principle—to enable the communist elements linked with the proletariat to imbue the proletariat with their own spirit, win its adherence, and open its eyes to the bourgeois deceit which we have been trying so long to eliminate. The People's Commissariat of Education has gone through a long struggle; for a long time the teachers' organisation resisted the socialist revolution. Bourgeois prejudices have struck very deep root among the teachers. There has been a long struggle in the form of direct sabotage and of tenacious bourgeois prejudices, and we have to fight for the communist positions slowly, step by step and win them. The Chief Committee for Political Education, which is concerned with extramural education, the work of educating and enlightening the masses, is faced with the clear task of combining Party leadership with the effort to gain the adherence of, to imbue with its spirit and to animate with its initiative, this half-million strong army of teachers, this vast institution which is now in the service of the workers. Education workers—the teachers—were trained in the spirit of bourgeois prejudices and habits, in a spirit hostile to the proletariat, with which they have had no ties whatever. We must now train a new army of teachers and instructors who must be in close touch with the Party and its ideas, be imbued with its spirit, and attract the masses of workers, instilling the spirit of communism into them and arousing their interest in what is being done by the Communists.

Since the old customs, habits and ideas must be discarded, the Chief Committee for Political Education and its personnel are faced with a most important task, which they must keep uppermost in their minds. Here we indeed have a dilemma: how can we establish a link between the teachers, most of whom are of the old school, with Party members, with the Communists? That is an extremely difficult problem, one that will require a considerable amount of thought.

Let us consider the means of establishing organisational links between people who are so different. In principle, we cannot for a moment doubt the need of the Communist Party's primacy. Consequently, the purpose of political culture, of political instruction, is to train genuine Communists capable of stamping out falsehood and prejudices and helping the working masses to vanquish the old system and build up a state without capitalists, without exploiters, and without landowners. How can that be done? Only by acquiring the sum total of knowledge that the teachers have inherited from the bourgeoisie. Without this the technical achievements of communism will be impossible, and all hopes for those achievements would be pipe dreams. So the question arises: how are we to organise these people, who are not used to bringing politics into their work, especially the politics that is to our advantage, i.e., politics essential to communism? That, as I have said, is a very difficult problem. We have discussed the matter in the Central Committee, and in discussing it have tried to take into account the lessons of experience. We think that a congress like the one I am addressing today, a conference like yours, will be of great value in this respect. Every Party Committee now has to look from a new angle upon every propagandist, who used to be regarded merely as a man belonging to a definite circle, a definite organisation. Each of them belongs to a ruling party which directs the whole state, and the Soviet Russia's world struggle against the bourgeois system. He is a representative of a fighting class and of a party which runs, and must run, an enormous machine of state. Many a Communist who has been through the splendid school of underground work and has been tested and steeled in the struggle is unwilling or unable to understand the full significance of this change, of this transition, which turns the agitator and propagandist into a leader of agitators, a leader in a huge political organisation. The kind of title he is given, even if it is an embarrassing one—such as superintendent of general schools—does not matter much; what is important is that he should be capable of directing the mass of teachers.

It should be said that the hundreds of thousands of teachers constitute a body that must get the work moving, stimulate thought, and combat the prejudices that to this day still persist among the masses. The heritage of capitalist culture, the fact that the mass of the teachers are imbued with its defects, which prevent them from being Communists, should not deter us from admitting these teachers into the ranks of the political education workers, for these teachers possess the knowledge without which we cannot achieve our aim.

We must put hundreds of thousands of useful people to work in the service of communist education. That is a task that was accomplished at the front, in our Red Army, into which tens of thousands of representatives of the old army were incorporated. In the lengthy process of re-education, they became welded with the Red Army, as they ultimately proved by their victories. This is an example that we must follow in our cultural and educational work. True, this work is not so spectacular, but it is even more important. We need every agitator and propagandist; he will be doing his job if he works in a strictly Party spirit but at the same time does not limit himself to Party work, and remembers that it is his duty to direct hundreds of thousands of teachers, whet their interest, overcome their old bourgeois prejudices, enlist them in the work we are doing, and make them realise the immensity of our work. It is only by tackling that job that we can lead this mass of people, whom capitalism suppressed and drew away from us, along the right path.

Such are the aims that every agitator and propagandist working in the sphere of extra-mural education must pursue and constantly keep in sight. A host of practical difficulties will be encountered in the process, and you must help the cause of communism by becoming representatives and leaders, not only of Party study circles, but of the entire state administration, which is now in the hands of the working class.

We must overcome resistance from the capitalists in all its forms, not only in the military and the political spheres, but also ideological resistance, which is the most deep-seated and the strongest. It is the duty of our educational workers to accomplish the re-education of the masses. The interest, the thirst for education and knowledge of communism which are to be seen among them are a guarantee of our victory in this field too, although, perhaps, not as rapid as at the front and only after great difficulties and at times even reverses. However, we shall ultimately win.

Last, I should like to dwell on one more point. Perhaps the title of Chief Committee for Political Education is not properly understood. Inasmuch as it makes mention of the political concept, politics is the main thing here.

But how is politics to be understood? If politics is understood in the old sense, one may fall into a grave and profound error. Politics means a struggle between classes; means the relations of the proletariat in its struggle for its emancipation, against the world bourgeoisie. However, in our struggle two aspects of the matter stand out: on the one hand, there is the task of destroying the heritage of the bourgeois system, of foiling the repeated attempts of the whole bourgeoisie to crush the Soviet state. This task has absorbed most of our attention hitherto and has prevented us from proceeding to the other task, that of construction. According to the bourgeois world-outlook, politics was divorced, as it were, from economics. The bourgeoisie said: peasants, you must work for your livelihood; workers, you must work to secure your means of subsistence on the market; as for economic policy, that is the business of your masters. That, however, is not so; politics should be the business of the people, the business of the proletariat. Here we must emphasise the fact that nine-tenths of our time and our work is devoted to the struggle against the bourgeoisie. The victories over Wrangel, of which we read yesterday, and of which you will read today and probably tomorrow, show that one stage of the struggle is coming to an end and that we have secured peace with a number of Western countries; every victory on the war front leaves our hands freer for the internal struggle, for the politics of state organisation. Every step that brings us closer to victory over the whiteguards gradually shifts the focus of the struggle to economic policy. Propaganda of the old type describes and illustrates what communism is. This kind of propaganda is now useless, for we have to show in practice how socialism is to be built. All our propaganda must be based on the political experience of economic development. That is our principal task; whoever interprets it in the old sense will show himself to be a retrograde, one who is incapable of conducting propaganda work among the masses of the peasants and workers. Our main policy must now be to develop the state economically, so as to gather in more poods of grain and mine more poods of coal, to decide how best to utilise these poods of grain and coal and preclude starvation—that is our policy. All our agitation and propaganda must be focussed on this aim. There must be less fine talk, for you cannot satisfy the working people with fine words. As soon as the war enables us to shift the focus from the struggle against the bourgeoisie, from the struggle against Wrangel and the whiteguards, we shall turn to economic policy. And then agitation and propaganda will play a role of tremendous and ever growing importance.

Every agitator must be a state leader, a leader of all the peasants and workers in the work of economic development. He must tell them what one should know, what pamphlets and books one should read to become a Communist.

That is the way to improve our economic life and make it more secure, more social; that is the way to increase production, improve the food situation and distribution of the goods produced, increase coal output, and restore industry without capitalism and without the capitalist spirit.

What does communism consist in? All propaganda for communism must be conducted in a way that will amount to practical guidance of the state's development. Communism must be made comprehensible to the masses of the workers so that they will regard it as their own cause. That task is being poorly accomplished, and thousands of mistakes are being made. We make no secret of the fact. However, the workers and the peasants must themselves build up and improve our apparatus, with our assistance, feeble and inadequate as it is. To us, that is no longer a programme, a theory, or a task to be accomplished; it has become a matter of actual and practical development. Although we suffered some cruel reverses in our war, we have at least learnt from these reverses and won complete victory. Now, too, we must learn a lesson from every defeat and must remember that the workers and peasants have to be instructed by taking the work already performed as an example. We must point out what is bad, so as to avoid it in future.

By taking constructive work as an example, by repeating it time and again, we shall succeed in turning inefficient communist managers into genuine builders, and, in the first place, into builders of our economic life. We shall achieve our targets and overcome all the obstacles which we have inherited from the old system and cannot be eliminated at a single stroke. We must re-educate the masses; they can be re-educated only by agitation and propaganda. The masses must be brought, in the first place, into the work of building the entire economic life. That must be the principal and basic object in the work of each agitator and propagandist, and when he realises this, the success of his work will be assured. (*Loud applause.*)

TENTH CONGRESS OF THE R.C.P.(B.)[294]
MARCH 8-16, 1921

PRELIMINARY DRAFT RESOLUTION
OF THE TENTH CONGRESS OF THE R.C.P.
ON PARTY UNITY

1. The congress calls the attention of all members of the Party to the fact that the unity and cohesion of the ranks of the Party, the guarantee of complete mutual confidence among Party members and genuine team-work that really embodies the unanimity of will of the vanguard of the proletariat, are particularly essential at the present time, when a number of circumstances are increasing the vacillation among the petty-bourgeois population of the country.

2. Notwithstanding this, even before the general Party discussion on the trade unions, certain signs of factionalism had been apparent in the Party—the formation of groups with separate platforms, striving to a certain degree to segregate and create their own group discipline. Such symptoms of factionalism were manifested, for example, at a Party conference in Moscow (November 1920) and at a Party conference in Kharkov, by the so-called Workers' Opposition[295] group, and partly by the so-called Democratic Centralism[296] group.

All class-conscious workers must clearly realise that factionalism of any kind is harmful and impermissible, for no matter how members of individual groups may desire to safeguard Party unity, factionalism in practice inevitably leads to the weakening of team-work and to intensified and repeated attempts by the enemies of the governing Party, who have wormed their way into it, to widen the cleavage and to use it for counter-revolutionary purposes.

The way the enemies of the proletariat take advantage of every deviation from a thoroughly consistent communist line was perhaps most strikingly shown in the case of the Kronstadt mutiny,[297] when the bourgeois counter-revolutionaries and whiteguards in all countries of the world immediately expressed their readiness to accept the slogans of the Soviet system, if only they might thereby secure the overthrow of the dictatorship of the proletariat in

Russia, and when the Socialist-Revolutionaries and the bourgeois counter-revolutionaries in general resorted in Kronstadt to slogans calling for an insurrection against the Soviet Government of Russia ostensibly in the interest of the Soviet power. These facts fully prove that the whiteguards strive, and are able, to disguise themselves as Communists, and even as the most Left-wing Communists, solely for the purpose of weakening and destroying the bulwark of the proletarian revolution in Russia. Menshevik leaflets distributed in Petrograd on the eve of the Kronstadt mutiny likewise show how the Mensheviks took advantage of the disagreements and certain rudiments of factionalism in the Russian Communist Party actually in order to egg on and support the Kronstadt mutineers, the Socialist-Revolutionaries and the whiteguards, while claiming to be opponents of mutiny and supporters of the Soviet power, only with supposedly slight modifications.

3. In this question, propaganda should consist, on the one hand, in a comprehensive explanation of the harmfulness and danger of factionalism from the standpoint of Party unity and of achieving unanimity of will among the vanguard of the proletariat as the fundamental condition for the success of the dictatorship of the proletariat; and, on the other hand, in an explanation of the peculiar features of the latest tactical devices of the enemies of the Soviet power. These enemies, having realised the hopelessness of counter-revolution under an openly whiteguard flag, are now doing their utmost to utilise the disagreements within the Russian Communist Party and to further the counter-revolution in one way or another by transferring power to a political group which is outwardly closest to recognition of the Soviet power.

Propaganda must also teach the lessons of preceding revolutions, in which the counter-revolution made a point of supporting the opposition to the extreme revolutionary party which stood closest to the latter, in order to undermine and overthrow the revolutionary dictatorship and thus pave the way for the subsequent complete victory of the counter-revolution, of the capitalists and landowners.

4. In the practical struggle against factionalism, every organisation of the Party must take strict measures to prevent all factional actions. Criticism of the Party's shortcomings, which is absolutely necessary, must be conducted in such a way that every practical proposal shall be submitted immediately, without any delay, in the most precise form possible, for consideration and decision to the leading local and central bodies of the Party. Moreover, every critic must see to it that the form of his criticism takes account of the position of the Party, surrounded as it is by a ring of enemies, and that the content of his criticism is such that, by directly participating in Soviet and Party work, he can test the rectification

of the errors of the Party or of individual Party members in practice. Analyses of the Party's general line, estimates of its practical experience, check-ups of the fulfilment of its decisions, studies of methods of rectifying errors, etc., must under no circumstances be submitted for preliminary discussion to groups formed on the basis of "platforms", etc., but must in all cases be submitted for discussion directly to all the members of the Party. For this purpose, the congress orders a more regular publication of *Diskussionny Listok*[298] and special symposiums to promote unceasing efforts to ensure that criticism shall be concentrated on essentials and shall not assume a form capable of assisting the class enemies of the proletariat.

5. Rejecting in principle the deviation towards syndicalism and anarchism, which is examined in a special resolution,[299] and instructing the Central Committee to secure the complete elimination of all factionalism, the congress at the same time declares that every practical proposal concerning questions to which the so-called Workers' Opposition group, for example, has devoted special attention, such as purging the Party of non-proletarian and unreliable elements, combating bureaucratic practices, developing democracy and workers' initiative, etc., must be examined with the greatest care and tested in practice. The Party must know that we have not taken all the necessary measures in regard to these questions because of various obstacles, but that, while ruthlessly rejecting impractical and factional pseudo-criticism, the Party will unceasingly continue—trying out new methods—to fight with all the means at its disposal against the evils of bureaucracy, for the extension of democracy and initiative, for detecting, exposing and expelling from the Party elements that have wormed their way into its ranks, etc.

6. The congress, therefore, hereby declares dissolved and orders the immediate dissolution of all groups without exception formed on the basis of one platform or another (such as the Workers' Opposition group, the Democratic Centralism group, etc.). Non-observance of this decision of the congress shall entail unconditional and instant expulsion from the Party.

7. In order to ensure strict discipline within the Party and in all Soviet work and to secure the maximum unanimity in eliminating all factionalism, the congress authorises the Central Committee, in cases of breach of discipline or of a revival or toleration of factionalism, to apply all Party penalties, including expulsion, and in regard to members of the Central Committee, reduction to the status of alternate members and, as an extreme measure, expulsion from the Party. A necessary condition for the application of such an extreme measure to members of the Central Committee, alternate members of the Central Committee and members of the Control

Commission is the convocation of a Plenary Meeting of the Central Committee, to which all alternate members of the Central Committee and all members of the Control Commission shall be invited. If such a general assembly of the most responsible leaders of the Party deems it necessary by a two-thirds majority to reduce a member of the Central Committee to the status of alternate member, or to expel him from the Party, this measure shall be put into effect immediately.[300]

First published in 1923
in the magazine
Prozhektor No. 22

Collected Works, Vol. 32

TENTH ALL-RUSSIA CONFERENCE OF THE R.C.P.(B.)[301]
MAY 26-28, 1921

SPEECH IN CLOSING THE CONFERENCE
MAY 28

Comrades, I think that I can confine myself to a very short speech. As you are aware, we convened this special conference mainly for the purpose of achieving complete understanding on economic policy[302] between the centre and the localities, among Party and all Soviet workers. I think that the conference has fully achieved its object. Some speakers noted that Comrade Osinsky gave the correct expression to the feelings of very many, probably, the majority of local Party workers when he said that we must remove all doubt about the fact that the policy adopted by the Tenth Party Congress and subsequently reinforced by decrees and orders has unquestionably been accepted by the Party in earnest and for a long time. This is what the conference most emphatically expressed and amplified by a number of points. When the comrades return to their localities, not the slightest possibility of wrong interpretation will remain. Of course, in adopting a policy to be pursued over a number of years we do not for a moment forget that everything may be altered by the international revolution, its rate of development and the circumstances accompanying it. The current international situation is such that some sort of a temporary, unstable equilibrium, but equilibrium for all that, has been established; it is the kind of equilibrium under which the imperialist powers have been compelled to abandon their desire to hurl themselves at Soviet Russia, despite their hatred for her, because the disintegration of the capitalist world is steadily progressing, unity is steadily diminishing, while the onslaught of the forces of the oppressed colonies, which have a population of over a thousand million, is increasing from year to year, month to month, and even week to week. But we can make no conjectures on this score. We are now exercising our main influence on the international revolution through our economic policy. The working people of all countries without exception and without exaggeration are looking to the Soviet Russian Republic. This much has been achieved. The capitalists cannot hush up or conceal anything. That is why they so eagerly catch at our every economic mistake and weakness. The struggle in this field has now become global. Once we solve this problem, we shall have certainly and finally won on an international scale. That is why for us questions of economic development become of absolutely exceptional importance. On this front, we must achieve victory by a steady rise and progress which must be gradual and necessarily slow. I think that as a result of the work of our conference we shall certainly achieve this goal. (*Applause.*)

Published in *Pravda* No. 119,   *Collected Works*, Vol. 32
     June 2, 1921

THIRD CONGRESS OF THE COMMUNIST INTERNATIONAL[303]
JUNE 22-JULY 12, 1921

THESES FOR A REPORT ON THE TACTICS
OF THE R.C.P.

1. THE INTERNATIONAL POSITION OF THE R.S.F.S.R.

The international position of the R.S.F.S.R. at present is distinguished by a certain equilibrium, which, although extremely unstable, has nevertheless given rise to a peculiar state of affairs in world politics.

This peculiarity is the following. On the one hand, the international bourgeoisie is filled with furious hatred of, and hostility towards, Soviet Russia, and is prepared at any moment to fling itself upon her in order to strangle her. On the other hand, all attempts at military intervention, which have cost the international bourgeoisie hundreds of millions of francs, ended in complete failure, in spite of the fact that the Soviet power was then weaker than it is now and that the Russian landowners and capitalists had whole armies on the territory of the R.S.F.S.R. Opposition to the war against Soviet Russia has grown considerably in all capitalist countries, adding fuel to the revolutionary movement of the proletariat and extending to very wide sections of the petty-bourgeois democrats. The conflict of interests between the various imperialist countries has become acute, and is growing more acute every day. The revolutionary movement among the hundreds of millions of oppressed peoples of the East is growing with remarkable vigour. The result of all these conditions is that international imperialism has proved unable to strangle Soviet Russia, although it is far stronger, and has been obliged for the time being to grant her recognition, or semi-recognition, and to conclude trade agreements with her.

The result is a state of equilibrium which, although highly unstable and precarious, enables the Socialist Republic to exist—not for long, of course—within the capitalist encirclement.

2. THE INTERNATIONAL ALIGNMENT
OF CLASS FORCES

This state of affairs has given rise to the following international alignment of class forces.

The international bourgeoisie, deprived of the opportunity of waging open war against Soviet Russia, is waiting and watching for the moment when circumstances will permit it to resume the war.

The proletariat in all the advanced capitalist countries has already formed its vanguard, the Communist Parties, which are growing, making steady progress towards winning the majority of the proletariat in each country, and destroying the influence of the old trade union bureaucrats and of the upper stratum of the working class of America and Europe, which has been corrupted by imperialist privileges.

The petty-bourgeois democrats in the capitalist countries, whose foremost sections are represented by the Second and Two-and-a-Half Internationals,[304] serve today as the mainstay of capitalism, since they retain an influence over the majority, or a considerable section, of the industrial and commercial workers and office employees who are afraid that if revolution breaks out they will lose the relative petty-bourgeois prosperity created by the privileges of imperialism. But the growing economic crisis is worsening the condition of broad sections of the people everywhere, and this, with the looming inevitability of new imperialist wars if capitalism is preserved, is steadily weakening this mainstay.

The masses of the working people in the colonial and semi-colonial countries, who constitute the overwhelming majority of the population of the globe, were roused to political life at the turn of the twentieth century, particularly by the revolutions in Russia, Turkey, Persia and China. The imperialist war of 1914-18 and the Soviet power in Russia are completing the process of converting these masses into an active factor in world politics and in the revolutionary destruction of imperialism, although the educated philistines of Europe and America, including the leaders of the Second and Two-and-a-Half Internationals, stubbornly refuse to see this. British India is at the head of these countries, and there revolution is maturing in proportion, on the one hand, to the growth of the industrial and railway proletariat, and on the other, to the increase in the brutal terrorism of the British, who with ever greater frequency resort to massacres (Amritsar),[305] public floggings, etc.

3. THE ALIGNMENT OF CLASS FORCES IN RUSSIA

The internal political situation in Soviet Russia is determined by the fact that here, for the first time in history, there have been, for a number of years, only two classes—the proletariat, trained for decades by a very young, but modern, large-scale machine industry, and the small peasantry, who constitute the overwhelming majority of the population.

In Russia, the big landowners and capitalists have not vanished, but they have been subjected to total expropriation and crushed politically as a class, whose remnants are hiding out among Soviet government employees. They have preserved their class organisation abroad, as émigrés, numbering probably from 1,500,000 to 2,000,000 people, with over 50 daily newspapers of all bourgeois and "socialist" (i.e., petty-bourgeois) parties, the remnants of an army, and numerous connections with the international bourgeoisie. These émigrés are striving, with might and main, to destroy the Soviet power and restore capitalism in Russia.

4. THE PROLETARIAT AND THE PEASANTRY IN RUSSIA

This being the internal situation in Russia, the main task now confronting her proletariat, as the ruling class, is properly to determine and carry out the measures that are necessary to lead the peasantry, establish a firm alliance with them and achieve the transition, in a series of gradual stages, to large-scale, socialised, mechanised agriculture. This is a particularly difficult task in Russia, both because of her backwardness, and her extreme state of ruin as a result of seven years of imperialist and civil war. But apart from these specific circumstances, this is one of the most difficult tasks of socialist construction that will confront all capitalist countries, with, perhaps, the sole exception of Britain. However, even in regard to Britain it must not be forgotten that, while the small tenant farmers there constitute only a very small class, the percentage of workers and office employees who enjoy a petty-bourgeois standard of living is exceptionally high, due to the actual enslavement of hundreds of millions of people in Britain's colonial possessions.

Hence, from the standpoint of development of the world proletarian revolution as a single process, the epoch Russia is passing through is significant as a practical test and a verification of the policy of a proletariat in power towards the mass of the petty bourgeoisie.

5. THE MILITARY ALLIANCE BETWEEN THE PROLETARIAT AND THE PEASANTRY IN THE R.S.F.S.R.

The basis for proper relations between the proletariat and the peasantry in Soviet Russia was created in the period of 1917-21 when the invasion of the capitalists and landowners, supported by the whole world bourgeoisie and all the petty-bourgeois, democratic parties (Socialist-Revolutionaries and Mensheviks), caused the proletariat and the peasantry to form, sign and seal a military alliance to defend the Soviet power. Civil war is the most intense form of class struggle, but the more intense it is, the more rapidly its flames consume all petty-bourgeois illusions and prejudices, and the more clearly experience proves even to the most backward strata of the peasantry that only the dictatorship of the proletariat can save it, and that the Socialist-Revolutionaries and Mensheviks are in fact merely the servants of the landowners and capitalists.

But while the military alliance between the proletariat and the peasantry was—and had perforce to be—the primary form of their firm alliance, it could not have been maintained even for a few weeks without an economic alliance between the two classes. The peasants received from the workers' state all the land and were given protection against the landowners and the kulaks; the workers have been receiving from the peasants loans of food supplies until large-scale industry is restored.

6. THE TRANSITION TO PROPER ECONOMIC RELATIONS BETWEEN THE PROLETARIAT AND THE PEASANTRY

The alliance between the small peasants and the proletariat can become a correct and stable one from the socialist standpoint only when the complete restoration of transport and large-scale industry enables the proletariat to give the peasants, in exchange for food, all the goods they need for their own use and for the improvement of their farms. With the country in ruins, this could not possibly be achieved at once. The surplus appropriation system was the best measure available to the insufficiently organised state to maintain itself in the incredibly arduous war against the landowners. The crop failure and the fodder shortage in 1920 particularly increased the hardships of the peasantry, already severe enough, and made the immediate transition to the tax in kind imperative.

The moderate tax in kind will bring about a big improvement in the condition of the peasantry at once, and will at the same time stimulate them to enlarge crop areas and improve farming methods.

The tax in kind signifies a transition from the requisition of all the peasants' surplus grain to regular socialist exchange of products between industry and agriculture.

7. THE CONDITIONS UNDER WHICH THE SOVIET GOVERNMENT CAN PERMIT CAPITALISM AND CONCESSIONS, AND THE SIGNIFICANCE THEREOF

Naturally, the tax in kind means freedom for the peasant to dispose of his after-tax surplus at his own discretion. Since the state cannot provide the peasant with goods from socialist factories in exchange for all his surplus, freedom to trade with this surplus necessarily means freedom for the development of capitalism.

Within the limits indicated, however, this is not at all dangerous for socialism as long as transport and large-scale industry remain in the hands of the proletariat. On the contrary, the development of capitalism, controlled and regulated by the proletarian state (i.e., "state" capitalism in *this* sense of the term), is advantageous and necessary in an extremely devastated and backward small-peasant country (within certain limits, of course), inasmuch as it is capable of hastening the *immediate* revival of peasant farming. This applies still more to concessions: without denationalising anything, the workers' state leases certain mines, forest tracts, oilfields, and so forth, to foreign capitalists in order to obtain from them extra equipment and machinery that will enable us to accelerate the restoration of Soviet large-scale industry.

The payment made to the concessionaires in the form of a share of the highly valuable products obtained is undoubtedly tribute, which the workers' state pays to the world bourgeoisie; without in any way glossing this over, we must clearly realise that we stand to gain by paying this tribute, so long as it accelerates the restoration of our large-scale industry and substantially improves the condition of the workers and peasants.

8. THE SUCCESS OF OUR FOOD POLICY

The food policy pursued by Soviet Russia in 1917-21 was undoubtedly very crude and imperfect, and gave rise to many abuses. A number of mistakes were made in its implementation. But as a whole, it was the only possible policy under the conditions prevailing at the time. And it did fulfil its historic mission: it saved the proletarian dictatorship in a ruined and backward country. There can be no doubt that it has gradually improved. In the first year that we had full power (August 1, 1918 to August 1, 1919) the state collected 110 million poods of grain; in the second year it collected 220 million poods, and in the third year—over 285 million poods.

Now, having acquired practical experience, we have set out, and expect, to collect 400 million poods (the tax in kind is expected to bring in 240 million poods). Only when it is actually in possession of an adequate stock of food will the workers' state be able to stand firmly on its own feet economically, secure the steady, if slow, restoration of large-scale industry, and create a proper financial system.

9. THE MATERIAL BASIS OF SOCIALISM AND THE PLAN FOR THE ELECTRIFICATION OF RUSSIA

A large-scale machine industry capable of reorganising agriculture is the only material basis that is possible for socialism. But we cannot confine ourselves to this general thesis. It must be made more concrete. Large-scale industry based on the latest achievements of technology and capable of reorganising agriculture implies the electrification of the whole country. We had to undertake the scientific work of drawing up such a plan for the electrification of the R.S.F.S.R. and we have accomplished it. With the co-operation of over two hundred of the best scientists, engineers and agronomists in Russia, this work has now been completed; it was published in a large volume and, as a whole, endorsed by the Eighth All-Russia Congress of Soviets in December 1920. Arrangements have now been made to convene an all-Russia congress of electrical engineers in August 1921 to examine this plan in detail, before it is given final government endorsement.[306] The execution of the first part of the electrification scheme is estimated to take ten years, and will require about 370 million man-days.

In 1918, we had eight newly-erected power stations (with a total capacity of 4,757 kw); in 1919, the figure rose to 36 (total capacity of 1,648 kw), and in 1920, it rose to 100 (total capacity of 8,699 kw).

Modest as this beginning is for our vast country, a start has been made, work has begun and is making steady progress. After the imperialist war, after a million prisoners of war in Germany had become familiar with modern up-to-date technique, after the stern but hardening experience of three years of civil war, the Russian peasant is a different man. With every passing month he sees more clearly and more vividly that only the guidance given by the proletariat is capable of leading the mass of small farmers out of capitalist slavery to socialism.

10. THE ROLE OF "PURE DEMOCRACY", THE SECOND AND TWO-AND-A-HALF INTERNATIONALS, THE SOCIALIST-REVOLUTIONARIES AND THE MENSHEVIKS AS THE ALLIES OF CAPITAL

The dictatorship of the proletariat does not signify a cessation of the class struggle, but its continuation in a new form and with new weapons. This dictatorship is essential as long as classes exist, as long as the bourgeoisie, overthrown in one country, intensifies tenfold its attacks on socialism on an international scale. In the transition period, the small farmer class is bound to experience certain vacillations. The difficulties of transition, and the influence of the bourgeoisie, inevitably cause the mood of this mass to change from time to time. Upon the proletariat, enfeebled and to a certain extent declassed by the destruction of the large-scale machine industry, which is its vital foundation, devolves the very difficult but paramount historic task of holding out in spite of these vacillations, and of carrying to victory its cause of emancipating labour from the yoke of capital.

The policy pursued by the petty-bourgeois democratic parties, i.e., the parties affiliated to the Second and Two-and-a-Half Internationals, represented in Russia by the S.R. (Socialist-Revolutionary) and Menshevik parties, is the political expression of the vacillations of the petty bourgeoisie. These parties now have their headquarters and newspapers abroad, and are actually in a bloc with the whole of the bourgeois counter-revolution and are serving it loyally.

The shrewd leaders of the Russian big bourgeoisie headed by Milyukov, the leader of the Cadet (Constitutional-Democratic) Party, have quite clearly, definitely and openly appraised this role of the petty-bourgeois democrats, i.e., the Socialist-Revolutionaries and Mensheviks. In connection with the Kronstadt mutiny, in which the Mensheviks, Socialist-Revolutionaries and whiteguards joined forces, Milyukov declared in favour of the "Soviets without the Bolsheviks" slogan. Elaborating on the idea, he wrote that the Socialist-Revolutionaries and Mensheviks "are welcome to try" (*Pravda* No. 64, 1921, quoted from the Paris *Posledniye Novosti*[307]), because upon them devolves the task of *first taking* power away from the Bolsheviks. Milyukov, the leader of the big bourgeoisie, has correctly appraised the lesson taught by all revolutions, namely, that the petty-bourgeois democrats are incapable of holding power, and always serve merely as a screen for the dictatorship of the bourgeoisie, and a stepping stone to its undivided power.

The proletarian revolution in Russia again and again confirms this lesson of 1789-94 and 1848-49, and also what Frederick Engels said in his letter to Bebel of December 11, 1884.

... "Pure democracy ... when the moment of revolution comes, acquires a temporary importance ... as the final sheet-anchor of the whole bourgeois and even feudal economy.... Thus between March and September 1848 the whole feudal-bureaucratic mass strengthened the liberals in order to hold down the revolutionary masses.... In any case our sole adversary on the day of the crisis and on the day after the crisis will be the whole of the reaction which will group around pure democracy, and this, I think, should not be lost sight of." (Published in Russian in *Kommunisticheski Trud*[308] No. 360, June 9, 1921, in an article by Comrade V. Adoratsky: "Marx and Engels on Democracy". In German, published in the book, Friedrich Engels, *Politisches Vermächtnis*, Internationale Jugend-Bibliothek, Nr. 12, Berlin, 1920, S. 19.)

N. Lenin

Moscow, Kremlin, June 13, 1921

Published in pamphlet form in 1921 by the Comintern Press Department

Collected Works, Vol. 32

FOURTH ANNIVERSARY OF THE OCTOBER REVOLUTION

The fourth anniversary of October 25 (November 7) is approaching.

The farther that great day recedes from us, the more clearly we see the significance of the proletarian revolution in Russia, and the more deeply we reflect upon the practical experience of our work as a whole.

Very briefly and, of course, in very incomplete and rough outline, this significance and experience may be summed up as follows.

The direct and immediate object of the revolution in Russia was a bourgeois-democratic one, namely, to destroy the survivals of medievalism and sweep them away completely, to purge Russia of this barbarism, of this shame, and to remove this immense obstacle to all culture and progress in our country.

And we can justifiably pride ourselves on having carried out that purge with greater determination and much more rapidly, boldly and successfully, and, from the point of view of its effect on the masses, much more widely and deeply, than the great French Revolution over one hundred and twenty-five years ago.

Both the anarchists and the petty-bourgeois democrats (i.e., the Mensheviks and the Socialist-Revolutionaries, who are the Russian counterparts of that international social type) have talked and are still talking an incredible lot of nonsense about the relation between the bourgeois-democratic revolution and the socialist (*that is,* proletarian) revolution. The last four years have proved to the hilt that our interpretation of Marxism on this point, and our estimate of the experience of former revolutions were correct. We have *consummated* the bourgeois-democratic revolution as nobody had done before. We are *advancing* towards the socialist revolution consciously, firmly and unswervingly, knowing that it is not separated from the bourgeois-democratic revolution by a Chinese Wall, and knowing too that (in the last analysis) *struggle alone* will determine how far we shall advance, what part of this immense and lofty task we shall accomplish, and to what extent we shall succeed in consolidating our victories. Time will show. But we see even now that a tremendous amount—tremendous for this ruined, exhausted and backward country—has already been done towards the socialist transformation of society.

Let us, however, finish what we have to say about the bourgeois-democratic content of our revolution. Marxists must understand what that means. To explain, let us take a few striking examples.

The bourgeois-democratic content of the revolution means that the social relations (system, institutions) of the country are purged of medievalism, serfdom, feudalism.

What were the chief manifestations, survivals, remnants of serfdom in Russia up to 1917? The monarchy, the system of social estates, landed proprietorship and land tenure, the status of women, religion, and national oppression. Take any one of these Augean stables, which, incidentally, were left largely uncleansed by all the more advanced states when they accomplished *their* bourgeois-democratic revolutions one hundred and twenty-five, two hundred and fifty and more years ago (1649 in England); take any of these Augean stables, and you will see that we have cleansed them thoroughly. In a matter of *ten weeks*, from October 25 (November 7), 1917 to January 5, 1918, when the Constituent Assembly was dissolved, we accomplished a thousand times more in this respect than was accomplished by the bourgeois democrats and liberals (the Cadets) and by the petty-bourgeois democrats (the Mensheviks and the Socialist-Revolutionaries) *during the eight months* they were in power.

Those poltroons, gas-bags, vainglorious Narcissuses and petty Hamlets[309] brandished their wooden swords—but did not even destroy the monarchy! We cleansed out all that monarchist muck as nobody had ever done before. We left not a stone, not a brick of that ancient edifice, the social-estate system (even the most advanced countries, such as Britain, France and Germany, have not completely eliminated the survivals of that system to this day!), standing. We tore out the deep-seated roots of the social-estate system, namely, the remnants of feudalism and serfdom in the system of landownership, to the last. "One may argue" (there are plenty of quill-drivers, Cadets, Mensheviks and Socialist-Revolutionaries abroad to indulge in such arguments) as to what "in the long run" will be the outcome of the agrarian reform effected by the Great October Revolution. We have no desire at the moment to waste time on such controversies, for we are deciding this, as well as the mass of accompanying controversies, by struggle. But the fact cannot be denied that the petty-bourgeois democrats "compromised" with the landowners, the custodians of the traditions of serfdom, for eight months, while we completely swept the landowners and all their traditions from Russian soil in a few weeks.

Take religion, or the denial of rights to women, or the oppression and inequality of the non-Russian nationalities. These are all problems of the bourgeois-democratic revolution. The vulgar petty-bourgeois democrats talked about them for eight months. In not a *single* one of the most advanced countries in the world have *these* questions been *completely* settled on *bourgeois-democratic* lines. In our country they have been settled completely by the legislation of the October Revolution. We have fought and are fighting religion in earnest. We have granted *all* the non-Russian nationalities *their own* republics or autonomous regions. We in Russia no longer have the base, mean and infamous denial of rights to women or inequality of the sexes, that disgusting survival of feudalism and medievalism, which is being renovated by the avaricious bourgeoisie and the dull-witted and frightened petty bourgeoisie in every other country in the world without exception.

All this goes to make up the content of the bourgeois-democratic revolution. A hundred and fifty and two hundred and fifty years ago the progressive leaders of that revolution (or of those revolutions, if we consider each national variety of the one general type) promised to rid mankind of medieval privileges, of sex inequality, of state privileges for one religion or another (or "religious *ideas*", "the church" in general), and of national inequality. They promised, but did not keep their promises. They could not keep them, for they were hindered by their "respect"—for the "sacred right of private property". Our proletarian revolution was not afflicted with this accursed "respect" for this thrice-accursed medievalism and for the "sacred right of private property".

But in order to consolidate the achievements of the bourgeois-democratic revolution for the peoples of Russia, we were obliged to go farther; and we did go farther. We solved the problems of the bourgeois-democratic revolution in passing, as a "by-product" of our main and genuinely *proletarian*-revolutionary, socialist activities. We have always said that reforms are a by-product of the revolutionary class struggle. We said—and proved it by deeds— that bourgeois-democratic reforms are a by-product of the proletarian, i.e., of the socialist revolution. Incidentally, the Kautskys, Hilferdings, Martovs, Chernovs, Hillquits, Longuets, MacDonalds, Turatis and other heroes of "Two-and-a-Half" Marxism were incapable of understanding *this* relation between the bourgeois-democratic and the proletarian-socialist revolutions. The first develops into the second. The second, in passing, solves the problems of the first. The second consolidates the work of the first. Struggle, and struggle alone, decides how far the second succeeds in outgrowing the first.

The Soviet system is one of the most vivid proofs, or manifestations, of how the one revolution develops into the other. The Soviet system provides the maximum of democracy for the workers and peasants; at the same time, it marks a break with *bourgeois* democracy and the rise of a *new,* epoch-making *type* of democracy, namely, proletarian democracy, or the dictatorship of the proletariat.

Let the curs and swine of the moribund bourgeoisie and of the petty-bourgeois democrats who trail behind them heap imprecations, abuse and derision upon our heads for our reverses and mistakes in the work of building up *our* Soviet system. We do not forget for a moment that we have committed and are committing numerous mistakes and are suffering numerous reverses. How can reverses and mistakes be avoided in a matter so new in the history of the world as the building of an unprecedented *type* of state edifice! We shall work steadfastly to set our reverses and mistakes right and to improve our practical application of Soviet principles, which is still very, very far from being perfect. But we have a right to be and are proud that to us has fallen the good fortune to *begin* the building of a Soviet state, and thereby to *usher in* a new era in world history, the era of the rule of a *new* class, a class which is oppressed in every capitalist country, but which everywhere is marching forward towards a new life, towards victory over the bourgeoisie, towards the dictatorship of the proletariat, towards the emancipation of mankind from the yoke of capital and from imperialist wars.

The question of imperialist wars, of the international policy of finance capital which now dominates the whole world, a policy that must *inevitably* engender new imperialist wars, that must inevitably cause an extreme intensification of national oppression, pillage, brigandry and the strangulation of weak, backward and small nationalities by a handful of "advanced" powers—that question has been the keystone of all policy in all the countries of the globe since 1914. It is a question of life and death for millions upon millions of people. It is a question of whether 20,000,000 people (as compared with the 10,000,000 who were killed in the war of 1914-18 and in the supplementary "minor" wars that are still going on) are to be slaughtered in the next imperialist war, which the bourgeoisie are preparing, and which is growing out of capitalism before our very eyes. It is a question of whether in that future war, which is inevitable (if capitalism continues to exist), 60,000,000 people are to be maimed (compared with the 30,000,000 maimed in 1914-18). In this question, too, our October Revolution marked the beginning of a new era in world history. The lackeys of the bourgeoisie and its yes-men—the Socialist-Revolutionaries and the Mensheviks, and the petty-bourgeois, allegedly "socialist", democrats all over the world—derided our slogan "convert the imperialist war into a civil war". But that slogan proved to be the *truth*—it was the only truth, unpleasant, blunt, naked and brutal, but nevertheless the *truth,* as against the host of most refined jingoist and pacifist lies. Those lies are being dispelled. The Brest peace has been exposed. And with every passing day the significance and consequences of a peace that is even worse than the Brest peace—the peace of Versailles—are being more relentlessly exposed. And the millions who are thinking about the causes of the recent war and of the approaching future was are more and more clearly realising the grim and inexorable truth that it is impossible to escape imperialist war, and imperialist peace (if the old orthography were still in use, I would have written the word *mir* in two ways, to give it both its meanings)* which inevitably engenders imperialist war, that it is impossible to escape that inferno, *except by a Bolshevik struggle and a Bolshevik revolution.*

Let the bourgeoisie and the pacifists, the generals and the petty bourgeoisie, the capitalists and the philistines, the pious Christians and the knights of the Second and the Two-and-a-Half Internationals vent their fury against that revolution. No torrents of abuse, calumnies and lies can enable them to conceal the historic fact that for the first time in hundreds and thousands of years the slaves have replied to a war between slave-owners by openly proclaiming the slogan: "Convert this war between slave-owners for the division of their loot into a war of the slaves of all nations against the slave-owners of all nations."

For the first time in hundreds and thousands of years that slogan has grown from a vague and helpless waiting into a clear and definite political programme, into an effective struggle waged by millions of oppressed people under the leadership of the proletariat; it has grown into the first victory of the proletariat, the first victory in the struggle to abolish war and to unite the workers of all countries against the united bourgeoisie of different nations, against the bourgeoisie that makes peace and war at the expense of the slaves of capital, the wage-workers, the peasants, the working people.

This first victory is *not yet the final victory,* and it was achieved by our October Revolution at the price of incredible difficulties and hardships, at the price of unprecedented suffering, accompanied by a series of serious reverses and mistakes on our part. How could a single backward people be expected to frustrate the imperialist wars of the most powerful and most developed countries

---

* In Russian, the word *mir* has two meanings (*world* and *peace*) and had two different spellings in the old orthography.—*Ed.*

of the world without sustaining reverses and without committing mistakes! We are not afraid to admit our mistakes and shall examine them dispassionately in order to learn how to correct them. But the fact remains that for the first time in hundreds and thousands of years the promise "to reply" to war between the slave-owners by a revolution of the slaves directed *against* all the slave-owners *has been completely fulfilled*—and is being fulfilled despite all difficulties.

We have made the start. When, at what date and time, and the proletarians of which nation will complete this process is not important. The important thing is that the ice has been broken; the road is open, the way has been shown.

Gentlemen, capitalists of all countries, keep up your hypocritical pretence of "defending the fatherland"—the Japanese fatherland against the American, the American against the Japanese, the French against the British, and so forth! Gentlemen, knights of the Second and Two-and-a-Half Internationals, pacifist petty bourgeoisie and philistines of the entire world, go on "evading" the question of how to combat imperialist wars by issuing new "Basle Manifestos" (on the model of the Basle Manifesto of 1912). *The first Bolshevik revolution* has wrested *the first hundred million people* of this earth from the clutches of imperialist war and the imperialist world. Subsequent revolutions will deliver the rest of mankind from such wars and from such a world.

Our last, but most important and most difficult task, the one we have done least about, is economic development, the laying of economic foundations for the new, socialist edifice on the site of the demolished feudal edifice and the semi-demolished capitalist edifice. It is in this most important and most difficult task that we have sustained the greatest number of reverses and have made most mistakes. How could anyone expect that a task so new to the world could be begun without reverses and without mistakes! But we have begun it. We shall continue it. At this very moment we are, by our New Economic Policy, correcting a number of our mistakes. We are learning how to continue erecting the socialist edifice in a small-peasant country without committing such mistakes.

The difficulties are immense. But we are accustomed to grappling with immense difficulties. Not for nothing do our enemies call us "stone-hard" and exponents of a "firm-line policy". But we have also learned, at least to some extent, another art that is essential in revolution, namely, flexibility, the ability to effect swift and sudden changes of tactics if changes in objective conditions demand them, and to choose another path for the achievement of our goal if the former path proves to be inexpedient or impossible at the given moment.

Borne along on the crest of the wave of enthusiasm, rousing first the political enthusiasm and then the military enthusiasm of the people, we expected to accomplish economic tasks just as great as the political and military tasks we had accomplished by relying directly on this enthusiasm. We expected—or perhaps it would be truer to say that we presumed without having given it adequate consideration—to be able to organise the state production and the state distribution of products on communist lines in a small-peasant country directly as ordered by the proletarian state. Experience has proved that we were wrong. It appears that a number of transitional stages were necessary—state capitalism and socialism—in order to *prepare*—to prepare by many years of effort —for the transition to communism. Not directly relying on enthusiasm, but aided by the enthusiasm engendered by the great revolution, and on the basis of personal interest, personal incentive and business principles, we must first set to work in this small-peasant country to build solid gangways to socialism by way of state capitalism. Otherwise we shall never get to communism, we shall never bring scores of millions of people to communism. That is what experience, the objective course of the development of the revolution, has taught us.

And we, who during these three or four years have learned a little to make abrupt changes of front (when abrupt changes of front are needed), have begun zealously, attentively and sedulously (although still not zealously, attentively and sedulously enough) to learn to make a new change of front, namely, the New Economic Policy. The proletarian state must become a cautious, assiduous and shrewd "businessman", a punctilious *wholesale merchant*— otherwise it will never succeed in putting this small-peasant country economically on its feet. Under existing conditions, living as we are side by side with the capitalist (for the time being capitalist) West, there is no other way of progressing to communism. A wholesale merchant seems to be an economic type as remote from communism as heaven from earth. But that is one of the contradictions which, in actual life, lead from a small-peasant economy via state capitalism to socialism. Personal incentive will step up production; we must increase production first and foremost and at all costs. Wholesale trade economically unites millions of small peasants: it gives them a personal incentive, links them up and leads them to the next step, namely, to various forms of association and alliance in the process of production itself. We have already started the necessary changes in our economic policy and already have some successes to our credit; true, they are small and partial, but nonetheless they are successes. In this new field of "tuition" we are already finishing our preparatory class. By persistent and assiduous study, by making practical experience the test of every step we take, by not fearing to alter over and over again what we have already begun, by correcting our mistakes and most carefully analysing their significance, we shall pass to the higher classes. We shall go through the whole "course", although the present state of world economics and world politics has made that course much longer and much more difficult than we would have liked. No matter at what cost, no matter how severe the hardships of the transition period may be—despite disaster, famine and ruin—we shall not flinch; we shall triumphantly carry our cause to its goal.

October 14, 1921

Pravda No. 234,
October 18, 1921
Signed: *N. Lenin*

Collected Works, Vol. 33

THE IMPORTANCE OF GOLD NOW
AND AFTER THE COMPLETE VICTORY OF SOCIALISM

The best way to celebrate the anniversary of a great revolution is to concentrate attention on its unsolved problems. It is particularly appropriate and necessary to celebrate the revolution in this way at a time when we are faced with fundamental problems that the revolution has not yet solved, and when we must master something new (from the point of view of what the revolution has accomplished up to now) for the solution of these problems.

What is new for our revolution at the present time is the need for a "reformist", gradual, cautious and round-about approach to the solution of the fundamental problems of economic development. This "novelty" gives rise to a number of questions, perplexities and doubts in both theory and practice.

A theoretical question. How can we explain the transition from a series of extremely revolutionary actions to extremely "reformist" actions in the same field at a time when the revolution as a whole is making victorious progress? Does it not imply a "surrender of positions", an "admission of defeat", or something of that sort? Of course, our enemies—from the semi-feudal type of reactionaries to the Mensheviks or other knights of the Two-and-a-Half International—say that it does. They would not be enemies if they did not shout something of the sort on every pretext, and even without any pretext. The touching unanimity that prevails on this question among all parties, from the feudal reactionaries to the Mensheviks, is only further proof that all these parties constitute "one reactionary mass" opposed to the proletarian revolution (as Engels foresaw in his letters to Bebel of 1875 and 1884—be it said in parenthesis).

But there is "perplexity", shall we say, among friends, too.

Restore large-scale industry, organise the direct exchange of its goods for the produce of small-peasant farming, and thus assist the socialisation of the latter. For the purpose of restoring large-scale industry, borrow from the peasants a certain quantity of foodstuffs and raw materials by requisitioning—this was the plan (or method, system) that we followed for more than three years, up to the spring of 1921. This was a revolutionary approach to the problem—to break up the old social-economic system completely at one stroke and to substitute a new one for it.

Since the spring of 1921, instead of this approach, plan, method, or mode of action, we have been adopting (we have not yet "adopted" but are still "adopting", and have not yet fully realised it) a totally different method, a reformist type of method: not to *break up* the old social-economic system—trade, petty production, petty proprietorship, capitalism—but to *revive* trade, petty proprietorship, capitalism, while cautiously and gradually getting the upper hand over them, or making it possible to subject them to state regulation *only to the extent* that they revive.

That is an entirely different approach to the problem.

Compared with the previous, revolutionary, approach, it is a reformist approach (revolution is a change which breaks the old order to its very foundations, and not one that cautiously, slowly and gradually remodels it, taking care to break as little as possible).

The question that arises is this. If, after trying revolutionary methods, you find they have failed and adopt reformist methods, does it not prove that you are declaring the revolution to have been a mistake in general? Does it not prove that you should not have started with the revolution but should have started with reforms and confined yourselves to them?

That is the conclusion which the Mensheviks and others like them have drawn. But this conclusion is either sophistry, a mere fraud perpetrated by case-hardened politicians, or it is the childishness of political tyros. The greatest, perhaps the only danger to the genuine revolutionary is that of exaggerated revolutionism, ignoring the limits and conditions in which revolutionary methods are appropriate and can be successfully employed. True revolutionaries have mostly come a cropper when they began to write "revolution" with a capital R, to elevate "revolution" to something almost divine, to lose their heads, to lose the ability to reflect, weigh and ascertain in the coolest and most dispassionate manner at what moment, under what circumstances and in which sphere of action you must act in a revolutionary manner, and at what moment, under what circumstances and in which sphere you must turn to reformist action. True revolutionaries will perish (not that they will be defeated from outside, but that their work will suffer internal collapse) only if they abandon their sober outlook and take it into their heads that the "great, victorious, world" revolution can and must solve all problems in a revolutionary manner under all circumstances and in all spheres of action. If they do this, their doom is certain.

Whoever gets such ideas into his head is lost because he has foolish ideas about a fundamental problem; and in a fierce war (and revolution is the fiercest sort of war) the penalty for folly is defeat.

What grounds are there for assuming that the "great, victorious, world" revolution can and must employ only revolutionary methods? There are none at all. The assumption is a pure fallacy; this can be proved by purely theoretical propositions if we stick to Marxism. The experience of our revolution also shows that it is a fallacy. From the theoretical point of view—foolish things are done in time of revolution just as at any other time, said Engels,[310] and he was right. We must try to do as few foolish things as possible, and rectify those that are done as quickly as possible, and we must, as soberly as we can, estimate which problems can be solved by revolutionary methods at any given time and which cannot. From the point of view of our practical experience the Brest peace was an example of action that was not revolutionary at all; it was reformist, and even worse, because it was a retreat, whereas, as a general rule, reformist action advances slowly, cautiously, gradually, and does not move backward. The proof that our tactics in concluding the Brest peace were correct is now so complete, so obvious to all and generally admitted, that there is no need to say any more about it.

Our revolution has completed only its bourgeois-democratic work; and we have every right to be proud of this. The proletarian or socialist part of its work may be summed up in three main points: (1) The revolutionary withdrawal from the imperialist world war; the exposure and *halting* of the slaughter organised by the two world groups of capitalist predators—for our part we have done this in full; others could have done it only if there had been a revolution in a number of advanced countries. (2) The establishment of the Soviet system, as a form of the dictatorship of the proletariat. An epoch-making change has been made. The era of bourgeois-democratic parliamentarism has come to an end. A new chapter in world history—the era of proletarian dictatorship—has been opened. The Soviet system and all forms of proletarian dictatorship will have the finishing touches put to them and be completed only by the efforts of a number of countries. There is still a great deal we have not done in this field. It would be unpardonable to lose sight of this. Again and again we shall have to improve the work, redo it, start from the beginning. Every step onward and upward that we take in developing our productive forces and our culture must be accompanied by the work of improving and altering our Soviet system—we are still low in the scale of economics and culture. Much will have to be altered, and to be "embarrassed" by this would be absurd (if not worse). (3) The creation of the economic basis of the socialist system; the main features of what is most important, most fundamental, have not yet been completed. This, however, is our soundest basis, soundest from the point of view of principle and from the practical point of view, from the point of view of the R.S.F.S.R. today and from the international point of view.

Since the main features of this basis have not yet been completed we must concentrate all our attention upon it. The difficulty here lies in the form of the transition.

In April 1918, in my *Immediate Tasks of the Soviet Government,* I wrote:

"It is not enough to be a revolutionary and an adherent of socialism or a Communist in general. You must be able at each particular moment to find the particular link in the chain which you must grasp with all your might in order to hold the whole chain and to prepare firmly for the transition to the next link; the order of the links, their form, the manner in which they are linked together, their difference from each other in the historical chain of events are not as simple and not as senseless as those in an ordinary chain made by a smith."*

At the present time, in the sphere of activity with which we are dealing, this link is the revival of home *trade* under proper state regulation (direction). Trade is the "link" in the historical chain of events, in the transitional forms of our socialist construction in 1921-22, which we, the proletarian government, we, the ruling Communist Party, "*must grasp with a l l our might*". If we "grasp" this link firmly enough *now* we shall certainly control the *whole* chain in the very near future. If we do not, we shall not control the whole chain, we shall not create the foundation for socialist social and economic relations.

Communism and trade?! It sounds strange. The two seem to be unconnected, incongruous, poles apart. But if we study it from the point of view of *economics,* we shall find that the one is no more remote from the other than communism is from small-peasant, patriarchal farming.

When we are victorious on a world scale I think we shall use gold for the purpose of building public lavatories in the streets of some of the largest cities of the world. This would be the most "just" and most educational way of utilising gold for the benefit of those generations which have not forgotten how, for the sake of gold, ten million men were killed and thirty million maimed in the "great war for freedom", the war of 1914-18, the war that was waged to decide the great question of which peace was the worst, that of Brest or that of Versailles; and how, for the sake of this same gold, they certainly intend to kill twenty million men and to maim sixty million in a war, say, in 1925, or 1928, between, say,

---

* See pp. 427-29 of the present volume.—*Ed.*

Japan and the U.S.A., or between Britain and the U.S.A., or something like that.

But however "just", useful, or humane it would be to utilise gold for this purpose, we nevertheless say that we must work for another decade or two with the same intensity and with the same success as in the 1917-21 period, only in a much wider field, in order to reach this stage. Meanwhile, we must save the gold in the R.S.F.S.R., sell it at the highest price, buy goods with it at the lowest price. When you live among wolves, you must howl like a wolf, while as for exterminating all the wolves, as should be done in a rational human society, we shall act up to the wise Russian proverb: "Boast not before but after the battle."

Trade is the only possible economic link between the scores of millions of small farmers and large-scale industry if ... if there is not alongside these farmers an excellently equipped large-scale machine industry with a network of power transmission lines, an industry whose technical equipment, organisational "superstructures" and other features are sufficient of enable it to supply the small farmers with the best goods in larger quantities, more quickly and more cheaply than before. On a world scale this "if" *has already been achieved,* this condition already exists. But the country, formerly one of the most backward capitalist countries, which tried alone directly and at one stroke to create, to put into use, to organise practically the *new* links between industry and agriculture, failed to achieve this task by "direct assault", and must now try to achieve it by a number of slow, gradual, and cautious "siege" operations.

The proletarian government can control trade, direct it into definite channels, keep it within certain limits. I shall give a small, a very small example. In the Donets Basin a slight, still very slight, but undoubted revival in the economy has commenced, partly due to a rise in the productivity of labour at the large state mines, and partly due to the leasing of small mines to peasants. As a result, the proletarian government is receiving a small additional quantity (a miserably small quantity compared with what is obtained in the advanced countries, but an appreciable quantity considering our poverty-stricken condition) of coal at a cost of, say, 100; and it is selling this coal to various government departments at a price of, say, 120, and to private individuals at a price of, say, 140. (I must say in parenthesis that my figures are quite arbitrary, first because I do not know the exact figures, and, secondly, I would not now make them public even if I did.) This looks as if we are *beginning,* if only in very modest dimensions, to control *exchange* between industry and agriculture, to control wholesale trade, to cope with the task of taking in hand the available, small, backward industry, or large-scale but weakened and ruined industry; of reviving trade on the *present* economic basis; of making the ordinary middle peasant (and that is the typical peasant, the peasant in the mass, the true representative of the petty-bourgeois milieu) feel the benefit of the economic revival; of taking advantage of it for the purpose of more systematically and persistently, more widely and successfully restoring large-scale industry.

We shall not surrender to "sentimental socialism", or to the old Russian, semi-aristocratic, semi-muzhik and patriarchal mood, with their supreme contempt for trade. We can use, and, since it is necessary, we *must* learn to use, all transitional economic forms for the purpose of strengthening the link between the peasantry and the proletariat, for the purpose of immediately reviving the economy of our ruined and tormented country, of improving industry, and facilitating such future, more extensive and more deepgoing, measures as electrification.

Marxism alone has precisely and correctly defined the relation of reforms to revolution, although Marx was able to see this relation only from one aspect—under the conditions preceding the first to any extent permanent and lasting victory of the proletariat, if only in one country. Under those conditions, the basis of the proper relation was that reforms are a by-product of the revolutionary class struggle of the proletariat. Throughout the capitalist world this relation is the foundation of the revolutionary tactics of the proletariat—the ABC, which is being distorted and obscured by the corrupt leaders of the Second International and the half-pedantic and half-finicky knights of the Two-and-a-Half International. After the victory of the proletariat, if only in one country, something new enters into the relation between reforms and revolution. In principle, it is the same as before, but a change in form takes place, which Marx himself could not foresee, but which can be appreciated only on the basis of the philosophy and politics of Marxism. Why were we able to carry out the Brest retreat successfully? Because we had advanced so far that we had room in which to retreat. At such dizzy speed, *in a few weeks,* from October 25, 1917, to the Brest peace, we built up the Soviet state, withdrew from the imperialist war in a revolutionary manner and completed the bourgeois-democratic revolution so that *even* the great backward movement (the Brest peace) left us sufficient room in which to take advantage of the "respite" and to march forward victoriously against Kolchak, Denikin, Yudenich, Pilsudski and Wrangel.

Before the victory of the proletariat, reforms are a by-product of the revolutionary class struggle. After the victory (while still remaining a "by-product" on an international scale) they are, in addition, for the country in which victory has been achieved, a necessary and legitimate breathing space when, after the utmost exertion of effort, it becomes obvious that sufficient strength is lacking for the revolutionary accomplishment of some transition or another. Victory creates such a "reserve of strength" that it is possible to hold out even in a forced retreat, hold out both materially and morally. Holding out materially means preserving a sufficient superiority of forces to prevent the enemy from inflicting utter defeat. Holding out morally means not allowing oneself to become demoralised and disorganised, keeping a sober view of the situation, preserving vigour and firmness of spirit, even retreating a long way, but not too far, and in such a way as to stop the retreat in time and revert to the offensive.

We retreated to state capitalism, but we did not retreat too far. We are now retreating to the state regulation of trade, but we shall not retreat too far. There are visible signs that the retreat is coming to an end; there are signs that we shall be able to stop this retreat in the not too distant future. The more conscious, the more unanimous, the more free from prejudice we are in carrying out this necessary retreat, the sooner shall we be able to stop it, and the more lasting, speedy and extensive will be our subsequent victorious advance.

November 5, 1921

Pravda No. 251,
November 6-7, 1921
Signed: *N. Lenin*

Collected Works, Vol. 33

ON THE SIGNIFICANCE OF MILITANT MATERIALISM[311]

Comrade Trotsky has already said everything necessary, and said it very well, about the general purposes of *Pod Znamenem Marksizma* in issue No. 1-2 of that journal. I should like to deal with certain questions that more closely define the content and programme of the work which its editors have set forth in the introductory statement in this issue.

This statement says that not all those gathered round the journal *Pod Znamenem Marksizma* are Communists but that they are all consistent materialists. I think that this alliance of Communists and non-Communists is absolutely essential and correctly defines the purposes of the journal. One of the biggest and most dangerous mistakes made by Communists (as generally by revolutionaries who have successfully accomplished the beginning of a great revolution) is the idea that a revolution can be made by revolutionaries alone. On the contrary, to be successful, all serious revolutionary work requires that the idea that revolutionaries are capable of playing the part only of the vanguard of the truly virile and advanced class must be understood and translated into action. A vanguard performs its task as vanguard only when it is able to avoid being isolated from the mass of the people it leads and is able really to lead the whole mass forward. Without an alliance with non-Communists in the most diverse spheres of activity there can be no question of any successful communist construction.

This also applies to the defence of materialism and Marxism, which has been undertaken by *Pod Znamenem Marksizma*. Fortunately, the main trends of advanced social thinking in Russia have a solid materialist tradition. Apart from G. V. Plekhanov, it will be enough to mention Chernyshevsky, from whom the modern Narodniks (the Popular Socialists,[312] Socialist-Revolutionaries, etc.) have frequently retreated in quest of fashionable reactionary philosophical doctrines, captivated by the tinsel of the so-called last word in European science, and unable to discern beneath this tinsel some variety of servility to the bourgeoisie, to bourgeois prejudice and bourgeois reaction.

At any rate, in Russia we still have—and shall undoubtedly have for a fairly long time to come—materialists from the non-communist camp, and it is our absolute duty to enlist all adherents of consistent and militant materialism in the joint work of combating philosophical reaction and the philosophical prejudices of so-called educated society. Dietzgen senior—not to be confused with his writer son, who was as pretentious as he was unsuccessful—correctly, aptly and clearly expressed the fundamental Marxist view of the philosophical trends which prevail in bourgeois countries and enjoy the regard of their scientists and publicists, when he said that in effect the professors of philosophy in modern society are in the majority of cases nothing but "graduated flunkeys of clericalism".

Our Russian intellectuals, who, like their brethren in all other countries, are fond of thinking themselves advanced, are very much averse to shifting the question to the level of the opinion expressed in Dietzgen's words. But they are averse to it because they cannot look the truth in the face. One has only to give a little thought to the governmental and also the general economic, social and every other kind of dependence of modern educated people on the ruling bourgeoisie to realise that Dietzgen's scathing description was absolutely true. One has only to recall the vast majority of the fashionable philosophical trends that arise so frequently in European countries, beginning for example with those connected with the discovery of radium and ending with those which are now seeking to clutch at the skirts of Einstein, to gain an idea of the connection between the class interests and the class position of the bourgeoisie and its support of all forms of religion on the one hand, and the ideological content of the fashionable philosophical trends on the other.

It will be seen from the above that a journal that sets out to be a militant materialist organ must be primarily a militant organ, in the sense of unflinchingly exposing and indicting all modern "graduated flunkeys of clericalism", irrespective of whether they act as representatives of official science or as free lances calling themselves "democratic Left or ideologically socialist" publicists.

In the second place, such a journal must be a militant atheist organ. We have departments, or at least state institutions, which are in charge of this work. But the work is being carried on with extreme apathy and very unsatisfactorily, and is apparently suffering from the general conditions of our truly Russian (even though Soviet) bureaucratic ways. It is therefore highly essential that in addition to the work of these state institutions, and in order to improve and infuse life into that work, a journal which sets out to propagandise militant materialism must carry on untiring atheist propaganda and an untiring atheist fight. The literature on the subject in all languages should be carefully followed and everything at all valuable in this sphere should be translated, or at least reviewed.

Engels long ago advised the contemporary leaders of the proletariat to translate the militant atheist literature of the late eighteenth century[313] for mass distribution among the people. We have not done this up to the present, to our shame be it said (this is one of the numerous proofs that it is much easier to seize power in a revolutionary epoch than to know how to use this power properly). Our apathy, inactivity and incompetence are sometimes excused on all sorts of "lofty" grounds, as, for example, that the old atheist literature of the eighteenth century is antiquated, unscientific, naïve, etc. There is nothing worse than such pseudo-scientific sophistry, which serves as a screen either for pedantry or for a complete misunderstanding of Marxism. There is, of course, much that is unscientific and naïve in the atheist writings of the eighteenth century revolutionaries. But nobody prevents the publishers of these writings from abridging them and providing them with brief postscripts pointing out the progress made by mankind in the scientific criticism of religions since the end of the eighteenth century, mentioning the latest writings on the subject, and so forth. It would be the biggest and most grievous mistake a Marxist could make to think that the millions of the people (especially the peasants and artisans), who have been condemned by all modern society to darkness, ignorance and superstition, can extricate themselves from this darkness only along the straight line of a purely Marxist education. These masses should be supplied with the most varied atheist propaganda material, they should be made familiar with facts from the most diverse spheres of life, they should be approached in every possible way, so as to interest them, rouse them from their religious torpor, stir them from the most varied angles and by the most varied methods, and so forth.

The keen, vivacious and talented writings of the old eighteenth-century atheists wittily and openly attacked the prevailing clericalism and will very often prove a thousand times more suitable for arousing people from their religious torpor than the dull and dry paraphrases of Marxism, almost completely unillustrated by skilfully selected facts, which predominate in our literature and which (it is no use hiding the fact) frequently distort Marxism. We have translations of all the major works of Marx and Engels. There are absolutely no grounds for fearing that the old atheism and old materialism will remain unsupplemented by the corrections introduced by Marx and Engels. The most important thing—and it is this that is most frequently overlooked by those of our Communists who are supposedly Marxists, but who in fact mutilate Marxism—is to know how to awaken in the still undeveloped masses an intelligent attitude towards religous questions and an intelligent criticism of religions.

On the other hand, take a glance at modern scientific critics of religion. These educated bourgeois writers almost invariably "supplement" their own refutations of religious superstitions with arguments which immediately expose them as ideological slaves of the bourgeoisie, as "graduated flunkeys of clericalism".

Two examples. Professor R. Y. Wipper published in 1918 a little book entitled *Vozniknovenie Khristianstva* (The Origin of Christianity—Pharos Publishing House, Moscow). In his account of the principal results of modern science, the author not only refrains from combating the superstitions and deception which are the weapons of the church as a political organisation, not only evades these questions, but makes the simply ridiculous and most reactionary claim that he is above both "extremes"—the idealist and the materialist. This is toadying to the ruling bourgeoisie, which all over the world devotes to the support of religion hundreds of millions of rubles from the profits squeezed out of the working people.

The well-known German scientist, Arthur Drews, while refuting religious superstitions and fables in his book, *Die Christusmythe* (The Christ Myth), and while showing that Christ never existed, at the end of the book declares in favour of religion, albeit a renovated, purified and more subtle religion, one that would be capable of withstanding "the daily growing naturalist torrent" (fourth German edition, 1910, p. 238). Here we have an outspoken and deliberate reactionary, who is openly helping the exploiters to replace the old, decayed religious superstitions by new, more odious and vile superstitions.

This does not mean that Drews should not be translated. It means that while in a certain measure effecting an alliance with the progressive section of the bourgeoisie, Communists and all consistent materialists should unflinchingly expose that section when it is guilty of reaction. It means that to shun an alliance with the representatives of the bourgeoisie of the eighteenth century, i.e., the period when it was revolutionary, would be to betray Marxism and materialism; for an "alliance" with the Drewses, in one form or another and in one degree or another, is essential for our struggle against the predominating religious obscurantists.

Pod Znamenem Marksizma, which sets out to be an organ of militant materialism, should devote much of its space to atheist propaganda, to reviews of the literature on the subject and to correcting the immense shortcomings of our governmental work in this field. It is particularly important to utilise books and pamphlets

which contain many concrete facts and comparisons showing how
the class interests and class organisations of the modern bourgeoisie
are connected with the organisations of religious institutions and
religious propaganda.

All material relating to the United States of America, where the
official, state connection between religion and capital is less manifest, is extremely important. But, on the other hand, it becomes
all the clearer to us that so-called modern democracy (which the
Mensheviks, the Socialist-Revolutionaries, partly also the anarchists,
etc., so unreasonably worship) is nothing but the freedom to preach
whatever is to the advantage of the bourgeoisie, to preach, namely,
the most reactionary ideas, religion, obscurantism, defence of the
exploiters, etc.

One would like to hope that a journal which sets out to be a
militant materialist organ will provide our reading public with
reviews of atheist literature, showing for which circle of readers
any particular writing might be suitable and in what respect, and
mentioning what literature has been published in our country (only
decent translations should be given notice, and they are not so
many), and what is still to be published.

———

In addition to the alliance with consistent materialists who do
not belong to the Communist Party, of no less and perhaps even
of more importance for the work which militant materialism should
perform is an alliance with those modern natural scientists who
incline towards materialism and are not afraid to defend and
preach it as against the modish philosophical wanderings into
idealism and scepticism which are prevalent in so-called educated
society.

The article by A. Timiryazev on Einstein's theory of relativity
published in *Pod Znamenem Marksizma* No. 1-2 permits us to hope
that the journal will succeed in effecting this second alliance too.
Greater attention should be paid to it. It should be remembered
that the sharp upheaval which modern natural science is undergoing very often gives rise to reactionary philosophical schools
and minor schools, trends and minor trends. Unless, therefore, the
problems raised by the recent revolution in natural science are
followed, and unless natural scientists are enlisted in the work of
a philosophical journal, militant materialism can be neither militant
nor materialism. Timiryazev was obliged to observe in the first
issue of the journal that the theory of Einstein, who, according to
Timiryazev, is himself not making any active attack on the foundations of materialism, has already been seized upon by a vast number
of bourgeois intellectuals of all countries; it should be noted that

this applies not only to Einstein, but to a number, if not to the majority, of the great reformers of natural science since the end of the nineteenth century.

For our attitude towards this phenomenon to be a politically conscious one, it must be realised that no natural science and no materialism can hold its own in the struggle against the onslaught of bourgeois ideas and the restoration of the bourgeois world outlook unless it stands on solid philosophical ground. In order to hold his own in this struggle and carry it to a victorious finish, the natural scientist must be a modern materialist, a conscious adherent of the materialism represented by Marx, i.e., he must be a dialectical materialist. In order to attain this aim, the contributors to *Pod Znamenem Marksizma* must arrange for the systematic study of Hegelian dialectics from a materialist standpoint, i.e., the dialectics which Marx applied practically in his *Capital* and in his historical and political works, and applied so successfully that now every day of the awakening to life and struggle of new classes in the East (Japan, India, and China)—i.e., the hundreds of millions of human beings who form the greater part of the world population and whose historical passivity and historical torpor have hitherto conditioned the stagnation and decay of many advanced European countries— every day of the awakening to life of new peoples and new classes serves as a fresh confirmation of Marxism.

Of course, this study, this interpretation, this propaganda of Hegelian dialectics is extremely difficult, and the first experiments in this direction will undoubtedly be accompanied by errors. But only he who never does anything never makes mistakes. Taking as our basis Marx's method of applying materialistically conceived Hegelian dialectics, we can and should elaborate this dialectics from all aspects, print in the journal excerpts from Hegel's principal works, interpret them materialistically and comment on them with the help of examples of the way Marx applied dialectics, as well as of examples of dialectics in the sphere of economic and political relations, which recent history, especially modern imperialist war and revolution, provides in unusual abundance. In my opinion, the editors and contributors of *Pod Znamenem Marksizma* should be a kind of "Society of Materialist Friends of Hegelian Dialectics". Modern natural scientists (if they know how to seek, and if we learn to help them) will find in the Hegelian dialectics, materialistically interpreted, a series of answers to the philosophical problems which are being raised by the revolution in natural science and which make the intellectual admirers of bourgeois fashion "stumble" into reaction.

Unless it sets itself such a task and systematically fulfils it, materialism cannot be militant materialism. It will be not so much the fighter as the fought,[314] to use an expression of Shchedrin's.

Without this, eminent natural scientists will as often as hitherto be helpless in making their philosophical deductions and generalisations. For natural science is progressing so fast and is undergoing such a profound revolutionary upheaval in all spheres that it cannot possibly dispense with philosophical deductions.

In conclusion, I will cite an example which has nothing to do with philosophy, but does at any rate concern social questions, to which *Pod Znamenem Marksizma* also desires to devote attention.

It is an example of the way in which modern pseudo-science actually serves as a vehicle for the grossest and most infamous reactionary views.

I was recently sent a copy of *Ekonomist* No. 1[315] (1922), published by the Eleventh Department of the Russian Technical Society. The young Communist who sent me this journal (he probably had no time to read it) rashly expressed considerable agreement with it. In reality the journal is—I do not know to what extent deliberately—an organ of the modern feudalists, disguised of course under a cloak of science, democracy and so forth.

A certain Mr. P. A. Sorokin publishes in this journal an extensive, so-called "sociological", inquiry on "The Influence of the War". This learned article abounds in learned references to the "sociological" works of the author and his numerous teachers and colleagues abroad. Here is an example of his learning.

On page 83, I read:

"For every 10,000 marriages in Petrograd there are now 92.2 divorces—a fantastic figure. Of every 100 annulled marriages, 51.1 had lasted less than one year, 11 per cent less than one month, 22 per cent less than two months, 41 per cent less than three to six months and only 26 per cent over six months. These figures show that modern legal marriage is a form which conceals what is in effect extra-marital sexual intercourse, enabling lovers of 'strawberries' to satisfy their appetites in a 'legal' way" (*Ekonomist* No. 1, p. 83).

Both this gentleman and the Russian Technical Society, which publishes this journal and gives space to this kind of talk, no doubt regard themselves as adherents of democracy and would consider it a great insult to be called what they are in fact, namely, feudalists, reactionaries, "graduated flunkeys of clericalism".

Even the slightest acquaintance with the legislation of bourgeois countries on marriage, divorce and illegitimate children, and with the actual state of affairs in this field, is enough to show anyone interested in the subject that modern bourgeois democracy, even in all the most democratic bourgeois republics, exhibits a truly feudal attitude in this respect towards women and towards children born out of wedlock.

This, of course, does not prevent the Mensheviks, the Socialist-Revolutionaries, a part of the anarchists and all the corresponding parties in the West from shouting about democracy and how it is being violated by the Bolsheviks. But as a matter of fact the Bolshevik revolution is the only consistently democratic revolution in respect to such questions as marriage, divorce and the position of children born out of wedlock. And this is a question which most directly affects the interests of more than half the population of any country. Although a large number of bourgeois revolutions preceded it and called themselves democratic, the Bolshevik revolution was the first and only revolution to wage a resolute struggle in this respect both against reaction and feudalism and against the usual hypocrisy of the ruling and propertied classes.

If 92 divorces for every 10,000 marriages seem to Mr. Sorokin a fantastic figure, one can only suppose that either the author lived and was brought up in a monastery so entirely walled off from life that hardly anyone will believe such a monastery ever existed, or that he is distorting the truth in the interest of reaction and the bourgeoisie. Anybody in the least acquainted with social conditions in bourgeois countries knows that the real number of actual divorces (of course, not sanctioned by church and law) is everywhere immeasurably greater. The only difference between Russia and other countries in this respect is that our laws do not sanctify hypocrisy and the debasement of the woman and her child, but openly and in the name of the government declare systematic war on all hypocrisy and all debasement.

The Marxist journal will have to wage war also on these modern "educated" feudalists. Not a few of them, very likely, are in receipt of government money and are employed by our government to educate our youth, although they are no more fitted for this than notorious perverts are fitted for the post of superintendents of educational establishments for the young.

The working class of Russia proved able to win power; but it has not yet learned to utilise it, for otherwise it would have long ago very politely dispatched such teachers and members of learned societies to countries with a bourgeois "democracy." That is the proper place for such feudalists.

But it will learn, given the will to learn.

March 12, 1922

Pod Znamenem Marksizma No. 3,
March 1922
Signed: *N. Lenin*

Collected Works, Vol. 33

ON THE TENTH ANNIVERSARY OF "PRAVDA"

It is ten years since *Pravda*, the legal—legal even under *tsarist* law—Bolshevik daily paper, was founded. This decade was preceded by, approximately, another decade: nine years (1903-12) since the emergence of Bolshevism, or thirteen years (1900-12), if we count from the founding in 1900 of the "Bolshevik-oriented" old *Iskra*.

The tenth anniversary of a Bolshevik daily published in Russia.... Only ten years have elapsed! But measured in terms of our struggle and movement they are equal to a hundred years. For the pace of social development in the past five years has been positively staggering if we apply the old yardstick of European philistines like the heroes of the Second and Two-and-a-Half Internationals. These civilised philistines are accustomed to regard as "natural" a situation in which hundreds of millions of people (over a thousand million, to be exact) in the colonies and in semi-dependent and poor countries tolerate the treatment meted out to Indians or Chinese, tolerate incredible exploitation, and outright depredation, and hunger, and violence, and humiliation, all in order that "civilised" men might "freely", "democratically", according to "parliamentary procedure", decide whether the booty should be divided up peacefully, or whether ten million or so must be done to death in this division of the imperialist booty, yesterday between Germany and Britain, tomorrow between Japan and the U.S.A. (with France and Britain participating in one form or another).

The basic reason for this tremendous acceleration of world development is that new hundreds of millions of people have been drawn into it. The old bourgeois and imperialist Europe, which was accustomed to look upon itself as the centre of the universe, rotted and burst like a putrid ulcer in the first imperialist holocaust. No matter how the Spenglers and all the enlightened philistines, who are capable of admiring (or even studying) Spengler, may lament it, this decline of the old Europe is but an episode in the history of the downfall of the world bourgeoisie, oversatiated by imperialist rapine and the oppression of the majority of the world's population.

That majority has now awakened and has begun a movement which even the "mightiest" powers cannot stem. They stand no chance. For the present "victors" in the first imperialist slaughter have not the strength to defeat small—tiny, I might say—Ireland, nor can they emerge victorious from the confusion in currency and finance issues that reigns in their own midst. Meanwhile, India and China are seething. They represent over 700 million people, and together with the neighbouring Asian countries, that are in all ways similar to them, over half of the world's inhabitants. Inexorably and with mounting momentum they are approaching their 1905, with the essential and important difference that in 1905 the revolution in Russia could still proceed (at any rate at the beginning) in isolation, that is, without other countries being immediately drawn in. But the revolutions that are maturing in India and China are being drawn into—have already been drawn into—the revolutionary struggle, the revolutionary movement, the world revolution.

The tenth anniversary of *Pravda*, the legal Bolshevik daily, is a clearly defined marker of this great acceleration of the greatest world revolution. In 1906-07, it seemed that the tsarist government had completely crushed the revolution. A few years later the Bolshevik Party was able—*in a different form, by a different method*—to penetrate into the very citadel of the enemy and daily, "legally", proceed with its work of undermining the accursed tsarist and landowner autocracy from within. A few more years passed, and the proletarian revolution, organised by Bolshevism, triumphed.

Some ten or so revolutionaries shared in the founding of the old *Iskra* in 1900, and only about forty attended the birth of Bolshevism at the illegal congresses in Brussels and London in 1903.

In 1912-13, when the legal Bolshevik *Pravda* came into being it had the support of hundreds of thousands of workers, who by their modest contributions were able to overcome both the oppression of tsarism and the competition of the Mensheviks, those pettybourgeois traitors to socialism.

In November 1917, nine million electors out of a total of thirty-six million voted for the Bolsheviks in the elections to the Constituent Assembly. But if we take the actual struggle,· and not merely the elections, at the close of October and in November 1917, the Bolsheviks had the support of the *majority* of the proletariat and class-conscious peasantry, as represented by the majority of the delegates at the Second All-Russia Congress of Soviets,[316] and by the majority of the most active and politically conscious section of the working people, namely, the twelve-million-strong army of that day.

These few figures illustrating the "acceleration" of the world revolutionary movement in the past twenty years give a very small and very incomplete picture. They afford only a very approximate idea of the history of no more than 150 million people, whereas in these twenty years the revolution has developed into an invincible force in countries with a total population of over a thousand million (the whole of Asia, not to forget South Africa, which recently reminded the world of its claim to *human* and not slavish existence, and by methods which were not altogether "parliamentary").

Some infant Spenglers—I apologise for the expression—may conclude (every variety of nonsense can be expected from the "clever" leaders of the Second and Two-and-a-Half Internationals) that this estimate of the revolutionary forces fails to take into account the European and American proletariat. These "clever" leaders always argue as if the fact that birth comes nine months after conception necessarily means that the exact hour and minute of birth can be defined beforehand, also the position of the infant during delivery, the condition of the mother and the exact degree of pain and danger both will suffer. Very "clever"! These gentry cannot for the life of them understand that from the point of view of the development of the international revolution the transition from Chartism[317] to Henderson's servility to the bourgeoisie, or the transition from Varlin to Renaudel, from Wilhelm Liebknecht and Bebel to Südekum, Scheidemann and Noske, can only be likened to an automobile passing *from* a smooth highway stretching for hundreds of miles *to* a dirty stinking puddle of a few yards in length on that highway.

Men are the makers of history. But the Chartists, the Varlins and the Liebknechts applied their minds and hearts to it. The leaders of the Second and Two-and-a-Half Internationals apply other parts of the anatomy: they fertilise the ground for the appearance of new Chartists, new Varlins and new Liebknechts.

At this *most difficult* moment it would be most harmful for revolutionaries to indulge in self-deception. Though Bolshevism *has become* an international force, though in *all* the civilised and advanced countries new Chartists, new Varlins, new Liebknechts have been born, and are growing up as legal (just as legal as our *Pravda* was under the tsars ten years ago) Communist Parties, nonetheless, for the time being, the international bourgeoisie still remains incomparably stronger than its class enemy. This bourgeoisie, which has done everything in its power to hamper the birth of proletarian power in Russia and to multiply tenfold the dangers and suffering attending its birth, is still in a position to condemn millions and tens of millions to torment and death through its whiteguard and imperialist wars, etc. That is something we must not forget. And we must skilfully adapt our tactics to this specific situation. The bourgeoisie is still able freely to torment, torture and kill. But it cannot halt the inevitable and—from the standpoint of world history—not far distant triumph of the revolutionary proletariat.

May 2, 1922

Pravda No. 98,
May 5, 1922
Signed: *N. Lenin*

Collected Works, Vol. 33

DRAFT DECISION
OF THE ALL-RUSSIA CENTRAL EXECUTIVE COMMITTEE ON THE REPORT OF THE DELEGATION TO THE GENOA CONFERENCE[318]

The All-Russia Central Executive Committee's draft resolution on Joffe's report should be drawn up approximately as follows:

1. The delegation of the All-Russia Central Executive Committee has carried out its task correctly in upholding the full sovereignty of the R.S.F.S.R., opposing attempts to force the country into bondage and restore private property, and in concluding a treaty with Germany.[319]

2. The international political and economic situation is characterised by the following features.

Political: the absence of peace and the danger of fresh imperialist wars [Ireland, India, China and others; worsening of relations between Britain and France, between Japan and the United States, *etc.*, *etc.* ((in greater detail))].

3. Economic: the "victor" countries, exceedingly powerful and enriched by the war (= by plunder), have not been able to re-establish even the former capitalist relations three and a half years after the war [currency chaos; non-fulfilment of the Treaty of Versailles and the impossibility of its fulfilment; non-payment of debts to the United States, *etc.*, *etc.* (*in greater detail*)].

4. Therefore, § 1 of the Cannes resolutions,[320] by recognising the *equality* of the two *property systems* (capitalist or private property, and communist property, *so far* accepted only in the R.S.F.S.R.), is thus compelled to recognise, even if only indirectly, the collapse, the bankruptcy of the first property system and the inevitability of its coming to an *agreement* with the second, on terms of equality.

5. The other §§ of the Cannes terms, as well as the memoranda, etc., of the powers at Genoa, are in contradiction to this and are, therefore, still-born.

6. True equality of the two property systems—*if only as a temporary state, until such time as the entire world abandons* private property and the *economic chaos* and wars engendered by it for the higher property system—is found only in the Treaty of Rapallo.

The All-Russia Central Executive Committee, therefore:

welcomes the Treaty of Rapallo as the only correct way out of the difficulties, chaos and danger of wars (as long as there remain two property systems, one of them as obsolete as capitalist property);

recognises *only* this type of treaty as normal for relations between the R.S.F.S.R. and capitalist countries;

— instructs the Council of People's Commissars and the People's Commissariat of Foreign Affairs to pursue a policy along these lines;

— instructs the Presidium of the All-Russia Central Executive Committee to confirm it by agreement with all republics that are in federal relations with the R.S.F.S.R.;

— instructs the People's Commissariat of Foreign Affairs and the Council of People's Commissars to permit deviations from the Rapallo-type treaty only in exceptional circumstances that gain very special advantages for the working people of the R.S.F.S.R., etc.

Written May 15 or 16, 1922   *Collected Works*, Vol. 33

First published in 1950
in the 4th Russian edition
of Lenin's *Collected   Works*,
                    Vol. 33

SPEECH AT A PLENARY SESSION OF THE MOSCOW SOVIET
NOVEMBER 20, 1922[321]

(*Stormy applause. "The Internationale" is sung.*) Comrades, I regret very much and apologise that I have been unable to come to your session earlier. As far as I know you intended a few weeks ago to give me an opportunity of attending the Moscow Soviet. I could not come because after my illness, from December onwards, I was incapacitated, to use the professional term, for quite a long time, and because of this reduced ability to work had to postpone my present address from week to week. A very considerable portion of my work which, as you will remember, I had first piled on Comrade Tsyurupa, and then on Comrade Rykov, I also had to pile additionally on Comrade Kamenev. And I must say that, to employ a simile I have already used, he was suddenly burdened with two loads. Though, to continue the simile, it should be said that the horse has proved to be an exceptionally capable and zealous one. (*Applause.*) All the same, however, nobody is supposed to drag two loads, and I am now waiting impatiently for Comrades Tsyurupa and Rykov to return, and we shall divide up the work at least a little more fairly. As for myself, in view of my reduced ability to work it takes me much more time to look into matters than I should like.

In December 1921, when I had to stop working altogether, it was the year's end. We were effecting the transition to the New Economic Policy, and it turned out already then that, although we had embarked upon this transition in the beginning of 1921, it was quite a difficult, I would say a very difficult, transition. We have now been effecting this transition for more than eighteen months, and one would think that it was time the majority took up new places and disposed themselves according to the new conditions, particularly those of the New Economic Policy.

As to foreign policy, we had the fewest changes in that field. We pursued the line that we had adopted earlier, and I think I can say with a clear conscience that we pursued it quite consistently and with enormous success. There is no need, I think, to deal with that in detail; the capture of Vladivostok, the ensuing demonstration and the declaration of federation which you read in the press the other day have proved and shown with the utmost clarity that no changes are necessary in this respect.[322] The road we are on is absolutely clearly and well defined, and has ensured us success in face of all the countries of the world, although some of them are still prepared to declare that they refuse to sit at one table with us. Nevertheless, economic relations, followed by diplomatic relations, are improving, must improve, and certainly will improve. Every country which resists this risks being late, and, perhaps in some quite substantial things, it risks being at a disadvantage. All of us see this now, and not only from the press, from the newspapers. I think that in their trips abroad comrades are also finding the changes very great. In that respect, to use an old simile, we have not changed to other trains, or to other conveyances.

But as regards our home policy, the change we made in the spring of 1921, which was necessitated by such extremely powerful and convincing circumstances that no debates or disagreements arose among us about it—that change continues to cause us some difficulties, great difficulties, I would say. Not because we have any doubts about the need for the turn—no doubts exist in that respect—not because we have any doubts as to whether the test of our New Economic Policy has yielded the successes we expected. No doubts exist on that score—I can say this quite definitely— either in the ranks of our Party or in the ranks of the huge mass of non-Party workers and peasants.

In this sense the problem presents no difficulties. The difficulties we have stem from our being faced with a task whose solution very often requires the services of new people, extraordinary measures and extraordinary methods. Doubts still exist among us as to whether this or that is correct. There are changes in one direction or another. And it should be said that both will continue for quite a long time. "The New Economic Policy!" A strange title. It was called a New Economic Policy because it turned things back. We are now retreating, going back, as it were; but we are doing so in order, after first retreating, to take a running start and make a bigger leap forward. It was on this condition alone that we retreated in pursuing our New Economic Policy. Where and how we must now regroup, adapt and reorganise in order to start a most stubborn offensive after our retreat, we do not yet know. To carry out all these operations properly we need, as the proverb says, to look not ten but a hundred times before we leap. We must do so in order to cope with the incredible difficulties we encounter in dealing with all our tasks and problems. You know perfectly well what sacrifices have been made to achieve what has been achieved; you know how long the Civil War has dragged on and what effort it has cost. Well now, the capture of Vladivostok has shown all of us (though Vladivostok is a long way off, it is after all one of our own towns) (*prolonged applause*) everybody's desire to join us, to join in our achievements. The Russian Soviet Federative Socialist Republic now stretches from here to there. This desire has rid us both of our civil enemies and of the foreign enemies who attacked us. I am referring to Japan.

We have won quite a definite diplomatic position, recognised by the whole world. All of you see it. You see its results, but how much time we needed to get it! We have now won the recognition of our rights by our enemies both in economic and in commercial policy. This is proved by the conclusion of trade agreements.

We can see why we, who eighteen months ago took the path of the so-called New Economic Policy, are finding it so incredibly difficult to advance along that path. We live in a country devastated so severely by war, knocked out of anything like the normal course of life, in a country that has suffered and endured so much, that willy-nilly we are beginning all our calculations with a very, very small percentage—the pre-war percentage. We apply this yardstick to the conditions of our life, we sometimes do so very impatiently, heatedly, and always end up with the conviction that the difficulties are vast. The task we have set ourselves in this field seems all the more vast because we are comparing it with the state of affairs in any ordinary bourgeois country. We have set ourselves this task because we understood that it was no use expecting the wealthy powers to give us the assistance usually forthcoming under such circumstances. After the Civil War we have been subjected to very nearly a boycott, that is, we have been told that the economic ties that are customary and normal in the capitalist world will not be maintained in our case.

Over eighteen months have passed since we undertook the New Economic Policy, and even a longer period has passed since we concluded our first international treaty. Nonetheless, this boycott of us by all the bourgeoisie and all governments continues to be felt. We could not count on anything else when we adopted the new economic conditions; yet we had no doubt that we had to make the change and achieve success single-handed. The further we go, the clearer it becomes that any aid that may be rendered to us, that will be rendered to us by the capitalist powers, will, far from eliminating this condition, in all likelihood and in the overwhelming majority of cases intensify it, accentuate it still further. "Single-handed"—we told ourselves. "Single-handed"—we are told by almost every capitalist country with which we have concluded any deals, with which we have undertaken any engagements, with which we have begun any negotiations. And that is where the special difficulty lies. We must realise this difficulty. We have built up our own political system in more than three years of work, incredibly hard work that was incredibly full of heroism. In the position in which we were till now we had no time to see whether we would smash something needlessly, no time to see whether there would be many sacrifices, because there were sacrifices enough, because the struggle which we then began (you know this perfectly well and there is no need to dwell on it) was a life-and-death struggle against the old social system, against which we fought to forge for ourselves a right to existence, to peaceful development. And we have won it. It is not we who say this, it is not the testimony of witnesses who may be accused of being partial to us. It is the testimony of witnesses who are in the camp of our enemies and who are naturally partial—not in our favour, however, but against us. These witnesses were in Denikin's camp. They directed the occupation. And we know that their partiality cost us very dear, cost us colossal destruction. We suffered all sorts of losses on their account, and lost values of all kinds, including the greatest of all values—human lives—on an incredibly large scale. Now we must scrutinise our tasks most carefully and understand that the main task will be not to give up our previous gains. We shall not give up a single one of our old gains. (*Applause.*) Yet we are also faced with an entirely new task; the old may prove a downright obstacle. To understand this task is most difficult. Yet it must be understood, so that we may learn how to work when, so to speak, it is necessary to turn ourselves inside out. I think, comrades, that these words and slogans are understandable, because for nearly a year, during my enforced absence, you have had in practice, handling the jobs on hand, to speak and think of this in various ways and on hundreds of occasions, and I am confident that your reflections on that score can only lead to one conclusion, namely, that today we must display still more of the flexibility which we employed till now in the Civil War.

We must not abandon the old. The series of concessions that adapt us to the capitalist powers is a series of concessions that enables them to make contact with us, ensures them a profit which is sometimes bigger, perhaps, than it should be. At the same time, we are conceding but a little part of the means of production, which are held almost entirely by our state. The other day the papers discussed the concession proposed by the Englishman Urquhart,[323] who has hitherto been against us almost throughout the Civil War. He used to say: "We shall achieve our aim in the Civil War against Russia, against the Russia that has dared to deprive us of this and of that." And after all that we had to enter into negotiations with him. We did not refuse them, we undertook them with the greatest joy, but we said: "Beg your pardon, but we shall not give up what we have won. Our Russia is so big, our economic potentialities are so numerous, and we feel justified in not rejecting your kind proposal, but we shall discuss it soberly, like businessmen." True, nothing came of our first talk, because we could not agree to his proposal for political reasons. We had to reject it. So long as the British did not entertain the possibility of our participating in the negotiations on the Straits, the Dardanelles,[324] we had to reject it, but right after doing so we had to start examining the matter in substance. We discussed whether or not it was of advantage to us, whether we would profit from concluding this concession agreement, and if so, under what circumstances it would be profitable. We had to talk about the price. That, comrades, is what shows you clearly how much our present approach to problems should differ from our former approach. Formerly the Communist said: "I give my life", and it seemed very simple to him, although it was not always so simple. Now, however, we Communists face quite another task. We must now take all things into account, and each of you must learn to be prudent. We must calculate how, in the capitalist environment, we can ensure our existence, how we can profit by our enemies, who, of course, will bargain, who have never forgotten how to bargain and will bargain at our expense. We are not forgetting that either, and do not in the least imagine commercial people anywhere turning into lambs and, having turned into lambs, offering us blessings of all sorts for nothing. That does not happen, and we do not expect it, but count on the fact that we, who are accustomed to putting up a fight, will find a way out and prove capable of trading, and profiting, and emerging safely from difficult economic situations. That is a very difficult task. That is the task we are working on now. I should like us to realise clearly how great is the abyss between the old and the new tasks. However great the abyss may be, we learned to manoeuvre during the war, and we must understand that the manoeuvre we now have to perform, in the midst of which we now are, is the most difficult one. But then it seems to be our last manoeuvre. We must test our strength in this field and prove that we have learned more than just the lessons of yesterday and do not just keep repeating the fundamentals. Nothing of the kind. We have begun to relearn, and shall relearn in such a way that we shall achieve definite and obvious success. And it is for the sake of this relearning, I think, that we must again firmly promise one another that under the name of the New Economic Policy we have turned back, but turned back in such a way as to surrender nothing of the new, and yet to give the capitalists such advantages as will compel any state, however hostile to us, to establish contacts and to deal with us. Comrade Krasin, who has had many talks with Urquhart, the head and backbone of the whole intervention, said that Urquhart, after all his attempts to foist the old system on us at all costs, throughout Russia, seated himself at the same table with him, with Krasin, and began asking: "What's the price? How much? For how many years?" (*Applause.*) This is still quite far from our concluding concession deals and thus entering into treaty relations that are perfectly precise and binding—from the viewpoint of bourgeois society—but we can already see that we are coming to it, have nearly come to it, but have not quite arrived. We must admit that, comrades, and not be swell-headed. We are still far from having fully achieved the things that will make us strong, self-reliant and calmly confident that no capitalist deals can frighten us, calmly confident that however difficult a deal may be we shall conclude it, we shall get to the bottom of it and settle it. That is why the work—both political and Party—that we have begun in this sphere must be continued, and that is why we must change from the old methods to entirely new ones.

We still have the old machinery, and our task now is to remould it along new lines. We cannot do so at once, but we must see to it that the Communists we have are properly placed. What we need is that they, the Communists, should control the machinery they are assigned to, and not, as so often happens with us, that the machinery should control them. We should make no secret of it, and speak of it frankly. Such are the tasks and the difficulties that confront us—and that at a moment when we have set out on our practical path, when we must not approach socialism as if it were an icon painted in festive colours. We need to take the right direction, we need to see that everything is checked, that the masses, the entire population, check the path we follow and say: "Yes, this is better than the old system." That is the task we have set ourselves. Our Party, a little group of people in comparison with the country's total population, has tackled this job. This tiny nucleus has set itself the task of remaking everything, and it will do so. We have proved that this is no utopia but a cause which people live by. We have all seen this. This has already been done. We must remake things in such a way that the great majority of the masses, the peasants and workers, will say: "It is not you who praise yourselves, but we. We say that you have achieved splendid results, after which no intelligent person will ever dream of returning to the old." We have not reached that point yet. *That is why NEP remains the main, current, and all-embracing slogan of today.* We shall not forget a single one of the slogans we learned yesterday. We can say that quite calmly, without the slightest hesitation, say it to anybody, and every step we take demonstrates it. But we still have to adapt ourselves to the New Economic Policy. We must know how to overcome, to reduce to a definite minimum all its negative features, which there is no need to enumerate and which you know perfectly well. We must know how to arrange everything shrewdly. Our legislation gives us every opportunity to do so. Shall we be able to get things going properly? That is still far from being settled. We are making a study of things. Every issue of our Party newspaper offers you a dozen articles which tell you that at such-and-such a factory, owned by so-and-so, the rental terms are such-and-such, whereas at another, where our Communist comrade is the manager, the terms are such-and-such. Does it yield a profit or not, does it pay its way or not? We have approached the very core of the everyday problems, and that is a tremendous achievement. Socialism is no longer a matter of the distant future, or an abstract picture, or an icon. Our opinion of icons is the same—a very bad one. We have brought socialism into everyday life and must here see how matters stand. That is the task of our day, the task of our epoch. Permit me to conclude by expressing confidence that difficult as this task may be, new as it may be compared with our previous task, and numerous as the difficulties may be that it entails, we shall all—not in a day, but in a few years—all of us together fulfil it whatever the cost, so that NEP Russia will become socialist Russia. (*Stormy, prolonged applause.*)

Pravda No. 263   *Collected Works*, Vol. 33
November 21, 1922

LETTER TO THE CONGRESS[325]

I

I would urge strongly that at this Congress a number of changes be made in our political structure.

I want to tell you of the considerations to which I attach most importance.

At the head of the list I set an increase in the number of Central Committee members to a few dozen or even a hundred. It is my opinion that without this reform our Central Committee would be in great danger if the course of events were not quite favourable for us (and that is something we cannot count on).

Then, I intend to propose that the Congress should on certain conditions invest the decisions of the State Planning Commission with legislative force, meeting, in this respect, the wishes of Comrade Trotsky—to a certain extent and on certain conditions.

As for the first point, i.e., increasing the number of C.C. members, I think it must be done in order to raise the prestige of the Central Committee, to do a thorough job of improving our administrative machinery and to prevent conflicts between small sections of the C.C. from acquiring excessive importance for the future of the Party.

It seems to me that our Party has every right to demand from the working class 50 to 100 C.C. members, and that it could get them from it without unduly taxing the resources of that class.

Such a reform would considerably increase the stability of our Party and ease its struggle in the encirclement of hostile states, which, in my opinion, is likely to, and must, become much more acute in the next few years. I think that the stability of our Party would gain a thousandfold by such a measure.

Lenin

December 24, 1922
Taken down by M. V.

II

Continuation of the notes.
December 24, 1922

By stability of the Central Committee, of which I spoke above, I mean measures against a split, as far as such measures can at all be taken. For, of course, the whiteguard in *Russkaya Mysl*[326] (it seems to have been S. S. Oldenburg) was right when, first, in the whiteguards' game against Soviet Russia he banked on a split in our Party, and when, secondly, he banked on grave differences in our Party to cause that split.

Our Party relies on two classes and therefore its instability would be possible and its downfall inevitable if there were no agreement between those two classes. In that event this or that measure, and generally all talk about the stability of our C.C., would be futile. No measures of any kind could prevent a split in such a case. But I hope that this is too remote a future and too improbable an event to talk about.

I have in mind stability as a guarantee against a split in the immediate future, and I intend to deal here with a few ideas concerning personal qualities.

I think that from this standpoint the prime factors in the question of stability are such members of the C.C. as Stalin and Trotsky. I think relations between them make up the greater part of the danger of a split, which could be avoided, and this purpose, in my opinion, would be served, among other things, by increasing the number of C.C. members to 50 or 100.

Comrade Stalin, having become Secretary, has unlimited authority concentrated in his hands, and I am not sure whether he will always be capable of using that authority with sufficient caution. Comrade Trotsky, on the other hand, as his struggle against the C. C. on the question of the People's Commissariat for Communications has already proved, is distinguished not only by outstanding ability. He is personally perhaps the most capable man in the present C.C., but he has displayed excessive self-assurance and shown excessive preoccupation with the purely administrative side of the work.

These two qualities of the two outstanding leaders of the present C.C. can inadvertently lead to a split, and if our Party does not take steps to avert this, the split may come unexpectedly.

I shall not give any further appraisals of the personal qualities of other members of the C.C. I shall just recall that the October episode with Zinoviev and Kamenev[327] was, of course, no accident, but neither can the blame for it be laid upon them personally, and more than non-Bolshevism can upon Trotsky.

Speaking of the young C.C. members, I wish to say a few words about Bukharin and Pyatakov. They are, in my opinion, the most outstanding figures (among the youngest ones), and the following must be borne in mind about them: Bukharin is not only a most valuable and major theorist of the Party; he is also rightly considered the favourite of the whole Party, but his theoretical views can be classified as fully Marxist only with great reserve, for there is something scholastic about him (he has never made a study of dialectics and, I think, never fully understood it).

December 25. As for Pyatakov, he is unquestionably a man of outstanding will and outstanding ability, but shows too much zeal for administrating and the administrative side of the work to be relied upon in a serious political matter.

Both of these remarks, of course, are made only for the present, on the assumption that both these outstanding and devoted Party workers fail to find an occasion to enhance their knowledge and amend their one-sidedness.

Lenin

December 25, 1922
Taken down by M. V.

ADDITION TO THE LETTER OF DECEMBER 24, 1922

Stalin is too rude and this defect, although quite tolerable in our midst and in dealings among us Communists, becomes intolerable in a Secretary General. That is why I suggest that the comrades think about a way of removing Stalin from that post and appointing another man in his stead who in all other respects differs from Comrade Stalin in having only one advantage, namely, that of being more tolerant, more loyal, more polite and more considerate to the comrades, less capricious, etc. This circumstance may appear to be a negligible detail. But I think that from the standpoint of safeguards against a split and from the standpoint of what I wrote above about the relationship between Stalin and Trotsky it is not a detail, or it is a detail which can assume decisive importance.

Lenin

Taken down by L. F.
January 4, 1923

III

Continuation of the notes.
December 26, 1922

The increase in the number of C.C. members to 50 or even 100 must, in my opinion, serve a double or even a treble purpose: the more members there are in the C.C., the more men will be trained in C.C. work and the less danger there will be of a split due to some indiscretion. The enlistment of many workers to the

C.C. will help the workers to improve our administrative machinery, which is pretty bad. We inherited it, in effect, from the old regime, for it was absolutely impossible to reorganise it in such a short time, especially in conditions of war, famine, etc. That is why those "critics" who point to the defects of our administrative machinery out of mockery or malice may be calmly answered that they do not in the least understand the conditions of the revolution today. It is altogether impossible in five years to reorganise the machinery adequately, especially in the conditions in which our revolution took place. It is enough that in five years we have created a new type of state in which the workers are leading the peasants against the bourgeoisie; and in a hostile international environment this in itself is a gigantic achievement. But knowledge of this must on no account blind us to the fact that, in effect, we took over the old machinery of state from the tsar and the bourgeoisie and that now, with the onset of peace and the satisfaction of the minimum requirements against famine, all our work must be directed towards improving the administrative machinery.

I think that a few dozen workers, being members of the C.C., can deal better than anybody else with checking, improving and remodelling our state apparatus. The Workers' and Peasants' Inspection[328] on whom this function devolved at the beginning proved unable to cope with it and can be used only as an "appendage" or, on certain conditions, as an assistant to these members of the C.C. In my opinion, the workers admitted to the Central Committee should come preferably not from among those who have had long service in Soviet bodies (in this part of my letter the term workers everywhere includes peasants), because those workers have already acquired the very traditions and the very prejudices which it is desirable to combat.

The working-class members of the C.C. must be mainly workers of a lower stratum than those promoted in the last five years to work in Soviet bodies; they must be people closer to being rank-and-file workers and peasants, who, however, do not fall into the category of direct or indirect exploiters. I think that by attending all sittings of the C.C. and all sittings of the Political Bureau, and by reading all the documents of the C.C., such workers can form a staff of devoted supporters of the Soviet system, able, first, to give stability to the C.C. itself, and second, to work effectively on the renewal and improvement of the state apparatus.

Lenin

Taken down by L. F.
December 26, 1922

First published in 1956
in the magazine *Kommunist*
No. 9

Collected Works, Vol. 36

PAGES FROM A DIARY

The recent publication of the report on literacy among the population of Russia, based on the census of 1920 (*Literacy in Russia*, issued by the Central Statistical Board, Public Education Section, Moscow, 1922), is a very important event.

Below I quote a table from this report on the state of literacy among the population of Russia in 1897 and 1920.

	Literates per thousand males		Literates per thousand females		Literates per thousand population	
	1897	1920	1897	1920	1897	1920
1. European Russia . .	326	422	136	255	229	330
2. North Caucasus . . .	241	357	56	215	150	281
3. Siberia (Western) . .	170	307	46	134	108	218
Overall average . . .	318	409	131	244	223	319

At a time when we hold forth on proletarian culture and the relation in which it stands to bourgeois culture, facts and figures reveal that we are in a very bad way even as far as bourgeois culture is concerned. As might have been expected, it appears that we are still a very long way from attaining universal literacy, and that even compared with tsarist times (1897) our progress has been far too slow. This should serve as a stern warning and reproach to those who have been soaring in the empyreal heights of "proletarian culture". It shows what a vast amount of urgent spade-work we still have to do to reach the standard of an ordinary West-European civilised country. It also shows what a vast amount of work we have to do today to achieve, on the basis of our proletarian gains, anything like a real cultural standard.

We must not confine ourselves to this incontrovertible but too theoretical proposition. The very next time we revise our quarterly budget we must take this matter up in a practical way as well. In the first place, of course, we shall have to cut down the expenditure of government departments other than the People's Commissariat of Education, and the sums thus released should be assigned for the latter's needs. In a year like the present, when we are relatively well supplied, we must not be chary in increasing the bread ration for schoolteachers.

Generally speaking, it cannot be said that the work now being done in public education is too narrow. Quite a lot is being done to get the old teachers out of their rut, to attract them to the new problems, to rouse their interest in new methods of education, and in such problems as religion.

But we are not doing the main thing. We are not doing anything—or doing far from enough—to raise the schoolteacher to the level that is absolutely essential if we want any culture at all, proletarian or even bourgeois. We must bear in mind the semi-Asiatic ignorance from which we have not yet extricated ourselves, and from which we cannot extricate ourselves without strenuous effort—although we have every opportunity to do so, because nowhere are the masses of the people so interested in real culture as they are in our country; nowhere are the problems of this culture tackled so thoroughly and consistently as they are in our country; in no other country is state power in the hands of the working class which, in its mass, is fully aware of the deficiencies, I shall not say of its culture, but of its literacy; nowhere is the working class so ready to make, and nowhere is it actually making, such sacrifices to improve its position in this respect as in our country.

Too little, far too little, is still being done by us to adjust our state budget to satisfy, as a first measure, the requirements of elementary public education. Even in our People's Commissariat of Education we all too often find disgracefully inflated staffs in some state publishing establishment, which is contrary to the concept that the state's first concern should not be publishing houses but that there should be people to read, that the number of people able to read is greater, so that book publishing should have a wider political field in future Russia. Owing to the old (and bad) habit, we are still devoting much more time and effort to technical questions, such as the question of book publishing, than to the general political question of literacy among the people.

If we take the Central Vocational Education Board,[329] we are sure that there, too, we shall find far too much that is superfluous and inflated by departmental interests, much that is ill-adjusted to the requirements of broad public education. Far from everything that we find in the Central Vocational Education Board can be justified by the legitimate desire first of all to improve and give a practical slant to the education of our young factory workers. If we examine the staff of the Central Vocational Education Board carefully we shall find very much that is inflated and is in that respect fictitious and should be done away with. There is still very much in the proletarian and peasant state that can and must be economised for the purpose of promoting literacy among the people; this can be done by closing institutions which are playthings of a semi-aristocratic type, or institutions we can still do without and will be able to do without, and shall have to do without, for a long time to come, considering the state of literacy among the people as revealed by the statistics.

Our schoolteacher should be raised to a standard he has never achieved, and cannot achieve, in bourgeois society. This is a truism and requires no proof. We must strive for this state of affairs by working steadily, methodically and persistently to raise the teacher to a higher cultural level, to train him thoroughly for his really high calling and—mainly, mainly and mainly—to improve his position materially.

We must systematically step up our efforts to organise the schoolteachers so as to transform them from the bulwark of the bourgeois system that they still are in all capitalist countries without exception, into the bulwark of the Soviet system, in order, through their agency, to divert the peasantry from alliance with the bourgeoisie and to bring them into alliance with the proletariat.

I want briefly to emphasise the special importance in this respect of regular visits to the villages; such visits, it is true, are already being practised and should be regularly promoted. We should not stint money—which we all too often waste on the machinery of state that is almost entirely a product of the past historical epoch—on measures like these visits to the villages.

For the speech I was to have delivered at the Congress of Soviets in December 1922 I collected data on the patronage undertaken by urban workers over villagers. Part of these data was obtained for me by Comrade Khodorovsky, and since I have been unable to deal with this problem and give it publicity through the Congress, I submit the matter to the comrades for discussion now.

Here we have a fundamental political question—the relations

between town and country—which is of decisive importance for
the whole of our revolution. While the bourgeois state methodically concentrates all its efforts on doping the urban workers,
adapting all the literature published at state expense and at the
expense of the tsarist and bourgeois parties for this purpose, we
can and must utilise our political power to make the urban worker
an effective vehicle of communist ideas among the rural proletariat.

I said "communist", but I hasten to make a reservation for
fear of causing a misunderstanding, or of being taken too literally.
Under no circumstances must this be understood to mean that
we should immediately propagate purely and strictly communist
ideas in the countryside. As long as our countryside lacks the
material basis for communism, it will be, I should say, harmful, in
fact, I should say, fatal, for communism to do so.

That is a fact. We must start by establishing contacts between
town and country without the preconceived aim of implanting
communism in the rural districts. It is an aim which cannot be
achieved at the present time. It is inopportune, and to set an aim
like that at the present time would be harmful, instead of useful,
to the cause.

But it is our duty to establish contacts between the urban
workers and the rural working people, to establish between them
a form of comradeship which can easily be created. This is one
of the fundamental tasks of the working class which holds power.
To achieve this we must form a number of associations (Party,
trade union and private) of factory workers, which would devote
themselves regularly to assisting the villages in their cultural
development.

Is it possible to "attach" all the urban groups to all the village
groups, so that every working-class group may take advantage
regularly of every opportunity, of every occasion to serve the cultural needs of the village group it is "attached" to? Or will it be
possible to find other forms of contact? I here confine myself
solely to formulating the question in order to draw the comrades'
attention to it, to point out the available experience of Western
Siberia (to which Comrade Khodorovsky drew my attention)
and to present this gigantic, historic cultural task in all its
magnitude.

We are doing almost nothing for the rural districts outside our
official budget or outside official channels. True, in our country
the nature of the cultural relations between town and village is
automatically and inevitably changing. Under capitalism the town
introduced political, economic, moral, physical, etc., corruption
into the countryside. In our case, towns are automatically beginning to introduce the very opposite of this into the countryside.

But, I repeat, all this is going on automatically, spontaneously, and can be improved (and later increased a hundredfold) by doing it consciously, methodically and systematically.

We shall begin to advance (and shall then surely advance a hundred times more quickly) only after we have studied the question, after we have formed all sorts of workers' organisations— doing everything to prevent them from becoming bureaucratic— to take up the matter, discuss it and get things done.

January 2, 1923

Pravda No. 2
January 4, 1923
Signed: *N. Lenin*

Collected Works, Vol. 33

ON CO-OPERATION

I

It seems to me that not enough attention is being paid to the co-operative movement in our country. Not everyone understands that now, since the time of the October Revolution and quite apart from NEP (on the contrary, in this connection we must say—because of NEP), our co-operative movement has become one of great significance. There is a lot of fantasy in the dreams of the old co-operators. Often they are ridiculously fantastic. But why are they fantastic? Because people do not understand the fundamental, the rock-bottom significance of the working-class political struggle for the overthrow of the rule of the exploiters. We have overthrown the rule of the exploiters, and much that was fantastic, even romantic, even banal in the dreams of the old co-operators is now becoming unvarnished reality.

Indeed, since political power is in the hands of the working class, since this political power owns all the means of production, the only task, indeed, that remains for us is to organise the population in co-operative societies. With most of the population organised in co-operatives, the socialism which in the past was legitimately treated with ridicule, scorn and contempt by those who were rightly convinced that it was necessary to wage the class struggle, the struggle for political power, etc., will achieve its aim automatically. But not all comrades realise how vastly, how infinitely important it is now to organise the population of Russia in co-operative societies. By adopting NEP we made a concession to the peasant as a trader, to the principle of private trade; it is precisely for this reason (contrary to what some people think) that the co-operative movement is of such immense importance. All we actually need under NEP is to organise the population of Russia in co-operative societies on a sufficiently large scale, for we have now found that degree of combination of private interest, of private commercial interest, with state supervision and control of this interest, that degree of its subordination to the common interests which was formerly the stumbling-block for very many socialists. Indeed, the power of the state over all large-scale means of production, political power in the hands of the proletariat, the alliance of this proletariat with the many millions of small and very small peasants, the assured proletarian leadership of the peasantry, etc.—is this not all that is necessary to build a complete socialist society out of co-operatives, out of co-operatives alone, which we formerly ridiculed as huckstering and which from a certain aspect we have the right to treat as such now, under NEP? Is this not all that is necessary to build a complete socialist society? It is still not the building of socialist society, but it is all that is necessary and sufficient for it.

It is this very circumstance that is underestimated by many of our practical workers. They look down upon our co-operative societies, failing to appreciate their exceptional importance, first, from the standpoint of principle (the means of production are owned by the state), and, second, from the standpoint of transition to the new system by means that are the *simplest, easiest and most acceptable to the peasant.*

But this again is of fundamental importance. It is one thing to draw up fantastic plans for building socialism through all sorts of workers' associations, and quite another to learn to build socialism in practice in such a way that *every* small peasant could take part in it. That is the very stage we have now reached. And there is no doubt that, having reached it, we are taking too little advantage of it.

We went too far when we introduced NEP, but not because we attached too much importance to the principle of free enterprise and trade—we went too far because we lost sight of the co-operatives, because we now underrate the co-operatives, because we are already beginning to forget the vast importance of the co-operatives from the above two points of view.

I now propose to discuss with the reader what can and must at once be done practically on the basis of this "co-operative" principle. By what means can we, and must we, start at once to develop this "co-operative" principle so that its socialist meaning may be clear to all?

Co-operation must be politically so organised that it will not only generally and always enjoy certain privileges, but that these privileges should be of a purely material nature (a favourable bank-rate, etc.). The co-operatives must be granted state loans that are greater, if only by a little, than the loans we grant to private enterprises, even to heavy industry, etc.

A social system emerges only if it has the financial backing of a definite class. There is no need to mention the hundreds of millions of rubles that the birth of "free" capitalism cost. At present we have to realise that the co-operative system is the social system we must now give more than ordinary assistance, and we must actually give that assistance. But it must be assistance in the real sense of the word, i.e., it will not be enough to interpret it to mean assistance for any kind of co-operative trade; by assistance we must mean aid to co-operative trade in which *really large masses of the population actually take part*. It is certainly a correct form of assistance to give a bonus to peasants who take part in co-operative trade; but the whole point is to verify the nature of this participation, to verify the awareness behind it, and to verify its quality. Strictly speaking, when a co-operator goes to a village and opens a co-operative store, the people take no part in this whatever; but at the same time guided by their own interests they will hasten to try to take part in it.

There is another aspect to this question. From the point of view of the "enlightened" (primarily, literate) European there is not much left for us to do to induce absolutely everyone to take not a passive, but an active part in co-operative operations. Strictly speaking, there is *"only"* one thing we have left to do and that is to make our people so "enlightened" that they understand all the advantages of everybody participating in the work of the co-operatives, and organise this participation. *"Only"* that. There are now no other devices needed to advance to socialism. But to achieve this "only", there must be a veritable revolution—the entire people must go through a period of cultural development. Therefore, our rule must be: as little philosophising and as few acrobatics as possible. In this respect NEP is an advance, because it is adjustable to the level of the most ordinary peasant and does not demand anything higher of him. But it will take a whole historical epoch to get the entire population into the work of the co-operatives through NEP. At best we can achieve this in one or two decades. Nevertheless, it will be a distinct historical epoch, and without this historical epoch, without universal literacy, without a proper degree of efficiency, without training the population sufficiently to acquire the habit of book-reading, and without the material basis for this, without a certain sufficiency to safeguard against, say, bad harvests, famine, etc.—without this we shall not achieve our object. The thing now is to learn to combine the wide revolutionary range of action, the revolutionary enthusiasm which we have displayed, and displayed abundantly, and crowned with complete success— to learn to combine this with (I am almost inclined to say) the ability to be an efficient and capable trader, which is quite enough to be a good co-operator. By ability to be a trader I mean the ability to be a cultured trader. Let those Russians, or peasants, who imagine that since they trade they are good traders, get that well into their heads. This does not follow at all. They do trade, but that is far from being cultured traders. They now trade in an Asiatic manner, but to be a good trader one must trade in the European manner. They are a whole epoch behind in that.

In conclusion: a number of economic, financial and banking privileges must be granted to the co-operatives— this is the way our socialist state must promote the new principle on which the population must be organised. But this is only the general outline of the task; it does not define and depict in detail the entire content of the practical task, i.e., we must find what form of "bonus" to give for joining the co-operatives (and the terms on which we should give it), the form of bonus by which we shall assist the co-operatives sufficiently, the form of bonus that will produce the civilised co-operator. And given social ownership of the means of production, given the class victory of the proletariat over the bourgeoisie, the system of civilised co-operators is the system of socialism.

January 4, 1923

II

Whenever I wrote about the New Economic Policy I always quoted the article on state capitalism* which I wrote in 1918. This has more than once aroused doubts in the minds of certain young comrades. But their doubts were mainly on abstract political points.

It seemed to them that the term "state capitalism" could not be applied to a system under which the means of production were owned by the working class, a working class that held political power. They did not notice, however, that I used the term "state capitalism", *firstly*, to connect historically our present position with the position adopted in my controversy with the so-called Left Communists; also, I argued at the time that state capitalism would be superior to our existing economy. It was important for me to show the continuity between ordinary state capitalism and the unusual, even very unusual, state capitalism to which I referred in introducing the reader to the New Economic Policy. *Secondly*, the practical purpose was always important to me. And the practical purpose of our New Economic Policy was to lease out concessions. In the prevailing circumstances, concessions in our country would unquestionably have been a pure type of state capitalism. That is how I argued about state capitalism.

But there is another aspect of the matter for which we may need state capitalism, or at least a comparison with it. It is the question of co-operatives.

---

* See pp. 432-55 of the present volume.—*Ed.*

In the capitalist state, co-operatives are no doubt collective capitalist institutions. Nor is there any doubt that under our present economic conditions, when we combine private capitalist enterprises —but in no other way than on natonalised land and in no other way than under the control of the working-class state—with enterprises of a consistently socialist type (the means of production, the land on which the enterprises are situated, and the enterprises as a whole belonging to the state), the question arises about a third type of enterprise, the co-operatives, which were not formerly regarded as an independent type differing fundamentally from the others. Under private capitalism, co-operative enterprises differ from capitalist enterprises as collective enterprises differ from private enterprises. Under state capitalism, co-operative enterprises differ from state capitalist enterprises, firstly, because they are private enterprises, and, secondly, because they are collective enterprises. Under our present system, co-operative enterprises differ from private capitalist enterprises because they are collective enterprises, but do not differ from socialist enterprises if the land on which they are situated and the means of production belong to the state, i.e., the working class.

This circumstance is not considered sufficiently when co-operatives are discussed. It is forgotten that owing to the special features of our political system, our co-operatives acquire an altogether exceptional significance. If we exclude concessions, which, incidentally, have not developed on any considerable scale, co-operation under our conditions nearly always coincides fully with socialism.

Let me explain what I mean. Why were the plans of the old co-operators, from Robert Owen onwards, fantastic? Because they dreamed of peacefully remodelling contemporary society into socialism without taking account of such fundamental questions as the class struggle, the capture of political power by the working class, the overthrow of the rule of the exploiting class. That is why we are right in regarding as entirely fantastic this "co-operative" socialism, and as romantic, and even banal, the dream of transforming class enemies into class collaborators and class war into class peace (so-called class truce) by merely organising the population in co-operative societies.

Undoubtedly we were right from the point of view of the fundamental task of the present day, for socialism cannot be established without a class struggle for political power in the state.

But see how things have changed now that political power is in the hands of the working class, now that the political power of the exploiters is overthrown and all the means of production (except those which the workers' state voluntarily abandons on specified terms and for a certain time to the exploiters in the form of concessions) are owned by the working class.

Now we are entitled to say that for us the mere growth of co-operation (with the "slight" exception mentioned above) is identical with the growth of socialism, and at the same time we have to admit that there has been a radical modification in our whole outlook on socialism. The radical modification is this; formerly we placed, and had to place, the main emphasis on the political struggle, on revolution, on winning political power, etc. Now the emphasis is changing and shifting to peaceful, organisational, "cultural" work. I should say that emphasis is shifting to educational work, were it not for our international relations, were it not for the fact that we have to fight for our position on a world scale. If we leave that aside, however, and confine ourselves to internal economic relations, the emphasis in our work is certainly shifting to education.

Two main tasks confront us, which constitute the epoch—to reorganise our machinery of state, which is utterly useless, and which we took over in its entirety from the preceding epoch; during the past five years of struggle we did not, and could not, drastically reorganise it. Our second task is educational work among the peasants. And the economic object of this educational work among the peasants is to organise the latter in co-operative societies. If the whole of the peasantry had been organised in co-operatives, we would by now have been standing with both feet on the soil of socialism. But the organisation of the entire peasantry in co-operative societies presupposes a standard of culture among the peasants (precisely among the peasants as the overwhelming mass) that cannot, in fact, be achieved without a cultural revolution.

Our opponents told us repeatedly that we were rash in undertaking to implant socialism in an insufficiently cultured country. But they were misled by our having started from the opposite end to that prescribed by theory (the theory of pedants of all kinds), because in our country the political and social revolution preceded the cultural revolution, that very cultural revolution which nevertheless now confronts us.

This cultural revolution would now suffice to make our country a completely socialist country; but it presents immense difficulties of a purely cultural (for we are illiterate) and material character (for to be cultured we must achieve a certain development of the material means of production, must have a certain material base).

January 6, 1923

First published in *Pravda*
Nos. 115 and 116,
May 26 and 27, 1923
Signed: *N. Lenin*

Collected Works, Vol. 33

OUR REVOLUTION

(APROPOS OF N. SUKHANOV'S NOTES[330])

I

I have lately been glancing through Sukhanov's notes on the revolution. What strikes one most is the pedantry of all our petty-bourgeois democrats and of all the heroes of the Second International. Apart from the fact that they are all extremely faint-hearted, that when it comes to the minutest deviation from the German model even the best of them fortify themselves with reservations—apart from this characteristic, which is common to all petty-bourgeois democrats and has been abundantly manifested by them throughout the revolution, what strikes one is their slavish imitation of the past.

They all call themselves Marxists, but their conception of Marxism is impossibly pedantic. They have completely failed to understand what is decisive in Marxism, namely, its revolutionary dialectics. They have even absolutely failed to understand Marx's plain statements that in times of revolution the utmost flexibility[331] is demanded, and have even failed to notice, for instance, the statements Marx made in his letters—I think it was in 1856—expressing the hope of combining a peasant war in Germany, which might create a revolutionary situation, with the working-class movement[332] —they avoid even this plain statement and walk round and about it like a cat around a bowl of hot porridge.

Their conduct betrays them as cowardly reformists who are afraid to deviate from the bourgeoisie, let alone break with it, and at the same time they disguise their cowardice with the wildest rhetoric and braggartry. But what strikes one in all of them even from the purely theoretical point of view is their utter inability to grasp the following Marxist considerations: up to now they have seen capitalism and bourgeois democracy in Western Europe follow a definite path of development, and cannot conceive that this path can be taken as a model only *mutatis mutandis*, only with certain amendments (quite insignificant from the standpoint of the general development of world history).

First—the revolution connected with the first imperialist world war. Such a revolution was bound to reveal new features, or variations, resulting from the war itself, for the world has never seen such a war in such a situation. We find that since the war the bourgeoisie of the wealthiest countries have to this day been unable to restore "normal" bourgeois relations. Yet our reformists—petty bourgeois who make a show of being revolutionaries—believed, and still believe, that normal bourgeois relations are the limit (thus far shalt thou go and no farther). And even their conception of "normal" is extremely stereotyped and narrow.

Secondly, they are complete strangers to the idea that while the development of world history as a whole follows general laws it is by no means precluded, but, on the contrary, presumed, that certain periods of development may display peculiarities in either the form or the sequence of this development. For instance, it does not even occur to them that because Russia stands on the border-line between the civilised countries and the countries which this war has for the first time definitely brought into the orbit of civilisation—all the Oriental, non-European countries—she could and was, indeed, bound to reveal certain distinguishing features; although these, of course, are in keeping with the general line of world development, they distinguish her revolution from those which took place in the West-European countries and introduce certain partial innovations as the revolution moves on to the countries of the East.

Infinitely stereotyped, for instance, is the argument they learned by rote during the development of West-European Social-Democracy, namely, that we are not yet ripe for socialism, that, as certain "learned" gentlemen among them put it, the objective economic premises for socialism do not exist in our country. It does not occur to any of them to ask: but what about a people that found itself in a revolutionary situation such as that created during the first imperialist war? Might it not, influenced by the hopelessness of its situation, fling itself into a struggle that would offer it at least some chance of securing conditions for the further development of civilisation that were somewhat unusual?

"The development of the productive forces of Russia has not attained the level that makes socialism possible." All the heroes of the Second International, including, of course, Sukhanov, beat the drums about this proposition. They keep harping on this incontrovertible proposition in a thousand different keys, and think that it is the decisive criterion of our revolution.

But what if the situation, which drew Russia into the imperialist world war that involved every more or less influential West-European country and made her a witness of the eve of the revolutions maturing or partly already begun in the East, gave rise to circum-

stances that put Russia and her development in a position which
enabled us to achieve precisely that combination of a "peasant war"
with the working-class movement suggested in 1856 by no less a
Marxist than Marx himself as a possible prospect for Prussia?

What if the complete hopelessness of the situation, by stimulating
the efforts of the workers and peasants tenfold, offered us the opportunity to create the fundamental requisites of civilisation in a
different way from that of the West-European countries? Has that
altered the general line of development of world history? Has that
altered the basic relations between the basic classes of all the
countries that are being, or have been, drawn into the general
course of world history?

If a definite level of culture is required for the building of socialism (although nobody can say just what that definite "level of
culture" is, for it differs in every West-European country), why
cannot we begin by first achieving the prerequisites for that definite
level of culture in a revolutionary way, and *then*, with the aid of
the workers' and peasants' government and the Soviet system,
proceed to overtake the other nations?

January 16, 1923

II

You say that civilisation is necessary for the building of socialism. Very good. But why could we not first create such prerequisites of civilisation in our country as the expulsion of the landowners and the Russian capitalists, and then start moving towards
socialism? Where, in what books, have you read that such variations of the customary historical sequence of events are impermissible or impossible?

Napoleon, I think, wrote: "*On s'engage et puis ... on voit.*" Rendered freely this means: "First engage in a serious battle and then
see what happens." Well, we did first engage in a serious battle in
October 1917, and then saw such details of development (from the
standpoint of world history they were certainly details) as the
Brest peace, the New Economic Policy, and so forth. And now
there can be no doubt that in the main we have been victorious.

Our Sukhanovs, not to mention Social-Democrats still farther to
the right, never even dream that revolutions could be made otherwise. Our European philistines never even dream that the subsequent revolutions in Oriental countries, which possess much vaster
populations and a much vaster diversity of social conditions, will
undoubtedly display even greater distinctions than the Russian
revolution.

It need hardly be said that a textbook written on Kautskyan lines was a very useful thing in its day. But it is time, for all that, to abandon the idea that it foresaw all the forms of development of subsequent world history. It would be timely to say that those who think so are simply fools.

January 17, 1923

First published in
Pravda No. 117,
May 30, 1923
Signed: *Lenin*

Collected Works, Vol. 33

BETTER FEWER, BUT BETTER

In the matter of improving our state apparatus, the Workers' and Peasants' Inspection should not, in my opinion, either strive after quantity or hurry. We have so far been able to devote so little thought and attention to the efficiency of our state apparatus that it would now be quite legitimate if we took special care to secure its thorough organisation, and concentrated in the Workers' and Peasants' Inspection a staff of workers really abreast of the times, i.e., not inferior to the best West-European standards. For a socialist republic this condition is, of course, too modest. But our experience of the first five years has fairly crammed our heads with mistrust and scepticism. These qualities assert themselves involuntarily when, for example, we hear people dilating at too great length and too flippantly on "proletarian" culture. For a start, we should be satisfied with real bourgeois culture; for a start, we should be glad to dispense with the cruder types of pre-bourgeois culture, i.e., bureaucratic culture or serf culture, etc. In matters of culture, haste and sweeping measures are most harmful. Many of our young writers and Communists should get this well into their heads.

Thus, in the matter of our state apparatus we should now draw the conclusion from our past experience that it would be better to proceed more slowly.

Our state apparatus is so deplorable, not to say wretched, that we must first think very carefully how to combat its defects, bearing in mind that these defects are rooted in the past, which, although it has been overthrown, has not yet been overcome, has not yet reached the stage of a culture that has receded into the distant past. I say culture deliberately, because in these matters we can only regard as achieved what has become part and parcel of our culture, of our social life, our habits. We might say that the good in our social system has not been properly studied, understood, and

taken to heart; it has been hastily grasped at; it has not been verified or tested, corroborated by experience, and not made durable,
etc. Of course, it could not be otherwise in a revolutionary epoch,
when development proceeded at such breakneck speed that in
a matter of five years we passed from tsarism to the Soviet
system.

It is time we did something about it. We must show sound scepticism for too rapid progress, for boastfulness, etc. We must give
thought to testing the steps forward we proclaim every hour, take
every minute and then prove every second that they are flimsy,
superficial and misunderstood. The most harmful thing here would
be haste. The most harmful thing would be to rely on the assumption that we know at least something, or that we have any considerable number of elements necessary for the building of a really
new state apparatus, one really worthy to be called socialist, Soviet, etc.

No, we are ridiculously deficient of such an apparatus, and even
of the elements of it, and we must remember that we should
not stint time on building it, and that it will take many, many
years.

What elements have we for building this apparatus? Only two.
First, the workers who are absorbed in the struggle for socialism.
These elements are not sufficiently educated. They would like to
build a better apparatus for us, but they do not know how. They
cannot build one. They have not yet developed the culture required
for this; and it is culture that is required. Nothing will be achieved
in this by doing things in a rush, by assault, by vim or vigour, or
in general, by any of the best human qualities. Secondly, we have
elements of knowledge, education and training, but they are
ridiculously inadequate compared with all other countries.

Here we must not forget that we are too prone to compensate
(or imagine that we can compensate) our lack of knowledge by
zeal, haste, etc.

In order to renovate our state apparatus we must at all costs
set out, first, to learn, secondly, to learn, and thirdly, to learn, and
then see to it that learning shall not remain a dead letter, or a
fashionable catch-phrase (and we should admit in all frankness
that this happens very often with us), that learning shall really
become part of our very being, that it shall actually and fully become a constituent element of our social life. In short, we must not
make the demands that are made by bourgeois Western Europe,
but demands that are fit and proper for a country which has set out
to develop into a socialist country.

The conclusions to be drawn from the above are the following:
we must make the Workers' and Peasants' Inspection a really exemplary institution, an instrument to improve our state apparatus.

In order that it may attain the desired high level, we must follow the rule: "Measure your cloth seven times before you cut."

For this purpose, we must utilise the very best of what there is in our social system, and utilise it with the greatest caution, thoughtfulness and knowledge, to build up the new People's Commissariat.

For this purpose, the best elements that we have in our social system—such as, first, the advanced workers, and, second, the really enlightened elements for whom we can vouch that they will not take the word for the deed, and will not utter a single word that goes against their conscience—should not shrink from admitting any difficulty and should not shrink from any struggle in order to achieve the object they have seriously set themselves.

We have been bustling for five years trying to improve our state apparatus, but it has been mere bustle, which has proved useless in these five years, or even futile, or even harmful. This bustle created the impression that we were doing something, but in effect it was only clogging up our institutions and our brains.

It is high time things were changed.

We must follow the rule: Better fewer, but better. We must follow the rule: Better get good human material in two or even three years than work in haste without hope of getting any at all.

I know that it will be hard to keep to this rule and apply it under our conditions. I know that the opposite rule will force its way through a thousand loopholes. I know that enormous resistance will have to be put up, that devilish persistence will be required, that in the first few years at least work in this field will be hellishly hard. Nevertheless, I am convinced that only by such effort shall we be able to achieve our aim; and that only by achieving this aim shall we create a republic that is really worthy of the name of Soviet, socialist, and so on, and so forth.

Many readers probably thought that the figures I quoted by way of illustration in my first article[333] were too small. I am sure that many calculations may be made to prove that they are. But I think that we must put one thing above all such and other calculations, i.e., our desire to obtain really exemplary quality.

I think that the time has at last come when we must work in real earnest to improve our state apparatus and in this there can scarcely be anything more harmful than haste. That is why I would sound a strong warning against inflating the figures. In my opinion, we should, on the contrary, be especially sparing with figures in this matter. Let us say frankly that the People's Commissariat of the Workers' and Peasants' Inspection does not at present enjoy the slightest authority. Everybody knows that no other institutions are worse organised than those of our Workers' and Peasants' Inspection, and that under present conditions nothing can be expected from this People's Commissariat. We must have this firmly fixed in our minds if we really want to create within a few years an institution that will, first, be an exemplary institution, secondly, win everybody's absolute confidence, and, thirdly, prove to all and sundry that we have really justified the work of such a highly placed institution as the Central Control Commission.[334] In my opinion, we must immediately and irrevocably reject all general figures for the size of office staffs. We must select employees for the Workers' and Peasants' Inspection with particular care and only on the basis of the strictest test. Indeed, what is the use of establishing a People's Commissariat which carries on anyhow, which does not enjoy the slightest confidence, and whose word carries scarcely any weight? I think that our main object in launching the work of reconstruction that we now have in mind is to avoid all this.

The workers whom we are enlisting as members of the Central Control Commission must be irreproachable Communists, and I think that a great deal has yet to be done to teach them the methods and objects of their work. Furthermore, there must be a definite number of secretaries to assist in this work, who must be put to a triple test before they are appointed to their posts. Lastly, the officials whom in exceptional cases we shall accept directly as employees of the Workers' and Peasants' Inspection must conform to the following requirements:

First, they must be recommended by several Communists.

Second, they must pass a test for knowledge of our state apparatus.

Third, they must pass a test in the fundamentals of the theory of our state apparatus, in the fundamentals of management, office routine, etc.

Fourth, they must work in such close harmony with the members of the Central Control Commission and with their own secretariat that we could vouch for the work of the whole apparatus.

I know that these requirements are extraordinarily strict, and I am very much afraid that the majority of the "practical" workers in the Workers' and Peasants' Inspection will say that these requirements are impracticable, or will scoff at them. But I ask any of the present chiefs of the Workers' and Peasants' Inspection, or anyone associated with that body, whether they can honestly tell me the practical purpose of a People's Commissariat like the Workers' and Peasants' Inspection. I think this question will help them recover their sense of proportion. Either it is not worth while having another of the numerous reorganisations that we have had of this hopeless affair, the Workers' and Peasants' Inspection, or we must really set to work, by slow, difficult and unusual methods, and by testing these methods over and over again, to create something really exemplary, something that will win the respect of all and sundry for its merits, and not only because of its rank and title.

If we do not arm ourselves with patience, if we do not devote several years to this task, we had better not tackle it at all.

In my opinion we ought to select a minimum number of the higher labour research institutes, etc., which we have baked so hastily, see whether they are organised properly, and allow them to continue working, but only in a way that conforms to the high standards of modern science and gives us all its benefits. If we do that it will not be utopian to hope that within a few years we shall have an institution that will be able to perform its functions, to work systematically and steadily on improving our state apparatus, an institution backed by the trust of the working class, of the Russian Communist Party, and the whole population of our Republic.

The spade-work for this could be begun at once. If the People's Commissariat of the Workers' and Peasants' Inspection accepted the present plan of reorganisation, it could now take preparatory steps and work methodically until the task is completed, without haste, and not hesitating to alter what has already been done.

Any half-hearted solution would be extremely harmful in this matter. A measure for the size of the staff of the Workers' and Peasants' Inspection based on any other consideration would, in fact, be based on the old bureaucratic considerations, on old prejudices, on what has already been condemned, universally ridiculed, etc.

In substance, the matter is as follows:

Either we prove now that we have really learned something about state organisation (we ought to have learned something in five years), or we prove that we are not sufficiently mature for it. If the latter is the case, we had better not tackle the task.

I think that with the available human material it will not be immodest to assume that we have learned enough to be able systematically to rebuild at least one People's Commissariat. True, this one People's Commissariat will have to be the model for our entire state apparatus.

We ought at once to announce a contest in the compilation of two or more textbooks on the organisation of labour in general, and on management in particular. We can take as a basis the book already published by Yermansky, although it should be said in parentheses that he obviously sympathises with Menshevism and is unfit to compile textbooks for the Soviet system.

We can also take as a basis the recent book by Kerzhentsev,[335] and some of the other partial textbooks available may be useful too.

We ought to send several qualified and conscientious people to Germany, or to Britain, to collect literature and to study this question. I mention Britain in case it is found impossible to send people to the U.S.A. or Canada.

We ought to appoint a commission to draw up the preliminary programme of examinations for prospective employees of the Workers' and Peasants' Inspection; ditto for candidates to the Central Control Commission.

These and similar measures will not, of course, cause any difficulties for the People's Commissar or the collegium of the Workers' and Peasants' Inspection, or for the Presidium of the Central Control Commission.

Simultaneously, a preparatory commission should be appointed to select candidates for membership of the Central Control Commission. I hope that we shall now be able to find more than enough candidates for this post among the experienced workers in all departments, as well as among the students of our Soviet higher schools. It would hardly be right to exclude one or another category beforehand. Probably preference will have to be given to a mixed composition for this institution, which should combine many qualities, and dissimilar merits. Consequently, the task of drawing up the list of candidates will entail a considerable amount of work. For example, it would be least desirable for the staff of the new People's Commissariat to consist of people of one type, only of officials, say, or for it to exclude people of the propagandist type, or people whose principal quality is sociability or the ability to penetrate into circles that are not altogether customary for officials in this field, etc.

* * *

I think I shall be able to express my idea best if I compare my plan with that of academic institutions. Under the guidance of their Presidium, the members of the Central Control Commission should systematically examine all the papers and documents of the Political Bureau. Moreover, they should divide their time correctly between various jobs in investigating the routine in our institutions, from the very small and privately-owned offices to the highest state institutions. And lastly, their functions should include the study of theory, i.e., the theory of organisation of the work they intend to devote themselves to, and practical work under the guidance either of older comrades or of teachers in the higher institutes for the organisation of labour.

I do not think, however, that they will be able to confine them-selves to this sort of academic work. In addition, they will have to prepare themselves for work which I would not hesitate to call training to catch, I will not say rogues, but something like that, and working out special ruses to screen their movements, their approach, etc.

If such proposals were made in West-European government institutions they would rouse frightful resentment, a feeling of moral indignation, etc.; but I trust that we have not become so bureaucratic as to be capable of that. NEP has not yet succeeded in gaining such respect as to cause any of us to be shocked at the idea that somebody may be caught. Our Soviet Republic is of such recent construction, and there are such heaps of the old lumber still lying around that it would hardly occur to anyone to be shocked at the idea that we should delve into them by means of ruses, by means of investigations sometimes directed to rather remote sources or in a roundabout way. And even if it did occur to anyone to be shocked by this, we may be sure that such a person would make himself a laughing-stock.

Let us hope that our new Workers' and Peasants' Inspection will abandon what the French call *pruderie*, which we may call ridiculous primness, or ridiculous swank, and which plays entirely into the hands of our Soviet and Party bureaucracy. Let it be said in parentheses that we have bureaucrats in our Party offices as well as in Soviet offices.

When I said above that we must study and study hard in institutes for the higher organisation of labour, etc., I did not by any means imply "studying" in the schoolroom way, nor did I confine myself to the idea of studying only in the schoolroom way. I hope that not a single genuine revolutionary will suspect me of refusing, in this case, to understand "studies" to include resorting to some semi-humorous trick, cunning device, piece of trickery or something of that sort. I know that in the staid and earnest states of Western Europe such an idea would horrify people and that not a single decent official would even entertain it. I hope, however, that we have not yet become as bureaucratic as all that and that in our midst the discussion of this idea will give rise to nothing more than amusement.

Indeed, why not combine pleasure with utility? Why not resort to some humorous or semi-humorous trick to expose something ridiculous, something harmful, something semi-ridiculous, semi-harmful, etc.?

It seems to me that our Workers' and Peasants' Inspection will gain a great deal if it undertakes to examine these ideas, and that the list of cases in which our Central Control Commission and its colleagues in the Workers' and Peasants' Inspection achieved a few of their most brilliant victories will be enriched by not a few exploits of our future Workers' and Peasants' Inspection and Central Control Commission members in places not quite mentionable in prim and staid textbooks.

* * *

How can a Party institution be amalgamated with a Soviet institution? Is there not something improper in this suggestion?

I do not ask these questions on my own behalf, but on behalf of those I hinted at above when I said that we have bureaucrats in our Party institutions as well as in the Soviet institutions.

But why, indeed, should we not amalgamate the two if this is in the interests of our work? Do we not all see that such an amalgamation has been very beneficial in the case of the People's Commissariat of Foreign Affairs, where it was brought about at the very beginning? Does not the Political Bureau discuss from the Party point of view many questions, both minor and important, concerning the "moves" we should make in reply to the "moves" of foreign powers in order to forestall their, say, cunning, if we are not to use a less respectable term? Is not this flexible amalgamation of a Soviet institution with a Party institution a source of great strength in our politics? I think that what has proved its usefulness, what has been definitely adopted in our foreign politics and has become so customary that it no longer calls forth any doubt in this field, will be at least as appropriate (in fact, I think it will be much more appropriate) for our state apparatus as a whole. The functions of the Workers' and Peasants' Inspection cover our state apparatus as a whole, and its activities should affect all and every state institution without exception: local, central, commercial, purely administrative, educational, archive, theatrical, etc.—in short, all without any exception.

Why then should not an institution, whose activities have such wide scope, and which moreover requires such extraordinary flexibility of forms, be permitted to adopt this peculiar amalgamation of a Party control institution with a Soviet control institution?

I see no obstacles to this. What is more, I think that such an amalgamation is the only guarantee of success in our work. I think that all doubts on this score arise in the dustiest corners of our government offices, and that they deserve to be treated with nothing but ridicule.

* * *

Another doubt: is it expedient to combine educational activities with official activities? I think that it is not only expedient, but necessary. Generally speaking, in spite of our revolutionary attitude towards the West-European form of state, we have allowed ourselves to become infected with a number of its most harmful and ridiculous prejudices; to some extent we have been deliberately infected with them by our dear bureaucrats, who counted on being able again and again to fish in the muddy waters of these prejudices. And they did fish in these muddy waters to so great an extent that only the blind among us failed to see how extensively this fishing was practised.

In all spheres of social, economic and political relationships we are "frightfully" revolutionary. But as regards precedence, the observance of the forms and rites of office management, our "revolutionariness" often gives way to the mustiest routine. On more than one occasion, we have witnessed the very interesting phenomenon of a great leap forward in social life being accompanied by amazing timidity whenever the slightest changes are proposed.

This is natural, for the boldest steps forward were taken in a field which was long reserved for theoretical study, which was promoted mainly, and even almost exclusively, in theory. The Russian, when away from work, found solace from bleak bureaucratic realities in unusually bold theoretical constructions, and that is why in our country these unusually bold theoretical constructions assumed an unusually lopsided character. Theoretical audacity in general constructions went hand in hand with amazing timidity as regards certain very minor reforms in office routine. Some great universal agrarian revolution was worked out with an audacity unexampled in any other country, and at the same time the imagination failed when it came to working out a tenth-rate reform in office routine; the imagination, or patience, was lacking to apply to this reform the general propositions that produced such brilliant results when applied to general problems.

That is why in our present life reckless audacity goes hand in hand, to an astonishing degree, with timidity of thought even when it comes to very minor changes.

I think that this has happened in all really great revolutions, for really great revolutions grow out of the contradictions between the old, between what is directed towards developing the old, and the very abstract striving for the new, which must be so new as not to contain the tiniest particle of the old.

And the more abrupt the revolution, the longer will many of these contradictions last.

* * *

The general feature of our present life is the following: we have destroyed capitalist industry and have done our best to raze to the ground the medieval institutions and landed proprietorship, and thus created a small and very small peasantry, which is following the lead of the proletariat because it believes in the results of its revolutionary work. It is not easy for us, however, to keep going until the socialist revolution is victorious in more developed countries merely with the aid of this confidence, because economic necessity, especially under NEP, keeps the productivity of labour of the small and very small peasants at an extremely low level. Moreover, the international situation, too, threw Russia back and, by and large, reduced the labour productivity of the people to a level considerably below pre-war. The West-European capitalist powers, partly deliberately and partly unconsciously, did everything they could to throw us back, to utilise the elements of the Civil War in Russia in order to spread as much ruin in the country as possible. It was precisely this way out of the imperialist war that seemed to have many advantages. They argued somewhat as follows: "If we fail to overthrow the revolutionary system in Russia, we shall, at all events, hinder its progress towards socialism." And from their point of view they could argue in no other way. In the end, their problem was half solved. They failed to overthrow the new system created by the revolution, but they did prevent it from at once taking the step forward that would have justified the forecasts of the socialists, that would have enabled the latter to develop the productive forces with enormous speed, to develop all the potentialities which, taken together, would have produced socialism; socialists would thus have proved to all and sundry that socialism contains within itself gigantic forces and that mankind had now entered into a new stage of development of extraordinarily brilliant prospects.

The system of international relationships which has now taken shape is one in which a European state, Germany, is enslaved by the victor countries. Furthermore, owing to their victory, a number of states, the oldest states in the West, are in a position to make some insignificant concessions to their oppressed classes—concessions which, insignificant though they are, nevertheless retard the revolutionary movement in those countries and create some semblance of "class truce".

At the same time, as a result of the last imperialist war, a number of countries of the East, India, China, etc., have been completely jolted out of the rut. Their development has definitely shifted to general European capitalist lines. The general European ferment has begun to affect them, and it is now clear to the whole world that they have been drawn into a process of development that must lead to a crisis in the whole of world capitalism.

Thus, at the present time we are confronted with the question— shall we be able to hold on with our small and very small peasant production, and in our present state of ruin, until the West-

European capitalist countries consummate their development towards socialism? But they are consummating it not as we formerly expected. They are not consummating it through the gradual "maturing" of socialism, but through the exploitation of some countries by others, through the exploitation of the first of the countries vanquished in the imperialist war combined with the exploitation of the whole of the East. On the other hand, precisely as a result of the first imperialist war, the East has been definitely drawn into the revolutionary movement, has been definitely drawn into the general maelstrom of the world revolutionary movement.

What tactics does this situation prescribe for our country? Obviously the following. We must display extreme caution so as to preserve our workers' government and to retain our small and very small peasantry under its leadership and authority. We have the advantage that the whole world is now passing to a movement that must give rise to a world socialist revolution. But we are labouring under the disadvantage that the imperialists have succeeded in splitting the world into two camps; and this split is made more complicated by the fact that it is extremely difficult for Germany, which is really a land of advanced, cultured, capitalist development, to rise to her feet. All the capitalist powers of what is called the West are pecking at her and preventing her from rising. On the other hand, the entire East, with its hundreds of millions of exploited working people, reduced to the last degree of human suffering, has been forced into a position where its physical and material strength cannot possibly be compared with the physical, material and military strength of any of the much smaller West-European states.

Can we save ourselves from the impending conflict with these imperialist countries? May we hope that the internal antagonisms and conflicts between the thriving imperialist countries of the West and the thriving imperialist countries of the East will give us a second respite as they did the first time, when the campaign of the West-European counter-revolution in support of the Russian counter-revolution broke down owing to the antagonisms in the camp of the counter-revolutionaries of the West and the East, in the camp of the Eastern and Western exploiters, in the camp of Japan and the U.S.A.?

I think the reply to this question should be that the issue depends upon too many factors, and that the outcome of the struggle as a whole can be forecast only because in the long run capitalism itself is educating and training the vast majority of the population of the globe for the struggle.

In the last analysis, the outcome of the struggle will be determined by the fact that Russia, India, China. etc., account for the overwhelming majority of the population of the globe. And during the past few years it is this majority that has been drawn into the struggle for emancipation with extraordinary rapidity, so that in this respect there cannot be the slightest doubt what the final outcome of the world struggle will be. In this sense, the complete victory of socialism is fully and absolutely assured.

But what interests us is not the inevitability of this complete victory of socialism, but the tactics which we, the Russian Communist Party, we, the Russian Soviet Government, should pursue to prevent the West-European counter-revolutionary states from crushing us. To ensure our existence until the next military conflict between the counter-revolutionary imperialist West and the revolutionary and nationalist East, between the most civilised countries of the world and the Orientally backward countries which, however, comprise the majority, this majority must become civilised. We, too, lack enough civilisation to enable us to pass straight on to socialism, although we do have the political requisites for it. We should adopt the following tactics, or pursue the following policy, to save ourselves.

We must strive to build up a state in which the workers retain the leadership of the peasants, in which they retain the confidence of the peasants, and by exercising the greatest economy remove every trace of extravagance from our social relations.

We must reduce our state apparatus to the utmost degree of economy. We must banish from it all traces of extravagance, of which so much has been left over from tsarist Russia, from its bureaucratic capitalist state machine.

Will not this be a reign of peasant limitations?

No. If we see to it that the working class retains its leadership over the peasantry, we shall be able, by exercising the greatest possible thrift in the economic life of our state, to use every saving we make to develop our large-scale machine industry, to develop electrification, the hydraulic extraction of peat, to complete the Volkhov Power Project,[336] etc.

In this, and in this alone, lies our hope. Only when we have done this shall we, speaking figuratively, be able to change horses, to change from the peasant, muzhik horse of poverty, from the horse of an economy designed for a ruined peasant country, to the horse which the proletariat is seeking and must seek—the horse of large-scale machine industry, of electrification, of the Volkhov Power Station, etc.

That is how I link up in my mind the general plan of our work, of our policy, of our tactics, of our strategy, with the functions of the reorganised Workers' and Peasants' Inspection. This is what, in my opinion, justifies the exceptional care, the exceptional attention that we must devote to the Workers' and Peasants' Inspection in raising it to an exceptionally high level, in giving it a leadership with Central Committee rights, etc., etc.

And this justification is that only by thoroughly purging our government machine, by reducing to the utmost everything that is not absolutely essential in it, shall we be certain of being able to keep going. Moreover, we shall be able to keep going not on the level of a small-peasant country, not on the level of universal limitation, but on a level steadily advancing to large-scale machine industry.

These are the lofty tasks that I dream of for our Workers' and Peasants' Inspection. That is why I am planning for it the amalgamation of the most authoritative Party body with an "ordinary" People's Commissariat.

March 2, 1923

Pravda No. 49,
March 4, 1923
Signed: *N. Lenin*   *Collected Works*, Vol. 33

NOTES

[1] Lenin wrote this article on the 30th anniversary of the death of Karl Marx.
p. 17

[2] This is a reference to the bourgeois-democratic and bourgeois revolutions of 1848-49 in France, Italy, Germany, Austria and Hungary.
p. 17

[3] *The Paris Commune* was the revolutionary government of the working class set up by the proletarian revolution in Paris in 1871. History's first government of the dictatorship of the proletariat, it existed for 73 days, from March 18 to May 28.
p. 17

[4] *Narodism* was a petty-bourgeois trend in the Russian revolutionary movement. It took shape in the 1870s. The Narodniks sought to destroy the autocracy and transfer the landed estates to the peasants. At the same time, they refused to recognise that the development of capitalist relations in Russia was a law-governed process and, consequently, considered the peasants and not the proletariat as the main revolutionary force, seeing the embryo of socialism in the village commune. In an effort to stir the peasants to fight the autocracy, they went to the villages, to the people (*narod*), hence their name. But they found no support there.

In the 1880-90s they reconciled themselves to tsarism, expressing the interests of the kulaks and bitterly opposing Marxism.
p. 17

[5] Founded by Marx in 1864, this was the first mass international revolutionary association of the proletariat in history. It laid the foundation for an international organisation of workers and for the world proletarian struggle for socialism. This, essentially, completed its function. Although it was officially disbanded in 1876, it ceased to exist in 1872.
p. 18

[6] The Russian revolution of 1905-07 gave tremendous impetus to the national liberation movement in a number of countries. Under the impact of this revolution, the bourgeois-revolutionary movement which started in Turkey at the end of the 19th century reached the peak of its intensity in 1908. The mutiny engineered in the Turkish Army by the Young Turks ended with the restoration of the 1876 Constitution and the creation of a parliament.

In Iran (Persia) the anti-feudal and anti-imperialist revolutionary movement gained further momentum after the 1905-07 revolution in Russia. This movement, led by the merchant-industrial bourgeoisie, resulted in the setting up of Iran's first-ever parliament and the adoption of the 1906 Constitution. With certain amendments, this Constitution is in operation to this day. The revolution in Persia was crushed through the intervention of foreign imperialists, and Britain and Russia divided Persia into zones of influence and eradicated the gains of the revolution.

In China, the bourgeoisie led a movement in 1905-11 for a Constitution and provincial autonomy and advanced the slogan of struggle against imperialism. Those years witnessed a mounting revolutionary movement among the peasants and workers as well. In 1911 the Manchu dynasty was deposed and China was proclaimed a republic. The revolutionary democrat Sun Yat-sen was elected provincial President, but under pressure of the counter-revolution he was forced to relinquish this post, which was taken over by the adventurer Yuan Shih-kai, who established a counter-revolutionary military dictatorship.   p. 19

[7] This article was written by Lenin on the 30th anniversary of the death of Karl Marx.   p. 20

[8] A reference to Engels's *Anti-Dühring. Herr Eugen Dühring's Revolution in Science.*   p. 21

[9] The Left or Young Hegelians constituted the Left wing of the idealistic Hegelian philosophy in Germany.

Marx and Engels, who, early in their revolutionary activities, were associated with the Young Hegelians, subsequently subjected the philosophy of the Young Hegelians to a withering criticism, revealing its class roots and showing its complete scientific hollowness.   p. 25

[10] *Proudhonism* was an unscientific trend of petty-bourgeois socialism which was hostile to Marxism. It derived its name from its ideologist, the French anarchist Pierre Joseph Proudhon. Criticising big capitalist ownership from the petty-bourgeois standpoint, Proudhon sought to perpetuate petty private ownership, suggesting the creation of "people's" and "exchange" banks, which, he claimed, would enable workers to acquire implements of production, become artisans and ensure the "just" marketing of their products. He failed to appreciate the historic role of the proletariat and adopted a negative attitude to the class struggle, the proletarian revolution and the dictatorship of the proletariat. As an anarchist he held that there was no need for a state as such. Proudhonism is scathingly criticised in Marx's *The Poverty of Philosophy.*   p. 25

[11] *Bakuninism*—a trend named after Mikhail Bakunin, an ideologist of anarchism and a rabid enemy of Marxism and scientific socialism. This trend was opposed to a state of any kind and failed to understand the historic role of the proletariat. Their idea was that a secret revolutionary society consisting of "outstanding" personalities should lead the people's uprisings that were to be accomplished forthwith. Their tactics of conspiracy, immediate revolts and terrorism were adventurist and hostile to the Marxist teaching on the state, and this brought Bakuninism close to Droudhonism.

Bakunin attempted to foist his views on the entire international working-class movement, joined the First International and sought to seize control of its General Council. For his disorganising activities he was expelled from the First International at the Hague Congress in 1872.   p. 26

[12] *Neo-Kantians* belonged to a reactionary trend in bourgeois philosophy which appeared in the mid-19th century in Germany. They adopted the most reactionary and idealistic aspects of Kantian philosophy and rejected all

elements of materialism in it. Under the slogan of "Back to Kant" they championed a revival of Kantian idealism and opposed dialectical and historical materialism. p. 26

13 In 1908-09 Lenin wrote his *Materialism and Empirio-Criticism*, in which he subjected revisionism to annihilating criticism, upheld the theoretical principles of Marxism and showed that all the latest achievements of science, particularly of the natural sciences, confirmed the teaching on dialectical materialism. p. 27

14 *The Constitutional-Democratic Party* (Cadet)—the principal political organisation of the liberal-monarchist bourgeoisie in Russia, was set up in October 1905. Its membership consisted of representatives of the bourgeoisie, Zemstvo officials from among the landowners, and bourgeois intellectuals. The Cadets limited themselves to demanding a constitutional monarchy. During the First World War they actively supported the predatory foreign policy of the tsarist government. When the bourgeois-democratic revolution broke out in February 1917 they attempted to save the monarchy. The Cadets were prominent in the bourgeois Provisional Government and pursued an anti-popular, counter-revolutionary policy. p. 30

15 *Millerandism* (Ministerialism)—an opportunist trend in the Social-Democratic movement. It derived its name from Alexandre Millerand, the French Social-Reformist, who in 1899 received a cabinet appointment in the reactionary bourgeois government of France and supported its anti-popular policy. Characterising Millerandism as revisionism and apostasy, Lenin pointed out that the Social-Reformists in the bourgeois government were becoming a screen for the capitalists and an instrument which that government was using to deceive the masses. p. 30

16 *Guesdists*—members of a revolutionary Marxist trend in the French socialist movement at the close of the 19th and beginning of the 20th century. This movement was headed by Jules Guesde and Paul Lafargue. In 1882, after the split in the Workers' Party of France at the Saint-Etienne Congress, the Guesdists organised an independent party which adopted the old name.

In 1901, led by Guesde, supporters of the revolutionary class struggle united in the Socialist Party of France (whose members were likewise called Guesdists). In 1905 the Guesdists united with the reformist French Socialist Party. During the imperialist war of 1914-18 this party's leaders betrayed the working class by adopting a social-chauvinist stand.

The *Jaurèsists* were supporters of Jean Jaurès, the French socialist, who headed the Right, reformist wing of the French socialist movement. Under the guise of the slogan "Freedom of criticism", the Jaurèsists demanded a revision of the basic principles of Marxism and preached class co-operation between the proletariat and the bourgeoisie. In 1902 they formed the reformist French Socialist Party.

Broussists or Possibilists (Paul Brousse, Benoît Malon and others)—a petty-bourgeois, reformist trend, which emerged in the French socialist movement in the 1880s and distracted the proletariat from revolutionary methods of struggle. The Possibilists rejected the revolutionary programme and tactics of the proletariat, glossed over the socialist objectives of the working-class movement and recommended limiting the struggle of the workers to what was "possible", hence the name of the party. The influence of the Possibilists spread chiefly in the economically backward regions of France and over the less developed sections of the working class.

Most of the Possibilists subsequently joined the reformist French Social-ist Party, founded in 1902 under the leadership of Jean Jaurès.   p. 30

[17] *The Social-Democratic Federation* of Britain was founded in 1884. Along with reformists and anarchists, the membership of this Federation included a group of revolutionary Social-Democrats, adherents of Marxism who formed the Left wing of the socialist movement in Britain. Engels criticised the Federation for its dogmatism and sectarianism, its isolation from the working-class movement in the country and its disregard of the features of this movement. In 1907 the Federation took a new name—Social-Democratic Party. In 1911, jointly with Left-wing elements in the Independent Labour Party, it formed the British Socialist Party. In 1920, alongside the Com-munist Unity group this party played the principal role in forming the Com-munist Party of Great Britain.   p. 30

[18] *Independent Labour Party* in Great Britain—a reformist organisation founded by the leaders of the "new trade unions" in 1893 during a revival of the strike struggle and a growth of the movement for the independence of the British working class from the bourgeois parties. The Independent Labour Party was joined by members of the "new trade unions" and a number of the old trade unions, as well as intellectuals and petty-bourgeoisie influenced by the Fabians. The Party was headed by James Keir Hardie. While laying claim to political independence from the bourgeois parties, the Independent Labour Party was " 'independent' only of socialism, but very dependent on liberalism" (V. I. Lenin, *Collected Works*, Vol. 18, p. 360). During the First World War it held Centrist views, but later slid into social-chauvinism.   p. 30

[19] *The Integralists* vere advocates of "integral" socialism, a variety of petty-bourgeois socialism. During the first decade of the 20th century, the Integral-ists, being a Centrist trend in the Italian Socialist Party, opposed the reform-ists, who held extremely opportunist views and co-operated with the reac-tionary bourgeoisie.   p. 30

[20] *The Mensheviks* represented an opportunist trend in the Russian Social-Democratic movement, being an offshoot of international opportunism. This trend was given shape in 1903 at the Second Congress of the R.S.D.L.P. by the opponents of Lenin's *Iskra*. At that congress the Leninists received the majority of the votes in the elections to the Party's central organs and were called Bolsheviks, while the opportunists, who were in the minority, became known as Mensheviks.

The Mensheviks came out against the Party's revolutionary programme. They opposed the hegemony of the proletariat in the revolution, the alliance of the working class with the peasants, and wanted agreement with the liberal bourgeoisie.

Following the defeat of the revolution of 1905-07 they sought to abolish the illegal revolutionary Party of the proletariat. They were expelled from the R.S.D.L.P. in January 1912 by the Sixth All-Russia Party Conference.

In 1917 Mensheviks held portfolios in the bourgeois Provisional Govern-ment. After the Great October Socialist Revolution the Mensheviks joined the other counter-revolutionary parties in fighting Soviet rule.   p. 30

[21] *Revolutionary syndicalism* was a petty-bourgeois semi-anarchist trend that appeared in the working-class movement of some West-European coun-tries at the close of the 19th century.

It maintained that the working class did not have to wage a political struggle and rejected the idea that the Party had to play the leading role and that there should be a dictatorship of the proletariat. It considered that by organising a general strike, the trade unions (syndicates) could overthrow capitalism without a revolution and take over the management of production.   p. 31

[22] *The Hannover Congress* of the German Social-Democratic Party sat on October 9-14, 1899. The report on the main item on the agenda—"The Attack on the Fundamental Views and Tactics of the Party"—was delivered by August Bebel. Lenin wrote that his speech would long remain "a model of the defence of Marxist views and of struggle for the truly socialist character of the workers' party." However, this congress, which came out against the revisionist views of Bernstein, refrained from subjecting Bernsteinism to extended criticism.   p. 34

[23] *Rabochaya Mysl* (Workers' Thought), mouthpiece of the Economists (see Note 26), was in existence from October 1897 to December 1902. Altogether 16 issues were put out.   p. 35

This is a reference to the strikes staged by St. Petersburg workers, primarily in the textile industry, in 1895 and, in particular, in 1896, under the leadership of the League of Struggle for the Emancipation of the Working Class. (See Note 262.) These strikes helped to promote the working-class movement in Moscow and other towns in Russia and compelled the government to expedite its revision of the factory laws and publish the law of June 2 (14), 1897, which shortened the working day at factories to eleven and a half hours.   p. 36

[25] This reference is to the Manifesto of the Russian Social-Democratic Labour Party, published in 1898 on the instructions of the First Congress of the R.S.D.L.P. and on its behalf by the Central Committee of the R.S.D.L.P. This Manifesto advanced the struggle for political freedom and the overthrow of the autocracy to the forefront of the Russian Social-Democratic movement, and linked the political struggle with the general objectives of the working-class movement.   p. 36

[26] *The Economist—Economism* was an opportunist trend in the Russian Social-Democratic movement of the end of the 19th and beginning of the 20th century, a Russian variety of international opportunism. The mouthpieces of the Economists were the newspaper *Rabochaya Mysl* (1897-1902) in Russia and the journal *Rabocheye Dyelo* (Workers' Cause) (1899-1902) abroad.

The Economists wanted the working class to confine itself to an economic struggle for higher wages, improved working conditions and so forth, holding that the political struggle should be left to the liberal bourgeoisie. They were opposed to the Party of the working class playing the leading role, considering that its functions should be solely to contemplate the spontaneous process of the movement and register developments. Economism held the threat of diverting the working class from the class revolutionary road and turning it into a political adjunct of the bourgeoisie.

A large role was played by Lenin's *Iskra* in the struggle against Economism. The ideological coup de grâce was dealt Economism by Lenin in the book *What Is To Be Done?*   p. 37

[27] *Rabocheye Dyelo*—journal of the Economists and non-periodic organ of the Union of Russian Social-Democrats Abroad. It was published in Geneva

from April 1899 to February 1902. Altogether 12 issues were put out. This journal was the foreign centre of the Economists and it waged an open struggle against the *Iskra* plan of setting up a party, called for a trade unionist policy, discounted the revolutionary potentialities of the peasantry, and so forth. p. 37

[28] *Listok Rabochego Dyela* (Rabocheye Dyelo Supplement) was published in Geneva from June 1900 to July 1901; altogether eight issues were put out. p. 37

[29] *Iskra*—the first all-Russia illegal Marxist newspaper, was founded by Lenin in 1900. It played the decisive role in organising a revolutionary Marxist Party of the working class.

The first issue of *Iskra* was published in December 1900 in Leipzig; subsequent issues appeared in print in Munich, London and Geneva.

The editors were V. I. Lenin, G. V. Plekhanov, Y. O. Martov, P. B. Axelrod, A. N. Potresov and V. I. Zasulich. Lenin was virtually the Editor-in-Chief and head of the newspaper.

Iskra became the rallying and training centre of Party cadres.

On Lenin's initiative and with his direct participation the *Iskra* editorial board drew up a draft Party programme and made the preparations for the Second Congress of the R.S.D.L.P., which was held in July-August 1903. This congress laid the foundation for a really revolutionary, Marxist Party in Russia. Soon after the congress the Mensheviks seized control of *Iskra*. As of its 52nd issue the newspaper ceased being the organ of revolutionary Marxism. Lenin called it the new, opportunist *Iskra* to distinguish it from the old revolutionary newspaper (up to issue No. 52). p. 38

[30] This refers to the mass revolutionary action of students and workers: political demonstrations, meetings and strikes that took place in February-March 1901 in St. Petersburg, Moscow, Kiev, Kharkov, Kazan, Yaroslavl, Warsaw, Belostok, Tomsk, Odessa and other towns in Russia.

The student movement of the 1900-01 school year, which sprang up on the soil of academic demands, acquired the nature of revolutionary political action against the reactionary policy of the autocracy. It was supported by foremost workers and roused a response in all sections of Russian society.

The direct cause for the demonstrations and strikes of February and March 1901 was the conscription into the army of 183 students of Kiev University for participation in a student political meeting. The government clamped down on the participants in the revolutionary actions. The reprisals were particularly severe in the case of the participants in the demonstration of March 4 (17), 1901 in the square before the Kazan Cathedral in St. Petersburg. The events of February-March 1901 showed that the wave of revolution was mounting in Russia. The fact that workers took part in the movement under political slogans was of great significance. p. 40

[31] A reference to Lenin's book *What Is To Be Done? Burning Questions of Our Movement*. This book was first put out by the Dietz Publishing House in Stuttgart in March 1902. p. 40

[32] *Zemstvos*—local self-government bodies headed by the nobility. They were set up in the central gubernias of tsarist Russia in 1864. Their powers were confined to purely local economic problems (the running of hospitals, the building of roads, statistics, insurance), and they were controlled by the gubernia governors and the Ministry for Internal Affairs, which could waive any decision the government found disagreeable. p. 42

[33] *Yuzhny Rabochy* (Southern Worker)—a Social-Democratic newspaper published illegally from January 1900 to April 1903 by a group calling itself by the same name; 12 issues were published. This newspaper opposed Economism and terrorism and advocated the need for a mass revolutionary movement.

The *Yuzhny Rabochy* group conducted extensive revolutionary work in Russia, but it displayed opportunist tendencies in the question of the attitude to the liberal bourgeoisie and to the peasant movement, and nurtured a separatist plan for setting up an all-Russia newspaper parallel to *Iskra*.
p. 44

[34] The First Congress of the R.S.D.L.P. was held in 1898. p. 47

[35] *The Emancipation of Labour group*—the first Russian Marxist group, it was organised by Georgi Plekhanov in 1883 in Switzerland. It did much to popularise Marxism in Russia. The two drafts of the programme of the Russian Social-Democrats (1883 and 1885), written by Plekhanov and published by the Emancipation of Labour group, were an important step towards the formation of a Social-Democratic Party in Russia. The Emancipation of Labour group established contact with the international working-class movement and represented the Russian Social-Democratic movement at all the congresses of the Second International, beginning with the First Congress, which was held in Paris in 1889. But the group erred gravely in a number of questions: it overestimated the role of the liberal bourgeoisie and underestimated the revolutionary peasants as a reserve of the proletarian revolution. These errors were the embryos of the future Menshevik views of Plekhanov and other members of the group. p. 49

[36] Lenin wrote *Two Tactics of Social-Democracy in the Democratic Revolution* in June-July 1905 after the Third Congress of the R.S.D.L.P. and the Menshevik Conference which sat in Geneva at the same time. On the importance of this book Lenin wrote: "It is a systematic statement of the *fundamental* tactical differences with the Mensheviks. These differences were fully formulated in the resolutions of the Third (Spring) R.S.D.L.P. (Bolshevik) Congress in London and the Menshevik Conference in Geneva and established the *basic* divergence between the Bolshevik and Menshevik appraisals of our bourgeois revolution as a whole from the standpoint of the proletariat's tasks" (V. I. Lenin, *Collected Works*, Vol. 13, p. 111). The publication of this book was a major event in the life of the Party. p. 50

[37] The mutiny on the armoured cruiser *Potemkin* broke out on June 14 (27), 1905. The mutineers sailed the battleship to Odessa where a general strike was in progress. But the favourable conditions for joint action by the workers of Odessa and by the sailors were not utilised. After eleven days at sea the mutineers, finding themselves running out of food and coal, were forced to sail to Rumania and surrender to the Rumanian authorities. Most of the sailors remained abroad. Those who returned to Russia were taken into custody and tried.

The *Potemkin* mutiny ended in failure, but the fact that the crew of this large naval vessel went over to the side of the revolution was an important step in the struggle against the autocracy. p. 50

[38] *Proletary*—an illegal Bolshevik weekly. Central organ of the R.S.D.L.P., it was set up by decision of the Third Party Congress. On April 27 (May 10), 1905, the Central Committee of the Party appointed Lenin Editor-in-Chief of this newspaper. *Proletary* was published in Geneva from May 14 (27) to

November 12 (25), 1905; 26 issues were put out. The newspaper continued the line of the old, Leninist *Iskra*.

Lenin wrote some 90 articles and notes for this newspaper. He conducted extensive work as the newspaper's head and editor. The newspaper was closely linked up with the Russian working-class movement. It printed articles and notes by workers who were directly participating in the revolutionary movement. p. 50

[39] The programme of the Socialist-Revolutionary Party was adopted at that party's first congress, which was held in Finland from December 29, 1905 to January 6, 1906.

The Socialist-Revolutionaries were members of a petty-bourgeois party of the same name in Russia. It was formed at the end of 1901 or the beginning of 1902 through the merging of various Narodnik groups and circles.

The Socialist-Revolutionaries did not see the class distinctions between the proletariat and the peasantry, slurred over the class stratification and contradictions within the peasantry and refused to concede the leading role in the revolution to the proletariat.

Their agrarian programme envisaged the abolition of private ownership of land and its transfer to the communities on the basis of equalitarian use, and the promotion of all kinds of co-operatives. There was nothing socialist in this programme, which the Socialist-Revolutionaries sought to present as a programme of the "socialisation of land", because the abolition only of private ownership of land, as Lenin pointed out, without the establishment of working-class rule and the transfer of all the basic means of production (banks, large factories, railways) into the hands of the working class could not destroy capitalist rule and put an end to the poverty of the masses. The realistic, historically progressive element of the Socialist-Revolutionary agrarian programme was that it demanded the abolition of the landed estates. This demand objectively mirrored the interests and aspirations of the peasantry in the period of the bourgeois-democratic revolution.

During the imperialist world war most of the Socialist-Revolutionaries embraced social-chauvinistic views.

After the bourgeois-democratic revolution of February 1917, the Socialist-Revolutionaries, together with the Mensheviks, were the mainstay of the bourgeois-landowner Provisional Government, and the party's leaders (Kerensky, Avksentyev, Chernov) were members of that Government. In this period the Socialist-Revolutionary Party refused to support the peasants' demand for the abolition of the landed estates, and the Socialist-Revolutionary ministers of the Provisional Government sent punitive expeditions against peasants who had seized landed estates.

At the close of November 1917 the Left wing of the Socialist-Revolutionaries formed the independent Left Socialist-Revolutionary Party.

During the foreign intervention and the Civil War the Socialist-Revolutionaries engaged in counter-revolutionary activities, actively helped the interventionists and whiteguards, took part in counter-revolutionary conspiracies and organised acts of terrorism against leaders of the Soviet Government and the Communist Party. p. 50

[40] *Osvobozhdeniye* (Emancipation)—a fortnightly journal published abroad under the editorship of P.B. Struve from June 18 (July 1), 1902 to October 5 (18), 1905. It was the mouthpiece of the Russian liberal bourgeoisie and consistently advocated moderate monarchist liberalism. A group, calling itself the League of Emancipation, which existed until October 1905, formed round this journal in 1903 (and took final shape in January 1904). In October

1905, together with the Zemstvo-Constitutionalists, the League of Emancipation formed the nucleus of the Constitutional-Democratic Party, which became the principal bourgeois party in Russia (see Note 14).   p. 52

[41] *New-Iskrists* were supporters of the new, opportunist *Iskra,* controlled by the Mensheviks (see Note 20).   p. 52

[42] The Third Congress of the R.S.D.L.P. was held in London on April 12-27 (April 25-May 10), 1905. It was prepared by the Bolsheviks and sat under Lenin's leadership. The Mensheviks refused to attend it and held their own conference in Geneva.

This congress reviewed the basic problems of the revolution in Russia and defined the tasks of the proletariat and its Party.

It charted the strategy and tactics of the Party in the bourgeois-democratic revolution. The immediate and most important objective set by the congress was that of organising the armed uprising. The congress pointed out that the armed uprising must be followed by the setting up of a provisional revolutionary government which would have to crush the resistance of the counter-revolution, carry out the minimum programme of the R.S.D.L.P. (see Note 57) and prepare the conditions for the transition to the socialist revolution.

The congress denounced the actions of the Mensheviks and their opportunism in questions of organisation and tactics. It set up the newspaper *Proletary* as the new central organ. At a plenary meeting of the Central Committee on April 27 (May 10), 1905, Lenin was appointed Editor-in-Chief of *Proletary.*

The significance of this congress was that it was the first congress of the Bolshevik Party and that it gave the Party and the working class a militant programme of struggle for the democratic revolution.   p. 52

[43] *The Bulygin Commission* was an extraordinary conference convened by order of the tsar on February 18 (March 3), 1905 under the chairmanship of A. G. Bulygin, Minister for Internal Affairs. It included big landowners and representatives of the reactionary nobility. Its purpose was to draw up a law on the convocation of a consultative State Duma.

The elections to the Bulygin Duma were not held and the government never convened it. The idea of convening it was shelved in face of the mounting revolution and the October political strike.   p. 54

[44] On January 9, 1905, by order of the tsar, troops fired on a peaceful demonstration of St. Petersburg workers who, led by the priest Gapon, were on their way to the Winter Palace to hand a petition to the tsar. This shooting down of unarmed workers triggered mass political strikes and demonstrations throughout Russia under the slogan "Down with the autocracy". It marked the beginning of the first Russian revolution of 1905-07.   p. 63

[45] This was the All-German National Assembly, which was convened after the revolution of March 1848 in Germany and began its sitting in Frankfort on May 18, 1848. Its main objective was to put an end to political dismemberment and draw up an all-German Constitution. However, because of the cowardice and vacillation of the liberal majority, and the indecision and inconsistency of the petty-bourgeois Left wing, the Assembly hesitated to assume supreme power in the country and failed to take a firm stand on the basic issues of the German revolution of 1848-49. In June 1849 the Assembly was dispersed by troops of the Württemberg Government.   p. 64

[46] The *Neue Rheinische Zeitung* was published in Cologne from June 1, 1848 to May 19, 1849. It was directed by Marx and Engels, with Marx as the Editor-in-Chief. To use Lenin's words, this was "the finest and unsurpassed organ of the revolutionary proletariat".   p. 64

[47] *The Sotsial-Demokrat*—a Georgian language Menshevik newspaper published in Tiflis from April 7 (20) to November 13 (26), 1906; altogether six issues appeared in print. This newspaper was headed by N. Jordania, leader of the Georgian Mensheviks.   p. 65

[48] A reference to a project for a state system drawn up by D. N. Shipov, a moderate liberal who headed the Right wing of the local self-government bodies (the Zemstvos). Seeking to limit the revolution and, at the same time, secure some concessions from the tsarist government in favour of the Zemstvos, Shipov recommended forming a consultative representative body under the tsar. The liberals hoped that by putting through this deal they would deceive the masses, preserve the monarchy and obtain some political rights for themselves.   p. 67

[49] *Russkaya Starina* (The Russian Antiquary)—a monthly historical journal published in St. Petersburg from 1870 to 1918.   p. 71

[50] *Theses on Feuerbach* by Marx (K. Marx, F. Engels, *Selected Works*, Vol. II, Moscow, 1962, pp. 403-405).

[51] *"General Redistribution"*—a popular slogan among the peasants of tsarist Russia which expressed their desire for a general redistribution of land.   p. 75

[52] *Russkiye Vedomosti* (Russian Recorder)—a newspaper which expressed the views of the moderate liberal intelligentsia. It was published in Moscow from 1863 to 1918.
Syn Otechestva (Son of the Fatherland)—a liberal newspaper published in St. Petersburg from 1856 to 1900 and then from November 18 (December 1), 1904 to December 2 (15), 1905.
Nasha Zhizn (Our Life)—a daily liberal newspaper published in St. Petersburg with intervals from November 6 (19), 1904 to July 11 (24), 1906.
Nashi Dni (Our Days)—a daily liberal newspaper published in St. Petersburg from December 18 (31), 1904 to February 5 (18), 1905; publication of this newspaper was resumed on December 7 (20), 1905, but only two issues came out in print.   p. 78

[53] *Man in the muffler*—a personage in a Chekhov story of the same name. Used in literature to characterise a narrow-minded philistine who is afraid of change and initiative.   p. 79

[54] K. Marx, F. Engels, *Selected Works*, Vol. I, Moscow, 1962, p. 67.   p. 84

[55] *Girondists and Jacobins* were members of two political groups of the bourgeoisie during the French bourgeois revolution of the end of the 18th century. The Girondists expressed the interests of the moderate bourgeoisie, which vacillated between the revolution and the counter-revolution and bargained with the monarchy.
The Jacobins represented the most determined section of the bourgeoisie, the revolutionary democrats who consistently demanded the abolition of

absolutism and feudalism. They headed the popular uprising of May 31-
June 2, 1793, which established the Jacobin dictatorship.

Lenin called the Mensheviks the Girondists of the Social-Democratic
movement. p. 84

56 A reference to the audience given by Nikolai II to a Zemstvo delegation on
June 6 (19), 1905. The delegation presented a petition to the tsar requesting
him to convene people's representatives with the purpose of establishing, in
agreement with him, a "renewed state system". p. 84

57 The Second Congress of the R.S.D.L.P., held in 1903, adopted a Party Programme consisting of two parts—a maximum and a minimum programme.
The maximum programme called for the triumph of the socialist revolution and the establishment of a proletarian dictatorship in order to build a
socialist society. The minimum programme covered the Party's immediate
demands: the overthrow of the autocracy, the establishment of a democratic
republic, the introduction of an eight-hour working day and the eradication
of all survivals of serfdom in the countryside. p. 84

58 This is a reference to the resolution on the attitude to be adopted towards
Liberals, submitted by A. N. Potresov and passed by the Second Congress of
the R.S.D.L.P. p. 85

59 The naval battle off Tsushima, on May 14-15 (27-28), 1905, during the Russo-
Japanese War. The battle ended with the defeat of the Russian fleet. p. 86

60 The expression "parliamentary cretinism" is used repeatedly by Lenin, and
was used by Marx and Engels.

Lenin applied it to the opportunists, who held that the parliamentary
system was all-powerful and that parliamentary activity was the only and
main form of political struggle under all conditions. p. 88

61 The draft agrarian programme submitted to the congress of the German
Social-Democratic Party in Breslau on October 6-12, 1895, contained grave
errors, in particular, betraying a trend to turn the proletarian Party into a
general "people's" party. The supporters of this draft, in addition to the
opportunists, included A. Bebel and W. Liebknecht. K. Kautsky, C. Zetkin
and other Social-Democrats sharply criticised this project, and it was
rejected by a majority vote. p. 90

62 *The Black Hundreds* were monarchist gangs organised by the tsarist police
to fight the revolutionary movement. They murdered revolutionaries, attacked
progressive intellectuals and staged Jewish pogroms. p. 94

63 *Frankfurter Zeitung*—a daily newspaper of the big German stock-market
manipulators, was published in Frankfort from 1856 to 1943. In 1949 it
changed its name to *Frankfurter Allgemeine* and became the mouthpiece of
the West-German monopolists. p. 95

64 Lenin refers to the programme published in 1874 by the London group of
Blanquists, former members of the Paris Commune.

Blanquism, a trend in the French socialist movement, was headed by
the outstanding revolutionary and leader of French utopian communism
Louis Auguste Blanqui.

The Blanquists expected, as Lenin wrote, "that mankind will be emancipated from wage-slavery not by the proletarian class struggle, but through
a conspiracy hatched by a small minority of intellectuals" (V. I. Lenin,

Collected Works, Vol. 10, p. 392). Rejecting action by a revolutionary party in favour of action by a secret handful of conspirators, they took no account of the specific situation necessary for the triumph of an uprising and scorned contact with the masses. p. 101

[65] Versailles, a suburb of Paris, where the counter-revolutionary Thiers government had its headquarters during the Paris Commune of 1871. p. 102

[66] *The Erfurt Programme* of the German Social-Democratic Party was adopted in October 1891 at a congress in Erfurt. Compared with the Gotha Programme (1875), it marked a step forward; it was founded on the Marxist theory of the inevitable downfall of the capitalist mode of production and its replacement by the socialist mode; it stressed that the working class had to engage in political struggle, underlined the Party's role as leader of this struggle, and so forth; but it also contained major concessions to opportunism. Engels gave an extended criticism of the draft Erfurt Programme in his *Contribution to the Critique of the Draft Social-Democratic Programme of 1891*. Lenin considered that its main drawback was its cowardly concession to opportunism, namely, that it passed the dictatorship of the proletariat over in silence. p. 106

[67] See F. Engels, *Die künftige italienische Revolution und die Socialistische Partei*. Bd. 22, S. 439-42, Dietz Verlag, Berlin, 1963. p. 106

[68] *Credo*—symbol of faith, a programme, the setting forth of a viewpoint. In 1899 a group of Economists published a document of that title. It advocated the opportunist views of the Economists, who refused to recognise that the proletariat played an independent role in politics and that there was a need for a political Party of the working class (see Note 26). p. 113

[69] A reference to a statement by Marx in his *Zur Kritik der Hegelschen Rechtsphilosophie* (Marx/Engels, *Werke*, Bd. I, S. 380, Dietz Verlag, Berlin, 1956). p. 114

[70] *L'Humanité*—a daily newspaper founded in 1904 by Jean Jaurès as the organ of the French Socialist Party. In 1905 it hailed the revolution that broke out in Russia. During the First World War, it was controlled by the extreme chauvinist Right wing of the French Socialist Party.

In December 1920, following the split in the French Socialist Party in Tours and the founding of the Communist Party of France, the newspaper became the latter's central organ. p. 115

[71] A reference to the Russo-Japanese War of 1904-05, in which tsarist Russia suffered defeat. p. 116

[72] Lenin refers to the participation of Louis Eugéne Varlin, prominent figure of the French working-class movement and the First International, in the Council of the Paris Commune in 1871 (see Note 15). p. 122

[73] *The Second Congress of the R.S.D.L.P.* was held on July 17 (30)-August 10 (23), 1903. It was prepared by *Iskra*, which under Lenin's leadership conducted extensive work in uniting the Russian Social-Democrats on the foundation of revolutionary Marxism.

The opportunists savagely attacked the draft Party Programme, which was debated at the congress. This draft was drawn up by the editors of *Iskra*. They levelled their attacks particularly on the proposition about the leading role played by the Party in the working-class movement, and the point about the need for the dictatorship of the proletariat. The congress gave a rebuff to the opportunists and endorsed the Party Programme, in which were formulated the immediate objectives of the proletariat in the pending bourgeois-democratic revolution (minimum programme) and its tasks stemming from the victory of the socialist revolution and the establishment of the proletarian dictatorship (maximum programme).   p. 123

[74] This was a Menshevik plan of supporting the Zemstvo campaign sponsored by bourgeois liberals in the period from the autumn of 1904 to January 1905. This campaign involved congresses, meetings and banquets at which speeches were made and resolutions, couched in moderate constitutional terms, were adopted.   p. 124

[75] K. Marx, F. Engels, *Selected Works*, Vol. I, Moscow, 1962, p. 271.   p. 125

[76] By mentioning the Brentano class struggle, Lenin has in mind the views of Lujo Brentano (1844-1931), the German bourgeois economist who preached a "social peace" in capitalist society, and believed that the social contradictions of capitalism could be surmounted without a class struggle, and that the working-class problem could be settled and the interests of the workers and capitalists reconciled through the organisation of reformist trade unions and the adoption of factory legislation.   p. 131

[77] The reformist Hirsch-Duncker trade unions in Germany were set up in 1868 by M. Hirsch and F. Duncker, leaders of the bourgeois Progressist Party. They preached "harmony" of interests between labour and capital and considered that capitalists could be admitted to membership in the trade unions alongside workers, and had no use for the strike struggle. The activities of the trade unions were confined chiefly to mutual aid funds and cultural-educational organisations.   p. 131

[78] *Rassvet* (Dawn)—a daily legal liberal newspaper, which was published in St. Petersburg from March 1 (14) to November 29 (December 12), 1905. p. 131

[79] *Zarya* (Dawn)—a Marxist scientific and political journal was published legally in Stuttgart in 1901-02 by the *Iskra* editorial office. It criticised international and Russian revisionism and upheld the theoretical principles of Marxism.
                                                                          p. 135

[80] *Moskovskiye Vedomosti* (Moscow Recorder)—a newspaper whose publication was started by Moscow University in 1756. In 1863-87 it was the organ of the monarchist-nationalists, who championed the views of the most reactionary sections of the landowners and clergy. In 1905 it became one of the main organs of the Black Hundreds. It was published until the Great October Socialist Revolution of 1917.   p. 137

[81] K. Marx, *Die Krisis und Konterrevolution* (Marx/Engels, *Werke*, Bd. 5, S. 398-404, Dietz Verlag, Berlin, 1959).   p. 140

[82] K. Marx, F. Engels, *Programme der radikal-demokratischen Partei und der Linken zu Frankfurt* (Marx/Engels, *Werke*, Bd. 5, S. 39-43, Dietz Verlag, Berlin, 1959).   p. 140

[83] K. Marx, F. Engels, *Programme der radikal-demokratischen Partei und der Linken zu Frankfurt* (Marx/Engels, *Werke*, Bd. 5, S. 39-43, Dietz Verlag, Berlin, 1959).   p. 141

[84] Lenin quotes from *Die Frankfurter Versammlung* an article by Engels (Marx/Engels, *Werke*, Bd. 5, S. 14-17, Dietz Verlag, Berlin, 1959).   p. 141

[85] F. Engels, *Die Berliner Debatte über die Revolution* (Marx/Engels, *Werke*, Bd. 5, S. 64-77, Dietz Verlag, Berlin, 1959).   p. 142

[86] K. Marx, *Der Gesetzentwurf über die Aufhebungen der Feudallasten* (Marx/Engels, *Werke*, Bd. 5, S. 278-83, Dietz Verlag, Berlin, 1959).   p. 143

[87] This organ of the Cologne Workers' League was first called *Zeitung des Arbeiter-Vereins zu Köln* (Newspaper of the Cologne Workers' League) with the sub-heading *Freiheit, Brüderlichkeit, Arbeit* (Freedom, Fraternity, Labour). The 40 issues that came out in print were published in the period from April to October 1848. They reported on the activities of the Cologne Workers' League and other working-class unions in Rhine Province. When publication was resumed on October 26, the newspaper was called *Freiheit, Brüderlichkeit, Arbeit*, under which name it carried on with a small interval until June 24, 1849. Altogether 32 issues appeared in print.   p. 144

[88] *The Communist League* was the first international organisation of the revolutionary proletariat. It was founded in London in the summer of 1847 at a congress of delegates from revolutionary proletarian organisations. Marx and Engels were its organisers and leaders, and on its instruction wrote the *Manifesto of the Communist Party*. The League existed until 1852, and prominent figures in it later played a leading role in the First International.
                                                                              p. 146

[89] *Tovarishch* (Comrade)—a daily bourgeois newspaper that was published in St. Petersburg from March 15 (28), 1906 to December 30, 1907 (December 12, 1908). Formally it was not affiliated to any party, but was controlled by the Left Constitutional-Democrats. Its contributors included Mensheviks. p. 146

[90] K. Marx, F. Engels, *Selected Works*, Vol. II, Moscow, 1962, p. 352.   p. 147

[91] A reference to the all-Russia political strike of October 1905.   p. 148

[92] *Izvestia Soveta Rabochikh Deputatov* (Bulletin of the Soviet of Workers' Deputies), official organ of the St. Petersburg Soviet of Workers' Deputies, was published from October 17 (30) to December 14 (27), 1905.   p. 148

[93] *Sotsial-Demokrat*—illegal newspaper of the R.S.D.L.P. It was published from February 1908 to January 1917. After the first issue, the newspaper was printed abroad. Of the 58 issues that appeared in print, five had supplements.

By decision of the Central Committee of the R.S.D.L.P., elected at the Fifth Congress (London), the newspaper's editorial staff consisted of Bolsheviks, Mensheviks and Polish Social-Democrats. To all intents and purposes the newspaper was directed by Lenin, whose articles were given prominence. He contributed more than 80 articles and notes, and became the newspaper's Editor-in-Chief in December 1911.

During the years of reaction and the period of the new uplift of the revolutionary movement, the *Sotsial-Demokrat* was an important instrument of the Bolsheviks in their struggle against the liquidators, Trotskyites and otzovists, for the preservation of the illegal Marxist Party, the enhancement of its unity and the strengthening of its ties with the masses.

During the First World War the *Sotsial-Demokrat*, as the central organ of the Bolshevik Party, played an exceedingly important role in popularising the Bolshevik slogans on questions of war, peace and revolution.   p. 153

[94] *The Conference of the R.S.D.L.P. Groups Abroad* was held in Berne on February 14-19 (February 27-March 4), 1915. It was convened on Lenin's initiative and played the role of an all-Party conference. The war and the Party's tasks were the main point on the agenda. The report on these questions was delivered by Lenin.

In the resolutions which it adopted on Lenin's report, the Berne Conference defined the Bolshevik Party's objectives and tactics in the situation brought about by the imperialist war.   p. 153

[95] *The Dreyfus case* was a provocation organised in 1894 by reactionary monarchist groups among the French military against an officer of the French General Staff. Dreyfus, a Jew, was falsely accused of espionage and high treason, and sentenced to life imprisonment. This frame-up was used by reactionary circles in France to stir up anti-Semitism and attack the Republican regime and democratic liberties. Dreyfus was pardoned in 1899 through the pressure of public opinion, and in 1906 he was exonerated by a court of appeal and reinstated in the army.   p. 159

[96] *The Zabern incident* took place in the town of Zabern, Alsace, in November 1913. A Prussian officer insulted Alsatian civilians and this caused an outburst of indignation among the local population, who were mostly French, against Prussian military oppression.   p. 159

[97] *The cultural-national autonomy*—an opportunist programme in the national question. It was proposed in the 1890s by the Austrian Social-Democrats Otto Bauer and Karl Renner. Its substance was that in each given country people of one and the same nationality, regardless of their place of residence, should form an autonomous national union, which would have complete jurisdiction over schools (separate schools for children of different nationalities) and other spheres of education and culture. Had it been implemented, this programme would have strengthened the influence of the clergy and of reactionary ideology within each national group, impeded the organisation of the working class and divided workers into national groups.

In a number of articles Lenin sharply criticised this autonomy, pointing out that underlying it was a "thoroughly bourgeois and thoroughly false" idea, namely, "securing the separation of all nations from one another by means of a special state institution" (V. I. Lenin, *Collected Works*, Vol. 20, p. 35).   p. 160

[98] See Letter from Marx to Engels of November 2, 1867 (K. Marx, F. Engels, *Selected Correspondence*, Moscow, 1965, p. 194).   p. 162

[99] *Augean stables*—according to Greek mythology these were enormous stables belonging to Augeas, King of Elis. They remained uncleaned for many years. Hercules cleaned them in one day. Hence a synonym for filth and corruption.   p. 162

100 *Die Glocke* (The Bell)—a journal published in Munich and then in Berlin in 1915-25 by the social-chauvinist Parvus (A. L. Gelfand), a member of the German Social-Democratic Party.   p. 163

101 *The Fabians* were members of the Fabian Society, a reformist organisation founded in Britain in 1844. It took its name from the Roman general Fabius Maximus, called Cunctator (the Delayer) for his military strategy of avoiding decisive battles against Hannibal in the 3rd century B.C. The members of this society were mostly bourgeois intellectuals—scientists, writers and politicians (Sidney and Beatrice Webb, Ramsay MacDonald, Bernard Shaw and others)—who scorned the necessity for the class struggle and the proletariat and the socialist revolution and maintained that the transition from capitalism to socialism could be effected solely by petty reforms and gradual changes in society. In 1900 the Fabian Society was incorporated in the Labour Party.   p. 164

102 *Die Neue Zeit* (New Times)—theoretical journal of the German Social-Democratic Party, was published in Stuttgart from 1883 to 1923. Prior to October 1917 it was edited by Kautsky and then by H. Cunow. Some of the works of Marx and Engels were first printed in this journal. Engels helped the editors with advice and now and then criticised them for divergences from Marxism. Its contributors included A. Bebel, W. Liebknecht, R. Luxemburg, F. Mehring, C. Zetkin, G. V. Plekhanov, P. Lafargue and other prominent figures of the German and international working-class movement of the close of the 19th and beginning of the 20th century. In the second half of the 1890s, after the death of Engels, the journal systematically printed articles by revisionists, including a series of articles by E. Bernstein on *Problems of Socialism*, which started the revisionist crusade against Marxism. During the First World War the journal adopted a Centrist stand and virtually gave its support to the social-chauvinists.   p. 164

103 This is a reference to the Sixth (Prague) All-Russia Conference of the R.S.D L.P., which was held on January 5-17 (18-30), 1912. It played the role of a congress and was instrumental in the further building up of the Bolshevik Party as a Party of the new type, and in strengthening its unity. Lenin directed the proceedings at this conference. He delivered reports on the contemporary situation and the Party's tasks, and on the work of the International Socialist Bureau, and spoke on a number of other points. He drew up the draft resolutions on all the major questions discussed by the conference. The Party Central Committee was elected at the conference, which summed up the results of an entire period of struggle by the Bolsheviks against the Mensheviks and consolidated the triumph of the Bolsheviks. The liquidators were expelled from the R.S.D.L.P. The conference strengthened the Party as an all-Russia organisation. Its decisions rallied the Party organisations in the different localities and determined the Party's political line and tactics in the situation marked by a fresh revolutionary upsurge.   p. 166

104 Lenin refers to the resolution on the national question, drawn up by him and adopted at a meeting of the Central Committee of the R.S.D.L.P. with Party officials on September 23-October 1 (October 6-14), 1913 in the small town of Poronin near Cracow.   p. 166

105 *Nashe Dyelo* (Our Cause)—a monthly journal of the Menshevik-liquidators. The first issue came out in print in January 1915 in place of the journal *Nasha Zarya*, which was closed down in October 1914. It was the main

mouthpiece of the social-chauvinists in Russia, and altogether six issues were printed. p. 166

106 The Zimmerwald or First International Socialist Conference sat on September 5-8, 1915. It was attended by 38 delegates from the socialists of 11 European countries: Germany, France, Italy, Russia, Poland, Rumania, Bulgaria, Sweden, Norway, Holland and Switzerland. The delegation from the Central Committee of the R.S.D.L.P. was led by Lenin.

The conference adopted a manifesto "To the Workers of Europe", which, thanks to the insistence of Lenin and the Left Social-Democrats, included a number of basic propositions of revolutionary Marxism. Moreover, the conference adopted the general statement of the German and French delegations, a resolution sympathising with the war victims and with people persecuted for their political activities, and elected an International Socialist Commission.

The Zimmerwald Left group was formed at this conference. It consisted of representatives of the Central Committee of the R.S.D.L.P. with Lenin at their head, the territorial board of the Social-Democratic Party of the Kingdom of Poland and Lithuania, the Central Committee of the Social-Democratic Party of the Latvian Territory, the Swedish, Norwegian and Swiss Lefts, and a group of International Socialists of Germany. At the conference, the Zimmerwald Left group actively opposed the Centrist majority. Only the representatives of the Bolshevik Party occupied a consistent stand. p. 166

107 *The Bulletin. Internationale Sozialistische Kommission zu Bern*—journal of the executive organ of the Zimmerwald group, was published from September 1915 to January 1917 in English, French and German. Altogether six issues were put out. p. 167

108 *The Second International*—an international association of socialist parties, was founded in 1889. When the epoch of imperialism was ushered in, opportunist trends began to gain the upper hand in it. In 1914, when the world war broke out, the opportunist leaders of the Second International openly championed the imperialist policy of the bourgeois governments of their countries. Finally this association broke up. p. 167

109 *Imperialism, the Highest Stage of Capitalism* was written in January-June 1916 in Zurich for the Parus Publishing House, which was founded in Petrograd in December 1915.

Lenin had noted the new phenomena in capitalist development long before the outbreak of the First World War. He brought to light and analysed some of the features of the epoch of imperialism, and closely followed and studied the latest literature on capitalism.

He began his comprehensive study of the monopoly stage of capitalism when the First World War broke out. The *Notebooks on Imperialism,* which were the preparatory material for *Imperialism, the Highest Stage of Capitalism,* comprise nearly 50 folios and contain notes from 148 books (including 106 German, 23 French and 17 English books, and two Russian translations) and 232 articles.

In mid-1917 the book was printed under the title *Imperialism, the Latest Stage of Capitalism (A Popular Outline).* The foreword, also written by Lenin, bore the date April 26, 1917. p. 169

110 This is a reference to the Peace Treaty signed by Soviet Russia and the Quadruple Alliance (Germany, Austria-Hungary, Bulgaria, Turkey) on March 3, 1918 at Brest-Litovsk and ratified by the Fourth Extraordinary All-Russia

Congress of Soviets on March 15. The peace terms were extremely onerous for Soviet Russia. They placed Poland, almost the entire Baltic area and part of Byelorussia under the suzerainty of Germany and Austria-Hungary. The Ukraine was separated from Soviet Russia and turned into a state dependent on Germany. Turkey obtained the towns of Kars, Batum and Ardagan. In August 1918, Germany imposed on Soviet Russia an additional treaty and a financial agreement, which contained further predatory demands.

On November 13, 1918, after the revolution in Germany in November 1918, when the monarchy was deposed, the All-Russia Central Executive Committee annulled the predatory, unjust Brest Treaty.   p. 172

111 *The Versailles Peace Treaty*, which ended the imperialist world war of 1914-18, was signed on June 28, 1919 by the U.S.A., the United Kingdom, France, Italy, Japan and their allies, on the one hand, and Germany on the other. Its purpose was to consolidate the redivision of the capitalist world in favour of the victors, and to create a system of relations among countries which would be directed towards the strangulation of Soviet Russia and the crushing of the revolutionary movement throughout the world.   p. 172

112 *Wilsonism* derived its name from Woodrow Wilson, U.S. President in 1913-21. During the first year of his presidency Wilson passed a series of laws (on a progressive income tax, and anti-trust bill and others), which he demagogically called the era of "new freedom". He and his supporters camouflaged the predatory policy of U.S. imperialism behind demagogic slogans and words about "democracy" and an "alliance of nations". As soon as Soviet power was established, Wilson was one of the first inspirers and organisers of intervention against Soviet Russia. With the aim of counteracting the deep impact of the Soviet Government's peaceful policy, Wilson advanced a demagogic 14-point "peace programme", which was designed as a screen for the U.S. policy of aggression. American propaganda and the European bourgeois press created for Wilson the oreole of a peace fighter. This was a false oreole, and very soon the hypocrisy of the petty-bourgeois phrasemongering of Wilson and the "Wilsonians" was exposed by the anti-labour policy pursued within the U.S.A. and the policy of aggression with regard to other countries.   p. 173

113 *The Basle Manifesto* of the Second International was adopted on November 25, 1912 by the Extraordinary International Socialist Congress, which sat in Basle on November 24-25, 1912. It warned the peoples of the threat of a world war, showed the predatory objectives of this war and urged the workers of all countries to wage a determined struggle for peace, "to pit against the might of capitalist imperialism the international solidarity of the working class". It included a point, formulated by Lenin, of the resolution of the Stuttgart Congress of 1907, which stated that if an imperialist war broke out socialists had to use the war-induced economic and political crisis to move forward the struggle for the socialist revolution.

The leaders of the Second International voted for the adoption of the anti-war manifesto, but when the war broke out they buried it in oblivion together with the other decisions of international socialist congresses on the struggle against war, and went over to the side of their imperialist governments.   p. 173

114 Lenin has in mind the Second (Berne) International that was set up at a conference of Socialist parties in Berne in February 1919 by the leaders of the West-European Socialist parties. It was designed to take the place of the Second International that ceased to exist at the outbreak of the First World War. Essentially speaking, it played the role of a servitor of the international bourgeoisie. p. 174

115 *The Independent Social-Democratic Party of Germany*, set up in April 1917, was a Centrist party. Behind a screen of Centrist phraseology its members preached "unity" with the social-chauvinists, sliding into renunciation of the class struggle. The core of this party consisted of the Kautskyan Arbeitergemeinschaft.

A split occurred in this party at a congress held in October 1920 in Halle. In December 1920 most of its members joined the Communist Party of Germany. The Right-wing elements formed a separate party under the old name of Independent Social-Democratic Party of Germany, and as such it existed until 1922. p. 174

116 *The Third Communist International* was an international revolutionary proletarian organisation which united Communist Parties of different countries. It was in existence from 1919 to 1943.

The establishment of the Third International became historically necessary after the split caused in the working-class movement by the betrayal of socialism by the opportunist leaders of the Second International at the outbreak of the First World War and the subsequent collapse of the Second International. Lenin played the leading role in founding the Communist International.

Its First Congress was held in Moscow on March 2-6, 1919, when it adopted a Manifesto to the workers of the whole world, in which it was pointed out that the Comintern was the heir to the ideals of Marx and Engels as expressed in the *Manifesto of the Communist Party*.

The Comintern restored and strengthened the links between the working people of all countries and helped to expose opportunism in the international working-class movement, consolidate the then young Communist Parties and frame the strategy and tactics of the international communist movement.

In May 1943, finding that the form of organisation satisfying the requirements of a passed stage has become outdated, the Comintern Executive Committee passed a decision to dissolve the Communist International. p. 174

117 *The Spartacus group,* a revolutionary organisation of German Left Social-Democrats, was formed at the outbreak of the First World War by Karl Liebknecht, Rosa Luxemburg, Franz Mehring, Clara Zetkin, Julian Marchlewski, Léon Jogiches (Tyszka) and Wilhelm Pieck. The members of this group spread revolutionary propaganda, organised mass anti-war actions, directed strikes and exposed the imperialist nature of the world war and the treachery of the opportunist Social-Democratic leaders. However, they went astray in questions of theory and politics: they underestimated the role of the proletarian Party in the struggle of the working class, feared a split with the opportunists, failed to appreciate the need for an alliance between the working class and the peasants and the importance of the national liberation movements, and opposed the right of nations to self-determination up to secession and the formation of independent states.

In April 1917 they joined the Centrist Independent Social-Democratic Party of Germany while retaining their organisational independence. In November 1918, in the course of the revolution in Germany, they formed the Spartacus Union and after publishing their programme in December 1918 they broke with the Independents. At the Inaugural Congress on December 30, 1918-January 1, 1919, they founded the Communist Party of Germany.

p. 174

[118] The *Versaillais* were supporters of the French counter-revolutionary bourgeois government headed by Louis Adolphe Thiers, which set up its headquarters at Versailles after the Paris Commune was formed in 1871. When the Commune was crushed the Versaillais took unheard-of reprisals against the Communards, so much so that their name has become a synonym of brutal counter-revolution.

p. 175

[119] *The Spanish-American War of 1898* was the first imperialist war with the objective of redividing the world.

The U.S. imperialists had their eye on Spanish colonies in Central America—Cuba and Puerto Rico—and also the Philippine Islands, which belonged to Spain. In that war Spain lost her most important colonies. The Philippine Islands, Puerto Rico and other islands passed to the U.S.A. Cuba was made independent, but in actual fact she became a semi-colony of the U.S.A.

The Anglo-Boer War (October 1899-May 1902) was a predatory war fought by Britain against two South African republics—the Transvaal Republic and the Orange Free State—as a result of which the latter lost their independence and became British colonies.

p. 176

[120] A reference to the resolution of the Chemnitz Congress of the German Social-Democratic Party on the question of imperialism and the attitude of socialists to the war. This resolution, passed on September 20, 1912, denounced imperialist policy and stressed the importance of the struggle for peace.

p. 176

[121] *Die Bank*—a journal of the German financiers. It was published in Berlin from 1908 to 1943.

p. 186

[122] K. Marx, *Capital,* Vol. III, Moscow, 1966, pp. 606-07.

p. 193

[123] *The Gründer scandals* took place during the rapid growth of the number of joint-stock companies in Germany during the early 1870s. This growth was accompanied by frenzied speculation in land and stocks on the stock-exchange which brought great wealth to the bourgeois operatives.

p. 194

[124] A reference to G. V. Plekhanov.

p. 202

[125] *Produgol*—abbreviation of the Russian Association for Trade in Mineral Fuel of the Donets Basin, a syndicate founded in 1906. *Prodamet* was the abbreviated name of the Association for the sale of Products of Russian Metallurgical Plants, founded in 1901.

p. 206

[126] *French Panama*—a term coined following the exposure in 1892-93 of glaring abuses and corruption among statesmen, politicians, civil servants and newspapers bribed by the French Panama Canal Company.

p. 209

[127] *Liquidationism* was an extreme Right, opportunist trend among the Mensheviks. It became rife in the Russian Social-Democratic Party in 1908-12, after the defeat of the first Russian revolution. The liquidators rejected

the programme and tactics of the Marxist Party, sought to abolish the proletarian revolutionary Party and organise their own reformist party and adapt it to the conditions prevailing under the tsarist regime.   p. 248

128 K. Marx, *Capital*, Vol. III, Moscow, 1966, pp. 118-19.   p. 252

129 This is a reference to the "final protocol" signed on September 7, 1901 by the imperialist powers (Britain, Austria-Hungary, Belgium, France, Germany, Italy, Japan, Russia, Holland, Spain and the U.S.A.) and China following the crushing of the Boxer uprising of 1899-1901. This protocol gave capitalism fresh possibilities of exploiting and plundering China.   p. 256

130 The Boxer uprising was a people's anti-imperialist revolt in China in 1899-1901. It was led by the I Ho T'uan society. This uprising was ruthlessly suppressed by a joint expeditionary corps of the imperialist powers. Its commander was the German General Count Alfred von Waldersee. The German, Japanese, British, American and Russian imperialists took part in crushing the uprising. In 1901 China was forced to sign the so-called "final protocol", under which she became a semi-colony of foreign imperialism.   p. 257

131 *Fashoda* (Kodok), a town in Eastern Sudan. In September 1898 a clash between British and French colonial troops at Fashoda gave rise to an acute crisis in international relations. This mirrored the struggle between Britain and France for domination in the Sudan and ended the division of Africa.   p. 257

132 *The State and Revolution. The Marxist Theory of the State and the Tasks of the Proletariat in the Revolution*, was written by Lenin in August-September 1917 when he was hiding from persecution by the bourgeois Provisional Government.

In Zurich in the autumn of 1916 and early in 1917 Lenin worked extensively in a library, studying the writings of Marx and Engels on the problem of the state. He wrote his notes in a small hand in a blue notebook, which he entitled *Marxism on the State*. These notes consisted of quotations from Marx and Engels as well as excerpts from books and articles by K. Kautsky, A. Pannekoek and E. Bernstein with critical commentaries, conclusions and generalisations by Lenin. This material served as the basis for the brilliant *The State and Revolution*. However, much of it was not used.

Originally Lenin planned seven chapters for *The State and Revolution*, but the last, seventh chapter—*The Experience of the Russian Revolutions of 1905 and 1917*—remained unwritten. Lenin left behind a detailed plan of this chapter and a plan for the *Conclusion. The State and Revolution* was published in 1918.

The second edition, with a new section—*The Presentation of the Question by Marx in 1852*—in Chapter 2 was published in 1919.

The State and Revolution was widely read in the U.S.S.R. and abroad.   p. 264

133 K. Marx, F. Engels, *Selected Works*, Vol. II, Moscow, 1962, pp. 318-19. Further below Lenin quotes from the same work (op. cit., pp. 319-22).   p. 267

[134] The gentile or clan organisation of society, i.e., the primitive communal system was the first socio-economic formation in human history. It was a community of blood relatives united by economic and social ties. Its relations of production were founded on social ownership of the means of production and an egalitarian distribution of products. In the main, this conformed to the low level and nature of the productive forces in that period.
p. 268

[135] *Bonapartism* (named after the two Bonaparte emperors) is a term used to designate a government that seeks to give the impression of being non-partisan and utilise the sharp struggle between the parties of the capitalists and the working class. While actually serving the interests of the capitalists, such a government, more than any other, deceives the workers with promises and paltry doles.
p. 272

[136] K. Marx, F. Engels, *Anti-Dühring*, Moscow, 1962, pp. 384-85.
p. 274

[137] *The Thirty Years' War of 1618-48* was the first general European war caused by an aggravation of contradictions between various groups of European states. These contradictions took the shape of a struggle between Protestants and Catholics. Germany became the main arena of this struggle, an object of military plunder and predatory claims. This war terminated with the conclusion of the Peace of Westphalia, which legalised the political dismemberment of Germany.
p. 277

[138] K. Marx, F. Engels, *Anti-Dühring*, Moscow, 1962, pp. 253-54.
p. 277

[139] This was the programme adopted in 1875 by the Socialist Labour Party of Germany at a congress in Gotha where the two then existing German Socialist parties merged. These were the Eisenachers (led by Bebel and Liebknecht and ideologically influenced by Marx and Engels) and the Lassalleans. The programme suffered from eclecticism and was opportunist; on major issues the Eisenachers made concessions to the Lassalleans and accepted their formulations. Marx (in the *Critique of the Gotha Programme*) and Engels (in a letter to Bebel on March 18-28, 1875), levelled annihilating criticism at the draft Gotha Programme, regarding it as a considerable step backwards compared with the Eisenach Programme of 1869.
p. 278

[140] K. Marx, F. Engels, *The Poverty of Philosophy*, Moscow, 1966, p.151. p. 279

[141] K. Marx, F. Engels, *Selected Works*, Vol. I, Moscow, 1962, pp. 45, 53.
p. 279

[142] K. Marx, F. Engels, *Selected Works*, Vol. I, Moscow, 1962, pp. 332-33.
p. 282

[143] Lenin refers to the bourgeois-democratic revolution in Russia of February 27 (March 12), 1917, which deposed the autocracy and led to the formation of a bourgeois Provisional Government.
p. 284

[144] In a statement made on March 2 (15), 1917 the Provisional Government announced that it would convene a Constituent Assembly. Elections were set for September 17 (30), 1917. However, it was soon announced that

the elections were postponed until November 12 (25). The Constituent Assembly was convened by the Soviet Government in Petrograd on January 5 (18), 1918. The elections were held according to the electoral lists drawn up before the Great October Socialist Revolution. On January 6 (19), 1918, after the Constituent Assembly refused to endorse the decrees of the Second Congress of Soviets on peace, on land and on the transfer of power to the Soviets, it was dissolved by decision of the All-Russia Central Executive Committee.   p. 284

145 K. Marx, F. Engels, *Selected Works*, Vol. I, Moscow, 1962, pp. 245-46.
p. 285

146 K. Marx, F. Engels, *Selected Correspondence*, Moscow, 1965, p. 69.
p. 287

147 K. Marx, F. Engels, *Selected Works*, Vol. I, Moscow, 1962, p. 22.   p. 289

148 K. Marx, F. Engels, *Selected Correspondence*, Moscow, 1965, pp. 262-63.
p. 290

149 This is a reference to the 1910 revolution in Portugal, where the monarchy was overthrown and a republic proclaimed on October 5, 1910.   p. 291

150 K. Marx, F. Engels, *Selected Works*, Vol. I, Moscow, 1962, pp. 516-20, 519-22.
p. 293

151 *Dyelo Naroda* (People's Cause), a daily newspaper published by the Socialist-Revolutionary Party from March 1917 to July 1918 in Petrograd. It advocated defencism and conciliation and supported the bourgeois Provisional Government.   p. 296

152 F. Engels, *The Housing Question*. Further below Lenin quoted from the same work. See also K. Marx, F. Engels, *Selected Works*, Vol. I, Moscow, 1962, pp. 570-71, 629, 613.   p. 304

153 A reference to *Der politische Indifferentismus*, an article by Marx, and "On Authority", an article by Engels.   p. 306

154 K. Marx, *Der politische Indifferentismus* (Marx/Engels, *Werke*, Bd. 18, S. 299-304, Dietz Verlag, Berlin, 1962).   p. 306

155 F. Engels, "On Authority" (K. Marx, F. Engels, *Selected Works*, Vol. I, Moscow, 1962, p. 638).   p. 307

156 F. Engels, "On Authority" (K. Marx, F. Engels, *Selected Works*, Vol. I, Moscow, 1962, pp. 638-39).   p. 308

157 K. Marx, *Critique of the Gotha Programme*, Moscow, 1966.   p. 309

158 K. Marx, F. Engels, *Selected Correspondence*, Moscow, 1965, pp. 293-94.
p. 309

[159] F. Engels, *Zur Kritik des sozial-demokratischen Programmentwurfes 1891* (Marx/Engels, *Werke*, Bd. 22, S. 227-43, Dietz Verlag, Berlin, 1962). Further below Lenin quotes from the same work.   p. 311

[160] In 1878 the Bismarck government in Germany passed an Anti-Socialist Law with the purpose of combating the workers and the socialist movement. This law banned all organisations of the Social-Democratic Party, mass workers' organisations and the working-class press; socialist literature was confiscated. More than 1,500 Social-Democrats were taken into custody. These repressions did not break the Social-Democratic Party. It reorganised its activities, going underground: its central organ was published abroad, while in Germany the Social-Democratic organisations and groups were revived illegally and were headed by the underground Central Committee. At the same time, the Party made good use of legal possibilities of strengthening its ties with the masses, and its influence grew steadily. Extensive assistance was rendered to the German Social-Democrats by Marx and Engels. The Anti-Socialist Law was repealed in 1890 under pressure from the growing mass working-class movement.   p. 313

[161] A reference to the Austro-Prussian War of 1866 and the Franco-Prussian War of 1870-71, which ended with Germany's unification under the Prussian Junkers.   p. 315

[162] *Pravda*—legal daily Bolshevik newspaper. The first issue was printed in St. Petersburg on April 22 (May 5), 1912. Funds to finance the newspaper were donated by the workers, and its circulation reached 40,000 copies, while some issues had a circulation of 60,000 copies. Lenin characterised the organisation of the newspaper's day-to-day work as an epoch-making accomplishment of the St. Petersburg workers. *Pravda* kept the Party in constant touch with the masses and had a large army of worker-correspondents. It was directed by Lenin, who wrote for it almost every day, guided the work of its editorial staff and maintained its militant, revolutionary spirit.

The newspaper was subjected to constant police persecution. On July 8 (21), 1914 it was closed down, and publication was renewed only after the bourgeois-democratic revolution of February 1917. It was persecuted by the Provisional Government and this compelled it to change its name time and again. On October 27 (November 9), 1917, publication was resumed under the old name—*Pravda*.   p. 316

[163] K. Marx, F. Engels, *Selected Works*, Vol. I, Moscow, 1962, pp. 474-75, 479, 483, 484-85.   p. 317

[164] *Los-von-Kirche-Bewegung* (movement for separation from the church) or *Kirchenaustrittbewegung* (movement for withdrawal from the church) became a mass movement in Germany on the eve of the First World War. During the debates on the attitude of the Social-Democratic Party to this issue, leading figures in the German Social-Democratic movement did not oppose the Social-Democrat Göhre, who held that the Party should be neutral and forbid its members to carry on anti-religious and anti-clerical propaganda on behalf of the Party.   p. 318

[165] The figures given by Lenin for possible salaries are in the paper currency of the second half of 1917. During the First World War the Russian paper ruble depreciated considerably.   p. 319

[166] *Der Volksstaat*—central organ of the German Social-Democratic Party (Eisenachers), was published in Leipzig in 1869-76. The Editor-in-Chief was Wilhelm Liebknecht, and Marx and Engels were among the contributors.
p. 321

[167] The Lassalleans were supporters and followers of the German petty-bourgeois Socialist Ferdinand Lassalle. They belonged to the General Association of German Workers, which was founded in 1863 at a congress of workers' societies in Leipzig. Its first president was Lassalle, who charted its programme and tactics. Its political programme called for a drive for universal suffrage, and its economic programme demanded the setting up of state-subsidised workers' production associations. The Lassalleans supported Bismarck's Great-Power policy. Marx and Engels repeatedly and sharply criticised the Lassallean theory, tactics and organisational principles as being an opportunist trend in the German working-class movement.
p. 321

[168] Frederick Engels, *Vorwort zur Broschüre "Internationales aus dem 'Volksstaat' (1871-1875)"*, Marx/Engels, *Werke*, Bd. 22, S. 417-18. Dietz Verlag, Berlin, 1963. p. 321

[169] This is a reference to the Second Congress of the R.S.D.L.P., which was held from July 17 (30) to August 10 (23), 1903. The first sittings took place in Brussels, but police persecution forced the congress to move to London. Lenin's supporters won the majority during the voting to the Party's central organs and became known as Bolsheviks, while the opportunists, who found themselves in the minority, were called Mensheviks. p. 322

[170] K. Marx, F. Engels, *Selected Works*, Vol. II, Moscow, 1962, pp. 32-3, 23, 24.
p. 325

[171] K. Marx, F. Engels, *Selected Works*, Vol. I, Moscow, 1962, p. 53. p. 326

[172] K. Marx, F. Engels, *Selected Correspondence,* Moscow, 1965, p. 294. p. 327

[173] Shylock, a personage in Shakespeare's comedy *The Merchant of Venice*, was a ruthless, callous usurer, who under the terms of a promissory note demanded a pound of flesh from one of his debtors. p. 333

[174] Seminary students whose crude customs were described by the Russian writer N. G. Pomyalovsky in *Sketches of Seminary Life*. p. 333

[175] K. Marx, F. Engels, *Selected Works*, Vol. II, Moscow, 1962, p. 14. p. 338

[176] *The Hague Congress of the First International* took place on September 2-7, 1872. It witnessed the culmination of the long struggle waged by Marx and Engels and their supporters against all forms of petty-bourgeois sectarianism. M. A. Bakunin, D. Guillaume and other anarchist leaders were expelled from the International.
Marx and Engels guided the decisions and the entire proceedings at the congress, which flatly rejected the petty-bourgeois views of the anarchists and laid the foundations for the setting up of future independent national political parties of the working class. p. 339

[177] A reference to the Fifth International Congress of the Second International, which was held in Paris on September 23-27, 1900. On the basic issue of the conquest of political power and an alliance with bourgeois parties, which was raised in connection with Alexandre Millerand's acceptance of a portfolio in the reactionary Waldeck-Rousseau cabinet, the majority voted for a resolution moved by Kautsky. This resolution stated that "the acceptance of a portfolio by an individual socialist in a bourgeois government must be regarded not as a normal beginning of the conquest of political power but as a forced temporary and extraordinary means in the struggle with difficult circumstances". Subsequently, this point was frequently quoted by opportunists to justify co-operation with the bourgeoisie.   p. 339

[178] K. Marx, F. Engels, *Selected Works*, Vol. I, Moscow, 1962, p. 519.   p. 343

[179] K. Marx, F. Engels, *Address of the Central Committee to the Communist League* (K. Marx, F. Engels, *Selected Works*, Vol. I, Moscow, 1962, p. 115).
p. 346

[180] K. Marx, *The Civil War in France* (K. Marx, F. Engels, *Selected Works*, Vol. I, Moscow, 1962, p. 519).   p. 347

[181] K. Marx, F. Engels, *Selected Works*, Vol. I, Moscow, 1962, p. 53.   p. 349

[182] *Sozialistische Monatshefte*—mouthpiece of the German opportunists and an organ of international revisionism, was published in Berlin from 1897 to 1933. During the First World War it preached social-chauvinist views.
p. 350

[183] F. Engels, *Fluchtlingsliteratur. II. Programme der Blanquistischen Kommuneflüchtlinge*. Marx/Engels, *Werke*, Bd. 18, S. 528-35, Dietz Verlag, Berlin, 1962.   p. 352

[184] *The State Duma* was a representative body which the tsarist government was compelled to convene as a result of the revolutionary developments of 1905. Formally it was a legislative body, but it had no real power. The elections were indirect, unequal and non-universal. The suffrage of the working classes as well as of the non-Russian nationalities inhabiting Russia was substantially curtailed, and a considerable section of the workers and peasants had no suffrage at all. Under the electoral law of December 11 (24), 1905, the vote of a landowner was equal to the votes of three urban bourgeois, 15 peasants or 45 workers.
The First (April-July 1906) and the Second Duma (February-June 1907) were dissolved by the government. Accomplishing a coup on June 3, 1907, the government passed a new electoral law, which still further cut the rights of workers, peasants and the urban petty bourgeoisie and ensured the complete supremacy of the reactionary bloc of landowners and big capitalists in the Third (1907-12) and the Fourth Duma (1912-17).
The Bolsheviks stood for elections to the Third and the Fourth Duma, winning seats in them.   p. 352

[185] Lenin has in mind the political developments of April-August 1917, which accelerated the revolutionary process. On April 21-22 (May 4-5) a hundred thousand workers and soldiers demonstrated in Petrograd, protesting

against the Note of the Foreign Minister Milyukov, in which he pledged Russia's continued participation in the war until victory. This demonstration precipitated a political crisis, and a coalition Provisional Government was formed consisting of Constitutional-Democrats, Socialist-Revolutionaries and Mensheviks.

At a conference with workers' and soldiers' representatives, the Bolshevik Party set the demonstration for June 10 (23). The plan was that the demonstration would show the First All-Russia Congress of Soviets the will of the workers and soldiers of Petrograd, who demanded the transfer of all power to the Soviets. The Mensheviks and Socialist-Revolutionaries decided to ban the demonstration and on June 9 (22) forced through a resolution forbidding it. Wishing to avoid opposing the Congress of Soviets, the Central Committee of the Bolshevik Party called off the demonstration.

The Menshevik-Socialist-Revolutionary leadership of the Congress of Soviets decided to organise a demonstration on June 18 (July 1), hoping that it would express trust in the Provisional Government.

Nearly half a million people turned out for the demonstration on June 18 (July 1). Most of them marched under the revolutionary slogans of the Bolshevik Party, demanding the expulsion of capitalist ministers and the transfer of all power to the Soviets. The demonstration showed the mounting tide of revolution and the tremendous influence of the Bolsheviks.

Mass actions took place spontaneously among the workers, soldiers and sailors in Petrograd on July 3-4 (16-17), 1917. Their indignation was aroused by the Provisional Government's policy of continuing the imperialist war.

In this period the Bolshevik Party was opposed to armed action, because the revolutionary crisis had yet to mature. However, taking the mood of the masses into consideration the Central Committee, the Petrograd Committee and the Military Organisation of the Bolshevik Party decided to take part in the demonstration of July 4 (17) with the purpose of ensuring its peaceableness and organisation.

With the approval of the Menshevik-Socialist-Revolutionary Central Executive Committee, the Provisional Government ordered troops to fire on the peaceful demonstrators, and after the demonstration was dispersed the government continued repressions, aiming the main blow at the Bolshevik Party. After the July developments, the Bolsheviks removed the slogan "All power to the Soviets" because the Socialist-Revolutionary and Menshevik leaders of the Soviets had openly defected to the counter-revolution.

A counter-revolutionary revolt was started by General Kornilov on August 25, 1917 with the purpose of restoring the monarchy that had been overthrown by the people in February. He marched on revolutionary Petrograd at the head of an army. The revolt was smashed by the workers and peasants under the leadership of the Bolsheviks. Pressed by the masses, the Provisional Government ordered the arrest and trial of Kornilov and his accomplices. p. 353

186 On September 1 (14), 1917 the Provisional Government decided to form a directorate of five persons. The Constitutional Democrats held no official post in this government, but it was set up as a result of a back-stage deal with them. The Mensheviks and Socialist-Revolutionaries passed a resolution supporting the new government. Thus, behind a façade of statements about their rupture with the Constitutional-Democrats, the Mensheviks and Socialist-Revolutionaries helped the landowners and capitalists to retain power. p. 356

[187] *The All-Russia Democratic Conference* was convened by the Menshevik Socialist-Revolutionary Central Executive Committee of Soviets for the purpose of deciding the question of power. It was held on September 14-22 (September 27-October 5), 1917 in Petrograd. The leaders of the Mensheviks and Socialist-Revolutionaries took steps to curtail the number of representatives from the workers and peasants and increase the number of deputies from petty-bourgeois and bourgeois organisations.

The Bolsheviks attended this conference with the purpose of using its rostrum to expose the Mensheviks and Socialist-Revolutionaries.

The conference passed a resolution on the setting up of a consultative Pre-parliament (Provisional Council of the Republic) in an attempt to give the impression that Russia had adopted a parliamentary system.

On October 7 (20), when the Pre-parliament was opened, the Bolsheviks walked out after reading their statement. p. 359

[188] *Alexandrinka*—the Alexandrinsky Theatre in Petrograd where the Democratic Conference was held.

The Peter and Paul Fortress is situated opposite the Winter Palace on the far bank of the Neva. The tsars used it for political prisoners. It had a huge arsenal and was an important strategical point in Petrograd. Today it is a museum of the history of the Revolution. p. 361

[189] Officer cadets at military schools in tsarist Russia. p. 361

[190] *The Savage Division*, formed during the First World War, consisted of volunteers from the Caucasian peoples. General Kornilov attempted to use this division as his assault force in the offensive against revolutionary Petrograd. p. 361

[191] *Rech* (Speech)—daily newspaper of the Constitutional-Democrats, was published in St. Petersburg from February 23 (March 8), 1906 to August 1918. After the bourgeois-democratic revolution of February 1917 it actively supported the home and foreign policy of the Provisional Government and baited Lenin and the Bolshevik Party.

Novaya Zhizn (New Life), a daily semi-Menshevik newspaper that was published in Petrograd from April 18 (May 1), 1917 to July 1918. Characterising the supporters of this newspaper Lenin noted that the dominant mood among them was "intellectual scepticism, which conceals and expresses lack of principle" (V. I. Lenin, *Collected Works*, Vol. 25, p. 271). p. 363

[192] The incident mentioned by Lenin took place at a sitting of the First All-Russia Congress of Soviets on June 4 (17), 1917. When the Menshevik Tsereteli, a Minister in the Provisional Government, who was speaking from the rostrum, declared that in Russia there was no political party willing to take all the power in the country into its hands, Lenin, on behalf of the Bolshevik Party, cried out that there was such a party. He then took the floor and declared that the Bolshevik Party was prepared to assume full powers at any time. p. 363

[193] *Rabochy Put* (Workers' Path)—one of the names of *Pravda* in 1917. p. 365

[194] Quotation from N. A. Nekrasov's poem *Blessed Is the Unmalicious Poet*. p. 367

195 A personage in N. V. Gogol's *Dead Souls*.   p. 367

196 *Znamya Truda* (Banner of Labour)—a daily newspaper of the Petrograd Committee of the Socialist-Revolutionary Party. It was published from August 23 (September 5), 1917 to July 1918.   p. 369

197 *Volya Naroda* (People's Will)—a daily newspaper of the Right wing of the Socialist-Revolutionary Party. It was published in Petrograd from April 29 to November 1917.

Yedinstvo (Unity), a newspaper of the extreme Right-wing group of Menshevik-defencists in Petrograd, published from March to November 1917. From December 1917 to January 1918 it was published as *Nashe Yedinstvo* (Our Unity). It supported the Provisional Government and the coalition with the bourgeoisie, and demanded the continuation of the imperialist war "until final victory".   p. 371

198 In mentioning April 4, 1917, Lenin refers to his article *The Tasks of the Proletariat in the Present Revolution,* better known as the *April Theses.*
                                                                            p. 372

199 The Menshevik internationalists were a small wing of the Menshevik Party. During the First World War they inconsistently held internationalist, Centrist views. While criticising the social-chauvinists they feared an organisational rupture with them. They opposed the basic propositions of the Bolshevik Party's Leninist tactics on questions of war, peace and revolution.
                                                                            p. 373

200 *Tit Titych Bruskov*—a stupid and wilful merchant in A. N. Ostrovsky's comedy *Shouldering Another's Troubles.*   p. 377

201 During the Franco-Prussian War of 1870-71, the whole French army led by Napoleon III was surrounded at Sedan and taken prisoner.   p. 377

202 *Izvestia*—a daily newspaper whose publication was started on February 28 (March 13), 1917. At first it came out as the *Izvestia Petrogradskogo Soveta Rabochikh i Soldatskikh Deputatov (of the Petrograd Soviet of Workers' and Soldiers' Deputies)* and then as *Izvestia Tsentralnogo Ispolnitelnogo Komiteta Sovetov Rabochikh i Soldatskikh Deputatov (of the Central Executive Committee of the Soviets of Workers' and Soldiers' Deputies)*. It was controlled by the Mensheviks and the Socialist-Revolutionaries. After the Great October Socialist Revolution it became the official organ of the Soviet government.   p. 379

203 *Vendée*—a Department of France and scene of a counter-revolution during the French bourgeois revolution of the 18th century. Became a synonym of counter-revolution.   p. 390

204 *Trudoviki* (Labour Group), were petty-bourgeois democrats who comprised a small group of peasant deputies in the State Duma of April 1906. During the First World War they held chauvinistic views. In 1917, they merged with the Popular Socialists (see Note 312) and actively supported the bourgeois Provisional Government. After the October Socialist Revolution they sided with the bourgeois counter-revolution.   p. 393

205 *Kulak*—in tsarist Russia a wealthy peasant exploiting the labour of others.
p. 394

206 *"Moderation and punctuality"* is how Molchalin, a careerist and toady in A. S. Griboyedov's comedy *Wit Works Woe*, defined his virtues. Lenin frequently used this expression to characterise the liberal bourgeoisie and social-opportunists. p. 397

207 By giving these dates Lenin refers to the following: February 28 (March 13)—the date of the February bourgeois-democratic revolution; September 30 (October 13)—the date initially set by the Provisional Government for the Constituent Assembly; this assembly was postponed to November 28 (December 11), 1917. p. 400

208 Lenin quotes the words of the Menshevik Sukhanov.
As from August 1917 the Smolny Institute was the headquarters of the Bolshevik sections of the All-Russia Central Executive Committee and the Petrograd Soviet of Workers' and Soldiers' Deputies. In October the Revolutionary Military Committee likewise moved into it. p. 400

209 In manuscript Lenin's work *The Immediate Tasks of the Soviet Government* was called *Theses on the Tasks of the Soviet Government at Present*.
Lenin's *Theses* were debated by the Party Central Committee on April 26, 1917. They were unanimously approved and a decision was taken to publish them as an article in *Pravda* and *Izvestia*, and as a separate pamphlet. More than 10 printings of this pamphlet were published in 1918; moreover in that same year it was printed in English in New York and in French in Geneva. An abridged German edition was put out in Zurich by F. Platten under the title *Am Tage nach der Revolution (The Day after the Revolution)*. p. 401

210 A reference to the Peace Treaty of Brest-Litovsk. p. 401

211 Lenin refers to the Decree on Land published on October 26 (November 8), 1917. It proclaimed the confiscation of the landed estates and the abolition of private ownership of land. p. 404

212 The year 1793 was when the Jacobin dictatorship, a dictatorship of the most revolutionary section of the bourgeoisie, was established in France.
The Paris Commune, the first government of the proletarian dictatorship in history, was set up in 1871. p. 406

213 On November 18 (December 1), 1917, acting on Lenin's recommendations, the Council of People's Commissars adopted a decision on the salaries of People's Commissars and senior employees and officials. Under this decision, the top monthly salary for a People's Commissar was 500 rubles with the addition of 100 rubles for every member of his family who was incapable of work. This was approximately the average wage of a worker. On January 2 (15), 1918 the Council of People's Commissars explained that the decree did not forbid paying specialists a salary above the fixed ceiling, thereby giving its sanction for higher salaries for scientists and engineers. p. 409

214 After the October Revolution piece-rate payment for work was replaced by fixed salaries and wages almost at all enterprises. This adversely affected labour productivity and discipline.

Piece-rate payment, which most fully accorded with the socialist principle of distribution according to the quantity and quality of labour, was first reintroduced at nationalised enterprises. Subsequently, it became widespread in industry.   p. 416

215 *The Left Socialist-Revolutionaries* (internationalists) were members of the Left Socialist-Revolutionary Party, which was founded at its First All-Russia Congress on November 19-28 (December 2-11), 1917. Prior to this congress the Left Socialist-Revolutionaries formed the Left wing of the Socialist-Revolutionary Party (See Note 39), which was set up during the First World War. At the Second All-Russia Congress of Soviets they joined the Bolsheviks in the voting on the key points on the agenda, but rejected the invitation of the Bolsheviks to accept posts in the Soviet Government.

After long wavering, the Left Socialist-Revolutionaries who were anxious to retain their influence among the peasants, reached agreement with the Bolsheviks and were given posts on the collegiums of a number of People's Commissariats. While co-operating with the Bolsheviks, they disagreed with them on basic issues of socialist construction, and opposed the dictatorship of the proletariat. In January-February 1918, the Central Committee of the Left Socialist-Revolutionary Party started a campaign against the signing of the Brest-Litovsk Peace Treaty. After the treaty was signed and then ratified by the Fourth Congress of Soviets in March 1918, the Left Socialist-Revolutionaries withdrew from the Council of People's Commissars, but remained in the collegiums of the People's Commissariats and in local organs of power. Anti-Soviet sentiments began to grow among the Left Socialist-Revolutionaries during the socialist revolution in the countryside. In July 1918 their Central Committee organised the assassination of the German ambassador in Moscow in the hope that this would lead to war between Soviet Russia and Germany, and started an armed revolt against Soviet power. After the revolt was crushed, the Fifth All-Russia Congress of Soviets expelled from the Soviets all Left Socialist-Revolutionaries who shared the views of their leaders.   p. 423

216 *Vperyod* (Forward), a Menshevik daily newspaper that was published with intervals in 1917-19.   p. 425

217 *Nash Vek* (Our Age), one of the names under which the newspaper *Rech* was printed (see Note 191).   p. 425

218 A reference to and quotation from Engels's *Anti-Dühring*.   p. 428

219 *The "Left Communists"* were an anti-Party group that was formed early in 1918 over the question of the signing of a peace treaty with Germany (the Treaty of Brest-Litovsk). Taking cover behind Left phraseology about a revolutionary war, the "Left Communists" urged the adventurist policy of drawing the Soviet Republic which did not have an army into a war against imperialist Germany and thereby threatened the very existence of Soviet power. Lenin and his supporters had to wage a difficult struggle in the Central Committee against Trotsky and the "Left Communists" in order to secure a decision on the signing of the peace treaty with Germany and save the young Soviet Republic.

Moreover, the "Left Communists" adopted an erroneous stand on a number of problems of economic development.

In May-June 1918 they lost the last vestiges of influence in the Party. *Kommunist*, a monthly journal and factional organ of the "Left Communists". It was published in Moscow from April 20 to June 1918, and altogether four issues appeared in print. p. 432

[220] Lenin refers to the Extraordinary Seventh Congress of the R.C.P.(B.), which was the first Party Congress after the Great October Socialist Revolution. It was held in Petrograd on March 6-8, 1918 and was convened for the purpose of taking a final decision on a peace treaty with Germany, a question which sparked off a tense struggle within the Party.

Lenin directed all the proceedings at the congress and delivered the political report of the Central Committee. The congress unanimously endorsed this report and by name voting with 30 in favour, 12 against and four abstentions approved Lenin's resolution on war and peace which recognised the need for endorsing the Brest Peace Treaty.

This treaty was ratified by the Extraordinary Fourth All-Russia Congress of Soviets, which was held on March 14-16. p. 433

[221] On March 13, 1918, in the voting on the resolution to ratify the Brest-Litovsk Peace Treaty, in the Communist faction at the Extraordinary Fourth All-Russia Congress, 453 votes were cast in favour and 36 votes against the treaty. p. 433

[222] Lenin refers to the following passage in the political report of the Central Committee which he delivered at the Extraordinary Seventh Party Congress on March 7, 1918: "...Their newspaper bears the title *Kommunist*, but it should bear the title *Szlachcic* because it looks at things from the point of view of the szlach*c*ic who, dying in a beautiful pose, sword in hand, said: 'Peace is disgraceful, war is honourable' " (V. I. Lenin, *Collected Works*, Vol. 27, p. 105).

Kommunist—a daily newspaper and factional mouthpiece of the "Left Communists", was published in Petrograd from March 5 to 19, 1918 as the organ of the St. Petersburg Committee and St. Petersburg District Committee of the R.S.D.L.P. Its publication was stopped by decision of the Petrograd City Party Conference. p. 435

[223] The name derives from Nozdryov, a personage in N. V. Gogol's *Dead Souls*: synonym for prattle and boasting. p. 436

[224] Lenin quotes a statement by Marx given by Engels in *The Peasant Question in France and Germany* (K. Marx, F. Engels, *Selected Works*, Vol. II, Moscow, 1962, p. 438). p. 446

[225] *Liberdans*—an ironical nickname of the Menshevik leaders M. I. Liber and F. I. Dan and their supporters after the publication of a feuilleton entitled *Liberdan* by Demyan Byedny. p. 450

[226] Lenin quotes A. S. Pushkin's epigram about a mediocre poet who dedicated his verse to Phoebus (in Greek mythology Apollo, the sun god and patron of arts). The epigram ends with the lines:

> And while he read, the yawning Phoebus asked
> What age this rhymster had attained,
> How long such rumbling odes composed?
> "He is fifteen," Erato made reply.
> "But fifteen years?"—"No more, my lord."
> "Then shall the birch be his reward!"

p. 452

227 *Letter to American Workers* was published in English (with some abbreviation) in December 1918 in organs of the Left wing of the Socialist Party of America—*The Class Struggle*, the journal which was published in New York, and the weekly *The Revolutionary Age*, which was published in Boston with the participation of John Reed and Sen Katayama. Later it was printed as a separate pamphlet and appeared time and again in the American and West-European periodical press.   p. 456

228 In April 1898, the U.S. imperialists took advantage of the national liberation movement against the Spanish colonialists in Cuba and the Philippines and started a war against Spain. On the pretext of "assisting" the Philipino people, who had proclaimed the independence of the Philippine Republic, U.S. troops landed in the Philippines. Under the peace treaty, signed in Paris on December 10, 1898, defeated Spain renounced her claim to the Philippines in favour of the U.S.A. In February 1899 the U.S. imperialists perfidiously began military operations against the Philippine Republic. A partisan movement directed against the invaders embraced the Philippines. In 1901 the national liberation movement on the islands was crushed and the Philippines became a U.S. colony.   p. 457

229 A reference to the Decree on Peace passed by the Second All-Russia Congress of Soviets on October 26 (November 8), 1917.   p. 458

230 The Civil War of 1861-65 in the U.S.A. was a war between the Northern and Southern States, a struggle of the North against the slave-owning South, which sought to preserve and spread slavery.   p. 462

231 *Appeal to Reason*—a newspaper of the American Socialists that was founded in 1895 in the town of Girard, Kansas. It spread socialist ideas and was extremely popular with workers. During the First World War it adopted an internationalist stand.
Eugene Debs' article was printed in this newspaper on September 11, 1915. The heading, cited by Lenin probably from memory, was: *When I Shall Fight*.   p. 462

232 A reference to the English bourgeois revolution of the 17th century and the French bourgeois revolution of the end of the 18th century.   p. 463

233 In Soviet Russia the land was nationalised under the Decree on Land of October 26 (November 8), 1917, which proclaimed the confiscation of the landed estates and abolished private ownership of land.   p. 465

234 *Jupiter* and *Minerva* were Roman gods. Jupiter, the god of the sky, light and rain, and lightning-hurler; subsequently became the chief deity of the Roman Empire. Minerva—goddess of war and patroness of handicrafts, sciences and arts. She is fabled to have sprung from the head of Jupiter. p. 465

235 The Constitution of the R.S.F.S.R. was approved by the Fifth All-Russia Congress of Soviets on July 10, 1918. It was drawn up with Lenin's active participation.   p. 466

236 Lenin began writing *The Proletarian Revolution and the Renegade Kautsky* early in October 1918, immediately after he read Kautsky's pamphlet *The Dictatorship of the Proletariat*, in which the ideological leader of the

Second International misrepresented and vulgarised the Marxist theory of the proletarian revolution and slandered the Soviet state.   p. 468

[237] *The Socialist Review*—a monthly journal and organ of the reformist Independent Labour Party in Great Britain (see Note 18); published in London from 1908 to 1934.   p. 468

[238] A reference to the counter-revolutionary revolt of a Czechoslovak army corps. This rising was organised by the Entente imperialists with the assistance of Mensheviks and Socialist-Revolutionaries. The corps, consisting of Czech and Slovak prisoners of war, was formed in Russia before the Great October Socialist Revolution. The Soviet Government gave the corps permission to leave Russia via Vladivostok on condition that it surrendered its weapons. However, at the close of May 1918, the counter-revolutionary command of the corps provoked an armed revolt against Soviet Russia. Acting in close contact with the whiteguards and kulaks, the White Czechs seized considerable territory in the Urals, the Volga country and Siberia, restoring bourgeois rule in these areas.

Many of the troops saw through the lies of their counter-revolutionary commanders and deserted from the corps, refusing to fight against Soviet Russia. Some 12,000 Czechs and Slovaks joined the Red Army.

The revolt was finally smashed in 1919.   p. 471

[239] These words were said by Molchalin, a personage in A. S. Griboyedov's comedy *Wit Works Woe*.   p. 473

[240] *Longuetists*—supporters of a minority, led by Jean Longuet in the French Socialist Party. During the imperialist world war of 1914-18 the Longuetists urged conciliation with the social-chauvinists, rejecting the revolutionary struggle and preaching the "defence of the fatherland" in the imperialist war. After the October Socialist Revolution they made themselves out to be supporters of the proletarian dictatorship while actually remaining its opponents. In December 1920, together with the candid reformists, the Longuetists broke away from the Party and aligned themselves with the so-called Two-and-a-Half International (see Note 304).
                                    p. 473

[241] *The Entente* was a bloc of imperialist powers (Britain, France and Russia) that was formed early in the 20th century and directed against the imperialists of the Tripartite Alliance (Germany, Austria-Hungary and Italy). It obtained its name from the 1904 Anglo-French Entente cordiale. During the First World War the Entente was joined by the U.S.A., Japan and other countries. After the Great October Socialist Revolution, the principal members of this bloc—Britain, France, the U.S.A. and Japan—inspired, organised and took part in the military intervention against Soviet Russia.
                                    p. 474

[242] The recording of Lenin's speeches on gramophone records was organised by the Tsentropechat. Sixteen of his speeches were recorded in 1919-21. This speech and the speeches on *The Middle Peasants* and *The Tax in Kind* were in great demand.   p. 476

[243] Lenin refers to the plot to surrender Petrograd. This plot was directed by the counter-revolutionary "national centre", which united the activities of a number of anti-Soviet groups and underground espionage organisations. On the night of June 13, 1919, the plotters started a revolt at the Krasnaya

Gorka Fort, which was one of the key approaches of Petrograd. Troops of a shore defence group, vessels of the Baltic Fleet, aircraft, and volunteer detachments were sent against the insurgents. During the night of June 15-16, the shore defence group captured the fort. The counter-revolutionary organisation that led the conspiracy was uncovered and liquidated.

p. 484

244 The battle at the village of Sadowa (now a town) in Hradec Kralove Region, Czechoslovakia, was fought on July 3, 1866. In this battle Prussia defeated Austria and decided the outcome of the Austro-Prussian War.

p. 488

245 In Russia serfdom was abolished in 1861.

p. 489

246 A reference to the Party Programme adopted at the Eighth Congress of the R.C.P.(B.) in March 1919.

p. 491

247 By a decree passed by the Council of People's Commissars on March 16, 1919, the consumer co-operatives were united and reorganised into a single distributive organ with the name of Consumers' Commune. However, this name led to confusion in interpreting the decree. Taking this into account, the All-Russia Central Executive Committee passed a decision "On Worker-Peasant Consumer Societies" on June 30, 1919, in which it approved the decree but changed the name Consumer Commune into Consumers' Societies.

p. 494

248 The Constitution of the R.S.F.S.R., adopted at the Fifth All-Russia Congress of Soviets in July 1918, gave the working class advantages in the elections to the Soviets. Deputies to the All-Russia Congress of Soviets were elected under the following representation quotas: one deputy per 25,000 voters of the urban population and one deputy per 125,000 rural inhabitants.

This ruling remained in force until 1936 when the Eighth Congress of Soviets of the U.S.S.R. adopted a new Constitution, which gave all citizens equal rights to elect and be elected to the Soviets.

p. 503

249 This article was not completed.

p. 505

250 *The Second All-Russia Congress of Communist Organisations of the Peoples of the East,* convened by the Central Bureau of Communist Organisations of the Peoples of the East at the Central Committee of the R.C.P.(B.), was held in Moscow from November 22 to December 3, 1919. On the first day of the congress Lenin delivered a report on current developments. The congress charted the tasks of Party and government work in the East, and elected a new Central Bureau of Communist Organisations of the Peoples of the East at the Central Committee of the R.C.P.(B.).

p. 506

251 A reference to the whiteguard Socialist-Revolutionary Menshevik government in Samara (now Kuibyshev)—the so-called Committee of Members of the Constituent Assembly or the "Samara Assembly". It was formed on June 8, 1918 after Samara was captured by the insurgent Czechoslovak Corps. By August 1918, aided by units of this corps, the Assembly extended its rule over a number of gubernias along the Volga and the cis-Urals. In the autumn of the same year this counter-revolutionary government ceased to exist.

p. 507

[252] *"Left-wing" Communism—an Infantile Disorder* was written by Lenin to coincide with the opening of the Second Congress of the Communist International.

Most of this book was written in April 1920. Lenin personally kept an eye on the progress of the typesetting and printing to make sure that it would appear in print when the Second Comintern Congress opened. The book was published on June 12, 1920 and almost simultaneously, in July, it was printed in Soviet Russia in French and in English. It was distributed to all the delegates at the Second Comintern Congress, whose decisions were based on its key propositions and conclusions.

In the course of the second half of 1920 this book was published in German in Berlin and Hamburg, in English in London and New York, in French in Paris and in Italian in Milan. p. 516

[253] The pamphlet *Weltrevolution* (*World Revolution*) was written by Otto Bauer. p. 517

[254] A reference to the Mensheviks in the R.S.D.L.P. who comprised the Right, opportunist wing of the Social-Democratic movement, and to the Socialist-Revolutionary Party. p. 520

[255] This is a reference to the shooting down of unarmed workers during the strike at the Lena goldfields in Siberia on April 4 (17), 1912.

The news of this tragedy aroused the working class of Russia. A wave of street demonstrations, meetings and protest strikes swept across the country. Lenin wrote: "The Lena shooting led to the revolutionary temper of the masses developing into a revolutionary upswing of the masses" (V. I. Lenin, *Collected Works*, Vol. 18, p. 103). p. 522

[256] Here Lenin means the Bolshevik deputies to the Fourth State Duma— A. E. Badayev, M. K. Muranov, G. I. Petrovsky, F. N. Samoilov and N. R. Shagov. At a sitting of the Duma on July 26 (August 8), 1914, the Bolshevik faction made a strong protest against tsarist Russia's involvement in the imperialist war. They refused to vote for war credits and launched on revolutionary propaganda among the people. In November 1914 they were arrested, and in February 1915 sentenced to exile for life in Turukhansk region (Eastern Siberia). p. 522

[257] A reference to the otzovists and ultimatumists. The struggle against them began in 1908, and in 1909 it led to the expulsion of their leader, A. Bogdanov, from the Bolshevik Party. Behind a façade of revolutionary phrasemongering, the otzovists demanded the recall of the Social-Democratic deputies from the Third State Duma and the Party's withdrawal from the trade unions, co-operatives and other legal organisations. Ultimatumism was a variety of otzovism. The ultimatumists failed to appreciate the need for persevering and painstaking work with Socialist-Democratic deputies, for training them as consistent revolutionary parliamentarians, and urged that the Social-Democratic faction in the Duma should be presented with an ultimatum demanding their implicit subordination to the decisons of the Party's Central Committee, and in the event they failed to comply with these decisions that they should be recalled from the Duma. At an extended meeting in June 1909, the editors of the Bolshevik newspaper *Proletary* passed a resolution which stated that as a definite trend in the R.S.D.L.P. Bolshevism had nothing in common with otzovism or ultimatumism. p. 527

258 The tsarist Manifesto on the establishment of the State Duma and the rules of the elections to it were published on August 6 (19), 1905. This Duma became known as the Bulygin Duma after A. G. Bulygin, Minister for Internal Affairs, who was instructed by the tsar to draw up the plan for it.   p. 527

259 A reference to the all-Russia political strike of October 1905. More than two million people took part in this strike, which showed the strength and power of the working-class movement, gave an impetus to the revolutionary struggle in the countryside, the Army and the Navy, and led the proletariat to an armed uprising.   p. 527

260 *Labourites*—members of the Labour Party of Britain, which was founded in 1900 with the purpose of sending workers' representatives to Parliament (Labour Representation Committee). In 1906 this Committee was renamed as the Labour Party, which initially took shape as a working-class party (subsequently it admitted a considerable number of petty-bourgeois elements). By its ideology and tactics it is an opportunist organisation. From the very beginning its leaders have been pursuing a policy of class co-operation with the bourgeoisie.   p. 529

261 *Kommunistische Arbeiterzeitung*—organ of the anarcho-syndicalist group of German "Left Communists", was published in Hamburg from 1919 to 1927.   p. 534

262 A reference to the League of Struggle for the Emancipation of the Working Class, founded by Lenin in the autumn of 1895. The League united about twenty Marxist circles in St. Petersburg. At the head of the League was the Central Group. The entire organisation was subdivided into district groups. Foremost, politically conscious workers acted as contacts between these groups and the factories.

Lenin described the St. Petersburg League as the embryo of a political party relying on the working-class movement and leading the class struggle of the proletariat.   p. 535

263 *The Ninth Congress of the R.C.P.(B.)* was held in Moscow from March 29 to April 5, 1920.

Much of its attention was focussed on the organisation of production management. In the resolution on this question it was pointed out that an efficient, firm and energetic leadership had to be set up along the lines of one-man management. Acting on Lenin's recommendations, the congress laid special emphasis on the fact that it was in the interests of socialist economy to draw as many old specialists as possible into production management.

At this congress, the Party line in economic development was opposed by the anti-Party "democratic centralism" group. Bandying words about democratic Centralism while in reality distorting this principle, the "democratic Centralists" held that there was no necessity for one-man management in production and came out against firm Party and state discipline, falsely asserting that there was no collective leadership in the Central Committee. The congress strongly condemned and rejected the anti-Party recommendations of the "democratic-Centralists".   p. 535

264 *The Communist International*—a journal and organ of the Executive Committee of the Communist International. It was published in Russian, Ger-

man, French, English, Spanish and Chinese. The first issue appeared in print on May 1, 1919. This journal printed theoretical articles and documents of the Comintern. A number of Lenin's articles were published in it. Publication was stopped in 1943. p. 541

265 *Folkets Dagblad Politiken*—newspaper of the Left Social-Democratic Party of Sweden. It was published in Stockholm from April 1916 to May 1945, at first every other day and then as a daily (prior to November 1917 it was called *Politiken*). p. 542

266 *The Industrial Workers of the World (I.W.W.)*—a workers' organisation in the U.S.A., was founded in 1905 and united mainly unskilled and low-paid workers of various trades. Those who helped to found it included Daniel De Leon, Eugene Debs and William Haywood. During the First World War this organisation sponsored a series of mass anti-war working-class actions. Some features of anarcho-syndicalism appeared in the activities of this organisation: it did not recognise the political struggle of the proletariat, rejected the leading role of the Party and the need for a dictatorship of the proletariat and refused to conduct any work among members of trade unions affiliated to the American Federation of Labour. As a result of the opportunist policy of its leadership, the Industrial Workers of the World became a sectarian organisation with no influence in the working-class movement. p. 543

267 Lenin has in mind the Peasant Mandate on the Land, which was framed on the basis of 242 local peasant mandates and became a component of the Decree on Land drawn up by him. p. 550

268 *Il Soviet*—a newspaper published in Naples by the Italian Socialist Party from 1918 to 1922; in 1920 it became the organ of the Communist-abstentionist faction in the Italian Socialist Party. p. 551

269 *Comunismo*—a fortnightly journal of the Italian Socialist Party; published in Milan from 1919 to 1922 under the editorship of G. Serrati. p. 551

270 Hungary was proclaimed a Soviet Republic on March 21, 1919. The socialist revolution in Hungary was relatively peaceful. The terms of the Communist Party—formation of a Soviet Government, the disarming of the bourgeoisie, the setting up of a Red Army and a people's militia, the confiscation of the landed estates, the nationalisation of industry, the conclusion of an alliance with Soviet Russia, and so forth—were accepted at the talks between the leaders of the Social-Democratic and Communist parties. At the same time an agreement was signed on the merging of the two parties into the Socialist Party of Hungary. During the process of this merging errors were committed which made themselves felt later: it was a mechanical merging which did not exclude reformist elements. A land reform law was passed, under which all landed estates with a land area of more than 57 hectares were confiscated and turned into large state farms, but they remained in control of the same overseers. The poorest section of the peasantry, which had hoped to receive land from the Soviet authorities, found their hopes blighted. This prevented the establishment of a firm alliance between the proletariat and the peasants and undermined Soviet power in Hungary.

The Soviet Government in Hungary was overthrown on August 1, 1919 as a result of the concerted actions of foreign imperialist intervention and the internal counter-revolution. p. 551

271 *The League of Nations* existed in the period between the first and the second world wars. It was set up in 1919 at the Paris Peace Conference by the victor powers. Its Covenant was drawn up with an eye to creating the impression that its purpose was to combat aggression, achieve a reduction of armaments and strengthen peace and security. In reality, the League's leaders pandered to aggressors and encouraged the arms race and the preparations for another world war.

On September 15, 1934, following the lead given by French diplomacy, 34 League member-states invited the Soviet Union to join the League. The U.S.S.R. took this step in order to help strengthen peace. However, the Soviet Union's efforts to create a peace front were resisted by reactionary circles in the West. When the Second World War broke out the League ceased its activities and it was formally dissolved in April 1946.   p. 554

272 A reference to the international socialist conferences at Zimmerwald and Kienthal, Switzerland.

The Zimmerwald or First International Socialist Conference was held on September 5-8, 1915.

The Kienthal or Second International Socialist Conference was held on April 24-30, 1916.

These conferences helped to unite the Left elements in the European Social-Democratic movement on the ideological foundation of Marxism-Leninism.   p. 556

273 *The Revolutionary Communists* were a Narodnik group who withdrew from the Left Socialist-Revolutionary Party and finally broke with it after the Left Socialist-Revolutionary uprising of July 1918. In September 1918 they formed the Party of Revolutionary Communism, which co-operated with Soviet power, and in September 1920 it merged with the R.C.P.(B.)   p. 556

274 *The British Socialist Party* was founded in Manchester in 1911 as a result of the merging of the Social-Democratic Party with other socialist groups. It carried on agitation in the spirit of Marxist ideals and was "not opportunist and ... really independent of the Liberals" (V. I. Lenin, *Collected Works*, Vol. 19, p. 273).

It welcomed the Great October Socialist Revolution and its members played a leading part in the popular movement in defence of Soviet Russia against foreign intervention. In 1919 the vast majority of this Party's organisations (98 against 4) voted for membership in the Communist International. Together with the Communist Unity group, the British Socialist Party played the main role in founding the Communist Party of Great Britain. At its first unity congress, the overwhelming majority of the local B.S.P. organisations merged in the Communist Party.   p. 560

275 *The Socialist Labour Party* was a revolutionary Marxist organisation formed in 1903 in Scotland by a group of Left Social-Democrats, mostly Scots, who had broken away from the Social-Democratic Federation.

The South Wales Socialist Society was a small group of mainly revolutionary Welsh miners. It originated from a movement for mining reform, which gradually gained momentum on the eve of the First World War.

The Workers' Socialist Federation was a small organisation that in May 1918 sprang from the Society for the Protection of Women's Suffrage Rights and consisted chiefly of women.

When the Communist Party of Great Britain (whose Inaugurating Congress was held on July 31-August 1, 1920) was formed and included in its programme points about the Party's participation in parliamentary elections and entry into the Labour Party, the above-named organisations, which had committed errors of a sectarian nature, did not join it. In January 1921 the South Wales Socialist Society and the Workers' Socialist Federation, which had by that time adopted the name "Communist Party (British Section of the Third International)", merged with the Communist Party of Great Britain. The leaders of the Socialist Labour Party refused to join the Communist Party of Great Britain.   p. 561

276 *Workers Dreadnought* was published in London from March 1914 to June 1924; until July 1917 it was published as *Woman's Dreadnought*. In 1918, with the formation of the Workers' Socialist Federation, it became that Federation's mouthpiece.   p. 561

277 *Manchester Guardian*—a bourgeois-liberal organ and one of the largest and most influential bourgeois newspapers in Britain. Founded in 1821.   p. 563

278 A reference to the military-monarchist coup known as the Kapp putsch, which was accomplished by reactionary German military. The organisers were the monarchists Kapp, Ludendorff, Sekt and Lüttwitz. They had the obvious support of the Social-Democratic government. On March 13, 1920 the insurgent generals led troops into Berlin and without opposition from the government proclaimed a military dictatorship. The workers of Germany called a general strike and on March 17 the Kapp government was deposed; the Social-Democrats returned to power.   p. 573

279 Lenin refers to the repressions organised by the bourgeois Provisional Government against the Bolsheviks after the dispersal of the peaceful workers' demonstration in Petrograd on July 3-4, 1917 (see Note 185).   p. 579

280 *The Communist Workers' Party of Germany* was formed by a group of "Left" Communists, who broke away from the Communist Party of Germany in October 1919; among them were many anarcho-syndicalist elements. This party, which became an independent organisation in April 1920, held sectarian views, was opposed to the use of parliament, refused to work in trade unions and rejected the leading role of the Communist Party in the proletarian revolution. It sent a delegation to the Third Congress of the Communist International, but it did not fulfil the decisions of that congress, which required that it should renounce its sectarian tactics and join the Communist Party of Germany. Following its expulsion from the Comintern it degenerated into a tiny group that was hostile to the communist movement.   p. 582

281 *Die Rote Fahne*—a newspaper founded by Karl Liebknecht and Rosa Luxemburg as the central organ of the Spartacus League. It later became the organ of the Communist Party of Germany. The publication of this newspaper was started in Berlin on November 9, 1918. It was persecuted and repeatedly banned by the German authorities. Ernst Thaelmann, Chairman of the Central Committee of the Communist Party of Germany, was

a frequent contributor. When the nazi dictatorship was set up, the newspaper was banned but continued publication illegally. In 1935 it was printed in Prague, Czechoslovakia, and from October 1936 to the autumn of 1939 it was printed in Brussels, Belgium. p. 584

[282] *Die Rote Fahne*—central organ of the Communist Party of Austria; the publication of this newspaper was started in Vienna in November 1918, as *Weckruf*. In January 1919 its name was changed to *Die Soziale Revolution*, and in July 1919 to *Die Rote Fahne*. In 1933 it had to go underground, and as from February 21, 1957 publication was resumed under the name *Volkstimme*. p. 585

[283] *Die Freiheit*—an organ of the Independent Social-Democratic Party of Germany. It was published in Berlin from November 1918 to October 1922. p. 585

[284] A reference to the collegiums of lawyers that were instituted in February 1918 at the Soviets of Workers', Soldiers', Peasants' and Cossacks' Deputies. Many of these collegiums were strongly influenced by bourgeois lawyers, who distorted and abused the principles of Soviet legal proceedings. p. 589

[285] In conformity with this instruction by Lenin, the expression "Dutch Tribunists" in *"Left-Wing" Communism—an Infantile Disorder* has everywhere been substituted with the words "certain members of the Dutch Communist Party". p. 590

[286] Initially the rough draft of the theses on the agrarian question was endorsed by the Executive Committee of the Communist International as "Theses of the Executive Committee of the Communist International on the Agrarian Problem". These theses were adopted by the Second Comintern Congress and passed on to a commission with instructions to draft a resolution on the agrarian question. This commission, whose work was directed by Lenin, introduced a number of amendments into the initial draft of the theses, and on August 4, 1920 they were endorsed by the congress. p. 592

[287] Lenin refers to Marchlewski's article "The Agrarian Question and the World Revolution", which was printed in the journal *The Communist International*, No. 12, July 20, 1920. Lenin read this article before it was printed. p. 592

[288] *The Second Congress of the Communist International* which laid down the programmatic, tactical and organisational principles of the Comintern, was held on July 19-August 7, 1920. It was attended by more than 200 delegates representing Communist Parties and workers' organisations in 37 countries.

The report on the international situation and on the basic aims of the Comintern was delivered at the first session of the congress by Lenin. At subsequent sessions he delivered a speech on the Communist Party, a report on the national and colonial questions, and a speech on parliamentarism and other questions. He took an active part in the proceedings of most of the congress commissions.

Underlying the congress decisions were the ideas expounded by Lenin in his classical "*Left-Wing*" *Communism—an Infantile Disorder*. The congress endorsed Lenin's *Theses on the Fundamental Tasks of the 2nd Congress of the Communist International* as its resolution on the first question of the agenda. One of the basic questions debated at the congress was the role played by the Communist Party in the proletarian revolution and the relations between the Party and the working class. In the resolution "On the Role of the Communist Party in the Proletarian Revolution" the congress noted that the Communist Party is the main and basic weapon for the emancipation of the working class. Lenin's theses on the national, colonial and agrarian questions were approved by the congress as its resolutions on these questions.

It adopted Lenin's 21 conditions for admittance to the Communist International. This was of tremendous importance in setting up and strengthening parties of the new type in the working-class movement of the capitalist countries.

The congress did much to promote the international communist movement. After the congress, Lenin pointed out that "communism has become the focal issue of the working-class movement as a whole".   p. 602

[289] *Jingoism*—militant chauvinism, which advocated aggressive imperialist policies. The term derived from the chorus of an English chauvinistic song of the 1870s.   p. 606

[290] *The Third All-Russia Congress of the Russian Young Communist League* was held in Moscow on October 2-10, 1920. It was attended by about 600 delegates. Lenin delivered a speech at its first sitting in the evening of October 2.

In line with Lenin's instructions, it emphasised the following programmatic proposition: "The basic aim of the R.Y.C.L. is to educate young working people in a spirit of communism, in which theoretical education is closely linked up with active participation in the life, work, struggle and creative endeavour of the masses. The practical activities of the R.Y.C.L. in all spheres must be subordinated to the task of the communist education of young people, to the training of energetic and skilful builders of socialist economy, defenders of the Soviet Republic and organisers of the new society."   p. 607

[291] A reference to members of the Proletarian Culture Organisation known by its abbreviated name *Proletcult*. Founded as early as in September 1917 as an independent workers' organisation, Proletcult continued to insist on its "independence" after the October Revolution, thereby counterposing itself to the proletarian state. The members of this organisation virtually rejected the importance of the cultural heritage of the past, fenced themselves off from mass cultural activities and sought to create a special "proletarian culture" in isolation from life, by "laboratory means". Proletcult was not a homogeneous organisation. Along with bourgeois intellectuals, who controlled many of the Proletcult bodies, the membership included young workers who sincerely strove to help promote cultural development in the country. Proletcult reached its heyday in 1919, and in the early twenties it declined, finally ceasing to exist in 1932.   p. 610

[292] Lenin drafted the resolution "On Proletarian Culture" in connection with the First All-Russia Proletcult Congress that was held in Moscow on

October 5-12, 1920. The Communist faction at that congress was instructed to adopt an organisational resolution on the subordination of the Prolet-cult bodies in the centre and in the localities to the People's Commissariat of Education. This resolution, drawn up in the spirit of Lenin's direct instructions, was unanimously passed by the congress.   p. 621

293 *The All-Russia Conference of Political Education Workers of Gubernia and Uyezd Education Departments* was held in Moscow on November 2-8, 1920 and was attended by 283 delegates. The proceedings centred around questions linked up with the setting up of a Central Political Education Committee of the Republic. The agenda also included questions connected with the food campaign, political education, production propaganda (linked up with economic rehabilitation), the abolition of illiteracy and other items.
p. 623

294 *The Tenth Congress of the R.C.P.(B.)* was held in Moscow on March 8-16, 1921. Its proceedings were directed by Lenin, who delivered the opening and closing speeches and reports on the political activity of the Central Committee, the replacement of surplus food requisitioning by a tax in kind, Party unity and the anarcho-syndicalist deviation, the trade unions and the fuel question. He drafted the key resolutions.

In the report on the activity of the Central Committee and on the replacement of surplus food requisitioning by a tax in kind, Lenin gave profound theoretical and political reasons for the need to go over to the New Economic Policy (see Note 302). Following the debate on these reports the congress passed historic decisions on the replacement of surplus food requisitioning by a tax in kind and on the transition from war communism to the New Economic Policy.

Party unity was given considerable attention. The resolution "On Party Unity", proposed by Lenin, required the immediate dissolution of all fac-tions which weakened the Party and undermined its unity. The congress passed a resolution "On the Syndicalist and Anarchist Deviation in Our Party", which was likewise drafted by Lenin.

The role of the trade unions in economic development were closely reviewed at the congress. Summing up the debate on the trade unions, the congress emphatically condemned the views of the "Workers' Opposition" and the "democratic Centralism" and other opportunist groups, and by an overwhelming majority approved Lenin's platform, in which the role of the trade unions was defined as that of a school of communism, and charted steps to extend trade union democracy.

In its decision on the national question, drafted by a commission headed by Lenin, the congress put forward the task of completely eradicating the actual inequality of the formerly oppressed peoples and drawing them into active participation in the building of socialism. The congress denounced anti-Party deviations in the national question—Great Power chauvinism and local nationalism.   p. 631

295 *The "Workers' Opposition"* was an anti-Party anarcho-syndicalist factional group that took final shape during the discussions on the trade unions in 1920-21. It recommended placing the management of the economy in the hands of an "All-Russia Congress of Producers" united in trade unions. This opposition demanded that all economic administrative bodies should be elected solely by the corresponding trade unions and that Party and government bodies should not have the right to challenge the candidatures nominated by the trade unions. Compliance with these demands would

have been tantamount to negating the leading role of the Party and the dictatorship of the proletariat as the basic vehicle of socialist construction. The "Workers' Opposition" counterposed the trade unions to the Soviet Government and the Communist Party, considering them and not the Party as the highest form of organisation of the working class. Its platform on inner-Party issues consisted of slanderous accusations that the Party leadership was "isolated from the Party masses", that it "underestimated the creative forces of the working class" and that it was "degenerating".

The congress dealt crushing blows at the views of the "Workers' Opposition". In the resolution "On the Syndicalist and Anarchist Deviation in Our Party", moved by Lenin, the congress declared that any propagation of the ideas of the "Workers' Opposition" was incompatible with membership in the Communist Party.   p. 631

296 *The "Democratic Centralism"* group first came forward at the Eighth Congress of the R.C.P.(B.) in March 1919. It published its factional platform during the trade union discussion in 1920-21. The "democratic Centralists" did not recognise the Party's leading role in the Soviets and trade unions, opposed one-man leadership and personal responsibility in the management of enterprises, spurned the principles worked out by Lenin in questions of organisation and demanded freedom for factions and groups. They had no influence among the Party masses.

In 1923 this group fell apart.   p. 631

297 *The Kronstadt counter-revolutionary mutiny* against Soviet power was organised by the whiteguards, Socialist-Revolutionaries, Mensheviks, anarchists and agents of the imperialist powers. The mutiny began on February 28, 1921. In that mutiny the class enemy employed new tactics in an effort to disguise its desire to restore capitalism. It put forward the slogan "Soviets without Communists" with the intention of deceiving the masses. The counter-revolutionaries planned to remove the Communists from the leadership in the Soviets and establish a bourgeois dictatorship and capitalist orders. The mutiny was put down on March 18.   p. 631

298 *Diskussionny Listok* was a non-periodical publication of the Central Committee of the R.C.P.(B.). It was published by decision of the Ninth All-Russia Conference of the R.C.P.(B.). Two issues were put out before the Tenth Congress. Subsequently, publication was resumed during discussions and before Party congresses.   p. 633

299 A reference to the resolution "On the Syndicalist and Anarchist Deviation in Our Party".   p. 633

300 By decision of the congress, the seventh point of the resolution "On Party Unity" was not published at the time. It was published in 1924 by decision of the Thirteenth conference of the R.C.P.(B.).   p. 634

301 *The Tenth All-Russia Conference of the R.C.P.(B.)* was held in Moscow on May 26-28, 1921. The main question on its agenda was that of the New Economic Policy. The proceedings were directed by Lenin. He opened the conference, spoke on the question of the agenda, delivered the report on the food tax and made the concluding speech closing the debate on this

question. He took the floor several times during the debate on the conference resolution "On Economic Policy". "The basic political task of the
moment," it was emphasised in this resolution, "is that all Party and
government workers should fully master and precisely fulfil the New
Economic Policy."   p. 635

302 *The New Economic Policy* was adopted by the proletarian state in the
period of transition from capitalism to socialism. Its principles were worked
out by Lenin as far back as in the spring of 1918, but its implementation
was held up by the foreign military intervention and the Civil War of
1918-20. It was called "new" to distinguish it from the economic policy
that was pursued during the period of the foreign military intervention
and the Civil War and known as "war communism". The "war communism"
policy, imposed by the war, was characterised by extreme centralisation
of production and distribution, the banning of free trade, and food requisitioning under which the peasants delivered all their surplus products to
the state.
    When the foreign military intervention and the Civil War ended, food
requisitioning was abolished and a food tax was introduced. This gave the
peasants the possibility of freely disposing their surplus products, selling
them in the market and, through the market, acquiring manufactured
goods.
    The purpose of the New Economic Policy, which, for a certain period,
allowed the limited existence of capitalist elements while retaining the key
economic positions in the hands of the proletarian state, was to promote
the country's productive forces, achieve an upswing in agriculture and
lay the economic foundations for the transition to socialism.   p. 635

303 *The Third Congress of the Communist International* was held in Moscow
on June 22-July 12, 1921. It was attended by 605 delegates from 103 organisations in 52 countries. The R.C.P.(B.) delegation was led by Lenin,
who directed the preparations for and the proceedings at the congress.
He was elected honorary chairman of the congress, delivered a report on
the tactics of the R.C.P.(B.), spoke on several questions, and helped to
draft all the main decisions.
    The Third Congress is known in the history of the world communist
movement as the congress that laid the foundations for the tactics of
Communist Parties and set the task of winning the masses over to the
side of the proletariat, achieving unity of the working class and imple·
menting united front tactics. The principle feature of the congress decisions, Lenin declared, was "more careful, more thorough preparation for
fresh and more decisive battles, both defensive and offensive..." (V. I. Lenin,
Collected Works, Vol. 32, p. 521).   p. 637

304 *The Two-and-a-Half* or *Vienna International* (officially known as the International Association of Socialist Parties) was set up at the conference in
Vienna in February 1921. Its leaders criticised the Second International but
pursued an opportunist, splitting policy on all major issues of the proletarian movement and strove to utilise their organisation to counter the growing
influence enjoyed by the Communists among the worker masses.
    In May 1923 the Second and the Two-and-a-Half Internationals merged
into the so-called Socialist Labour International.   p. 638

305 On April 13, 1919, British troops opened fire on a mass rally in Amritsar,
a major industrial centre in the Punjab. The rally had attracted thousands

of people who protested against the reign of terrorism instituted by colonialists. Nearly a thousand people were killed and about two thousand were wounded. An uprising broke out and disturbances spread to other regions of India in response to the Amritsar slaughter. The uprising in the Punjab was ruthlessly suppressed by the British colonialists.   p. 638

[306] This is a reference to the Eighth All-Russia Congress of Electrical Engineers that was held in Moscow on October 1-9, 1921. It was attended by leading scientists, business executives and other specialists, and numerous representatives of electrical engineering plants. The congress passed a resolution on the general plan of electrification of the R.S.F.S.R. Its recommendations were taken into consideration when the GOELRO plan (of the State Commission for the Electrification of Russia) was adopted by the Eighth Congress of Soviets and during the practical implementation of that plan.
                                                                          p. 642

[307] *Posledniye Novosti* (Latest News)—a white émigré daily newspaper and organ of the counter-revolutionary Constitutional-Democratic Party, was published in Paris from April 1920 to July 1940.   p. 643

[308] *Kommunisticheski Trud* (Communist Labour)—a daily newspaper published by the Moscow Committee of the R.C.P.(B.) and the Moscow Soviet of Workers' and Peasants' Deputies. Its publication was started on March 18, 1920, and at present it is published as *Moskovskaya Pravda*.   p. 644

[309] *Hamlet*, hero of the tragedy of the same name by Shakespeare.   p. 646

[310] F. Engels, *Flüchtlingsliteratur*.   p. 655

[311] The article "On the Significance of Militant Materialism" was written for the journal *Pod Znamenem Marksizma* No. 3, which was scheduled to be printed in time for the Eleventh Party Congress (held in Moscow on March 27-April 2, 1922).
    Pod Znamenem Marksizma (Under the Banner of Marxism), a philosophical and socio-economic monthly journal. It was published in Moscow from January 1922 to June 1944 (in 1933-35 it was published once in two months).
                                                                          p. 660

[312] *Popular Socialists* were members of the petty-bourgeois Trudovik Popular Socialist Party, which stemmed from the Right wing of the Socialist-Revolutionary Party in 1906. The Popular Socialists formed a bloc with the Constitutional-Democrats. After the bourgeois-democratic revolution of February 1917 they actively supported the bourgeois Provisional Government and held posts in it. After the October Socialist Revolution they were involved in counter-revolutionary plots and armed action against Soviet power.   p. 660

[313] F. Engels, *Flüchtlingsliteratur*.   p. 662

[314] Lenin borrowed this expression from M. E. Saltykov-Shchedrin's *The History of a Town*.
                                                                          p. 665

315 *Economist*—journal published by the Industrial and Economic Department of the Russian Technical Society, whose members included bourgeois technical intellectuals and former industrialists who were hostile to Soviet power. It was published in Petrograd from December 1921 to June 1922. p. 666

316 *The Second All-Russia Congress of Soviets of Workers' and Soldiers' Deputies,* which took place on October 25-26 (November 7-8), 1917 in Petrograd, heard the report on the taking of the Winter Palace and the detention of the Provisional Government. It adopted an appeal, written by Lenin, "To Workers, Soldiers and Peasants", in which it proclaimed the transfer of power to the Soviets of Workers', Soldiers' and Peasants' Deputies.

The congress endorsed the historic decrees on peace and on land, which were drafted by Lenin, and formed a Workers' and Peasants' Government, the Council of People's Commissars with Lenin at its head. p. 670

317 *Chartism* was a mass revolutionary movement of British workers. It was called forth by the economic difficulties of the workers and their dissatisfaction with the parliamentary reform of 1832, which extended the political rights solely of the bourgeoisie. The movement began at the close of the 1830s with huge rallies and demonstrations and continued with intervals until the beginning of the 1850s.

The principal reason for the failure of the Chartist movement was the absence of a precise programme and tactics and also of a consistent revolutionary proletarian leadership. However, the Chartists had a tremendous impact on the political history of Britain as well as on the international working-class movement. Lenin characterised Chartism as the "first broad, truly mass and politically organised proletarian revolutionary movement" (V. I. Lenin, *Collected Works*, Vol. 29, p. 309). p. 670

318 *The Genoa Economic and Financial Conference* was held on April 10-May 19, 1922 with the participation of representatives of 29 countries.

The Soviet delegation submitted an extended programme aimed at strengthening peace and economic co-operation and establishing business-like trade relations between Soviet Russia and capitalist countries. An important point of this programme concerned a general reduction of armaments.

At this conference the imperialist powers made every effort to take advantage of Soviet Russia's economic difficulties to impose on her an agreement containing onerous terms. They demanded the payment of all the tsarist debts, including pre-war debts, the return of nationalised enterprises to their former foreign owners, and so forth.

In line with the directives of the Party Central Committee and Lenin's instructions, the Soviet delegation flatly rejected the insolent demands of the imperialists and gave a rebuff to the encroachments on the sovereignty of the Soviet state. Due to the hostility of France and Britain towards Soviet Russia, the conference was cut short. At its last plenary sitting on May 19, it adopted a decision to form two commissions of experts (a Soviet and a Western commission) which met in June 1922 at the Hague for further talks on issues that remained outstanding at Genoa. The Hague Conference was likewise fruitless. p. 672

319 A reference to the treaty signed by Soviet Russia and Germany at Rapallo (near Genoa) on April 16, 1922 while the Genoa Conference was in progress.

Under this treaty the two countries relinquished mutual claims arising from the First World War. The German Government renounced its demand for the return to German nationals of enterprises nationalised by the Soviet Government providing the Soviet Government would not satisfy similar claims by other states. At the same time, the two countries established diplomatic relations and most favoured nation treatment in economic relations. The signing of the Rapallo Treaty was a major success for Soviet diplomacy for it strengthened Soviet Russia's international position and wrecked the attempts to create a united anti-Soviet front.   p. 672

320 A reference to the first paragraph of the resolution to convene an international economic conference at Genoa, adopted on January 6, 1922 at a conference of the Supreme Allied Council (held at Cannes, France, on January 6-13, 1922). This resolution contained the terms, whose acceptance, in the view of the Supreme Allied Council, was necessary for the fruitful work of the planned conference. These terms, as set forth in the first paragraph, were: "The nations may not arrogate to themselves the right to dictate to each other the principles by which they organise their internal property regime, their economy and their government. It is for each nation to choose for itself the system it prefers in this respect".

321 A plenary session of the Moscow Soviet, which sat jointly with the plenary meetings of all of Moscow's District Soviets in the Bolshoi Theatre, heard a report on the activities of the Presidium and Executive Committee of the Moscow Soviet before the re-election of deputies to the City and District Soviets.
This was Lenin's last public appearance.   p. 674

322 Lenin refers to the resolution on the reunification of the Far Eastern Republic with the R.S.F.S.R. adopted by the People's Assembly of the Far Eastern Republic on November 14, 1922. This resolution was made public on the next day.   p. 675

323 In the period from the end of October to early November 1922 *Pravda* printed a series of articles discussing the conclusion of an agreement with John Leslie Urquhart.
The talks on granting a mining concession to the British industrialist and financier John Leslie Urquhart took place in 1921-22. A preliminary agreement was drawn up and it was subject to approval by the Council of People's Commissars within a month after the date on which it was signed. When Lenin scrutinised the agreement he found that it was clearly disadvantageous to the Soviet state and opposed its approval.
The preliminary agreement was rejected by the Central Committee of the R.C.P.(B.) at a plenary meeting on October 5 and by the Council of People's Commissars on October 6, 1922.   p. 677

324 A reference to Lausanne Conference, which Britain, France and Italy convened to discuss the situation in the Near East in connection with the failure of the Anglo-Greek intervention in Turkey. The imperialist powers announced that they would admit Soviet Russia to the conference only for the discussion of the question of the Dardanelles.   p. 678

325 *Letter to the Congress* includes notes dictated by Lenin on December 23, 24, 25 and 26, 1922 and on January 4, 1923.
The recommendations made by Lenin in the notes of December 23 and developed by him in the articles *How We Should Reorganise the Workers' and Peasants' Inspection* and *Better Fewer, But Better* were used as the basis of the resolution adopted on the question of organisation by the Party Central Committee for the Twelfth Congress of the R.C.P.(B.).   p. 681

[326] *Russkaya Mysl* (Russian Thought)—a journal published in Prague in 1922 under the editorship of P. B. Struve.   p. 682

[327] A reference to the capitulatory behaviour of G. Y. Zinoviev and L. B. Kamenev at sittings of the Party Central Committee on October 10 (23) and 16 (29), 1917, when they spoke and voted against Lenin's resolution on immediate preparations for an armed uprising. Receiving a resolute rebuff, Kamenev, acting in his own name and on behalf of Zinoviev, printed a statement in the Menshevik newspaper *Novaya Zhizn* to the effect that the Bolsheviks were preparing an uprising and that they (Kamenev and Zinoviev) considered this an adventurist gamble. They thereby leaked the Central Committee's decision to organise an uprising in the immediate future to Kerensky.
                                                                       p. 682

[328] People's Commissariat for the Workers' and Peasants' Inspection of the R.S.F.S.R.   p. 684

[329] Central Administration of Vocational and Polytechnical Schools and Institutions of Higher Learning of the People's Commissariat of Education. p. 687

[330] Lenin wrote his article *Our Revolution* in connection with the third and fourth books entitled *Notes on the Revolution* by the Menshevik N. Sukhanov.
                                                                       p. 696

[331] Lenin evidently has in mind the assessment of the Paris Commune as having been an extremely flexible political form in K. Marx's *The Civil War in France* and the high evaluation of the "flexibility of the Parisians" given by Marx in a letter to L. Kugelmann on April 12, 1871 (K. Marx, F. Engels, *Selected Correspondence*, Moscow, 1965, pp. 262-63).   p. 696

[332] Lenin refers to the following passage in a letter from Marx to Engels on April 16, 1856: "The whole thing in Germany will depend on the possibility of backing the proletarian revolution by some second edition of the Peasant War. Then the affair will be splendid..." (K. Marx, F. Engels, *Selected Correspondence*, Moscow, 1965, p. 92).   p. 696

[333] A reference to the article *How We Should Reorganise the Workers' and Peasants' Inspection (Recommendation to the Twelfth Party Congress)*. p. 702

[334] Central Control Commission of the R.C.P.(B.).   p. 703

[335] Lenin refers to the following books: *Scientific Organisation of Labour and Production and the Taylor System* by O. A. Yermansky, and *Principles of Organisation* by P. M. Kerzhentsev (published by Gosizdat in 1922). p. 705

[336] *Volkhovstroi*—the Volkhov Power Project. It was commissioned at the close of 1926.   p. 711

NAME INDEX

A

Adler, Friedrich (1879-1960)—Austrian Right Social-Democrat.—497, 517, 523, 529

Adoratsky, V. V. (1878-1945)—an outstanding propagandist of Marxism, prominent Soviet scientist.—644

Agahd, E.—a German petty-bourgeois economist.—204, 205, 210, 250

Aguinaldo (Aguivinaldo), Emilio (b. 1869)—a political figure in the Philippines. Took part in the popular uprising in the Philippines, which was directed against Spanish domination. President of the newly formed Philippine Republic (1899). Subsequently pursued American policy the Philippine Islands.—250

Akimov (Makhnovets*), V P (1872-1921)—a Social-Democrat, outstanding representative of "Economism", extreme opportunist.—52, 90, 130

Alexinsky, G. A. (b. 1879)—a Social-Democrat. In 1917, while in Russia he was a counter-revolutionary. In 1918 he fled abroad and joined the extreme reactionary camp.—397

Aristophanes (c. 446-385 B.C.)—the great comic dramatist of Ancient Greece.—214

Arnim-Suchow, Heinrich Alexander (1798-1861)—a Prussian statesman, moderate liberal, Minister of Foreign Affairs (March-June 1848).—142

Asquith, Herbert Henry (1852-1928)— a British political figure and statesman, one of the Liberal Party leaders.—563, 567

Austerlitz, Friedrich (1862-1931)—one of the leaders of the Austrian Social-Democratic Party.—168, 523

Avksentyev, N. D. (1878-1943)—one of the leaders of the Socialist-Revolutionary Party and member of its Central Committee. After the February bourgeois-democratic revolution in 1917 he was chairman of the All-Russia Council of Peasants' Deputies and held a number of responsible posts in the bourgeois Provisional Government. Following the October Socialist Revolution he was one of the organisers of counter-revolutionary revolts and later emigrated.—296, 365

Axelrod, P. B. (1850-1928)—one of the Menshevik leaders. From 1900 onwards a member of the *Iskra* editorial board. After the February bourgeois-democratic revolution in 1917 he supported the bourgeois Provisional Government and was hostile towards the October Socialist Revolution. Later, when abroad, he advocated armed intervention against Soviet Russia.—248, 556

---

* Real name is given in parentheses.—*Ed.*

came out against the Comintern tactics of establishing a united anti-fascist front.—551, 586

Born, Stefan (Simon Buttermilch) (1824-1898)—one of the representatives of the reformist trend in the German working-class movement.—144, 145, 146, 147

Bracke, Wilhelm (1842-1880)—a German Socialist, one of the founders and leaders of the German Social-Democratic Workers' Party (1869)—309, 323

Branting (Carl Hjalmar) (1860-1925) —a leader of the Social-Democratic Party of Sweden, one of the Second International leaders, an opportunist.—295, 350

Breshko-Breshkovskaya, Y. K. (1844-1934)—one of the organisers and leaders of the Socialist-Revolutionary Party, who belonged to its extreme Right wing. After the February bourgeois democratic revolution in 1917 she supported the bourgeois Provisional Government. Following the October Socialist Revolution she opposed Soviet power.—264, 371, 381, 382, 392, 393, 394

Briand, Aristide (1862-1932)—a French statesman and diplomat. For a short while he belonged to the Socialist Left wing. In 1902 he became a member of Parliament and reactionary bourgeois politician openly hostile towards the working class. Prime Minister (1913, 1915-17; 1921-22).—376

Brouckère, Louis de (b. 1870)—one of the leaders and theoreticians of the Workers' Party of Belgium. During the First World War he took up an outspokenly social-chauvinist stand.—30

Bukharin, N. I. (1888-1938)—a publicist and economist. Member of the R.S.D.L.P. from 1906 onwards. On a number of questions, such as: the state, the dictatorship of the proletariat, the right of nations to self-determination and others he opposed Lenin. After the October Socialist Revolution, he repeatedly came out against Leninist Party policy. In 1918 when the discussion of the Brest peace

took place he headed the anti-Party group of "Left Communists". During the discussion that took place in the Party on trade unions (1920-21) he occupied at the beginning a "buffer" position, and later on joined the Trotsky anti-Leninist group. After 1928 he headed the Right-wing opposition in the Party and in 1929 was removed from the Politbureau of the Central Committee and the Presidium of the Executive Committee of the Comintern. In 1937 he was expelled from the Party for his anti-Party activities.—198, 446, 448, 449, 453, 454, 455, 528, 683

Bulygin, A. G. (1851-1919)—a statesman in tsarist Russia, big landlord. Since January 20, 1905 Minister of the Interior. On the tsar's instructions he was put in charge of drafting a bill on the convening of a consultative State Duma.—54, 83, 86, 88, 368, 388, 394

C

Calwer, Richard (1868-1927)—a prominent German economist, representative of reformism and revisionism in the German Social-Democratic Party.—237

Camphausen, Ludolph (1803-1890)—a Prussian statesman, one of the leaders of the Rhine liberal bourgeoisie. From March to June 1848 he headed the Prussian bourgeois-liberal government.—140, 142

Canitz, August (1783-1852)—a Prussian general, representative of the reactionary nobility and bureaucracy. During May and June 1848 he was War Minister in Camphausen's cabinet.—142

Carnegie, Andrew (1835-1919)—an American millionaire, a Scot. In 1848 he went to the United States of America. In 1901 Carnegie amalgamated his enterprises with P. Morgan's Steel Trust.—245

Cavaignac, Louis Eugène (1802-1857) —a French general, reactionary political figure. After the February

1848 revolution he headed a
military dictatorship and with
extreme severity suppressed the
Paris workers' uprising in June
1848.—420, 442
Chamberlain, Josef (1836-1914)—a
British statesman and political
leader; he actively pursued colonial annexation policy and was
one of the chief inspirers of the
Boer War (1899-1902).—225
Chernyshevsky, N. G. (1828-1889)—a
great Russian revolutionary
democrat and Utopian socialist,
scientist, writer and literary critic;
one of the outstanding predecessors of Russian Social-Democracy.
—429, 461, 555, 660
Chernenkov, B. N. (b. 1883)—a
Socialist-Revolutionary.—496
Chernov, V. M. (1876-1952)—one of
the leaders and theoreticians of
the Socialist-Revolutionary Party.
From May to August 1917, he was
Minister of Agriculture in the
bourgeois Provisional Government
and pursued a policy of brutal
reprisals against the peasants who
seized landlords' lands. After the
October Socialist Revolution he
was one of the organisers of the
anti-Soviet mutinees. He fled
abroad in 1920 where he continued
his anti-Soviet activities.—264,
272, 296, 297, 321, 334, 349, 358,
359, 371, 374, 389, 392, 403, 421,
502, 503, 556, 647
Chkheidze, V. S. (1864-1926)—one of
the Menshevik leaders. In 1917
he was chairman of the Petrograd
Soviet of Workers' and Soldiers'
Deputies, chairman of the Central
Executive Committee (First Convocation), and actively supported
the bourgeois Provisional Government. After the October Socialist
Revolution he became chairman of
the Georgian Constituent Assembly, the counter-revolutionary
Menshevik government, and later
emigrated.—248
Chkhenkeli, A. I. (b. 1874)—a Social-
Democrat and Menshevik. After
the February bourgeois-democratic
revolution in 1917 he was the
representative of the bourgeois
Provisional Government in the
Transcaucasus. He later became
Minister of Foreign Affairs of the
Menshevik Government in Georgia
(1918-21) and then emigrated.—
248
Churchill, Winston (1874-1965)—an
English political leader, Conservative. From 1918 to 1921 as War
Minister he was one of the inspirer
of the armed intervention against
Soviet Russia.—511, 566, 567, 569,
574
Clausewitz, Karl (1780-1831)—a Prussian general, most prominent bourgeois military theoretician, author
of a number of works on the
history of Napoleonic and other
wars.—438
Clynes, John Robert (1869-1949)—an
English political figure, one of the
leaders of the Labour Party.—
562, 563
Cornelissen, Christian—a Dutch anarchist, P. A. Kropotkin's follower; an
opponent of Marxism.—334
Crispien, Arthur (1875-1946)—one of
the leaders of the German Social-
Democratic movement, publicist.
He led the Right-wing group in
the Independent Social-Democratic
Party of Germany (1917-22). In
1920 as a delegate of the Party
of "Independents" he attended
the Second Congress of the Comintern. Upon his return to Germany he opposed affiliation to
the Comintern.—526, 557, 584, 585
Cunow, Heinrich (1862-1936)—a German Right-wing Social-Democrat,
historian, sociologist and ethno-
grapher, professor. At the beginning of his career he supported
the Marxists but subsequently became a revisionist and falsifier of
Marxism.—164, 236

D

Dan (Gurwich), F. I. (1871-1947)—one
of the Menshevik leaders. After
the October Socialist Revolution
he opposed Soviet power. In 1922
he was sent out of the country
as a sworn enemy of the Soviet
state.—374, 471
Danton, George Jacques (1759-1794)—
one of the prominent leaders of

the French bourgeois revolution in the late XVIIIth century.—397

David, Eduard (1863-1930)—one of the leaders of the Right wing of the German Social-Democratic movement.—226, 264, 295, 350 469

Davydov, L. F.—a director of the St. Petersburg (Leningrad) credit office; a businessman.—210

Debs, Eugene Victor (1855-1926)—an outstanding figure of the labour movement in the U.S.A.; one of the founders of the Social-Democratic Party. During world imperialist war an internationalist. Debs welcomed the victorious October Socialist Revolution. In 1918 he was sentenced to ten years' imprisonment for his anti-imperialist propaganda. In 1921 he was acquitted.—462, 463, 472

De Leon, Daniel (1852-1914)—a prominent figure in the labour movement in the U.S.A. After the 1890's he became a leader and ideologist of the Socialist Workers' Party; was a publicist and one of the founders of the Industrial Workers of the World (I.W.W.) (1905).—541

Denikin, A. I. (1872-1947)—a tsarist general, during Civil War—one of the ringleaders of the whiteguard movement, commander-in-chief of the anti-Soviet armed forces in the south of Russia. After his armies were defeated by Soviet troops, he emigrated.—174, 478, 507, 508, 509, 512, 530, 536, 537, 548, 617, 658

Deschanel, Paul (1855-1922)—a French statesman and publicist.—215

Dietzgen, Eugen (1862-1930)—son of I. Dietzgen and publisher of his works.—661

Dietzgen, Josef (1828-1888)—a German worker, tanner, Social-Democrat, philosopher, who independently arrived at dialectical materialism. Marx pointed out, that Dietzgen, despite some of his errors and inaccuracies in understanding dialectical materialism, expressed many splendid ideas—the result of independent thinking on the part of an astonishingly farsighted worker.—549, 661

Disraeli, Benjamin (Earl of Beaconsfield) (1804-1881)—an English reactionary statesman, leader of the Conservative Party and one of the ideologists of nascent imperialist bourgeoisie.—225

Dobrolyubov, N. A. (1836-1861)—a great Russian revolutionary democrat, outstanding literary critic and philosopher-materialist. Together with A. I. Herzen, V. G. Belinsky and N. G. Chernyshevsky he was a predecessor of revolutionary Social-Democrats in Russia.—429

Drews, Arthur (1865-1935)—a German reactionary bourgeois historian of early Christianity. In his works Drews refuted the historicity of Christ's existence; church dogma and religious prejudices he criticised from an idealistic point of view.—663

Dreyfus, Alfred (1859-1935)—an officer of the French General Staff, a Jew, who was innocently condemned to life imprisonment on a false charge of high treason in 1894. Thanks to the democratic section of the population of France who waged a struggle in Dreyfus' defence, the latter was pardoned in 1899, and in 1906 rehabilitated.—159, 472, 576

Driault, J. Edouard—a French bourgeois historian.—231

Dubasov—non-Party officer, frontline soldier.—400

Dugoni, Enrico (1874-1945)—an Italian socialist, who belonged to the Turati-Trèves reformist group.—586

Dühring, Eugen (1833-1921)—a German philosopher and economist. Dühring's confused views on questions of philosophy, political economy and socialism, Engels subjected to criticism in his book Anti-Dühring. Herr Eugen Dühring's Revolution in Science (1877-1878)—21, 26, 27, 274, 277, 305

Dutov, A. I. (1864-1921)—a colonel of the tsarist army, ataman of the Orenburg Cossack troops, one of the leaders in the cossack counter-revolution of 1918-19.—407, 425, 427, 471

of Justice, Minister of War and Minister of the Navy; later deputy-chairman of the bourgeois Provisional Government and Supreme Commander-in-Chief. After the October Socialist Revolution he fought against Soviet power and in 1918 fled abroad.— 272, 316, 356, 358, 369-71, 375, 387-90, 395, 399, 400, 403, 405, 407, 415, 419, 425, 445, 449, 450, 473, 530, 557, 565, 578

Kerzhentsev (Lebedev). P. M. (1881-1940)—a Soviet statesman and Party figure, historian, publicist. Member of the R.S.D.L.P. from 1904, Bolshevik.—705

Kestner, Fritz—a German economist. —184-85

Kolb Wilhelm (1870-1918)—a German Social-Democrat, extreme opportunist and revisionist.—350, 469

Kolchak, A. V. (1873-1920)—admiral of the tsarist navy, monarchist, one of the chief leaders of the Russian counter-revolution in 1918-19 and a protégé of the Entente. After the October Socialist Revolution, supported by the U.S.A. imperialists and the Entente, he proclaimed himself Supreme ruler of Russia and headed the military bourgeois-landlord dictatorship in the Urals, Siberia and the Far East. The blows delivered by the Red Army and the growth of the revolutionary guerilla movement brought about Kolchak's destruction.—174, 478, 479, 507, 508, 511, 530, 548, 617, 625, 658

Koltzov, D. (Ginsburg, B. A.) (1863-1920)—a Social-Democrat and active Menshevik.—146

Kornilov, L. G. (1870-1918)—general of the tsarist army, monarchist. In July-August 1917 he was supreme commander-in-chief of the Russian army. He headed the counter-revolutionary revolt in August. After the revolt was crushed he was arrested and sent to jail from which he escaped and fled to the Don where he became one of the organisers and commander-in-chief of the white-guard "voluntary army". He was killed in battle not far from Yeka-

terinodar (now Krasnodar).—355, 358, 363, 373, 375, 388, 389, 390, 395, 398, 399, 413, 415, 419, 420, 421, 422, 425

Krasin, L. B. (1870-1926)—an outstanding Soviet statesman. He participated in the Social-Democratic movement from 1890s; a Bolshevik. From 1919 he worked as a diplomat. In 1921 he became People's Commissar of Foreign Trade.—678-79

Krasnov, P. N. (1869-1947)—a general of the tsarist army, who took an active part in the Kornilov revolt that was organised in August 1917. In 1918-19 he led the white Cossack army on the Don. Fled abroad in 1919.—407, 471

Krichevsky, B. N. (1866-1919)—a Social-Democrat, publicist, one of the proponents of "Economism". After the Second Congress of the R.S.D.L.P. he withdrew from the Social-Democratic movement.—90

Kropotkin, P. A. (1842-1921)—one of the chief leaders and theoreticians of anarchism, a prince. He opposed K. Marx's teaching on the class struggle and the dictatorship of the proletariat. During the world imperialist war he took up a chauvinist stand. Upon his return to Russia from emigration in 1917 he adhered to his anarchist views.—334, 348

Krupp—the dynasty of magnates of war-metallurgical industry in Germany—one of the main arsenals of German imperialism. The leaders of the Trust took an active part in the preparation of the first and second world wars as a result of which they received enormous profits. According to the Yalta and Potsdam decisions of 1945, the military works of this Trust were to be liquidated. In West Germany these decisions were not carried out, and the works of the Krupp family continue to produce arms for the revanchist army of the Federal Republic of Germany.—215, 254

Kugelmann, Ludwig (1830-1902)—a German Social-Democrat, friend of K. Marx, participant of the

1848-49 Revolution in Germany and member of the First International.—289

Kuskova, Y. D. (1869-1958)—a Russian bourgeois public figure and publicist. Kuskova called on the workers to repudiate the revolutionary struggle, trying to subordinate the workers' movement to the political leadership of the liberal bourgeoisie. She was a follower of the Left Constitutional Democrats. After the October Socialist Revolution she came out against Soviet power.—365

L

L. L.—see Herman, Ladislaus.

Labriola, Arturo (b. 1873)—an Italian political leader, lawyer and economist; one of the leaders of the syndicalist movement in Italy. —31

Lagardelle, Juber (b. 1874)—a French petty-bourgeois political figure, anarcho-syndicalist.—31

Lansburgh, Alfred (b. 1872)—a German bourgeois economist.—190, 192, 209, 243, 250, 252, 253, 254

Lassalle, Ferdinand (1825-1864)—a German petty-bourgeois socialist, father of one of the varieties of opportunism in the German working-class movement—Lassalleanism.—49, 321, 324, 329, 330, 331

Laufenberg, Heinrich (Erler), Karl (1872-1932)—a German Left Social-Democrat and publicist. After the November revolution of 1918 he joined the Communist Party of Germany and soon headed the "Left" opposition. In 1919 he was expelled from the Communist Party of Germany.— 533, 559

Ledebour, Georg (1850-1947)—a German Social-Democrat, from 1900 to 1918; he represented German Social-Democrats in the Reichstag and was a member of the German Independent Social-Democratic Party which supported the blatant chauvinists.—526, 557

Legien, Karl (1861-1920)—a German Right Social-Democrat, one of the leaders of the German trade unions; revisionist.—264, 295, 297, 349, 526, 540, 543

Lenin, V. I. (N.) (Ulyanov, V. I.) (1870-1924)—53, 89, 127, 128, 133, 139, 175, 361, 362, 388, 400, 446, 681, 683, 684

Lansbury, George (1859-1940)—one of the leaders of the British Labour Party.—528, 552

Lensch, Paul (1873-1926)—a German Social-Democrat, chauvinist. In 1922 on the demand of the rank-and-file members of the Social-Democratic Party of Germany he was expelled from its ranks.—163

Leo XIII (Vincenzo Gioacchino Pecci) (1810-1903)—he was elected Pope in 1878.—137

Levy, Hermann (b. 1881)—a German bourgeois economist and professor: author of a number of works on questions of finance capital.— 179

Lieber (Goldman), M. I. (1880-1937)— one of the Menshevik leaders. After the February bourgeois-democratic revolution in 1917 he became a member of the Executive Committee of the Petrograd Soviet of Workers' and Soldiers' Deputies and of the Presidium of the Central Executive Committee (First Convocation), where he adopted a Menshevik stand. He opposed the October Socialist Revolution. Later he devoted himself to economic work.—374

Liebknecht, Wilhelm (1826-1900)—a prominent leader of the German and international working-class movement, one of the founders and leaders of the German Social-Democratic Party. He took an active part in the work of the First International and the founding of the Second International.— 37, 311, 312, 670

Liebknecht, Karl (1871-1919)—an outstanding leader of the German and international working-class movement. He fought actively against opportunism and militarism. From the outset of the First World War he came out resolutely against supporting "one's own" government in the predatory war.

In the Reichstag he alone voted against war credits (December 2, 1914). One of the organisers and leaders of the revolutionary "Spartacus League". During the November revolution in Germany together with R. Luxemburg he led the revolutionary vanguard of the German workers; one of the founders of the Communist Party of Germany and leader of the Berlin workers' uprising that took place in January 1919. After the uprising was crushed he was brutally assassinated by Noske's hirelings.—472, 544, 550

Liebman, F. (Gersh, P. L.) (b. 1882) —a well-known Bundist.—164

Liefmann, Robert (1874-1941)—a German bourgeois economist, professor. Author of a number of works on economic and social problems. —186, 187, 189, 200, 201, 202, 222

Lincoln, Abraham (1809-1865)—an outstanding American statesman; President of the U.S.A. (1861-65). In the course of the Civil War under the influence of the popular masses he carried out a number of important bourgeois-democratic reforms which led to the transition to revolutionary methods of conducting the war. In 1865 he was killed by one of the slave-owners' agents.—250

Lloyd George, David (1863-1945)—an English statesman and diplomat, leader of the Liberal Party. He played an important role in launching the First World War. Prime Minister (1916-22). After the October Socialist Revolution in Russia he was one of the inspirers and organisers of the military intervention and blockade, directed against the Soviet state.—213, 563, 564, 566, 567, 568, 569, 574

Longuet, Jean (1876-1938)—an outstanding leader of the French Socialist Party and the Second International, publicist; son of Charles Longuet and Jenny Marx. He actively contributed to the French and international socialist press. He was one of the leaders of the Centrist wing of the French Socialist Party. In the 1930s he advocated unity of action between socialists and communists against fascism and took part in international organisations that fought against fascism and war. —473, 497, 523, 529, 582, 599, 647

Lubersac, Jean—an officer of the French army, count, monarchist and a member of the French Military Mission in Russia in 1917-18.—460

Lunacharsky, A. V. (1875-1933)—a professional revolutionary, outstanding Soviet state and Party worker. After the Second Congress of the R.S.D.L.P. he became a Bolshevik. Following the October Socialist Revolution and up to 1929 he was People's Commissar of Education. In 1930 he became an Academician. He was a publicist, playwright and the author of a number of books on art and literature.—622

Lüttwitz, Walther (1859-1942)—a general, baron, one of the representatives of the German imperialist militarists. In March 1920 he was one of the leaders of a so-called "Kapp putsch"—counter-revolutionary revolt—organised by the German militarists with the aim of restoring monarchy and establishing a military dictatorship in Germany.—584, 585

Luxemburg, Rosa (1871-1919)—a prominent leader of the international working-class movement, one of the leaders of the Left wing of the Second International, and one of the founders of the Polish Social-Democratic movement. From 1897 onwards she actively participated in the German Social-Democratic movement. From the outset of the imperialist war she took up an internationalist stand and was one of the initiators of organising an "International" group, which later on was named "Spartacus" group and finally the "Spartacus League". After the November 1918 revolution in Germany she played a leading part in the Inaugural Congress of the Communist Party of Germany. In January 1919 on the instructions of Scheidemann's

of Leninist "Iskra". After the Second Congress of the R.S.D.L.P. (1903) he wrote articles for Menshevik periodicals.—93

Nakhimson, M. I. (Spectator) (b. 1880)—an economist and publicist, a Bundist.—251, 252, 254

Napoleon I (Bonaparte) (1769-1821)—an outstanding French Commander-in-Chief, first Consul of the French Republic (1799-1804) and French Emperor (1804-1814 and 1815).—282, 442, 472, 698

Napoleon III (Bonaparte, Louis; Louis Napoleon) (1808-1873)—French Emperor (1852-1870), cousin of Napoleon I. After the defeat of the 1848 Revolution he was elected President of the French Republic; on the eve of December 2, 1851 he effected a coup d'état.—282

Natanson, M. A. (1850-1919)—a representative of revolutionary Narodism, who subsequently became a Socialist-Revolutionary. After the February bourgeois-democratic revolution in 1917 he became one of the organisers of the Left Socialist-Revolutionary Party. In 1918 he condemned the revolt that was organised against the Soviet power by the Left Socialist-Revolutionaries.—556

Neymarck, Alfred—a French bourgeois economist, statistician.—211, 213, 250

Nikitin, A. M. (b. 1876)—a Menshevik, after the July events in 1917 he became minister in the bourgeois Provisional Government.—375, 389

Nicholas II (Romanov) (Bloody) (1868-1918)—last Russian emperor, who reigned from 1894 to 1917. On the decision of the Urals Regional Soviet of Workers' and Soldiers' Deputies he was shot on July 17, 1918 in Yekaterinburg (Sverdlovsk).—84, 88, 136

Noske, Gustav (1868-1946)—one of the opportunist leaders of the German Social-Democratic Party, War Minister (1919-20) and organiser of reprisals against the Berlin workers and the assassination of K. Liebknecht and R. Luxemburg.—174, 523, 562, 563, 579, 670

O

Oldenburg, S. S. (d. 1940)—political observer and one of the most regular contributors to the whiteguard magazine *Russkaya Mysl* (Russian Thought), that came out in 1922 in Prague.—682

Osinsky, N. (Obolensky V.V.) (1887-1938)—a member of the Bolshevik Party since 1907. After the October Socialist Revolution he became a leading figure in the Soviet and Party apparatuses. "Left Communist" in 1918. He took an active part in the anti-Party "democratic Centralism" group (1920-21); in 1923 he joined the Trotskyite opposition.—451, 452

Owen, Robert (1771-1858)—a great English Utopian socialist.—694

Owens, Michael Joseph (1859-1923)—an American who invented a bottle-making machine, subsequently an industrialist in this sphere.—241

P

Paish, George (1867-1957)—an English bourgeois economist and statistician, pacifist. Author of a number of works on world economic and political problems.—213, 216

Palchinsky, P. I. (d. 1930)—an engineer and organiser of the "Produgol" (Coal) syndicate, who was closely connected with banking circles. After the February revolution of 1917 he became member of the bourgeois Provisional Government and instigator of industrialists' sabotage.—272

Pankhurst, Sylvia Estella (1882-1960)—a leading figure in the English labour movement. After the October Socialist Revolution she called for the withdrawal of military intervention of the imperialist states against Soviet Russia. She took part in the Second Congress of the Comintern. In 1921 she joined the Communist Party of Great Britain, but very soon was expelled from its ranks for her refusal to subordinate to Party discipline.—561, 563, 565, 569

October Socialist Revolution he emigrated.—130, 142, 143

Rodzyanko, M. V. (1859-1924)—a big landlord, one of the leaders of the Party of big bourgeoisie, the Octobrists; a monarchist. In March 1911 he became Chairman of the Third and later on of the Fourth State Duma. After the October Socialist Revolution joined Denikin, attempted to muster all counter-revolutionary forces for the struggle against Soviet power, eventually he fled abroad.—536

Rothschild—a dynasty of powerful West-European finance magnates. —219

Roy, Manabendra Nat (1892-1948)—an Indian political leader and member of the Communist Party. Delegate to the Second, Third, Fourth and Fifth congresses of the Comintern; in 1922 he became a candidate member of the Executive Committee of the Communist International and in 1924, a full member. Later he withdrew from the Communist Party.—602

Rubanovich, I. A. (1860-1920)—one of the leaders of the Socialist-Revolutionaries and a member of the International Socialist Bureau. After the October Socialist Revolution he opposed Soviet power.—166, 264

Ruge, Arnold (1802-1880)—a German publicist, Young Hegelian and bourgeois Radical; one of the leaders of German petty-bourgeois émigrés in England.—49

Rusanov, N. S. (b. 1859)—a publicist, Narodovolets and subsequently a Socialist-Revolutionary. After the October Socialist Revolution he emigrated.—297

Rykov, A. I. (1881-1938)—joined the Bolshevik Party in 1899. After the February bourgeois-democratic revolution in 1917 he opposed the Party's Leninist line with regard to the socialist revolution. After the October Socialist Revolution he was People's Commissar of the Interior, chairman of the Supreme Council of National Economy, deputy chairman of the Council of People's Commis-

sars and of the Council of Labour and Defence, chairman of the Council of People's Commissars of the U.S.S.R. and the R.S.F.S.R. and was member of the Central Committee's Politbureau. He repeatedly opposed the Party's Leninist policy; in November 1917 he advocated the creation of a coalition government with the participation of the Mensheviks and the Socialist-Revolutionaries. On declaring that he disagreed with the Party's policy, he withdrew from the Central Committee and the Government and later became one of the leaders of the Right opportunist deviation in the Party (1928). In 1937 he was expelled from the Party because of his anti-Party activities.—674

S

Sadoul, Jacques (1881-1956)—a French officer; in 1917 he was sent to Russia as a member of the French Military Mission. Under the influence of the October Socialist Revolution in 1917 he adopted communist views, joined the French section of the R.C.P.(B.) and the Red Army as a volunteer. He attended the First Congress of the Comintern.—460

Saint-Simon, Henri Claude (1760-1825)—a great French Utopian Socialist.—263

Sartorius von Waltershausen, August (b. 1852)—a German bourgeois economist and the author of books on world economics and politics. —242

Savinkov, B. V. (1879-1925)—a prominent figure of the Socialist-Revolutionary Party, who took an active part in terrorist activity. After the October Revolution he became the organiser of a number of counter-revolutionary revolts and military intervention against the Soviet Republic.—407, 422, 471

Schapper, Karl (1812-1870)—a well-known leader of the German and international working-class movement; member of the Central Com-

Revolutionary. After the October Socialist Revolution he became an organiser of anti-Soviet revolts and aided the armed intervention against Soviet Russia.—365

Thiers, Adolphe (1797-1877)—a French bourgeois statesman and historian and one of the main organisers of the Civil War and the Paris Commune suppression.—137

Thomas, Albert (1878-1932)—a French political figure and social-reformist. From 1910—one of the leaders of the Parliamentary group of the Socialist Party.—173

Timiryazev, A. K. (1880-1955)—a professor, Doctor of Physical and Mathematical Sciences, he joined the R.C.P.(B.) in 1921.—664

Trèves, Claudio (1868-1933)—one of the reformist leaders of the Italian Socialist Party.—350, 586

Trotsky (Bronstein), L. D. (1879-1940)—the most malicious enemy of Leninism. At the Sixth Congress of the R.S.D.L.P.(B.) in 1917 he became a member of the Bolshevik Party. After the October Socialist Revolution he held a number of posts in the Government. From 1923 he waged a fierce factional struggle against the Party's general policy and the Leninist programme for the construction of socialism and preached the impossibility of a victory of socialism in the U.S.S.R. The Communist Party exposed Trotskyism as a petty-bourgeois trend in the Party, defeated it on the ideological and organisational fronts. In 1927 Trotsky was expelled from the Party. In 1929 he was deported from the U.S.S.R. for his anti-Soviet activities and in 1932 he was deprived of Soviet citizenship. Abroad he continued his struggle against the Soviet state, the Communist Party and the international communist movement.—52, 90, 388, 682. 683

Trubetskoi, S. N. (1862-1905)—prince, liberal and idealist philosopher. He attempted to strengthen tsarism by introducing a moderate constitution.—130, 143

Tschierschky, Sigfried (b. 1872)—a German bourgeois economist.—193

Tsereteli, I. G. (1882-1959)—one of the Menshevik leaders. After the February bourgeois-democratic revolution in 1917 he became a member of the Petrograd Soviet Executive Committee and the Central Executive Committee of the Soviet (First Convocation). In May 1917 he entered the bourgeois Provisional Government; was one of the inspirers of the reprisals against the Bolsheviks. After the October Socialist Revolution he became one of the leaders in the counter-revolutionary Menshevik government in Georgia; later he went into emigration.—264, 272, 296, 297, 317, 321, 334, 349, 358, 363, 368, 374, 375, 381, 382, 388, 389, 392, 398, 403, 421, 450

Tsyurupa, A. D. (1870-1928)—Party member since 1898, professional revolutionary and a prominent leader of the Communist Party and the Soviet state. At the end of 1921 he became Deputy Chairman of the Council of People's Commissars and Council of Labour and Defence.—674

Tugan-Baranovsky, M. I. (1865-1919)—a Russian bourgeois economist. During the 1905-07 revolution he was a member of the Constitutional-Democratic Party. After the October Socialist Revolution he was an active counter-revolutionary in the Ukraine.—331

Turati, Filippo (1857-1932)—a reformist leader of the Italian working-class movement and one of the organisers (1892) of the Italian Socialist Party. He pursued a policy of class collaboration between the proletariat and the bourgeoisie. During the First World War he adopted Centrist views. He was hostile towards the October Socialist Revolution and the revolutionary movement of the Italian working people.—98, 106, 350, 473, 523, 551, 586, 647

Turgenev, I. S. (1818-1883)—a great Russian writer.—429

U

Urquhart, J. L. (1874-1933)—a British financier and industrialist: chairman of the "Russian-Asian Amalgamated Society" and owner of large mining enterprises in Russia. In 1921-22 he negotiated in an attempt to regain his former enterprises as concessions.—678

V

Vaillant, Edouard Marie (1840-1915) —a French socialist, member of the First International's General Council. Later on one of the leaders of the Second International. One of the founders of the French Socialist Party (1901). In 1905 after the Socialist Party amalgamated with the reformist French Socialist Party, Vaillant, on the most important issues, adopted an opportunist stand.— 552

Vandervelde, Emile (1866-1938)—a leader of the Workers' Party of Belgium, President of the International Socialist Bureau of the Second International, who held extreme opportunist views.—30, 164, 264, 295, 297, 349, 350

Varlin, Louis Eugen (1839-1871)—a French revolutionary, outstanding leader of the Paris Commune (1871), Left Proudhonist; a bookbinder by trade. In 1865 he became a member of the First International. In the period of the Paris Commune he joined the Commune's left minority, fought heroically on the barricades. On May 28 was seized by the Versaillais, tortured and shot.—121, 670

Völker—a German government official, who subsequently headed the German Steel Industry Trust.—210

Vogelstein, Theodor—a German economist.—221

W

Webb, Beatrice (1858-1943) and **Sidney** (1859-1947)—well-known English public figures, reformists, and members of Fabian Society; they wrote a number of works on the history and theory of the British labour movement; during the First World War they adopted a social-chauvinist stand.—474

Wendel, Friedrich (1886-1960)—a German Left Social-Democrat, satirist and publicist. After the November 1918 Revolution in Germany he became a member of the Communist Party and joined the Left opposition group; in 1919 he was expelled from the German Communist Party.—534

Weydemeyer, Joseph (1818-1866)—an outstanding leader of the German and American labour movement, friend and comrade-in-arms of K. Marx and F. Engels. He was a member of the "Communist League" and took part in the 1848-49 Revolution in Germany. After the defeat of the revolution he emigrated to the U.S.A., where he participated in the Civil War on the Northerners' side.—286

Wijnkoop, David (1877-1941)—a Dutch Left Social-Democrat, subsequently a Communist.—590

Wilhelm II (Hohenzollern) (1859-1941)—German emperor and King of Prussia (1888-1918)—168, 209, 474

Wilson (Woodrow) (1856-1924)—President of the U.S.A. (1913-20); one of the chief organisers of the military intervention by the imperialist states against Soviet Russia. —173, 463, 474

Wipper, R. Y. (1859-1954)—a well-known historian, Professor of Moscow University; since 1943 Academician.—663

Wolffheim, Fritz—a German Left Social-Democrat, publicist. Towards the end of 1918 he joined the Communist Party of Germany, in which together with Laufenberg he led the "Left" opposition. In 1919 the "Left" opposition group was expelled from the German Communist Party.—533

Wrangel, P. N. (1878-1928)—a general of the tsarist army, baron, rabid monarchist. During the foreign military intervention and Civil

War he was a hireling of the Anglo-French and American imperialists; one of the leaders of the counter-revolution in the south of Russia. From April to November 1920 he was commander-in-chief of the whiteguard "armed forces" in the south of Russia; after they were routed by the Red Army he fled abroad.—658

Y

Yermansky, A. (Kogan, O. A.) (1866-1941)—a Social-Democrat, Menshevik. In 1921 he left the Menshevik party and devoted himself to research work.—704

Yudenich, N. N. (1862-1933)—a general in the tsarist army. After the October Socialist Revolution he was commander-in-chief of the whiteguard northwestern army. In 1919 he attempted twice to seize Petrograd (Leningrad), but both times was unsuccessful. Defeated by the Red Army in November 1919 he retreated to Estonia.—507, 508, 511, 512, 537, 625, 658

Yurkevich, L. (1885-1918)—a Ukrainian bourgeois nationalist, opportunist. Member of the Central Committee of the Ukrainian Social-Democratic Workers' Party.—164

Z

Zasulich, V. I. (1849-1919)—an outstanding participant of the Narod-nik and subsequently the Social-Democratic movement in Russia. In 1900 she was a member of the editorial staff of the newspaper Iskra. After the Second Congress of the R.S.D.L.P. she became one of the Menshevik leaders. —556

Zenzinov, V. M. (b. 1881)—one of the leaders of the Socialist-Revolutionary Party and its Central Committee member. In 1917 he became a member of the Executive Committee of the Petrograd Soviet and supported a bloc with the bourgeoisie. After the October Socialist Revolution he emigrated. —297

Zinoviev (Radomyslsky), G. Y. (1883-1936)—member of the Bolshevik Party from 1901. During the preparation for carrying out the October Socialist Revolution his allegiance vacillated and he opposed the armed uprising. After the October Socialist Revolution he held leading state and Party posts and was chairman of the Executive Committee of the Comintern. For his factional activities he was expelled from the Party. —682

Zubatov, S. V. (1864-1917)—a gendarmerie colonel, inspirer and organiser of "police socialism" (Zubatovshchina). From 1901 to 1903 he organised police workers' unions with the aim of diverting the workers from the revolutionary struggle.—44, 45, 49, 543

SUBJECT INDEX